1 Peter, 2 Peter, and Jude

1 Peter, 2 Peter, and Jude

Worship Matters

John Paul Heil

CASCADE Books • Eugene, Oregon

1 PETER, 2 PETER, AND JUDE
Worship Matters

Copyright © 2013 John Paul Heil. All rights reserved. Except for brief quotations in critical publications or reviews, no part of this book may be reproduced in any manner without prior written permission from the publisher. Write: Permissions, Wipf and Stock Publishers, 199 W. 8th Ave., Suite 3, Eugene, OR 97401.

Cascade Books
An Imprint of Wipf and Stock Publishers
199 W. 8th Ave., Suite 3
Eugene, OR 97401

www.wipfandstock.com

ISBN 13: 978-1-62032-437-0

Cataloging-in-Publication data:

Heil, John Paul

    1 Peter, 2 Peter, and Jude : worship matters / John Paul Heil

    viii + 228 p. ; 23 cm. Includes bibliographical references and indexes.

    ISBN 13: 978-1-62032-437-0

    1. Bible. Peter—Criticism, interpretation, etc. 2. Bible. Peter—Commentaries. 3. Bible. Jude—Criticism, interpretation, etc. 4. Bible. Jude—Commentaries. 5. Worship—Biblical teaching. I. Title.

BS2795.53 H35 2013

Manufactured in the U.S.A.

Contents

Abbreviations — vii

1. Introduction — 1
2. 1 Peter 1:1–13 — 27
3. 1 Peter 1:14–25 — 47
4. 1 Peter 2:1–17 — 64
5. 1 Peter 2:18–21a — 83
6. 1 Peter 2:21b–25 — 89
7. 1 Peter 3:1–7 — 98
8. 1 Peter 3:8–17 — 110
9. 1 Peter 3:18–22 — 126
10. 1 Peter 4:1–11 — 137
11. 1 Peter 4:12–19 — 154
12. 1 Peter 5:1–14 — 167
13. Summary and Conclusion on 1 Peter — 185
14. Introduction to 2 Peter — 191
15. 2 Peter 1:1–15 — 206
16. 2 Peter 1:16–21 — 230
17. 2 Peter 2:1–16 — 240
18. 2 Peter 2:17–22 — 258
19. 2 Peter 3:1–18 — 268
20. Summary and Conclusion on 2 Peter — 291
21. Introduction to Jude — 295
22. Jude 1:1–4 — 303
23. Jude 1:5–11 — 309
24. Jude 1:12–20 — 318

25	Jude 1:21–25 — 330	
26	Summary and Conclusion on Jude — 340	

Bibliography   —   343
Scripture Index   —   351
Author Index   —   1

Abbreviations

AB	Anchor Bible
AcT	*Acta theologica*
AnBib	Analecta biblica
ANTC	Abingdon New Testament Commentaries
BBR	*Bulletin for Biblical Research*
BDAG	Danker, F. W., W. Bauer, W. F. Arndt, and F. W. Gingrich. *Greek-English Lexicon of the New Testament and Other Early Christian Literature*. 3rd ed. Chicago, 2000
BECNT	Baker Exegetical Commentary on the New Testament
BHGNT	Baylor Handbook on the Greek New Testament
Bib	*Biblica*
BL	*Bibel und Liturgie*
BSac	*Bibliotheca sacra*
BTB	*Biblical Theology Bulletin*
BTZ	*Berliner Theologische Zeitschrift*
BTCB	Brazos Theological Commentary on the Bible
BZ	*Biblische Zeitschrift*
BZNW	Beihefte zur Zeitschrift für die neutestamentliche Wissenschaft
CBQ	*Catholic Biblical Quarterly*
CBQMS	Catholic Biblical Quarterly Monograph Series
CCSS	Catholic Commentary on Sacred Scripture

Abbreviations

ConBNT	Coniectanea biblica: New Testament Series
CTJ	Calvin Theological Journal
CTR	Criswell Theological Review
EDNT	*Exegetical Dictionary of the New Testament.* Edited by H. Balz, G. Schneider. ET. Grand Rapids. 1990–1993
EstBíb	Estudios bíblicos
EvQ	Evangelical Quarterly
ExpTim	Expository Times
HBT	Horizons in Biblical Theology
Hen	Henoch
HTR	Harvard Theological Review
IBS	Irish Biblical Studies
Int	Interpretation
IVPNTC	The InterVarsity Press New Testament Commentary Series
JBL	Journal of Biblical Literature
JETS	Journal of the Evangelical Theological Society
JSNT	Journal for the Study of the New Testament
JSNTSup	Journal for the Study of the New Testament: Supplement Series
LNTS	Library of New Testament Studies
LTP	Laval théologique et philosophique
NAC	New American Commentary
Neot	Neotestamentica
NICNT	New International Commentary on the New Testament
NTL	New Testament Library
Notes	Notes on Translation
NovT	Novum Testamentum
NTS	New Testament Studies
PzB	Protokolle zur Bibel
RevExp	Review and Expositor

Abbreviations

SBLDS	Society of Biblical Literature Dissertation Series
SBLECL	Society of Biblical Literature: Early Christianity and Its Literature
SBLMS	Society of Biblical Literature Monograph Series
SBLSCS	Society of Biblical Literature Septuagint and Cognate Studies
SNTSMS	Society for New Testament Studies Monograph Series
SNTSU	*Studien zum Neuen Testament und seiner Umwelt*
SP	Sacra pagina
THNTC	Two Horizons New Testament Commentary
WUNT	Wissenschaftliche Untersuchungen zum Neuen Testament
WBC	Word Biblical Commentary
WTJ	*Westminster Theological Journal*
ZNW	*Zeitschrift für die neutestamentliche Wissenschaft und die Kunde der älteren Kirche*

1

Introduction

1 Peter, 2 Peter, and Jude: Worship Matters

THIS BOOK WILL PRESENT new proposals for the structures and main themes regarding worship of three closely related letters in the New Testament—1 Peter, 2 Peter, and Jude. The first thirteen chapters will be devoted to 1 Peter. Chapters 14–20 will examine 2 Peter, while chapters 21–26 will treat Jude.

Chiastic Structures and 1 Peter, 2 Peter, and Jude

My investigation of the chiastic structures of 1 Peter, 2 Peter, and Jude will be guided by the following list of criteria for detecting an extended chiasm:

1. There must be a problem in perceiving the structure of the text in question, which more conventional outlines fail to resolve.
2. There must be clear examples of parallelism between the two "halves" of the hypothesized chiasm, to which commentators call attention even when they propose quite different outlines for the text overall.
3. Linguistic (or grammatical) parallelism as well as conceptual (or structural) parallelism should characterize most if not all of the corresponding pairs of subdivisions.
4. The linguistic parallelism should involve central or dominant imagery or terminology important to the rhetorical strategy of the text.
5. Both linguistic and conceptual parallelism should involve words and ideas not regularly found elsewhere within the proposed chiasm.

6. Multiple sets of correspondences between passages opposite each other in the chiasm as well as multiple members of the chiasm itself are desirable.
7. The outline should divide the text at natural breaks which would be agreed upon even by those proposing very different structures to account for the whole.
8. The central or pivotal as well as the final or climactic elements normally play key roles in the rhetorical strategy of the chiasm.
9. Ruptures in the outline should be avoided.[1]

An important and distinctive feature of this investigation is that all of the proposed chiasms are determined mainly by precise linguistic parallels with an objective basis in the text, rather than on thematic or conceptual parallels, which can often be subjective. Indeed, the main criterion for the establishment of chiasms in this investigation is the demonstration of these linguistic parallels. I will seek to determine how the subsequent occurrence(s) of a paralleled word or phrase develops the first occurrence after a central unparalleled element or central parallel elements serve as a pivot from the first to the second half of the chiasm.

Since they are based strictly on linguistic parallels, some of the proposed chiasms may or may not exhibit a balance in the length of the various parallel elements or units—one parallel element or unit may be much longer or much shorter than its corresponding parallel. This may seem odd to a modern audience, but an ancient audience would presumably be attuned to the key linguistic parallels that are heard rather than the balance of length between the elements or units of a given chiasm. The main presupposition of this investigation is that if there are demonstrable linguistic parallels with a pivotal section between them, then a chiasm is operative regardless of a certain lack of balance between various elements or units.

Furthermore, some of the linguistic parallels involve what might be considered by a modern audience as rather ordinary or trivial words, unlikely to be key words in chiastic parallels. But it should be kept in mind that what may seem to be insignificant words or phrases on the surface to

---

1. For a slightly different and more detailed version of this list, as well as an example of an extended biblical chiasm, see Blomberg, "Structure of 2 Corinthians 1–7," 4–8. For more on chiastic structures in 2 Corinthians, see also Milinovich, *Now Is the Day*. And for more discussion of criteria and more biblical examples of extended chiasms, see Brouwer, *Literary Development*. See also Welch, "Chiasmus," 211–49; idem, "Criteria," 157–74; Thomson, *Chiasmus in the Pauline Letters*, 13–45; Wilson, *Victor Sayings in the Book of Revelation*, 3–8; deSilva, "Chiasmus in Macro-Structural Analyses of Revelation," 343–71.

Introduction

a modern audience may have been very significant indeed to the particular rhetorical strategy of the author and the particular situation of the original audience as they listened to the entire oral performances of 1 Peter, 2 Peter, and Jude. In some cases the parallels may be between cognates or between synonyms, antonyms, and/or alliterative terms. And in some cases an identical grammatical form of a word determines the chiastic parallel.

Not all of the proposed chiasms have the same number of elements or units. Some chiasms may exhibit a single unparalleled central element, e.g., A-B-C-B'-A', while others may exhibit dual, parallel central, or pivotal elements, e.g., A-B-C-C'-B'-A'. Nevertheless, both of these types operate as chiasms in the ears of the implied audience, since they both involve a pivot from the first to the second half of the chiasm. In one type a central unparalleled element serves as the pivot, whereas in the other type two parallel elements together serve as the pivot to the second half of parallel elements. In addition it may often be more accurate to speak of the central element or elements as the pivotal point of the chiasm and the final A' element as the climax. This is important to keep in mind, lest one think that chiastic patterns are a type of circular or merely repetitive argument rather than exhibiting an ongoing, dynamic development.

Chiastic patterns serve to organize the content to be heard and not only aid the memory of the one delivering or performing a document but also make it easier for the implied audience to follow and remember the content. A chiasm works by leading its audience through introductory elements to a central, pivotal point or points, and then reaching its conclusion by recalling and developing, via the chiastic parallels, aspects of the initial elements that led to the central, pivotal point or points. Since chiasms were very common in ancient oral-auricular and rhetorical cultures,[2] the original audience may and need not necessarily have been consciously identifying any of these chiasms as they heard them. They unconsciously experienced the chiastic phenomenon as an organizing dynamic, which had a subtle but purposeful effect on how they received and perceived the content.[3] But a discovery, delineation, and bringing to consciousness of the underlying chiastic structures of ancient documents can greatly aid the modern audience to a more accurate interpretation of them by providing a visual guide to the way the original audience heard them.

---

2. For some of the evidence of this see Brouwer, *Literary Development*, 23–27.
3. On chiasms as an aid to both listener and performer, see Dewey, "Mark as Aural Narrative," 50–52.

1 Peter, 2 Peter, and Jude

1 Peter: Worship for Life through the Sufferings of Jesus Christ

I aim to contribute to a better understanding of the First Letter of Peter in a twofold way. First, I will demonstrate a completely new and comprehensive text-centered structure for 1 Peter, based on its nature as an epistolary homily or sermon composed of rhetorical strategies meant for an oral performance to be heard by its audience gathered together as a worshiping assembly.[4] This structure consists of a series of eleven microchiastic units arranged in a cohesive and coherent macrochiastic framework embracing the entire letter. Many previous discussions of the structure of 1 Peter simply propose general outlines of the contents of the letter, often assigning labels to sections of the letter based upon its epistolary (prescript, thanksgiving, body of the letter, closing greetings) or rhetorical (exordium, propositio, peroratio) character.[5] Rather than imposing such thematic or conceptually based labels upon the text of the letter, my proposal seeks to be as rigorously text-centered as possible. It begins with and is governed by a close reading of or listening to the text, and thus is strictly based upon linguistic criteria within the text itself.

The chiastic phenomenon appears to have been a quite common way of organizing and punctuating material to be delivered orally in antiquity. The repetitive patterns of chiastic structures evidently guided audiences to a better understanding and remembrance of what they heard. I have demonstrated similar chiastic structures for several other NT letters.[6] The identification of them provides a visual aid to guide the interpretation of modern audiences. Based on my identification of the chiastic structures comprising 1 Peter, I will provide an interpretation focused on how the implied audience are to respond to the rhetorical strategies presented by the dynamics of these chiastic structures as they listen to them.[7]

---

4. On the importance of recognizing the oral and rhetorical culture of NT writings, see Witherington, *New Testament Rhetoric*, 1–9; idem, *What's in the Word*, 7–17. On translating 1 Peter with an ear attuned to orality, see Thomas and Thomas, *Structure*.

5. For recent discussions of the structure and proposals for the outline of 1 Peter, see Donelson, *I & II Peter*, 17–19; Horrell, *1 Peter*, 9–20; Witherington, *Letters*, 45–51; Jobes, *1 Peter*, 56–57; Schreiner, *1, 2 Peter*, 46–48; Senior, *1 Peter*, 10–11; Elliott, *1 Peter*, 80–83; Achtemeier, *1 Peter*, 73–74.

6. Heil, "Chiastic Structure," 178–206; idem, *Ephesians*; idem, *Philippians*; idem, *Colossians*; idem, *Hebrews*; idem, *Letter of James*.

7. The collective noun "audience" will be used as a plural noun, so that it conforms to the Greek text of 1 Peter, which employs plural terms in reference to its audience, who are conceived of as a group composed of individual members with responsibilities toward one another.

Second, I will present a new proposal for the unifying or organizing theme of 1 Peter in accord with its comprehensive chiastic structure as a key to its interpretation. The subtitle I have chosen for 1 Peter, "worship for life through the sufferings of Jesus Christ," articulates what the whole of 1 Peter, as an epistolary homily or sermon, is encouraging its audience to maintain. The term "worship" is to be understood comprehensively as including not only liturgical or cultic worship but also the ethical or moral behavior that complements it, so that the result is a holistic way of worshiping God. The phrase "for life" indicates the goal of this worship as a participation in the risen life of Jesus Christ, for which believers have been given a new birth by God (1 Pet 1:3, 23). They have thus already begun to live this eternal life as they look forward to its full and final manifestation at the revelation of Jesus Christ at the end of time (1:5, 7, 13). And the phrase "through the sufferings of Jesus Christ" indicates that the suffering and death of Jesus Christ is both the model and means by which this worship for eternal life takes place.[8]

In the rest of this chapter I will introduce and explain the text-centered, linguistically based chiastic structures of 1 Peter, and then I will provide preliminary indications of its unifying main theme of worship. In subsequent chapters I will present a comprehensive interpretation in accord with the chiastic structures, which illustrate and confirm that 1 Peter is encouraging its implied audience to remain firm in the worship of God for eternal life through the sufferings of Jesus Christ.

The Eleven Microchiastic Units of 1 Peter

In what follows I will first demonstrate how the text of 1 Peter naturally divides itself into eleven distinct literary units based upon their microchiastic structures as determined by very precise linguistic parallels found objectively in the text. Where applicable I will point out how other lexical and grammatical features often confirm the integrity of these units. Second, I will demonstrate how these eleven units form a macrochiastic pattern based upon very precise linguistic parallels found objectively in the text of the parallel chiastic units.[9] Third, I will point out the various transitional words

---

8. For discussions and past proposals for the main purpose and themes of 1 Peter, see Achtemeier, *1 Peter*, 64–66; Elliott, *1 Peter*, 103–9; Jobes, *1 Peter*, 42–53. None of the past proposals for the main concerns of 1 Peter focus on the dynamics of worship, as understood in its most comprehensive sense, to the extent that I am proposing in this study. My proposal is distinctive in its concerted focus upon all of the dimensions of worship operative in 1 Peter.

9. On the interpretive significance of chiastic structures, see Man, "Value of Chiasm," 146–57; Breck, "Biblical Chiasmus," 70–74.

that connect a unit to the unit that immediately precedes it. These various transitional words, which occur at the conclusion of one unit and at the beginning of the following unit, indicate that the chiastic units are heard as a cohesive sequence. These various transitional words are italicized in the translations of the units below.

1. Peace in Attaining the Salvation To Be Revealed by God (1:1-13)

In God and for Jesus Christ you are exulting[10]

A   1:1 Peter, apostle [ἀπόστολος] of Jesus Christ [Ἰησοῦ Χριστοῦ], to the chosen sojourners of the diaspora, of Pontus, Galatia, Cappadocia, Asia, and Bithynia, ² according to the foreknowledge of God the Father in [ἐν] the holiness [ἁγιασμῷ] of the Spirit [πνεύματος] for [εἰς] obedience and sprinkling of the blood of Jesus Christ [Ἰησοῦ Χριστοῦ]. May grace [χάρις] to you [ὑμῖν] and peace be multiplied! ³ Blessed the God and Father of our Lord Jesus Christ [Ἰησοῦ Χριστοῦ], who according to his great mercy has given us new birth for [εἰς] a living hope [ἐλπίδα] through the resurrection of Jesus Christ [Ἰησοῦ Χριστοῦ] from the dead, ⁴ for [εἰς] an inheritance imperishable and undefiled and unfading, kept in [ἐν] heaven [οὐρανοῖς] for you [εἰς ὑμᾶς], ⁵ who in [ἐν] the power of God are guarded through faith for [εἰς] a salvation [σωτηρίαν] ready to be revealed [ἀποκαλυφθῆναι] in [ἐν] the last time [καιρῷ]. ⁶ In [ἐν] whom you are exulting [ἀγαλλιᾶσθε], though briefly now [ἄρτι] if necessary, saddened in [ἐν] various trials,

B   ⁷ᵃ so that the refinement [δοκίμιον] of your faith,

     C   ⁷ᵇ more precious than gold that is passing away,

B′   ⁷ᶜ yet through fire is refined [δοκιμαζομένου],

A′   ⁷ᵈ may be found for [εἰς] praise and glory and honor at [ἐν] the revelation [ἀποκαλύψει] of Jesus Christ [Ἰησοῦ Χριστοῦ], ⁸ whom, not having seen, you love; for [εἰς] whom, now [ἄρτι] not seeing, but believing, you are exulting [ἀγαλλιᾶσθε] with a joy indescribable and glorified, ⁹ attaining the end of your faith, salvation [σωτηρίαν] of souls. ¹⁰ Concerning which salvation [σωτηρίας] prophets sought out and searched out, who, concerning the grace [χάριτος] that is for you [εἰς ὑμᾶς], having

---

10. The main heading of each unit is intended to summarize the unit as it relates to its parallel unit within the overall macrochiastic structure of the letter, while the subheading of each unit is intended to summarize or characterize the microchiastic dimension of each unit.

Introduction

prophesied, ¹¹ probing for [εἰς] what certain person or what sort of time [καιρόν] the Spirit [πνεῦμα] of Christ in [ἐν] them was indicating, testifying beforehand to the sufferings for [εἰς] Christ and the glories after these things, ¹² to whom it was revealed [ἀπεκαλύφθη] that not to themselves but to you [ὑμῖν] they were serving the very things which now have been announced to you [ὑμῖν] through those who proclaimed good news unto you [ὑμᾶς] by the Holy [ἁγίῳ] Spirit [πνεύματι] sent [ἀποσταλέντι] from heaven [οὐρανοῦ], for [εἰς] which things angels are longing to catch a glimpse. ¹³ Therefore, having girded up the loins of *your mind*, being sober, completely hope [ἐλπίσατε] upon the grace [χάριν] that is to be borne to you [ὑμῖν] at [ἐν] the revelation [ἀποκαλύψει] of Jesus Christ (Ἰησοῦ Χριστοῦ).¹¹

An A-B-C-B'-A' chiastic pattern secures the integrity and distinctness of this first unit (1:1–13). Several linguistic occurrences constitute the parallelism between the A (1:1–6) and A' (1:7d–13) elements of this chiasm. First of all, these elements contain the only occurrences in 1 Peter of expressions for being sent—"apostle" (ἀπόστολος) in 1:1 and "sent" (ἀποσταλέντι) in 1:12, and of the adverb "now"— ἄρτι in 1:6, 8.

And these elements contain the only occurrences in this unit of "Jesus Christ" in 1:1, 2, 3, 7, 13; of the preposition "in/at"—ἐν in 1:2, 4, 5, 6, 7, 11, 13; of "holiness" and "holy"— ἁγιασμῷ in 1:2 and ἁγίῳ in 1:12; of the "Spirit"—πνεύματος in 1:2, πνεῦμα in 1:11, and πνεύματι in 1:12; of "grace"— χάρις in 1:2, χάριτος in 1:10, and χάριν in 1:13; of the second person plural dative pronoun "you"—ὑμῖν in 1:2, 12, 13; of the preposition "for"—εἰς in 1:2, 3, 4, 5, 7d, 8, 10, 11, 12; of "hope"—ἐλπίδα in 1:3 and ἐλπίσατε in 1:13; of "heaven"—οὐρανοῖς in 1:4 and οὐρανοῦ in 1:12; of the second person plural accusative pronoun "you"—ὑμᾶς in 1:4, 10, 12; of "salvation"— σωτηρίαν in 1:5, 9 and σωτηρίας in 1:10; of "reveal"—ἀποκαλυφθῆναι in 1:5, ἀποκαλύψει in 1:7d, 13, and ἀπεκαλύφθη in 1:12; of "time"—καιρῷ in 1:5 and καιρόν in 1:11; and of "exult"—ἀγαλλιᾶσθε in 1:6, 8.¹²

The only occurrences in 1 Peter of cognate expressions for "refine"— "the refinement [δοκίμιον] of your faith" in 1:7a and "through fire is refined [δοκιμαζομένου]" in 1:7c—determine the parallelism between the B (1:7a)

---

11. The translation of this and all subsequent units is my own, presenting what I call an "exegetical" translation. The aim is to present a strictly literal translation that attempts, as far as possible, to follow the Greek word order and to render the same Greek words with the same English equivalents. The translation also attempts to render some of the alliterative dimensions of the Greek text when possible.

12. Some of these chiastic elements, especially the longer ones, form chiastic sub-units in themselves, which will be illustrated in the subsequent exegetical chapters of this study.

and the B′ (1:7c) elements. Finally, the unparalleled central and pivotal C (1:7b) element contains the only occurrences in 1 Peter of "more precious" (πολυτιμότερον) and "passing away" (ἀπολλυμένου).

2. Through Christ You Are Faithful for God with Purified Souls (1:14–25)

Through the risen and glorified Christ your faith and hope are for God

A   [14] As [ὡς] children of obedience [ὑπακοῆς], not being conformed, as before, in *your ignorance*, to the desires, [15] but, according to the Holy One who called you, become holy also yourselves in all conduct, [16] because [διότι] it is written, "You shall be holy, for I am holy" (Lev 19:2). [17] And if you call upon as Father the one who impartially judges according to the work of each one, in fear conduct the time of your sojourning, [18] knowing that not [οὐ] with perishable [φθαρτοῖς] things, silver or gold, have you been ransomed from your futile conduct inherited from fathers [19] but with the precious blood of Christ as [ὡς] of a lamb flawless and faultless, [20] foreknown before the foundation of the world but manifested at the last of these times for the sake of you,

B   [21a] who through him are faithful [πιστούς] for God [εἰς θεόν],

C   [21b] who raised him from the dead and gave him glory,

B′   [21c] so that your faith [πίστιν] and hope are for God [εἰς θεόν].

A′   [22] Your souls having purified in the obedience [ὑπακοῇ] to the truth for sincere brotherly affection, from a clean heart love one another constantly, [23] having been given new birth not [οὐκ] from a seed perishable [φθαρτῆς] but imperishable [ἀφθάρτου], through a living word of God, indeed abiding, [24] because [διότι] "*all* flesh is as [ὡς] grass and *all* its glory as [ὡς] a flower of the grass; the grass withers and the flower wilts; [25] but the pronouncement of the Lord abides for eternity" (Isa 40:6, 8). This is the pronouncement that was proclaimed as good news for you.

The expression "your ignorance" (ἀγνοίᾳ ὑμῶν) toward the beginning of this unit in 1:14 recalls its linguistically related antonym, "your mind" (διανοίας ὑμῶν), toward the conclusion of the preceding unit in 1:13. These expressions referring to the understanding of the audience, which occur only here in 1 Peter, serve as the transitional words linking the first unit (1:1–13) to the second unit (1:14–25).

An A-B-C-B′-A′ chiastic pattern secures the integrity and distinctness of this second unit (1:14–25). The following linguistic occurrences constitute the parallelism between the A (1:14–20) and A′ (1:22–25) elements of this chiasm: the only occurrences in this unit of the subordinating conjunction "as"—ὡς in 1:14, 19, 24(2x); of "obedience"—ὑπακοῆς in 1:14 and ὑπακοῇ in 1:22; of the subordinating conjunction "because"—διότι in 1:16, 24; and of expressions referring to what is not perishable—"not [οὐ] with perishable [φθαρτοῖς] things" in 1:18 and "not [οὐκ] from perishable [φθαρτῆς] but imperishable [ἀφθάρτου] seed" in 1:23. The only occurrences in this unit of expressions referring to faith and of the phrase "for God"—"faithful [πιστούς] for God [εἰς θεόν]" in 1:21a and "your faith [πίστιν] and hope are for God [εἰς θεόν]" in 1:21c—determine the parallelism between the B (1:21a) and the B' (1:21c) elements. Finally, the unparalleled central and pivotal C (1:21b) element contains the only occurrence in 1 Peter of the verb "raised"—"raised [ἐγείραντα] him from the dead."

3. Offer Up Spiritual Sacrifices Acceptable to God through Jesus Christ (2:1-17)

Keep your conduct among Gentiles praiseworthy that they may glorify God

A 2:1 Having removed then *all* evil [κακίαν] and *all* deceit and hypocrisies and envies and *all* slanders [καταλαλιάς], ² as [ὡς] newborn infants long for the pure milk of the word, so that by it you may grow up for salvation, ³ if you have tasted that benevolent is the Lord [κύριος] (Ps 33:9 LXX). ⁴ Before whom approaching, a living stone by human beings [ἀνθρώπων] rejected but in the sight of God chosen, esteemed, ⁵ also yourselves as [ὡς] living stones are being built up as a spiritual house for a holy priesthood to offer up spiritual sacrifices acceptable to God through Jesus Christ. ⁶ Because it stands in scripture, "Behold I am setting in Zion a stone, a cornerstone, chosen, esteemed, and whoever believes in it will never be put to shame" (Isa 28:16). ⁷ Its honor [τιμή] then is for you who believe, but for those who do not believe "the stone which the builders rejected, this has become the head of the corner" (Ps 117:22 LXX), ⁸ and "a stone of stumbling and rock of offense" (Isa 8:14). They stumble, disobeying the word, for which indeed they were set.
⁹ᵃ But you are a chosen race, a royal priesthood, a holy nation [ἔθνος],
B ⁹ᵇ a people [λαός] for possession,
  C ⁹ᶜ so that you may proclaim the virtues of the one who called you out of darkness for his marvelous light,
B' ¹⁰ who were once not a people [λαός] but now are God's people [λαός], who had not received mercy but now have received mercy.

A′ ⁱⁱ Beloved, I encourage you as [ὡς] aliens and sojourners to keep away from fleshly desires that are waging war against the soul, ¹² keeping your conduct among the Gentiles [ἔθνεσιν] praiseworthy, so that in what they slander [καταλαλοῦσιν] you as [ὡς] evildoers, observing from the praiseworthy works, they may glorify God on the day of visitation. ¹³ Be subject to every human institution on account of the Lord [κύριον], whether to a king as [ὡς] being in authority, ¹⁴ whether to governors as [ὡς] sent through him for the punishment of evildoers but the praise of good doers, ¹⁵ for thus it is the will of God that those doing good silence the ignorance of foolish human beings [ἀνθρώπων], ¹⁶ as [ὡς] free but not keeping freedom as [ὡς] a cover for evil [κακίας], but rather as [ὡς] slaves of God. ¹⁷ Honor [τιμήσατε] all, love the brotherhood, *fear* God, honor [τιμᾶτε] the king.

The triple occurrence of the adjective "all" at the beginning of this unit in 2:1—"having put away then all [πᾶσαν] evil and all [πάντα] deceit and hypocrisies and envies and all [πάσας] slanders"—echoes the double occurrence of the same adjective toward the conclusion of the preceding unit in 1:24—"all [πᾶσα] flesh is like grass and all [πᾶσα] its glory like a flower of the grass." These multiple occurrences of "all" serve as the transitional words linking the second unit (1:14–25) to the third unit (2:1–17).

An A-B-C-B′-A′ chiastic pattern secures the integrity and distinctness of this third unit (2:1–17). The following linguistic occurrences constitute the parallelism between the A (2:1–9a) and A′ (2:11–17) elements of this chiasm: the only occurrences in 1 Peter of the noun "evil"—"having removed then all evil [κακίαν]" in 2:1 and "not keeping freedom as a cover for evil [κακίας]" in 2:16; the only occurrences in this unit of "slander"—"all slanders [καταλαλιάς]" in 2:1 and "slander [καταλαλοῦσιν] you" in 2:12; of the subordinating conjunction "as"—ὡς in 2:2, 5, 11, 12, 13, 14, 16(3x); of "Lord"—"benevolent is the Lord [κύριος]" in 2:3 and "on account of the Lord [κύριον]" in 2:13; of "human beings"—"by human beings [ἀνθρώπων] rejected" in 2:4 and "the ignorance of foolish human beings [ἀνθρώπων]" in 2:15; of "honor"—"its honor [τιμή] then is for you" in 2:7, "honor [τιμήσατε] all" in 2:17, and "honor [τιμᾶτε] the king" in 2:17; of "nation/Gentiles"— "holy nation [ἔθνος]" in 2:9a and "among the Gentiles [ἔθνεσιν]" in 2:12.

The only occurrences in 1 Peter of "people"—"a people [λαός] for possession" in 2:9b and "who were once not a people [λαός] but now are God's people [λαός]" in 2:10—determine the parallelism between the B (2:9b) and the B′ (2:10) elements. Finally, the unparalleled central and pivotal C (2:9c) element contains the only occurrence in 1 Peter of the statement "so that

Introduction

you may proclaim the virtues of the one who called you out of darkness for his marvelous light."

4. Endure Unjust Suffering on account of a Conscience toward God (2:18-21a)

Enduring suffering for doing good is grace with God

A   ¹⁸ House servants being subject in all *fear* to masters, not only to the good and kind but also to the perverse. ^{19a} for this [τοῦτο] is grace [χάρις], if on account of a conscience toward God [θεοῦ] anyone bears up,
B   ^{19b} suffering [πάσχων] sorrows unjustly. ^{20a} For what credit is it if, sinning and being mistreated, you endure [ὑπομενεῖτε]?
B'   ^{20b} But if, doing good and *suffering* [πάσχοντες], you endure [ὑπομενεῖτε],
A'   ^{20c} this [τοῦτο] is grace [χάρις] in the sight of God [θεῷ], ^{21a} for to this [τοῦτο] you were called.

The noun "fear" at the beginning of this unit in 2:18—"house servants being subject in all fear [φόβῳ] to masters"—echoes the verb "fear" at the conclusion of the preceding unit in 2:17—"fear [φοβεῖσθε] God." These cognate terms for fear serve as the transitional words linking the third unit (2:1-17) to the fourth unit (2:18-21a).

An A-B-B'-A' chiastic pattern secures the integrity and distinctness of this fourth unit (2:18-21a). The following linguistic occurrences constitute the parallelism between the A (2:18-19a) and A' (2:20c-21a) elements of this chiasm: the only occurrences in this unit of the demonstrative pronoun "this," of "grace," and of "God"—"for this [τοῦτο] is grace [χάρις], if on account of a conscience toward God [θεοῦ]" in 2:19a and "this [τοῦτο] is grace [χάρις] in the sight of God [θεῷ], for to this [τοῦτο] you were called" in 2:20c-21a. And the only occurrences in this unit of the verb "suffering"— "suffering [πάσχων] sorrows unjustly" in 2:19b and "doing good and suffering [πάσχοντες]" in 2:20b—and in 1 Peter of the verb "you endure" (ὑπομενεῖτε) in 2:20a, 20b determine the parallelism between the B (2:19b-20a) and the B' (2:20b) elements at the pivotal center of this chiastic unit.

5. Christ Did No Sin or Deceit So That to Righteousness We Might Live (2:21b-25)

Christ offered up our sins so that having died to sins we might live to righteousness

A ²¹ᵇ For also Christ *suffered* on behalf of you [ὑμῶν], to you leaving a model that you may closely follow in his footsteps,
    B ²² "who did not do sin [ἁμαρτίαν] nor was deceit found in his mouth [ἐν τῷ στόματι αὐτοῦ]" (Isa 53:9),
        C ²³ who, being insulted did not return insult, suffering, he did not threaten, but handed himself over to the one who judges righteously,
    B' ²⁴ᵃ who the sins [ἁμαρτίας] of us he himself offered up in his body [ἐν τῷ σώματι αὐτοῦ] upon the tree, so that to sins [ἁμαρτίαις] having died, to righteousness we might live,
A' ²⁴ᵇ by whose wound you have been healed. ²⁵ For like sheep you were being led astray, but you have turned now to the shepherd and overseer of *your* [ὑμῶν] souls.

The verb "suffer" at the beginning of this unit in 2:21b—"Christ also suffered [ἔπαθεν] on behalf of you"—echoes the same verb toward the conclusion of the preceding unit in 2:20b—"doing good and suffering [πάσχοντες]." These successive occurrences of the verb "suffer" thus serve as the transitional words linking the fourth unit (2:18–21a) to the fifth unit (2:21b–25).

An A-B-C-B'-A' chiastic pattern secures the integrity and distinctness of this fifth unit (2:21b-25). The only occurrences in this unit of the second person plural genitive pronoun—"on behalf of you [ὑμῶν]" in 2:21b and "overseer of your [ὑμῶν] souls" in 2:25—constitute the parallelism between the A (2:21b) and A' (2:24b-25) elements of this chiastic unit. The only occurrences in this unit of the noun "sin"—"who did not do sin [ἁμαρτίαν]" in 2:22 and "who the sins [ἁμαρτίας] of us he himself offered up" in 2:24a, as well as the only occurrence in 1 Peter of the alliterative phrases "in his mouth [ἐν τῷ στόματι αὐτοῦ]" in 2:22 and "in his body [ἐν τῷ σώματι αὐτοῦ]" in 2:24a determine the parallelism between the B (2:22) and B' (2:24a) elements. Finally, the unparalleled central and pivotal C (2:23) element contains the only occurrence in 1 Peter of the statement "who, being insulted did not return insult, suffering, he did not threaten, but handed himself over to the one who judges righteously."

6. The Inner Human Being of the Heart Is of Great Value before God (3:1-7)

Honor wives as fellow heirs of the grace of life so that prayers are not hindered

A   3:1 Likewise [ὁμοίως], wives [γυναῖκες], being subject to their own husbands [ὑποτασσόμεναι τοῖς ἰδίοις ἀνδράσιν], so that even if some are disobeying the word, through the conduct of the wives [γυναικῶν] without a word they will be gained, ² observing *your* [ὑμῶν] conduct that is pure in fear [φόβῳ].

B   ³ Of whom let the adornment not be [ἔστω] the external one of braiding of hair and of wearing of gold things or of dressing in fine clothes,

C   ⁴ᵃ but rather the inner human being of the heart in the imperishableness of the gentle and quiet spirit,

B'   ⁴ᵇ which is [ἐστιν] before God of great value,

A'   ⁵ for thus formerly also the holy wives [γυναῖκες] who hoped for God adorned themselves, being subject to their own husbands [ὑποτασσόμεναι τοῖς ἰδίοις ἀνδράσιν], ⁶ as Sarah obeyed Abraham, calling him "lord," whose children you become, doing good and not fearing [φοβούμεναι] any intimidation. ⁷ The husbands [ἄνδρες] likewise [ὁμοίως], fellow dwellers according to knowledge as to the more delicate vessel, the feminine, showing honor as also to *fellow heirs* of the grace of life so that your [ὑμῶν] prayers may not be hindered.

The second person plural genitive pronoun toward the beginning of this unit in 3:2—"observing your [ὑμῶν] conduct"—recalls "overseer of your [ὑμῶν] souls" at the conclusion of the preceding unit in 2:25. These successive occurrences of the same form of the pronoun serve as the transitional words linking the fifth unit (2:21b-25) to the sixth unit (3:1-7).

An A-B-C-B'-A' chiastic pattern secures the integrity and distinctness of this sixth unit (3:1-7). The following linguistic occurrences constitute the parallelism between the A (3:1-2) and A' (3:5-7) elements of this chiasm: the only occurrences in this unit of the adverb "likewise" (ὁμοίως) in 3:1, 7; in 1 Peter of "wives" (γυναῖκες/γυναικῶν) in 3:1, 5; in 1 Peter of the clause "being subject to their own husbands" (ὑποτασσόμεναι τοῖς ἰδίοις ἀνδράσιν) in 3:1, 5; in this unit of the second person plural genitive pronoun "your" (ὑμῶν) in 3:2, 7; and in this unit of expressions for "fear"—"pure in fear [φόβῳ]" in 3:2 and "not fearing [φοβούμεναι] any intimidation" in 3:6. The only occurrences in this unit of the verb "to be"—"let the adornment not be [ἔστω] the external one" in 3:3 and "which is [ἐστιν] before God of great value" in 3:4b—determine the parallelism between the B (3:3) and B' (3:4b) elements. Finally, the unparalleled central and pivotal C (3:4a) element has a statement unique in 1 Peter—"but rather the inner human being of the heart in the imperishableness of the gentle and quiet spirit."

7. Do Not Speak Deceit or Do Evil But Do Good on account of Righteousness (3:8–17)

Hold holy the Christ as Lord in your hearts
by suffering for doing good if God wills it

A   **8** At the end, all [πάντες] harmonious, sympathetic, having brotherly affection, compassionate, humble, **9** not returning evil [κακόν] for evil [κακοῦ] or insult for insult, but instead blessing, **10** for to this you were called so that you might *inherit* a blessing, for let the one who wants [θέλων] to love life and see good [ἀγαθάς] days separate the tongue from evil [κακοῦ] and lips from speaking deceit, **11** let him turn away from evil [κακοῦ] and do [ποιησάτω] good [ἀγαθόν], let him seek peace and pursue it, **12** for the eyes of the Lord [κυρίου] are upon the righteous and his ears for their supplication, but the face of the Lord is [κυρίου] upon those doing [ποιοῦντας] evil [κακά] things (Ps 33:13–17 LXX). **13** And who is going to cause you evil [κακώσων], if for the good [ἀγαθοῦ] you become zealots?

B   **14a** But even if you should suffer on account of righteousness, you are blessed. But the fear [φόβον] for them

B'   **14b** do not fear [φοβηθῆτε] or be terrified,

A'   **15** but as Lord [κύριον] hold holy the Christ in your hearts, always ready for an answer to all [παντί] who ask you a word concerning the hope within you, **16** but with gentleness and fear, keeping a good [ἀγαθήν] conscience, so that when you are spoken against, shame may come against those mistreating your good [ἀγαθήν] in Christ conduct. **17** For it is better to *suffer* for doing good [ἀγαθοποιοῦντας], if the will of God wants [θέλοι] it, than for doing evil [κακοποιοῦντας].

The verb "you might inherit" (κληρονομήσητε) toward the beginning of this unit in 3:9 recalls its cognate noun "fellow heirs" (συγκληρονόμοις) at the conclusion of the preceding unit in 3:7. These successive occurrences of linguistically related expressions for "inherit/heirs" serve as the transitional words linking the sixth unit (3:1–7) to the seventh unit (3:8–17).

Introduction

An A-B-B'-A' chiastic pattern secures the integrity and distinctness of this seventh unit (3:8–17). The following linguistic occurrences constitute the parallelism between the A (3:8–13) and A' (3:15–17) elements of this chiasm: the only occurrences in this unit of "all"—πάντες in 3:8 and παντί in 3:15; in 1 Peter of the following expressions for "evil"—κακόν in 3:9, κακοῦ in 3:9, 10, 11, ποιοῦντας κακά in 3:12, κακώσων in 3:13, and κακοποιοῦντας in 3:17; in 1 Peter of the verb "wants"—"the one who wants [θέλων] to love life" in 3:10 and "if the will of God wants [θέλοι] it" in 3:17; in this unit of "good"—ἀγαθάς in 3:10, ποιησάτω ἀγαθόν in 3:11, ἀγαθοῦ in 3:13, ἀγαθήν twice in 3:16, and ἀγαθοποιοῦντας in 3:17; in this unit of "Lord"—κυρίου twice in 3:12 and κύριον in 3:15. The pivot between the noun and the cognate verb for "fear" in 3:14—"but the fear [φόβον] for them do not fear [φοβηθῆτε]"—determines the parallelism between the B (3:14a) and B' (3:14b) elements at the center of this chiastic unit.

8. The Saving Water of Baptism Is a Pledge of a Good Conscience for God (3:18–22)

Christ suffered to lead you to God through the saving water of baptism

A   [18] For also Christ [Χριστός] once concerning sins *suffered*, the righteous one on behalf of the unrighteous, so that he might lead you to God [θεῷ], having been put to death in the flesh [σαρκί], but having been brought to life in the Spirit, [19] in which, also to the spirits in prison having gone [πορευθείς], he made proclamation, [20] to those having disobeyed formerly when the patience of God [θεοῦ] awaited in the days of Noah as an ark was being furnished for the purpose of which a few, that is [ἔστιν] eight souls,

B   [20b] were saved [διεσώθησαν] through water,

B'   [21a] which also as an antitype of baptism now saves [σῴζει] you,

A'   [21b] not a removal of the dirt of flesh [σαρκός] but a pledge of a good conscience for God [θεόν], through the resurrection of Jesus *Christ* [Χριστοῦ], [22] who is [ἔστιν] at the right of God [θεοῦ], having gone [πορευθείς] into heaven, angels and authorities and powers having been subjected to him.

The verb "suffer" at the beginning of this unit in 3:18—"Christ also suffered [ἔπαθεν] once concerning sins"—echoes the same verb at the conclusion of the preceding unit in 3:17—"it is better to suffer [πάσχειν] for doing good." These successive occurrences of the verb "suffer" thus serve as the transitional words linking the seventh unit (3:8–17) to the eighth unit (3:18–22).

An A-B-B'-A' chiastic pattern secures the integrity and distinctness of this eighth unit (3:18–22). The following linguistic occurrences constitute the parallelism between the A (3:18–20a) and A' (3:21b-22) elements of this chiasm: the only occurrences in this unit of "Christ" in 3:18, 21; of "God" in 3:18, 20, 21, 22; of "flesh"—σαρκί in 3:18 and σαρκός in 3:21b; in 1 Peter of the aorist passive participle "having gone" (πορευθείς) in 3:19, 22; and in this unit of the verb "is" (ἐστιν) in 3:20a, 22. The only occurrences in this unit of verbs for "save"—"were saved [διεσώθησαν] through water" in 3:20b and "now saves [σῴζει] you" in 3:21a—determine the parallelism between the B (3:20b) and the B' (3:21a) elements at the pivotal center of this chiastic unit.

9. In All Things God May Be Glorified for Eternity through Jesus Christ (4:1–11)

In love live in accord with and glorify God through Jesus Christ

A   4:1 *Christ* [Χριστοῦ] then having suffered in the flesh, you also arm yourselves with the same attitude, for the one suffering in the flesh is separated from sin, ² so as not in the desires of human beings but in the will of God [θεοῦ], the in the flesh remaining time to spend, ³ for sufficient time has passed for you to accomplish the purpose of the Gentiles, having gone in debaucheries, desires, drunkenness, carousing, drinking bouts, and wanton idolatries, ⁴ in which they are surprised that you are not running together into the same flood of dissipation, as they go on blaspheming, ⁵ but they will return a word [of reckoning] to the one who keeps ready to judge the living and the dead, ⁶ for to this [purpose] even to the dead good news was proclaimed, so that though they were judged according to human beings in the flesh, they may live according to God [θεόν] in the Spirit.

  B   ⁷ The end of all things has come near. Be serious then and sober for prayers. ⁸ᵃ Above all things, keeping love [ἀγάπην] for each other constant,

  B'   ⁸ᵇ because love [ἀγάπη] covers a multitude of sins.

A'   ⁹ Be hospitable for one another without complaining, ¹⁰ just as each has received a gift, serving it for each other, as praiseworthy stewards of the varied grace of God [θεοῦ]. ¹¹ If anyone speaks—as sayings of God [θεοῦ], if anyone serves—as from the strength which God [θεός] supplies, so that in all things God [θεός] may be glorified through Jesus *Christ* [Χριστοῦ], to whom is the glory and the might for the ages of the ages, amen!

Introduction

The term "Christ" at the beginning of this unit in 4:1—"Christ [Χριστοῦ] then having suffered in the flesh"—recalls the same term toward the conclusion of the preceding unit in 3:21—"through the resurrection of Jesus Christ [Χριστοῦ]." These successive occurrences of the same form of the term "Christ" thus serve as the transitional words linking the eighth unit (3:18-22) to the ninth unit (4:1-11).

An A-B-B'-A' chiastic pattern secures the integrity and distinctness of this ninth unit (4:1-11). The only occurrences in this unit of "Christ" (Χριστοῦ) in 4:1, 11 and of "God"—θεοῦ in 4:2, 10, 11, θεόν in 4:6, and θεός twice in 4:11—constitute the parallelism between the A (4:1-6) and the A' (4:9-11) elements of this chiasm. And the only occurrences in this unit of the noun "love"—"keeping love [ἀγάπην] for each other constant" in 4:8a and "because love [ἀγάπη] covers a multitude of sins" in 4:8b—determine the parallelism between the B (4:7-8a) and the B' (4:8b) elements at the pivotal center of this chiastic unit.

10. The Suffering Entrust to the Faithful Creator Their Souls in Doing Good (4:12-19)

Glorify God for suffering in the name of Christ

A   ¹² Beloved, do not be surprised at the burning among you, occurring to you for a trial, as if something strange were happening to you, ¹³ but to the degree that you are sharing in the sufferings of the *Christ* rejoice, so that at the revelation of his glory [δόξης] you may rejoice, exulting. ¹⁴ If you are reproached in the name [ὀνόματι] of Christ, blessed are you, because the Spirit of glory [δόξης] and of God [θεοῦ] rests upon you.

B   ¹⁵ᵃ For do not [μή] let anyone of you suffer

C   ¹⁵ᵇ as [ὡς] a murderer or thief or evildoer or as [ὡς] a troublemaker.

C'   ¹⁶ᵃ But if as [ὡς] a Christian

B'   ¹⁶ᵇ do not [μή] be ashamed,

A'   ¹⁶ᶜ let him glorify [δοξαζέτω] God [θεόν] in this name [ὀνόματι], ¹⁷ because it is the time to begin the judgment from the house of God [θεοῦ]. If the first is from us, what is the end for those disobeying the gospel of God [θεοῦ]? ¹⁸ "And if the righteous one is with difficulty saved, where will the ungodly and sinful one appear?" (Prov 11:31 LXX). ¹⁹ So then let those who are *suffering* according to the will of God [θεοῦ] entrust to the faithful Creator their souls in good-doing.

The term "Christ" toward the beginning of this unit in 4:13—"the sufferings of the Christ [Χριστοῦ]"—recalls the same term at the conclusion of the preceding unit in 4:11—"through Jesus Christ [Χριστοῦ]." These successive occurrences of the same form of the term "Christ" thus serve as the transitional words linking the ninth unit (4:1–11) to the tenth unit (4:12–19).

An A-B-C-C'-B'-A' chiastic pattern secures the integrity and distinctness of this tenth unit (4:12–19). The following linguistic occurrences constitute the parallelism between the A (4:12–14) and A' (4:16c–19) elements of this chiasm: the only occurrences in this unit of the noun "glory" and its cognate verb "glorify"—"at the revelation of his glory [δόξης]" in 4:13, "the Spirit of glory [δόξης]" in 4:14, and "let him glorify [δοξαζέτω] God" in 4:16c; in 1 Peter of the noun "name" (ὀνόματι) in 4:14, 16c; and in this unit of "God"—θεοῦ in 4:14, twice in 4:17, and in 4:19, and θεόν in 4:16c. The only occurrences in this unit of the particle "not"—"do not [μή] let anyone of you suffer" in 4:15a and "do not [μή] be ashamed" in 4:16b—determine the parallelism between the B (4:15a) and the B' (4:16b) elements. Finally, the pivot between the occurrences of the subordinating conjunction "as"— "as [ὡς] a murderer or thief or evildoer or as [ὡς] a troublemaker" in 4:15b and "as [ὡς] a Christian" in 4:16a—establish the parallelism between the C (4:15b) and C' (4:16a) elements at the center of this chiastic unit.

11. Peace in Attaining the Eternal Glory To Be Revealed by God (5:1–14)

The true grace of God for which you are to remain firm in Christ

A   5:1 The elders then among you [ὑμῖν] I encourage [παρακαλῶ], as a fellow elder and witness [μάρτυς] of the *sufferings* [παθημάτων] of Christ [Χριστοῦ], and a sharer in the glory [δόξης] that is going to be revealed, ² shepherd the flock of God among you [ὑμῖν], overseeing not as under compulsion but willingly according to God, not for shameful profit but eagerly, ³ not as lording it over the ones allotted, but becoming examples to the flock, ⁴ and when the chief shepherd is manifested, you will attain the unfading crown of the glory [δόξης]. ⁵ᵃ Likewise, you who are younger, be subjected to the elders.

B   ⁵ᵇ And all of you clothe yourselves with humility [ταπεινοφροσύνην] toward one another, for "God opposes [ἀντιτάσσεται] the proud but to the humble [ταπεινοῖς] gives grace" (Prov 3:34 LXX).

B'   ⁶ Be humbled [ταπεινώθητε] then under the mighty hand of God, so that he may exalt you in time, ⁷ casting all your anxiety upon him, because from him there is care concerning you. ⁸ Be sober, be watchful. Your opponent [ἀντίδικος] the devil, roaring like a lion, is

Introduction

    going around seeking someone to devour, [9a] whom you are to oppose [ἀντίστητε], as strong in the faith,

A' [9b] knowing that the same kinds of sufferings [παθημάτων] are being undergone by your brotherhood throughout the world. [10] The God of all grace, who called you for his eternal glory [δόξαν] in Christ [Χριστῷ] Jesus, after you have suffered briefly, will himself restore, confirm, strengthen, establish. [11] To him be the might for the ages, amen! [12] Through Silvanus, to you [ὑμῖν] the faithful brother, as I reckon, through a few things I have written, encouraging [παρακαλῶν] and bearing witness [ἐπιμαρτυρῶν] that this is the true grace of God for which you are to remain firm. [13] The chosen together in Babylon greet you and Mark my son. [14] Greet one another with a kiss of love. Peace to you [ὑμῖν] all who are in Christ [Χριστῷ].

    The noun "suffering" at the beginning of this unit in 5:1—"the sufferings [παθημάτων] of Christ"—resonates with the verb "suffer" at the conclusion of the preceding unit in 4:19—"those who are suffering [πάσχοντες] according to the will of God." These successive occurrences of cognate expressions for suffering thus serve as the transitional words linking the tenth unit (4:12-19) to the eleventh unit (5:1-14).

    An A-B-B'-A' chiastic pattern secures the integrity and distinctness of this final eleventh unit (5:1-14). The following linguistic occurrences constitute the parallelism between the A (5:7-9a) and A' (5:10-11) elements of this chiasm: the only occurrences in this unit of the second person dative plural pronoun "you" (ὑμῖν) in 5:1, 2, 12, 14; of the verb "encourage"—"I encourage" (παρακαλῶ) in 5:1 and "encouraging" (παρακαλῶν) in 5:12; in 1 Peter of cognate expressions for "witness"—"witness [μάρτυς] of the sufferings of Christ" in 5:1 and "bearing witness [ἐπιμαρτυρῶν] that this is the true grace of God" in 5:12; in 1 Peter of the genitive plural "sufferings" (παθημάτων) in 5:1, 9b; in this unit of "Christ"—Χριστοῦ in 5:1 and Χριστῷ in 5:10, 14; and in this unit of "glory"—δόξης in 5:1, 4 and δόξαν in 5:10.

    And the following linguistic occurrences determine the parallelism between the B (5:5b) and B' (5:6-9a) elements at the pivotal center of this chiastic unit: the only occurrences in 1 Peter of expressions for "humility/humble"—"with humility [ταπεινοφροσύνην] toward one another" and "to the humble" (ταπεινοῖς) in 5:5b, "be humbled" (ταπεινώθητε) in 5:6; and of expressions for "oppose/opponent"—"God opposes [ἀντιτάσσεται] the proud" in 5:5b, "your opponent [ἀντίδικος] the devil" in 5:8, and "whom you are to oppose [ἀντίστητε]" in 5:9a.

1 Peter, 2 Peter, and Jude

The Macrochiastic Structure of 1 Peter

Having illustrated the sequence of the various microchiastic structures operative in the eleven distinct units of 1 Peter, I will now demonstrate how these eleven main units form an A-B-C-D-E-F-E'-D'-C'-B'-A' macrochiastic structure unifying and organizing the entire letter.

A: *Peace* in *Attaining* the Salvation *To Be Revealed* by God (1:1-13)
A': *Peace* in *Attaining* the Eternal Glory *To Be Revealed* by God (5:1-14)

Repetitions of several significant terms indicate the parallelism between the opening A unit (1:1-13) and the closing A' unit (5:1-14) within the macrochiastic structure of 1 Peter. The A' unit commences with the author's description of himself as "a sharer in the glory that is going to be revealed [ἀποκαλύπτεσθαι]" (5:1). This resonates with the author's description in the A unit of the prophets as those "to whom it was revealed [ἀπεκαλύφθη] that not to themselves but to you they were serving the very things which now have been announced to you" (1:12) and of the audience as those "who in the power of God are protected through faith for a salvation ready to be revealed [ἀποκαλυφθῆναι] in the last time" (1:5). That these are the only occurrences in 1 Peter of the verb "reveal" enhances the distinctiveness of this chiastic parallelism.

Furthermore, the A and A' units contain the only occurrences in 1 Peter of the verb "attain"—"attaining [κομιζόμενοι] the end of your faith" (1:9) and "you will attain [κομιεῖσθε] the unfading crown of the glory" (5:4), and of the adverb "briefly"—"though briefly [ὀλίγον] now if necessary, saddened in various trials" (1:6) and "after you have suffered briefly [ὀλίγον]" (5:10). The final greeting from "the chosen together [συνεκλεκτή] in Babylon" (5:13) at the conclusion of the A' unit resonates with the description of the letter's recipients as "the chosen [ἐκλεκτοῖς] sojourners of the diaspora" (1:1) at the beginning of the A unit.[13] And finally, the A and A' units contain the only occurrences in 1 Peter of the noun "peace" in a prayer greeting—"may grace to you and peace [εἰρήνη] be in abundance" (1:2) and "peace [εἰρήνη] to you all in Christ" (5:14).[14]

B: Through Christ You Are *Faithful* for God with Purified *Souls* (1:14-25)
B': The Suffering Entrust Their *Souls* to the *Faithful* Creator in Doing Good (4:12-19)

Repetitions of the terms "faithful" and "souls" provide the chiastic parallels between the B (1:14-25) and the B' (4:12-19) units. The B' unit concludes

---

13. The adjective "chosen" (ἐκλεκτός) occurs also in 2:4, 6, 9.

14. The only other occurrence of the noun "peace" in 1 Peter is in 3:11, but not in a prayer greeting.

with the exhortation that "those who are suffering according to the will of God entrust their souls to the faithful Creator in good-doing" (4:19). The reference to God as "the faithful [πιστῷ] Creator" recalls the only previous occurrence in 1 Peter of the adjective "faithful" in the description of the audience as those "who through him [Christ] are faithful [πιστούς] for God" in the B unit (1:21).[15] And the B and B' units contain the only occurrences in 1 Peter of the noun "souls" in the accusative plural—"having purified your souls [ψυχάς]" (1:22) and "entrust their souls [ψυχάς]" (4:19).[16]

    C: Offer Up Spiritual Sacrifices Acceptable to God *through Jesus Christ* (2:1-17)

    C': In All Things God May Be Glorified for Eternity *through Jesus Christ* (4:1-11)

Repetitions of the phrase "through Jesus Christ" and of the terms "nation/Gentiles," "desires," and "human beings" provide the chiastic parallels between the C (2:1-17) and the C' (4:1-11) units. The statement "that in all things God may be glorified through Jesus Christ [διὰ Ἰησοῦ Χριστοῦ]" (4:11) in the C' unit recalls and resonates with the only other occurrence in 1 Peter of "through Jesus Christ" in the C unit—"to offer spiritual sacrifices acceptable to God through Jesus Christ [διὰ Ἰησοῦ Χριστοῦ]" (2:5). And the C and C' units contain the only occurrences in 1 Peter of the term "nation/Gentiles"—"a holy nation [ἔθνος]" (2:9), "keeping your conduct among the Gentiles [ἔθνεσιν] praiseworthy" (2:12), and "to accomplish the purpose of the Gentiles [ἐθνῶν]" (4:3).

The double occurrence of the noun "desires [ἐπιθυμίαις]" (4:2, 3) in the C' unit recalls and resonates with the previous occurrence in 1 Peter of this noun in the C unit—"fleshly desires [ἐπιθυμῶν] that are waging war against the soul" (2:11).[17] And finally, the C and C' units contain the only occurrences in 1 Peter of the term "human beings" in the plural. The "desires of human beings [ἀνθρώπων]" (4:2) and "judged according to human beings [ἀνθρώπους] in the flesh" (4:6) in the C' unit recall and resonate with "a living stone by human beings [ἀνθρώπων] rejected" (2:4) and "the ignorance of foolish human beings [ἀνθρώπων]" (2:15) in the C unit.[18]

    D: Endure Unjust Suffering on account of a *Conscience* toward *God* (2:18-21a)

    D': The Saving Water of Baptism Is an Pledge of a Good *Conscience* for *God* (3:18-22)

---

15. There is a subsequent occurrence of the adjective "faithful" in 5:12.
16. Other forms of the noun "soul" occur in 1:9; 2:11, 25; 3:20.
17. The only other occurrence of the noun "desires" in 1 Peter is in 1:14.
18. The term "human being" occurs in the singular in 3:4.

1 Peter, 2 Peter, and Jude

The only occurrences in 1 Peter of expressions involving a conscience that is explicitly oriented toward God provide the chiastic parallels between the D (2:18–21a) and the D' (3:18–22) units. "A pledge of a good conscience [συνειδήσεως] for God [εἰς θεόν]" (3:21) in the D' unit recalls and resonates with "on account of a conscience toward God [συνείδησιν θεοῦ]" (2:19) in the D unit.[19]

> E: Christ *Did* No Sin or *Deceit* So That to *Righteousness* We Might Live (2:21b–25)
>
> E': Do Not Speak *Deceit* or *Do* Evil But *Do* Good on account of *Righteousness* (3:8–17)

Repetitions of the verb "do," of the nouns "deceit" and "righteousness," as well as of expressions involving not returning insults provide the chiastic parallels between the E (2:21b–25) and the E' (3:8–17) units. "Not returning evil for evil or insult for insult [λοιδορίαν ἀντὶ λοιδορίας]" (3:9) in the E' unit recalls and resonates with the only other occurrence in 1 Peter of an expression of not returning an insult—"who (Christ), being insulted did not return insult [λοιδορούμενος οὐκ ἀντελοιδόρει]" (2:23) in the E unit. "Let him do [ποιησάτω] good" (3:11) and "doing [ποιοῦντας] evil things" (3:12) in the E' unit recall and resonate with the only other occurrence of the verb "do" in 1 Peter in the E unit—"who did not do [ἐποίησεν] sin" (2:22). And the E and E' units contain the only occurrences in 1 Peter of the noun "righteousness"—"to righteousness [δικαιοσύνῃ] we might live" (2:24) and "on account of righteousness [δικαιοσύνην]" (3:14), as well as the final two occurrences in 1 Peter of the noun "deceit"—"nor was deceit [δόλος] found in his mouth" (2:22) and "lips from speaking deceit [δόλον]" (3:10).[20]

> F: The Inner Human Being of the Heart Is of Great Value before God (3:1–7)

The F unit (3:1–7) functions as the unparalleled central and pivotal unit within the macrochiastic structure of 1 Peter. As the only unit in 1 Peter dealing with the relationship between wives and their husbands, this central unit provides the pivot from the model of the suffering Christ in the E unit (2:21b–25) to the exhortation for the audience to adopt Christ's model of suffering in the E' unit (3:8–17).

---

19. The expression "good conscience" occurs in 3:16 but without an explicit reference to God.

20. The only other occurrence of the noun "deceit" in 1 Peter is in 2:1.

Introduction

Outline of the Macrochiastic Structure of 1 Peter

A: 1:1-13: *Peace* in *Attaining* the Salvation *To Be Revealed* by God
　B: 1:14-25: Through Christ You Are *Faithful* for God with Purified *Souls*
　　C: 2:1-17: Offer Up Spiritual Sacrifices Acceptable to God *through Jesus Christ*
　　　D: 2:18-21a: Endure Unjust Suffering on account of a *Conscience* toward *God*
　　　　E: 2:21b-25: Christ *Did* No Sin or *Deceit* So That to *Righteousness* We Might Live
　　　　　F: 3:1-7: The Inner Human Being of the Heart Is of Great Value before God
　　　　E': 3:8-17: Do Not Speak *Deceit* or *Do* Evil But *Do* Good on account of *Righteousness*
　　　D': 3:18-22: The Saving Water of Baptism Is a Pledge of a Good *Conscience* for *God*
　　C': 4:1-11: In All Things God May Be Glorified for Eternity *through Jesus Christ*
　B': 4:12-19: The Suffering Entrust Their *Souls* to the *Faithful* Creator in Doing Good
A': 5:1-14: *Peace* in *Attaining* the Eternal Glory *To Be Revealed* by God

Preliminary Indications of Worship as the Main Theme of 1 Peter

As mentioned above, the subtitle chosen for 1 Peter, "worship for life through the sufferings of Jesus Christ," articulates what I am proposing as the main theme of 1 Peter. In this section I will present an introductory overview of the indications that worship, understood in its most comprehensive and dynamic sense as including not only liturgical but ethical worship, serves as the main theme that organizes and unifies the whole of 1 Peter.[21]

First of all, as a circular letter addressed "to the chosen sojourners of the diaspora, of Pontus, Galatia, Cappadocia, Asia, and Bithynia" (1:1), 1 Peter was intended to be publicly read throughout these five regions of Asia Minor to communities gathered together as worshiping assemblies. That 1 Peter was an epistolary homily or sermon meant to encourage and exhort

---

21. For a brief consideration of worship in 1 Peter, see Borchert, *Worship*, 189-97. Past theories proposing that 1 Peter is a baptismal liturgy have been convincingly rejected by recent commentators; see Witherington, *Letters*, 47.

worshiping assemblies is indicated by the author's statement of the letter's purpose. He has written the letter, "encouraging and bearing witness that this is the true grace of God for which you are to remain firm" (5:12).[22] As I will show later, the letter presents "the true grace of God" as the motivation for its audiences to maintain their worship of God even in the midst of and through their sufferings. That 1 Peter was intended to be listened to by audiences gathered for worship is confirmed by its concluding directive to "greet one another with a kiss of love" (5:14), a ritualistic gesture usually performed within a context of worship.[23]

Second, the author of 1 Peter performs acts of worship within the letter itself. After the epistolary prescript (1:1–2a), the author pronounces a prayer greeting for the audience: "May grace to you and peace be multiplied!" (1:2b). The letter concludes with a similar prayer greeting, "Peace to you all in Christ!" (5:14), thus enveloping 1 Peter within a framework of prayer on behalf of the audience. After the introductory prayer greeting, with another act of epistolary worship, the author draws the audience and all believers into a benediction of God: "Blessed the God and Father of our Lord Jesus Christ, who according to his great mercy having given us new birth for a living hope through the resurrection of Jesus Christ from the dead" (1:3). Twice the author leads the audience in communal doxologies: "God may be glorified through Jesus Christ, to whom is the glory and the might for the ages of the ages, amen!" (4:11) and "to him be the might of the ages, amen!" (5:11). Furthermore, the letter's cultic terminology, hymnlike formulations, and OT citations and allusions add to its worship character.[24]

22. "The consistency and coherence of its language, style, themes, arrangement, and line of argumentation indicate that 1 Peter from the outset was conceived, composed, and dispatched as an integral, genuine letter.... The hortatory aim (5:12) and mood of 1 Peter, along with its inclusion of much hortatory and parenetic material clearly qualify it as a 'parenetic/hortatory letter', where 'parenetic' refers to its aim and mood (hortatory)" (Elliott, *1 Peter*, 11).

23. "The fact that such a liturgical kiss later became a regular part of the eucharistic celebration may indicate such was the setting that the author envisioned for the public reading of this letter. Yet since worship would normally be the only time a Christian community assembled, one could suppose a context of that sort for the reading of the letter whether or not the liturgical kiss was a part of the eucharistic celebration at this time" (Achtemeier, *1 Peter*, 356). "The author's encouragement of this greeting may suggest the presumption that the letter would be read during a worship assembly. Reference to the kiss in combination with the reading of letters, probably during the worship assembly, is found already in 1 Cor 16:19–20 and 1 Thess 5:26–27; cf. also Acts 20:37" (Elliott, *1 Peter*, 891).

24. On the cultic terminology in 1 Peter, see Mbuvi, *Temple*, 70–126. "The liturgical tradition, like the Christological and kerygmatic traditions and OT citations and allusions, was cited to affirm the concepts, traditions, and practices that the senders and recipients had *in common* and thus to demonstrate and affirm the *bonds of belief*

Introduction

And third, an overview of the concepts key to the subtitle chosen for 1 Peter provide additional preliminary indications of this letter's prevalent concern for the dynamics of worship. The letter begins by designating its audience as recipients of the grace of God that motivates their worship. They are sojourners of the diaspora chosen according to the foreknowledge of God the Father (1:1-2a). After the initial greeting that prays for an abundance of this "grace" (χάρις) from God (1:2b), the audience are led to bless God in an act of worship motivated by the grace whose preeminent content is the "new birth for a living hope through the resurrection of Jesus Christ from the dead," a grace which God has given to all believers (1:3). The grace of God (1:2, 10, 13; 3:7; 4:10; 5:5, 10) not only motivates, but can be an expression of the worship of God: "But if, doing good and suffering, you endure, this is grace [χάρις] in the sight of God" (2:20; cf. 2:19). The letter was written to encourage and bear witness "that this is the true grace [χάριν] of God" for which its audience are to remain firm in and through their worship (5:12).

Another aspect of this "grace of life [χάριτος ζωῆς]" (3:7), God's gift of new birth (1:3, 23) for the risen, eternal life of Jesus Christ, is the "glory" (δόξαν) God gave the Christ whom he raised from the dead (1:21), the "eternal glory [δόξαν]" (5:10) that is the focus of the "living hope [ἐλπίδα ζῶσαν]" (1:3) for the risen, eternal life of Christ motivating worship in 1 Peter. Similar to "grace," the "glory" given by God not only motivates (1:7, 11; 4:13, 14; 5:1, 4, 10), but can be an expression of the worship of God: "God may be glorified [δοξάζηται] through Jesus Christ, to whom is the glory [δόξα] and the might for the ages of the ages, amen!" (4:11; cf. 2:12; 4:16). Thus, "worship for life" in 1 Peter means that worship has the grace (1:13) and eternal glory (5:10) of the risen, eternal life of Christ as both its motivation and ultimate goal.

That the sufferings of Christ function as both a model and means for worship indicates that the worship of God for life is "through the sufferings of Jesus Christ." According to 1 Peter, Christ "suffered" (ἔπαθεν) as a model to be followed (2:21; cf. 4:1). By "suffering [πάσχων]" (2:23), he performed an act of cultic worship as he offered up our sins as a sacrifice (2:24; cf. 3:18), providing the model and means for the ethical worship of the audience as "a holy priesthood to offer spiritual sacrifices acceptable to God through Jesus Christ" (2:5). Sharing in the "sufferings" (παθήμασιν) of Christ (cf. 1:11; 5:1, 9, 10) enables the audience to perform the liturgical worship of rejoicing now, so that at the future and final revelation of his glory they may rejoice, "exulting [ἀγαλλιώμενοι]" (4:13) as the complement of their

---

and worship that united the Christians in Rome with those in Asia Minor [emphases original]" (Elliott, *1 Peter*, 35).

present worship—"you are exulting [ἀγαλλιᾶσθε]" (1:6, 8). If anyone in the audience should "suffer [πασχέτω]" (4:15) as a Christian, such an individual may thereby perform the ethical worship of "glorifying" (δοξαζέτω) God in this name (4:16).

These preliminary indications that "worship for life through the sufferings of Jesus Christ" expresses the main theme and concern embracing the whole of 1 Peter will be confirmed by the remainder of my exegetical investigation into its chiastic structures in the chapters to follow.

Summary

1. There are eleven distinct units in 1 Peter with each exhibiting its own microchiastic structure.

2. The eleven units comprising 1 Peter operate as a macrochiastic structure with five pairs of parallel units and with the pivot of the entire macrochiastic structure occurring as the unparalleled central F unit in 3:1–7.

3. That 1 Peter was heard by its audiences in a setting of worship, contains epistolary acts of worship with references to liturgical traditions, uses cultic terminology, and is concerned with language and concepts involving the dynamics of both liturgical and ethical worship provide preliminary indications for worship as its main organizing and unifying theme. More specifically, the subtitle, "worship for life through the sufferings of Jesus Christ," expresses the central focus and main concern of 1 Peter.

2

1 Peter 1:1–13
Peace in Attaining the Salvation To Be Revealed by God (A)

In God and for Jesus Christ you are exulting

A   1:1 Peter, *apostle* of *Jesus Christ*, to the chosen sojourners of the diaspora, of Pontus, Galatia, Cappadocia, Asia, and Bithynia, ² according to the foreknowledge of God the Father *in* the holiness of the *Spirit for* obedience and sprinkling of the blood of *Jesus Christ*. May *grace* to *you* and peace be multiplied! ³ Blessed the God and Father of our Lord *Jesus Christ*, who according to his great mercy has given us new birth *for* a living *hope* through the resurrection of *Jesus Christ* from the dead, ⁴ *for* an inheritance imperishable and undefiled and unfading, kept *in* heaven *for you*, ⁵ who *in* the power of God are guarded through faith *for* a *salvation* ready to be *revealed in* the last *time*. ⁶ *In* whom you are *exulting*, though briefly *now* if necessary, saddened *in* various trials,

B   ⁷ᵃ so that the *refinement* of your faith,

C   ⁷ᵇ more precious than gold that is passing away,

B'   ⁷ᶜ yet through fire is *refined*,

A'   ⁷ᵈ may be found *for* praise and glory and honor *at* the *revelation* of *Jesus Christ*, ⁸ whom, not having seen, you love; *for* whom, *now* not seeing, but believing, you are *exulting* with a joy indescribable and glorified, ⁹ attaining the end of your faith, *salvation* of souls. ¹⁰ Concerning which *salvation* prophets sought out and searched out, who, concerning the *grace* that is *for you*, having prophesied, ¹¹ probing *for* what certain person or what sort of *time* the *Spirit* of Christ *in* them was indicating, testifying beforehand to the sufferings *for* Christ and the glories after these things,

¹² to whom it was *revealed* that not to themselves but to *you* they were serving the very things which now have been announced to *you* through those who proclaimed good news unto you by the Holy *Spirit sent* from *heaven, for* which things angels are desiring to catch a glimpse.
¹³ Therefore, having girded up the loins of your mind, being sober, completely *hope* upon the *grace* that is to be borne to *you at* the *revelation* of *Jesus Christ*.¹

Audience Response to 1:1–13

1:1–6 (A): Grace of New Birth to You for a Living Hope Through Jesus Christ

The audience hear the A element (1:1–6) of this chiastic unit as a chiastic pattern in itself:²

a) Peter, apostle of *Jesus Christ*, to the chosen sojourners of the diaspora, of Pontus, Galatia, Cappadocia, Asia, and Bithynia, *according* to the foreknowledge of *God* the *Father* in the holiness of the Spirit *for* obedience and sprinkling of the blood of *Jesus Christ* (1:1–2a).

b) May grace to you and peace be multiplied! (1:2b).

a') Blessed the *God* and *Father* of our Lord *Jesus Christ*, who *according* to his great mercy has given us new birth *for* a living hope through the resurrection of *Jesus Christ* from the dead, *for* an inheritance imperishable and undefiled and unfading, kept in heaven *for* you, who in the power of *God* are guarded through faith *for* a salvation ready to be revealed in the last time. In whom you are exulting, though briefly now if necessary, saddened in various trials (1:3–6).

The audience hear the prayer greeting, "May grace to you and peace be multiplied" (1:2b), as the unparalleled central and pivotal sub-element in this chiastic sub-unit. They then experience a pivot of parallels involving the only occurrences in this sub-unit of several terms. They hear the following progressions of chiastic parallels from the a) (1:1–2a) to the a') (1:3–6) sub-element: from "apostle of Jesus Christ [Ἰησοῦ Χριστοῦ]" (1:1) and "blood of Jesus Christ [Ἰησοῦ Χριστοῦ]" (1:2a) to "our Lord Jesus Christ [Ἰησοῦ Χριστοῦ]" (1:3) and "the resurrection of Jesus Christ [Ἰησοῦ Χριστοῦ]"

---

1. For the establishment of 1 Pet 1:1–13 as a chiasm, see ch. 1.

2. As mentioned previously in the first chapter, the term "audience" will be used throughout the work as a collective plural noun, since in the Greek text plural terms are used in reference to the audience, who are conceived of as a group composed of individual members with responsibilities toward one another.

1 Peter 1:1-13

(1:3); from "according [κατά] to the foreknowledge of God [θεοῦ] the Father [πατρός]" (1:2) to "blessed the God [θεός] and Father [πατήρ] . . . according [κατά] to his great mercy" (1:3) and "the power of God [θεοῦ]" (1:5); and from "for [εἰς] obedience" (1:2a) to "for [εἰς] a living hope" (1:3), "for [εἰς] an inheritance" (1:4), "for [εἰς] you" (1:4), and "for [εἰς] a salvation" (1:5). The audience hear the a) sub-element (1:1-2a) of this chiastic sub-unit (1:1-6) as yet another chiastic pattern in itself:

(a) Peter, apostle of *Jesus Christ*, to the chosen sojourners of the diaspora, of Pontus, Galatia, Cappadocia, Asia, and Bithynia (1:1),
(b) according to the foreknowledge of God the *Father* (1:2a)
(b') in the holiness of the *Spirit* (1:2b)
(a') for obedience and sprinkling of the blood of *Jesus Christ* (1:2c).

At the center of this chiastic sub-unit the audience experience a pivot of parallels involving the only occurrences in this sub-unit of alliterative expressions for divine persons. They hear a progression from "God the Father [πατρός]" in the (b) sub-element (1:2a) to "holiness of the Spirit [πνεύματος]" in the (b') sub-element (1:2b). They then experience a progression of parallels involving the only occurrences in this sub-unit of "Jesus Christ." "Apostle of Jesus Christ [Ἰησοῦ Χριστοῦ]" in the (a) sub-element (1:1) progresses to "blood of Jesus Christ [Ἰησοῦ Χριστοῦ]" in the (a') sub-element (1:2c).

This letter, a hortatory homily to be publicly read to a worshiping assembly, presents itself as sent by "Peter," describing himself as "apostle of Jesus Christ" (1:1). Undoubtedly this refers to the Simon Peter who, according to the Gospels, was a brother of Andrew (Matt 4:18; Mark 1:16; Luke 6:14; John 1:40) and who became the leader of the twelve apostles chosen by Jesus (Matt 10:2; Mark 3:16; Luke 6:14; John 6:68-70). This "Peter" is the implied author of the letter. Whether or not the historical Peter was the actual author, his apostolic authority and status stand behind the letter.[3] As

---

3. See the commentaries for discussions of the authorship of 1 Peter. "The number of prominent interpreters who continue to favor pseudonymous authorship may suggest that the issue has been settled. Although the case against Peter's authorship may at one time have seemed 'overwhelming,' it no longer appears to be so. Because the evidence used against Petrine authorship is not conclusive and because of further evidence that points the letter to the lifetime of Peter, many other prominent interpreters believe that an amanuensis wrote under Peter's personal direction" (Jobes, *1 Peter*, 19). On the role of Silvanus, named at 1 Pet 5:12, in the writing of the letter, Witherington (*Letters*, 50) notes: "It is difficult to judge how much Silvanus contributed to what we have here, but since he is not claimed as an 'author' *even at this juncture* (here Peter says, 'I wrote . . .'), we may assume that at most he simply played the role of scribe or amanuensis so far as the composition of the document is concerned. He may in addition have been its deliverer and interpreter" (emphasis original). See also Richards, "Silvanus," 417-32; Sargent, "Chosen," 117-20.

an "apostle" of, that is, one sent by, Jesus Christ, "Peter," the sender of this letter, functions as an authoritative representative of Jesus Christ himself.

The letter is sent to an audience characterized as "the chosen sojourners of the diaspora, of Pontus, Galatia, Cappadocia, Asia, and Bithynia" (1:1). The audience are thus led to realize and acknowledge that they are temporary "sojourners" (παρεπιδήμοις) in these five regions of Asia Minor, which represent neither the origin nor ultimate goal of their permanent residence.[4] They are to recognize that as "chosen" (ἐκλεκτοῖς) sojourners of the "diaspora" (διασπορᾶς) they are residing among non-Christian Gentiles in areas distinct from their true homeland as members of the chosen people of God.[5] That they have been chosen "according to the foreknowledge of God the Father" (1:2a) informs them that they, as chosen sojourners of the diaspora, have a role to play in the predetermined plan of God as Father of all.

The audience are to appreciate that they have been divinely chosen to play this role of being sojourners of the diaspora "in the holiness of the Spirit" (1:2b). While they reside physically as sojourners of the diaspora in Asia Minor, they are to realize that God has chosen them to be spiritually within the realm or sphere determined by the "holiness" or "sanctification" (ἁγιασμῷ) of God's Spirit. This indicates that they are to conduct themselves in a manner that demonstrates their separation and distinction from the secular, profane society of the diaspora, as those divinely chosen to be consecrated and dedicated to God by means of the holiness of God's own Spirit. Being within the realm of the holiness of the Spirit thus implies both their worthiness and responsibility to worship God as diaspora sojourners chosen to be God's holy people.

Finally, the audience are encouraged and exhorted that as sojourners of the diaspora they have been divinely chosen "for obedience and sprinkling of the blood of Jesus Christ" (1:2c). They have been chosen "for" (εἰς), that is, for the purpose or goal of being beneficiaries of both the obedience and sprinkling of the blood of Jesus Christ as divine gifts.[6] Through "obedience" (ὑπακοήν) to God's will as an act of ethical worship pleasing to God, Jesus Christ offered up his body in death as a sacrifice that resulted in the

---

4. On the possibility that the audiences to whom Peter writes were Christians from Rome who were deported to Roman colonies in Asia Minor in the first century, see Jobes, *1 Peter*, 28–41. On 1 Peter as a "diaspora letter," see Doering, "First Peter," 215–36.

5. "By drawing an analogy between the Jewish Diaspora and the situation of his readers, he [Peter] implies they should understand themselves as Christians in terms of God's people of the old covenant who were foreigners in the lands to which they had been scattered. The Diaspora experience provides a perspective through which they are to frame their experiences" (Jobes, *1 Peter*, 59).

6. For a recent refutation that the preposition εἰς means the cause ("by") rather than the goal ("for") of divine election, see Page, "Obedience," 291–98.

1 Peter 1:1-13

"sprinkling of blood" (ῥαντισμὸν αἵματος) as an act of cultic worship effecting atonement for and purification from sins.⁷ The encouragement of these divine benefits of Jesus Christ's obedience and sprinkling of blood also implies an exhortation for the audience to likewise worship and please God by their own obedience, even if it means suffering to the point of sprinkling their own blood.⁸ That Peter is an apostle of "Jesus Christ" (1:1) adds his apostolic authority and status to the assertion that his audiences were divinely chosen for the obedience and sprinkling of the blood of "Jesus Christ."

Peter's initial prayer greeting for the audience, "May grace to you and peace be multiplied!" (1:2d), confirms and reinforces the grace they have already received as sojourners chosen (1:1) according to the foreknowledge of God the Father (1:2a) in the holiness of God's Spirit (1:2b) for the divine benefits of the obedience and sprinkling of the blood of Jesus Christ (1:2c). It also prays for a future increase not only of this divine "grace" (χάρις) but of the "peace" (εἰρήνη) that is a further aspect of this grace. The prayer for the divine gift of peace, a comprehensive concept in the biblical tradition connoting an overall harmony and peace with God and fellow human beings, resonates with the peace implied as a result of the atonement and purification effected by the obedience and sprinkling of the blood of Jesus Christ. The audience hear the (a′) sub-element (1:3-6) of this chiastic sub-unit (1:1-6) as yet another chiastic pattern in itself:

[a] Blessed the *God* and Father of our Lord Jesus Christ, who according to his great mercy has given us new birth *for* a living hope *through* the resurrection of Jesus Christ from the dead, *for* an inheritance imperishable (1:3-4a),

[b] and *undefiled* (1:4b)

[b′] and *unfading* (1:4c),

[a′] kept in heaven *for* you, who in the power of *God* are guarded *through* faith *for* a salvation ready to be revealed in the last time. In whom

---

7. The sacrificial obedience and sprinkling of the blood of Jesus Christ receive fuller description in 2:21-24. "In the same way that the blood of the animals established the purification necessary for the connection with God, so now the blood of Jesus purifies the believers, enabling them to establish the new connection to God. And while the OT sacrifices and sprinkling took place on the altar at the sanctuary, the sacrifice of Jesus is on the cross (1.18-19) and the 'sprinkling' is on those that make up the new 'spiritual house' (2.5), the eschatological dwelling place of God" (Mbuvi, *Temple*, 74).

8. "In 1 Peter, Christ's subordination to God's will (2:22-23; 3:18) will serve as a model for the obedience enjoined upon his followers (1:14, 17, 22; 2:15, 17, 18-25; 3:14, 16; 5:2, 6)" (Elliott, *1 Peter*, 320). As Donelson (*I & II Peter*, 27) notes, "the only other reference to Christ's blood in 1 Peter clearly refers to atonement (1:18-19). Furthermore, given the constant call to suffering in the letter, it is difficult not to hear echoes of that suffering in the reference to blood. 'Sprinkling of the blood of Jesus Christ' may occur in the abuse that Christians endure when they follow in his footsteps (2:21)."

you are exulting, though briefly now if necessary, saddened in various trials (1:4d-6).

At the center of this chiastic sub-unit the audience experience a pivot of parallels involving the only occurrences in this sub-unit of alliterative expressions describing the inheritance. They hear a progression from "undefiled" (ἀμίαντον) in the [b] sub-element (1:4b) to "unfading" (ἀμάραντον) in the [b'] sub-element (1:4c). They then experience a progression of parallels involving the only occurrences in this sub-unit of "God" and the prepositions "for" and "through." "Blessed the God [θεός] and Father . . . for [εἰς] a living hope through [δι'] the resurrection . . . for [εἰς] an inheritance imperishable" in the [a] sub-element (1:3-4a) progresses to "kept in heaven for [εἰς] you, who in the power of God [θεοῦ] are guarded through [διά] faith for [εἰς] a salvation" in the [a'] sub-element (1:4d-6).

After the prayer greeting, an act of worship on the part of Peter, for an increase of grace and peace for the audience (1:2d), Peter then draws the audience into an act of communal worship, a benediction praising God for the grace not only the audience but all Christians have received.[9] It begins by declaring "blessed the God and Father of our Lord Jesus Christ" (1:3), thus praising the God who is not only the "Father" according to whose foreknowledge the audience were chosen to be sojourners of the diaspora (1:1-2), but "Father" of "our"—of Peter, the audience, and all Christians— Lord Jesus Christ. The benediction thus leads the audience to acknowledge that the Jesus Christ of whom Peter is an apostle (1:1), and for whose obedience and sprinkling of blood the audience were divinely chosen (1:2c), is the authoritative divine "Lord" to whom all Christians owe their obedience.

The audience, chosen to be sojourners of the diaspora (1:1) "according" (κατά) to the foreknowledge of God the Father (1:2a), are to bless the God and Father, who "according" (κατά) to his great mercy has given "us"—Peter, the audience, and all Christians—"new birth for a living hope through the resurrection of Jesus Christ from the dead" (1:3).[10] Whereas the audience were chosen "for" (εἰς) the purpose of receiving the divine grace of the obedience and sprinkling of the blood of Jesus Christ (1:2c), the audience, along with all

---

9. "To call God 'blessed' is not to make a theological pronouncement but to offer up to him one's praise" (Michaels, *1 Peter*, 15). "[I]t is important not to forget that the benediction is a *benediction*. Right from the start, the epistle's theology is placed in the context of *worship* . . . This worship is rooted in gratitude to God for his many gracious gifts, which the author catalogs [emphases original]" (Dryden, *Theology*, 86).

10. Miller, "Resurrection," 132-40. On "has given new birth" (ἀναγεννήσας), Dubis (*1 Peter*, 6) notes: "Although grammatically this is an adjectival participle, semantically it functions as a ground for the preceding mitigated command, i.e., the recipients should praise God because he has brought them to new life." On the metaphor of "new birth" here, see Green, *1 Peter*, 26-30.

Christians, have been given a new birth "for" (εἰς) the purpose of receiving the divine grace of a living hope through the resurrection of Jesus Christ from the dead. This "new birth" whose purpose and goal is a "living hope" thus gives the audience a hope that is "living" (ζῶσαν) because it is the hope of living the risen, eternal life of Jesus Christ.[11] As an epistolary act of worship, this benediction, then, begins to indicate that 1 Peter is concerned with the worship of God for life through the sufferings of Jesus Christ.[12]

This new birth given by God is "for" (εἰς) the goal not only of a living hope through the resurrection of Jesus Christ from the dead (1:3), but "for" (εἰς) the goal of an inheritance that is imperishable and undefiled and unfading, kept in heaven, whose goal is "for" (εἰς) you (1:4). This heavenly inheritance is surely for all Christians, but the audience, as chosen sojourners of the diaspora (1:1) and thus without an earthly inheritance, are especially to appreciate the heavenly inheritance which is emphatically "for you." Following upon the expressions "for" (εἰς) the obedience and sprinkling of the blood of Jesus Christ (1:2c), "for" (εἰς) a living hope (1:3), and "for" (εἰς) an inheritance (1:4a), the expression "for [εἰς] you" (1:4c) emphatically underlines that the audience, as chosen sojourners of the diaspora, are among the beneficiaries who are the intended goal for these divine gifts. The triple description of the immortal, pure, and permanent aspects of this heavenly inheritance as "imperishable and undefiled and unfading" indicates that it refers to the audience's share in the eternal, risen life of Jesus Christ.[13]

The audience, chosen sojourners of the diaspora (1:1) "in" (ἐν) the holiness of God's Spirit (1:2b) for an inheritance kept by God "in" (ἐν) heaven for them (1:4), are to appreciate that they are also "in" (ἐν) the power of God being guarded through faith for a salvation ready to be revealed by God "in" (ἐν) the last time (1:5). They are being guarded by and within the realm of the power of the God to be blessed for having given Christians

11. "The phrase 'through the resurrection of Jesus Christ' is linked most immediately with 'living hope,' thereby explaining the basis for and enlivened quality of Christian hope" (Elliott, *1 Peter*, 334). "[T]he word 'living' connects the hope to the resurrection" (Schreiner, *1, 2 Peter*, 62).

12. On 1 Pet 1:1-3 as the programmatic introduction to the entire letter, see Tite, "Compositional Function," 47-56.

13. "This 'inheritance' became in ancient Judaism, as also in early Christianity, a metaphor for the eschatological substance of salvation consisting of (eternal) life. The specification of the inheritance here through the three attributes formed with an α-*privativum* and also its formation of a parallel with the 'living hope' are consistent with this" (Feldmeier, *First Letter*, 71). "The three Greek adjectives modifying 'inheritance,' namely ἄφθαρτον ('imperishable'), ἀμίαντον ('undefiled'), and ἀμάραντον ('unfading'), form an alliterative triad of terms. Such alliterations occur frequently in this letter and are one example of the author's literary refinement; see also 1:6, 9–11a, 19; 2:12, 15, 18–20, 21; 3:17; 4:4" (Elliott, *1 Peter*, 335).

new birth for a living hope "through" (δι᾽) the resurrection of Jesus Christ from the dead (1:3). And it is "through" (διά) faith in the God whose power raised Jesus Christ from the dead that the audience are being guarded for a salvation from death to eternal life. The audience are thus to appreciate that, as sojourners of the diaspora chosen "for" (εἰς) obedience and sprinkling of the blood of Jesus Christ (1:2c), "for" (εἰς) a living hope (1:3), "for" (εἰς) an imperishable inheritance (1:4) kept in heaven "for" (εἰς) you (1:4), they are being guarded "for" (εἰς) a salvation to the eternal, risen life of Jesus Christ ready to be revealed by God at the last time.[14]

Peter impresses upon the audience that the God they have been led to bless in worship (1:3), as the God "in" (ἐν) whose power they are being guarded through faith for eschatological salvation (1:5), is the God "in [ἐν] whom you are exulting [ἀγαλλιᾶσθε]" as the focus of their worship (1:6a).[15] The audience may engage in the joyful worship of exulting in God, even though briefly now if necessary in accord with God's will, they are saddened in various trials (1:6b). Indeed, the audience, as chosen sojourners of the diaspora (1:1) "in" (ἐν) the holiness of God's Spirit (1:2b) for an inheritance kept by God "in" (ἐν) heaven for them (1:4), who "in" (ἐν) the power of God are guarded through faith for a salvation to be revealed by God "in" (ἐν) the last time (1:5), may continue to joyfully worship the God "in" (ἐν) whom they are exulting. And they may do so even though being briefly saddened now "in" (ἐν) the various trials that are a necessary part of God's salvific plan (1:6).[16]

1:7a (B): The Refinement of Your Faith

The audience begin to hear the divine purpose for their various trials (1:6) explained: "so that the refinement of your faith" (1:7a). As those who through

---

14. Feldmeier, "Salvation," 203-13; Williams, *Salvation*.

15. Although technically the antecedent of the prepositional phrase ἐν ᾧ at the beginning of 1:6 could be "in the last time" (ἐν καιρῷ ἐσχάτῳ) at the end of 1:5, this reference to a future time does not cohere well with the present tense of the verb "you are exulting" (ἀγαλλιᾶσθε). Furthermore, if "in the last time" were intended as the antecedent, one would expect this to be made clear by repeating the word "time" in 1:6—ἐν ᾧ καιρῷ, just as the antecedent of the phrase "concerning which" (περὶ ἧς) in 1:10 is made clear by repeating "salvation" from 1:9 (so Selwyn, *First Epistle*, 126). More likely the antecedent of the prepositional phrase ἐν ᾧ in 1:6 is "God" (θεοῦ) at the beginning of 1:5. "Similar syntax in the LXX argues against an adverbial sense for this prepositional phrase, especially in the Psalms, where the verb ἀγαλλιᾶσθε is often found with ἐν, which phrase expresses the grounds of the rejoicing, in this case represented by the relative pronoun ᾧ" (Jobes, *1 Peter*, 92).

16. "The idea is that the sufferings believers experience are not the result of fate or impersonal forces of nature. They are the will of God for believers" (Schreiner, *1, 2 Peter*, 67).

1 Peter 1:1-13

their "faith" (πίστεως) in the God who has the power to save them (1:5) from death for a new birth to the risen, eternal life of Jesus Christ (1:3), the audience are to be encouraged that their various trials are actually leading to something quite valuable—the refinement of their "faith" (πίστεως) in God.

1:7b (C): More Precious Than Gold That Is Passing Away

The refinement of the faith of the audience (1:7a) through their various trials (1:6) is "more precious than gold that is passing away" (1:7b). The comparison of the refinement of their faith as more precious than gold that is "passing away" or "perishing" (ἀπολλυμένου) and thus not lasting for eternity implies that such refinement is most precious precisely because it gives faith a quality oriented toward their new birth to eternal life (1:3). The audience are to appreciate that the precious refinement of their faith through their various trials will give them a faith with an enduring quality appropriate for the eternal inheritance being kept by God in heaven for them. The eternal character of this inheritance, which is unlike perishable gold, is emphatically underlined by means of an alliterative triplet of adjectives—it is "imperishable and undefiled and unfading [ἄφθαρτον καὶ ἀμίαντον καὶ ἀμάραντον]" (1:4).

1:7c (B'): Yet Through Fire Is Refined

The audience are reminded that the precious metal of gold, even though it is passing away (1:7b), "yet through fire is refined" (1:7c). At this point, after the unparalleled and central C element of this chiastic unit, "more precious than gold that is passing away" (1:7b), the audience experience a pivot of parallels from the B (1:7a) to the B' (1:7c) element. The "refinement" (δοκίμιον) of their faith progresses to the gold that through fire is "refined" (δοκιμαζομένου). The audience are thus to be encouraged that their various divinely necessary trials (1:6) are tantamount to the "fire" through which their faith is being refined into something more eternally precious in the sight of God than gold that is passing away.[17]

---

17. "The comparison in this verse, with its emphasis on the perishable (ἀπολλυμένου) nature of gold, implies an argument from the lesser to the greater: if perishable, and hence less valuable, gold must be so tested, how much more must faith, which is imperishable and hence of greater value. The emphasis here is not on faith itself so much as on the nature of the faith that results from such trials. It is that tested and proved character (δοκίμιον) of faith which is more precious (πολυτιμότερον) than gold and which brings approval from God at the last judgment" (Achtemeier, *1 Peter*, 102).

1 Peter, 2 Peter, and Jude

1:7d–13 (A'): Hope upon the Grace for You at the Revelation of Jesus Christ

The audience hear the A' element (1:7d–13) of this chiastic unit as a chiastic pattern in itself:

a) may be found for praise and *glory* and honor *at the revelation of Jesus Christ*, whom, not having seen, you love; *for whom*, now not seeing, but believing, you are exulting with a joy indescribable and *glorified*, attaining the end of your faith, salvation of souls (1:7d–9).

  b) *Concerning* which salvation *prophets* sought out and searched out (1:10a),

  b') who, *concerning* the grace that is for you, having *prophesied* (1:10b),

a') probing for what certain person or what sort of time the Spirit of *Christ* in them was indicating, testifying beforehand to the sufferings for *Christ* and the *glories* after these things. To whom it was revealed that not to themselves but to you they were serving the very things which now have been announced to you through those who proclaimed good news unto you by the Holy Spirit sent from heaven, *for which things* angels are desiring to catch a glimpse. Therefore, having girded up the loins of your mind, being sober, completely hope upon the grace that is to be borne to you *at the revelation of Jesus Christ* (1:11–13).

At the center of this chiastic sub-unit the audience experience a pivot of parallels involving the only occurrences in this sub-unit of "concerning" and in 1 Peter of "prophets/prophesy." They hear a progression from "concerning [περί] which salvation prophets [προφῆται] sought out" in the b) sub-element (1:10a) to "who, concerning [περί] the grace that is for you, having prophesied [προφητεύσαντες]" in the b') sub-element (1:10b). They then experience a progression of parallels involving the only occurrences in 1 Peter of "at the revelation of Jesus Christ [ἐν ἀποκαλύψει Ἰησοῦ Χριστοῦ]" (1:7d, 13), and in this sub-unit of "glory/glorified," of the preposition "for" with a relative pronoun, and of "Christ." "Glory [δόξαν]" (1:7d), "glorified [δεδοξασμένῃ]" (1:8), and "for whom [εἰς ὄν]" (1:8) in the a) sub-element (1:7d–9) progress to "glories [δόξας]" (1:11), "for which things [εἰς ἅ]" (1:12), "Spirit of Christ [Χριστοῦ]" (1:11), and "sufferings for Christ [Χριστόν]" (1:11) in the a') sub-element (1:11–13).

At this point the audience experience progressions, via the chiastic parallels, from the A (1:1–6) to the A' (1:7d–13) element of this chiastic unit. First of all, there is a key verbatim repetition of a verb involving worship: from "in whom [God] you are exulting [ἀγαλλιᾶσθε]" (1:6) to "for whom [Christ] . . . you are exulting [ἀγαλλιᾶσθε]" (1:8).

1 Peter 1:1-13

Then there are progressions of other terms: from "apostle [ἀπόστολος]" (1:1) to "sent [ἀποσταλέντι]" (1:12); from "apostle of Jesus Christ" (1:1), "blood of Jesus Christ" (1:2), "Lord Jesus Christ" (1:3), and "resurrection of Jesus Christ" (1:3) to "revelation of Jesus Christ" (1:7d, 13); from "holiness [ἁγιασμῷ] of the Spirit [πνεύματος]" (1:2)" to "Spirit [πνεῦμα] of Christ" (1:11), and "Holy [ἁγίῳ] Spirit [πνεύματι]" (1:12); from "grace [χάρις] to you" (1:2) to "concerning the grace [χάριτος]" (1:10), and "upon the grace [χάριν]" (1:13); from "living hope [ἐλπίδα]" (1:3) to "completely hope [ἐλπίσατε]" (1:13); from "in heaven [οὐρανοῖς]" (1:4) to "from heaven [οὐρανοῦ]" (1:12); from "salvation [σωτηρίαν]" (1:5) to "salvation [σωτηρίαν] of souls" (1:9), and "concerning which salvation [σωτηρίας]" (1:10); from "ready to be revealed [ἀποκαλυφθῆναι]" (1:5) to "it was revealed [ἀπεκαλύφθη]" (1:12), and "at the revelation [ἀποκαλύψει]" (1:7d, 13); from "in the last time [καιρῷ]" (1:5) to "what sort of time [καιρόν]" (1:11); and from "briefly now [ἄρτι]" (1:6) to "now [ἄρτι] not seeing" (1:8).

Noteworthy also are the progressions involving prepositions and the second person plural dative and accusative pronouns: from "in [ἐν] the holiness" (1:2), "in [ἐν] heaven" (1:4), "in [ἐν] the power" (1:5), "in [ἐν] the last time" (1:5), "in [ἐν] whom" (1:6), and "in [ἐν] various trials" (1:6) to "at [ἐν] the revelation" (1:7d, 13), and "in [ἐν] them" (1:11); from "for [εἰς] obedience" (1:2), "for [εἰς] a living hope" (1:3), "for [εἰς] an inheritance" (1:4), "for [εἰς] you" (1:4), and "for [εἰς] a salvation" (1:5) to "for [εἰς] praise" (1:7d), "for [εἰς] whom" (1:8), "for [εἰς] you" (1:10), "for [εἰς] what certain person" (1:11), "for [εἰς] Christ" (1:11), and "for [εἰς] which things" (1:12); from "grace to you [ὑμῖν]" (1:2) to "but to you [ὑμῖν]" (1:12), "announce to you [ὑμῖν]" (1:12), and "borne to you [ὑμῖν]" (1:13); and from "for you [ὑμᾶς]" (1:4) to "for you [ὑμᾶς]" (1:10) and "proclaimed good news unto to you [ὑμᾶς]" (1:12).[18]

The audience hear the a) sub-element (1:7d-9) of this chiastic sub-unit (1:7d-13) as yet another chiastic pattern in itself:

(a) may be found for praise and *glory* and honor at the revelation of Jesus Christ (1:7d),

(b) *whom*, not having *seen*, you love (1:8a);

(b') for *whom*, now not *seeing*, but believing, you are exulting with a joy indescribable (1:8b)

(a') and *glorified*, attaining the end of your faith, salvation of souls (1:8c-9).

At the center of this chiastic sub-unit the audience experience a pivot of parallels involving the only occurrences in this sub-unit of the accusative masculine singular relative pronoun "whom" and of the verb "see." "Whom

---

18. For a stylistic analysis of the uses of the prepositions εἰς and ἐν in 1 Pet 1:1-12, see Dupont-Roc, "Le jeu de prépositions," 201-12.

[ὄν], not having seen [ἰδόντες]" in the (b) sub-element (1:8a) progresses to "for whom [ὄν], now not seeing [ὁρῶντες]" in the (b') sub-element (1:8b). They then experience a progression of parallels involving the only occurrences in this sub-unit of cognate expressions for "glory"—from "glory" (δόξαν) in the (a) sub-element (1:7d) to "glorified" (δεδοξασμένῃ) in the (a') sub-element (1:8c-9).

The audience, who in the power of God are guarded through faith for a salvation ready to be revealed in the last time (1:5), are to be encouraged that the refinement of their faith (1:7a) in and through various trials (1:6) is so that it "may be found for praise and glory and honor at the revelation of Jesus Christ" (1:7d). The refinement of their faith "may be found" (εὑρεθῇ) by and before God (divine passive) "for" (εἰς) their praise, glory, and honor, as those chosen "for" (εἰς) the salvation from death to eternal life (1:3) ready to be "revealed" (ἀποκαλυφθῆναι) "in" (ἐν) the last time (1:5), "at" (ἐν) the "revelation" (ἀποκαλύψει) of Jesus Christ himself (1:7d).[19] The triplet of "praise" (ἔπαινον) and "glory" (δόξαν) and "honor" (τιμήν) God will give the audience in the end-time judgment at the revelation of Jesus Christ is simultaneously the praise, glory, and honor the audience's refinement of faith through the suffering of their trials will render to God as an act of worship.[20] In other words, God's approval at the last judgment of the refinement of the audience's faith through their sufferings will amount to worship pleasing to God.

The affirmation of the audience's love for the Jesus Christ whom they have not seen (1:8a) is motivated by the same divine gifts that are motivating their worship of the God in whom they are exulting (1:6). The person of

---

19. "The words 'may be found' refer to the final judgment when God examines the life of each person" (Schreiner, *1, 2 Peter*, 68). "The formulation is a divine passive indicating God as subject" (Elliott, *1 Peter*, 342). "The verb 'find' is used of the way in which people and their qualities are laid bare before God at the judgment and publicly shown to be of a certain kind" (Marshall, *1 Peter*, 41). "ἐν ἀποκαλύψει Ἰησοῦ Χριστοῦ is the personalized equivalent of 'the salvation about to be revealed at the last day' (v 5). The revealing of that salvation is the revealing of Jesus Christ himself (cf. v 13). The assumption of this epistle is not that Jesus is absent from his people, so that he must 'come.' Rather, he is present with them but invisible; therefore he must 'be revealed'" (Michaels, *1 Peter*, 32).

20. In the biblical tradition "praise," "glory," and "honor" can be given by God to human beings or by human beings to God; see BDAG, 257-58, 357, 1005. "It is God who crowns genuine faith with 'praise, glory, and honor' at the last day (cf. 5:4). Each term can be used either for that which human beings offer to God or for that which God confers on them. Because of the way in which God is understood in this epistle (and in the NT generally), the two alternatives are not to be set against each other but to be regarded as two sides of a single coin.... In honoring he is honored, in glorifying he receives glory, and in praising he is praised. There is a certain ambiguity in the three unmodified nouns, 'praise, glory, and honor,' with the hint of a double reference that cannot be overlooked" (Michaels, *1 Peter*, 31).

Jesus Christ represents the essential element and central focus of this divine grace. As sojourners of the diaspora, the audience have been chosen (1:1) to be recipients of the divine gift of the obedience and sprinkling of the blood of Jesus Christ (1:2). God has given them new birth for a living hope through the resurrection of Jesus Christ from the dead (1:3). And in the power of God they are being guarded through faith for a salvation to eternal life ready to be revealed (1:5) at the revelation of the Jesus Christ (1:7d) presently unable to be seen by the audience who nevertheless love him.

The Jesus Christ whom the audience, though not having seen, love (1:8a) is the one "for whom, now not seeing, but believing, you are exulting with a joy indescribable and glorified" (1:8b). The audience briefly "now" (ἄρτι) are saddened in various trials (1:6), as they are "now" (ἄρτι) not yet seeing the Jesus Christ to be revealed in the last time (1:5, 7d).[21] That they are nevertheless "believing" (πιστεύοντες) reaffirms the "faith" (πίστεως) through which they are being guarded for a salvation to be revealed in the last time (1:5). The refinement of their "faith" (πίστεως) in and through their various trials (1:6) will result in praise and glory and honor both as God's approval of them and as their worship of God at the revelation of Jesus Christ (1:7).

The audience's present worship of the God "in whom [ἐν ᾧ] you are exulting [ἀγαλλιᾶσθε]" (1:6) has been motivated by the divine grace given them as sojourners of the diaspora chosen (1:1) "for [εἰς] obedience and sprinkling of the blood of Jesus Christ" (1:2). And their worship has also been motivated by the new birth given to them as Christians by God "for" (εἰς) a living hope through the resurrection of Jesus Christ from the dead (1:3). The goals of this worship are "for" (εἰς) an inheritance kept in heaven and destined "for" (εἰς) you (1:4), "for" (εἰς) a salvation ready to be revealed in the last time (1:5), and "for" (εἰς) praise and glory and honor at the revelation of Jesus Christ (1:7d). Now the audience are to realize that the Jesus Christ "whom" (ὅν) they love without seeing (1:8a) represents, as the fundamental basis central to all these divine gifts, the ultimate goal of their

---

21. "Peter's intent is simply to make a generalization about the experience of all Christian believers. None of them (himself included) have ever seen Jesus Christ in the way they will see him at the time when he is revealed . . . but why the repetition of the theme of not seeing Jesus? . . . The real distinction in the two participles is perhaps that οὐκ ἰδόντες points to what is necessarily and universally the case—i.e., that Christ and the salvation he brings are hidden from human view until the moment of his revelation—while ἄρτι μὴ ὁρῶντες focuses more specifically on the 'various ordeals' (v 6) now confronting Peter and his readers. The phrase ἄρτι μὴ ὁρῶντες recalls the ὀλίγον ἄρτι . . . λυπηθέντες of v 6: the trials facing the Christian community are as burdensome as they are because Christ the Deliverer is not yet in sight" (Michaels, *1 Peter*, 32-33).

worship—"for whom" (εἰς ὅν) "you are exulting [ἀγαλλιᾶσθε] with a joy indescribable and glorified" (1:8b).²²

As the audience's worship of exulting "in" (ἐν) God (1:6) is further elaborated as an exulting "for" (εἰς) the Jesus Christ whom they love, it is intensified as an exulting "with a joy indescribable and glorified" (1:8). That their worship of exulting is accompanied by a joy that is humanly "indescribable" or "inexpressible" (ἀνεκλαλήτῳ) underlines that this joyful exultation is motivated by and oriented toward divine, heavenly gifts transcending what can be observed or articulated in human, earthly terms. And that the joy of this exultation is also "glorified" (δεδοξασμένῃ) by God (divine passive) underscores that it is motivated by and oriented toward the "glory" (δόξαν) to be given by and to God at the revelation of Jesus Christ (1:7d).²³

While they are exulting "in" God and "for" Jesus Christ (1:6-8), the audience are to appreciate that they are "attaining the end of your faith, salvation of souls" (1:9). As those who are "believing" (πιστεύοντες), the audience are attaining the end or goal of their "faith" (πίστεως), their "faith" (πίστεως) that is being refined so that it "may be found for praise and glory and honor at the revelation of Jesus Christ" (1:7). In the power of God the audience are being guarded through "faith" (πίστεως) "for a salvation [σωτηρίαν] ready to be revealed in the last time" (1:5). It is this "salvation [σωτηρίαν] of souls," the salvation of their persons from death to risen, eternal life, that the audience are in the process of attaining, as they are engaged in the worship of exulting for Jesus Christ (1:8), whose resurrection from the dead (1:3) provides the basis for this salvation to be fully attained at the final revelation of Jesus Christ (1:7d).²⁴

---

22. "Although the verb ἀγαλλιάομαι ('exult,' 'be glad,' 'be overjoyed') is unattested outside the Bible and the Christian literature, it is used frequently in the Psalms (41x) to express the jubilation of the individual or the worshiping community over the experience of God's goodness and mercy" (Elliott, *1 Peter*, 343).

23. "The glory that these Christians will enjoy at the revelation of Jesus Christ is already shining in this rejoicing" (Donelson, *I & II Peter*, 35).

24. "The sense is that Christians now obtain by faith what they will only fully enter into at the end; the power of the new age is already at work and allows Christians in their present plight nevertheless to experience something of the eschatological joy awaiting them" (Achtemeier, *1 Peter*, 104). "Peter now further defines the 'salvation' of v 5 as 'salvation of souls,' probably to avoid promising his readers exemption from physical suffering and death. σωτηρία by itself can mean physical deliverance, and he is offering no guarantees of that. Yet ψυχή here is not the 'soul' in distinction from the body but rather a person's whole life or self-identity.... Although the ψυχή Peter has in mind is bodily life, it is also a life transcending physical death. His terminology is not that of resurrection, yet the hope of personal resurrection (on the basis of the resurrection of Jesus, cf. vv 3, 21) is implied" (Michaels, *1 Peter*, 35-36).

The "salvation" (σωτηρίαν) the audience are attaining (1:9), the "salvation" (σωτηρίαν) ready to be revealed in the last time (1:5), represents the "salvation" (σωτηρίας) concerning which prophets of old, those who by special revelation relayed God's word or plan to others, "sought out and searched out" (ἐξεζήτησαν καὶ ἐξηραύνησαν)—an emphatic expression intensified by its alliteration (1:10a).[25] The salvation "concerning" (περί) which prophets sought out and searched out represents a dimension of the grace "concerning" (περί) which they prophesied (1:10b). That they prophesied "concerning the grace [χάριτος] that is for you [εἰς ὑμᾶς]" (1:10b) bolsters Peter's prayer greeting as a petition for this prophesied grace, "May grace [χάρις] to you [ὑμῖν] and peace be multiplied!" (1:2d). The audience are to appreciate that the grace of the inheritance to eternal life being kept by God in heaven emphatically and specifically "for you [εἰς ὑμᾶς]" (1:4) represents a dimension of this prophesied grace that is emphatically and specifically "for you [εἰς ὑμᾶς]" (1:10b).

The audience hear the a') sub-element (1:11-13) of this chiastic sub-unit (1:7d-13) as yet another chiastic pattern in itself:

(a) probing *for* what certain person or what sort of time the *Spirit* of Christ in them was indicating, testifying beforehand to the sufferings *for* Christ and the glories after these things, to whom it was *revealed* (1:11-12a)

(b) that not to themselves but to you they were serving the very things which now have been *announced* to you (1:12b)

(b') through those who *proclaimed good news* unto you (1:12c)[26]

(a') by the Holy *Spirit* sent from heaven, *for* which things angels are desiring to catch a glimpse. Therefore, having girded up the loins of your mind, being sober, completely hope upon the grace that is to be borne to you at the *revelation* of Jesus Christ (1:12d-13).

At the center of this chiastic sub-unit the audience experience a pivot of parallels involving the only occurrences in this sub-unit of alliterative expressions for "announce" or "proclaim." "The very things which now have been announced [ἀνηγγέλη] to you" in the (b) sub-element (1:12b) progresses to "through those who proclaimed good news [εὐαγγελισαμένων] unto you" in the (b') sub-element (1:12c). They then experience a progression of parallels from the (a) (1:11-12a) to the (a') (1:12d-13) sub-element

---

25. A "prophet" (προφήτης) was "a proclaimer or expounder of divine matters or concerns that could not ordinarily be known except by special revelation" (BDAG, 890). "First Peter describes the prophets as having 'searched' (ἐξεζήτησαν) and 'investigated diligently' (ἐξηραύνησαν), two verbs nearly identical in meaning but coupled to emphasize the intensity and diligence of the prophets' work" (Senior, *1 Peter*, 34).

26. The translation "unto you [ὑμᾶς]" in 1:12c was chosen to indicate the variation from "to you" (ὑμῖν) in 1:12b.

involving the only occurrences in this sub-unit of the preposition "for," "Spirit," "Christ," and expressions for revelation: "for [εἰς] what certain person" (1:11) and "for [εἰς] Christ" progress to "for [εἰς] which things" (1:12d); "Spirit [πνεῦμα] of Christ" (1:11) and "sufferings of Christ" (1:11) progress to "by the Holy Spirit [πνεύματι]" (1:12d) and "revelation of Jesus Christ" (1:13); and finally "to whom it was revealed [ἀπεκαλύφθη]" (1:12a) progresses to "at the revelation [ἀποκαλύψει]" (1:13).

The "certain person" (τίνα) "for" (εἰς) whom the prophets were probing (1:11) refers to the Jesus Christ "for whom" (εἰς ὅν) the audience are presently exulting as the eschatological goal of their joyful worship (1:8). And the sort of "time" (καιρόν) for which the prophets were probing (1:11) resonates with the last "time" (καιρῷ) in which the salvation "for" (εἰς) which the audience are being guarded is ready to be revealed (1:5). Whereas the prophets were probing for what sort of time the "Spirit" (πνεῦμα) of Christ "in" (ἐν) them was indicating (1:11), the audience have been chosen to be "in" (ἐν) the holiness of the "Spirit" (πνεύματος) "for" (εἰς) obedience and sprinkling of the blood of Jesus Christ (1:2). And whereas the prophets were testifying beforehand to the sufferings "for" (εἰς) Christ and the "glories" (δόξας) after these things (1:11), the faith of the audience is being refined in and through the various trials they are suffering so that it may be found for "glory" (δόξαν) at the revelation of Jesus Christ (1:7), "for" (εἰς) whom they are exulting with a joy indescribable and "glorified [δεδοξασμένη]" (1:8).[27]

The audience have been informed that an eternal inheritance is being kept by God in heaven emphatically for "you [ὑμᾶς]" (1:4), who in the power of God are being guarded for a salvation ready to be "revealed" (ἀποκαλυφθῆναι) by God in the last time (1:5), at the "revelation" (ἀποκαλύψει) of Jesus Christ (1:7d). They are thus to deepen their appreciation for this divine grace that motivates their worship of joyful exultation in God and for Jesus Christ (1:6, 8), since it was "revealed" (ἀπεκαλύφθη) by God to the prophets that not to themselves but to "you" (ὑμῖν) they were serving the very things which now have been announced to "you" (ὑμῖν) through those who proclaimed good news unto "you [ὑμᾶς]" (1:12).

That those who proclaimed good news to the audience did so by the "Holy" (ἁγίῳ) "Spirit [πνεύματι]" (1:12), in continuity with the "Spirit" (πνεῦμα) of Christ that was already in the prophets (1:11), underscores the privilege of the audience's reception of divine grace as those chosen to be in the "holiness" (ἁγιασμῷ) of the "Spirit [πνεύματος]" (1:2). The audience are to appreciate that Peter, as an "apostle" of, that is, one "sent" (ἀπόστολος) by,

---

27. "The glories likely include Christ's glorious resurrection but perhaps also the glorious things that have happened to believers and are yet to happen to believers (cf. 1 Pet 1:7–8)" (Witherington, *Letters*, 84).

1 Peter 1:1-13

Jesus Christ (1:1) is exercising, as the author of this letter, a divine authority in association with those who proclaimed good news to them by the Holy Spirit "sent" (ἀποσταλέντι) by God from heaven (1:12). The divine origin of the proclamation of this good news unto "you" (ὑμᾶς) from "heaven [οὐρανοῦ]" (1:12) reaffirms the good news that an eternal inheritance is being kept by God in "heaven" (οὐρανοῖς) for the audience—indeed emphatically for "you [ὑμᾶς]" (1:4).[28]

The audience are to appreciate that they have been divinely privileged to have proclaimed to them as good news not only the very "things" (ἅ) the prophets were serving for the benefit of the audience, but the "things" (ἅ) for which angels are desiring to catch a glimpse (1:12). The things "for" (εἰς) which angels are desiring to catch a glimpse refer to the divine eschatological gifts for which the audience have been divinely destined—"for" (εἰς) an inheritance imperishable and undefiled and unfading, kept in heaven "for you [εἰς ὑμᾶς]" (1:4), "for" (εἰς) a salvation ready to be revealed in the last time (1:5), and "for" (εἰς) the praise and glory and honor to be found at the revelation of Jesus Christ (1:7d). These are the divine eschatological gifts motivating the audience's worship as those who are exulting in God (1:6) and "for" (εἰς) Jesus Christ with a joy indescribable and glorified (1:8, 11), as they are attaining the eschatological goal of their faith, the salvation of their souls (1:9).[29]

The minds of the audience have been made conscious that it may be necessary for them, as chosen sojourners of the diaspora (1:1), briefly to suffer various trials (1:6). But such suffering will refine their faith with a precious value appropriate for the divine gifts they are destined to receive, the eschatological salvation (1:7-9) that the prophets of old prophesied and that angels are desiring to behold (1:10-12). With an emphatic "therefore" (διό), Peter then draws out the consequences of everything he has previously told the audience (1:1-12). "Having girded up the loins" of their mind, that is, mentally prepared themselves, and "being sober," that is, attentively focused, they are exhorted to "completely hope upon the grace that is to be borne to you at the revelation of Jesus Christ" (1:13).[30]

28. Herzer, "Alttestamentliche Prophetie," 14-22.

29. "What does seem to be implied is that this angelic desire points to the greatness of what Christians now hear announced to them, and further underlines one of the author's main purposes for writing the letter: the readers live in a time firmly under God's control when history is about to reach its climax. They therefore have reason rather to rejoice than to despair" (Achtemeier, *1 Peter*, 112).

30. "The girding of the loins is a common ancient image that is derived from the need to tie up one's robe before attempting any vigorous physical act. Here it means something like 'having gotten ready for action'" (Donelson, *I & II Peter*, 41). "An important ritual instance of the girding of loins in Israel took place in conjunction with the Passover festival commemorating God's liberation and redemption of his people

The audience are to hope "completely" or "to the end [τελείως]" (1:13), that is, with a hope fully and enduringly oriented toward the eschatological "end" or "completion" (τέλος) of their faith, the salvation of their souls (1:9). As among those to whom God has given a new birth for a living "hope" (ἐλπίδα) through the resurrection of Jesus Christ from the dead (1:3), the audience are to completely "hope" (ἐλπίσατε) upon the grace that is to be borne to them by God at the full and final revelation of Jesus Christ (1:13).[31] The audience are to completely hope upon the "grace" (χάριν) that is to be borne by God to "you" (ὑμῖν), the prophesied "grace" (χάριτος) that is for "you [ὑμᾶς]" (1:10), the "grace" (χάρις) that Peter has prayed for God to give and multiply to "you [ὑμῖν]" (1:2).[32]

The grace that is to be borne by God to the audience at the future and final "revelation" (ἀποκαλύψει) of Jesus Christ (1:13) includes the eternal inheritance being kept by God in heaven for them (1:4), their salvation from death to risen, eternal life ready to be fully and finally "revealed" (ἀποκαλυφθῆναι) in the last time (1:5), as well as the praise and glory and honor to be found as grace from God and worship of God at the "revelation" (ἀποκαλύψει) of Jesus Christ (1:7d). The audience, then, are to completely hope upon the future, eschatological grace to be borne to them by God, as they are presently engaged in the worship of exulting in God (1:6) and exulting for Christ with a joy indescribable and glorified (1:8).

Summary on 1:1-13

Peter's initial prayer greeting for the audience, "May grace to you and peace be multiplied!" (1:2d), confirms and reinforces the grace they have already

---

from Egyptian bondage (Exod 12:11)" (Elliott, *1 Peter*, 356). "Peter makes it clear that he is using the image as a metaphor by stating clearly 'mind,' which indicates not the intellectual processes in general, but a mental resolve and preparation" (Davids, *First Epistle*, 66). See also Watson, "Spiritual Sobriety," 539-42.

31. "ἐλπίσατε followed by ἐπί and the accusative (contrast 3:5, where the preposition is εἰς, and in the NT cf. only 1 Tim 5:5) shows the probable influence of the LXX, especially such passages as Pss 32 [33]:18; 51 [52]:10; 77 [78]:22; 146 [147]:11, which combine ἐλπίζειν with ἐπί to speak of hoping for God's salvation or mercy" (Michaels, *1 Peter*, 55). On the Septuagint textual tradition in 1 Peter, see Jobes, "Septuagint," 311-33.

32. "The object of the hope that Peter commands is 'the grace to be brought to you when Jesus Christ is revealed,' a phrase combining the ἐν ἀποκαλύψει Ἰησοῦ Χριστοῦ of v 7 with the 'grace to be given you' mentioned in v 10 ... The grace of which Peter speaks, however, does not 'come'; it is 'brought' or 'conferred' ... [This] underscores the sovereign action of God in bringing grace to his people at the 'revelation of Jesus Christ' (cf. the passive participles in vv 4 and 5 and the passive verbs in v 12 that similarly imply the initiative of God)" (Michaels, *1 Peter*, 55-56).

received as sojourners chosen (1:1) according to the foreknowledge of God the Father (1:2a) in the holiness of God's Spirit (1:2b) for the divine benefits of the obedience and sprinkling of the blood of Jesus Christ (1:2c). Through obedience to God's will as an act of ethical worship pleasing to God, Jesus Christ offered up his body in death as a sacrifice that resulted in the "sprinkling of blood" as an act of cultic worship effecting atonement for and purification from sins. The encouragement of these divine benefits of Jesus Christ implies an exhortation for the audience to likewise worship and please God by their own obedience, even if it means suffering to the point of sprinkling their own blood.

Peter draws the audience into an act of communal worship, a benediction praising God for the grace not only the audience but all Christians have received. In accord with his great mercy God has given "us" a new birth for a living hope through the resurrection of Jesus Christ from the dead (1:3). As an epistolary act of worship, this benediction begins to indicate that 1 Peter is concerned with the worship of God for life through the sufferings of Jesus Christ, the sufferings which led to his resurrection from the dead.

The audience are to appreciate that, as sojourners of the diaspora chosen "for" obedience and sprinkling of the blood of Jesus Christ (1:2c), "for" a living hope (1:3), "for" an imperishable inheritance (1:4) kept in heaven "for" you (1:4), they are being guarded "for" a salvation to the eternal, risen life of Jesus Christ ready to be revealed by God at the last time (1:5). Peter impresses upon them that the God they have been led to bless in worship (1:3), as the God "in" whose power they are being guarded through faith for eschatological salvation (1:5), is the God "in whom you are exulting" as the focus of their worship (1:6a). The audience, as chosen sojourners of the diaspora (1:1) "in" the holiness of God's Spirit (1:2b) for an inheritance kept by God "in" heaven for them (1:4), who "in" the power of God are being guarded through faith for a salvation to be revealed by God "in" the last time (1:5), may continue to joyfully worship the God "in" whom they are exulting. And they may do so even though being briefly saddened now "in" the various trials that are a necessary part of God's salvific plan (1:6).

The audience are to be encouraged that the refinement of their faith in and through various trials is so that it "may be found for praise and glory and honor at the revelation of Jesus Christ" (1:6-7). The refinement of their faith "may be found" by and before God (divine passive) "for" their praise, glory, and honor, as those chosen "for" the salvation from death to eternal life (1:3) ready to be "revealed" in the last time (1:5), at the "revelation" of Jesus Christ (1:7d). The triplet of "praise" and "glory" and "honor" that God will give the audience in the end-time judgment at the final revelation of Jesus Christ is simultaneously the praise, glory, and honor the audience's refinement of faith through the suffering of their trials will render to God as an act of worship. In other words, God's approval at the last judgment of the refinement of the audience's faith through their sufferings will amount to worship pleasing to God.

The audience's present worship of the God "in whom you are exulting" (1:6) has been motivated by all of the divine gifts they have received. The Jesus Christ "whom" they love without seeing (1:8a) represents, as the fundamental basis central to all of these divine gifts, the ultimate goal of their worship—"for whom you are exulting with a joy indescribable and glorified" (1:8b). It is this "salvation of souls," the salvation of their persons from death to risen, eternal life, that the audience are in the process of attaining (1:9), as they are engaged in the worship of exulting for Jesus Christ (1:8), whose resurrection from the dead (1:3) provides the basis for this salvation to be fully attained at the final revelation of Jesus Christ (1:7d).

The "salvation" the audience are attaining (1:9) represents the "salvation" concerning which prophets of old, those who by special revelation relayed God's word or plan to others, sought out and searched out (1:10a). The salvation "concerning" which prophets sought out and searched out represents a dimension of the grace "concerning" which they prophesied (1:10b). That they prophesied "concerning the grace that is for you" (1:10b) bolsters Peter's prayer greeting as a petition for this prophesied grace, "May grace to you and peace be multiplied!" (1:2d). The audience are to appreciate that the grace of the inheritance to eternal life being kept by God in heaven emphatically and specifically "for you" (1:4) represents a dimension of this prophesied grace that is emphatically and specifically "for you" (1:10b).

The minds of the audience have been made conscious that it may be necessary for them, as chosen sojourners of the diaspora (1:1), briefly to suffer various trials (1:6). But such suffering will refine their faith with a very precious value appropriate for the divine gifts they are destined to receive, the eschatological salvation (1:7–9) based upon the sufferings for Christ that the prophets of old testified to beforehand, the divine glory that angels are desiring to behold (1:10–12). With an emphatic "therefore," Peter then draws out the consequences of everything he has just affirmed for the audience (1:1–12). "Having girded up the loins" of their mind, that is, mentally prepared themselves, and "being sober," that is, attentively focused, they are exhorted to "completely hope upon the grace that is to be borne to you at the revelation of Jesus Christ" (1:13). The audience, then, are to completely hope upon the future, eschatological grace to be borne to them by God, as they are presently engaged in their communal worship of exulting in God (1:6) and exulting for Christ with a joy indescribable and glorified (1:8).

3

1 Peter 1:14–25
Through Christ You Are Faithful for God with Purified Souls (B)

Through the risen and glorified Christ your faith and hope are for God

A   ¹⁴ As children of *obedience*, not being conformed, as before, in your ignorance, to the desires, ¹⁵ but, according to the Holy One who called you, become holy also yourselves in all conduct, ¹⁶ *because* it is written, "You shall be holy, for I am holy" (Lev 19:2). ¹⁷ And if you call upon as Father the one who impartially judges according to the work of each one, in fear conduct the time of your sojourning, ¹⁸ knowing that *not* with *perishable* things, silver or gold, have you been ransomed from your futile conduct inherited from fathers ¹⁹ but with the precious blood of Christ *as* of a lamb flawless and faultless, ²⁰ foreknown before the foundation of the world but manifested at the last of these times for the sake of you,

B   ^{21a} who through him are *faithful for God*,

C   ^{21b} who raised him from the dead and gave him glory,

B'   ^{21c} so that your *faith* and hope are *for God*.

A'   ²² Your souls having purified in the *obedience* to the truth for sincere brotherly affection, from a clean heart love one another constantly, ²³ having been given new birth *not* from a seed *perishable* but *imperishable*, through a living word of God, indeed abiding, ²⁴ *because* "all flesh is *as* grass and all its glory *as* a flower of the grass; the grass withers and the flower wilts; ²⁵ but the pronouncement of the Lord abides for eternity" (Isa 40:6, 8). This is the pronouncement that was proclaimed as good news for you.[1]

Audience Response to 1:14-25

1:14-20 (A): As Children of Obedience Ransomed Not with Perishable Things

The audience hear the A element (1:14-20) of this chiastic unit as a chiastic pattern in itself:
a) As children of obedience, not being conformed, as *before*, in your *ignorance*, to the desires (1:14),
  b) *but*, according to the Holy One who *called* you, become holy also yourselves in all *conduct*, because it is written, "You shall be holy, for I am holy [Lev 19:2]" (1:15-16).
  b') And if you *call upon* as Father the one who impartially judges according to the work of each one, in fear *conduct* the time of your sojourning, knowing that not with perishable things, silver or gold, have you been ransomed from your futile *conduct* inherited from fathers, *but* with the precious blood of Christ as of a lamb flawless and faultless (1:17-19),
a') *foreknown before* the foundation of the world but manifested at the last of these times for the sake of you (1:20).

At the center of this chiastic sub-unit the audience experience a pivot of parallels involving the only occurrences in this sub-unit of the conjunction "but," expressions for "call" or "call upon," and expressions for "conduct." They hear a progression from "but [ἀλλά], according to the Holy One who called [καλέσαντα] you, become holy also yourselves in all conduct [ἀναστροφῇ]" in the b) sub-element (1:15-16) to "if you call upon [ἐπικαλεῖσθε] as Father... in fear conduct [ἀναστράφητε] the time... from your futile conduct [ἀναστροφῆς]... but [ἀλλά] with the precious blood of Christ" in the b') sub-element (1:17-19). They then hear a progression of parallels involving the only occurrences in 1 Peter of expressions of former knowledge or ignorance. "As before [πρότερον], in your ignorance [ἀγνοίᾳ]" in the a) sub-element (1:14) progresses to "foreknown [προεγνωσμένου] before [πρό]" in the a') sub-element (1:20).

---

1. For the establishment of 1 Pet 1:14-25 as a chiasm, see ch. 1.

1 Peter 1:14-25

That the audience are addressed "as" (ὡς) children of "obedience [ὑπακοῆς]" (1:14) resonates with their having been chosen, as sojourners of the diaspora (1:1), for "obedience" (ὑπακοήν) and sprinkling of the blood of Jesus Christ (1:2c).[2] It reminds them that they are the beneficiaries of the divine gift of the obedience of Jesus Christ, the obedience which led to their atonement and purification by the sprinkling of his blood, and to their being given by God the Father a new birth to a living hope through the resurrection of Jesus Christ from the dead (1:3). And it implies their own obedience of God, as newborn children of God the Father (1:2a, 3), in imitation of Jesus' own obedience.[3]

As children of obedience, the audience are not to be conformed to the desires of their former ignorance, the desires they had before their minds were enlightened in becoming Christians (1:14). With the phrase "in your ignorance [ἀγνοίᾳ ὑμῶν]," the audience hear the transitional words that link this unit (1:14-25) with the preceding unit (1:1-13), which concluded with a reference to "your mind [διανοίας ὑμῶν]" (1:13). For the audience to be conformed to the desires of their former ignorance would contradict their "having girded up the loins of your mind," as they completely hope upon the grace to be borne to them by God at the final revelation of Jesus Christ (1:13). And for them to be conformed to the desires of their former ignorance would indicate a lack of appreciation for the divine gifts they have received from God the Father as children of obedience, divine gifts so much greater than their former "desires" (ἐπιθυμίαις) that even angels are "desiring" (ἐπιθυμοῦσιν) to catch a glimpse of them (1:12).

Rather than being conformed to the desires of their former ignorance (1:14), the audience, "according" (κατά) to the "Holy One" (ἅγιον) who called them, are to become "holy" (ἅγιοι) themselves in all of their conduct (1:15), because in the authoritative scriptural word of God himself from Lev 19:2 it is written, "You shall be holy [ἅγιοι], for I am holy [ἅγιός]" (1:16). This reaffirms and begins to draw out the implications of the audience having been chosen (1:1) "according" (κατά) to the foreknowledge of God the Father in the "holiness" (ἁγιασμῷ) of the Spirit (1:2), and of the God and Father, "according" (κατά) to his great mercy, having given them new birth for a living

---

2. "The repeated use of the comparative particle ὡς is a stylistic characteristic of 1 Peter, occurring more often here (27x) than in any other NT writing. It serves not simply to introduce a comparison but often to mark an essential quality of the term or phrase that it precedes" (Elliott, *1 Peter*, 357).

3. "The image of 'obedient children' recalls the language of rebirth in 1:3 and anticipates the discussion of God as father in 1:17. In 1:2, obedience is portrayed as the proper destiny of the readers" (Donelson, *I & II Peter*, 42).

hope through the resurrection of Jesus Christ from the dead (1:3).[4] Not only are the audience to completely hope upon the grace God will give them at the revelation of Jesus Christ (1:13), as they are engaged in the worship of exulting in God (1:6) and for Christ (1:8), but this worship is to be complemented by their becoming holy, consecrating themselves to the God who is the Holy One, in all of their conduct as their ethical worship of God.[5]

The audience hear the b') sub-element (1:17-19) of this chiastic sub-unit (1:14-20) as yet another chiastic pattern in itself:

(a) And if you call upon as *Father* the one who impartially judges according to the work of each one, in fear *conduct* the time of *your* sojourning (1:17),

  (b) knowing that not with perishable things, silver or gold (1:18a),

(a') have you been ransomed from *your* futile *conduct inherited from fathers* but with the precious blood of Christ as of a lamb flawless and faultless (1:18b-19).

The audience hear the subordinate clause, "knowing that not with perishable things, silver or gold" (1:18a), as the unparalleled central and pivotal sub-element of this chiastic sub-unit. They then experience a pivot of parallels involving the only occurrences in this sub-unit of expressions for "father(s)," for "conduct," and of the second person plural pronoun. "Father" (πατέρα), "in fear conduct [ἀναστράφητε]," and "your [ὑμῶν] sojourning" in the (a) sub-element (1:17) progress to "your [ὑμῶν] futile conduct [ἀναστροφῆς] inherited from fathers [πατροπαραδότου]" in the (a') sub-element (1:18b-19).

The audience are to know that if in their worship "you call upon" (ἐπικαλεῖσθε) God as Father, the Holy One who "called" (καλέσαντα) them (1:15) to be children of obedience (1:14), the Father whom they worship is also the Father who impartially judges according to the work of each one (1:17a).[6] The audience, who as "sojourners" (παρεπιδήμοις) of the dias-

---

4. "κατά phrases are used repeatedly in this letter to indicate God as the source and norm of Christian blessings and behavior (1:2, 3, 15; 4:6, 19; 5:2)" (Elliott, *1 Peter*, 360).

5. "In the Bible, Yahweh was 'the Holy One' par excellence, and all that was dedicated, consecrated, or set apart for God and for use in cultic worship was considered holy" (Elliott, *1 Peter*, 360). "Holiness, which in many religious traditions epitomizes all that is set apart from the world and assigned to a distinctly ceremonial sphere of its own, is in Peter's terminology brought face to face with the world and the practical decisions and concerns of everyday life. A religious, almost numinous, quality characteristic of God and of priest, temples, and all kinds of cult objects is boldly translated here into positive ethical virtues: purity and reverence, and above all the doing of good in specific human relationships. In this way Peter begins to develop the ethical implications of the ἁγιασμὸς πνεύματος mentioned in v 2" (Michaels, *1 Peter*, 59).

6. "It is therefore likely that the verb ἐπικαλεῖσθε has the sense of 'calling upon' God the father in prayer" (Elliott, *1 Peter*, 365).

pora were divinely chosen (1:1), in fear are to conduct the time of their "sojourning [παροικίας]" (1:17b). In "fear" (φόβῳ), in both the respectful "fear" of the Father who judges them and the reverent "fear" of the Father they worship, "you are to conduct" (ἀναστράφητε) the time of sojourning before the attainment of the heavenly inheritance (1:4).⁷ They may thereby become holy as God is holy, "according" (κατά) to the Holy One who called them, in all of their "conduct [ἀναστροφῇ]" (1:15), devoting themselves to God in both their worship and in the work "according" (κατά) to which the Holy One will judge them. Such work may be found for the praise, glory, and honor that God will give and that will be given to God as worship at the last judgment (1:7d).⁸

In contrast to their former "ignorance [ἀγνοίᾳ]" (1:14), the audience are to be those "knowing" (εἰδότες) that not with perishable things, silver or gold, have they been ransomed from their futile conduct inherited from their ancestors (1:18). Not with perishable things, silver or "gold" (χρυσίῳ), the "gold" (χρυσίου) that is passing away (1:7b), have the audience been ransomed by God (divine passive) from "your [ὑμῶν] futile conduct [ἀναστροφῆς] inherited from fathers [πατροπαραδότου]."⁹ In place of this "futile" (ματαίας) conduct that connotes false or idol worship, as those who in reverent "fear" of the divine "Father" (πατέρα) they call upon in worship (1:17a), "you are to conduct" (ἀναστράφητε) the "time of your [ὑμῶν] sojourning" (1:17b). As they become holy, devoted to the God who is the Holy One, in all of their "conduct [ἀναστροφῇ]" (1:15), they will thereby replace their former futile conduct, which did not render proper worship to God, with conduct in reverent fear of the divine Father who will judge whether they are holy in all of their conduct, whether their work renders worship to the Holy One.¹⁰

7. "The phrase 'in fear' has occasioned debate because the Greek φόβος means both fear and reverence. In a given context φόβος can thus have either a negative or positive connotation. Both connotations seem to be in force in 1 Peter. God is both to be feared and revered" (Donelson, *I & II Peter*, 46).

8. "Work" (ἔργον) here includes all of the behavior in one's way of life; see Feldmeier, *First Letter*, 108n35.

9. "The reference to silver and gold may be mentioned because of their association with idolatry (Deut 29:17; Dan 5:23; Wis 13:10; Rev 9:20)" (Schreiner, *1, 2 Peter*, 85). "The second adjective, πατροπαράδοτος (lit., 'handed down from the fathers'), occurs nowhere else in the NT or LXX. But in Greco-Roman literature and inscriptions it designates the positive sense of values, traditions, and customs that are rooted in the past and transmitted by the fathers as a worthy heritage. Here in 1 Peter, however, in conjunction with μάταιος, it is employed in a negative sense of conduct encouraged by the fathers that was empty and aimless, conduct from which the believers have now been liberated" (Elliott, *1 Peter*, 370).

10. "While the general meaning of ματαία is 'vain' or 'foolish,' it is used in the LXX

1 Peter, 2 Peter, and Jude

The audience were exhorted not to be conformed to the desires of their former ignorance (1:14), "but" (ἀλλά) to become holy in all of their conduct (1:15). Now, they are to realize that not with perishable things have they been ransomed or redeemed by God from their futile conduct (1:18), "but" (ἀλλά) with the precious blood of Christ, as of a lamb flawless and faultless (1:19). That the audience have been ransomed or redeemed with the precious "blood" (αἵματι) of Christ deepens their appreciation of the obedience and sprinkling of the "blood" (αἵματος) of Christ (1:2c) for which they have been divinely chosen (1:1).

The obedience of Christ, the moral or ethical conduct involved in his submission to the will of God, was essential to the sacrificial worship of the sprinkling of his blood for the atonement and purification that enables the audience's own worship (1:2c). Similarly, the comparison of the precious blood of Christ with the sacrificial worship of a lamb employs the cultic terminology for a worthy sacrifice. "As [ὡς] of a lamb flawless and faultless" (1:19) metaphorically portrays Christ's obedient conduct as the sacrificial worship that rendered his blood precious for the redemption that has liberated the audience from their past futile conduct, which included their inadequate cultic and ethical worship. As an aural embellishment, the sonorous and resounding alliteration of a "lamb flawless and faultless" (ἀμνοῦ ἀμώμου καὶ ἀσπίλου) attracts the audience to the precious value of the shedding of the blood of Christ as an act of sacrificial worship.[11] The obedience that it implies serves as an implicit model for the audience's own worship, "as [ὡς] children of obedience" (1:14).[12]

---

to describe the gods of the Gentiles" (Achtemeier, *1 Peter*, 127). "In the NT the ματαία include every false worship directed toward the veneration of humankind rather than the true, living God" (Balz, "μάταιος," 396).

11. "While ἄσπιλος does not occur in the LXX, it is added here to emphasize the holiness and purity of Christ's sacrifice, given 1 Peter's melding the ideas of a faultless sacrificial lamb (Lev. 2.19-20) with the Isaianic silent lamb—the suffering servant (Isa. 53) . . . the concepts of purity and holiness in 1 Peter not only recall OT cultic purity rites, they expand them to incorporate all spheres of life" (Mbuvi, *Temple*, 84-85).

12. "To underline the *holiness* of Christ the lamb, the adjective describing flawless and therefore acceptable sacrifices in Israel's cult, ἄμωμος, is used as modifier, together with ἄσπιλος, a term of secular provenance meaning 'faultless' in either a physical or moral sense . . . The result of this blending in 1 Peter is a statement that is both rhetorically attractive and theologically impressive. Rhetorically, the phrase ἀμνός ἄμωμος καὶ ἄσπιλος illustrates the author's refined appreciation of alliteration [emphasis original]" (Elliott, *1 Peter*, 374-75. See also Michaels, *1 Peter*, 66. "In the larger context of 1:19, blood is connected once again to obedience. The readers were named 'obedient children' in 1:14, and the whole passage is a call to live the holy life. Thus most readers of 1 Peter connect the imagery of blood and ransom, not to the political sphere, but to the cultic, wherein obedience and blood are constantly connected" (Donelson, *I & II Peter*, 48).

1 Peter 1:14-25

The audience have been ransomed or redeemed from their futile conduct not with perishable silver or gold (1:18) but with the precious blood that resulted from the obedient suffering and death of Christ, the blood that has a "precious" (τιμίῳ) value beyond what is perishable, a value oriented to risen, eternal life (1:19).[13] This strengthens the resolve of the audience to suffer the various trials (1:6) that will refine their faith, bestowing it with an imperishable, eternal value "more precious" (πολυτιμότερον) than perishable gold (1:7b). At the final revelation of Jesus Christ such refinement of faith through suffering may be found for the praise, glory, and honor (1:7d) to be given both by God, the Father who judges the work of each one (1:17b), and as worship to the God the audience calls upon as Father (1:17a).

Rather than being conformed, as "before" (πρότερον), to the desires of their "ignorance [ἀγνοίᾳ]" (1:14), the audience are to be "knowing" (εἰδότες) that they have been ransomed by God from their former futile conduct (1:18) with the precious blood of the Christ "foreknown" (προεγνωσμένου) by God "before" (πρό) the foundation of the world (1:20a). That the Christ with whose precious blood the audience have been ransomed by God was "foreknown" by God closely associates the audience, chosen according to the "foreknowledge" (πρόγνωσιν) of God the Father for obedience and sprinkling of the blood of Jesus Christ (1:2), with Christ in God's plan of salvation.[14] Christ has been manifested for the sake of the audience in the "last" (ἐσχάτου) of these "times [χρόνων]" (1:20b), the end-time of God's salvific plan that has already begun to be completed, which includes the present "time" (χρόνον) of their sojourning (1:17), as they await the salvation to be fully and finally revealed in the "last" (ἐσχάτῳ) time (1:5).[15]

---

13. "The shedding of blood signifies death, the giving up of one's life. Blood is precious because without it no one can live (Lev 17:11) . . . the shedding of blood indicates that Christ poured out his life to death for sinners. What Peter teaches is that the blood of Christ is the means by which believers are redeemed" (Schreiner, *1, 2 Peter*, 85). "The word τίμιος with its sense of 'costly' and 'valuable' fits naturally with gold and silver. Hence, gold and silver, which might warrant the adjective 'precious,' instead acquire the adjective 'perishable.' And blood, which seems to be the most perishable of all things, instead is called 'precious'" (Donelson, *I & II Peter*, 47).

14. "The foreknowledge of Christ's redeeming death (1:19-20) corresponds to God's electing foreknowledge of those who would be redeemed by it (1:2). Thus God knew the complete program of redemption before the foundation of the world" (Jobes, *1 Peter*, 119).

15. "In v. 17, Peter writes of 'the time of your dwelling in a strange land,' while in v. 20 he writes of 'the end of the times (or ages).' The juxtaposition of these two descriptions is parabolic of the deeper reality to which his audience must attend, namely, that the last days, inaugurated by the death and resurrection of Jesus, can only be, for those who have been born anew, a time of living as strangers, never really at home" (Green, *1 Peter*, 43). "ἐπ᾽ ἐσχάτου τῶν χρόνων is not to be equated with the ἐν καιρῷ ἐσχάτῳ of

That Christ has been manifested by God in the last of these times for the sake of the audience (1:20) adds to the concerted focus, through emphatic expressions employing the accusative second person plural pronoun, on how divinely privileged they are. An inheritance imperishable and undefiled and unfading is being kept by God in heaven emphatically "for you [εἰς ὑμᾶς]" (1:4). The prophets prophesied concerning the divine grace that is emphatically "for you [εἰς ὑμᾶς]" (1:10). Good news was proclaimed unto "you [ὑμᾶς]" (1:12) and the Holy One has called "you [ὑμᾶς]" (1:15). Now, the audience are to appreciate that Christ has been manifested by God emphatically and especially "for the sake of you [δι' ὑμᾶς]."[16]

1:21a (B): Faithful for God

The benefit of Christ for the audience is then elaborated: "who through him are faithful for God" (1:21a). "Through him [δι' αὐτοῦ]," that is, through the Christ who has been manifested by God "for the sake of you [δι' ὑμᾶς]" (1:20), the audience are faithful for God.[17] The audience are to appreciate that it is through the sacrificial worship of Christ, with whose precious blood (1:19; cf. 1:2) they have been ransomed and liberated from the futile conduct that prevented a proper worship of God (1:18), that they are enabled to be faithful for God in their own worship. Through the sacrificial worship of Christ, essentially his ethical worship—his obedience (1:2), his "flawless and faultless" moral conduct (1:19), the audience are able to conduct the time of their sojourning as those faithful in the reverent fear for the God they call upon as Father in their liturgical worship, the God for whom their work is to be judged as worthy ethical worship (1:17). They are thus able to become holy, as God is holy (1:16), in all of their conduct which is to serve as worship in response to the Holy One who called them (1:15).

Through Christ the audience are "faithful" (πιστούς) for "God [θεόν]" (1:21a), as those "believing [πιστεύοντες]" (1:8), those who in the power of "God" (θεοῦ) are being guarded through their "faith" (πίστεως) for salvation

---

v 5. Rather it defines the 'now' that stands in contrast to the time 'before the beginning of the world'" (Michaels, *1 Peter*, 68). "[E]ven though the 'last of times' was ushered in with the life, death, and resurrection of Jesus, there remains a future point in time when a further, more universal revelation of Jesus Christ will occur" (Jobes, *1 Peter*, 119).

16. "The function of δι' ὑμᾶς is similar to that of εἰς ὑμᾶς in v 4b, the first direct address to the readers in the body of the epistle" (Michaels, *1 Peter*, 68). "This centering of the entire story of salvation upon 'you' is one of the central convictions of the letter" (Donelson, *I & II Peter*, 49).

17. "There is a certain stylistic symmetry to δι' ὑμᾶς and δι' αὐτοῦ despite the differing uses of διά" (Michaels, *1 Peter*, 69).

1 Peter 1:14-25

(1:5)—the end of their "faith [πίστεως]" (1:9), the "faith" (πίστεως) to be refined in their trials (1:7). Through Christ they are faithful for God as those who are to bless the "God" (θεός) and Father of our Lord Jesus Christ (1:3) in their communal worship, faithful as those chosen in the foreknowledge of "God" (θεοῦ) the Father (1:2). The audience are to realize that not only are they engaged in the joyous worship of exulting for Christ—"for whom [εἰς ὅν] you are exulting" (1:8), but also through Christ—"through him" (δι' αὐτοῦ)—they are able to be faithful "for God" (εἰς θεόν) as the ultimate goal of their worship. They are faithful "for" the God who chose them "for" (εἰς) obedience (1:2), "for" (εἰς) a living hope (1:3), "for" (εἰς) a heavenly inheritance (1:4), "for" (εἰς) salvation (1:5), and "for" (εἰς) divine praise, glory, and honor to be given by God and to God as worship (1:7).

1:21b (C): Who Raised Him from the Dead and Gave Him Glory

The God for whom the audience are faithful through Christ (1:21a) is the God "who raised him from the dead and gave him glory" (1:21b). That through Christ the audience are able to be faithful to the God who "raised" (ἐγείραντα) him "from the dead" (ἐκ νεκρῶν) recalls that God has given believers new birth for a living hope through the "resurrection" (ἀναστάσεως) of Jesus Christ "from the dead [ἐκ νεκρῶν]" (1:3b). This recall reinforces the motivation for the audience's participation in the epistolary worship inviting them to bless the God and Father of our Lord Jesus Christ (1:3a).

The "glory" (δόξαν) that God gave to Christ in raising him from the dead after his sufferings (1:21b) is preeminently included among the "glories" (δόξας) to come after the sufferings for Christ to which the prophets testified (1:11). That God gave Christ the glory of the resurrection after his sufferings further strengthens the resolve of the audience to suffer various trials (1:6) for the refinement of their faith, so that it may be found for praise and "glory" (δόξαν) and honor at the revelation of Jesus Christ (1:7). This implies that the audience, who are faithful for God through Christ (1:21a), will also receive the glory of the resurrection after their sufferings. It bolsters the motivation for their worship of exulting in God (1:6) and for Christ with a joy that is indescribable and "glorified [δεδοξασμένῃ]" (1:8), since it includes their hope of being given the "glory" of a risen, eternal life.[18]

---

18. "This honor and glory of the suffering Christ is thus a surety of the glory and honor in store for believers who remain faithful in adversity" (Elliott, *1 Peter*, 379).

1:21c (B'): Your Faith and Hope Are for God

The audience then hear the consequences of their being faithful through Christ for God (1:21a), who raised him from the dead and gave him glory (1:21b): "so that your faith and hope are for God" (1:21c).[19] At this point, after the central and unparalleled C element of this chiastic unit, "who raised him from the dead and gave him glory" (1:21b), the audience experience a pivot of parallels. "Faithful [πιστούς] for God [εἰς θεόν]" in the B element (1:21a) progresses to "faith [πίστιν] and hope are for God [εἰς θεόν]" in the B' (1:21c) element.

Not only the "faith" of the audience, who through Christ are "faithful" for God (1:21a), but their "hope" (ἐλπίδα) is fully focused on God as the ultimate goal of their worship (1:21c). This bolsters the exhortation for the audience to completely "hope" (ἐλπίσατε) upon the grace that is to be borne to them by God at the full and final revelation of Jesus Christ (1:13), whom God raised from the dead and gave glory (1:21b). Their hope for God is the living "hope" (ἐλπίδα) for which God gave believers a new birth through the resurrection of Jesus Christ from the dead (1:3). That their hope is "for God" reinforces their realization that their worship of exulting "in God" (1:6), their joyful exulting "for Christ" (1:8), is ultimately their worship "for God"—the God who raised Christ from the dead, so that the audience may worship God with the "living" hope for the glory of a risen, eternal life from and for God.[20]

1:22–25 (A'): Obedience to Truth Not from Perishable but Imperishable Seed

The audience hear the A' element (1:22–25) of this chiastic unit as a chiastic pattern in itself:

---

19. "While the absence of the article with ἐλπίδα has led to the suggestion that it stands in the predicate position and thus ought to be understood as meaning 'your faith is also hope in God,' the absent article is more likely due to style than substance, with the τήν before πίστιν understood also to apply to ἐλπίδα. As a result, the two nouns ought to be understood as coordinate, almost in the sense of a hendiadys" (Achtemeier, *1 Peter*, 133).

20. On the significance of hope in 1 Pet 1:17–21, see Beckman, "Live," 77–98. "According to 1 Peter, God has revealed himself in the fate of Christ as the one who can and will transform the lowness, suffering, and death of those who belong to him into triumph, glory, and eternal life" (Feldmeier, *First Letter*, 120). "Although Christian existence centers on Jesus, God the Father is its ultimate source and its ultimate goal . . . If there is a new element introduced with the mention of hope, it is the possible implication that the God who raised up Jesus and gave him glory will also raise and glorify those who hope in him" (Michaels, *1 Peter*, 70).

1 Peter 1:14-25

a) Your souls having purified in the obedience to the truth *for* sincere brotherly affection, from a clean heart love one another constantly,[21] having been given new birth not from a seed perishable but imperishable, through a living word of God, indeed *abiding* (1:22-23),

b) because, "All flesh is as *grass* and all its glory as a *flower* of the *grass* (1:24a);

b') the *grass* withers and the *flower* wilts (1:24b);

a') but the pronouncement of the Lord *abides* for eternity" (Isa 40:6, 8). This is the pronouncement that was proclaimed as good news *for* you (1:25).

At the center of this chiastic sub-unit the audience experience a pivot of parallels involving the only occurrences in 1 Peter of the terms "grass" and "flower." "Grass [χόρτος] and all its glory like a flower [ἄνθος] of the grass [χόρτου]" in the b) sub-element (1:24a) progresses to "grass [χόρτος] withers and the flower [ἄνθος] wilts" in the b') sub-element (1:24b). They then hear a progression of parallels involving the only occurrences in 1 Peter of the verb "abide" and in this sub-unit of the preposition "for." "For [εἰς] sincere brotherly affection" and "through a living word of God, indeed abiding [μένοντος]" in the a) sub-element (1:22-23) progress to "the pronouncement of the Lord abides [μένει] for eternity" and "the pronouncement that was proclaimed as good news for [εἰς] you" in the a') sub-element (1:25).

At this point the audience experience progressions, via the chiastic parallels, from the A (1:14-20) to the A' (1:22-25) element of this chiastic unit. "As [ὡς] children of obedience [ὑπακοῆς]" (1:14), "because [διότι]" (1:16), "not [οὐ] with perishable [φθαρτοῖς] things" (1:18), and "as [ὡς] of a lamb" (1:19) progress to "obedience [ὑπακοῇ] to the truth" (1:22), "not [οὐκ] from perishable [φθαρτῆς] but imperishable [ἀφθάρτου] seed" (1:23), "because [διότι]" (1:24), "as [ὡς] grass" (1:24), and "as [ὡς] a flower" (1:24).

The audience have purified their "souls [ψυχάς]" (1:22), the salvation of which "souls" (ψυχῶν) they are attaining as the end of their faith (1:9). They have "purified" (ἡγνικότες) and made their souls and thus their lives holy as those called to become "holy [ἅγιοι]" (1:15) as God is "holy [ἅγιός]" (1:16).[22] That they have purified their souls in the "obedience" (ὑπακοῇ) to the "truth" (ἀληθείας) for sincere brotherly affection (1:22) serves as the positive assertion to the negative statement that, as children of "obedience" (ὑπακοῆς), they are not conformed, in the falsehood of their "ignorance"

---

21. The words "your souls" are accentuated by their placement at the beginning of the statement and contrast "one another" at the end of the verse, according to Elliott, *1 Peter*, 383.

22. "This section opens with the perfect participle ἡγνικότες, suggesting thereby that the call to holiness has been and still is being accomplished" (Donelson, *1 & II Peter*, 51).

1 Peter, 2 Peter, and Jude

(ἀγνοίᾳ), to their former desires (1:14).[23] As sojourners of the diaspora chosen for the "obedience" (ὑπακοήν) that resulted in their cultic atonement and made possible not only their cultic but moral purification through the sacrificial sprinkling of the blood of Jesus Christ (1:2), the audience have purified their souls ethically in their "obedience" to the truth for sincere brotherly affection.[24]

As a consequence of the ethical purification of their souls in the obedience to the truth for sincere brotherly affection, the audience are exhorted, from a "clean" or "purified" (καθαρᾶς) heart, to love one another earnestly (1:22).[25] The audience have been addressed as those who, although not having seen, "you are loving" (ἀγαπᾶτε) Jesus Christ, for whom they are portrayed as presently engaged in the communal liturgical worship of exulting with a joy indescribable and glorified (1:8). Now, they are to complement this liturgical worship motivated by their love for Jesus Christ with the ethical worship of their "purified" souls and hearts, as "you are to love" (ἀγαπήσατε) one another constantly.

The audience's liturgical worship of blessing the God and Father of our Lord Jesus Christ was motivated by their being among those to whom God "has given new birth [ἀναγεννήσας]" (1:3). In a complementary manner, their ethical worship of loving one another constantly (1:22) is motivated by their "having been given new birth" (ἀναγεγεννημένοι) by God (1:23). Just as they have been ransomed by God from their former futile conduct with its false worship "not [οὐ] with perishable things [φθαρτοῖς]" (1:18), so they have been given new birth by God "not [οὐκ] from a seed perishable [φθαρτῆς] but imperishable [ἀφθάρτου]" (1:23).

Resonating with the "imperishable" (ἄφθαρτον) inheritance being kept by God in heaven for the audience (1:4), that the seed instigating this new birth is emphatically "imperishable [ἀφθάρτου]" (1:23) underscores

---

23. "The word ἁγνίζω usually carries a ceremonial referent both in the LXX and in the NT and is probably doing the same here, while the use of ἀληθείας is probably in contrast to ἀγνοίᾳ in v. 14 which defines the falsehood of unbelief" (Mbuvi, *Temple*, 83). "The verb ἁγνίζω ('purify') is used in the Old Testament to refer to ritual purification, but 1 Peter uses the term in reference to moral purification" (Senior, *1 Peter*, 47).

24. "The association of purification with obedience recalls Peter's opening greeting, and (especially in light of the reflection on Christ's 'precious blood' in v 19) suggests that the purification of the readers' souls has been accomplished in principle by 'sprinkling with the blood of Jesus' (v 2)" (Michaels, *1 Peter*, 75).

25. "Since they have purified their souls through ὑπακοῇ τῆς ἀληθείας ('obedience of truth'), their conduct should be dictated by their καθαρᾶς ('purified') hearts (1.22). For 1 Peter, obedience is an act of faith and not a prerequisite to faith meaning he is not calling for works righteousness but rather the expression of faith that demonstrates the believers' purification" (Mbuvi, *Temple*, 83–84).

for the audience how it is a birth to eternal, heavenly life. That the new birth from a seed imperishable is "through" (διά) a "living" (ζῶντος) word of God, which is indeed emphatically "abiding [μένοντος]" (1:23), further underscores that this is a birth to a risen, eternal life. It recalls that this new birth is for a "living" (ζῶσαν) hope "through" (διά) the resurrection of Jesus Christ from the dead (1:3).[26]

The exhortation for the audience to become holy as God is holy in all of their conduct (1:15), so that it may render not only liturgical but ethical worship to God, was reinforced by the divine authority of the scriptural word of God himself from Lev 19:2—"because" (διότι) it is written, "You shall be holy, for I am holy" (1:16). Similarly, the exhortation to love one another constantly (1:22) as part of their ethical worship is reinforced by the divine authority of the scriptural word of God from Isa 40:6, 8—"because" (διότι) "all flesh is as grass and all its glory as a flower of the grass; the grass withers and the flower wilts (1:24); but the pronouncement of the Lord abides for eternity" (1:25).[27]

That all flesh is perishable "as" (ὡς) grass and all its glory perishable "as" (ὡς) a flower of the grass (1:24) reinforces the implicit exhortation for the audience, "as" (ὡς) children of obedience (1:14) who have been given new birth for an imperishable life (1:23; cf. 1:3), to imitate the sacrificial obedience of Christ, which was "as" (ὡς) of a lamb flawless and faultless (1:19). In contrast to the "glory" (δόξαν) of eternal life which the audience hope to receive at the revelation of Jesus Christ (1:7d), the "glory" (δόξα) of all flesh is as a flower of the grass that withers and wilts, rather than "abiding" (μένει) for eternity like the pronouncement of the Lord, the "living" word of God, which is indeed "abiding" (μένοντος) eternally (1:23).[28]

---

26. "The two phrases thus express the double aspect of the word of God as seed: it is both the imperishable source and the enduring means of Christian rebirth" (Elliott, *1 Peter*, 389). "[T]he parallelism between ἀφθάρτου and μένοντος, each in the emphatic position in its clause, suggests that as ἀφθάρτου modifies σπορᾶς, so μένοντος is to modify λόγου" (Achtemeier, *1 Peter*, 140). See also LaVerdiere, "Grammatical Ambiguity," 92.

27. "It is possible that 'Lord' is used in order to affirm that it is the word of Jesus that endures forever. However, 'Lord' can refer to both God and Jesus" (Donelson, *I & II Peter*, 53). "The Isaian phrase ῥῆμα τοῦ θεοῦ ἡμῶν is a subjective genitive construction (the word that our God speaks). But our author's substitution of 'Lord' for 'God,' along with the echo of vv 10-12 in vv 24-25, suggest that he intended this as an objective genitive construction: the word *about* the Lord. From this perspective, the word that endures forever is the word about Jesus Christ, his suffering, and glorification. This constitutes the heart of the good news for his suffering audience and the word from which they are to draw constant nourishment (2:3) [emphasis original]" (Elliott, *1 Peter*, 391).

28. "Peter does not consciously choose the word δόξα ('glory') to refer to this outward beauty; his use of Isa 40:6 makes it inevitable. Yet its occurrence in the Scripture quotation creates an appropriate contrast with the eschatological 'glory' of Jesus Christ

1 Peter, 2 Peter, and Jude

The divine gifts announced to the audience through those who "proclaimed good news" (εὐαγγελισαμένων) unto "you [ὑμᾶς]" (1:12) motivates their communal liturgical worship of exulting in God (1:6) and exulting for Christ (1:8). Similarly, the divine gift of their new birth to eternal life (1:23) through the pronouncement that was "proclaimed as good news" (εὐαγγελισθέν) "for you [ὑμᾶς]" (1:25) motivates their ethical worship of loving one another constantly from purified souls and clean hearts (1:22).

The good news was proclaimed "for [εἰς] you" (1:25), the audience who have purified their souls in obedience to the truth "for" (εἰς) sincere brotherly affection (1:22). That the good news was proclaimed "for you [εἰς ὑμᾶς]" (1:25) continues the concerted focus upon the audience as the privileged recipients of divine grace, as it reaffirms not only the manifestation of Christ "for the sake of you [δι' ὑμᾶς]" (1:20), but the grace the prophets prophesied "for you [εἰς ὑμᾶς]" (1:10), and the eternal heavenly inheritance "for you [εἰς ὑμᾶς]" (1:4).[29] The living and abiding word of "God [θεοῦ]" (1:23) proclaimed as good news "for you" thus motivates the holistic worship—both the liturgical and the ethical—of the audience as those who through Christ are faithful in all of their conduct as worship "for God" (εἰς θεόν), as those whose faith and hope are ultimately "for God [εἰς θεόν]" (1:21). All of the divine grace that comes through Christ and is emphatically "for you" enables all of their conduct to serve as proper worship, through the sacrificial worship of Christ, which is emphatically and finally "for God."

Summary on 1:14-25

Rather than being conformed to the desires of their former ignorance, as children of obedience (1:14), the audience, according to the "Holy One" who called them, are to become "holy" themselves in all of their conduct (1:15), because in the authoritative scriptural word of God himself from Lev

---

made possible by his resurrection (vv 11, 21) and waiting to be revealed to those who trust in him (v 7; 4:13; 5:1, 4)" (Michaels, *1 Peter* 78).

29. "The final phrase εἰς ὑμᾶς could mean simply that the readers were the people to whom the gospel was preached, but its emphatic position in the sentence probably means it carries a greater significance, for example, 'for your benefit,' perhaps even implying 'for your salvation'" (Achtemeier, *1 Peter*, 142). "The placement of εἰς ὑμᾶς at the end of the section gives emphasis to what has been a major theme in the epistle's first chapter at least since the εἰς ὑμᾶς of v 4: everything that God planned from the beginning, everything that he accomplished through the death and resurrection of Jesus Christ, everything still waiting to be revealed, is for the sake of the Christians in Asia Minor who read Peter's words. From the εἰς ὑμᾶς of vv 4 and 10, to the δι' ὑμᾶς of v 20, to the εἰς ὑμᾶς of v 25, all of it, punctuated by the repetition of the pronouns ὑμῶν (vv 7, 9, 13, 14, 17, 18, 21, 22), ὑμῖν (vv 12, 13), and ὑμᾶς (vv 12, 15) is 'for you'" (Michaels, *1 Peter*, 79).

1 Peter 1:14–25

19:2 it is written, "You shall be holy, for I am holy" (1:16). The audience are to completely hope upon the grace God will give them at the revelation of Jesus Christ (1:13), as they are engaged in the communal liturgical worship of exulting in God (1:6) and for Christ (1:8). But their liturgical worship is to be complemented by their becoming holy, consecrating themselves to the God who is the Holy One, in all of their conduct, which includes not only their liturgical but ethical worship of God.

In "fear," in both the respectful "fear" of the Father who judges them and the reverent "fear" of the Father they worship, the audience are to "conduct" the time of their sojourning (1:17), the time before the attainment of their heavenly inheritance (1:4), as chosen sojourners of the diaspora (1:1). They may thereby become holy as God is holy, "according" to the Holy One who called them, in all of their "conduct" (1:15), devoting themselves to God in both their worship and in the work "according" to which the Holy One will judge them (1:17). Such work may be found for the praise, glory, and honor that God will give and that will be given to God as worship at the last judgment (1:7d).

The obedience of Christ, the moral or ethical conduct involved in his submission to the will of God, was essential to the sacrificial worship of the sprinkling of his blood for the atonement and purification that enables the audience's own worship (1:2c). Similarly, the comparison of the precious blood of Christ with the sacrificial worship of a lamb employs the cultic terminology for a worthy sacrifice. "As of a lamb flawless and faultless" (1:19) metaphorically portrays Christ's obedient conduct as the sacrificial worship that rendered his blood precious for the redemption that has liberated the audience from their past futile conduct, which included their inadequate cultic and ethical worship.

The audience have been ransomed or redeemed from their futile conduct not with perishable silver or gold (1:18) but with the precious blood that resulted from the obedient suffering and death of Christ, the blood that has a "precious" value beyond what is perishable, a value oriented to risen, eternal life (1:19). This strengthens the resolve of the audience to suffer the various trials (1:6) that will refine their faith, bestowing it with an imperishable, eternal value "more precious" than perishable gold (1:7b). At the final revelation of Jesus Christ such refinement of faith through suffering may be found for the praise, glory, and honor (1:7d) to be given both by God, the Father who judges the work of each one (1:17b), and as worship to the God the audience call upon as Father (1:17a) in their communal prayer.

Rather than being conformed, as "before," to the desires of their "ignorance" (1:14), the audience are to be "knowing" that they have been ransomed by God from their former futile conduct (1:18) with the precious

61

blood of the Christ "foreknown" by God "before" the foundation of the world (1:20a). That the Christ with whose precious blood the audience have been ransomed by God was "foreknown" by God closely associates the audience, chosen according to the "foreknowledge" of God the Father for obedience and sprinkling of the blood of Jesus Christ (1:2), with Christ in God's plan of salvation. Christ has been manifested for the sake of the audience in the "last" of these "times" (1:20b), the end-time of God's salvific plan that has already begun to be completed, which includes the present "time" of their sojourning (1:17), as they await the salvation to be fully and finally revealed in the "last" time (1:5).

Not only the "faith" of the audience, who through Christ are "faithful" for God (1:21a), but their "hope" is fully focused on God as the ultimate goal of their worship (1:21c). This bolsters the exhortation for the audience to completely "hope" upon the grace that is to be borne to them by God at the full and final revelation of Jesus Christ (1:13), whom God raised from the dead and gave glory (1:21b). Their hope for God is the living "hope" for which God gave believers a new birth through the resurrection of Jesus Christ from the dead (1:3). That their hope is "for God" reinforces their realization that their worship of exulting "in God" (1:6), their joyful exulting "for Christ" (1:8), is ultimately their worship "for God"—the God who raised Christ from the dead, so that the audience may worship God with the "living" hope for the glory of a risen, eternal life from and for God.

As a consequence of the ethical purification of their souls in the obedience to the truth for sincere brotherly affection, the audience are exhorted, from a "clean" or "purified" heart, to love one another constantly (1:22). The audience have been addressed as those who, although not having seen him, "you are loving" Jesus Christ, for whom they are portrayed as presently engaged in the communal liturgical worship of exulting with a joy indescribable and glorified (1:8). Now, they are to complement this liturgical worship motivated by their love for Jesus Christ with the ethical worship of their "purified" souls and hearts, as "you are to love" one another constantly.

The audience's liturgical worship of blessing the God and Father of our Lord Jesus Christ was motivated by their being among those to whom God "has given new birth" (1:3). In a complementary manner, their ethical worship of loving one another constantly (1:22) is motivated by their "having been given new birth" by God (1:23). Just as they have been ransomed or redeemed by God from their former futile conduct with its false worship "not with perishable things" (1:18), so they have been given new birth by God "not from a seed perishable but imperishable" (1:23).

The exhortation to love one another constantly (1:22) as part of their ethical worship is reinforced by the divine authority of the scriptural word

1 Peter 1:14–25

of God from Isa 40:6, 8—"because all flesh is like grass and all its glory like a flower of the grass; the grass withers and the flower wilts (1:24); but the pronouncement of the Lord abides for eternity" (1:25). In contrast to the "glory" of eternal life which the audience hope to receive at the revelation of Jesus Christ (1:7d), the "glory" of all flesh is like a flower of the grass that withers and wilts, rather than "abiding" for eternity like the pronouncement of the Lord, the "living" word of God, which is indeed "abiding" eternally (1:23).

The good news was proclaimed "for you" (1:25), the audience who have purified their souls in obedience to the truth "for" sincere brotherly love (1:22). That the good news was proclaimed "for you" continues the concerted focus upon the audience as the privileged recipients of divine grace, as it reaffirms not only the manifestation of Christ "for the sake of you" (1:20), but the grace the prophets prophesied "for you" (1:10), and the eternal heavenly inheritance "for you" (1:4). The living and abiding word of "God" (1:23) proclaimed as good news "for you" thus motivates the holistic worship—both the liturgical and the ethical—of the audience as those who through Christ are faithful in all of their conduct as worship "for God," as those whose faith and hope are ultimately "for God" (1:21). All of the divine grace that comes through Christ and is emphatically "for you" enables all of their conduct to serve as proper worship, through the sacrificial worship of Christ, which is emphatically and finally "for God."

4

1 Peter 2:1-17
Offer Up Spiritual Sacrifices Acceptable to God through Jesus Christ (C)

Keep your conduct among Gentiles praiseworthy that they may glorify God

A   2:1 Having removed then all *evil* and all deceit and hypocrisies and envies and all *slanders*, ² as newborn infants long for the pure milk of the word, so that by it you may grow up for salvation, ³ if you have tasted that benevolent is the *Lord* (Ps 33:9 LXX). ⁴ Before whom approaching, a living stone by *human beings* rejected but in the sight of God chosen, esteemed, ⁵ also yourselves as living stones are being built up as a spiritual house for a holy priesthood to offer up spiritual sacrifices acceptable to God through Jesus Christ. ⁶ Because it stands in scripture, "Behold I am setting in Zion a stone, a cornerstone, chosen, esteemed, and whoever believes in it will never be put to shame" (Isa 28:16). ⁷ Its *honor* then is for you who believe, but for those who do not believe "the stone which the builders rejected, this has become the head of the corner" (Ps 117:22 LXX), ⁸ and "a stone of stumbling and rock of offense" (Isa 8:14). They stumble, disobeying the word, for which indeed they were set. ⁹ᵃ But you are a chosen race, a royal priesthood, a holy *nation*,

  B   ⁹ᵇ a *people* for possession,

    C ⁹ᶜ so that you may proclaim the virtues of the one who called you out of darkness for his marvelous light,

  B′ ¹⁰ who were once not a *people* but now are God's *people*, who had not received mercy but now have received mercy.

A' **11** Beloved, I encourage you as aliens and sojourners to keep away from fleshly desires that are waging war against the soul, **12** keeping your conduct among the *Gentiles* praiseworthy, so that in what they *slander* you as *evildoers*, observing from the praiseworthy works, they may glorify God on the day of visitation. **13** Be subject to every *human* institution on account of the *Lord*, whether to a king as being in authority, **14** whether to governors as sent through him for the punishment of *evildoers* but the praise of good doers, **15** for thus it is the will of God that those doing good silence the ignorance of foolish *human beings*, **16** as free but not keeping freedom as a cover for *evil*, but rather as slaves of God. **17** *Honor* all, love the brotherhood, fear God, *honor* the king.[1]

Audience Response to 2:1–17

1. 1 Pet 2:1–9a (A): Benevolent Is the Lord Rejected by Human Beings

The audience hear the A element (2:1–9a) of this chiastic unit as a chiastic pattern in itself:

a) Having removed then all evil and all deceit and hypocrisies and envies and all slanders, as newborn infants long for the pure milk of the *word*, so that by it you may grow up for salvation, if you have tasted that benevolent is the Lord (Ps 33:9 LXX) (2:1–3).

  b) Before whom approaching, a living *stone* by human beings *rejected* but in the sight of *God chosen, esteemed*, also yourselves as living *stones* are being *built* up as a *spiritual* house for a holy priesthood (2:4–5a)

  b') to offer up *spiritual* sacrifices acceptable to *God* through Jesus Christ. Because it stands in scripture, "Behold I am setting in Zion a *stone*, a cornerstone, *chosen, esteemed*, and whoever believes in it will never be put to shame" (Isa 28:16). Its honor then is for you who believe, but for those who do not believe "the *stone* which the *builders rejected*, this has become the head of the corner" (Ps 117:22 LXX), and "a *stone* of stumbling and rock of offense" (Isa 8:14). They stumble (2:5b–8a),

a') disobeying the *word*, for which indeed they were set. But you are a chosen race, a royal priesthood, a holy nation (2:8b–9a).

At the center of this chiastic sub-unit the audience experience a pivot of parallels involving the only occurrences in 1 Peter of "stone," "rejected," "chosen, esteemed," "built," and "spiritual," and in this sub-unit of "God." "A living stone [λίθον] by human beings rejected [ἀποδεδοκιμασμένον]

---

1. For the establishment of 1 Pet 2:1–17 as a chiasm, see ch. 1.

but in the sight of God [θεῷ] chosen, esteemed [ἐκλεκτὸν ἔντιμον], also yourselves as living stones [λίθοι] are being built [οἰκοδομεῖσθε] up as a spiritual [πνευματικός] house" is heard in the b) sub-element (2:4-5a). This progresses to "offer up spiritual [πνευματικάς] sacrifices acceptable to God [θεῷ] . . . a stone [λίθον], a cornerstone, chosen, esteemed [ἐκλεκτὸν ἔντιμον] . . . the stone [λίθος] which the builders [οἰκοδομοῦντες] rejected [ἀπεδοκίμασαν] . . . a stone [λίθος] of stumbling" in the b') sub-element (2:5b-8a). They then hear a progression of parallels involving the only occurrences in this sub-unit of expressions for "word." "The pure milk of the word [λογικόν]" (2:2) in the a) sub-element (2:1-3) progresses to "disobeying the word [λόγῳ]" (2:8b) in the a') sub-element (2:8b-9a).

With the statement about having removed "all" (πᾶσαν) evil and "all" (πάντα) deceit and "all" (πάσας) slanders (2:1), the audience hear the transitional words that link this unit (2:1-17) with the preceding unit (1:14-25). Toward the conclusion of that unit the audience heard that "all" (πᾶσα) flesh is like grass and "all" (πᾶσα) its glory like a flower of the grass (1:24). They thus experience a transitional focus from the perishability of the total human condition to the totality of their former futile conduct inherited from their human fathers from which they have been ransomed not with perishable things but with the sacrificial blood of Christ precious for eternal life (1:18).

The audience, as "newborn [ἀρτιγέννητα] infants," are to long for the "pure milk" of the "word," literally, of "what pertains to the word [λογικόν]" (2:2a), as a consequence of their "having been given new birth" (ἀναγεγεννημένοι) by God not from a seed perishable but imperishable, through a living "word" (λόγου) of God (1:23).[2] Indeed, they are "newborn infants" as among those to whom God "has given new birth" (ἀναγεννήσας) for a living hope through the resurrection of Jesus Christ from the dead (1:3). As "newborn infants," they are to long for the metaphorical "milk" that is "pure," with a connotation of being "without deceit" (ἄδολον). This "pure milk" of the word of God stands in appropriate contrast to all of the "deceit" (δόλον) included in their former futile conduct, which they have removed (2:1) now that they are "infants" born into a new way of life.[3]

---

2. Dubis, *1 Peter*, 44; McCartney, "1Peter 2,2," 128-32. "Λογικός recalls the 'word' (λόγος) of 1:23, its synonym ῥῆμα (1:25), and its interpretation as the 'good news' in 1:25b—all portraying the means of Christian rebirth. In addition, it anticipates the further reference to this same 'word' (λόγος) in 2:8, where obedience-disobedience to the word is the point" (Elliott, *1 Peter*, 401). See also Achtemeier, *1 Peter*, 146-47.

3. "The undeceitful character of this milk imposes not only a contrast to the deceit that the recipients are to put away but also an association with the 'truth' that lies at the source of obedience (1:22)" (Donelson, *I & II Peter*, 57).

1 Peter 2:1-17

As "newborn infants," the audience are to long for the "pure milk" of the word, so that, in a continuation of their metaphorical infancy, by it they may "grow up" for salvation (2:2). In contrast to being conformed to their former "desires [ἐπιθυμίαις]" (1:14), the audience are exhorted that "you are to long for" (ἐπιποθήσατε) the "pure milk" of the word by which they may "grow up" for the salvation included among the divine gifts for which angels "are desiring" (ἐπιθυμοῦσιν) to catch a glimpse (1:12).[4] They are to grow up "for salvation" (εἰς σωτηρίαν) as the final goal of their new birth from God, the "salvation" (σωτηρίας) concerning which prophets sought out and searched out (1:10), the "salvation" (σωτηρίαν) of souls that they are attaining as the end of their faith (1:9). The audience are to grow up "for a salvation" (εἰς σωτηρίαν) ready to be revealed in the last time (1:5), a salvation from death to the risen, eternal life for which they have been given a new birth by God through the resurrection of Jesus Christ from the dead (1:3).

The provision, if "you have tasted that benevolent is the Lord [ἐγεύσασθε ὅτι χρηστὸς ὁ κύριος]" (2:3), affirms the audience's acceptance of the invitation given by the scriptural word of God in Ps 33:9 LXX: "Taste [γεύσασθε] and see that benevolent is the Lord [ὅτι χρηστὸς ὁ κύριος]." The subordinating conjunction "if" (εἰ) leads the audience to consider, but decisively to reject, the possibility that they have not tasted the benevolence of the Lord.[5] An alliterative wordplay underlines that the Lord who is "benevolent" (χρηστός) is the Lord who is Jesus "Christ [Χριστός]" (1:3; cf. 1:1, 2, 7, 11, 13, 19).[6]

As "newborn infants" who are to long for the "pure milk" of the word (2:2), the audience have already metaphorically "tasted," and thus began to experience, that benevolent is the "Lord [κύριος]" (2:3), when the pronouncement of the "Lord" (κυρίου), the pronouncement about the "Lord" (κυρίου) Jesus Christ (1:3), was proclaimed as good news to them (1:25; cf. 1:12). They have "tasted" the benevolence of the Lord in the pronouncement of the Lord that abides for eternity (1:25), the living and eternally abiding

---

4. "The imperative ἐπιποθήσατε is for Peter the recognition of legitimate 'desire,' the equivalent for Christian believers of the 'impulses' (ἐπιθυμίαι) that controlled them in the past (1:14; 2:11; 4:2–3), and (in a different way) of the unfulfilled 'desire' (ἐπιθυμοῦσιν, present indicative) of the angels trying to probe the mysteries of salvation (1:12)" (Michaels, *1 Peter*, 86).

5. "Peter wanted the readers to contemplate whether they have in fact experienced the kindness of the Lord, and he was confident that the answer would be affirmative. Translating the term 'if' by 'now' or 'since,' however, short-circuits the process, removing the contingency that the author wanted his readers to consider" (Schreiner, *1, 2 Peter*, 101).

6. Van Rensburg, "Referent," 103–19. "Interpreters through the ages have noted the possible wordplay between χρηστός and Χριστός in 1 Pet. 2:3. The difference between 'the Lord is good' and 'the Lord is Christ' is but one vowel" (Jobes, *1 Peter*, 137). See also Caulley, "The *Chrestos/Christos* Pun," 376–87.

word of God, the imperishable seed from which they were given a new birth (1:23) for eternal life. The audience are thus to long for the "pure milk" of the living and abiding word of God through which they have already "tasted" the "benevolence," which is the "Christ," in the pronouncement about the Lord Jesus Christ. By the nourishing "pure milk" of the word of God, which they hear proclaimed in their communal worship, the audience may "grow up" for the salvation of eternal life, their final goal as "newborn infants."[7]

In correspondence to the audience "having removed" (ἀποθέμενοι) and thus turned aside from all of the immorality (2:1) of their former futile conduct (1:18), they are now depicted as "approaching" (προσερχόμενοι), a term with a connotation of cultic worship, before the Lord Jesus Christ (2:4) whom they have already "tasted" as benevolent (2:3). The Jesus Christ "whom" (ὅν), not having seen, they are loving, and "for whom" (εἰς ὅν) they are engaged in the worship of exulting with a joy indescribable and glorified (1:8), is the Lord "before whom" (πρὸς ὅν) they are now, in a cultic way, "approaching" as a worshiping community.[8]

The Lord Jesus Christ (2:3) before whom the audience are approaching in their worship is metaphorically portrayed as a "living stone rejected by human beings but in the sight of God chosen, esteemed" (2:4). That the Lord Jesus Christ is a "living" (ζῶντα) stone resonates with the pronouncement about the Lord Jesus that abides for eternity (1:25), the "living" (ζῶντος) word of God through which the audience have been given a new birth for eternal life (1:23). This "living" stone provides the foundation for the "living" (ζῶσαν) hope through the resurrection of Jesus Christ from the dead, the living hope of eternal life for which God has given believers a new birth (1:3).[9]

Although as a "living stone" the Lord Jesus Christ was rejected by human beings, in the sight of God he was "chosen, esteemed" (2:4). That he was "chosen" (ἐκλεκτόν) in the sight of God recalls and resonates with the address of the audience as sojourners of the diaspora "chosen [ἐκλεκτοῖς]"

---

7. Tite, "Nurslings," 371–400. "Of all the sensory metaphors, tasting is the most intimate and the only one that involves ingestion. Seeing God, hearing God, even touching God, does not carry the powerful connotations that 'tasting' implies—making the experience of God internal to oneself" (Jobes, 1 Peter, 139). For a view that milk here does not refer to God's word, but to God's continuing grace, see Jobes, "Got Milk," 1–14.

8. "Προσέρχομαι is used cultically in 1 Pet 2:4 (come to Jesus, the 'living stone') [emphasis original]" (Palzkill, "προσέρχομαι," 164). "The content of the verse makes clear that the κύριος ('Lord') of v. 3, to which the ὅν refers, is to be understood as Christ rather than God, despite the fact that προσέρχομαι is used in the LXX of a priest's approach to God" (Achtemeier, 1 Peter, 153).

9. "If there is a common denominator in Peter's three uses of the participle 'living' (i.e., 'living hope,' 'living God,' 'living Stone'), it is the implied contrast with the hopelessness and idolatry of contemporary paganism" (Michaels, 1 Peter, 98).

1 Peter 2:1-17

(1:1) according to the foreknowledge of God the Father (1:2). This reaffirms the similar privileged positions both the Lord Jesus Christ and the audience have within God's plan of eternal salvation. That as a "living stone" the Lord Jesus Christ was "chosen" is emphatically intensified by his also being "esteemed" (ἔντιμον) in the sight of God. This resonates with his sacrificial blood being "precious [τιμίῳ]" (1:19), the blood with which the audience have been ransomed by God from their former futile conduct (1:18). God's "esteem" for the Lord Jesus Christ as a "living stone" provides a further foundation for the audience's hope of being found for praise, glory, and "honor" or "esteem" (τιμήν) at the revelation of Jesus Christ (1:7).

Not only is the Lord Jesus Christ a "living stone" (λίθον ζῶντα) chosen and esteemed in the sight of God (2:4), but the audience themselves—"also yourselves" (καὶ αὐτοί)—as "living stones" (λίθοι ζῶντες) are being built up by God (divine passive) as a spiritual house for a "holy" (ἅγιον) priesthood (2:5a).[10] This accords with the exhortation for the audience, according to the "Holy One" (ἅγιον) who called them, to become "holy" (ἅγιοι) "also yourselves" (καὶ αὐτοί) in all conduct (1:15), because it is written, "You shall be holy [ἅγιοι], for I am holy [ἅγιός]" (Lev 19:2 in 1:16). That "as" (ὡς) living stones "you are being built up" (οἰκοδομεῖσθε) by God as a spiritual "house" (οἶκος) "for" (εἰς) a holy priesthood reinforces the exhortation for the audience, "as" (ὡς) newborn infants, to long for the pure milk of the word of God, so that by this divine assistance "you may grow up" (αὐξηθῆτε) "for" (εἰς) eternal salvation (2:2).[11]

As living stones who are being built up as a "spiritual" (πνευματικός) house for a "holy" (ἅγιον) priesthood, the audience are to offer up "spiritual" (πνευματικάς) sacrifices acceptable to "God" (θεῷ) through Jesus Christ (2:5), a living stone by human beings rejected but in the sight of "God" (θεῷ) chosen, esteemed (2:4).[12] This accords with the status of the audience as

---

10. "We can summarize the verse as follows, You as a spiritual house are being built up 'to be a holy priesthood' (NRSV) . . . we should not be surprised that believers are both priests and the temple. They are God's dwelling place by the Spirit and his new priesthood. No internal contradiction is involved since Peter did not refer to believers as priests serving in a literal temple" (Schreiner, *1, 2 Peter*, 105–6). "Each person is not a priest; rather they together form a priesthood. Although the word ἱεράτευμα occurs only here and in 2:9 in the NT, the concept of a called people being a priesthood is a frequent part of OT covenant language. In both 2:5 and 2:9, then, 1 Peter seems to quote Exod 19:3–8 . . . the whole nation is called to function as a priesthood for the rest of humanity" (Donelson, *I & II Peter*, 62).

11. "While the word οἶκος can describe a building—the metaphor of stones would suggest that here—it can also describe the inhabitants of such a building" (Achtemeier, *1 Peter*, 155).

12. "'Spiritual' has its normal function of inscribing divine presence. Thus God's somewhat effaced presence in the passive 'you are being built up' emerges in the more

those chosen in the "holiness" (ἁγιασμῷ) of the divine "Spirit [πνεύματος]" (1:2), the "Spirit" (πνεῦμα) of Christ that was in the prophets (1:11), and the "Holy Spirit" (πνεύματι ἁγίῳ) by whom good news was proclaimed to them (1:12). They are to offer up these spiritual sacrifices acceptable to "God" (θεῷ) "through" (διά) Jesus Christ, as those who "through him" (δι' αὐτοῦ) are faithful for "God [θεόν]" (1:21). Through the cultic sacrificial worship of Jesus Christ, with whose precious blood (1:19) the audience have been ransomed from their former futile conduct with its false worship (1:18), the audience have been enabled to offer up "spiritual sacrifices," their conduct in reverence of God (1:17), as their ethical worship.[13]

The audience hear the remainder of the b') sub-element (2:5b–8a) of this chiastic sub-unit (2:1–9a) as yet another chiastic pattern in itself:

(a) Because it stands in scripture, "Behold I am setting in Zion a *stone*, a cornerstone, chosen, esteemed (2:6a),

  (b) and whoever *believes* in it will never be put to shame (Isa 28:16)" (2:6b).

  (b') Its honor then is for you who *believe*, but for those who do *not believe* (2:7a)

(a') "the *stone* which the builders rejected, this has become the head of the corner" (Ps 117:22 LXX), and "a *stone* of stumbling and rock of offense" (Isa 8:14). They stumble (2:7b–8a).

At the center of this chiastic sub-unit the audience experience a pivot of parallels involving the only occurrences in this sub-unit of expressions for "believing." "Whoever believes [πιστεύων] in it" in the (b) sub-element (2:6b) progresses to "you who believe [πιστεύουσιν], but for those who do not believe [ἀπιστοῦσιν]" in the (b') sub-element (2:7a). They then hear a progression of parallels involving the only occurrences in this sub-unit of the term "stone." "I am setting in Zion a stone [λίθον]" in the (a) sub-element

---

straightforward way in the adjective 'spiritual'" (Donelson, *I & II Peter*, 62).

13. "Therefore, the spiritual sacrifices in view may be understood as all behavior that flows from a transformation of the human spirit by the sanctifying work of the Holy Spirit (1:2)" (Jobes, *1 Peter*, 151). "1 Peter focuses on the spiritual *acts* of worship—not just prayer (1 Pet. 3.7) but also the equivalent of the sacrificial elements of the OT *cultus* (1 Pet. 1.18–20) [emphases original]" (Mbuvi, *Temple*, 108). "Because of the emphatic position of the phrase διὰ Ἰησοῦ Χριστοῦ at the end of the verse, it would appear most appropriate to understand that it is the entire act of offering acceptable sacrifices to God that depends on the prior enablement of Christ" (Achtemeier, *1 Peter*, 158). "In 1 Peter, as in Hebrews, the 'spiritual sacrifices' are first of all something offered up to God as worship and, second, a pattern of social conduct. The two aspects cannot be separated, and the priority is always the same . . . That the 'spiritual sacrifices' are 'acceptable to God through Jesus Christ' supports the view that they are above all acts of worship" (Michaels, *1 Peter*, 101–2).

(2:6a) progresses to "the stone [λίθος] which the builders rejected" (2:7b) and "a stone [λίθος] of stumbling" (2:8a) in the (a') sub-element (2:7b–8a).

That the Lord Jesus Christ is a living "stone" (λίθον) by human beings rejected but in the sight of God "chosen, esteemed [ἐκλεκτὸν ἔντιμον]" (2:4) the audience are to appreciate as part of God's plan of salvation. "Because" (διότι; cf. 1:16, 24) it stands in God's scriptural word, "Behold, I am setting in Zion a stone [λίθον], a cornerstone, chosen, esteemed [ἐκλεκτὸν ἔντιμον], and whoever believes in it will never be put to shame" (Isa 28:16 in 2:6). Since whoever "believes" (πιστεύων) in this "stone" will never be put to shame by God (divine passive), the audience, as those not seeing but "believing [πιστεύοντες]" (1:8), are assured that they will not be shamed by God in the last judgment. This is confirmed in more positive terms as the audience hear that the divine "honor" (τιμή) of this "stone" is for "you who believe [πιστεύουσιν]" (2:7), further bolstering the hope of the audience to be found for praise, glory, and "honor" (τιμήν) at the revelation of Jesus Christ (1:7).[14]

But for those who do not believe, in accord with God's scriptural word in Ps 117:22 LXX, "the stone which the builders rejected, this has become the head of the corner" (2:7). The audience are to realize that the builders who "rejected" (ἀπεδοκίμασαν) the "stone" (λίθος) are the nonbelieving human beings by whom the Lord Jesus Christ as a living "stone" (λίθον) was "rejected [ἀποδεδοκιμασμένον]" (2:4). In contrast to these human, nonbelieving "builders" (οἰκοδομοῦντες), the audience have heard that, as living "stones" (λίθοι), "you are being built up" (οἰκοδομεῖσθε) by God as a spiritual "house" (οἶκος) for a holy priesthood (2:5). That this rejected stone has become the "head of the corner" (κεφαλὴν γωνίας) resonates with its being a "cornerstone" (ἀκρογωνιαῖον), chosen and esteemed by God (2:6) as the foundation for the audience to be built up as a spiritual "house" to offer up spiritual sacrifices acceptable to God through Jesus Christ (2:5).[15] But for nonbelievers, in accord with God's scriptural word in Isa 8:14, this stone has become "a stone [λίθος] of stumbling and rock of offense" (2:8a).[16]

---

14. "The 'honor' or 'privilege' to which Peter refers is final vindication before God, the equivalent of never being put to shame; it is the same vindication already described more fully as 'praise, glory, and honor at the time when Jesus Christ is revealed' (1:7)" (Michaels, 1 Peter, 104).

15. "The term 'house' (οἶκος) alludes to the temple, which is commonly called a 'house' in the Old Testament and is also designated as a house in the New Testament. In particular, when the verb 'build' (οἰκοδομέω) is combined with 'house' (οἶκος) in the Septuagint, the temple is often in view" (Schreiner, 1, 2 Peter, 105). "The similarity between κεφαλὴ γωνίας and ἀκρογωνιαῖος in the context of 1 Peter favors their similar designation of *foundation* stones set at the farthest (and foremost) corner with which a building is begun [emphasis original]" (Elliott, 1 Peter, 429).

16. Siegert, "Christus," 139–46. "In Peter's imagery, Christ is included in the spiritual

In contrast to the believing audience who are being built up as a spiritual house (2:5) upon the foundation of the Lord Jesus Christ as a living stone (2:4), which is a cornerstone and head of the corner (2:6-7), nonbelievers "stumble" on this stone as a stone of stumbling and rock of offense, "disobeying the word, for which indeed they were set" (2:8). Whereas the audience are to long for the pure milk pertaining to the "word" (λογικόν) of God (2:2), the living "word" (λόγου) of God through which they were given new birth for eternal life (1:23), nonbelievers are disobeying the "word" (λόγῳ) of God. For which disobedience these nonbelievers were indeed "set" or "placed" (ἐτέθησαν) by God (divine passive) within God's plan of eternal salvation, just as the scriptural word of God declares that "I am setting" (τίθημι) in Zion a stone, a cornerstone, chosen, esteemed (2:6).[17]

But the audience are to appreciate that, as divinely "chosen" (ἐκλεκτοῖς) sojourners of the diaspora (1:1), they are a divinely "chosen" (ἐκλεκτόν) race (2:9; cf. Isa 43:20), like the divinely "chosen" (ἐκλεκτόν) and esteemed Lord Jesus Christ (2:4, 6).[18] And, as a royal "priesthood" (ἱεράτευμα), a "holy" (ἅγιον) nation (2:9; cf. Exod 19:6; 23:22), the audience as believers are being built up by God as a spiritual house for a "holy priesthood" (ἱεράτευμα ἅγιον) to offer up the conduct of their lives as spiritual sacrifices acceptable to God through Jesus Christ (2:5).[19] This enables them in reverence to conduct the time of their sojourning (1:17) as a time of offering ethical

---

temple alongside believers, but as the foundational, first, and preeminent stone in the new temple, a stone that holds a unique place. Christ is the foundation stone of this new temple; apart from him the new temple would not exist" (Jobes, *1 Peter*, 148).

17. "The role of God in all this is emphasized by the choice of the passive ἐτέθησαν (they were placed). This is the same verb used in verse 6b: 'I place in Zion a stone.' God is the one who places in Zion the stone, the people who trust it, and those who reject it. The entire gathering of forces and persons around the gospel of Jesus Christ is 'placed' by God" (Donelson, *I & II Peter*, 66). See also Panning, "1 Peter 2:8," 48-52; Howe, "Christ," 35-43.

18. "The first of the phrases, γένος ἐκλεκτόν ('elect race'), is drawn from Isa 43:20 and is placed first because it resumes the theme of Christians as elect. That theme was first announced in 1:1 and continued in this passage in v. 4 with the description of Christ, to whom Christians come, as the one elect and precious to God (see also 2:6). The word γένος implies common origin, a point about Christians already made in 1:3, 23" (Achtemeier, *1 Peter*, 163-64.)

19. "Peter drew on Exod 19:6, using the exact words found there in identifying the church as a 'royal priesthood' (βασίλειον ἱεράτευμα). In Exodus the title applies to Israel, with whom God enacts his covenant at Sinai. Israel's priesthood was such that they were to mirror to the nations the glory of Yahweh, so that all nations would see that no god rivals the Lord" (Schreiner, *1, 2 Peter*, 114). "The second and third pair (βασίλειον ἱεράτευμα, ἔθνος ἅγιον, 'royal priesthood, a holy nation') are drawn from Exod 19:6, and apply additional phrases to Christians that originally described Israel as God's elect people" (Achtemeier, *1 Peter*, 164).

1 Peter 2:1-17

worship to God through the Jesus Christ they believe in as a living stone and a cornerstone, which is chosen and esteemed by God (2:4, 6-7).[20]

2:9b (B): A People for Possession

The audience are assured that not only are they a "chosen race, a royal priesthood, a holy nation" (2:9a), but also "a people for possession" (2:9b).[21] They are to appreciate that they are a people destined for the possession of the eschatological salvation of eternal life they are to inherit as among those whom God has given a new birth. That they are a people "for possession" (εἰς περιποίησιν; cf. Isa 43:21; Mal 3:17; Hag 2:9) reaffirms and adds to previous expressions employing the preposition "for" (εἰς) to indicate their God-given future and final goal. By the pure milk of God's word they are to grow up "for" (εἰς) salvation (2:2). Their faith is to be refined in various trials, so that it may be found "for" (εἰς) praise, glory, and honor at the revelation of Jesus Christ (1:7). In the power of God they are being guarded through faith "for" (εἰς) a salvation ready to be revealed in the last time (1:5). And they are among those God has given a new birth "for" (εἰς) a living hope through the resurrection of Jesus Christ from the dead (1:3), "for" (εἰς) an eternal inheritance kept by God in heaven "for [εἰς] you" (1:4).[22]

---

20. Stenschke, "Geschlecht," 119-46; Abernathy, "1 Peter 2:7-9," 24-39; Seland, "Common Priesthood," 87-119.

21. "Of the four titles comprising v 9a, λαὸς εἰς περιποίησιν is the only one pointed distinctly toward the future. Once this is recognized, such traditional renderings as 'God's own people' (RSV) or 'a people belonging to God' (NIV) are shown to be inadequate. To Peter, it is already the case that the Christian community belongs to God as a unique possession; what still awaits is its final vindication against the unbelieving and disobedient" (Michaels, *1 Peter*, 109-10).

22. "This phrase [λαὸς εἰς περιποίησιν], together with the whole clause that follows, recalls Isa 43:21 LXX. Peter has changed Isaiah's λαόν μου ὃν περιεποιησάμην to the more future-oriented λαὸς εἰς περιποίησιν. In view of Peter's characteristic use of εἰς in various eschatological expressions in 1:3-5, and especially the εἰς σωτηρίαν of 1:5 and 2:2, περιποίησις could be plausibly understood as a synonym for σωτηρία in the sense of future or final salvation . . . the choice of περιποίησιν in place of σωτηρίαν, was probably dictated by Peter's desire to echo as much as possible the language of Isa 43:21 even while making his own independent statement (cf. the use of εἰς περιποίησιν by itself in Hag 2:9b and Mal 3:17 LXX). If not the precise equivalent of σωτηρία, περιποίησις is at least a closely parallel term for future divine vindication" (Michaels, *1 Peter*, 109). See also Horrell, "Race," 123-43.

2:9c (C): Proclaim the Virtues of the One Who Called You for His Light

As those already "a chosen race, a royal priesthood, a holy nation" (2:9a), the audience are a people of God destined for the future possession of the final salvation of eternal life (2:9b), "so that you may proclaim the virtues of the one who called you out of darkness for his marvelous light" (2:9c). In both their liturgical worship and in the conduct that serves as their ethical worship, the audience may proclaim the virtues of the God who "called" (καλέσαντος) them out of the darkness of their former futile conduct (1:14, 18) for the goal of the marvelous light of his salvation. Such liturgical and ethical "proclamation" provides a way for the audience, as a royal priesthood and holy nation, to become holy in all of their conduct, according to the Holy One who "called" (καλέσαντα) them (1:15) to be holy as he is holy (1:16).[23] As those who have been called "for" (εἰς) God's marvelous light, they are a people destined "for" (εἰς) the possession of the final salvation of eternal life for which this "marvelous light" is yet another expression.[24]

2:10 (B'): Once Not a People But Now God's People

The audience are then reminded that they are those "who were once not a people but now are God's people, who had not received mercy but now have received mercy" (2:10; cf. Hos 2:25). At this point, after the central and unparalleled C element of this chiastic unit, "so that you may proclaim the virtues of the one who called you out of darkness for his marvelous light" (2:9c), the audience experience a pivot of chiastic parallels. The focus on their inheritance of a future and final goal of salvation as "a people [λαός] for possession" in the B element (2:9b) progresses to an emphatic reaffirmation of their present privileged status as those "who were once not a people [λαός] but now are God's people [λαός]" in this B' element (2:10).

---

23. "The venue of collective worship would be one natural place for such public praise. But the author's concern with the witness that the believers are to give in society (2:11—15:11) suggests that this proclamation of God's honor is fitting not only within but also *beyond* the boundaries of the Christian community . . . in all circumstances, private and public [emphasis original]" (Elliott, *1 Peter*, 439–40).

24. "Thus as darkness connotes ruin and death so light salvation and life" (Feldmeier, *First Letter*, 141). "The 'marvelous light' to which the Christian community is called is nothing other than the 'glory' soon to be revealed in the coming of Jesus Christ (cf. 1:7–8; 4:13; 5:1). The elect community lives between the darkness of its pagan past and the light of its eschatological future" (Michaels, *1 Peter*, 112).

1 Peter 2:1-17

That the audience are "now" (νῦν) God's people and "now" (νῦν) have received divine mercy (2:10) corresponds to their present privileged status as those whom the prophets were serving the very things which "now" (νῦν) have been announced to them through those who proclaimed good news unto them (1:12). That they had not "received mercy" (ἠλεημένοι) but now have "received mercy [ἐλεηθέντες]" (2:10) emphatically reaffirms their present privileged status as being among those who according to his great "mercy" (ἔλεος) God has given new birth for a living hope through the resurrection of Jesus Christ from the dead (1:3).[25] And that they have now received the divine virtue of mercy as those who are now God's people further motivates their worship of publicly "proclaiming" the virtues of the God who called them out of darkness for his marvelous light (2:9c), as a people destined for possession (2:9b) of God's future and final salvation of eternal life.[26]

2:11-17 (A'): Be Subject to Every Human Institution on account of the Lord

The audience hear the A' element (2:11-17) of this chiastic unit as a chiastic pattern in itself:

a) *Beloved*, I encourage you as aliens and sojourners to keep away from fleshly desires that are waging war against the soul (2:11),

 b) *keeping* your conduct among the Gentiles praiseworthy (2:12a),

  c) so that in what they slander you as *evildoers*, observing from the praiseworthy works, they may glorify God on the day of visitation. Be subject to every *human* institution on account of the Lord (2:12b-13a),

   d) *whether* to a king *as* being in authority (2:13b),

---

25. "First Peter only uses the image of mercy in this verse and in 1:3. In both places 'mercy' reinforces the surety of salvation by locating its origin not in human behavior but in the character of God" (Donelson, *I & II Peter*, 67).

26. "While the content of the Christians' declaration, τὰς ἀρετάς, has the basic meaning 'virtues' or 'praises' in this context, it probably means rather 'mighty deeds' or 'saving acts,' particularly since the one whose ἀρεταί are to be announced is defined as one who has acted to save, such salvation in its turn being based on God's act of raising Christ from the dead (e.g., 1:3). The verb ἐξαγγέλλω is used only here in the NT; in the LXX it means 'tell forth' and is used primarily to mean the announcement of God's praise" (Achtemeier, *1 Peter*, 166). According to Balch, *Domestic Code*, 133, "in contexts where ἐξαγγέλλω refers to 'proclaiming' the praises, deeds, righteousness, or works of God, the proclaiming is always in worship." "Whether directed to God or to the worshipping community, the 'proclamation' involved in the verb ἐξαγγέλλειν belongs in the category of worship ... τὰς ἀρετάς does not refer to God's 'virtues' or ethical qualities in an abstract sense but to his praiseworthy deeds" (Michaels, *1 Peter*, 110).

d′) *whether* to governors *as* sent through him (2:14a)
c′) for the punishment of *evildoers* but the praise of good doers, for thus it is the will of God that those doing good silence the ignorance of foolish *human beings* (2:14b–15),
b′) as free but not *keeping* freedom as a cover for evil, but rather as slaves of God (2:16).
a′) Honor all, *love* the brotherhood, fear God, honor the king (2:17).

At the center of this chiastic sub-unit the audience experience a pivot of parallels involving the only occurrences in 1 Peter of the coordinating conjunction "whether" and in this sub-unit of the subordinating conjunction "as." "Whether [εἴτε] to a king as [ὡς] being in authority" in the d) sub-element (2:13b) progresses to "whether [εἴτε] to governors as [ὡς] sent through him" in the d′) sub-element (2:14a). Then they hear a progression of parallels involving the only occurrences in this sub-unit of the term "evildoer" and expressions for "human." "As evildoers [κακοποιῶν]" and "be subject to every human [ἀνθρωπίνῃ] institution" in the c) sub-element (2:12b–13a) progress to "the punishment of evildoers [κακοποιῶν]" and "the ignorance of foolish human beings [ἀνθρώπων]" in the c′) sub-element (2:14b–15).

The audience then hear a progression of parallels involving the only occurrences in this sub-unit of the term "keeping." "Keeping [ἔχοντες] your conduct" in the b) sub-element (2:12a) progresses to "keeping [ἔχοντες] freedom" in the b′) sub-element (2:16). And finally, they hear a progression of parallels involving the only occurrences in this sub-unit of expressions for "love." "Beloved" (ἀγαπητοί) in the a) sub-element (2:11) progresses to "love [ἀγαπᾶτε] the brotherhood" in the a′) sub-element (2:17).

At his point the audience experience several progressions, via the chiastic parallels, from the A (2:1–9a) to the A′ (2:11–17) element of this chiastic unit: from "all evil [κακίαν]" (2:1) to "as evildoers [κακοποιῶν]" (2:12b), "the punishment of evildoers [κακοποιῶν]" (2:14b), and "cover for evil [κακίας]" (2:16); from "slanders [καταλαλιάς]" (2:1) to "slander [καταλαλοῦσιν]" (2:12); from "as [ὡς] newborn infants" (2:2) and "as [ὡς] living stones" (2:5a) to "as [ὡς] aliens" (2:11), "as [ὡς] evildoers" (2:12b), "as [ὡς] being in authority" (2:13b), "as [ὡς] sent through him" (2:14a), "as [ὡς] free" (2:16), "as [ὡς] a cover" (2:16), and "as [ὡς] slaves" (2:16); from "benevolent is the Lord [κύριος]" (2:3) to "on account of the Lord [κύριον]" (2:13a); from "by human beings [ἀνθρώπων] rejected" (2:4) to "every human [ἀνθρωπίνῃ] institution" (2:13a) and "ignorance of foolish human beings [ἀνθρώπων]" (2:15); from "its honor [τιμή] then is for you" (2:7) to "honor [τιμήσατε] all" (2:17) and "honor [τιμᾶτε] the king" (2:17); and finally, from "a holy nation [ἔθνος]" (2:9a) to "among the Gentiles [ἔθνεσιν]" (2:12a).

1 Peter 2:1-17

Having been exhorted to "love" (ἀγαπήσατε) one another constantly (1:22), as those who "love" (ἀγαπᾶτε) the Jesus Christ they have not seen (1:8), the audience are now affectionately addressed as "beloved [ἀγαπητοί]" (2:11). They are thus reminded that they are beloved not only by one another and by the author but by God as God's chosen people who have received God's love in the form of divine mercy (2:9-10). Peter exhorts and encourages his beloved audience as "aliens and sojourners [παρεπιδήμους]" (2:11; cf. Gen 23:4 LXX), reaffirming their status as divinely chosen "sojourners" (παρεπιδήμοις) of the diaspora (1:1) in their present social situation on earth, as they await their heavenly inheritance (1:4).[27]

The audience are to keep away from "fleshly" (σαρκικῶν) "desires [ἐπιθυμιῶν]" (2:11), the "desires" (ἐπιθυμίαις) of the transitory "flesh [σάρξ]" (1:24) to which they were conformed in their pre-Christian ignorance (1:14). Such desires wage war against the "soul [ψυχῆς]" (2:11), in contradiction to the purification of their "souls" (ψυχάς) for brotherly affection (1:22), and to the salvation of "souls" (ψυχῶν) they are attaining as the end of their faith (1:9).

In appropriate correspondence to their status as God's holy "nation [ἔθνος]" (2:9a), the audience are to keep their conduct among the "Gentiles" or "nations" (ἔθνεσιν) praiseworthy (2:12a).[28] That they are to keep their "conduct" (ἀναστροφήν) praiseworthy reaffirms and develops the exhortation for them to become holy as God is holy in all "conduct [ἀναστροφῇ]" (1:15). As aliens and sojourners (2:11), in respectful and reverential fear of God they are to "conduct" (ἀναστράφητε) the time of their sojourning (1:17), since they have been ransomed from their former futile "conduct" (ἀναστροφῆς) with the precious blood of Christ (1:18).

In contrast to the audience, who are to remove all "slanders [καταλαλιάς]" (2:1), Gentiles may "slander" (καταλαλοῦσιν) them (2:12). But the audience are to keep their conduct among the Gentiles praiseworthy, so that when the Gentiles slander them as evildoers, their observation of the praiseworthy "works" (ἔργων), included in the "work" (ἔργον) according to which God judges each one (1:17), the Gentiles may glorify God on the day of God's final visitation (2:12).

---

27. "This first instance of the author speaking directly introduces a combination of exhortation and encouragement that dominates the remainder of the letter" (Elliott, *1 Peter*, 457).

28. On the translation "praiseworthy" for καλήν here, see BDAG, 504. "The term καλός has an aesthetic as well as a moral connotation. It denotes conduct that is both morally just and aesthetically attractive, thus behavior that is in all senses worthy of honor" (Elliott, *1 Peter*, 466).

1 Peter, 2 Peter, and Jude

The audience's praiseworthy works as part of their ethical worship will thus lead the Gentiles to their own worship, as they may "glorify" (δοξάσωσιν) God on the day of visitation. They may thus join the audience in their worship of offering praise, "glory" (δόξαν), and honor to God at the revelation of Jesus Christ (1:7). The audience, who are presently engaged in the worship of exulting for Jesus Christ with a joy indescribable and "glorified" (δεδοξασμένῃ) by God (1:8), may by their praiseworthy works induce the Gentiles to the worship of "glorifying" God.[29] "Observing" (ἐποπτεύοντες) from the audience's praiseworthy works, the Gentiles may glorify God on the day of God's "visitation," literally, God's "overseeing" (ἐπισκοπῆς), when God will watch over all in the final judgment.[30]

The audience are further exhorted on how they are to keep their conduct among the Gentiles praiseworthy (2:12). Despite the rejection by "human beings [ἀνθρώπων]" (2:4) of the "Lord" (κύριος) who is benevolent (2:3), they are to be subject to every "human" (ἀνθρωπίνῃ) institution on account of the "Lord [κύριον]" (2:13a). The human institutions to which the audience are to be subject include the king or emperor as being in authority (2:13b) as well as the governors sent through him for the punishment of evildoers but the praise of good doers (2:14). That governors are sent for the punishment of "evildoers" (κακοποιῶν) reinforces the exhortation for the audience to keep their conduct among the Gentiles praiseworthy, even if the Gentiles slander them as "evildoers [κακοποιῶν]" (2:12). The human "praise" (ἔπαινον) the audience will receive as good doers anticipates the divine praise they will receive when their faith, refined through various trials, is found for "praise" (ἔπαινον), glory, and honor at the revelation of Jesus Christ (1:7).

It is the will of "God" (θεοῦ) that the audience, as a people of "God [θεοῦ]" (2:10), who are to do good, silence the ignorance of foolish human beings (2:15). As children of obedience no longer conformed to the desires of their former "ignorance [ἀγνοίᾳ]" (1:14), the audience may silence the "ignorance" (ἀγνωσίαν) of foolish human beings.[31] By doing good, the

---

29. "'Glory,' 'glorify,' and their synonyms . . . belong to an accentuated theme of this letter. Relative to its length, 1 Peter contains more references to glory and glorification than any other writing of the NT" (Elliott, *1 Peter*, 470).

30. "The reference to the 'day of visitation' may be an echo of Isa 10:3 and refers to the time of final judgment" (Senior, *1 Peter*, 65). "The thrust of the verse is . . . that at the time of the final judgment nonbelievers will be brought to the realization that the Christians did what they did at God's behest and with divine approval, and thus be led to glorify God" (Achtemeier, *1 Peter*, 178).

31. "The outsiders' 'ignorance' of Christian virtue and of the God of the Christians is akin to the ignorance of the believers themselves prior to their conversion" (Elliott, *1 Peter*, 495).

1 Peter 2:1-17

audience may thus silence the ignorance of the foolish human beings who slander them as evildoers (2:12). That they may silence the ignorance of foolish "human beings" (ἀνθρώπων) by being subject to every "human" (ἀνθρωπίνῃ) institution on account of the "Lord [κύριον]" (2:13) further likens the audience to the "Lord [κύριος]" (2:3) Jesus Christ as the living stone rejected by what amounted to the ignorance of foolish "human beings [ἀνθρώπων]" (2:4).

The audience are to do good (2:15) as those who are free in society, but not keeping such freedom as a cover for evil (2:16). That they are not to be "keeping" (ἔχοντες) freedom "as" (ὡς) a cover for "evil" (κακίας), having removed all "evil [κακίαν]" (2:1), bolsters the exhortation for the audience to be "keeping" (ἔχοντες) their conduct among the Gentiles praiseworthy. This will give the Gentiles no basis for speaking against them "as" (ὡς) "evildoers [κακοποιῶν]" (2:12). The audience, a people of "God [θεοῦ]" (2:10), are rather to be "as" (ὡς) slaves of "God [θεοῦ]" (2:16), those who serve the will of "God [θεοῦ]" (2:15) by doing good and keeping their conduct praiseworthy.[32] As ethical worship, their praiseworthy works as slaves of God may thus lead the Gentiles to the worship of glorifying "God" (θεόν) on the day of visitation (2:12).

The exhortation for the audience as a whole to keep their conduct among Gentiles praiseworthy is then summarized with a comprehensive conclusion. They are to "honor all, love the brotherhood, fear God, honor the king" (2:17).[33] The audience are among the believers for whom is the divine "honor (τιμή)" (2:7) of Jesus Christ as the cornerstone, chosen and esteemed by God (2:6), the divine "honor" (τιμήν) they will receive at the revelation of Jesus Christ (1:7). As those to be honored by God, the audience are thus to "honor" (τιμήσατε) all human beings, and they are specifically to continue to "honor" (τιμᾶτε) the king. That they are to continue to "love" (ἀγαπᾶτε) the "brotherhood" (ἀδελφότητα) reinforces the exhortation for them to "love" (ἀγαπήσατε) one another earnestly for a sincere "brotherly love [φιλαδελφίαν]" (1:22), as those who "love" (ἀγαπᾶτε) Jesus Christ (1:8).[34]

---

32. "Being a slave of God denotes not only a command of obedience to God's will (2:15), but also the impossibility of being anyone else's slave" (Donelson, *I & II Peter*, 74).

33. "Perhaps the first imperative was attracted to the aorist tense of v. 13, while the remaining three indicate the author's intention that such activity become a regular and repeated part of Christian life" (Achtemeier, *1 Peter*, 187–88). "The single aorist imperative at the beginning of the series gives the entire series an unambiguous imperatival quality, but more important it has the quality of an effective or programmatic aorist: i.e., begin now to do all these things and keep doing them to the end" (Michaels, *1 Peter*, 130).

34. On the significance of "brotherhood" in 1 Peter, see Trebilco, *Self-Designations*, 60–62.

Finally, the audience are reminded that they are to continue to "fear" (φοβεῖσθε) the God (2:17) they worship both liturgically and ethically. In reverential and respectful "fear" (φόβῳ) of the God they call upon as Father in their liturgical worship, they are to conduct the time of their sojourning as a time for the ethical worship of the God who impartially judges according to the work of each one (1:17). They are to continue to fear "God" (θεόν) with the ethical worship of the praiseworthy works of their praiseworthy conduct, so that their own worship may induce the Gentiles to the worship of glorifying "God" (θεόν) on the day of visitation (2:12).

Summary on 2:1-17

As "newborn infants," the audience are to long for the metaphorical "milk" that is "pure," with a connotation of being "without deceit" (2:2). This "pure milk" of the word of God stands in appropriate contrast to all of the "deceit" included in their former futile conduct, which they have removed (2:1) now that they are "infants" born into a new way of life. The audience are thus to long for the "pure milk" of the living and abiding word of God through which they have already "tasted" the "benevolence," which is the "Christ" (2:3), in the pronouncement about the Lord Jesus Christ (1:25). By the nourishing "pure milk" of the word of God which they hear proclaimed in their communal worship, the audience may "grow up" for the salvation of eternal life, their final goal as "newborn infants."

As living stones who are being built up as a "spiritual" house for a "holy" priesthood, the audience are to offer up "spiritual" sacrifices acceptable to "God" through Jesus Christ (2:5), a living stone by human beings rejected but in the sight of "God" chosen, esteemed (2:4). They are to offer up these spiritual sacrifices acceptable to "God" "through" Jesus Christ, as those who "through him" are faithful for "God" (1:21). Through the cultic sacrificial worship of Jesus Christ, with whose precious blood (1:19) the audience have been ransomed from their former futile conduct with its false worship (1:18), the audience have been enabled to offer up "spiritual sacrifices," their conduct in reverence of God (1:17), as their ethical worship.

In contrast to the believing audience who are being built up as a spiritual house (2:5) upon the foundation of the Lord Jesus Christ as a living stone (2:4), which is a cornerstone and head of the corner (2:6-7), nonbelievers "stumble" on this stone as a stone of stumbling and rock of offense, "disobeying the word, for which indeed they were set" (2:8). Whereas the audience are to long for the pure milk pertaining to the "word" of God (2:2), the living "word" of God through which they were given new birth

1 Peter 2:1-17

for eternal life (1:23), nonbelievers are disobeying the "word" of God. For which disobedience these nonbelievers were indeed "set" or "placed" by God (divine passive) within God's plan of eternal salvation, just as the scriptural word of God declares that "I am setting" in Zion a stone, a cornerstone, chosen, esteemed (2:6).

But the audience are to appreciate that, as divinely "chosen" sojourners of the diaspora (1:1), they are a divinely "chosen" race (2:9; cf. Isa 43:20), like the divinely "chosen" and esteemed Lord Jesus Christ (2:4, 6). And, as a royal "priesthood," a "holy" nation (2:9; cf. Exod 19:6; 23:22), the audience as believers are being built up by God as a spiritual house for a "holy priesthood" to offer up the conduct of their lives as spiritual sacrifices acceptable to God through Jesus Christ (2:5). This enables them in reverence to conduct the time of their sojourning (1:17) as a time of offering ethical worship to God through the Jesus Christ they believe in as a living stone and a cornerstone, which is chosen and esteemed by God (2:4, 6-7).

In both their liturgical worship and in the conduct that serves as their ethical worship, the audience may proclaim the virtues of the God who "called" them out of the darkness of their former futile conduct (1:14, 18) for the goal of the marvelous light of his salvation (2:9). Such liturgical and ethical "proclamation" provides a way for the audience, as a royal priesthood and holy nation, to become holy in all of their conduct, according to the Holy One who "called" them (1:15) to be holy as he is holy (1:16). And that they have now received the divine virtue of mercy as those who are now God's people (2:10) further motivates their worship of publicly "proclaiming" the virtues of the God who called them out of darkness for his marvelous light, as a people destined for possession of God's future and final salvation of eternal life.

In appropriate correspondence to their status as God's holy "nation" (2:9a), the audience are to keep their conduct among the "Gentiles" or "nations" praiseworthy (2:12a). That they are to keep their "conduct" praiseworthy reaffirms and develops the exhortation for them to become holy as God is holy in all "conduct" (1:15). As aliens and sojourners (2:11), in respectful and reverential fear of God they are to "conduct" the time of their sojourning (1:17), since they have been ransomed from their former futile "conduct" with the precious blood of Christ (1:18).

The audience are to keep their conduct among the Gentiles praiseworthy, so that when the Gentiles speak against them as evildoers, their observation of the praiseworthy "works," included in the "work" according to which God judges each one (1:17), the Gentiles may glorify God on the day of visitation (2:12). The audience's praiseworthy works as part of their ethical worship will thus lead the Gentiles to their own worship, as they may "glorify" God on the day of God's final visitation. They may thus join the audience in their worship of offering praise, "glory," and honor to God at the revelation of Jesus Christ (1:7). The audience, who are presently engaged in the worship of exulting for Jesus Christ with a joy indescribable and "glorified" by God (1:8), may by their praiseworthy works induce the Gentiles to the worship of "glorifying" God. "Observing" from the audience's praiseworthy works, the Gentiles may glorify God on the day of God's "visitation," literally, God's "overseeing," when God will watch over all in the final judgment.

By doing good (2:14), the audience may silence the ignorance of the foolish human beings who slander them as evildoers (2:12). That they may silence the ignorance of foolish "human beings" by being subject to every "human" institution on account of the "Lord" (2:13) further likens the audience to the "Lord" (2:3) Jesus Christ as the living stone rejected by what amounted to the ignorance of foolish "human beings" (2:4). The audience, a people of "God" (2:10), are to be as slaves of "God" (2:16), those who serve the will of "God" (2:15) by doing good and keeping their conduct praiseworthy, so that it serves as their ethical worship.

Finally, the audience are reminded that they are to continue to "fear" the God (2:17) they worship both liturgically and ethically. In reverential and respectful "fear" of the God they call upon as Father in their liturgical worship, they are to conduct the time of their sojourning as a time for the ethical worship of the God who impartially judges according to the work of each one (1:17). They are to continue to fear "God" with the ethical worship of the praiseworthy works of their praiseworthy conduct, so that their own worship may induce the Gentiles to the worship of glorifying "God" on the day of his final visitation (2:12).

5

1 Peter 2:18-21a
Endure Unjust Suffering on account of a Conscience toward God (D)

Enduring suffering for doing good is grace with God

A   ¹⁸ House servants being subject in all fear to masters, not only to the good and kind but also to the perverse. ¹⁹ᵃ for *this* is *grace*, if on account of a conscience toward *God* anyone bears up,

B   ¹⁹ᵇ *suffering* sorrows unjustly. ²⁰ᵃ For what credit is it if, sinning and being mistreated, you *endure*?

B′   ²⁰ᵇ But if, doing good and *suffering*, you *endure*,

A′   ²⁰ᶜ *this* is *grace* in the sight of *God*, ²¹ᵃ for to *this* you were called.[1]

Audience Response to 2:18-21a

2:18-19a (A): This Is Grace on account of a Conscience toward God

As part of what it means for the audience as a whole to keep their conduct among the Gentiles praiseworthy as the ethical worship that may induce the Gentiles to their own worship of glorifying God (2:12), they were exhorted to be "subject" (ὑποτάγητε) to "every" (πάσῃ) human institution on account of the Lord (2:13). The audience now learn that this general "subjection" includes a portion of them, those who are house servants, "being subject" (ὑποτασσόμενοι) in "all" (παντί) fear to their human masters, not only to

---

1. For the establishment of 1 Pet 2:18-21a as a chiasm, see ch. 1.

the good and kind but also to the perverse (2:18).[2] But what is specifically addressed to those who are literally "house servants" (οἰκέται) has relevance for the audience as a whole, as those who are being built up by God as a spiritual "house" (οἶκος) for a holy priesthood to offer spiritual sacrifices acceptable to God through Jesus Christ (2:5), and as those who are to be "slaves" or "servants" (δοῦλοι) of God (2:16).[3]

With the description of the house servants as being subject in all "fear" (φόβῳ) to their human masters (2:18) at the beginning of this chiastic unit (2:18–21a) the audience hear the transitional term that links this unit with the previous one (2:1–17), whose conclusion included the general command to "fear [φοβεῖσθε] God" (2:17). The audience thus experience a transition from their fearing of God in general to the fearing of God by being subject to human masters as part of their ethical worship. This recalls the exhortation for them in "fear" (φόβῳ) of God to conduct the time of their sojourning (1:17).[4]

Previously the term "grace" has referred to the divine grace of which the audience are to be recipients. In the opening greeting of the letter Peter prayed that "grace" (χάρις) be to the audience in abundance (1:2). The prophets prophesied concerning the "grace" (χάριτος) that is for the audience (1:10). The audience are to hope upon the "grace" (χάριν) that is to be borne to them from God at the revelation of Jesus Christ (1:13).

But now the term "grace," like the terms "praise," "glory," and "honor" (1:7), refers both to what comes from God and to what is given in gratitude to God as an act of worship.[5] The audience now hear that "this is grace [χάρις],

---

2. "The Christian slave is no more to carry out the inappropriate commands of a good master than to refuse the appropriate commands of a bad master . . . subordination does not depend on the moral goodness of the master but on the will of God" (Achtemeier, *1 Peter*, 195).

3. "In fact, the only specific command to slaves comes in this verse in this general exhortation to submit. After this verse, the rest of the passage is couched in terms applicable to all Christians" (Donelson, *I & II Peter*, 80). "οἰκέτης is the more specific term for domestic slaves as opposed to slaves assigned to the fields, but it is also a generic term overlapping with δοῦλος, the term for 'slave' used in v. 16. Given the nature of slavery as an institutionalized form of marginality and Peter's characterization of his audience as people who, because of their loyalty to Jesus, inhabit the outer perimeters of honorable society, it is easy to find in vv. 18–20 an address to all Christians rather than to a subset" (Green, *1 Peter*, 77–78).

4. "[I]t is hardly conceivable that this 'fear' to which even Caesar is not entitled [1:17] now in 2:18 should be owed to masters and in 3:2 husbands, particularly since already in 1:17 the expression ἐν φόβῳ clearly refers to the fear of God" (Feldmeier, *First Letter*, 170). "The effect of παντί in the phrase ἐν παντὶ φόβῳ is to intensify rather than universalize the reverence of which Peter speaks, yielding the translation 'with deep reverence'" (Michaels, *1 Peter*, 138).

5. "χάρις in our lit. as a whole, in the sense *gratitude*, refers to appropriate response to the Deity for benefits conferred [emphasis original]" (BDAG, 1080).

1 Peter 2:18-21a

if on account of a conscience toward God anyone bears up" (2:19a). If the house servants bear up in being subject to even perverse masters (2:18), this may not only be considered possible as a result of grace previously given by God but will also win them a favorable response of additional grace from God. But such bearing up also amounts to grace given in gratitude to God as an act of ethical worship. That this is "grace," if on account of a conscience toward or consciousness of "God" (θεοῦ) anyone, not just house servants, but "anyone" (τις) at all bears up, further indicates the relevance of this specific exhortation to house servants for the ethical worship of the whole audience in general as slaves of "God [θεοῦ]" (2:16), who are to fear "God [θεόν]" (2:17).[6]

2:19b-20a (B): Suffering Sorrows Unjustly If You Endure

The audience hear the grace of bearing up on account of a conscience toward God (2:19a) further described as "suffering sorrows unjustly" (2:19b). This suffering of sorrows unjustly further indicates the relevance of this specific exhortation to the literal house servants among the audience for the whole audience in general. Such suffering of "sorrows" (λύπας) or afflictions unjustly recalls and resonates with the whole audience being "saddened" or "sorrowful" (λυπηθέντες) in the various trials it may be necessary for them to undergo (1:6) for the refinement of their faith (1:7).[7]

The house servants, as well as the audience in general, are then asked to ponder the question: "For what credit is it if, sinning and being mistreated, you endure?" (2:20a). This poignant and provocative rhetorical question makes the audience realize that they can expect no "credit" (κλέος), and thus no "grace [χάρις]" (2:19), to be received from or given to God as worship, if they are mistreated even by perverse masters for sinning.

---

6. "In the NT, συνείδησις has a range of meanings including both 'consciousness,' 'awareness of,' and 'conscience' in the sense of sensitivity to external norms or opinion. This conception of 'conscience,' it should be noted, differs markedly from the modern psychological notion of conscience as an interior moral faculty . . . In 1 Peter, as elsewhere in the NT, συνείδησις implies not merely knowledge of God but also sensitivity to the divine will concerning conduct, or 'compliance with God's will'" (Elliott, *1 Peter*, 519). "Finally, it may be noted that the author, by making the subject of the condition τις ('anyone'), clearly intends here to make a general statement, not one applicable to slaves alone. It is further indication of the paradigmatic nature of this address to slaves" (Achtemeier, *1 Peter*, 197).

7. "The 'afflictions' (λύπας) mentioned here are not limited to the beatings administered to slaves (cf. v 20) but are far more general in scope. Peter seems to have in mind the present necessity that his readers 'must suffer affliction (λυπηθέντες) in various ordeals' (1:6)" (Michaels, *1 Peter*, 140).

2:20b (B'): If Doing Good and Suffering You Endure

The audience are then presented with an alternate situation to the possibility of them sinning and enduring (2:20a): "But if, doing good and suffering, you endure" (2:20b). At this point the audience experience a progression of parallels from the B (2:19b–20a) to the B' (2:20b) element at the pivotal center of this chiastic unit. "Suffering [πάσχων] sorrows unjustly" (2:19b) and "sinning and being mistreated, you endure [ὑπομενεῖτε]" (2:20a) progress to "doing good and suffering [πάσχοντες], you endure [ὑπομενεῖτε]" (2:20b).

The audience have heard that they can expect to receive praise as "good doers [ἀγαθοποιῶν]" (2:14) and that it is the will of God that those "doing good" (ἀγαθοποιοῦντας) silence the ignorance of foolish human beings (2:15), especially those who would slander them as evildoers (2:12). The praise they receive as good doers may even induce their slanderers to the worship of glorifying God on the day of visitation (2:12). And now the audience hear that if not only the house servants but all of them endure while "doing good" (ἀγαθοποιοῦντες) and suffering (2:20b), even if any of them suffers sorrows unjustly (2:19b), they can expect a more positive outcome than if they endure while sinning and being mistreated (2:20a).

2:20c–21a (A'): This Is Grace in the Sight of God

The more positive outcome or "credit" (2:20a) the audience can expect for enduring if they do good yet suffer (2:20b) is then confirmed: "This is grace in the sight of God, for to this you were called" (2:20c–21a). At this point the audience experience a progression, via the chiastic parallels, from the A (2:18–19a) to the A' (2:20c–21a) element of this chiastic unit. "For this [τοῦτο] is grace [χάρις], if on account of a conscience toward God [θεοῦ]" (2:19a) progresses to "this [τοῦτο] is grace [χάρις] in the sight of God [θεῷ], for this [τοῦτο] you were called" (2:20c–21a).

The audience have been informed that it is "grace," that is, grace not only given by but to God as an act of worship, if on account of a conscience toward God anyone bears up, suffering sorrows unjustly (2:19). And now, that this "grace" is not only a gift of God but an act of worship given to God is emphatically confirmed, as the audience hear that if they suffer for doing good (2:20b), then "this is grace in the sight of God" (2:20c). That this is grace "in the sight of God" (παρὰ θεῷ) likens this kind of suffering on the part of Christians to the suffering of Christ as a living stone by human beings rejected "but in the sight of God" (παρὰ δὲ θεῷ) chosen, esteemed (2:4).

1 Peter 2:18-21a

And as the audience hear that "for to this you were called [ἐκλήθητε]" (2:21a), they are reminded that as God's own people they are to proclaim, in both their liturgical and ethical worship, the virtues of the God who "called" (καλέσαντος) them out of darkness for his marvelous light (2:9). Indeed, the audience, according to the Holy One who "called" (καλέσαντα) them, are to become holy, as God is holy (1:16), in all of their conduct (1:15), which includes both their liturgical and ethical worship. By enduring for doing good yet suffering, the audience may thus offer the ethical worship to which they were called by God, the ethical worship that is "grace" in the sight of God.[8]

Summary on 2:18–21a

If the house servants among the audience bear up in being subject to even perverse masters (2:18), this may not only be considered possible as a result of grace previously given by God but will also win them a favorable response of additional grace from God (2:19a). But such bearing up also amounts to grace given in gratitude to God as an act of ethical worship. That this is "grace," if on account of a conscience toward or consciousness of "God" anyone, not just house servants, but "anyone" at all bears up (2:19a), further indicates the relevance of this specific exhortation to house servants for the ethical worship of the whole audience in general as slaves of "God" (2:16), who are to fear "God" (2:17).

The suffering of "sorrows" unjustly (2:19b) recalls and resonates with the whole audience being "saddened" or "sorrowful" in the various trials it may be necessary for them to undergo (1:6) for the refinement of their faith (1:7). The poignant and provocative rhetorical question, "For what credit is it if, sinning and being mistreated, you endure?" (2:20a), makes the audience realize that they can expect no "credit," and thus no "grace" (2:19a), to be received from or given to God as worship, if they are mistreated even by perverse masters for sinning.

That the "grace" of bearing up on account of a conscience toward God, suffering sorrows unjustly (2:19), is not only grace from God but an act of worship given to God is emphatically confirmed, as the audience hear that if they suffer for doing good (2:20b), then "this is grace in the sight of God" (2:20c). This likens this kind of suffering on the part of Christians to the

---

8. "The verb ἐκλήθητε points to the readers' conversion from paganism; if the ultimate goal of that conversion is God's 'marvelous light' (2:9) or his 'eternal glory' (5:10), its nearer goal is holiness (1:15) or, as here, the doing of good even when it means suffering" (Michaels, *1 Peter*, 142).

suffering of Christ as a living stone by human beings rejected "but in the sight of God" chosen, esteemed (2:4). And as the audience hear that "for to this you were called" (2:21a), they are reminded that as God's own people they are to proclaim the virtues of the God who "called" them out of darkness for his marvelous light (2:9). Indeed, the audience, according to the Holy One who "called" them, are to become holy, as God is holy (1:16), in all of their conduct (1:15), which includes both their liturgical and ethical worship. By enduring for doing good yet suffering, the audience may thus offer the ethical worship to which they were called by God, the ethical worship that is "grace" in the sight of God.

6

1 Peter 2:21b-25
Christ Did No Sin or Deceit That to Righteousness We Might Live (E)

Christ offered up our sins so that having died to sins we might live to righteousness

A   ²¹ᵇ For also Christ suffered on behalf of *you*, to you leaving a model that you may closely follow in his footsteps,
B   ²² "who did not do *sin* nor was deceit found *in his mouth*" (Isa 53:9),
C   ²³ who, being insulted did not return insult, suffering, he did not threaten, but handed himself over to the one who judges righteously,
B'   ²⁴ who the *sins* of us he himself offered up *in his body* upon the tree, so that to *sins* having died, to righteousness we might live,
A'   ²⁴ by whose wound you have been healed. ²⁵ For like sheep you were being led astray, but you have turned now to the shepherd and overseer of *your* souls.[1]

Audience Response to 2:21b-25

2:21b (A): Christ Suffered on behalf of You

The audience are to appreciate how the suffering of Christ relates to their own suffering: "For also Christ suffered on behalf of you, to you leaving a model that you may closely follow in his footsteps" (2:21b). With the statement that Christ also "suffered" (ἔπαθεν) for them, the audience hear the transitional

---

1. For the establishment of 1 Pet 2:21b-25 as a chiasm, see ch. 1.

term that links this chiastic unit (2:21b-25) to the previous unit (2:18-21a), which refers to doing good and "suffering" (πάσχοντες) near its conclusion (2:20b). They thus experience a transition from their own "doing good and suffering," as well as "suffering [πάσχων] sorrows unjustly" (2:19b), to the suffering of Christ as a model for them to closely follow.[2]

How the model that Christ left them is especially relevant and closely related to the audience, to "you," is emphasized through a very striking alliteration in Greek. Literally, it states, "on behalf of you, to you leaving a model [ὑπὲρ ὑμῶν ὑμῖν ὑπολιμπάνων ὑπογραμμόν]" (2:21b). As "you" who were "called" (ἐκλήθητε) to endure suffering (2:21a), the audience are exhorted, enhanced through yet another alliteration linking the verbs addressed to them, to be the "you" who "closely follow" (ἐπακολουθήσητε) in the footsteps the suffering Christ left specifically for them. In contrast to the unbelievers who were "set" (ἐτέθησαν) by God to stumble over Christ as the rejected stone (2:7-8), the audience, as well as all believers, who are called by God to endure suffering, are to closely follow in the footsteps of the suffering Christ (2:21b).

2:22 (B): He Did Not Do Sin Nor Was Deceit Found in His Mouth

The model that the suffering Christ provides for the audience is elaborated by applying to Christ a scriptural quotation of the prophets (cf. 1:10-11) from Isa 53:9 regarding the "suffering servant" of God: "who did not do sin nor was deceit found in his mouth" (2:22).[3] That Christ suffered even though no deceit was "found" (εὑρέθη) in his mouth encourages the audience, whose faith is to be refined, as they are saddened by their own suffering in various trials (1:6), so that their faith may similarly be "found" (εὑρεθῇ) without deceit but rather for praise, glory, and honor at the revelation of Jesus Christ (1:7). And that no "deceit" (δόλος) was found in the mouth of the suffering Christ reinforces the exhortation for the audience to long for the pure milk of the word of God in

---

2. "The phrase 'follow closely in his footsteps' (ἐπακολουθήσητε τοῖς ἴχνεσιν αὐτοῦ) turns from the notion of imitating Christ's example or pattern to the more dynamic metaphor of following in his 'footsteps.' The prefix on the verb 'follow' (ἐπακολουθεῖν), instead of the more common New Testament term ἀκολουθεῖν, adds the sense of exactness or intensity, hence the translation 'follow closely'" (Senior, *1 Peter*, 75).

3. "The author of 1 Peter had already given the hermeneutical legitimation for this coupling of prophetic text and Passion in 1:10f. when he saw in the prophets the spirit of Christ at work, who testified beforehand to the suffering and glory of Christ" (Feldmeier, *First Letter*, 173).

1 Peter 2:21b–25

order to grow up for salvation (2:2), as those who, like the suffering Christ, have removed all "deceit [δόλον]" (2:1).[4]

2:23 (C): Suffering He Handed Himself Over to God Who Judges Righteously

The audience hear the model provided by the suffering Christ further described: "Who, being insulted did not return insult, suffering, he did not threaten, but handed himself over to the one who judges righteously" (2:23). That "suffering" (πάσχων), the Christ who "suffered [ἔπαθεν]" (2:21b) did not threaten those who insulted him provides the model for the audience in doing good and "suffering" (πάσχοντες) to endure (2:20b), and to bear up, "suffering" (πάσχων) sorrows unjustly (2:19). Such bearing up and enduring amounts to the "grace" of their ethical worship in the sight of God (2:20c).

That Christ handed himself over to the one God who "judges" (κρίνοντι) righteously serves as his ethical worship that the audience are to imitate.[5] As they call upon God as Father in their liturgical worship, they are likewise to hand themselves over to God as their ethical worship of the one God who impartially "judges" (κρίνοντα) according to the work of each one, so that in reverent fear of God they may conduct the time of their sojourning as a time of ethical worship (1:17). And anyone in the audience who may suffer sorrows "unjustly [ἀδίκως]" (2:19) is to imitate the suffering Christ who handed himself over to the God who judges "righteously" (δικαίως).

2:24 (B'): The Sins of Us He Himself Offered Up in His Body

The audience hear the B' element (2:24) of this chiastic unit as a chiastic pattern in itself:
a) who the *sins* of us he himself offered up (2:24a; cf. Isa 53:12)
   b) in his body upon the tree (2:24b; cf. Deut 21:23),
a') so that to *sins* having died, to righteousness we might live (2:24c).

After the central and unparalleled b) sub-element, "in his body upon the tree" (2:24b), the audience experience a pivot of parallels involving the only occurrences in this sub-unit of the term "sins." "The sins [ἁμαρτίας] of

---

4. That these are the only occurrences in 1 Peter of the terms "found" and "deceit" enhances these connections for the audience.

5. Although no explicit object is expressed for the verb "he handed over" (παρεδίδου) here, most translations supply "himself" as the implicit object; see Dubis, *1 Peter*, 78. "Since the object is unspecified, it would be a mistake to limit the object's sphere. Jesus kept 'handing over' to God every dimension of his life" (Schreiner, *1, 2 Peter*, 144).

1 Peter, 2 Peter, and Jude

us he himself offered up" in the a) sub-element (2:24a) progresses to "so that to sins [ἁμαρτίαις] having died" in the a') sub-element (2:24c). In addition, at this point the audience hear progressions, via the chiastic parallels, from the B to the B' element of this chiastic unit. "Who did not do sin [ἁμαρτίαν]" (2:22) progresses to "the sins [ἁμαρτίας] of us he himself offered up" (2:24a) and "so that to sins [ἁμαρτίαις] having died" (2:24c). And there is an alliterative progression of prepositional phrases from "in his mouth [ἐν τῷ στόματι αὐτοῦ]" (2:22) to "in his body [ἐν τῷ σώματι αὐτοῦ]" (2:24b).

The Christ who did not do sin (2:22), whom the audience, as among all of us believers, were invited to join in the liturgical worship of blessing as the Lord "of us [ἡμῶν]" (1:3), the sins "of us" (ἡμῶν) he himself offered up (2:24a).[6] The striking sequence of the personal pronoun in reference to the audience followed immediately by the emphatic personal pronoun in reference to Christ underscores what Christ has personally done for all of us believers. In other words, although they were the sins "of us" (ἡμῶν), "he himself" (αὐτός) offered them up.[7] That he himself "offered up" (ἀνήνεγκεν) the sins of us as an act of sacrificial worship makes it possible for the audience to "offer up" (ἀνενέγκαι) spiritual sacrifices acceptable to God as their ethical worship through Jesus Christ (2:5).[8] The audience are to appreciate that Christ "himself" (αὐτός) offered up the sins of us "in his body" (ἐν τῷ σώματι αὐτοῦ) upon the tree of his crucifixion (2:24b), that is, in his very own body rather than in the body of a sacrificial animal, even though he himself did not do sin nor was deceit found "in his mouth [ἐν τῷ στόματι αὐτοῦ]" (2:22).[9]

---

6. That these are the first two occurrences of the first person plural pronoun in 1 Peter enhances the significance of this connection for the audience.

7. "Of us" (ἡμῶν) corresponds to Isa 53:4; "he himself" (αὐτός) to Isa 53:11. See also Schreiner, *1, 2 Peter*, 145.

8. That these are the only occurrences in 1 Peter of this Greek verb for "offer up" (ἀναφέρω) enhances the significance of this connection for the audience.

9. "Peter adds two prepositional phrases, 'in his body' and 'on the tree,' an explicit reference to the death of Jesus by crucifixion. The latter phrase may be an allusion to Deut. 21:23, where God's curse is invoked on the one who is hung on a tree. In the context of Roman practices, the reference to crucifixion is a reminder that Jesus was executed unjustly as a criminal; Peter's readers might be similarly accused" (Jobes, *1 Peter*, 197). "The death of Jesus on the cross is here understood as a kind of sacrificial act (cf. Heb 9:14; 10:10) which effects the 'removal' of sins" (Kremer, "ἀναφέρω," 94). "The fact that Peter has already spoken of Jesus as a lamb in 1:19 encourages us to interpret the present verse in terms of sacrifice, but in any case the language of Isaiah 53 itself is definitely sacrificial" (Marshall, *1 Peter*, 96). Although 1 Pet 2:24a states that "the sins of us he himself offered up" (τὰς ἁμαρτίας ἡμῶν αὐτὸς ἀνήνεγκεν), the sacrifice is not actually the sins but Christ's body that bears the sins; see Schelkle, *Petrusbriefe*, 85. And see the similar sacrificial use of Isa 53:12 in Heb 9:28: "to offer up the sins [ἀνενεγκεῖν ἁμαρτίας] of many"; Heil, *Hebrews*, 256; idem, *Worship*, 156.

1 Peter 2:21b-25

As a result of Christ himself offering up the sins of us (2:24a), we believers have metaphorically "died" (ἀπογενόμενοι) to sins (2:24c) in the sense of having separated ourselves from them.[10] This resonates both alliteratively and conceptually with our having been "given new birth" (ἀναγεγεννημένοι) by God to eternal life (1:23), the God who according to his great mercy has "given new birth" (ἀναγεννήσας) to us (1:3). Our having died to sins means that we might live to "righteousness [δικαιοσύνῃ]" (2:24c), that is, that we might live by doing what is required by the God who judges "righteously [δικαίως]" (2:23). By his ethical worship of handing himself over to the one God who judges righteously (2:23), Christ shows himself to be the exemplar, and by his sacrificial worship of offering up our sins for atonement in his body (2:24), also the enabler for believers to offer the ethical worship of living in accord with the righteousness that pleases God.[11]

That to righteousness we believers might "live [ζήσωμεν]" (2:24c) reminds the audience that as "living" (ζῶντες) stones they are being built up by God as a spiritual house for a holy priesthood to offer up spiritual sacrifices as ethical worship acceptable to God through Jesus Christ (2:5), the stone rejected by human beings yet still "living" (ζῶντα) in the sight of God as chosen and esteemed (2:4). They have been given new birth through an eternally "living" (ζῶντος) word of God (1:23), a new birth for a "living" (ζῶσαν) hope of eternal life through the resurrection of Jesus Christ from the dead (1:3). Having died to sins (2:24c) then, the audience have been given a new birth so that they, along with all believers, might "live" presently and eternally by doing the righteousness that amounts to an ethical worship acceptable to God through the sacrificial worship of Jesus Christ.

2:24c–25 (A'): You Have Turned to the Shepherd and Overseer of Your Souls

After a focus on the significance of Christ's sacrificial worship for all believers, the audience are again addressed directly: "by whose wound you have been healed. For like sheep you were being led astray, but you have turned now to the shepherd and overseer of your souls" (2:24c–25; cf. Isa 53:5).[12] At this point, the audience experience a progression, via the chiastic parallels,

---

10. "In place of ἀποθνῄσκειν, the common verb for 'die,' ἀπογίνεσθαι serves Peter as a euphemism, with the meaning 'to be away' or 'to depart'" (Michaels, *1 Peter*, 148).

11. On Christ as both exemplar and enabler, see Elliott, *1 Peter*, 528.

12. Whereas Isa 53:5 LXX has the first person plural verb "we have been healed" (ἰάθημεν), 1 Pet 2:24 employs the second person plural verb "you have been healed" (ἰάθητε), thus emphatically applying the quotation directly to the audience.

from the A to the A' element of this chiastic unit. "Also Christ suffered on behalf of you [ὑμῶν]" (2:21b) progresses to the "overseer of your [ὑμῶν] souls" (2:25).

By the "wound" (μώλωπι), that is, the suffering and death Christ incurred in his sacrificial worship of offering up our sins in his body upon the tree, the audience are to appreciate that "you have been healed [ἰάθητε]" (2:24).[13] This resonates with the fact that "you have been ransomed [ἐλυτρώθητε]" from futile conduct inherited from ancestors, which includes false worship, with the precious blood of the sacrificial death of Christ (1:18). The audience have been "healed" or "cured" from being led astray like sheep before they became believers (2:25a).[14] That they have "now" (νῦν) been converted and turned to Christ as the shepherd and overseer of their souls (2:25b) resonates with the fact that they were once not a people but "now" (νῦν) are God's people (2:10), and that the things concerning their salvation which the prophets were serving have "now" (νῦν) been announced to them (1:12). A noteworthy alliteration involving the prepositional prefix ἐπί underscores their close dependence upon Christ—"you have turned [ἐπεστράφητε] now to [ἐπί] the shepherd and overseer [ἐπίσκοπον]" (2:25b).[15]

The resounding reaffirmation that the audience have now turned to Christ as the shepherd and overseer of their "souls [ψυχῶν]" (2:25) reinforces the exhortation for them to keep away from fleshly desires that are waging war against the "soul [ψυχῆς]" (2:11). They may thereby keep their conduct among Gentiles praiseworthy as the ethical worship that may induce Gentiles to the worship of glorifying God (2:12). That they have turned

---

13. "Peter spoke of being healed by Christ's wounds, and the wounds probably refer by metonymy to his death, though it is just possible that every dimension of the suffering leading to death is involved" (Schreiner, *1, 2 Peter*, 146). "Were we to adopt a view of disease at home in the world of 1 Peter, we would recognize that the two images—from death to life, and healing—speak to the same reality: cleansing for holiness" (Green, *1 Peter*, 90).

14. "In this Petrine construction, 'straying' does not imply Christian defection *after* conversion but, rather, estrangement from God *prior* to baptism and rebirth [emphasis original]" (Elliott, *1 Peter*, 538).

15. "The passive ἐπεστράφητε surely refers to divine initiative" (Achtemeier, *1 Peter*, 204n205). "This shift from atonement imagery to shepherding language is not in itself surprising, since the logic of sacrifice theology would be to include both. Processes of atonement should lead to a return to God's care. Not only is this sequence to be expected; a movement from atonement to shepherding also is crucial to the theology of 1 Peter" (Donelson, *I & II Peter*, 85). "While the word 'shepherd' is regularly used in the OT to refer to God, the absence of any reference to God as shepherd in the NT, the specific reference to Jesus as 'chief shepherd' in 1 Pet 5:10, and the connection of v. 24c with v. 25 by means of the explanatory conjunction γάρ, make it more likely that it here refers to Jesus" (Achtemeier, *1 Peter*, 204).

to Christ as the shepherd and overseer of "your souls" (ψυχῶν ὑμῶν) also recalls the exhortation for them to love one another as part of their ethical worship, "your souls" (ψυχὰς ὑμῶν) having purified in the obedience to the truth for sincere brotherly affection (1:22).

That the audience have now turned to Christ as the shepherd and overseer of their "souls [ψυχῶν]" (2:25) resonates with their worship of exulting with a joy indescribable and glorified (1:8), as they are attaining the end of their faith, salvation of "souls [ψυχῶν]" (1:9). And that they have "turned" (ἐπεστράφητε) now to the shepherd and overseer of "your" (ὑμῶν) souls bolsters the exhortation for them to "closely follow" (ἐπακολουθήσητε) the model of the Christ who suffered on behalf of "you [ὑμῶν]" (2:21b) as both the exemplar and enabler for their ethical worship.[16]

Summary on 2:21b-25

The audience experience a transition from their own "doing good and suffering" (2:20b), as well as "suffering sorrows unjustly" (2:19b), to the suffering of Christ as a model for them to closely follow (2:21b). As "you" who were "called" to endure suffering (2:21a), the audience are exhorted to be the "you" who "closely follow" in the footsteps the suffering Christ left specifically for them. In contrast to the unbelievers who were "set" by God to stumble over Christ as the rejected stone (2:7-8), the audience, as well as all believers, who are called by God to endure suffering, are to closely follow in the footsteps of the suffering Christ (2:21b).

That Christ suffered even though no deceit was "found" in his mouth encourages the audience, whose faith is to be refined, as they are saddened by their own suffering in various trials (1:6), so that their faith may similarly be "found" without deceit but rather for praise, glory, and honor at the revelation of Jesus Christ (1:7). And that no "deceit" was found in the mouth of the suffering Christ reinforces the exhortation for the audience to long for the pure milk of the word of God in order to grow up for salvation (2:2), as those who, like the suffering Christ, have removed all "deceit" (2:1).

That "suffering," the Christ who "suffered" (2:21b) did not threaten those who insulted him (2:23) provides the model for the audience in doing good and "suffering" to endure (2:20b), and to bear up, "suffering" sorrows unjustly

---

16. Jodoin, "Au coeur de la dispersion," 515-30. "The imagery of sheep following after the shepherd, following in his footsteps so to speak, forms a conceptual inclusion with 2:21, framing the entire Christological exposition with the image that walking in Jesus' footsteps, even through unjust suffering, is nevertheless the Shepherd's path of safety, protection, and deliverance" (Jobes, *1 Peter*, 199).

(2:19). Such bearing up and enduring amounts to the "grace" of their ethical worship in the sight of God (2:20c). That Christ handed himself over to the one God who "judges" righteously (2:23) serves as his ethical worship that the audience are to imitate. As they call upon God as Father in their liturgical worship, they are likewise to hand themselves over to God as their ethical worship of the one God who impartially "judges" according to the work of each one, so that in reverent fear of God they may conduct the time of their sojourning as a time of ethical worship (1:17). And anyone in the audience who may suffer sorrows "unjustly" (2:19) is to imitate the suffering Christ who handed himself over to the God who judges "justly."

The Christ who did not do sin (2:22), whom the audience, as among all of us believers, were invited to join in the liturgical worship of blessing as the Lord "of us" (1:3), the sins "of us" he himself offered up (2:24a). The striking sequence of the personal pronoun in reference to the audience followed immediately by the emphatic personal pronoun in reference to Christ underscores what Christ has personally done for all of us believers. In other words, although they were the sins "of us," "he himself" offered them up. That he himself "offered up" the sins of us as an act of sacrificial worship makes it possible for the audience to "offer up" spiritual sacrifices acceptable to God as their ethical worship through Jesus Christ (2:5). The audience are to appreciate that Christ "himself" offered up the sins of us "in his body" upon the tree of his crucifixion (2:24b), that is, in his very own body rather than in the body of a sacrificial animal, even though he himself did not do sin nor was deceit found "in his mouth" (2:22).

As a result of Christ himself offering up the sins of us (2:24a), we believers have metaphorically "died" to sins (2:24c) in the sense of having separated ourselves from them. This resonates with our having been "given new birth" by God to eternal life (1:23), the God who according to his great mercy has "given new birth" to us (1:3). Our having died to sins means that we might live to "righteousness" (2:24c), that is, that we might live by doing what is required by the God who judges "righteously" (2:23). By his ethical worship of handing himself over to the one God who judges righteously (2:23), Christ shows himself to be the exemplar, and by his sacrificial worship of offering up our sins for atonement in his body (2:24), also the enabler for believers to offer the ethical worship of living in accord with the righteousness that pleases God.

That to righteousness we believers might "live" (2:24c) reminds the audience that as "living" stones they are being built up by God as a spiritual house for a holy priesthood to offer up spiritual sacrifices as ethical worship acceptable to God through Jesus Christ (2:5), the stone rejected by human beings yet still "living" in the sight of God as chosen and esteemed

1 Peter 2:21b–25

(2:4). They have been given new birth through an eternally "living" word of God (1:23), a new birth for a "living" hope of eternal life through the resurrection of Jesus Christ from the dead (1:3). Having died to sins (2:24c) then, the audience have been given a new birth so that they, along with all believers, might "live" presently and eternally by doing the righteousness that amounts to an ethical worship acceptable to God through the sacrificial worship of Jesus Christ.

By the "wound," that is, the suffering and death Christ incurred in his sacrificial worship of offering up our sins in his body upon the tree, the audience are to appreciate that "you have been healed" (2:24). This resonates with the fact that "you have been ransomed" from futile conduct inherited from ancestors, which includes false worship, with the precious blood of the sacrificial death of Christ (1:18). The audience have been "healed" or "cured" from being led astray like sheep before they became believers (2:25a). That they have "now" been converted and turned to Christ as the shepherd and overseer of their souls (2:25b) resonates with the fact that they were once not a people but "now" are God's people (2:10), and that the things concerning their salvation which the prophets were serving have "now" been announced to them (1:12).

The resounding reaffirmation that the audience have now turned to Christ as the shepherd and overseer of their "souls" (2:25) reinforces the exhortation for them to keep away from fleshly desires that are waging war against the "soul" (2:11). They may thereby keep their conduct among Gentiles praiseworthy as the ethical worship that may induce Gentiles to the worship of glorifying God (2:12). That they have turned to Christ as the shepherd and overseer of "your souls" also recalls the exhortation for them to love one another as part of their ethical worship, "your souls" having purified in the obedience to the truth for sincere brotherly love (1:22). This also resonates with their worship of exulting with a joy indescribable and glorified (1:8), as they are attaining the end of their faith, salvation of "souls" (1:9). And that they have "turned" now to the shepherd and overseer of "your" souls bolsters the exhortation for them to "closely follow" the model of the Christ who suffered on behalf of "you" (2:21b) as both the exemplar and enabler for their ethical worship.

7

1 Peter 3:1-7

The Inner Human Being of the Heart Is of Great Value before God (F)

Honor wives as fellow heirs of the grace of life so that prayers are not hindered

A   3:1 *Likewise, wives, being subject to their own husbands*, so that even if some are disobeying the word, through the conduct of the *wives* without a word they will be gained, ² observing *your* conduct that is pure in *fear*.
    B   ³ Of whom let the adornment not *be* the external one of braiding of hair and of wearing of gold things or of dressing in fine clothes,
        C   ⁴ᵃ but rather the inner human being of the heart in the imperishableness of the gentle and quiet spirit,
    B′   ⁴ᵇ which *is* before God of great value,
A′   ⁵ for thus formerly also the holy *wives* who hoped for God adorned themselves, *being subject to their own husbands*, ⁶ as Sarah obeyed Abraham, calling him "lord," whose children you become, doing good and not *fearing* any intimidation. ⁷ The *husbands likewise*, fellow dwellers according to knowledge as to the more delicate vessel, the feminine, showing honor as also to fellow heirs of the grace of life so that *your* prayers may not be hindered.[1]

---

1. For the establishment of 1 Pet 3:1–7 as a chiasm, see ch. 1.

1 Peter 3:1-7

Audience Response to 3:1-7

3:1-2 (A): Wives Being Subject to Their Own Husbands

Those who are wives among the audience are then addressed: "Likewise, wives, being subject to their own husbands, so that even if some are disobeying the word, through the conduct of the wives without a word they will be gained, observing your conduct that is pure in fear" (3:1-2). As part of the general exhortation for the audience as a whole to "be subject" (ὑποτάγητε) to every human institution on account of the Lord (2:13), the house servants among the audience were addressed as "being subject" (ὑποτασσόμενοι) in all reverent fear of God to their human masters (2:18). And now, "likewise," wives are addressed as "being subject"(ὑποτασσόμεναι) to their own husbands (3:1).[2]

The wives are to be subject to their own husbands, so that even if some are "disobeying the word" (ἀπειθοῦσιν τῷ λόγῳ), thus aligning themselves with the nonbelievers who "stumble" over Christ, "disobeying the word [τῷ λόγῳ ἀπειθοῦντες]" (2:8), they may be "gained," becoming believers through the "conduct" (ἀναστροφῆς) of their wives "without a word [ἄνευ λόγου]" (3:1).[3] The wives thereby play their part in the audience's keeping of their "conduct" (ἀναστροφήν) among the Gentiles praiseworthy, so that, "observing" (ἐποπτεύοντες) from the praiseworthy works, they may be inspired to engage in the worship of glorifying God on the day of visitation (2:12).[4]

---

2. "Our Petrine author, like Xenophon and others, treats the marital relationship within the context of instruction on household management. Again, however, as in the case of the household slaves, he diverges from the Hellenistic household management tradition in *addressing wives directly* (rather than charging husbands with their instruction), thereby acknowledging these wives as intelligent and responsible moral agents in their own right [emphasis original]" (Elliott, *1 Peter*, 553-54).

3. "The first use of λόγος ('word') clearly means the Christian faith; whether the second does so as well has been disputed, but the intention is surely that the wife's Christian behavior will be an effective witness even without verbal reference to the gospel, not that she is to remain dumb in the presence of her husband as she lives her Christian life. It is thus to be understood as meaning 'without verbal reference to the gospel.' That the husband will be gained not as a compliant mate for the wife but as one converted to the Christian faith is implied in the verb κερδηθήσονται ('they shall be gained'), which belongs to the language of mission" (Achtemeier, *1 Peter*, 210). "All disobedience, of course, stems from unbelief, but the emphasis here is on the rebellion of husbands who refuse to adhere to the gospel" (Schreiner, *1, 2 Peter*, 149). "The play on words wherein husbands who are disobedient to the 'word' are won over without a 'word' underlines the irony of this silent proclamation" (Donelson, *I & II Peter*, 90).

4. "In Greco-Roman society it was expected that the wife would have no friends of her own and would worship the gods of her husband ... the husband and society would perceive the wife's worship of Jesus Christ as rebellion, especially if she worshipped Christ exclusively" (Jobes, *1 Peter*, 203).

1 Peter, 2 Peter, and Jude

The Gentile husbands will be gained as believers, "observing" (ἐποπτεύσαντες) the "conduct" (ἀναστροφήν) of their wives that is pure in the reverent "fear" (φόβῳ) of God (3:2), just as the house servants are subject to their masters in all "fear" (φόβῳ) of God (2:18). The wives thereby play their roles in the audience becoming holy as God is holy in all their "conduct [ἀναστροφῇ]" (1:15), as in "fear" (φόβῳ) of God "you," the audience, are to "conduct" (ἀναστράφητε) the time of their sojourning (1:17), in contrast to their futile "conduct" (ἀναστροφῆς) inherited from ancestors, which includes false worship (1:18). The conduct of the wives that is "pure" (ἁγνήν), which has cultic connotations, in the reverent fear of God resonates with the audience as a whole having "purified" (ἡγνικότες) their souls in the obedience to the truth for sincere brotherly love (1:22).[5] Such conduct amounts to their ethical worship that is part of the ethical worship of the audience as a whole, who are, in the reverent fear and thus worship of God, to conduct the time of their sojourning.

With the reference to the husbands as observing "your" (ὑμῶν) conduct, that is, the conduct of their wives (3:2), the audience hear the transitional term that links this chiastic unit (3:1–7) to the previous unit (2:21b–25), which concludes with a reference to Christ as the shepherd and overseer of "your" (ὑμῶν) souls (2:25). The transition thus shifts the focus from that of a concern for the souls of the audience as a whole to the exemplary conduct of the wives among the audience, as part of the praiseworthy conduct of the entire audience which leads Gentiles to the worship of glorifying God (2:12).[6]

3:3 (B): Let the Adornment Not Be the External One

The audience hear the conduct of the wives among them that is to be pure in the reverent fear of God (3:2) further described: "Of whom let the adornment not be the external one of braiding of hair and of wearing of gold things or of dressing in fine clothes" (3:3).[7] The imperative that the adorn-

---

5. "[T]he word ἁγνός does not simply mean 'purity' in the sense of 'chaste' but has a cultic sense of 'holy'" (Senior, *1 Peter*, 82).

6. Slaughter, "Submission of Wives," 63–74. As Elliott (*1 Peter*, 560–61) points out, "nonbelieving husbands are a particular instance of nonbelieving Gentiles in general." "A pagan married to a Christian woman must be able to see that his wife's conduct is 'reverent' and 'pure' by Roman standards even though she cannot join him in the worship of his gods. These virtues, while directed toward God and not toward her husband, are nonetheless for her husband's benefit" (Michaels, *1 Peter*, 158).

7. "While some of the activity described may have played a part in other cults, for example, the braiding of hair was especially important for women devotees of Isis

ment of the wives is not to "be" (ἔστω) an external one is part of what it means for the audience as a whole to be holy in all their conduct, including both their liturgical and ethical worship, as God is holy—"You shall be [ἔσεσθε] holy, for I am holy" (Lev 19:2 in 1:16).

The "adornment" (κόσμος)—the Greek term also means "world"—of the wives is not to be the external one that involves the wearing of perishable "gold things [χρυσίων]" (3:3). This follows from the fact that they have been ransomed from the futile conduct that includes false worship not with perishable things, silver or "gold [χρυσίῳ]" (1:18), but with the precious blood of Christ (1:19), foreknown before the foundation of the "world" (κόσμου) but manifested now for their sake (1:20). This exhortation regarding the external adornment/world of the wives thus reinforces the exhortation for the whole audience to be willing to undergo their various trials (1:6), so that the refinement of their faith, more precious than "gold" (χρυσίου) that is passing away, may be found for the worship of praise, honor, and glory at the revelation of Jesus Christ (1:7).[8]

3:4a (C): But Rather the Inner Human Being of the Heart

The adornment of the wives among the audience is not to be an external one (3:3), "but rather the inner human being of the heart in the imperishableness of the gentle and quiet spirit" (3:4a). That the adornment of the wives, whose conduct should be pure in fear (3:2), is not to be an external one (3:3) but rather the inner human being of the "heart" (καρδίας) follows closely from the exhortation for the whole audience to love one another constantly from a clean "heart [καρδίας]" (1:22). In contrast to the "external" (ἔξωθεν) one, the adornment of the wives is to be the "hidden" or "inner" (κρυπτός) one—the inner human being, the interior human character, of the heart. This adornment of the inner "human being" (ἄνθρωπος) of the heart recalls and resonates with the doing of good that will silence the ignorance of foolish "human beings [ἀνθρώπων]" (2:15), the kind of "human beings" (ἀνθρώπων) who rejected Christ as the living stone, who nevertheless was chosen and esteemed in the sight of God (2:4).[9]

---

and Artemis of Ephesus, there is no evidence that our author intended to counter such practices" (Achtemeier, 1 Peter, 212).

8. Batten, "Neither Gold," 484–501. "Whatever the source of the tradition upon which our author is drawing, it makes sense only if there were women among the readers of this letter who could afford the kind of expensive clothing and jewelry referred to" (Achtemeier, 1 Peter, 212).

9. "The inner human being of the heart" means that what is interior to the human being should be expressed exteriorly, that there should be coherence between the inner

That the adornment and thus the conduct of the wives is to be that of the inner human being of the heart in the "imperishableness" (ἀφθάρτῳ) of the gentle and quiet spirit (3:4a) coincides with their having been given a new birth for eternal life not from a seed perishable but "imperishable" (ἀφθάρτου), through a living and abiding word of God (1:23). This new birth includes a living hope through the resurrection of Jesus Christ from the dead (1:3), for an "imperishable" (ἄφθαρτον) heavenly inheritance (1:4).[10]

That the wives' adornment is to be that of the inner human being in the imperishableness of the gentle and quiet human "spirit [πνεύματος]" (3:4a) is appropriate to the holiness of the divine "Spirit [πνεύματος]" (1:2) in which the whole audience was chosen by God (1:1). This is the divine "Spirit" (πνεῦμα) of Christ that was in the prophets (1:11), the Holy "Spirit" (πνεύματι) by which the good news, the pronouncement of which abides for eternity (1:25), was proclaimed unto the audience (1:12). Thus, the audience as a whole are to appreciate that the gentle and quiet human spirit of the wives among them possesses an imperishableness that accords with their new birth for an imperishable, eternal life.

3:4b (B'): Which Is before God of Great Value

The wives' inner human being of the heart in the imperishableness of the gentle and quiet spirit (3:4a) is further described as an adornment (3:3), a conduct pure in fear (3:2), "which is before God of great value" (3:4b). At this point, after the central and unparalleled C element (3:4a), the audience experience a pivot of parallels from the B to the B' element of this chiastic unit. The exhortation to let the adornment of the wives not "be" (ἔστω) the external one (3:3) progresses to the assertion that the adornment of the inner human being of the heart (3:4a) "is" (ἐστιν) before God of great value (3:4b).

That the conduct with which the wives are to adorn themselves, that of the inner human being of the heart in the imperishableness of the gentle and quiet spirit (3:4a), is before "God" (τοῦ θεοῦ) of "great value [πολυτελές]"

---

and the outer person, according to Deselaers, "Der verborgene Mensch des Herzens," 281–84. "The 'secret person' in this context refers not so much to the general inner aspect of the human being as it does to the person who is determined by a faith that is visible directly only to God, and that is apparent to other human beings only by way of external acts" (Achtemeier, *1 Peter*, 213).

10. "The expression 'imperishable seed' in 1:23 suggests that the imperishable adornment mentioned here likewise is the result of a regeneration from hearing the word of the good news; see the other accents on imperishability in 1:4 (inheritance); 5:4 (crown); and the contrasts 'corruptible'—'flawless' (1:18–19) and 'perishable'—'imperishable' (1:23–25)" (Elliott, *1 Peter*, 565–66).

(3:4b) means that it serves as ethical worship acceptable to God. Such worship is made possible by the "precious" (τιμίῳ) blood of the sacrificial worship of Christ (1:19), the living stone by human beings rejected but in the sight of "God" (θεῷ) chosen, "esteemed [ἔντιμον]" (2:4). That such conduct by the wives "is before God" (ἐστιν ἐνώπιον τοῦ θεοῦ) of great value reaffirms that it "is the will of God" (ἐστὶν τὸ θέλημα τοῦ θεοῦ) that those doing good silence the ignorance of foolish human beings (2:15). The good doing on the part of the wives, through which they may gain their Gentile husbands as believers (3:1), thus contributes to the praiseworthy works of the praiseworthy conduct by which the whole audience may inspire Gentiles to the worship of glorifying God on the day of visitation (2:12).[11]

3:5–7 (A′): The Holy Wives Also Being Subject to Their Own Husbands

The audience hear the A′ element (3:5–7) of this chiastic unit as a chiastic pattern in itself:
a) for thus formerly also the holy *wives* who hoped for God adorned themselves (3:5a),
  b) being subject to their own *husbands* (3:5b),
    c) as Sarah obeyed Abraham, calling him "lord," whose children you become, doing good and not fearing any intimidation (3:6).
  b′) The *husbands* likewise, fellow dwellers according to knowledge (3:7a)
a′) as to the more delicate vessel, the *feminine*, showing honor as also to fellow heirs of the grace of life so that your prayers may not be hindered (3:7b).

After the central and unparalleled c) sub-element, "as Sarah obeyed Abraham, calling him 'lord,' whose children you become, doing good and not fearing any intimidation" (3:6), the audience experience a pivot of parallels from the b) to the b′) sub-element involving the only occurrences in this sub-unit of the term "husbands." "Being subject to their own husbands [ἀνδράσιν]" (3:5b) progresses to "the husbands [ἄνδρες] likewise" (3:7a).

---

11. Slaughter, "Winning Unbelieving Husbands to Christ," 199–211. "The wife, acting within the limits imposed on her by the social order that in this case urges a modesty in apparel also appropriate for Christians, must nevertheless have as her primary intention activity that is pleasing to God" (Achtemeier, *1 Peter*, 213). "The phrase ἐνώπιον τοῦ θεοῦ is what makes the difference... the accent here is on God's acceptance or positive verdict on a certain pattern of behavior... several of the passages in this category have to do with worship, or with ethical behavior regarded as a form of worship... God views a humble and quiet spirit as a 'lavish adornment'... in the sense of accepting it as a prayer from the heart or a generous sacrifice (cf. 2:5)" (Michaels, *1 Peter*, 163).

They then hear a progression from the a) to the a') sub-element involving the only occurrences in this sub-unit of terms referring to women. "Holy wives [γυναῖκες]" (3:5a) progresses to "the more delicate vessel, the feminine [γυναικείῳ]" (3:7b).

At this point, the audience also experience progressions, via the chiastic parallels, from the A (3:1-2) to the A' (3:5-7) element of this chiastic unit. "Likewise [ὁμοίως]" (3:1), "wives [γυναῖκες]" (3:1), "being subject to their own husbands [ὑποτασσόμεναι τοῖς ἰδίοις ἀνδράσιν]" (3:1), "the conduct of the wives [γυναικῶν]" (3:1), "your [ὑμῶν] conduct" (3:2), and "in fear [φόβῳ]" (3:2) occur in the A element. These occurrences progress to "holy wives [γυναῖκες]" (3:5), "being subject to their own husbands [ὑποτασσόμεναι τοῖς ἰδίοις ἀνδράσιν]" (3:5), "not fearing [φοβούμεναι] any intimidation" (3:6), "the husbands [ἄνδρες] likewise [ὁμοίως]" (3:7), and "your [ὑμῶν] prayers" (3:7).

Recalling that "for thus [οὕτως] it is the will of God [θεοῦ] that those doing good silence the ignorance of foolish human beings" (2:15), the audience now hear, "for thus [οὕτως] formerly also the holy wives who hoped for God [θεόν] adorned themselves" (3:5a). That these wives are "holy" (ἅγιαι) makes them a model for the audience to fulfill the command of the divine "Holy One" (ἅγιον) who called them to become "holy" (ἅγιοι) in all their conduct (1:15), because it is written, "You shall be holy [ἅγιοι], for I am holy [ἅγιός]" (Lev 19:2 in 1:16). That the holy wives of old are those who "hoped for God" (ἐλπίζουσαι εἰς θεόν) likens them to the audience, who through Christ are faithful "for God" (εἰς θεόν), so that their faith and "hope" (ἐλπίδα) are "for God [εἰς θεόν]" (1:21). These holy wives who hoped for God thus serve as a model for the whole audience to completely "hope" (ἐλπίσατε) upon the grace that is to be borne to them by God at the revelation of Jesus Christ (1:13).

That the holy "wives" (γυναῖκες) of old who hoped for "God" (θεόν) "adorned" (ἐκόσμουν) themselves, by "being subject to their own husbands [ὑποτασσόμεναι τοῖς ἰδίοις ἀνδράσιν]" (3:5), likens them also to the "wives" (γυναῖκες) among the audience, who are "being subject to their own husbands [ὑποτασσόμεναι τοῖς ἰδίοις ἀνδράσιν]" (3:1). With the holy wives of old as their model, the "adornment [κόσμος]" (3:3) of the wives among the audience is to be the inner human being of the heart in the imperishableness of the gentle and quiet spirit, which is before "God" (θεοῦ) of great value as their ethical worship (3:4).

The matriarch Sarah, as one of the holy wives of old who were being "subject" (ὑποτασσόμεναι) to their own husbands (3:5), obeyed her husband Abraham, calling him "lord [κύριον]" (3:6).¹² Sarah thus provides a stellar model not only for the wives among the audience being "subject" (ὑποτασσόμεναι) to their own husbands (3:1), but for the whole audience to be "subject" (ὑποτάγητε) to every human institution on account of the divine "Lord [κύριον]" (2:13). That the wives among the audience are to "become" (ἐγενήθητε) "children" (τέκνα) of the Sarah who "obeyed" (ὑπήκουσεν) her husband Abraham reinforces the exhortation for the whole audience, as "children of obedience [τέκνα ὑπακοῆς]" (1:14), to "become" (γενήθητε) holy in all of their conduct, in both their liturgical and ethical worship, as God is holy (1:15).¹³ Such becoming has its foundation in Christ who has "become" (ἐγενήθη) the head of the corner (2:7) of the spiritual house of the audience as a holy priesthood who have been built up to offer up the ethical worship of spiritual sacrifices acceptable to God through Jesus Christ (2:5).

The wives among the audience become children of the ideal wife Sarah by "doing good" (ἀγαθοποιοῦσαι), like the house servants who are to be "doing good" (ἀγαθοποιοῦντες) and suffering (2:20), and by not fearing any intimidation (3:6). They thereby reaffirm that it is the will of God that those "doing good" (ἀγαθοποιοῦντας) silence the ignorance of foolish human beings (2:15), so that in what the Gentiles may slander the audience as "evildoers" (κακοποιῶν), observing from the praiseworthy works of their good doing, they may offer the worship of glorifying God on the day of visitation (2:12). The wives are not to be "fearing" (φοβούμεναι) any intimidation (cf. Prov 3:25) from human beings, particularly from their husbands, but rather, like the house servants, are to be subject in all "fear" (φόβῳ) of God (2:18), just as the whole audience are in "fear" (φόβῳ) of God to conduct the time of their sojourning (1:17). The wives among the audience thereby provide a model for the whole audience to "fear" (φοβεῖσθε) God (2:17) in and through their liturgical and ethical worship of God.¹⁴

12. "The only explicit instance where Sarah calls Abraham 'Lord' is in Gen 18, where the three visitors promise to Abraham the birth of a son. In the Septuagint account of this event, Sarah 'laughed to herself, saying, "This has not yet happened to me even until now, and my lord [κύριος] is old"' (18:12 LXX). This is hardly an exemplary moment of submission, yet 1 Peter recalls this moment with the claim 'Sarah obeyed [ὑπήκουσεν] Abraham when she called him lord'" (Donelson, *I & II Peter*, 92). "LXX does not use any verb meaning 'obey' with respect to Sarah's relationship with Abraham . . . Nevertheless, the submission of Sarah to Abraham was a long-standing element of Jewish tradition" (Jobes, *1 Peter*, 205).

13. "This identification of Christian wives as the figurative 'children' of Sarah is unique in the Bible but is consistent with the depiction of all the believers as 'children of obedience' in 1:14" (Elliott, *1 Peter*, 572).

14. Kiley, "Like Sara," 689–92; Slaughter, "Sarah as a Model," 357–65; Spencer, "Peter's Pedagogical Method," 107–19; Forbes, "Children of Sarah," 105–9; Punt, "Subverting Sarah," 45–50. "The term πτόησις, with its connotations of passion and excitement,

1 Peter, 2 Peter, and Jude

Just as the whole audience are to be subject to every human institution on account of the Lord (2:13), "likewise" (ὁμοίως) "wives" (γυναῖκες) are to be subject to their own "husbands [ἀνδράσιν]" (3:1). But believing "husbands" (ἄνδρες) "likewise" (ὁμοίως), as fellow dwellers according to knowledge, are to show respect to their wives as to the more delicate vessel, the "feminine [γυναικείῳ]" (3:7).[15] Husbands are to dwell together with their wives in accord with their "knowledge" (γνῶσιν) not only that wives are more delicate, but of the significance of Christ in God's plan for believers. Christ was "foreknown" (προεγνωσμένου) by God before the foundation of the world but manifested at the last of these times for the sake of the believing audience (1:20), chosen sojourners according to the "foreknowledge" (πρόγνωσιν) of God for the obedience of Jesus Christ (1:2). Husbands are to show "honor" (τιμήν) to their believing wives (3:7), the "honor" (τιμή) of Christ that is for those who believe (2:7), which anticipates the "honor" (τιμήν) for which their refined faith may be found at the revelation of Jesus Christ (1:7).

The husbands are to show honor to their wives as also to fellow heirs of the "grace" (χάριτος) of "life [ζωῆς]" (3:7), that is, the "grace [χάρις]" (1:2) of the eternal life for which God has given us believers new birth for a "living" (ζῶσαν) hope through the resurrection of Jesus Christ from the dead (1:3).[16] This is so that "your" (ὑμῶν) prayers, the prayerful worship of the husbands, who observe "your" (ὑμῶν) conduct, that is, the conduct of their wives that is pure in the reverent fear of God (3:2), may not be hindered

---

may be referencing the sudden anger of husbands. In any case, the challenge to these wives is to not fear the dangerous behavior of their husbands. The implication is that they should fear not humans but God (1:17) and that by trusting God in the face of such violence, they are imitating Jesus (2:23; cf. 4:19)" (Donelson, *I & II Peter*, 93). "Only here and in 3:14, both OT allusions and both with cognate accusative, does the word φοβέω mean 'fear' with respect to human beings, rather than as normally in this letter, reverence for God" (Achtemeier, *1 Peter*, 216n156).

15. "The verb συνοικοῦντες ('live with,' 'dwell with') occurs only here in the NT but elsewhere of the cohabitation of husband and wife ... The considerateness or knowledge pertains not only to the assumed condition of wives as 'weaker feminine vessels' but also and especially to their special status as 'co-heirs of the grace of life'" (Elliott, *1 Peter*, 575). "The word σκεῦος ('vessel') was used in Greco-Roman and early Christian literature to refer to the body (e.g., 2 Cor 4:7; 1 Thess 4:4)" (Senior, *1 Peter*, 84).

16. "The genitive ζωῆς ('life') is probably epexegetic ('grace that consists in life') rather than qualitative or adjectival ('living grace'), and bears an eschatological implication: it refers to the new life awaiting the Christian subsequent to God's judgment of the world" (Achtemeier, *1 Peter*, 218). "The expression on the whole recalls 1:4, where the 'inheritance' of all of the believers is mentioned and anticipates 3:9, which also speaks of the blessing to be 'inherited' by all of the faithful. Thus, the motif of inheritance involved in the word 'co-heirs' links this passage with its broader context and the eschatological hope that pervades the letter" (Elliott, *1 Peter*, 580).

1 Peter 3:1–7

(3:7).[17] By observing the conduct that serves as the ethical worship of their wives, and showing them honor as fellow heirs of the grace of eternal life, the prayers of the husbands, and, by implication, also of their wives and of the whole audience, may not be hindered but rather enhanced as their own proper liturgical worship of God.[18]

Summary on 3:1–7

The wives among the audience are to be subject to their own husbands, so that even if some are "disobeying the word," thus aligning themselves with the nonbelievers who "stumble" over Christ, "disobeying the word" (2:8), they may be gained, becoming believers through the "conduct" of their wives "without a word" (3:1). The wives thereby play their part in the audience's keeping of their "conduct" among the Gentiles praiseworthy, so that, "observing" from the praiseworthy works, they may be inspired to engage in the worship of glorifying God on the day of visitation (2:12).

The Gentile husbands will be gained as believers, "observing" the "conduct" of their wives that is pure in the reverent "fear" of God (3:2), just as the house servants are subject to their masters in all "fear" of God (2:18). The wives thereby play their roles in the audience becoming holy as God is holy in all their "conduct" (1:15), as in "fear" of God "you," the audience, are to "conduct" the time of their sojourning (1:17), in contrast to their futile "conduct" inherited from ancestors, which includes false worship (1:18). The conduct of the wives that is "pure," which has cultic connotations, in the reverent fear of God resonates with the audience as a whole having "purified" their souls in the obedience to the truth for sincere brotherly love

---

17. "This final ὑμῶν draws together the whole unit dealing with marriage (vv 1–7) so that even wives married to unbelieving husbands (vv 1–2) may have a glimpse of what marriage can become in Christ—a household church, with husband and wife living together as a praying community and 'co-heirs' of salvation" (Michaels, *1 Peter*, 171).

18. Piper, "Beautiful Faith," 48–52. "The idea that the efficacy of prayers and worship in general depends upon ethics is prevalent in both Judaism and early Christianity" (Donelson, *I & II Peter*, 94). "This is the context within which the instructions of 1 Pet. 3.1–7 fall. They are to be framed by the eschatological understanding of the concept of χάρις as used in 1 Pet. 1.10, 13, making them more than mere instructions for moral or godly living. They are integrally entwined with the χάρις that awaits expectation in the revelation of the Lord Jesus Christ. As such, they serve not simply as motivators for good behavior but, even more, as the basis of true worship" (Mbuvi, *Temple*, 111). "This association between prayer and respectful conduct here in 1 Peter reflects the common Christian conviction that prayer, as an expression of one's relation to God and an act of praise, thanksgiving, confession, and petition, is directly affected by one's behavior toward other persons" (Elliott, *1 Peter*, 582).

(1:22). Such conduct amounts to their ethical worship that is part of the ethical worship of the audience as a whole, who are, in the reverent fear and thus worship of God, to conduct the time of their sojourning.

The "adornment"—the Greek term also means "world"—of the wives is not to be the external one that involves the wearing of perishable "gold things" (3:3). This follows from the fact that they have been ransomed from the futile conduct that includes false worship not with perishable things, silver or "gold" (1:18), but with the precious blood of Christ (1:19), foreknown before the foundation of the "world" but manifested now for their sake (1:20). This exhortation regarding the external adornment/world of the wives thus reinforces the exhortation for the whole audience to be willing to undergo their various trials (1:6), so that the refinement of their faith, more precious than "gold" that is passing away, may be found for the worship of praise, honor, and glory at the revelation of Jesus Christ (1:7).

That the conduct with which the wives are to adorn themselves, that of the inner human being of the heart in the imperishableness of the gentle and quiet spirit (3:4a), is before "God" of "great value" (3:4b) means that it serves as ethical worship acceptable to God. Such worship is made possible by the "precious" blood of the sacrificial worship of Christ (1:19), the living stone by human beings rejected but in the sight of "God" chosen, "esteemed" (2:4). That such conduct by the wives "is before God" of great value reaffirms that it "is the will of God" that those doing good silence the ignorance of foolish human beings (2:15). The good doing on the part of the wives, through which they may gain their Gentile husbands as believers (3:1), thus contributes to the praiseworthy works of the praiseworthy conduct by which the whole audience may inspire Gentiles to the worship of glorifying God on the day of visitation (2:12).

The preeminent matriarch Sarah, as one of the holy wives of old who were being "subject" to their own husbands (3:5), obeyed her husband Abraham, calling him "lord" (3:6). Sarah thus provides a stellar model not only for the wives among the audience being "subject" to their own husbands (3:1), but for the whole audience to be "subject" to every human institution on account of the divine "Lord" (2:13). That the wives among the audience are to "become children" of the Sarah who "obeyed" her husband Abraham reinforces the exhortation for the whole audience, as "children of obedience" (1:14), to "become" holy in all of their conduct, in both their liturgical and ethical worship, as God is holy (1:15). Such becoming has its foundation in Christ who has "become" the head of the corner (2:7) of the spiritual house of the audience as a holy priesthood who have been built up to offer up the ethical worship of spiritual sacrifices acceptable to God through Jesus Christ (2:5).

1 Peter 3:1-7

The wives among the audience become children of the ideal wife Sarah by "doing good," like the house servants who are to be "doing good" and suffering (2:20), and by not fearing any intimidation (3:6). They thereby reaffirm that it is the will of God that those "doing good" silence the ignorance of foolish human beings (2:15), so that in what the Gentiles may slander the audience as "evildoers," observing from the praiseworthy works of their good doing, they may offer the worship of glorifying God on the day of visitation (2:12). The wives are not to be "fearing" any intimidation from human beings, particularly from their husbands, but rather, like the house servants, are to be subject in all "fear" of God (2:18), just as the whole audience are in "fear" of God to conduct the time of their sojourning (1:17). The wives among the audience thereby provide a model for the whole audience to "fear" God (2:17) in and through their liturgical and ethical worship of God.

The husbands are to show honor to their wives as also to fellow heirs of the "grace" of "life" (3:7), that is, the "grace" (1:2) of the eternal life for which God has given us believers new birth for a "living" hope through the resurrection of Jesus Christ from the dead (1:3). This is so that "your" prayers, the prayerful worship of the husbands, who observe "your" conduct, that is, the conduct of their wives that is pure in the reverent fear of God (3:2), may not be hindered (3:7). By observing the conduct that serves as the ethical worship of their wives, and showing them honor as fellow heirs of the grace of eternal life, the prayers of the husbands, and, by implication, also of their wives and of the whole audience, may not be hindered but rather enhanced as their own proper liturgical worship of God.

8

1 Peter 3:8-17
Do Not Speak or Do Evil but Do Good on account of Righteousness (E′)

Hold holy the Christ as Lord in your hearts by suffering for doing good if God wills it

A   ⁸ At the end, *all* harmonious, sympathetic, having brotherly affection, compassionate, humble, ⁹ not returning *evil* for *evil* or insult for insult, but instead blessing, for to this you were called so that you might inherit a blessing, ¹⁰ for let the one who *wants* to love life and see *good* days separate the tongue from *evil* and lips from speaking deceit, ¹¹ let him turn away from *evil* and *do good*, let him seek peace and pursue it, ¹² for the eyes of the *Lord* are upon the righteous and his ears for their supplication, but the face of the *Lord* is upon those *doing evil* things (Ps 33:13-17 LXX). ¹³ And who is going to cause you *evil*, if for the *good* you become zealots?

   B   ¹⁴ᵃ But even if you should suffer on account of righteousness, you are blessed. But the *fear* for them

   B′   ¹⁴ᵇ do not *fear* or be terrified,

A′   ¹⁵ but as *Lord* hold holy the Christ in your hearts, always ready for an answer to *all* who ask you a word concerning the hope within you, ¹⁶ but with gentleness and fear, keeping a *good* conscience, so that when you are spoken against, shame may come against those mistreating your *good*, in Christ, conduct. ¹⁷ For it is better to suffer for *doing good*, if the will of God *wants* it, than for *doing evil*.¹

---

1. For the establishment of 1 Pet 3:8-17 as a chiasm, see ch. 1.

1 Peter 3:8–17

Audience Response to 3:8–17

At this point, after the central and unparalleled F unit (3:1–7), the audience experience a pivotal progression of macrochiastic parallels from the E (2:21b–25) to this E' (3:8–17) chiastic unit. In the E unit Christ is described as one who did not "do" (ἐποίησεν) sin nor was "deceit" (δόλος) found in his mouth (2:22), who, "being insulted did not return insult [λοιδορούμενος οὐκ ἀντελοιδόρει]" (2:23), so that to "righteousness" (δικαιοσύνῃ) we might live (2:24). This progresses to a description of the audience in the E' unit as not returning "insult for insult [λοιδορίαν ἀντὶ λοιδορίας]" (3:9). Furthermore, an individual should separate lips from speaking "deceit [δόλον]" (3:10) and "do" (ποιησάτω) good (3:11). Finally, the audience are warned that the face of the Lord is upon those "doing" (ποιοῦντας) evil (3:12), and informed that if they should suffer on account of "righteousness" (δικαιοσύνην), they are blessed (3:14).

3:8–13 (A): Let Him Turn Away from Evil and Do Good

The audience hear the A element (3:8–13) of this chiastic unit as a chiastic pattern in itself:
a) At the end, all harmonious, sympathetic, having brotherly love, compassionate, humble, not returning *evil* for *evil* or insult for insult, but instead blessing, for to this you were called so that you might inherit a blessing, for let the one who wants to love life and see *good* days separate the tongue from *evil* and lips from speaking deceit, let him turn away from *evil* and *do good* (3:8–11a),
b) let him seek peace and pursue *it* (3:11b),
c) for the eyes of the Lord are upon the righteous (3:12a)
b') and *his* ears for *their* supplication (3:12b),
a') but the face of the Lord is upon those *doing evil* things (Ps 33:13–17 LXX). And who is going to cause you *evil*, if for the *good* you become zealots (3:12c–13)?

After the central and unparalleled c) sub-element, "for the eyes of the Lord are upon the righteous" (3:12a), the audience experience a pivot of parallels from the b) to the b') sub-element involving the only occurrences of personal pronouns in this sub-unit. "Let him seek peace and pursue it [αὐτήν]" (3:11b) progresses to "his [αὐτοῦ] ears for their [αὐτῶν] supplication" (3:12b). They then hear a progression of parallels from the a) to the a') sub-element involving the only occurrences in 1 Peter of the term "evil" and in this sub-unit of expressions for doing good and doing evil. "Evil

1 Peter, 2 Peter, and Jude

[κακόν] for evil [κακοῦ]" (3:9), "good [ἀγαθάς] days" (3:10), "separate the tongue from evil [κακοῦ]" (3:10), and "turn away from evil [κακοῦ] and do good [ποιησάτω ἀγαθόν]" (3:11a) progress to "doing evil [ποιοῦντας κακά] things" (3:12c) and "who is going to cause you evil [κακώσων], if for the good [ἀγαθοῦ] you become zealots?" (3:13).

In addition, the audience hear the a) sub-element (3:8–11a) of this chiastic sub-unit as yet another chiastic pattern in itself:
(a) At the end, all harmonious, sympathetic, having brotherly affection, compassionate, humble, not returning *evil* for *evil* or insult for insult (3:8–9a),
  (b) but instead *blessing* (3:9b),
    (c) for to this you were called (3:9c)
  (b') so that you might inherit a *blessing* (3:9d),
(a') for let the one who wants to love life and see good days separate the tongue from *evil* and lips from speaking deceit, let him turn away from *evil* and do good (3:10–11a).

After the central and unparalleled (c) sub-element, "for this you were called" (3:9c), the audience experience a pivot of parallels from the (b) to the (b') sub-element involving the only occurrences in 1 Peter of expressions for "blessing." "But instead blessing [εὐλογοῦντες]" (3:9b) progresses to "so that you might inherit a blessing [εὐλογίαν]" (3:9d). They then hear a progression of parallels from the (a) to the (a') sub-element involving the only occurrences in this sub-unit of terms for "evil." "Not returning evil [κακόν] for evil [κακοῦ]" (3:9a) progresses to "separate the tongue from evil [κακοῦ]" (3:10) and "turn away from evil [κακοῦ]" (3:11a).

The first words of this unit, "at the end [τέλος]" (3:8a) remind the audience that they are attaining the "end" (τέλος) of their faith, salvation of souls (1:9), that will take place at the end of the world at the revelation of Jesus Christ (1:7, 13). In view of that end, they are all to be harmonious, sympathetic, having brotherly affection, compassionate, and humble (3:8), virtues which contribute to their ethical worship. That all in the audience are to have "brotherly affection" (φιλάδελφοι) reinforces the exhortation for them to have souls purified in the obedience to the truth for sincere "brotherly affection" (φιλαδελφίαν) and from a clean heart to love one another constantly (1:22). Such love with its cultic connotations of being performed by "purified" souls and from a "clean" heart amounts to ethical worship of the Holy One who called the audience to be holy in all conduct (1:15).[2]

---

2. "The adjective φιλάδελφος denotes here love of (i.e., emotional attachment and commitment to) fellow believers who are regarded, figuratively, as 'brothers' and 'sisters' in the faith" (Elliott, *1 Peter*, 604).

1 Peter 3:8-17

As an additional part of their ethical worship, the audience are not to be returning evil for evil or "insult for insult [λοιδορίαν ἀντὶ λοιδορίας]" (3:9a).³ By so doing, they will be following the model that the Christ who suffered on their behalf left for them (2:21b), the Christ, who, "being insulted did not return insult" (λοιδορούμενος οὐκ ἀντελοιδόρει), and suffering, he did not threaten, but offered the ethical worship of handing himself over to the One who judges righteously (2:23).⁴ Instead of returning evil or insult, the audience are to be "blessing [εὐλογοῦντες]" (3:9b) those who harm or insult them. This "blessing" consists of an act of worship whereby the audience invoke God's blessing upon their enemies. Such blessing complements the act of worship Peter invited the audience to perform at the beginning of the letter by declaring "blessed" (εὐλογητός) the God and Father of our Lord Jesus Christ (1:3).⁵

What concerned specifically the house servants among the audience (2:18) also applied to the audience in general as those being built up as a spiritual house for a holy priesthood to offer up spiritual sacrifices acceptable to God through Jesus Christ (2:5). If doing good and suffering, they endure, this is the grace of worship pleasing in the sight of God (2:20). For "to this" (εἰς τοῦτο) grace of worship "you were called" (ἐκλήθητε) by God (2:21a). Similarly, the audience now hear that "to this" (εἰς τοῦτο) worship of blessing (3:9b) "you were called" (ἐκλήθητε) by God (3:9c).⁶ They are

---

3. "This focus upon the verbal aspects of evil has suggested to many readers that the context of the conflict in 1 Peter is primarily verbal. Christians are being insulted and shamed by their Gentile neighbors. It is likely that the various trials (1:6) that Christians are enduring includes more than being insulted by neighbors, though it certainly includes such insults and the loss of social status that such abuse implies" (Donelson, *I & II Peter*, 99).

4. "The rehearsal of Christ's behavior in 2:22-23 was implicitly an appeal to the readers of the epistle to behave in much the same way. Now the appeal is made explicit. Nonretaliation becomes the crown of the household duty code and the centerpiece of the ethical teaching of the entire epistle" (Michaels, *1 Peter*, 178).

5. "Given the tendency of human nature to retaliate, coupled with the social expectation to do so, the Christian who refrains from verbal retaliation and instead offers blessing would give unbelievers pause" (Jobes, *1 Peter*, 217). "Although εὐλογοῦντες can have its etymological meaning of 'speaking well of,' it is likely that 1 Peter is being even more provocative than suggesting that these Christians respond to insults with praise. Since later in this verse εὐλογία has the sense of God's blessing, it probably does so here ... Believers are to respond to abuse by invoking God's blessings on those who are abusing them" (Donelson, *I & II Peter*, 99). "To 'bless' someone is to extend to that person the prospect of salvation, or the favor of God. It corresponds to praying for someone except that the words are directed to the person or persons involved rather than to God. The implied hope is that those who now insult Christian believers will 'glorify God on the day of visitation' (2:12)" (Michaels, *1 Peter*, 178).

6. "In 2:21a, εἰς τοῦτο can refer only to the conduct enjoined in 2:18-20, and this

thus again reminded that as God's own people they are to proclaim, in both their liturgical and ethical worship, the virtues of the God who "called" (καλέσαντος) them out of darkness for his marvelous light (2:9). Indeed, the audience, according to the Holy One who "called" (καλέσαντα) them, are to become holy, as God is holy (1:16), in all of their conduct (1:15), which includes both their liturgical and ethical worship.

The audience were called by God to the worship of blessing instead of returning evil or insult, so that they might inherit a blessing from God (3:9). With the verb "you might inherit" (κληρονομήσητε), the audience hear the transitional term that links this unit with the previous unit, which concluded with a reference to "fellow heirs [συγκληρονόμοις]" (3:7). As the audience are to appreciate, this "blessing" (εὐλογίαν) they are to inherit from God in reciprocation for their worship of "blessing" (εὐλογοῦντες) those who insult them is synonymous with the divine gift of eternal life. This blessing to be inherited from God is the same as the divine grace of eternal life of which the husbands and wives among the audience are "fellow heirs [συγκληρονόμοις]" (3:7). And it is the same as the imperishable heavenly "inheritance" (κληρονομίαν) of the eternal life for which God has given us new birth for a living hope through the resurrection of Jesus Christ from the dead (1:3; cf. 1:23).[7]

Any individual in the audience "who wants to love life and see good days is to separate the tongue from evil and lips from speaking deceit" (3:10). As those "beloved [ἀγαπητοί]" (2:11), the audience have been exhorted to "love" (ἀγαπᾶτε) the brotherhood of fellow believers (2:17), to "love" (ἀγαπήσατε) one another earnestly (1:22). They have been affirmed as those who "love" (ἀγαπᾶτε) the Jesus Christ they have not "seen [ἰδόντες]" (1:8). And now they hear what whoever wants to "love" (ἀγαπᾶν) "life" (ζωήν), the eternal "life [ζωῆς]" (3:7) for which God has given us new birth (1:3), and "see" (ἰδεῖν) the good "days" (ἡμέρας) of this life to be consummated on the "day" (ἡμέρᾳ) of visitation (2:12) is to do.[8] He or she is to separate the "tongue" from "evil" (κακοῦ), reinforcing the exhortation not to return "evil" (κακόν) for "evil [κακοῦ]" (3:9), and, as among the audience who have removed all "deceit [δόλον]" (2:1), to separate "lips" from speaking "deceit" (δόλον). Such individuals will thus imitate the ethical worship of the Christ who did not do sin nor was "deceit" (δόλος) found in his "mouth" (2:22).

---

argues for its similar retrospective function here in 3:9d as well. This yields the sense: 'you have been called to bless (or, less likely, to practice all of the conduct urged in vv 8-9c) in order that you yourselves may inherit a blessing'" (Elliott, *1 Peter*, 610).

7. "εὐλογία, or 'blessing,' is God's final pronouncement (i.e., bestowal) of eternal well-being on his people at the last day" (Michaels, *1 Peter*, 179).

8. As Feldmeier (*First Letter*, 187) notes, "the promise of life and of good days can in the context of 1 Peter only refer to eternal life with God."

1 Peter 3:8-17

In addition, whoever wants to love eternal life is not only to separate the tongue from "evil [κακοῦ]" (3:10), but to turn away from "evil [κακοῦ]" (3:11a), further reinforcing the exhortation not to return "evil" (κακόν) for "evil [κακοῦ]" (3:9). As appropriate for one wanting to see the "good" (ἀγαθάς) days of this eternal life (3:10), such an individual is to do "good [ἀγαθόν]" (3:11a), in accord with the ethical worship of the house servants who are to be subject in all fear of God to masters, not only to the "good" (ἀγαθοῖς) and kind but also to the perverse (2:18). That he or she is to "do" (ποιησάτω) good reinforces the exhortation for the audience to follow the model of the Christ who did not "do" (ἐποίησεν) sin (2:22), but handed himself over to the One who judges righteously as his ethical worship of God (2:23). Such an individual is also to seek "peace" (εἰρήνην) and pursue it (3:11b), the profound peace with one another and with God that is a gift from God and for which Peter offered the prayer greeting that introduced the letter—"May grace to you and peace [εἰρήνη] be in abundance!" (1:2d).

The audience are assured that their conduct of separating the "tongue" from evil and "lips" from speaking deceit, of turning away from evil and doing good, of seeking peace and pursuing it (3:10-11) serves as ethical worship, for the "eyes" of the Lord are upon the righteous (3:12a). That the eyes of the divine "Lord" (κυρίου) are upon the righteous resonates with the righteous Sarah calling Abraham her human "lord" (κύριον) as ethical worship of the divine Lord (3:6). It fortifies the exhortation for the audience to be subject to every human institution on account of the divine "Lord [κύριον]" (2:13), the divine "Lord" (κύριος) who is benevolent (2:3), as the pronouncement of this "Lord" (κυρίου) abides forever (1:25), the pronouncement about the divine "Lord" (κυρίου) Jesus Christ whose God and Father the audience have blessed in an act of worship (1:3). And that the eyes of the Lord are upon the "righteous" (δικαίους) supplies a further reason for the audience to imitate the ethical worship of the Christ who handed himself over to the One, the divine Lord, who judges "righteously [δικαίως]" (2:23).

The exhortation for individuals to seek peace and pursue it (3:11b) involves both the ethical and liturgical worship of the audience. Seeking and pursuing peace further delineates what it means to actively do good (3:11a). While achieving peace with one another and with God is something individuals must work at, profound peace is ultimately a gift of God for which the audience must pray. Indeed, Peter has already prayed that the audience may have peace in abundance (1:2d). That the eyes of the divine Lord are upon the righteous (3:12a), those doing good, and "his" (αὐτοῦ) ears for "their" (αὐτῶν) supplication (3:12b) assures the audience that their liturgical prayers of supplication in their ethical pursuit of "it" (αὐτήν), the peace they are to seek, will be heard.

1 Peter, 2 Peter, and Jude

Whereas the "eyes" of the divine "Lord" (κυρίου) look favorably upon the righteous (3:12a), who include everyone who is to "do" (ποιησάτω) good (3:11a), the "face" of the divine "Lord" (κυρίου) is set unfavorably upon those "doing" (ποιοῦντας) evil things (3:12c).[9] With these words the audience hear the conclusion of a scriptural allusion to Ps 33:13-17 LXX which began at 3:10.[10] But the scriptural allusion provocatively and ominously leaves unexpressed the implicit unfavorable consequences of the face of the Lord being upon those doing evil things—"to root out from the earth the memory of them" (Ps 33:17b LXX). Enhanced by the scriptural authority of the allusion to Psalm 33, that the "face" of the Lord is upon those doing "evil" (κακά) things reinforces the exhortations for the audience to turn away from "evil [κακοῦ]" (3:11a), to separate the tongue from "evil [κακοῦ]" (3:10), and not to return "evil" (κακόν) for "evil [κακοῦ]" (3:9a).[11]

If the eyes of the Lord are upon the righteous (3:12a), who include everyone in the audience who is to do "good [ἀγαθόν]" (3:11a), but the face of the Lord is upon those doing "evil" (κακά) things (3:12c), then the audience must appreciate that no one, including especially the divine Lord, is ultimately going to cause them "evil" (κακώσων), if for the "good" (ἀγαθοῦ) they become zealots (3:13). If for the good, "you," the audience "become" (γένησθε) zealots resonates with the assertion that "you," specifically the wives but by extension the whole audience, "become" (ἐγενήθητε) children

---

9. "Anthropomorphic references to the 'eyes,' 'ears,' and 'face' of the Lord concern imagined aspects of God's disposition. The face is the part of the anatomy through which one's attitudes are most clearly expressed . . . The combination of *eyes, ears* and *face* describes the full awareness and attentiveness of God to those who do right and those who do wrong, the divine blessing of the former and the divine opposition to the latter [emphases original]" (Elliott, *1 Peter*, 615).

10. For the differences between the text of 1 Pet 3:10-12 and Ps 33:13-17 LXX, see Achtemeier, *1 Peter*, 225n70. See also Jobes, "Septuagint," 326-28. "'The Lord,' who in the psalm is the God of Israel, is probably understood here as Jesus Christ, a reinterpretation characteristic of 1 Peter (cf. 2:3, alluding to v 9 of the very same psalm; also 3:15, based on Isa 8:13)" (Michaels, *1 Peter*, 181).

11. Gréaux, "Lord Delivers Us," 603-13. "If there is a conscious point to be made in citing the Psalter at this point, it would be that the surprising (cf. 4:12) necessity of suffering and the call to respond to such suffering with good deeds in not only patterned in Christ but also in the OT" (Donelson, *I & II Peter*, 101). "Peter directly applies the hopes and promises of Ps. 33 LXX to his contemporary readers. His logic appears to be that just as God delivered David from his sojourn among the Philistines, God will deliver the Asian Christians from the afflictions caused by their faith in Christ" (Jobes, *1 Peter*, 223). "Not only does the reference to God hearing prayers of the righteous in 3:12 echo the intent of 3:7b, but the language of 3:11a recalls the contrast between doing good and doing evil that has informed the entire paranesis which began with 2:11. Indeed, the theme of the psalm as a whole is God's deliverance of the oppressed, a point transparently appropriate to the readers of this epistle" (Achtemeier, *1 Peter*, 226).

1 Peter 3:8-17

of the holy matriarch Sarah by "doing good [ἀγαθοποιοῦσαι]" (3:6). It further bolsters the exhortation for the audience to "become" (γενήθητε) holy in all of their conduct, in both their liturgical and ethical worship, as God is holy (1:15). Such becoming has its foundation in Christ who has "become" (ἐγενήθη) the head of the corner (2:7) of the spiritual house of the audience as a holy priesthood who have been built up to offer up the ethical worship of spiritual sacrifices acceptable to God through Jesus Christ (2:5).

3:14a (B): But the Fear for Them

Having been exhorted to become zealots for the good (3:13), the audience are further encouraged regarding opposition from others: "But even if you should suffer on account of righteousness, you are blessed. But the fear for them" (3:14a). If "you," the audience, should "suffer" (πάσχοιτε) on account of "righteousness" (δικαιοσύνην), that is, on account of doing what is right in the eyes of God, resonates with anyone "suffering" (πάσχων) sorrows "unjustly" (ἀδίκως) on account of a conscience toward God (2:19). It reminds the audience that if, doing good and "suffering" (πάσχοντες) they endure, then this is grace that serves as ethical worship pleasing in the sight of God (2:20).

The audience are to realize that they should be able to suffer on account of righteousness, since Christ "suffered" (ἔπαθεν) on behalf of them, leaving them a model that they closely follow in his footsteps (2:21). In "suffering" (πάσχων), and not threatening those who insulted him, Christ handed himself over as ethical worship to the God who judges "righteously [δικαίως]" (2:23), that is, in accord with righteousness. Consequently, the audience and all believers might live to the "righteousness" (δικαιοσύνη) which amounts to ethical worship pleasing to God (2:24). This is confirmed by the affirmation that they are blessed by God, even if "you should suffer" (πάσχοιτε) on account of "righteousness [δικαιοσύνην]" (3:14a).[12]

---

12. "Righteousness in 1 Peter (cf. 2:24; 3:12) is equivalent to 'doing good' (3:11, 17; 4:19) and thus refers to the general virtuous character of the behavior of Jesus' followers. This beatitude, though it depends for its theological logic on the larger narratives of 1 Peter, functions as an effective summary of much of the letter. The beatitude gives the reason why 'you should not fear at all' those who mistreat you. It is not because they will not 'do bad to you' but because God will bless you" (Donelson, *I & II Peter*, 104). "The use of the rare optative mood here (πάσχοιτε) and in v 17 (θέλοι) is often urged as evidence that Peter has in view only a remote contingency . . . That such things are more than remote possibilities can be seen in this epistle as clearly in what has preceded (1:6-7; 2:18-20) as in what follows (4:12-19; 5:8-10) . . . the 'blessedness' of the readers derives from the certainty that they are to 'inherit blessing' (cf. 1:4) at the coming 'revelation of Jesus Christ' (cf. 1:7, 13)" (Michaels, *1 Peter*, 186).

The reference to the "fear" (φόβον) of them, that is, of those human beings who may cause the audience to suffer (3:14a), stands in sharp contrast to the previous references to the reverent fear of God that members of the audience are to demonstrate as part of their ethical worship. The conduct of wives is to be pure in "fear" (φόβῳ) of God (3:2). House servants are to be subject to their human masters in all "fear" (φόβῳ) of God (2:18). And in "fear" (φόβῳ) of God the audience are to conduct the time of their sojourning (1:17).

3:14b (B'): Do Not Fear or Be Terrified

With regard to the fear for those who may cause the audience to suffer (3:14a), they are exhorted, "do not fear or be terrified" (3:14b). At this point, the audience experience a pivot of parallels from the B to the B' element at the center of this chiastic unit. "But the fear [φόβον] for them" (3:14a) progresses to "do not fear [φοβηθῆτε] or be terrified" (3:14b; cf. Isa 8:12). That the audience are not to "fear" or be terrified of anyone who may cause them suffering bolsters the exhortation for the wives, and by implication all members of the audience, to become children of the holy matriarch Sarah by doing good and not "fearing" (φοβούμεναι) any intimidation (3:6). It also reinforces the exhortation for the audience, who are to honor all, love the brotherhood, and honor the king, above all also to reverently "fear" (φοβεῖσθε) God (2:17) in and through their worship.

3:15–17 (A'): It Is Better To Suffer for Doing Good than for Doing Evil

The audience hear the A' element (3:15–17) of this chiastic unit as a chiastic pattern in itself:
a) but as Lord hold holy the *Christ* in your hearts (cf. Isa 8:13), always ready for an answer to all who ask you a word concerning the hope within you (3:15),
  b) but with gentleness and fear, keeping a *good* conscience (3:16a),
    c) so that when you are spoken *against* (3:16b),
    c') shame may come *against* (3:16c),
  b') those mistreating your *good* (3:16d),
a') in *Christ*, conduct. For it is better to suffer for doing good, if the will of God wants it, than for doing evil (3:16e-17).[13]

---

13. On the use of Isaiah in 1 Pet 3:13–17, see Van Rensburg and Moyise, "Isaiah," 275–86.

1 Peter 3:8-17

At the center of this chiastic sub-unit the audience experience a pivot of parallels involving the only occurrences in this sub-unit of terms with the prefix "against" (κατα-). "When you are spoken against [καταλαλεῖσθε]" in the c) sub-element (3:16b) progresses to "shame may come against [καταισχυνθῶσιν]" in the c') sub-element (3:16c). They then hear a progression of parallels involving the only occurrences in this sub-unit of the adjective "good." "Keeping a good [ἀγαθήν] conscience" in the b) sub-element (3:16a) progresses to "those mistreating your good [ἀγαθήν]" in the b') sub-element (3:16d). Finally, they hear a progression of parallels involving the only occurrences in this sub-unit of "Christ." "As Lord hold holy the Christ [Χριστόν]" in the a) sub-element (3:15) progresses to "in Christ [Χριστῷ]" in the a') sub-element (3:16e-17).

In addition, the audience hear progressions, via the chiastic parallels, from the A (3:8-13) to the A' (3:15-17) element of this chiastic unit. "All [πάντες]" (3:8), "not returning evil [κακόν] for evil [κακοῦ]" (3:9), "the one who wants [θέλων] to love life and see good [ἀγαθάς] days" (3:10), "from evil [κακοῦ]" (3:10, 11), "do [ποιησάτω] good [ἀγαθόν]" (3:11), "eyes of the Lord [κυρίου]" (3:12), "face of the Lord [κυρίου]" (3:12), "doing [ποιοῦντας] evil [κακά] things" (3:12), "cause you evil [κακώσων]" (3:13), and "for the good [ἀγαθοῦ]" (3:13) occur in the A element. These occurrences progress to "Lord [κύριον]" (3:15), "to all [παντί]" (3:15), "good [ἀγαθήν] conscience" (3:16), "good [ἀγαθήν] conduct" (3:16), "doing good [ἀγαθοποιοῦντας]" (3:17), "God wants [θέλοι] it" (3:17), and "doing evil [κακοποιοῦντας]" (3:17).

In contrast to those doing evil things, upon whom is the face of the "Lord" (κυρίου), but as among the righteous upon whom are the eyes of the "Lord [κυρίου]" (3:12), the audience are to "sanctify" in the sense of "hold holy" (ἁγιάσατε) the Christ as "Lord" (κύριον) in their hearts (3:15).[14] The exhortation for the audience to hold holy the Christ as "Lord" in their "hearts" (καρδίαις) likens them to the wives among them whose adornment is to be the inner human being of the "heart [καρδίας]" (3:4). They are to become children of the matriarch Sarah, who, as among the "holy" (ἅγιαι) wives (3:5), obeyed Abraham, calling him "lord [κύριον]" (3:6). This bolsters the exhortation for the audience to perform the ethical worship of loving one another

---

14. "The point is not to make him holy, but to acknowledge that fact" (Achtemeier, *1 Peter*, 232n50). "The sequence κύριον δὲ τὸν Χριστόν can be read as predicative, 'Sanctify Christ as Lord,' or as appositional, 'Sanctify the Lord, that is, Christ.' While the syntax of Isaiah and the presence of δέ suggests an appositional reading, the presence of the article in τὸν Χριστόν indicates a predicative structure" (Donelson, *I & II Peter*, 102-3).

constantly from a clean "heart" (καρδίας), having "purified" (ἡγνικότες), akin to keeping holy, their souls in the obedience to the truth (1:22).[15]

The audience are to hold holy the "Christ" (Χριστόν) as "Lord" (κύριον) in their hearts (3:15). The matriarch Sarah prefigured this for the audience, as she obeyed Abraham, calling him "lord [κύριον]" (3:6). This reinforces the exhortation for them to be subject to every human institution on account of the "Lord [κύριον]" (2:13), the "Lord" (κύριος) they have tasted as benevolent (2:3), in accord with the pronouncement of the "Lord [κυρίου]" (1:25), that is, of our "Lord" (κυρίου) Jesus "Christ [Χριστοῦ]" (1:3).

They are to hold holy as Lord in "your" (ὑμῶν) hearts (3:15) the "Christ" (Χριστός) who suffered for "you" (ὑμῶν), leaving them a model to follow closely (2:21) for their ethical worship. That as Lord they are to "hold holy" (ἁγιάσατε) the Christ in their hearts accords with their being a "holy" (ἅγιον) nation (2:9), a "holy" (ἅγιον) priesthood to offer up the ethical worship of spiritual sacrifices acceptable to God through Jesus "Christ [Χριστοῦ]" (2:5). They will thereby become "holy" (ἅγιοι) according to the "Holy One" (ἅγιον) who called them (1:15) to be "holy" (ἅγιοι) as he is "holy [ἅγιός]" (1:16) in all their conduct, which includes their liturgical and ethical worship, through the precious blood of "Christ [Χριστοῦ]" (1:19).[16]

Aware that they are attaining a salvation "ready" (ἑτοίμην) to be revealed in the last time (1:5), the audience are always to be appropriately "ready" (ἕτοιμοι) for an answer to all who ask them a "word" (λόγον) concerning the "hope" (ἐλπίδος) within them (3:15).[17] The answer to such a request for a word regarding hope should involve the living "word" (λόγου) of God through which the audience have been given a new birth for eternal life (1:23), a new birth for a living "hope" (ἐλπίδα) through the resurrection of Jesus Christ from the dead (1:3). The audience can thus answer that their faith and "hope" (ἐλπίδα) are for the God (1:21) whom the Christ they are to hold holy in their hearts as Lord (3:15) has enabled them to offer fitting worship.

---

15. "We should not understand the heart as our inner and private lives, which are inaccessible to others. The heart is the origin of human behavior (cf. 1:22; 3:4), and from it flows everything people do. Hence, setting apart Christ as Lord in the heart is not merely a private reality but will be evident to all when believers suffer for their faith" (Schreiner, *1, 2 Peter*, 173–74).

16. "The verb ἁγιάζειν that is taken over from the LXX version of the Isaiah text is to be understood against the background of the discussion in 1 Peter 1:13–17 as a synonym for a lifestyle that accords with God" (Feldmeier, *First Letter*, 195). "The act of sanctifying Christ as Lord 'in your hearts' means both living the holy life in obedience to Christ and fearing God (and Christ) and no one else" (Donelson, *I & II Peter*, 104).

17. That these are the only occurrences of the adjective "ready" (ἕτοιμος) in 1 Peter enhances this connection.

1 Peter 3:8-17

In contrast to having "fear" (φόβον) for those who may cause them to suffer (3:14), the audience are always to be ready for an answer to all who ask them a word concerning the hope within them (3:15) with "gentleness" (πραΰτητος) and reverent "fear" (φόβου) of God (3:16a).[18] They are thus to imitate the wives whose conduct, characterized by a "gentle" (πραέως) and quiet spirit (3:4), is pure in reverent "fear" (φόβῳ) of God (3:2), and the house servants who are to be subject to their masters in all reverent "fear" (φόβῳ) of God (2:18). They will thereby in reverent "fear" (φόβῳ) of God conduct, through their liturgical and ethical worship of God, the time of their sojourning (1:17).[19]

The audience are to answer all those inquiring about their hope (3:15) with gentleness and fear, "having" or "keeping" (ἔχοντες) a good "conscience [συνείδησιν]" (3:16a), akin to keeping their "conscience" (συνείδησιν) toward God (2:19).[20] This reinforces the exhortation for the audience not to be "keeping" (ἔχοντες) their freedom as a cover for evil, but rather to be as slaves of God (2:16). And it bolsters the exhortation for the audience to be "keeping" (ἔχοντες) their conduct among the Gentiles praiseworthy, so that in what the Gentiles slander them as evildoers, observing the praiseworthy works of the audience, the Gentiles may offer the worship of glorifying God on the day of visitation (2:12).

That the audience are to be keeping a "good" (ἀγαθήν) conscience, so that when "you are spoken against [καταλαλεῖσθε]" (3:16), reminds them that the Gentiles may "speak against" or "slander" (καταλαλοῦσιν) them as evildoers (2:12), reinforcing the exhortation for the audience to remove all evil and all "slanders [καταλαλιάς]" (2:1). In contrast to the audience, who may be "spoken against," but as believers in Christ will never be "put to shame [καταισχυνθῇ]" (2:6), "shame may come against" (καταισχυνθῶσιν) those mistreating their "good" (ἀγαθήν), in Christ, conduct (3:16).[21] Their conduct

---

18. "The fear is not terror of the accuser but reverence for God" (Achtemeier, *1 Peter*, 234).

19. "Peter may simultaneously be urging reverence toward God and gentleness toward human beings (cf. 2:17). But more likely he has in view the same 'gentle (πραΰς) and quiet spirit' before God that should characterize Christian women (3:4). If so, πραΰτης is an inward quality or attitude of mind (cf. 3:3-4), a profound acknowledgment of the power of God, and of one's own poverty and dependence on Him (cf. Matt 5:5). Yet this God-centered quality of the heart finds expression also in one's behavior toward others" (Michaels, *1 Peter*, 189).

20. "The Christians have a 'good conscience' because they live with an interior awareness of God and God's protection of them that allows them to endure suffering and threat with serenity" (Senior, *1 Peter*, 96). "'Conscience' in 1 Peter involves a moral or spiritual awareness of God, and of oneself before God, whether explicitly (2:19; 3:21) or (as here) implicitly" (Michaels, *1 Peter*, 189).

21. "First Peter 2:12 and 3:16 do not contradict each other. They contemplate

in "Christ," the "Christ" they are to hold holy in their hearts as Lord (3:15), refers to their imitation of the "Christ" who suffered on behalf of them, leaving them a model of ethical worship they are to follow closely (2:21). The references to their "good" conduct and "good" conscience reinforce the exhortation for them to become zealots for the "good [ἀγαθοῦ]" (3:13), and to do "good [ἀγαθόν]" (3:11) in order to see the "good" (ἀγαθάς) days (3:10) of the eternal life for which they have been given new birth (1:3, 23).

The reference to the good, in Christ, "conduct" (ἀναστροφήν) the audience are to demonstrate (3:16) bolsters the implicit exhortation for them to imitate the "conduct" (ἀναστροφήν) of the wives that is pure in the reverent fear that offers worship to God (3:2), the "conduct" (ἀναστροφῆς) through which nonbelievers may become believers (3:1). It reinforces the exhortation for the audience to keep their "conduct" (ἀναστροφήν) among the Gentiles praiseworthy, so that the Gentiles may offer the worship of glorifying God (2:12). And it further strengthens the exhortation that, as those ransomed from past futile "conduct" (ἀναστροφῆς) with its false worship (1:18), they are to become holy as God is holy in all "conduct [ἀναστροφῇ]" (1:15), as in reverent fear they "conduct" (ἀναστράφητε) the time of their sojourning as a time of authentic worship, both liturgical and ethical (1:17).

That it is better for the audience to suffer for "doing good" (ἀγαθοποιοῦντας), if the will of God "wants" (θέλοι) it, than for "doing evil [κακοποιοῦντας]" (3:17) bolsters the exhortation for the one who "wants" (θέλων) to love eternal life and see its good days to separate the tongue from "evil [κακοῦ]" (3:10).[22] Each of them is to turn away from "evil" (κακοῦ) and "do good [ποιησάτω ἀγαθόν]" (3:11), for the face of the Lord is upon those "doing evil" (ποιοῦντας κακά) things (3:12). It reinforces the exhortation to become children of the holy matriarch Sarah by "doing good" (ἀγαθοποιοῦσαι) and not fearing any intimidation (3:6).

That it is better to "suffer" (πάσχειν) for doing good, if "the will of God" (τὸ θέλημα τοῦ θεοῦ) wants it, than for doing evil (3:17) reassures the audience that if "doing good" (ἀγαθοποιοῦντες) and "suffering" (πάσχοντες), even if one "suffers" (πάσχων) sorrows unjustly (2:19), they endure, this is the grace of worship pleasing in the sight of God (2:20). For it is "the will of God" (τὸ θέλημα τοῦ θεοῦ) that those "doing good" (ἀγαθοποιοῦντας) silence the ignorance of foolish human beings (2:15), in

---

different responses to the godly lives of believers; some unbelievers will see their good conduct and glorify God by believing the gospel (1 Pet 2:12), but others refuse to believe and will only admit the goodness of believers on the day that God judges them" (Schreiner, *1, 2 Peter*, 178).

22. That these are the only occurrences of the verb "want" (θέλω) in 1 Peter enhances this connection.

1 Peter 3:8-17

accord with the punishment of "evildoers" (κακοποιῶν) but the praise of "good doers [ἀγαθοποιῶν]" (2:14). Even if Gentiles slander them as "evildoers" (κακοποιῶν), when they observe the praiseworthy works of the audience, the Gentiles may offer the worship of glorifying God (2:12).[23]

That it is better to "suffer" (πάσχειν) for doing good than for doing evil (3:17) further reassures the audience that if "you should suffer" (πάσχοιτε) on account of righteousness, they are blessed by God (3:14). And it further fortifies the exhortation for the audience to follow closely the model of worship left for them by the Christ who "suffered" (ἔπαθεν) on behalf of them (2:21). While "suffering" (πάσχων), he did not threaten, but handed himself over as ethical worship to the God who judges righteously (2:23). This is the good, in Christ, conduct (3:16) the audience are to practice as their own ethical worship of the God who judges righteously.

Summary on 3:8–17

That all in the audience are to have "brotherly affection" (3:8) reinforces the exhortation for them to have souls purified in the obedience to the truth for sincere "brotherly affection" and from a clean heart to love one another constantly (1:22). Such love with its cultic connotations of being performed by "purified" souls and from a "clean" heart amounts to ethical worship of the Holy One who called the audience to be holy in all conduct (1:15).

By not returning "insult for insult" (3:9a), the audience will be following the model that the Christ who suffered on their behalf left for them (2:21b), the Christ, who, "being insulted did not return insult," and suffering, he did not threaten, but offered the ethical worship of handing himself over to the One who judges righteously (2:23). Instead of returning evil or insult, the audience are to be "blessing" (3:9b) those who harm or insult them. This "blessing" consists of an act of worship whereby the audience invoke God's blessing upon their enemies. Such blessing complements the act of worship Peter invited the audience to perform at the beginning of the letter by declaring "blessed" the God and Father of our Lord Jesus Christ (1:3).

The audience were called by God to the worship of blessing instead of returning evil or insult, so that they might inherit a blessing from God (3:9). This "blessing" they are to inherit from God in reciprocation for their worship of "blessing" those who insult them is synonymous with the divine gift of eternal life. This blessing to be inherited from God is the same

---

23. "The point is not that God wills suffering but that God *wills doing what is right* rather than doing what is wrong, even if and when this results in suffering [emphasis original]" (Elliott, *1 Peter*, 635).

as the divine grace of eternal life of which the husbands and wives among the audience are "fellow heirs" (3:7). And it is the same as the imperishable heavenly "inheritance" of the eternal life for which God has given us new birth for a living hope through the resurrection of Jesus Christ from the dead (1:3; cf. 1:23).

The exhortation for individuals to seek peace and pursue it (3:11b) involves both the ethical and liturgical worship of the audience. Seeking and pursuing peace further delineates what it means to actively do good (3:11a). While achieving peace with one another and with God is something individuals must work at, profound peace is ultimately a gift of God for which the audience must pray. Indeed, Peter has already prayed that the audience may have peace in abundance (1:2d). That the eyes of the divine Lord are upon the righteous (3:12a), those doing good, and "his" ears for "their" supplication (3:12b) assures the audience that their liturgical prayers of supplication in their ethical pursuit of "it," the peace they are to seek, will be heard.

If the eyes of the Lord are upon the righteous (3:12a), who include everyone in the audience who is to do "good" (3:11a), but the face of the Lord is upon those doing "evil" things (3:12c), then the audience must appreciate that no one, including especially the divine Lord, is ultimately going to cause them "evil," if for the "good" they become zealots (3:13). If for the good, "you," the audience "become" zealots further bolsters the exhortation for the audience to "become" holy in all of their conduct, in both their liturgical and ethical worship, as God is holy (1:15). Such becoming has its foundation in Christ who has "become" the head of the corner (2:7) of the spiritual house of the audience as a holy priesthood who have been built up to offer up the ethical worship of spiritual sacrifices acceptable to God through Jesus Christ (2:5).

The audience are to realize that they should be able to suffer on account of righteousness, since Christ "suffered" on behalf of them, leaving them a model that they closely follow in his footsteps (2:21). In "suffering," and not threatening those who insulted him, Christ handed himself over as ethical worship to the God who judges "righteously" (2:23), that is, in accord with righteousness. Consequently, the audience and all believers might live to the "righteousness" which amounts to ethical worship pleasing to God (2:24). This is confirmed by the affirmation that they are blessed by God, even if "you should suffer" on account of "righteousness" (3:14a).

That the audience are not to "fear" or be terrified of anyone who may cause them suffering (3:14b) bolsters the exhortation for the wives, and by implication all members of the audience, to become children of the holy matriarch Sarah by doing good and not "fearing" any intimidation (3:6). It also reinforces the exhortation for the audience, who are to honor all, love

1 Peter 3:8–17

the brotherhood, and honor the king, above all also to reverently "fear" God (2:17) in and through their worship.

The audience are to hold holy as Lord in "your" hearts the "Christ" (3:15) who suffered for "you," leaving them a model to follow closely (2:21) for their ethical worship. That as Lord they are to "hold holy" the Christ in their hearts accords with their being a "holy" nation (2:9), a "holy" priesthood to offer up the ethical worship of spiritual sacrifices acceptable to God through Jesus "Christ" (2:5). They will thereby become "holy," according to the "Holy One" who called them (1:15) to be "holy" as he is "holy" (1:16) in all their conduct, which includes their liturgical and ethical worship, through the precious blood of "Christ" (1:19).

The audience are to answer all those inquiring about their hope (3:15) with gentleness and fear, "keeping" a good "conscience" (3:16a), akin to keeping their "conscience" toward God (2:19). This reinforces the exhortation for the audience not to be "keeping" their freedom as a cover for evil, but rather to be as slaves of God (2:16). And it bolsters the exhortation for the audience to be "keeping" their conduct among the Gentiles praiseworthy, so that in what the Gentiles slander them as evildoers, observing the praiseworthy works of the audience, the Gentiles may offer the worship of glorifying God on the day of visitation (2:12).

The reference to the good, in Christ, "conduct" the audience are to demonstrate (3:16) bolsters the implicit exhortation for them to imitate the "conduct" of the wives that is pure in the reverent fear that offers worship to God (3:2), the "conduct" through which nonbelievers may become believers (3:1). It reinforces the exhortation for the audience to keep their "conduct" among the Gentiles praiseworthy, so that the Gentiles may offer the worship of glorifying God (2:12). And it further strengthens the exhortation that, as those ransomed from past futile "conduct" with its false worship (1:18), they are to become holy as God is holy in all "conduct" (1:15), as in reverent fear they "conduct" the time of their sojourning as a time of authentic worship, both liturgical and ethical (1:17).

That it is better to "suffer" for doing good than for doing evil (3:17) further reassures the audience that if "you should suffer" on account of righteousness, they are blessed by God (3:14). And it further fortifies the exhortation for the audience to follow closely the model of worship left for them by the Christ who "suffered" on behalf of them (2:21). While "suffering," he did not threaten, but handed himself over as ethical worship to the God who judges righteously (2:23). This is the good, in Christ, conduct (3:16) the audience are to practice as their own ethical worship of the God who judges righteously.

9

1 Peter 3:18–22

The Saving Water of Baptism Is a Pledge of a Good Conscience for God (D′)

Christ suffered to lead you to God
through the saving water of baptism

A   ¹⁸ For also *Christ* once concerning sins suffered, the righteous one on behalf of the unrighteous, so that he might lead you to *God*, having been put to death in the *flesh*, but having been brought to life in the Spirit, ¹⁹ in which, also to the spirits in prison *having gone*, he made proclamation, ^{20a} to those having disobeyed formerly when the patience of *God* awaited in the days of Noah as an ark was being furnished for the purpose of which a few, that *is* eight souls,

B   ^{20b} were *saved* through water,

B′   ^{21a} which also as an antitype of baptism now *saves* you,

A′   ^{21b} not a removal of the dirt of *flesh* but a pledge of a good conscience for God, through the resurrection of Jesus *Christ*, ²² who *is* at the right of *God, having gone* into heaven, angels and authorities and powers having been subjected to him.[1]

Audience Response to 3:18–22

At this point, the audience experience a progression of macrochiastic parallels from the D (2:18–21a) to this D′ (3:18–22) chiastic unit. "If on account

---

1. For the establishment of 1 Pet 3:18–22 as a chiasm, see ch. 1.

of a conscience toward God [συνείδησιν θεοῦ] anyone bears up" (2:19) occurs in the D unit. This progresses to "a pledge of a good conscience [συνειδήσεως] for God [θεόν]" (3:21) in the D' unit. In addition, with the statement that "Christ once concerning sins suffered [ἔπαθεν]" (3:18) at the beginning of this unit, the audience hear the transitional term that links this unit with the preceding unit (3:8–17), which concluded with the statement that "it is better to suffer [πάσχειν] for doing good" (3:17).

3:18–20a (A): Christ Suffered To Lead You to God

The audience hear the A element (3:18–20a) of this chiastic unit as a chiastic pattern in itself:

a) For also Christ once concerning sins suffered, the righteous one on behalf of the unrighteous, so that he might lead you to *God* (3:18a),
 b) having been put to death in the flesh, but having been brought to life in the *Spirit* (3:18b),
 b') in which, also to the *spirits* in prison having gone, he made proclamation (3:19),
a') to those having disobeyed formerly when the patience of *God* awaited in the days of Noah as an ark was being furnished for the purpose of which a few, that is eight souls (3:20a).[2]

At the center of this chiastic sub-unit the audience experience a pivot of parallels from the b) to the b') sub-element involving the only occurrences in this sub-unit of the term "spirit." "Having been brought to life in the Spirit [πνεύματι]" (3:18b) progresses to "also to the spirits [πνεύμασιν] in prison having gone" (3:19). They then hear a progression of parallels from the a) to the a') sub-element involving the only occurrences in this sub-unit of the term "God." "So that he might lead you to God [θεῷ]" (3:18a) progresses to "when the patience of God [θεοῦ] awaited" (3:20a).

Having been assured that "it is better to suffer [πάσχειν] for doing good, if the will of God [θεοῦ] wants it, than for doing evil" (3:17), the audience are immediately presented with the preeminent example of suffering for doing good. They hear that "also Christ once concerning sins suffered [ἔπαθεν], the righteous one on behalf of the unrighteous, so that he might lead you to God [θεῷ]" (3:18a). "For also Christ [ὅτι καὶ Χριστός] once concerning sins suffered [ἔπαθεν]" reverberates with the previously heard assertion, "for also Christ suffered [ὅτι καὶ Χριστὸς ἔπαθεν] on behalf of you," leaving the audience a model to closely follow in his footsteps (2:21b).

---

2. The prepositional phrase εἰς ἥν is here translated as "for the purpose of which" in accord with the telic sense of this preposition throughout 1 Peter.

That Christ once concerning "sins" (ἁμαρτιῶν) suffered reminds the audience that the Christ, who did not do "sin [ἁμαρτίαν]" (2:22), the "sins" (ἁμαρτίας) of us he himself offered up as sacrificial worship (2:24a) to the God who judges righteously (2:23), so that to "sins" (ἁμαρτίαις) having died, to righteousness we might live (2:24c). This is the righteousness that amounts to ethical worship pleasing to the God who judges righteously.

That Christ suffered as the righteous one "on behalf of" (ὑπέρ) the unrighteous (3:18a) reminds the audience that they were among the "unrighteous" (ἀδίκων) when Christ suffered "on behalf of" (ὑπέρ) you (2:21b).[3] But as the "righteous one" (δίκαιος) Christ has enabled the audience and all believers to become the "righteous" (δικαίους) upon whom are the eyes of the Lord, the Christ to be held holy as Lord (3:15), whose ears are attuned to answer their prayers of supplication offered in their liturgical worship (3:12).

Christ's sacrificial worship in suffering as atonement for our sins (2:24), so that he might "lead" (προσαγάγῃ) you to God, has cultic connotations of a leading oriented to the worship of God (3:18a).[4] That the Christ suffered so that he might lead to "God" (θεῷ) the audience "approaching" (προσερχόμενοι) him in worship (2:4) bolsters the exhortation for them to endure in doing good and suffering, since this is the grace of worship pleasing in the sight of "God [θεῷ]" (2:20). It reaffirms that the audience are being built up as a spiritual house for a holy priesthood to offer up as worship spiritual sacrifices acceptable to "God" (θεῷ) through Jesus Christ (2:5), the living stone chosen and esteemed in the sight of "God [θεῷ]" (2:4).[5] Christ's sacrificial worship has thus enabled not only the audience's liturgical worship but their ethical worship of living to righteousness (2:24) by closely following in the footsteps of Christ (2:21b). In other words, closely following in the footsteps of Christ by suffering for doing good (3:17), the audience are being led by Christ to the liturgical and ethical worship that is pleasing to God.[6]

---

3. That these are the only occurrences of the preposition "on behalf of" (ὑπέρ) in 1 Peter enhances this connection which identifies the audience as among those who were "unrighteous." "Indeed, Christ's suffering is the means by which the Petrine Christians were themselves brought to God, showing that they were formerly unrighteous and sinners" (Schreiner, *1, 2 Peter*, 182).

4. BDAG, 875-76. "The verb προσάγω means 'to procure access.' Christ's death provided access into the very presence of God. It is perhaps not an accident that this is the same term used to refer to the leading of the animals to sacrifice. Access comes through sacrifice, in this case the sacrifice Jesus offered in person" (Witherington, *Letters*, 181).

5. That these are the only occurrences of the dative form of "God" (θεῷ) in 1 Peter enhances these connections.

6. "Christ can lead 'you' to God by 'leaving for you a pattern, so that you might follow in his footsteps' (2:21). Such a reading connects nicely with the imagery of 4:1

1 Peter 3:18-22

The audience are to appreciate that Christ can lead them to an authentic worship (3:18a) that includes both liturgical and ethical dimensions, since, although he was put to death in the "flesh" (σαρκί), the "flesh" (σάρξ) that is perishable and not abiding for eternity (1:24), he was brought to life in the Spirit (3:18b). He was "brought to life" (ζῳοποιηθείς), that is, the eternal "life" (ζωήν) the audience are to love (3:10), the eternal "life" (ζωῆς) of which they are heirs (3:7; cf. 1:4). That Christ was brought to eternal life is the basis for our new birth for a "living" (ζῶσαν) hope through the resurrection of Jesus Christ from the dead (1:3), our new birth through a "living" (ζῶντος) word of God (1:23), which abides for eternity (1:25). Christ was brought to eternal life as the "living [ζῶντα]" (2:4) stone upon whom the audience as "living" (ζῶντες) stones are being built up as a spiritual house for a holy priesthood to offer up the worship of spiritual sacrifices acceptable to God through Jesus Christ (2:5). Thus, to the righteousness that pleases God as worship "we might live" (ζήσωμεν) both now and for eternity (2:24).

It is in the holiness of the divine "Spirit [πνεύματος]" (1:2) that the audience are chosen sojourners (1:1). And it is by the Holy "Spirit" (πνεύματι) sent from heaven that they have received the proclamation of the good news (1:12) of their new birth for eternal life (1:3). In this same divine "Spirit" (πνεύματι), in which Christ has been brought to eternal life (3:18b), he made proclamation, implicitly of his victory of life over death, to the evil, demonic "spirits" (πνεύμασιν) in prison within the heavenly realms where the risen Christ went (3:19).[7] These were the spirits ultimately respon-

---

that Christians arm themselves with the same way of thinking as did Christ. But Christ can also lead by opening an atoning door (cf. 2:24). The willingness of 1 Peter to combine both exemplary and atoning images in 2:21–25 suggests that both might be in place here" (Donelson, *I & II Peter*, 111).

7. According to Bandstra, "Making Proclamation to the Spirits," 120–24, 1 Pet 3:19 should be understood as follows: "And in that [resurrected] state, by means of [his] going further [into heaven], he made proclamation [of his victory] to the spirits in prison." "The author does not locate this 'prison' although a number of Jewish apocalyptic texts envisioned stages of ascent and located places where evil spirits abided even in the heavenly realm" (Senior, *1 Peter*, 103). "As a result of 'being made alive in the spirit,' Jesus Christ journeyed to the site of the imprisonment of those disobedient angels of Gen 6, who caused the Noachian flood, and there Jesus 'made proclamation' (ἐκήρυξεν). There is no definitive evidence in either the Jewish tradition or 1 Peter where this prison might be, but it does not have to be below. The content of the proclamation is not made explicit in this verse. However, the imagery of 3:22 and the example of Enoch suggests that Christ does not offer forgiveness but instead announces to the spirits their final defeat and subjugation. Perhaps the victories of Christ described in 3:18 and 3:22 provide the content" (Donelson, *I & II Peter*, 112). "Christ's ascension itself may have been the proclamation of their defeat" (Jobes, *1 Peter*, 244). "Usually in the New Testament what one 'heralds' is the gospel, but in this instance victory over demonic powers is heralded" (Schreiner, *1, 2 Peter*, 189). A "prison" (φυλακή) in itself was not necessarily a place of

sible for his death in the flesh (3:18b), as they were ultimately responsible for the devastation of death by the great flood that occurred at the time of Noah. That these evil, nonbelieving spirits "disobeyed" (ἀπειθήσασίν) formerly (3:20a) likens them to the nonbelieving husbands who are "disobeying" (ἀπειθοῦσιν) the word of the new birth to eternal life (3:1), and to the nonbelievers who stumble over Christ, the living stone, "disobeying" (ἀπειθοῦντες) that same word (2:8).[8]

In contrast to the Christ who suffered, so that he might lead the audience to "God [θεῷ]" (3:18a), the demonic disobedient spirits led people away from God when the patience of "God" (θεοῦ) awaited in the days of Noah as an ark was being furnished by God (divine passive) to save a few, that is eight souls, from death in the coming deluge (3:20).[9] The reference to the salvation of these eight "souls" (ψυχαί) reminds the audience that, although they were being led astray, they have turned now to the shepherd and overseer of their "souls [ψυχῶν]" (2:25), the Christ who is leading them to the worship of God. It reinforces the exhortation for the audience to keep away from the fleshly desires that are waging war against the "soul [ψυχῆς]" (2:11), and to purify their "souls" (ψυχάς) for the ethical worship of loving one another (1:22), as they are attaining the end of their faith, salvation of "souls [ψυχῶν]" (1:9).

3:20b (B): They Were Saved through Water

The audience then hear that the eight souls for whom an ark was furnished when the patience of God awaited in the days of Noah (3:20a) "were saved

---

punishment, but often a place to be guarded or held in custody. See Kratz, "φυλακή," 441; BDAG, 1067.

8. "The reference to the time of Noah need not lead one to understand those 'spirits' as human, since the Enoch literature, with which our author appears to have been acquainted, clearly associates Noah and the flood with the rebellious angels and their offspring, even to the point of attributing the flood to the evil angels whose taking for themselves human wives is understood as an act of disobedience, the meaning this word has in its other uses in this letter" (Achtemeier, *1 Peter*, 262-63).

9. "The mention of the number 'eight' probably has nothing to do with later Christian interpretations of the number as a holy number; rather, it is a simple counting of Noah, his wife, their three sons, and the three wives of those sons" (Donelson, *I & II Peter*, 113). "In this context, the reference to God's patience is probably to be understood as the reason why God has delayed, even if not for long, his final judgment, enduring for a time the evil of the contemporary society that opposes him in the form of opposing the Christian community . . . The use of ὀλίγοι to identify those saved reflects sayings of Jesus but is probably chosen here rather to encourage the readers who, although they were also a small minority in the midst of the hostile Greco-Roman world, could similarly look forward to their salvation" (Achtemeier, *1 Peter*, 263, 265).

through water" (3:20b). That the eight souls were "saved" (διεσώθησαν) from death through water, literally, "brought safely through," reminds the audience of their need to grow up for "salvation" (σωτηρίαν) from death to the eternal life into which they have been newly born (2:2). It adds to the hope of the audience attaining the end of their faith, "salvation" (σωτηρίαν) of souls (1:9), the "salvation" (σωτηρίας) concerning which the prophets of old sought out and searched out (1:10). This is the "salvation" (σωτηρίαν) from death to eternal life that is ready to be revealed in the last time, and for which the audience in the power of God are being guarded through their faith (1:5).

3:21a (B'): Which Also as an Antitype of Baptism Now Saves You

The significance for the audience of the water through which the eight souls were saved from death is then explained: "which also as an antitype of baptism now saves you" (3:21a). At this point, the audience experience the pivot from the B to the B' element at the center of this chiastic unit. That they "were saved [διεσώθησαν] through water" (3:20b) progresses to "now saves [σῴζει] you" (3:21a). The audience are to appreciate that, as an antitype of the water through which the eight souls at the time of Noah were saved, the water involved in the ritual of their baptism now saves them, since it was in this initiation ritual that they were given the new birth for eternal life through the resurrection of Jesus Christ from the dead (1:3, 5, 8–9, 23; cf. 3:21c). The water of baptism now saves "you" (ὑμᾶς), the audience, from death and for eternal life, so that, consequently, Christ might lead "you" (ὑμᾶς) to the worship of God (3:18).[10]

That the water of baptism "now" (νῦν) saves the audience (3:21a) continues the expressions of their current privileged status as recipients of the divine grace of salvation. Like sheep they were being led astray, but have turned "now" (νῦν) to the shepherd and overseer of their souls (2:25) for their salvation (1:9). They were once not a people but "now" (νῦν) are God's people, who had not received mercy but "now" (νῦν) have received

---

10. "The very water that threatened to kill Noah and his family was at the same time the means of their deliverance. The two corresponding διά phrases are not 'through [διά] water' and 'through [διά] baptism' but 'through water' (3:20) and 'through the resurrection of Jesus Christ' (3:21). The parallelism of the syntax supports taking διά as instrumental in both phrases . . . The efficacy of water baptism is completely dependent on Christ's resurrection" (Jobes, 1 Peter, 252–53, 256). "Thus, as Noah was rescued through water (i.e., the flood) from an evil world and subsequently entered into a new and cleansed world, so the Christians are rescued through water (i.e., their baptism) from the evil world that surrounds them and are delivered into the new world of the Christian community" (Achtemeier, 1 Peter, 266).

1 Peter, 2 Peter, and Jude

mercy from God (2:10). The prophets of old were serving the very things regarding the divine grace of salvation which "now" (νῦν) have been announced to the audience (1:12).

3:21b-22 (A'): A Good Conscience for God through the Resurrection of Christ

The audience hear the A' element (3:21b-22) of this chiastic unit as a chiastic pattern in itself:
a) not a removal of the dirt of flesh but a pledge of a good conscience for *God* (3:21b),
b) through the resurrection of Jesus Christ (3:21c),
a') who is at the right of *God*, having gone into heaven, angels and authorities and powers having been subjected to him (3:22).

After the unparalleled b) sub-element at the center of this chiastic sub-unit, "through the resurrection of Jesus Christ" (3:21c), the audience experience a progression from the a) to the a') sub-element, involving the only occurrences in this sub-unit of the term "God." "A good conscience for God [θεόν]" (3:21b) progresses to "the right of God [θεοῦ]" (3:22).

In addition, the audience hear progressions, via the chiastic parallels, from the A (3:18-20a) to the A' (3:21b-22) element of this chiastic unit. "Christ [Χριστός]" (3:18), "to God [θεῷ]" (3:18), "in the flesh [σαρκί]" (3:18), "having gone [πορευθείς]" (3:19), "patience of God [θεοῦ]" (3:20a), and "that is [ἔστιν] eight souls" (3:20a) occur in the A element. These occurrences progress to "the dirt of flesh [σαρκός]" (3:21b), "for God [θεόν]" (3:21b), "the resurrection of Jesus Christ [Χριστοῦ]" (3:21c), "who is [ἐστιν] at the right of God [θεοῦ]" (3:22), and "having gone [πορευθείς] into heaven" (3:22).

As those "having removed" (ἀποθέμενοι) the immoral conduct of all evil and all deceit and hypocrisies and envies and all slanders (2:1), the audience are reminded that the baptism which saves them is not in itself a "removal" (ἀπόθεσις) of the dirt, the immoral conduct, of the "flesh [σαρκός]" (3:21b), the perishable "flesh" (σαρκί) in the realm of which Christ was put to death (3:18b).[11] This reinforces the exhortation for the audience to keep away from the "fleshly" (σαρκικῶν) desires that are waging war against the

---

11. "The statement about the removal of dirt is made so that believers will not understand baptism mechanically or superficially. They must attend to what is really happening in baptism" (Schreiner, *1, 2 Peter*, 195). "[T]he noun ῥύπος (filth) is a strong word that occurs only here in the NT. In the LXX it occurs four times (Job 9:31; 11:15; 14:4; Isa. 4:4), where three of those occurrences refer to moral filth" (Jobes, *1 Peter*, 254). "ῥύπος, the only NT occurrence of this term, means 'filth,' 'dirt' or, metaphorically, moral 'uncleanness'" (Elliott, *1 Peter*, 678).

1 Peter 3:18-22

soul (2:11). Baptism, rather, is a ritualistic pledge on the part of the one baptized to keep a "good conscience" (συνειδήσεως ἀγαθῆς) for "God [θεόν]" (3:21b).[12] This bolsters the exhortation for the audience to be keeping a "good conscience" (συνείδησιν ἀγαθήν) appropriate for their ethical worship in Christ (3:16). Indeed, if on account of a "conscience toward God" (συνείδησιν θεοῦ) anyone bears up (2:19), this is the grace of giving ethical worship pleasing in the sight of God (2:20).[13]

That baptism is a ritualistic pledge to keep a good conscience "for God [εἰς θεόν]" (3:21b) fortifies the exhortation for the audience, by performing the ethical worship of doing good and not fearing any intimidation (3:6), to become children of the matriarch Sarah, one of the holy wives of old who hoped "for God [εἰς θεόν]" (3:5). That this baptismal pledge of a good conscience "for God" is "through the resurrection of Jesus Christ [δι' ἀναστάσεως Ἰησοῦ Χριστοῦ]" (3:21c) reaffirms that it is "through" (δι') him, Christ, that the audience are faithful "for God" (εἰς θεόν), who raised him from the dead and gave him glory, so that their faith and hope are "for God [εἰς θεόν]" (1:21). It recalls that it is "through the resurrection of Jesus Christ" (δι' ἀναστάσεως Ἰησοῦ Χριστοῦ) from the dead that believers have been given a new birth for a living hope of eternal life (1:3). And it reaffirms that it is "through Jesus Christ" (διὰ Ἰησοῦ Χριστοῦ) that the audience are to offer up the ethical worship of spiritual sacrifices acceptable to God (2:5).

That the risen Christ is at the right of "God [θεοῦ]" (3:22; cf. Ps 109:1 LXX) underscores his ability to lead the audience to "God" (θεῷ) for worship (3:18a), with a good conscience for "God [θεόν]" (3:21b), aware that the patience of "God" (θεοῦ) awaited for people to come to him in the days of Noah (3:20a). Christ's "having gone" (πορευθείς) into heaven (3:22) confirms the implication of his "having gone" (πορευθείς) to the evil spirits while they were in prison within the heavenly realm (3:19).[14] The audience

---

12. "The noun ἐπερώτημα is found in the papyri on the occasion of sealing a legal contract to refer both to a formal question of willingness from one party *and* a positive response from the other . . . Peter is reminding his readers that when they were baptized, a question was asked about their faith in Christ, to which they gave a positive response. They were then baptized in water as a sacrament of that pledge of faithfulness made to God [emphasis original]" (Jobes, *1 Peter*, 255). "[T]he baptisand pledges to God that he or she will maintain a 'good conscience,' that is, a consciousness of God and a good and decent conduct both within and without the Christian community" (Achtemeier, *1 Peter*, 271-72).

13. "Thus in 1 Peter the realm of baptism is not ritual purity but moral commitment" (Donelson, *I & II Peter*, 114). "The noun συνείδησις, literally, 'consciousness,' 'awareness,' here, as in 2:19 and 3:16, denotes *mindfulness* of God and compliance with God's will [emphasis original]" (Elliott, *1 Peter*, 681).

14. "The lack of any explicit connection between the ascension and the ensuing reference to the subjugation of the superhuman powers is due to the fact that the

are to appreciate that Christ went into "heaven" (οὐρανόν), as it was from "heaven" (οὐρανοῦ) that the Holy Spirit by whom they received the good news of their new birth for eternal life was sent (1:12). Indeed, it is in "heaven" (οὐρανοῖς) that the imperishable inheritance of this eternal life is being kept by God for the audience (1:4).

Whereas wives are being "subject" (ὑποτασσόμεναι) to their own husbands (3:1, 5) and house servants are being "subject" (ὑποτασσόμενοι) to their human masters (2:18), "angels" (ἀγγέλων) and authorities and powers have been "subjected" (ὑποταγέντων) by God to the risen Christ (3:22; cf. Ps 8:7 LXX).[15] This recalls that "angels" (ἄγγελοι) are desiring to catch a glimpse of the things the audience have been privileged to receive through the risen Christ (1:12). That these heavenly beings have been subjected to "him" (αὐτῷ), the risen Christ, further describes the glory that the God who raised him from the dead gave to "him [αὐτῷ]" (1:21). It strengthens the exhortation for the audience to be "subject" (ὑποτάγητε) to every human institution on account of their divine risen Lord Jesus Christ (2:13) as part of their praiseworthy ethical worship that may lead nonbelieving Gentiles to the worship of glorifying God on the day of visitation (2:12).[16]

Summary on 3:18–22

Christ's sacrificial worship in suffering as atonement for our sins (2:24), so that he might "lead" you to God, has cultic connotations of a leading oriented to the worship of God (3:18a). That the Christ suffered so that he might lead to "God" the audience "approaching" him in worship (2:4) bolsters the

---

same event is envisioned here as was described in v. 19, where the same verb was used (πορευθείς) to describe Christ's journey, and the mode of subjugation there was described as his proclamation to those powers" (Achtemeier, *1 Peter*, 273).

15. According to Donelson, *I & II Peter*, 115, the angels and authorities and powers in 3:22 "refer to cosmic powers that oppose God and threaten the Christian community. They are evil, spiritual, cosmic forces. It is not, however, possible to identify precisely the face and duty of each of these powers. The three terms together do not identify a generally acknowledged division of the cosmic powers into three categories. Rather, the three names create a sense of comprehensiveness." "Through the combination of *angels* with *authorities* and *powers*, the author thus appears to have included the disobedient angelic spirits in v 19 among the powers subordinated to the rule of the resurrected Christ [emphases original]" (Elliott, *1 Peter*, 688).

16. Campbell and Van Rensburg, "Interpretation of 1 Pet 3:18-22," 73-96; Pierce, "Reexamining Christ's Proclamation," 27-42; Klumbies, "Verkündigung," 207-28. According to Engel, "Christus Victor," 137-47, there is an underlying hymn in 1 Pet 3:18-22 which had its origin in the context of the worship of a Hellenistic Gentile Christian community.

1 Peter 3:18-22

exhortation for them to endure in doing good and suffering, since this is the grace of worship pleasing in the sight of "God" (2:20). It reaffirms that the audience are being built up as a spiritual house for a holy priesthood to offer up as worship spiritual sacrifices acceptable to "God" through Jesus Christ (2:5), the living stone chosen and esteemed in the sight of "God" (2:4). Christ's sacrificial worship has thus enabled not only the audience's liturgical worship but their ethical worship of living to righteousness (2:24) by closely following in the footsteps of Christ (2:21b). In other words, closely following in the footsteps of Christ by suffering for doing good (3:17), the audience are being led by Christ to the liturgical and ethical worship that is pleasing to God.

The audience are to appreciate that Christ can lead them to an authentic worship (3:18a) that includes both liturgical and ethical dimensions, since, although he was put to death in the "flesh," the "flesh" that is perishable and not abiding for eternity (1:24), he was brought to life in the Spirit (3:18b). He was "brought to life," that is, the eternal "life" the audience are to love (3:10), the eternal "life" of which they are heirs (3:7; cf. 1:4). That Christ was brought to eternal life is the basis for our new birth for a "living" hope through the resurrection of Jesus Christ from the dead (1:3), our new birth through a "living" word of God (1:23), which abides for eternity (1:25). Christ was brought to eternal life as the "living" (2:4) stone upon whom the audience as "living" stones are being built up as a spiritual house for a holy priesthood to offer up the worship of spiritual sacrifices acceptable to God through Jesus Christ (2:5). Thus, to the righteousness that pleases God as worship "we might live" both now and for eternity (2:24).

In contrast to the Christ who suffered, so that he might lead the audience to "God" (3:18a), the demonic disobedient spirits (3:19) led people away from God when the patience of "God" awaited in the days of Noah as an ark was being furnished by God (divine passive) to save a few, that is eight souls, from death in the coming deluge (3:20). The reference to the salvation of these eight "souls" reminds the audience that, although they were being led astray, they have turned now to the shepherd and overseer of their "souls" (2:25), the Christ who is leading them to the worship of God. It reinforces the exhortation for the audience to keep away from the fleshly desires that are waging war against the "soul" (2:11), and to purify their "souls" for the ethical worship of loving one another (1:22), as they are attaining the end of their faith, salvation of "souls" (1:9).

As those "having removed" the immoral conduct of all evil and all deceit and hypocrisies and envies and all slanders (2:1), the audience are reminded that the baptism which saves them is not in itself a "removal" of the dirt, the immoral conduct, of the "flesh" (3:21), the perishable "flesh" in the realm of which Christ was put to death (3:18b). This reinforces the exhortation for the audience to keep away from the "fleshly" desires that are waging war against the soul (2:11). Baptism, rather, is a ritualistic pledge on the part of the one baptized to keep a "good conscience" for "God" (3:21b). This bolsters the exhortation for the audience to be keeping a "good conscience" appropriate for their ethical worship in Christ (3:16). Indeed, if on account of a "conscience toward God" anyone bears up (2:19), this is the grace of giving ethical worship pleasing in the sight of God (2:20).

That baptism is a ritualistic pledge to keep a good conscience "for God" (3:21) fortifies the exhortation for the audience, by performing the ethical worship of doing good and not fearing any intimidation (3:6), to become children of the matriarch Sarah, one of the holy wives of old who hoped "for God" (3:5). That this baptismal pledge of a good conscience "for God" is "through the resurrection of Jesus Christ" (3:21) reaffirms that it is "through" him, Christ, that the audience are faithful "for God," who raised him from the dead and gave him glory, so that their faith and hope are "for God" (1:21). It recalls that it is "through the resurrection of Jesus Christ" from the dead that believers have been given a new birth for a living hope of eternal life (1:3). And it reaffirms that it is "through Jesus Christ" that the audience are to offer up the ethical worship of spiritual sacrifices acceptable to God (2:5).

Whereas wives are being "subject" to their own husbands (3:1, 5) and house servants are being "subject" to their human masters (2:18), angels and authorities and powers have been "subjected" by God to the risen Christ (3:22). That these heavenly beings have been subjected to "him," the risen Christ, further describes the glory that the God who raised him from the dead gave to "him" (1:21). It strengthens the exhortation for the audience to be "subject" to every human institution on account of their divine risen Lord Jesus Christ (2:13) as part of their praiseworthy ethical worship that may lead nonbelieving Gentiles to the worship of glorifying God on the day of visitation (2:12).

10

1 Peter 4:1-11
In All Things God May Be Glorified for Eternity through Jesus Christ (C')

*In love live in accord with
and glorify God through Jesus Christ*

A   4:1 *Christ* then having suffered in the flesh, you also arm yourselves with the same attitude, for the one suffering in the flesh is separated from sin, ² so as not in the desires of human beings but in the will of *God*, the in the flesh remaining time to spend, ³ for sufficient time has passed for you to accomplish the purpose of the Gentiles, having gone in debaucheries, desires, drunkenness, carousing, drinking bouts, and wanton idolatries, ⁴ in which they are surprised that you are not running together into the same flood of dissipation, as they go on blaspheming, ⁵ but they will return a word (of reckoning) to the one who keeps ready to judge the living and the dead, ⁶ for to this (purpose) even to the dead good news was proclaimed, so that though they were judged according to human beings in the flesh, they may live according to *God* in the Spirit.

B   ⁷ The end of all things has come near. Be serious then and sober for prayers. ⁸ᵃ Above all things, keeping *love* for each other constant,

B'   ⁸ᵇ because *love* covers a multitude of sins.

A'   ⁹ Be hospitable for one another without complaining, ¹⁰ just as each has received a gift, serving it for each other, as praiseworthy stewards of the varied grace of *God*. ¹¹ If anyone speaks—as sayings of *God*, if anyone serves—as from the strength which *God* supplies, so that in all things

1 Peter, 2 Peter, and Jude

God may be glorified through Jesus *Christ*, to whom is the glory and the might for the ages of the ages, amen![1]

Audience Response to 4:1-11

At this point, the audience experience a progression of macrochiastic parallels from the C (2:1-17) to this C' (4:1-11) chiastic unit. "A living stone by human beings [ἀνθρώπων] rejected" (2:4) and "the ignorance of foolish human beings [ἀνθρώπων]" (2:15) progress to "the desires of human beings [ἀνθρώπων]" (4:2) and "judged according to human beings [ἀνθρώπους]" (4:6). "Spiritual sacrifices acceptable to God through Jesus Christ [διὰ Ἰησοῦ Χριστοῦ]" (2:5) progresses to "God may be glorified through Jesus Christ [διὰ Ἰησοῦ Χριστοῦ]" (4:11). "A holy nation [ἔθνος]" (2:9) and "among the Gentiles [ἔθνεσιν]" (2:12) progress to "the purpose of the Gentiles [ἐθνῶν]" (4:3). And "fleshly desires [ἐπιθυμιῶν]" (2:11) progresses to "the desires [ἐπιθυμίαις] of human beings" (4:2) and "desires [ἐπιθυμίαις]" (4:3). In addition, with the reference to "Christ [Χριστοῦ]" (4:1) at the beginning of this unit, the audience hear the transitional term that links this unit with the preceding unit (3:18-22), which referred to "the resurrection of Jesus Christ [Χριστοῦ]" (3:21) near its conclusion.

4:1-6 (A): Christ Suffered so the Dead May Live according to God in the Spirit

The audience hear the A element (4:1-6) of this chiastic unit as a chiastic pattern in itself:

a) Christ then having suffered in the *flesh*, you also arm yourselves with the same attitude, for the one suffering in the *flesh* is separated from sin, so as not in the *desires* of *human beings* but in the will of *God*, the in the *flesh* remaining (4:1-2b)

  b) *time* to spend (4:2c),

  b') for sufficient *time* has passed for you to accomplish the purpose of the Gentiles (4:3a),

a') having gone in debaucheries, *desires*, drunkenness, carousing, drinking bouts, and wanton idolatries, in which they are surprised that you are not running together into the same flood of dissipation, as they go on blaspheming, but they will return a word (of reckoning) to the one who keeps ready to judge the living and the dead, for to this (purpose)

---

1. For the establishment of 1 Pet 4:1-11 as a chiasm, see ch. 1.

even to the dead good news was proclaimed, so that though they were judged according to *human beings* in the *flesh*, they may live according to *God* in the Spirit (4:3b-6).

At the center of this chiastic sub-unit the audience experience a pivot of parallels from the b) to the b') sub-element involving the only occurrences in this sub-unit of the term "time." "Time [χρόνον] to spend" (4:2c) progresses to "sufficient time [χρόνος]" (4:3a). They then hear a progression of several parallels from the a) to the a') sub-element involving the only occurrences in this sub-unit of the terms "flesh," "desires," "human beings," and "God." "Suffered in the flesh [σαρκί]" (4:1), "suffering in the flesh [σαρκί]" (4:1), and "in the flesh [σαρκί] remaining" (4:2b) progress to "according to human beings in the flesh [σαρκί]" (4:6). "The desires [ἐπιθυμίαις] of human beings" (4:2a) progresses to "desires [ἐπιθυμίαις]" (4:3b). "The desires of human beings [ἀνθρώπων]" (4:2a) progresses to "according to human beings [ἀνθρώπους] in the flesh" (4:6). And "the will of God [θεοῦ]" (4:2a) progresses to "according to God [θεόν]" (4:6).

In addition, the audience hear the a) sub-element (4:1-2b) of this chiastic sub-unit as yet another chiastic pattern in itself:
(a) Christ then having suffered in the *flesh*, you also arm yourselves with the same attitude, for the one suffering in the *flesh* is separated from sin (4:1),
(b) so as not in the desires of human beings but in the will of God (4:2a),
(a') the in the *flesh* remaining (4:2b).

After the unparalleled (b) sub-element at the center of this chiastic sub-unit, "so as not in the desires of human beings but in the will of God" (4:2a), the audience experience a pivot of parallels from the (a) to the (a') sub-element involving the only occurrences in this sub-unit of the term "flesh." "Suffered in the flesh [σαρκί]" (4:1) and "suffering in the flesh [σαρκί]" (4:1) progress to "in the flesh [σαρκί] remaining" (4:2b).

"Christ [Χριστοῦ] then having suffered [παθόντος] in the flesh [σαρκί]" (4:1) reminds the audience that the "Christ" (Χριστός) who was put to death in the "flesh" (σαρκί) once concerning "sins" (ἁμαρτιῶν) "suffered" (ἔπαθεν), so that he might lead the audience to the worship of God (3:18).[2] Consequently, the audience are to arm themselves with the same attitude, for the one "suffering" (παθών) in the "flesh" (σαρκί) is separated from "sin [ἁμαρτίας]" (4:1)—the sinfulness which prevents proper worship of God. This reinforces the exhortation for the audience to closely follow in the footsteps of the "Christ" (Χριστός) who "suffered" (ἔπαθεν) on behalf of them (2:21b). He did not do "sin [ἁμαρτίαν]" (2:22), but "suffering

2. "Already in the earlier passage, Christ's suffering and death were virtually indistinguishable, so that now the one verb 'suffer,' embraces both ideas without risk of misunderstanding" (Michaels, *1 Peter*, 225).

[πάσχων]" (2:23), he offered up our "sins" (ἁμαρτίας) as an act of sacrificial worship, so that to "sins" (ἁμαρτίαις) having died, to the righteousness that pleases God as ethical worship we might live (2:24). His atonement of our sins through his sacrificial worship thus makes it possible for the audience to be separated from sin, in order to properly worship God.³

That anyone in the audience suffering in the flesh, is "separated" (πέπαυται) from sin (4:1), as a result of the exemplary ethical and atoning sacrificial worship of Christ (2:21b-25), reinforces the exhortation for everyone who wants to love eternal life to "separate" (παυσάτω) the tongue from sinful evil and lips from speaking sinful deceit (3:10).⁴ That the audience, "you also," are to "arm" (ὁπλίσασθε) themselves metaphorically for war with the same attitude as the Christ who suffered in the "flesh" (σαρκί), as they suffer in the "flesh [σαρκί]" (4:1), resonates with the exhortation to keep away from "fleshly" (σαρκικῶν) "desires" (ἐπιθυμιῶν) that are "waging war" (στρατεύονται) against the soul (2:11).⁵ Indeed, they are not in the "desires" (ἐπιθυμίαις) of human beings but in the will of God to spend their time remaining in the "flesh [σαρκί]" (4:2). Such praiseworthy conduct—their ethical worship, may inspire nonbelieving Gentiles to the worship of glorifying God on the day of visitation (2:12).

Not in the desires of "human beings" (ἀνθρώπων) but in the "will of God" (θελήματι θεοῦ) the audience are to spend the time they have remaining in the flesh (4:2). This reaffirms that it is the "will of God" (θέλημα τοῦ θεοῦ) for the audience, as those for whom it is better to suffer for doing good, if the "will of God" (θέλημα τοῦ θεοῦ) wants it (3:17), to silence the ignorance of foolish "human beings [ἀνθρώπων]" (2:15). It recalls that the Christ, before whom the audience are approaching as worshipers, was a living stone rejected by "human beings" (ἀνθρώπων) but in the sight of God chosen and esteemed (2:4). The remaining "time" (χρόνον) they have refers to the "time" (χρόνον) of their earthly sojourning (1:17) toward the goal of

---

3. "By taking on Christ's 'way of thinking' the Christian who 'suffers in the flesh' is also empowered by Christ to be free from the tyranny of sin" (Senior, *1 Peter*, 114). "From what the author has already stated, this mind-set could have involved Christ's subordination to the divine will during his innocent suffering (1:2c; 2:21-23 [as God's servant]; 3:17-18), his resistance to wrongdoing and retaliation (2:22-23b), and his trusting commitment of his cause to God (2:23c)" (Elliott, *1 Peter*, 713).

4. That these are the only occurrences of the verb "separate" (παύω) in 1 Peter enhances this connection.

5. "The emphatic καὶ ὑμεῖς ('you also') underlines the applicability of Christ's human suffering to the situation of the readers" (Achtemeier, *1 Peter*, 277). "Conflict and war metaphors are commonly used in the New Testament as a characteristic of Christian existence... Here, as the following verses 4:3f. show, the arming serves the fight against the desires (cf. 2:11)" (Feldmeier, *First Letter*, 212).

1 Peter 4:1-11

their heavenly inheritance (1:4). They are to conduct this time in reverent fear of the God they call upon as Father in their liturgical worship, the God whom, as the one who impartially judges according to the work of each one, they seek to please by their ethical worship (1:17).

Sufficient "time" (χρόνος), the "time" (χρόνον) remaining in the flesh (4:2), has already passed for the audience to accomplish the sinful purpose of the Gentiles (4:3a). In the past the audience have gone in the way of such sinful conduct as debaucheries, "desires" (ἐπιθυμίαις), the "desires" (ἐπιθυμίαις) of human beings against the will of God (4:2a), drunkenness, carousing, drinking bouts, and, in the final emphatic and epitomizing position, wanton idolatries (4:3b). In other words, all of this immoral behavior amounts to false liturgical and ethical worship.[6] The Gentiles are surprised that the audience are no longer running together with them into the same flood of dissipation, and so they go on "vilifying" or "blaspheming" (βλασφημοῦντες) the audience (4:4).[7]

Although the audience are those "having gone" (πεπορευμένους) into the sinful behavior which amounts to false worship (4:3b), Christ is the one "having gone" (πορευθείς) into heaven to make proclamation of his victory over the evil spirits ultimately responsible for such sinful behavior (3:19).[8] He is the one "having gone" (πορευθείς) to be at the right of God to mediate the worship of the audience (3:22). Rather than accomplish the purpose of the "Gentiles [ἐθνῶν]" (4:3a), the audience, as a holy "nation (ἔθνος)" (2:9) and priesthood, are to offer up the worship of spiritual sacrifices acceptable to God through the mediation of Jesus Christ (2:5). Such praiseworthy conduct among the nonbelieving "Gentiles" (ἔθνεσιν) may lead them away from blaspheming (4:4) and speaking against the audience (2:12). Instead,

---

6. "The sequence of 'drunkenness, inebriating feasts, drinking parties' recalls the infamous dining and drinking parties that dominated much of Roman life. Romans and Greeks formed all kinds of associations and clubs for all kind of purposes, ranging from business interests to religious devotion to burial. Almost all of these had religious overtones... They were also acts of idolatry since these meals often included homage to gods and goddesses" (Donelson, *I & II Peter*, 121-22). "The association of three words for drinking, followed by the mention of idolatry, may reflect the pervasiveness of drinking, and drink offerings, in pagan worship" (Achtemeier, *1 Peter*, 282). "In its present final and emphatic position here in v 3, 'idolatries' serves to summarize in one condemning expression the futility and fatuity of life lived in opposition to God" (Elliott, *1 Peter*, 724).

7. "Rather than following the Christians' good example, pagan friends malign them because they do God's will, and thereby pagans implicitly blaspheme God" (Jobes, *1 Peter*, 269).

8. With regard to the participle "having gone" (πεπορευμένους) in 4:3b, Dubis (*1 Peter*, 134) states: "The referent/agent of this participle is an implied ὑμᾶς, accusative subject of κατειργάσθαι, which explains the accusative plural form of πεπορευμένους."

they may be led to the worship of glorifying God, together with the audience(1:7), on the day of visitation (2:12).⁹

At this point, the audience hear the remainder (4:5-6) of the a') sub-element (4:3b-6) in the chiastic sub-unit which comprises the A element (4:1-6) of this chiastic unit (4:1-11) as yet another chiastic pattern in itself:
(a) but they will return a word (of reckoning) to the one who keeps ready to *judge* the *living* (4:5a)
  (b) and the *dead* (4:5b)
    (c) for to this (purpose) (4:6a)
  (b') even to the *dead* good news was proclaimed (4:6b),
(a') so that though they were *judged* according to human beings in the flesh, they may *live* according to God in the Spirit (4:6c).

After the unparalleled (c) sub-element at the center of this chiastic sub-unit, "for to this (purpose)" (4:6a), the audience experience a pivot of parallels from the (b) to the (b') sub-element involving the only occurrences in this sub-unit of the term "dead." "And the dead [νεκρούς]" (4:5b) progresses to "even to the dead [νεκροῖς] good news was proclaimed" (4:6b). They then hear a progression from the (a) to the (a') sub-element involving the only occurrences in this sub-unit of the verbs "judge" and "live." "The one who keeps ready to judge [κρῖναι] the living [ζῶντας]" (4:5a) progresses to "they were judged" (κριθῶσι) and "they may live [ζῶσι]" (4:6c).

In contrast to the audience who are not to be "returning" (ἀποδιδόντες) evil for evil or insult for insult as part of their ethical worship (3:9), the blaspheming Gentiles (4:4) will be required to "return" (ἀποδώσουσιν) a word of reckoning to the God who keeps ready to judge the living and the dead (4:5).¹⁰ The audience are to be always "ready" (ἕτοιμοι) for an answer to all who ask them a "word" (λόγον) concerning the hope within them (3:15), alluding to the living "word" (λόγος) of God giving a living hope (1:3) for eternal life (1:23; 2:8; 3:1). In ironic contrast, the blaspheming Gentiles

---

9. "It is striking that Peter refers to all unbelievers as 'Gentiles' when writing to Christian readers who themselves may have been ethnically Gentile. The apostles used terms, familiar to the Jewish tradition, that divided all humanity into God's covenant people and the rest of humanity, who were referred to as ἔθνη, the nations, or Gentiles. The Christian apostles kept the language but redrew the line, redefining God's covenant people to be those who believe in Christ and referring to all others as 'Gentiles.' In this letter Peter writes to Christian readers *as if they were* Jews who are now scattered among the nations (Gentiles), as the ethnic Jews had historically been in the Diaspora (1 Pet. 1:1). This helps to explain why modern interpreters have been unable to decide with certainty whether the original readers were Jewish or Gentile converts; Peter wants his readers to think of themselves as God's true covenant people without distinction [emphasis original]" (Jobes, *1 Peter*, 267).

10. That these are the only occurrences of the verb "return" (ἀποδίδωμι) in 1 Peter enhances this connection.

1 Peter 4:1-11

will return a "word" (λόγον) to the God who keeps "ready" (ἑτοίμως) to judge the living and the dead.¹¹ Whereas the audience are to be "keeping" (ἔχοντες) their conduct among Gentiles praiseworthy (2:12), not "keeping" (ἔχοντες) their freedom as a cover for evil (2:16), and "keeping" (ἔχοντες) a good conscience (3:16) toward God (2:19), God "keeps" (ἔχοντι) ready to judge the living and the dead.

The one God who keeps ready to "judge" (κρῖναι) the living and the dead (4:5) is the one who "judges" (κρίνοντι) righteously, to whom the suffering Christ, who did not return insult or threaten, handed himself over in ethical worship (2:23). God is the one who impartially "judges" (κρίνοντα) according to the work of each one, so that the audience are to conduct the time of their sojourning in the reverent fear of their ethical worship of this God (1:17).

Even to the "dead" (νεκροῖς) who are now among the "dead" (νεκρούς) God is ready to judge (4:5), "good news was proclaimed [εὐηγγελίσθη]" (4:6), while they were still among the "living" (ζῶντας) whom God is to judge (4:5). Those now deceased were privileged during their lifetime, along with the audience, to have "good news proclaimed" (εὐαγγελισαμένων) unto them (1:12). Indeed, "proclaimed as good news" (εὐαγγελισθέν) for them was the pronouncement (1:25) of the living word of God through which they were given new birth for eternal life (1:23). While still living, those now dead were "judged" (κριθῶσι) according to "human beings" (ἀνθρώπους) in the flesh (4:6), according to the desires of "human beings" (ἀνθρώπων) that contradict the will of "God [θεοῦ]" (4:2), the one to finally "judge" (κρῖναι) the living and the dead (4:5).¹² Although they were judged in the "flesh" (σαρκί), the "flesh" (σαρκί) in which one suffering like Christ is separated from sin (4:1-2), they may now "live" (ζῶσι) according to "God" (θεόν) in the Spirit (4:6).¹³

---

11. That these are the only occurrences in 1 Peter of the adjective and its corresponding adverb for "ready" (ἕτοιμος- ἑτοίμως) enhances this connection. "Peter's language indeed suggests a reversal of the circumstances imagined in 3:15 16... In the future, the tables will be turned. Those who now ask the questions will have to come up with some answers of their own" (Michaels, *1 Peter*, 234).

12. "The closest parallel in 1 Peter itself to the contrast here between human judgment and the judgment of God is the reference in 2:4 to Christ the living Stone, 'rejected indeed by people generally but in God's sight choice and precious'" (Michaels, *1 Peter*, 239).

13. "The issue here may be the same as or similar to that of 1 Thess 4:13-18, which addresses the problem of Christians who have died before the final judgment. Christians, who have heard the gospel and perhaps been abused by Gentiles, have died. This verse affirms that God judges and saves not only the living but also the dead. The force of the gospel is not undone by death ... Thus the first sequence of the clause asserts that dead Christians in their mortal lives were judged negatively and slandered by the Gentiles according to the standards of the Gentiles. But the second sequence affirms

That the "dead" (νεκροῖς) to whom good news was proclaimed may now "live" (ζῶσι) according to God in the Spirit (4:6) bolsters the hope for all believers, having died to sins, to the righteousness that pleases God as worship "we might live" (ζήσωμεν) now and for eternity (2:24). It reinforces the exhortation for the audience, as "living" (ζῶντες) stones built up as a spiritual house for a holy priesthood upon Christ as the "living" (ζῶντα) stone (2:4), to offer up the worship of spiritual sacrifices acceptable to God through Jesus Christ (2:5). And it reassures them of their new birth for eternal life through the "living" (ζῶντος) word of God (1:23) for a "living" (ζῶσαν) hope through the resurrection of Jesus Christ from the "dead [νεκρῶν]" (1:3, 21). Indeed, because Christ was put to death by human beings in the "flesh" (σαρκί), but "brought to life" (ζωοποιηθείς) by God in the "Spirit [πνεύματι]" (3:18), the dead who were judged according to human beings in the "flesh" (σαρκί) may now likewise "live" (ζῶσι) according to God in the "Spirit [πνεύματι]" (4:6).[14]

4:7–8a (B): Keeping Love for Each Other Constant

The audience continue to be exhorted with regard to their worship: "The end of all things has come near. Be serious then and sober for prayers. Above all things, keeping love for each other constant" (4:7–8a). Having been assured that they are attaining the "end" (τέλος) of their faith, salvation of souls (1:9), and exhorted that at the "end" (τέλος) all of them are to have brotherly affection (3:8), the audience are now reminded that the "end" (τέλος) of all things has come near (4:7a). Consequently, "you are to be serious and sober [νήψατε] for prayers" (4:7b). This reinforces and develops the exhortation for them, having girded up the loins of their mind, being "sober" (νήφοντες), to completely hope upon the grace that is to be borne to them by God at the end-time revelation of Jesus Christ (1:13).[15] That they are to

---

that this is not the end. Ultimately these same Christians will 'live in the spirit according to God's standards.' The imagery is that of the resurrection. God will bestow life on these dead followers of the gospel" (Donelson, *I & II Peter*, 124–25).

14. Giesen, "Christi Leiden," 176–218. "The contrast between the 'flesh' and the 'spirit' here is parallel to 1 Pet 3:18, for Christ also died in terms of his flesh, but he was raised to life by the Holy Spirit. A similar destiny awaits believers. They die physically but will be raised to life by the Holy Spirit" (Schreiner, *1, 2 Peter*, 209). As Elliott (*1 Peter*, 738) notes, "the verb ζάω, as elsewhere in 1 Peter, denotes the life of resurrection conferred by God."

15. As Donelson (*I & II Peter*, 128) notes, "the call to 'be sober for prayers' recalls the insobriety and idolatry of their former lives (4:3) . . . Christian worship is not ordered by the insanity of drunkenness, and the God who judges all is not praised thereby. Christian worship is ordered by moderation and is offered with complete control of the mind and body."

be sober for "prayers" (προσευχάς) in their liturgical worship resonates with the implicit exhortation for them to imitate the mutual respect of husbands and wives so that their "prayers" (προσευχάς) may not be hindered (3:7).[16]

As the end of "all things" (πάντων) has come near (4:7a), above "all things" (πάντων) the audience are to be keeping love for each other constant (4:8a).[17] The exhortation for the audience to be keeping "love" (ἀγάπην) for each other "constant" (ἐκτενῆ) reinforces the exhortations for them to "love" (ἀγαπᾶτε) the brotherhood of their fellow believers as correlative with their "fear" or reverent worship of God (2:17), and with a clean heart to "love" (ἀγαπήσατε) one another "constantly [ἐκτενῶς]" (1:22). Their ethical worship of loving each other is thus to complement their liturgical worship in which they are joyfully exulting for the Jesus Christ whom "you love [ἀγαπᾶτε]" (1:8).

That the audience are to be "keeping" (ἔχοντες) love for each other constant (4:8a) resonates with their "keeping" (ἔχοντες) a good conscience (3:16) toward God (2:19), and as slaves of God, not "keeping" (ἔχοντες) freedom as a cover for evil (2:16). It bolsters the exhortation for them to be "keeping" (ἔχοντες) their conduct among the Gentiles praiseworthy as ethical worship, so that, observing the praiseworthy works, they may offer their own worship of glorifying God on the day of visitation (2:12).

4:8b (B'): Because Love Covers a Multitude of Sins

The audience are to be keeping love for each other constant (4:8a), "because love covers a multitude of sins" (4:8b). At this point, the audience experience a pivot of parallels at the center of this chiastic unit. "Keeping love [ἀγάπην] for each other constant" in the B element (4:7-8a) progresses to "love [ἀγάπη] covers a multitude of sins" in this B' element.

The constant love of the audience for each other, as part of their ethical worship, covers over a multitude of the "sins" (ἁμαρτιῶν) that prevent proper worship (4:8b).[18] This further fortifies the exhortation for them to

---

16. That these are the only occurrences of the term "prayer" (προσευχή) in 1 Peter enhances this connection.

17. "The phrase 'above all' (πρὸ πάντων) seems to be a word play on the opening phrase of v. 7 (πάντων δὲ τὸ τέλος)" (Senior, *1 Peter*, 119).

18. "The phrase 'covers a multitude of sins' is apparently from a saying familiar to Peter's readers, probably coming from Prov. 10:12 (cf. James 5:20)" (Jobes, *1 Peter*, 278). "When believers lavish love on others, the sins and offenses of others are overlooked" (Schreiner, *1, 2 Peter*, 212-13). Senior (*1 Peter*, 120) suggests that "the general sense may simply be that when Christians exercise the primary value of love God is pleased and reconciliation takes place—for all concerned." "Whether the 'covering' or forgiveness

1 Peter, 2 Peter, and Jude

imitate the exemplary ethical worship of the suffering Christ made possible by the atonement for sins that the suffering Christ effected by his sacrificial worship. Anyone in the audience suffering in the flesh, as Christ suffered in the flesh, is separated from "sin [ἁμαρτίας]" (4:1). Christ once concerning "sins" (ἁμαρτιῶν) suffered so that he might lead the audience to the worship of God (3:18). The "sins" (ἁμαρτίας) of us Christ himself offered up in sacrificial worship for their atonement, so that to "sins" (ἁμαρτίαις) having died, to the righteousness that pleases God as ethical worship we might live (2:24). The Christ who did not do "sin [ἁμαρτίαν]" (2:22), but instead handed himself over in ethical worship to the God who judges righteously (2:23), thus left the audience a model to follow closely (2:21b) in their own ethical worship of loving each other constantly.

4:9–11 (A'): So That in All Things God May Be Glorified through Jesus Christ

The audience hear the A' element (4:9–11) of this chiastic unit as a chiastic pattern in itself:
a) Be hospitable *for* one another without complaining, just as each has received a gift, serving it *for* each other, as praiseworthy stewards of the varied grace of God (4:9–10),
  b) *If anyone* speaks—*as* sayings of God (4:11a),
  b') *if anyone* serves—*as* from the strength which God supplies (4:11b),
a') so that in all things God may be glorified through Jesus Christ, to whom is the glory and the might *for* the ages of the ages, amen! (4:11c).

At the center of this chiastic sub-unit the audience experience a pivot of parallels from the b) to the b') sub-element involving the only occurrences in this sub-unit of the expression "if anyone" and the conjunction "as." "If anyone [εἴ τις] speaks as [ὡς]" (4:11a) progresses to "if anyone [εἴ τις] serves as [ὡς[" (4:11b). They then hear a progression of parallels from the a) to the a') sub-element involving the only occurrences in this sub-unit of the preposition "for." "For [εἰς] one another" (4:9) and "for [εἰς] each other" (4:10) progress to "for [εἰς] the ages of the ages" (4:11c).

At this point, the audience also experience a progression of parallels from the A (4:1–6) to the A' (4:9–11) element of this chiastic unit. "Christ

---

involves the sins of the one who loves or of those loved is not a relevant issue here, since the mutuality of Christian relations is in view and the forgiving of *all* sins is implied. As a loving God has covered (forgiven) believers' sins, so they are to cover (forgive) the sins of their brothers and sisters [emphasis original]" (Elliott, *1 Peter*, 751). "The meaning of 'cover' in its context in 1 Peter is neither to conceal sin illegitimately, nor precisely to atone for it, but rather to obliterate it or make it disappear" (Michaels, *1 Peter*, 247).

[Χριστοῦ] having suffered" (4:1), "the will of God [θεοῦ]" (4:2), and "according to God [θεόν]" (4:6) progress to "the varied grace of God [θεοῦ]" (4:10), "sayings of God [θεοῦ]" (4:11a), "the strength which God [θεός] supplies" (4:11b), and "God [θεός] may be glorified through Jesus Christ [Χριστοῦ]" (4:11c).

That in their constant love for each other (4:8) the audience are to be hospitable to "one another [ἀλλήλους]" (4:9) further specifies and thus intensifies the exhortation for them from a clean heart to love "one another" (ἀλλήλους) constantly as part of their ethical worship (1:22).[19] The conduct of the wives among the audience in being subject to their husbands "without" (ἄνευ) a word (3:1) is part of their conduct that is to be pure in the reverent fear that serves as their ethical worship of God (3:2). Similarly, the audience's hospitality for one another "without" (ἄνευ) complaining is to be part of their ethical worship of God.[20]

The acknowledgment that "each" (ἕκαστος) member of the audience has received a "gift [χάρισμα]" (4:10), that is, a specific manifestation of the more general "grace" (χάρις) of God (1:2, 10, 13), reminds them that the God upon whom they call as Father in their liturgical worship is the one who impartially judges according to the work of "each" (ἑκάστου) one (1:17).[21] In other words, God will judge them according to the work each of them performs as ethical worship with the divine gift each has received. As the prophets were "serving" (διηκόνουν) the audience the divine gift of the very things which now have been announced to them as good news (1:12), so the audience are to be "serving" (διακονοῦντες) each other with the divine gift each has received (4:10). And that the audience are to be serving their divine gifts "for each other" (εἰς ἑαυτούς) further specifies and thus intensifies the exhortation for them to be keeping love "for each other" (εἰς ἑαυτούς) constant as part of their ethical worship (4:8).

Even though the audience may be saddened in "various" (ποικίλοις) trials (1:6), they are to serve each other as praiseworthy stewards of the "varied" (ποικίλης) grace of God that counters those trials (4:10).[22] That they are to be praiseworthy "stewards," literally "house-stewards" (οἰκονόμοι),

---

19. "Peter may be expecting his readers to open their homes for the purpose of Christian worship and fellowship, since at that time the local church had to meet in the homes of its members" (Jobes, 1 Peter, 280).

20. That these are the only occurrences of the preposition "without" (ἄνευ) in 1 Peter enhances this connection.

21. That these are the only occurrence of the adjective "each" (ἕκαστος) in 1 Peter enhances this connection.

22. That these are the only occurrences of the adjective "varied" (ποικίλος) in 1 Peter enhances this connection. See also Jobes, 1 Peter, 281.

resonates with their being "built up" (οἰκοδομεῖσθε) as a spiritual "house" (οἶκος) for a holy priesthood to offer up the worship of spiritual sacrifices acceptable to God through Jesus Christ (2:5).[23] As "praiseworthy" (καλοί) stewards of this household for worship, the audience will keep their conduct, their ethical worship, among the Gentiles "praiseworthy" (καλήν), so that observing the "praiseworthy" (καλῶν) works, they may offer the worship of glorifying God (2:12). By serving each other as praiseworthy stewards of the varied "grace" (χάριτος) of God, the "grace" (χάριτος) of eternal life (3:7), the audience will be giving the "grace" (χάρις) that amounts to worship pleasing in the sight of God (2:19, 20) in response to the "grace" (χάρις) they have received (1:2, 19; 4:10) and will receive from God (1:13).

If anyone who has received a spiritual gift "speaks" (λαλεῖ) in the worship of the community as a spiritual house (2:5), he should speak the sayings of God (4:11a), rather than "speaking" (λαλῆσαι) deceit (3:10).[24] If anyone "serves" (διακονεῖ), as part of "serving" (διακονοῦντες) a gift for each other (4:10), he should do so as from the strength which God supplies (4:11b). Consequently, in view of the fact that the end of "all things" (πάντων) has come near (4:7) and that above "all things" (πάντων) the audience are to keep love for each other constant (4:8), then in "all things" (πᾶσιν) which they do as their ethical worship God may be glorified through Jesus Christ (4:11c).[25] That in all things God may be glorified "through Jesus Christ" (διὰ Ἰησοῦ Χριστοῦ) resonates with the audience offering up the worship of spiritual sacrifices acceptable to God "through Jesus Christ [διὰ Ἰησοῦ Χριστοῦ]" (2:5).[26]

As a result of the praiseworthy conduct, the ethical worship, of the audience, nonbelieving Gentiles may eventually "glorify" (δοξάσωσιν) God

---

23. "Used here metaphorically of all believers, οἰκονόμοι is a particularly appropriate characterization of those who serve one another in a community symbolized as the 'household [οἶκος] of God' (2:5; 4:17)" (Elliott, *1 Peter*, 757).

24. That these are the only occurrences of the verb "speak" (λαλέω) in 1 Peter enhances this connection. "The point seems to be that when people speak in the household of God, they speak not their own words but sacred words that belong to and come from God" (Donelson, *I & II Peter*, 130). "While the gift of speech could be understood as any instance in which someone speaks, the reference to the 'oracle of God' suggests that the author particularly has in mind preaching or teaching in the public assembly or worship" (Senior, *1 Peter*, 121). "In effect, Peter is broadening traditional understandings of prophecy so as to include all the teaching and exhortation that goes on in connection with Christian worship. 'Whoever speaks' should speak as if delivering the very oracles of God" (Michaels, *1 Peter*, 250).

25. "The phrase 'in all things' (ἐν πᾶσιν) embraces all of the actions and aspects of congregational life described in the foregoing verses" (Elliott, *1 Peter*, 761).

26. "That such ascription of glory to God is done διὰ Ἰησοῦ Χριστοῦ ('through Jesus Christ') means not that Christ praises God, but that Christ makes it possible for Christians to do so through the exercise of their gifts" (Achtemeier, *1 Peter*, 299).

1 Peter 4:1-11

on the day of visitation (2:12). Such worship will be complemented by all the things the audience do as their ethical worship in which God may be "glorified" (δοξάζηται) through Jesus Christ (4:11c). Such glorifying of God serves as an appropriate reciprocal response for the joy indescribable and "glorified" (δεδοξασμένῃ) by God (divine passive), with which the audience are engaged in their liturgical worship of exulting for Jesus Christ (1:8).[27]

In all things the audience do as ethical worship God may be glorified through Jesus Christ, to whom (either God or Jesus Christ) is the "glory" (δόξα) and the might for the "ages" (αἰῶνας) of the "ages" (αἰώνων), amen! (4:11c).[28] This doxological worship of glory for eternity stands in contrast to the perishable "glory" (δόξα) of all flesh (1:24), which does not abide for "eternity [αἰῶνα]" (1:25). It serves as an appropriate reciprocal response, acknowledging and reaffirming the "glory" (δόξαν) God gave to the Christ he raised from the dead (1:21). And it anticipates the "glory" (δόξαν) for which the refined faith of the audience may be found at the revelation of Jesus Christ (1:7). The concluding climactic, exuberant and emphatic "amen!" invites the audience to make this act of epistolary doxological worship their own in and through both their liturgical and ethical worship.[29]

Summary on 4:1-11

"Christ then having suffered in the flesh" (4:1) reminds the audience that the "Christ" who was put to death in the "flesh" once concerning "sins suffered," so that he might lead the audience to the worship of God (3:18).

---

27. "To 'glorify God' is to praise or worship God. The point of the doxology is that the ministry of Christians to one another counts as authentic worship toward God as well, if it is done with 'words from God' or 'out of the strength God provides'" (Michaels, *1 Peter*, 252).

28. Jobes (*1 Peter*, 283) points out that "the apparent ambiguity of the antecedent of the relative pronoun does not seem to trouble the author as much as it does modern interpreters, perhaps because he understands Christ and the Father to share such praiseworthy attributes." "Here again in 1 Peter, then, we find ourselves in the company of an affirmation of Jesus' divinity—not in ontological or functional terms (since these categories would be anachronistic), but in terms of Jesus' sharing in the identity of God" (Green, *1 Peter*, 147).

29. "The conclusion of the doxology with the word ἀμήν follows a practice attested in the OT and other Jewish literature, where the word can be used to affirm what has been said, but is more commonly employed as a response, public or private, to a curse, to a prayer, to a blessing or praise of God, whether public or private, or to a doxology. These uses are then carried over into the NT: affirmation, praise, prayer, but the chief use of the word as response is, as in this verse, at the conclusion of doxologies" (Achtemeier, *1 Peter*, 300). "'Amen' is the congregation's Hebrew response to words preached or worship given. It means 'So be it'" (Witherington, *Letters*, 206).

Consequently, the audience are to arm themselves with the same attitude, for the one "suffering" in the "flesh" is separated from "sin" (4:1)—the sinfulness which prevents proper worship of God. This reinforces the exhortation for the audience to closely follow in the footsteps of the "Christ" who "suffered" on behalf of them (2:21b). He did not do "sin" (2:22), but "suffering" (2:23), he offered up our "sins" as an act of sacrificial worship, so that to "sins" having died, to the righteousness that pleases God as ethical worship we might live (2:24). His atonement of our sins through his sacrificial worship thus makes it possible for the audience to be separated from sin, in order to properly worship God.

That anyone in the audience suffering in the flesh, is "separated" from sin (4:1), as a result of the exemplary ethical and atoning sacrificial worship of Christ (2:21b–25), reinforces the exhortation for everyone who wants to love eternal life to "separate" the tongue from sinful evil and lips from speaking sinful deceit (3:10). That the audience are to "arm" themselves metaphorically for war with the same attitude as the Christ who suffered in the "flesh," as they suffer in the "flesh" (4:1), resonates with the exhortation to keep away from "fleshly desires" that are "waging war" against the soul (2:11). Indeed, they are not in the "desires" of human beings but in the will of God to spend their time remaining in the "flesh" (4:2). Such praiseworthy conduct—their ethical worship, may inspire nonbelieving Gentiles to the worship of glorifying God on the day of visitation (2:12).

That not in the desires of "human beings" but in the "will of God" the audience are to spend the time they have remaining in the flesh (4:2) reaffirms that it is the "will of God" for the audience, as those for whom it is better to suffer for doing good, if the "will of God" wants it (3:17), to silence the ignorance of foolish "human beings" (2:15). It recalls that the Christ, before whom the audience are approaching as worshipers, was a living stone rejected by "human beings" but in the sight of God chosen and esteemed (2:4). The remaining "time" they have refers to the "time" of their earthly sojourning (1:17) toward the goal of their heavenly inheritance (1:4). They are to conduct this time in reverent fear of the God they call upon as Father in their liturgical worship, the God whom, as the one who impartially judges according to the work of each one, they seek to please by their ethical worship (1:17).

Although the audience are those "having gone" into the sinful behavior which amounts to false worship (4:3b), Christ is the one "having gone" into heaven to make proclamation of his victory over the evil spirits ultimately responsible for such sinful behavior (3:19). He is the one "having gone" to be at the right of God to mediate the worship of the audience (3:22). Rather than accomplish the purpose of the "Gentiles" or "nations" (4:3a), the

1 Peter 4:1-11

audience, as a holy "nation" (2:9) and priesthood, are to offer up the worship of spiritual sacrifices acceptable to God through the mediation of Jesus Christ (2:5). Such praiseworthy conduct among the nonbelieving "Gentiles" may lead them away from blaspheming (4:4) and speaking against the audience (2:12). Instead, they may be led to the worship of glorifying God, together with the audience (1:7), on the day of visitation (2:12).

Even to the "dead" who are now among the "dead" God is ready to judge (4:5), "good news was proclaimed" (4:6), while they were still among the "living" whom God is to judge (4:5). Those now deceased were privileged during their lifetime, along with the audience, to have "good news proclaimed" unto them (1:12). Indeed, "proclaimed as good news" for them was the pronouncement (1:25) of the living word of God through which they were given new birth for eternal life (1:23). While still living, those now dead were "judged" according to "human beings" in the flesh (4:6), according to the desires of "human beings" that contradict the will of "God" (4:2), the one to finally "judge" the living and the dead (4:5). Although they were judged in the "flesh," the "flesh" in which one suffering like Christ is separated from sin (4:1-2), they may now "live" according to "God" in the Spirit (4:6).

That the "dead" to whom good news was proclaimed may now "live" according to God in the Spirit (4:6) bolsters the hope for all believers, having died to sins, to the righteousness that pleases God as worship "we might live" now and for eternity (2:24). It reinforces the exhortation for the audience, as "living" stones built up as a spiritual house for a holy priesthood upon Christ as the "living" stone (2:4), to offer up the worship of spiritual sacrifices acceptable to God through Jesus Christ (2:5). And it reassures them of their new birth for eternal life through the "living" word of God (1:23) for a "living" hope through the resurrection of Jesus Christ from the "dead" (1:3, 21). Indeed, because Christ was put to death by human beings in the "flesh," but "brought to life" by God in the "Spirit" (3:18), the dead who were judged according to human beings in the "flesh" may now likewise "live" according to God in the "Spirit" (4:6).

That the audience are to be serious and "sober" for prayers (4:7) reinforces and develops the exhortation for them, having girded up the loins of their mind, being "sober," to completely hope upon the grace that is to be borne to them by God at the end-time revelation of Jesus Christ (1:13). That they are to be sober for "prayers" in their liturgical worship resonates with the implicit exhortation for them to imitate the mutual respect of husbands and wives so that their "prayers" may not be hindered (3:7). The exhortation for the audience to be keeping "love" for each other "constant" (4:8a) reinforces the exhortations for them to "love" the brotherhood of their fellow believers as correlative with their "fear" or reverent worship of God (2:17), and with a

151

clean heart to "love" one another "constantly" (1:22). Their ethical worship of loving each other is thus to complement their liturgical worship in which they are joyfully exulting for the Jesus Christ whom "you love" (1:8).

The constant love of the audience for each other, as part of their ethical worship, covers over a multitude of the "sins" that prevent proper worship (4:8b). This further fortifies the exhortation for them to imitate the exemplary ethical worship of the suffering Christ made possible by the atonement for sins that the suffering Christ effected by his sacrificial worship. Anyone in the audience suffering in the flesh, as Christ suffered in the flesh, is separated from "sin" (4:1). Christ once concerning "sins" suffered so that he might lead the audience to the worship of God (3:18). The "sins" of us Christ himself offered up in sacrificial worship for their atonement, so that to "sins" having died, to the righteousness that pleases God as ethical worship we might live (2:24). The Christ who did not do "sin" (2:22), but instead handed himself over in ethical worship to the God who judges righteously (2:23), thus left the audience a model to follow closely (2:21b) in their own ethical worship of loving each other constantly.

That the audience are to be praiseworthy "stewards," literally "house-stewards," resonates with their being "built up" as a spiritual "house" for a holy priesthood to offer up the worship of spiritual sacrifices acceptable to God through Jesus Christ (2:5). As "praiseworthy" stewards of this household for worship, the audience will keep their conduct, their ethical worship, among the Gentiles "praiseworthy," so that observing the "praiseworthy" works, they may offer the worship of glorifying God (2:12). By serving each other as praiseworthy stewards of the varied "grace" of God, the "grace" of eternal life (3:7), the audience will be giving the "grace" that amounts to worship pleasing in the sight of God (2:19, 20) in response to the "grace" they have received (1:2, 19; 4:10) and will receive from God (1:13). And that in all things God may be glorified "through Jesus Christ" (4:11c) resonates with the audience offering up the worship of spiritual sacrifices acceptable to God "through Jesus Christ" (2:5).

As a result of the praiseworthy conduct, the ethical worship, of the audience, nonbelieving Gentiles may eventually "glorify" God on the day of visitation (2:12). Such worship will be complemented by all the things the audience do as their ethical worship in which God may be "glorified" through Jesus Christ (4:11c). Such glorifying of God serves as an appropriate reciprocal response for the joy indescribable and "glorified" by God (divine passive), with which the audience are engaged in their liturgical worship of exulting for Jesus Christ (1:8).

In all things the audience do as ethical worship God may be glorified through Jesus Christ, to whom (either God or Jesus Christ) is the "glory" and

1 Peter 4:1–11

the might for the "ages" of the "ages," amen! (4:11c). This doxological worship of glory for eternity stands in contrast to the perishable "glory" of all flesh (1:24), which does not abide for "eternity" (1:25). It serves as an appropriate reciprocal response, acknowledging and reaffirming the "glory" God gave to the Christ he raised from the dead (1:21). And it anticipates the "glory" for which the refined faith of the audience may be found at the revelation of Jesus Christ (1:7). The concluding climactic, exuberant and emphatic "amen!" invites the audience to make this act of epistolary doxological worship their own in and through both their liturgical and ethical worship.

11

1 Peter 4:12–19
The Suffering Entrust to the Faithful Creator Their Souls in Doing Good (B′)

Glorify God for suffering in the name of Christ

A ¹² Beloved, do not be surprised at the burning among you, occurring to you for a trial, as if something strange were happening to you, ¹³ but to the degree that you are sharing in the sufferings of the Christ rejoice, so that at the revelation of his *glory* you may rejoice, exulting. ¹⁴ If you are reproached in the *name* of Christ, blessed are you, because the Spirit of *glory* and of *God* rests upon you.
  B ¹⁵ᵃ For do *not* let anyone of you suffer
    C ¹⁵ᵇ *as* a murderer or thief or evildoer or *as* a troublemaker.
    C′ ¹⁶ᵃ But if *as* a Christian
  B′ ¹⁶ᵇ do *not* be ashamed,
A′ ¹⁶ᶜ let him *glorify God* in this *name*, ¹⁷ because it is the time to begin the judgment from the house of *God*. If the first is from us, what is the end for those disobeying the gospel of *God*?
¹⁸ "And if the righteous one is with difficulty saved, where will the ungodly and sinful one appear?" (Prov 11:31 LXX). ¹⁹ So then let those who are suffering according to the will of *God* entrust to the faithful Creator their souls in good-doing.[1]

---

1. For the establishment of 1 Pet 4:12–19 as a chiasm, see ch. 1.

1 Peter 4:12-19

Audience Response to 4:12-19

At this point, the audience experience a progression of macrochiastic parallels from the B (1:14-25) to this B' (4:12-19) chiastic unit. "Who through him are faithful [πιστούς] for God" (1:21) and "your souls [ψυχάς] having purified" (1:22) progress to "entrust their souls [ψυχάς] to the faithful [πιστῷ] Creator in good-doing" (4:19). In addition, with the reference to "Christ [Χριστοῦ]" (4:13) near the beginning of this unit, the audience hear the transitional term that links this unit with the preceding unit (4:1-11), which referred to "through Jesus Christ [Χριστοῦ]" (4:11) near its conclusion.

4:12-14 (A): In Name of Christ the Spirit of Glory and of God Rests upon You

The audience hear the A element (4:12-14) of this chiastic unit as a chiastic pattern in itself:
a) Beloved, do not be surprised at the burning among *you*, occurring to *you* for a trial, as if something strange were happening to *you* (4:12),
  b) but to the degree that you are sharing in the sufferings of the *Christ* rejoice, so that at the revelation of his *glory* you may rejoice, exulting (4:13).
  b') If you are reproached in the name of *Christ*, blessed are you, because the Spirit of *glory* (4:14a)
a') and of God rests upon *you* (4:14b).

At the center of this chiastic sub-unit the audience experience a pivot of parallels from the b) to the b') sub-element involving the only occurrences in this sub-unit of the terms "Christ" and "glory." "The sufferings of Christ [Χριστοῦ]" and "the revelation of his glory [δόξης]" (4:13) progress to "the name of Christ [Χριστοῦ]" and "the Spirit of glory [δόξης]" (4:14a). They then hear a progression of several parallels from the a) to the a') sub-element involving the only occurrences in this sub-unit of the pronoun "you." "The burning among you [ὑμῖν]," "occurring to you [ὑμῖν]," and "happening to you [ὑμῖν]" (4:13) progress to "rests upon you [ὑμᾶς]" (4:14b).

The audience were previously addressed as "beloved" (ἀγαπητοί) before being encouraged by the author in their situation of being aliens and sojourners (2:11) among nonbelieving Gentiles (2:12). Now they are again addressed as "beloved [ἀγαπητοί]" (4:12)—those loved by God (2:10), by the author, and by one another (4:8). And now, in contrast to the nonbelieving Gentiles who are "surprised" (ξενίζονται) that the audience are no longer joining them in immoral and idolatrous behavior (4:4), the audience are encouraged that "you not be surprised [ξενίζεσθε]" (4:12).[2] They are not to be surprised at the "burning" (πυρώσει) among them, occurring to them for a "trial" (πειρασμόν), as if something "strange" or "surprising" (ξένου) were happening to them (4:12). This reaffirms the encouragement for them as those saddened in various "trials [πειρασμοῖς]" (1:6), but whose faith through "fire" (πυρός) is being refined, so that it may be found for praise and glory and honor at the final revelation of Jesus Christ (1:7).[3]

To the degree that the audience are sharing in the "sufferings" (παθήμασιν) of the Christ, the "sufferings" (παθήματα) for Christ to which the prophets testified (1:11), they are to rejoice, so that at the revelation of "his glory" (δόξης αὐτοῦ), the "glory" (δόξαν) God gave to "him" (αὐτῷ) in raising him from the dead (1:21), they may rejoice, exulting (4:13). That they are to rejoice at the "revelation" (ἀποκαλύψει) of the glory of the risen Jesus Christ reinforces the exhortation for them to hope upon the grace that is to be borne to them at the "revelation" (ἀποκαλύψει) of Jesus Christ (1:13). And it reaffirms the encouragement that their faith is being refined so that it may be found for praise, honor, and the "glory" (δόξαν) of risen, eternal life at the "revelation" (ἀποκαλύψει) of Jesus Christ (1:7). That they are to "rejoice" (χαίρετε), so that at the revelation of his glory, "you may rejoice" (χαρῆτε), "exulting" (ἀγαλλιώμενοι), thus resonates with their present worship in which "you are exulting" (ἀγαλλιᾶσθε) with a "joy" (χαρᾷ) indescribable and "glorified" (δεδοξασμένη) for Jesus Christ (1:8) and in God (1:6).[4]

If the audience are reproached in the name of "Christ," the "Christ" in whose sufferings they are sharing (4:13), they are "blessed [μακάριοι]" (4:14a), recalling that if they should suffer on account of righteousness, they are "blessed" (μακάριοι) by God (3:14).[5] They are blessed because the Spirit

2. Holloway, "1 Pet 4.12ff.," 433-48. "By using the same verb (ξενίζω) that was used in 4:4, the author tells his readers that their reaction to the non-Christians' behavior must not be the same as non-Christians' reaction to their behavior, primarily since suffering for those who are followers of Christ in a world that rejects him is inevitable" (Achtemeier, *1 Peter*, 305).

3. That these are the only occurrences in 1 Peter of the terms "trial" (πειρασμός) and "fire" (πῦρ)/"burning" (πύρωσις) enhances this connection. "At this point in 1 Peter, the burning of suffering connects the person to Christ and demonstrates the genuineness (1:7) of a person's faith" (Donelson, *I & II Peter*, 134-35).

4. "The verb ἀγαλλιάομαι, appearing also in the parallel unit of 1:6-9, is used in the OT of the eschatological jubilation of the redeemed" (Elliott, *1 Peter*, 777).

5. That these are the only occurrences of the term "blessed" (μακάριος) in 1 Peter enhances this connection. "Beatitudes in Judaism, the New Testament, and early Christianity tend to bless people who do not appear to be blessed. Thus they often provide an explanation for why such an apparently unblessed person is actually blessed" (Donelson, *I & II Peter*, 136).

1 Peter 4:12-19

of "glory" (δόξης), the "glory" (δόξης) of the risen Christ (4:13), and of God rests upon "you [ὑμᾶς]" (4:14)—the "you" (ὑμῖν) among whom is the burning occurring to "you" (ὑμῖν) for a trial that is not something strange happening to "you [ὑμῖν]" (4:12).[6]

Those to whom good news was proclaimed but have now died may live eternally according to "God" (θεόν) in the "Spirit [πνεύματι]" (4:6), the "Spirit" (πνεύματι) in whom Christ was brought to risen, eternal life (3:18). Similarly, the audience, as those reproached in the name of Christ, are blessed because the "Spirit" (πνεῦμα) of the glory of risen, eternal life and of "God" (θεοῦ), rests upon them (4:14). That the Spirit of glory and of God rests "upon you" (ἐφ᾽ ὑμᾶς) recalls that the eyes of the Lord are "upon the righteous" (ἐπὶ δικαίους) and his ears for their supplication (3:12). It thus reassures the suffering audience that, as those who are among the righteous through their ethical worship of doing good, their liturgical prayers of supplication are receiving a favorable hearing by God.[7]

4:15a (B): For Do Not Let Anyone of You Suffer

Each individual among the audience is then addressed: "For do not let anyone of you suffer" (4:15a). Not anyone of "you" (ὑμῶν), the "you" (ὑμᾶς) upon whom, if reproached in the name of Christ, the Spirit of glory and of God rests (4:14), is to suffer. That no one of them is to "suffer" (πασχέτω) recalls that they are not to "suffer" (πάσχειν) for doing evil but for doing good (3:17). Not "anyone" (τις) of them is to suffer for doing evil, because if "anyone" (τις) bears up, "suffering" (πάσχων) sorrows unjustly (2:19), then this is the grace of ethical worship that is pleasing in the sight of God (2:20).

---

6. "The situation envisioned here, as elsewhere in the letter, is not one of formally organized, legal persecution or prosecution but the informal and sporadic public shaming of those who follow the Christ and bear his name" (Elliott, *1 Peter*, 779).

7. "The phrase 'the Spirit of glory and of God rests upon you' is probably an allusion to Isa. 11:2 LXX ... Peter understands that it was the Spirit of Christ who spoke to the prophets, such as Isaiah, revealing the sufferings of the Messiah and the glories that would follow (1 Pet. 1:10-12). In 4:14, Peter claims that the same Spirit of God predicted to rest upon the Messiah also rests on the believer who is willing to suffer for Jesus Christ" (Jobes, *1 Peter*, 288). "Peter's point was that they were blessed because they possessed even now the glory that would be theirs at the end time and also that the eschatological gift of the Spirit even now rested upon them" (Schreiner, *1, 2 Peter*, 222).

4:15b (C): As a Murderer or Thief or Evildoer or As a Troublemaker

Not anyone in the audience is to suffer (4:15a) "as a murderer or thief or evildoer or as a troublemaker" (4:15b).[8] That no one of them is to suffer as an "evildoer" (κακοποιός) reinforces the exhortation for them to be subject to every human institution on account of the Lord, whether to a king as being in authority (2:13), whether to governors as sent through him for the punishment of "evildoers" (κακοποιῶν) but the praise of good doers (2:14). And it bolsters the exhortation for them to keep their conduct, their ethical worship, among the nonbelieving Gentiles praiseworthy, so that in what they slander the audience as "evildoers" (κακοποιῶν), observing their praiseworthy works, they may offer the worship of glorifying God on the day of visitation (2:12).

4:16a (C′): But If As a Christian

The audience then hear how they are to suffer: "But if as a Christian" (4:16a). At this point, the audience experience the pivot of parallels from the C to this C′ element at the center of this chiastic unit. "As [ὡς] a murderer" and "as [ὡς] a troublemaker" (4:15b) progress to "as [ὡς] a Christian" (4:16a). "If" (εἰ) anyone in the audience suffers as a "Christian" (Χριστιανός) recalls that "if" (εἰ) the audience are reproached in the name of "Christ" (Χριστοῦ), they are blessed, because the Spirit of glory and of God rests upon them (4:14).[9]

4:16b (B′): Do Not Be Ashamed

If anyone in the audience suffers as a Christian (4:16a), then "do not be ashamed" (4:16b). At this point, the audience experience a progression,

---

8. Brown, "Just a Busybody?," 549–68. "The word ἀλλοτριεπίσκοπος is apparently composed of ἀλλότριος and ἐπίσκοπος, which etymologically should mean something like 'overseer of another person's affairs.' While we do not have exact parallels in ancient literature to this word, the partial parallels we do have suggest either the rather benign meaning of a busybody, a meddler in the affairs of others , a 'mischief-maker,' or a more egregious meaning of one who defrauds others. Of the two, the more benign 'mischief-maker' has the better parallels in meaning" (Donelson, *I & II Peter*, 133).

9. Horrell, "The Label Χριστιανός," 361–81. "Believers in Jesus Christ are referred to as 'Christians' elsewhere in the NT only in Acts 11:26 and 26:28. All three instances appear to reflect the viewpoint of Jewish and pagan outsiders toward those who followed and worshiped Jesus . . . Peter's language does not imply that being a 'Christian' was in itself a punishable offense at the time the epistle was written" (Michaels, *1 Peter*, 268). See also Trebilco, *Self-Designations*, 283–85.

1 Peter 4:12-19

via the chiastic parallels, from the B to this B' element in this chiastic unit. "Do not [μή] let anyone of you suffer" (4:15a) progresses to "do not [μή] be ashamed" (4:16b). Anyone who suffers as a Christian is not to be "ashamed" (αἰσχυνέσθω), because when the audience are spoken against, "shame may come against" (καταισχυνθῶσιν) those mistreating their good, in Christ, conduct (3:16). Indeed, the audience are to be assured, through the scriptural authority of God's word in Isa 28:16, that anyone of them who suffers as a believer in Christ, "will never be put to shame [καταισχυνθῇ]" by God (divine passive) now or in the future, final judgment (2:6).[10]

4:16c-19 (A'): Let Him Glorify God in This Name

The audience hear the A' element (4:16c-19) of this chiastic unit as a chiastic pattern in itself:
a) let him glorify *God* in this name, because it is the time to begin the judgment from the house of *God* (4:16c-17a).
b) *If* the first is from us, what is the end for those disobeying (4:17b)
   c) the gospel of God (4:17c)?
b') "And *if* the righteous one is with difficulty saved, where will the ungodly and sinful one appear" (Prov 11:31 LXX)? (4:18).
a') So then let those who are suffering according to the will of *God* entrust to the faithful Creator their souls in good-doing (4:19).

After the central and unparalleled c) sub-element, "the gospel of God" (4:17c), which contains the only occurrence in 1 Peter of the noun "gospel" (εὐαγγέλιον), the audience experience a pivot of parallels from the b) to the b') sub-element involving the only occurrences in this sub-unit of the conjunction "if." "If [εἰ] the first is from us" (4:17b) progresses to "if [εἰ] the righteous one" (4:18). Finally, they hear a progression of parallels from the a) to the a') sub-element involving the first and final occurrences in this sub-unit of the term "God." "Glorify God [θεόν]" (4:16c) and "house of God [θεοῦ]" (4:17a) progress to "will of God [θεοῦ]" (4:19).

In addition, the audience hear progressions, via the chiastic parallels, from the A (4:12-14) to the A' (4:16c-19) element of this chiastic unit. "Glory [δόξης]" (4:13, 14), "name [ὀνόματι]" (4:14), and "of God [θεοῦ]" (4:14) progress to "glorify God [δοξαζέτω δὲ τὸν θεόν]" (4:16c), "name [ὀνόματι]" (4:16c), and "of God [θεοῦ]" (4:17, 19).

---

10. "The addressees' appropriate response to attempts at shaming them, as the remainder of this verse indicates, is to acknowledge God's honor and glory, even with the very name by which they are reproached and caused to suffer" (Elliott, *1 Peter*, 795).

1 Peter, 2 Peter, and Jude

The exhortation for any believer who suffers to "glorify" (δοξαζέτω) "God" (θεόν) in this "name [ὀνόματι]" (4:16c), that is as a Christian (4:16a), or in the "name" (ὀνόματι) of Christ (4:14a), accords with the author's previous prayer that in all things "God" (θεός) may be "glorified" (δοξάζηται) through Jesus Christ (4:11). Such worship of glorifying God on the part of a suffering believer complements the worship whereby nonbelieving Gentiles, who may cause believers to suffer, may nevertheless be led by the praiseworthy conduct, the ethical worship, of believers to "glorify" (δοξάσωσιν) "God" (θεόν) on the day of visitation (2:12).[11]

The audience have been assured that in the power of God they are being guarded through faith for a salvation ready to be revealed in the last "time [καιρῷ]" (1:5). They have heard that concerning this salvation (1:10) prophets probed for what certain person or what sort of "time" (καιρόν) the Spirit of Christ in them was indicating, testifying beforehand to the sufferings for Christ and the glories after these things (1:11). And now they, as those sharing in the sufferings of Christ (4:13), are informed that it is the "time" (καιρός) to begin the judgment from the house of God (4:17a). The "judgment" (κρίμα) that it is time to begin is that of the God who keeps ready to "judge" (κρῖναι) the living and the dead (4:5). It is that of the God to whom Christ handed himself over as the one who "judges" (κρίνοντι) righteously (2:23). And it is that of the God who impartially "judges" (κρίνοντα) the work of each one (1:17).[12]

That the judgment of God will begin from the "house" (οἴκου) of God (4:17a) means that it will begin with the audience, who as living stones are being built up by God as a spiritual "house" (οἶκος) for a holy priesthood to offer up the worship of spiritual sacrifices acceptable to God through Jesus Christ (2:5). This implies that each member of the audience, who are the house of "God" (θεοῦ) upon whom the Spirit of glory and of "God" (θεοῦ) rests (4:14), will be judged by God on his or her ethical worship of glorifying

---

11. "Thus the call 'to glorify God' has two edges. First, readers should not give in to shame over the name 'Christian' but take glory in it. The name 'Christian' is one of high status, not low. Second, these Christians who are tempted to deny their faith should instead give glory to God. While the phrase 'glorify God' can refer to all kinds of specific deeds, it must include here claiming the name 'Christian' and the behavior that goes with it" (Donelson, *I & II Peter*, 137). "The concern for glorifying or honoring God, especially through an honorable way of life, is a continuing theme of the letter (2: 9, 12; 4:11) but now is related to the experience of reproach and stigmatization with the contemptuous label 'Christian'" (Elliott, *1 Peter*, 796). As Michaels (*1 Peter*, 269) notes, "glorification of God depends on attitudes and behavior toward other people."

12. "Present suffering—the abuse and ridicule of the community by outsiders, which tempts, tests, and refines the community—is the first act of final judgment. It is not simply that this test will issue in a favorable report on the final day; this test is the final-day test" (Donelson, *I & II Peter*, 138).

1 Peter 4:12-19

"God" (θεόν) in the name of Christ (4:16), as one who shares in the sufferings of Christ (4:13). The audience will thus be judged by God on whether in all the things they do as their ethical worship "God" (θεός) has been glorified through Jesus Christ (4:11), and whether they have indeed offered up the ethical worship of spiritual sacrifices acceptable to "God" (θεῷ) through Jesus Christ (2:5).

The audience are to be serious and sober for prayers, since the "end" (τέλος) of all things has come near (4:7). At this "end" (τέλος) of all things the entire audience of believers are to be harmonious, sympathetic, having brotherly affection, compassionate, and humble (3:8). And the audience are on the way to attaining the "end" (τέλος) of their faith, the salvation of souls (1:9). Consequently, they are asked the poignant rhetorical question that if they, as obedient believers, are the first to be judged, what is the "end" (τέλος) for those disobeying the gospel of God? (4:17). The implicit answer that the end for those disobeying the gospel of God may be a judgment not as favorable as for the audience who are to be judged first bolsters the exhortation for the audience not to be ashamed for suffering as Christians (4:16), but rather to rejoice to the degree that they share in the sufferings of Christ (4:13a). Indeed, they are to rejoice now, so that at the final revelation of Christ's glory at the last judgment they may rejoice and continue their worship of exulting for Christ (4:13b; 1:8).

Those "disobeying" (ἀπειθούντων) the gospel of God (4:17) include the evil spirits who "disobeyed" (ἀπειθήσασίν) formerly (3:20), some husbands who are "disobeying" (ἀπειθοῦσιν) the word (3:1), and the nonbelieving human beings who have rejected Christ, "disobeying" (ἀπειθοῦντες) the word of the gospel (2:8). The reference to the "gospel" (εὐαγγελίῳ) of God recalls that to the living who have now died "good news was proclaimed [εὐηγγελίσθη]" (4:6). And the pronouncement of the Lord which abides for eternity was "proclaimed as good news" (εὐαγγελισθέν) for the audience (1:25), through those who "proclaimed good news" (εὐαγγελισαμένων) unto them by the Holy Spirit sent from heaven (1:12). The audience may thus be encouraged that they, as Christians who have obeyed the gospel (1:14, 22), can expect to be favorably judged by God.

The audience's appreciation that as suffering Christians they are among those being saved is then enhanced with a scriptural quotation from Prov 11:31 LXX: "And if the righteous one is with difficulty saved, where will the ungodly and sinful one appear?" (4:18). The audience were among the unrighteous on behalf of whom Christ, as the "righteous one" (δίκαιος), suffered once concerning sins (3:18). Consequently, they are now among the "righteous" (δικαίους) upon whom are the eyes of the Lord and his ears attentive for their prayers of supplication in their liturgical worship (3:12).

1 Peter, 2 Peter, and Jude

In addition, even if the audience should suffer on account of "righteousness" (δικαιοσύνην), they are blessed by God (3:14). And because of Christ's sacrificial atonement of our sins, to "righteousness" (δικαιοσύνῃ) the audience may live now and for eternity (2:24). They are thus to appreciate that each of them is now a "righteous one" (δίκαιος) who is, although with difficulty, nevertheless being saved.[13]

Each member of the audience is a righteous one who is being "saved [σῴζεται]" (4:18), because the ritual act of baptism now "saves" (σῴζει) them through the resurrection of Jesus Christ (3:21). As those given new birth, they may grow up for the "salvation" (σωτηρίαν) of eternal life (2:2), the "salvation" (σωτηρίας) concerning which prophets sought and searched (1:10), the "salvation" (σωτηρίαν) of souls they are attaining as the end of their faith (1:9), and the "salvation" (σωτηρίαν) ready to be revealed in the last time (1:5). Each member of the audience is among the righteous being saved, rather than a "sinful one [ἁμαρτωλός]" (4:18), because their constant love for one another covers a multitude of "sins [ἁμαρτιῶν]" (4:8). As those suffering, they are separated from "sin [ἁμαρτίας]" (4:1), since Christ once concerning "sins" (ἁμαρτιῶν) suffered (3:18). Indeed, Christ, who did not do "sin [ἁμαρτίαν]" (2:22), offered up our "sins" (ἁμαρτίας) in the sacrificial worship of his crucifixion, so that to "sins" (ἁμαρτίαις) having died, to righteousness we may live as those saved for eternal life (2:24).

As those who are suffering according to the will of God, the audience are exhorted to entrust to the faithful Creator their souls in the ethical worship of good-doing (4:19). That they are "suffering" (πάσχοντες) according to the "will of God" (θέλημα τοῦ θεοῦ) bolsters the exhortation for each one who is "suffering [παθών]" (4:1) to spend the time remaining not in the desires of human beings but in the "will of God [θελήματι θεοῦ]" (4:2). It recalls that it is better to "suffer" (πάσχειν) for doing good, if the "will of God" (θέλημα τοῦ θεοῦ) wants it, than for doing evil (3:17), for it is the "will of God" (θέλημα τοῦ θεοῦ) that those doing good silence the ignorance of foolish human beings (2:15). But if, doing good and "suffering"

---

13. "Peter's point is not that salvation is difficult for God to achieve, though the sufferings of Christ were certainly no easy means of atonement ... The thought is that the world's response makes it difficult for Christians to remain faithful to Christ to the end" (Jobes, *1 Peter*, 294). "The difficulty envisioned is the suffering believers must endure in order to be saved. God saves his people by refining and purifying them through suffering. It is implied here that salvation is eschatological, a gift that believers will receive after enduring suffering (cf. 1:5,9)" (Schreiner, *1, 2 Peter*, 228–29). "In the context of 1 Peter, the emphasis of the words μόλις σῴζεται is on σῴζεται: whatever the difficulty, and whether or not they suffer physical death, the 'just' will be saved (cf. 1:5, 9–10; 2:2; 3:21)" (Michaels, *1 Peter*, 272).

1 Peter 4:12-19

(πάσχοντες), they endure, then this is the grace of an ethical worship pleasing in the sight of God (2:20).

"So then" (ὥστε) the audience are to entrust to God as the "faithful" (πιστῷ) Creator their souls in doing good (4:19), since through Christ they are "faithful" (πιστούς) for God, who raised him from the dead and gave him glory, "so that" (ὥστε) their faith and hope are for God (1:21). They are to "entrust" (παρατιθέσθωσαν) to God as the faithful Creator their souls in the ethical worship of doing good as part of following the model of Christ, who "handed himself over" (παρεδίδου) in ethical worship to God as the one who judges righteously (2:23).[14]

That they, as among those being saved (4:18), are to entrust to the faithful Creator their "souls" (ψυχάς) in good-doing (4:19) likens them to the eight "souls" (ψυχαί) in Noah's ark who were saved through water (3:20). It resonates with the affirmation that they have turned now to Christ as the shepherd and overseer of their "souls [ψυχῶν]" (2:25), and with the exhortation that they are to keep away from fleshly desires that are waging war against the "soul [ψυχῆς]" (2:11). It reinforces the exhortation for them, as those having purified their "souls" (ψυχάς) in the obedience to the truth, to do the good of loving one another constantly as part of their ethical worship (1:22). And it reaffirms their liturgical worship of exulting for Christ (1:8) and in God (1:6), as they are attaining the end of their faith, salvation of "souls [ψυχῶν]" (1:9).

The audience, as those who are suffering according to the will of God, are to entrust to the faithful Creator their souls in "good-doing [ἀγαθοποιΐᾳ]" (4:19), since it is better to suffer for "doing good" (ἀγαθοποιοῦντας), if the will of God wants it, than for doing evil (3:17). This resonates with the exhortation for them to become children of Sarah as those "doing good" (ἀγαθοποιοῦσαι) and not fearing any intimidation (3:6). It reaffirms the assertion that if, "doing good" (ἀγαθοποιοῦντες) and suffering, they endure, then this is the grace of ethical worship pleasing in the sight of God (2:20). And it reinforces the exhortation for them, as those "doing good" (ἀγαθοποιοῦντας), to silence the ignorance of foolish human beings (2:15), so that, rather than speaking against them as evildoers, nonbelieving Gentiles will be inspired to offer the worship of glorifying God on the day of visitation (2:12).[15]

---

14. "The reference to God as Creator implies his sovereignty, for the Creator of the world is also sovereign over it. Therefore believers can be confident that he will not allow them to suffer beyond their capacity and that he will provide the strength needed to endure" (Schreiner, 1, 2 Peter, 229).

15. Dubis, Messianic Woes. "The participle of the verb ἀγαθοποιεῖν has dominated the ethical teaching of the entire epistle (2:15, 20; 3:6, 17; cf. 2:12, 14; 3:11–12, 13),

Summary on 4:12-19

To the degree that the audience are sharing in the "sufferings" of the Christ, the "sufferings" for Christ to which the prophets testified (1:11), they are to rejoice, so that at the revelation of "his glory," the "glory" God gave to "him" in raising him from the dead (1:21), they may rejoice, exulting (4:13). That they are to rejoice at the "revelation" of the glory of the risen Jesus Christ reinforces the exhortation for them to hope upon the grace that is to be borne to them at the "revelation" of Jesus Christ (1:13). And it reaffirms the encouragement that their faith is being refined so that it may be found for praise, honor, and the "glory" of risen, eternal life at the "revelation" of Jesus Christ (1:7). That they are to "rejoice," so that at the revelation of his glory, "you may rejoice," "exulting," thus resonates with their present worship in which "you are exulting" with a "joy" indescribable and "glorified" for Jesus Christ (1:8) and in God (1:6).

Those to whom good news was proclaimed but have now died may live eternally according to "God" in the "Spirit" (4:6), the "Spirit" in whom Christ was brought to risen, eternal life (3:18). Similarly, the audience, as those reproached in the name of Christ, are blessed because the "Spirit" of the glory of risen, eternal life and of "God," rests upon them (4:14). That the Spirit of glory and of God rests "upon you" recalls that the eyes of the Lord are "upon the righteous" and his ears for their supplication (3:12). It thus reassures the suffering audience that, as those who are among the righteous through their ethical worship of doing good, their liturgical prayers of supplication are receiving a favorable hearing by God.

The exhortation for any believer who suffers to "glorify" "God" in this "name" (4:16c), that is as a Christian (4:16a), or in the "name" of Christ (4:14a), accords with the author's previous prayer that in all things "God" may be "glorified" through Jesus Christ (4:11). Such worship of glorifying God on the part of a suffering believer complements the worship whereby

---

and it is no surprise to find 'the doing of good' standing so emphatically at the end of the author's summary of the proper response to slander and suffering" (Michaels, *1 Peter*, 274). "The eloquent combination of exhortation and consolation contained in this final verse expresses quintessentially the spirit and substance of the entire letter: innocent suffering and perseverance in doing good in fidelity to God's will are possible for those who trust in God's care and entrust themselves, as did Jesus (2:23), to God as a trustworthy Creator" (Elliott, *1 Peter*, 807). "Christian suffering that occurs as part of God's plan of universal judgment is to lead Christians to continue to entrust themselves to the creator God who is faithful to his creatures who trust him and who show that trust by doing what he wants, despite the suffering that may entail. It also assures the Christians that such suffering is not due to human arbitrariness, or a sign that God has abandoned them; rather it is the result of activity pleasing to God, and so is in accord with the divine will" (Achtemeier, *1 Peter*, 319).

nonbelieving Gentiles, who may cause believers to suffer, may nevertheless be led by the praiseworthy conduct, the ethical worship, of believers to "glorify" "God" on the day of visitation (2:12).

That the judgment of God will begin from the "house" of God (4:17a) means that it will begin with the audience, who as living stones are being built up by God as a spiritual "house" for a holy priesthood to offer up the worship of spiritual sacrifices acceptable to God through Jesus Christ (2:5). This implies that each member of the audience, who are the house of "God" upon whom the Spirit of glory and of "God" rests (4:14), will be judged by God on his or her ethical worship of glorifying "God" in the name of Christ (4:16), as one who shares in the sufferings of Christ (4:13). The audience will thus be judged by God on whether in all the things they do as their ethical worship "God" has been glorified through Jesus Christ (4:11), and whether they have indeed offered up the ethical worship of spiritual sacrifices acceptable to "God" through Jesus Christ (2:5).

Each member of the audience is a righteous one who is being "saved" (4:18), because the ritual act of baptism now "saves" them through the resurrection of Jesus Christ (3:21). As those given new birth, they may grow up for the "salvation" of eternal life (2:2), the "salvation" concerning which prophets sought and searched (1:10), the "salvation" of souls they are attaining as the end of their faith (1:9), and the "salvation" ready to be revealed in the last time (1:5). Each member of the audience is among the righteous being saved, rather than a "sinful one" (4:18), because their constant love for one another covers a multitude of "sins" (4:8). As those suffering, they are separated from "sin" (4:1), since Christ once concerning "sins" suffered (3:18). Indeed, Christ, who did not do "sin" (2:22), offered up our "sins" in the sacrificial worship of his crucifixion, so that to "sins" having died, to the righteousness that serves as ethical worship we may live as those saved for eternal life (2:24).

As those who are suffering according to the will of God, the audience are exhorted to entrust to the faithful Creator their souls in the ethical worship of good-doing (4:19). That they are "suffering" according to the "will of God" bolsters the exhortation for each one who is "suffering" (4:1) to spend the time remaining not in the desires of human beings but in the "will of God" (4:2). It recalls that it is better to "suffer" for doing good, if the "will of God" wants it, than for doing evil (3:17), for it is the "will of God" that those doing good silence the ignorance of foolish human beings (2:15). But if, doing good and "suffering," they endure, then this is the grace of an ethical worship pleasing in the sight of God (2:20).

That they, as among those being saved (4:18), are to entrust to the faithful Creator their "souls" in good-doing (4:19) likens them to the eight "souls" in Noah's ark who were saved through water (3:20). It resonates with the affirmation that they have turned now to Christ as the shepherd and overseer of their "souls" (2:25), and with the exhortation that they are to keep away from fleshly desires that are waging war against the "soul" (2:11). It reinforces the exhortation for them, as those having purified their "souls" in the obedience to the truth, to do the good of loving one another constantly as part of their ethical worship (1:22). And it reaffirms their liturgical worship of exulting for Christ (1:8) and in God (1:6), as they are attaining the end of their faith, salvation of "souls" (1:9).

The audience, as those who are suffering according to the will of God, are to entrust to the faithful Creator their souls in "good-doing" (4:19), since it is better to suffer for "doing good," if the will of God wants it, than for doing evil (3:17). This resonates with the exhortation for them to become children of Sarah as those "doing good" and not fearing any intimidation (3:6). It reaffirms the assertion that if, "doing good" and suffering, they endure, then this is the grace of ethical worship pleasing in the sight of God (2:20). And it reinforces the exhortation for them, as those "doing good," to silence the ignorance of foolish human beings (2:15), so that, rather than speaking against them as evildoers, nonbelieving Gentiles will be inspired to offer the worship of glorifying God on the day of visitation (2:12).

12

1 Peter 5:1–14
Peace in Attaining the Eternal Glory To Be Revealed by God (A′)

The true grace of God for which you are to remain firm in Christ

A 5:1 The elders then among *you* I *encourage*, as a fellow elder and *witness* of the *sufferings* of *Christ*, and a sharer in the *glory* that is going to be revealed, ² shepherd the flock of God among *you*, overseeing not as under compulsion but willingly according to God, not for shameful profit but eagerly, ³ not as lording it over the ones allotted, but becoming examples to the flock, ⁴ and when the chief shepherd is manifested, you will attain the unfading crown of the *glory*, ⁵ᵃ Likewise, you who are younger, be subjected to the elders.

B ⁵ᵇ And all of you clothe yourselves with *humility* toward one another, for "God *opposes* the proud but to the *humble* gives grace" (Prov 3:34 LXX).

B′ ⁶ Be *humbled* then under the mighty hand of God, so that he may exalt you in time, ⁷ casting all your anxiety upon him, because from him there is care concerning you. ⁸ Be sober, be watchful. Your *opponent* the devil, roaring like a lion, is going around seeking someone to devour, 9a whom you are to *oppose*, as strong in the faith,

A′ ⁹ᵇ knowing that the same kinds of *sufferings* are being undergone by your brotherhood throughout the world. ¹⁰ The God of all grace, who called you for his eternal *glory* in *Christ* Jesus, after you have suffered briefly, will himself restore, confirm, strengthen, establish. ¹¹ To him be the might for the ages, amen! ¹² Through Silvanus, to *you* the faithful brother, as I reckon, through a few things I have written, *encouraging* and *bearing witness* that this is the true grace of God for which you are to remain firm. ¹³ The chosen together in Babylon greet you and Mark my son. ¹⁴ Greet one another with a kiss of love. Peace to *you* all who are in *Christ*![1]

Audience Response to 5:1-14

At this point, the audience experience a progression of macrochiastic parallels from the A (1:1-13) to this A' (5:1-14) chiastic unit. "Chosen [ἐκλεκτοῖς] sojourners" (1:1), "grace to you and peace [εἰρήνη]" (1:2), "ready to be revealed [ἀποκαλυφθῆναι]" (1:5), "though briefly [ὀλίγον] now" (1:6), "attaining [κομιζόμενοι] the end of your faith" (1:9), and "to whom it was revealed [ἀπεκαλύφθη]" (1:12) occur in the A unit. These progress to "the glory that is going to be revealed [ἀποκαλύπτεσθαι]" (5:1), "you will attain [κομιεῖσθε] the unfading crown" (5:4), "suffered briefly [ὀλίγον]" (5:10), "chosen together [συνεκλεκτή]" (5:13), and "peace [εἰρήνη] to you" (5:14) in the A' unit. In addition, with the reference to "sufferings [παθημάτων]" (5:1) near the beginning of this unit, the audience hear the transitional term that links this unit with the preceding unit (4:12-19), which referred to "suffering [πάσχοντες]" (4:19) near its conclusion.

5:1-5a (A): Encouragement as Witness of the Sufferings of Christ

The audience hear the A element (5:1-5a) of this chiastic unit as a chiastic pattern in itself:

a) The *elders* then among you I encourage, as a fellow elder and witness of the sufferings of Christ, and a sharer in the *glory* that is going to be revealed (5:1),

  b) *shepherd* the *flock* of God among you, overseeing not as under compulsion but willingly according to God, not for shameful profit but eagerly, not as lording it over the ones allotted (5:2-3a),

  b') but becoming examples to the *flock*, and when the *chief shepherd* is manifested (5:3b-4a),

a') you will attain the unfading crown of the *glory*. Likewise, you who are younger, be subjected to the *elders* (5:4b-5a).

---

1. For the establishment of 1 Pet 5:1-14 as a chiasm, see ch. 1.

1 Peter 5:1-14

At the center of this chiastic sub-unit the audience experience a pivot of parallels from the b) to the b') sub-element involving the only occurrences in 1 Peter of the terms "shepherd" and "flock." "Shepherd [ποιμάνατε] the flock [ποίμνιον]" (5:2) progresses to "becoming examples to the flock [ποιμνίου]" (5:3b) and "when the chief shepherd [ἀρχιποίμενος] is manifested" (5:4a). They then hear a progression of parallels from the a) to the a') sub-element involving the only occurrences in 1 Peter of the term "elders" and in this sub-unit of the term "glory." "The elders [πρεσβυτέρους]" and "a sharer in the glory [δόξης]" (5:1) progress to "crown of the glory [δόξης]" (5:4b) and "elders [πρεσβυτέροις]" (5:5a).

Recalling the hope for eternal life (1:3, 21) that is "within you [ἐν ὑμῖν]" (3:15), but also the burning of suffering "among you [ἐν ὑμῖν]" (4:12), the audience now hear Peter address the elders, the leaders of the communities, "among you" (ἐν ὑμῖν) with the exhortation, "I encourage [παρακαλῶ]" (5:1a).[2] He had previously addressed the whole audience with the exhortation, "I encourage [παρακαλῶ] you as aliens and sojourners to keep away from fleshly desires that are waging war against the soul" (2:11). In continuity with the prophets, in whom the Spirit of "Christ" (Χριστοῦ) was "testifying beforehand" (προμαρτυρόμενον) to the "sufferings" (παθήματα) for "Christ" (Χριστόν) and the "glories" (δόξας) after them (1:11), it is as a fellow elder and "witness" (μάρτυς) of the "sufferings" (παθημάτων) of "Christ [Χριστοῦ]" (5:1b) that Peter addresses the elders among his audience.[3]

Peter is not only a witness of the sufferings of Christ (5:1b) but also a "sharer" (κοινωνός) in the "glory" (δόξης) that is going to be "revealed [ἀποκαλύπτεσθαι]" (5:1c). This recalls his exhortation for the audience, as "you" who are "sharing" (κοινωνεῖτε) in the "sufferings" (παθήμασιν) of "Christ" (Χριστοῦ), to "rejoice" (χαίρετε), so that at the "revelation" (ἀποκαλύψει) of his "glory" (δόξης) "you" may continue the worship of "rejoicing" (χαρῆτε) and exulting (4:13). It reaffirms that the audience in the power of God through faith are being guarded for a salvation ready to be "revealed" (ἀποκαλυφθῆναι) in the last time (1:5). Consequently, the audience are even now to continue to be engaged in the liturgical worship of exulting not only in God (1:6) but for Christ with a "joy" (χαρᾷ) indescribable and "glorified" (δεδοξασμένῃ) by God (1:8).

---

2. For a discussion of elders in early Christianity, see Campbell, *Elders*.

3. "By appealing to the 'elders' as 'co-elder,' he affirms a collegiality that puts him on an equal rather than superior footing with the elders in respect to leadership and responsibility. This in turn provides a common and courteous basis for the exhortation that follows. He is thus exhorting fellow-leaders as peers, with perhaps the further implication that they too are witnesses to the suffering of the Christ and sharers in the glory to be revealed" (Elliott, *1 Peter*, 818).

1 Peter, 2 Peter, and Jude

Peter encourages the elders "among you [ἐν ὑμῖν]" (5:1a) to "shepherd" (ποιμάνατε) the "flock" (ποίμνιον) of God "among you" (ἐν ὑμῖν), "overseeing" (ἐπισκοποῦντες) not as under compulsion but willingly according to God, not for shameful profit but eagerly (5:2), not as lording it over the ones allotted, but becoming examples to the "flock [ποιμνίου]" (5:3). This implies that the elders are to imitate and extend the shepherding role of Christ, as it recalls the affirmation that the audience like sheep were being led astray, but have turned now to Christ as the "shepherd" (ποιμένα) and "overseer" (ἐπίσκοπον) of their souls (2:25). As those now dead, to whom the gospel had been proclaimed, may live "according to God" (κατὰ θεόν) in the Spirit (4:6), so the elders are to shepherd the flock of God "according to God" (κατὰ θεόν), rather than "lording it over" (κατακυριεύοντες) them. As the suffering Christ left the audience a model to closely follow in his footsteps (2:21), so the elders are to become examples for the flock to follow.

By "becoming" (γινόμενοι) examples to the flock (5:3), the elders can play their role in guiding the audience to "become" (γένησθε) zealots for the good (3:13), so that the prayerful supplications of their liturgical worship may be heard by the Lord (3:12). The examples the elders are to become may also aid the audience to "become" (ἐγενήθητε) children of the exemplary Sarah by performing the ethical worship of doing good and not fearing any intimidation (3:6). And, by becoming examples, the elders may lead the audience to "become" (γενήθητε) holy as God is holy in all of their conduct (1:15), which serves as ethical worship, as in reverent fear of God they conduct the time of their sojourning (1:17).

Christ was foreknown by God before the foundation of the world but "manifested" (φανερωθέντος) at the last of these times for the sake of the audience (1:20). And so the elders, who are to "shepherd" (ποιμάνατε) the flock which is the audience (5:2), are promised that when Christ, as the "chief shepherd" (ἀρχιποίμενος), is "manifested" (φανερωθέντος) in the future, they will attain the unfading crown of the "glory [δόξης]" (5:4), the "glory" (δόξης) that is going to be revealed and of which Peter is a sharer (5:1). That "you will attain" (κομιεῖσθε) the unfading and thus eternal crown of glory, the "glory" (δόξαν) of eternal life God gave to the risen Christ (1:21), resonates with the audience as a whole "attaining" (κομιζόμενοι) the end of their faith, salvation of souls (1:9). It assures the elders that their faith will be found for the worship of praise, "glory" (δόξαν), and honor at the final revelation of Jesus Christ (1:7).[4]

---

4. "The other uses of 'glory' in 1 Peter make it clear, in fact, that the 'crown of glory' promised here is not for elders alone, but for all who share in the Christian hope" (Michaels, *1 Peter*, 287).

"Likewise" (ὁμοίως; cf. 3:1, 7), those in the audience who are younger are exhorted to be subjected to the "elders [πρεσβυτέροις]" (5:5a), the "elders [πρεσβυτέρους]" (5:1) who are to shepherd them as members of the flock of God (5:2). That "you are to be subjected" (ὑποτάγητε) to the elders associates those who are younger with the wives who are "being subject" (ὑποτασσόμεναι) to their husbands (3:1, 5), and with the house servants who are "being subject" (ὑποτασσόμενοι) to their masters in all reverent fear or worship of God (2:18). It resonates with the exhortation for the whole audience to "be subject" (ὑποτάγητε) to every human institution on account of the Lord (2:13), as part of their ethical worship of offering up spiritual sacrifices acceptable to God through Jesus Christ (2:5), who is at the right of God with angels, authorities, and powers having been "subjected" (ὑποταγέντων) to him (3:22).

5:5b (B): God Opposes the Proud but to the Humble Gives Grace

The audience as a whole are again exhorted: "And all of you clothe yourselves with humility toward one another, for 'God opposes the proud but to the humble gives grace [Prov 3:34 LXX]'" (5:5b). That all in the audience are to clothe themselves with humility toward "one another" (ἀλλήλοις) resonates with the exhortations for the audience to be hospitable for "one another" (ἀλλήλους) without complaining (4:9), and to love "one another" (ἀλλήλους) constantly (1:22) as part of their ethical worship. That to the humble God "gives" (δίδωσιν) "grace" (χάριν) was confirmed and exemplified when God raised Christ from the dead and "gave" (δόντα) him the glory of eternal life (1:21).[5] It bolsters the exhortation for the audience to completely hope upon the "grace" (χάριν) that is to be borne to them by God at the revelation of Jesus Christ (1:13). And it reinforces the exhortation for husbands to show honor to their wives as fellow heirs of the "grace" (χάριτος) of eternal life that is given by God, so that the prayers that are part of the audience's liturgical worship may not be hindered (3:7).

5:6–9a (B'): Be Humbled under God and Oppose Your Opponent the Devil

The exhortation regarding the humility of the audience (5:5b) continues: "Be humbled then under the mighty hand of God, so that he may exalt you

---

5. That these are the only occurrences of the verb "give" (δίδωμι) in 1 Peter enhances this connection.

in time, casting all your anxiety upon him, because from him there is care concerning you. Be sober, be watchful. Your opponent the devil, roaring like a lion, is going around seeking someone to devour, whom you are to oppose, as strong in the faith" (5:6-9a). At this point, the audience experience a pivot of parallels from the B (5:5b) to the B' (5:6-9a) element at the center of this chiastic unit. "With humility [ταπεινοφροσύνην]" and "God opposes [ἀντιτάσσεται] the proud but to the humble [ταπεινοῖς] gives grace" (5:5b) progress to "be humbled [ταπεινώθητε]" (5:6), "your opponent [ἀντίδικος] the devil" (5:8), and "whom you are to oppose [ἀντίστητε]" (5:9a).

The audience, who are to clothe themselves with "humility" toward one another (5:5b), are also to be "humbled" under the "mighty" (κραταιάν) hand of God (5:6a). This recalls how they have been led to join Peter in doxological worship by professing that in all things that they do as their ethical worship God may be glorified through Jesus Christ, to whom is the glory and the "might" (κράτος) for the ages of the ages, amen!" (4:11). The mighty God may thus exalt the humble audience "in time [ἐν καιρῷ]" (5:6b), that is, "in the last time" (ἐν καιρῷ ἐσχάτῳ) when salvation to eternal life (1:3) is ready to be revealed for the audience, who in the power of God are being guarded through faith (1:5).[6]

That the audience are to cast all their anxiety "upon him" (ἐπ' αὐτόν), God (cf. Ps 54:23 LXX), because from "him" (αὐτῷ) there is care concerning them (5:7) resonates with the affirmation that the audience have turned now "to the shepherd" (ἐπὶ τὸν ποιμένα) and overseer of their souls (2:25), namely Christ as their divine Lord (3:15). It also resonates with the scriptural assertion that whoever believes "in it" (ἐπ' αὐτῷ), that is, in Christ as the cornerstone chosen and esteemed by God, will never be put to shame by God (2:6).

In contrast to the idolatrous conduct of the Gentiles, which includes drunkenness and drinking bouts (4:3), the audience are to "be sober" (νήψατε) and watchful (5:8a). This reinforces the exhortation for them to be serious and "be sober" (νήψατε) for the prayers that are part of their liturgical worship (4:7). It coincides with the exhortation for them, "being sober" (νήφοντες), to completely hope upon the grace to be borne to them by God at the revelation of Jesus Christ (1:13). The audience's opponent the devil, roaring like a lion, is going around "seeking" (ζητῶν) someone to devour (5:8b).[7] In contrast, each member of the audience is to "seek" (ζητησάτω)

---

6. "First Peter offers no respite from abuse and humble status within the normal sequences of history. God will lift up these Christians only on the last day" (Donelson, *I & II Peter*, 149). "Thus, in the context of this letter, to be exalted is equivalent to being raised, honored, glorified, saved, and receiving a crown of glory" (Elliott, *1 Peter*, 851).

7. Paschke, "Historical Background for 1 Peter 5.8," 489-500. "The context in 1 Peter suggests that the devil 'devours someone' by tempting them away from their

1 Peter 5:1-14

peace and pursue it (3:11), for the eyes of the Lord are upon the righteous and his ears attuned and attentive for the prayerful supplication that is part of the audience's liturgical worship (3:12).[8]

Just as God "opposes" (ἀντιτάσσεται) the proud (5:5b), the audience, as those strong in the "faith" (πίστει), are to "oppose" [ἀντίστητε]" (5:9a) the "opponent" (ἀντίδικος), the devil (5:8). This reminds the audience that their "faith" (πίστιν) and hope are for God (1:21), that they are attaining the end of their "faith" (πίστεως), salvation of souls (1:9), and that they are in the power of God being guarded through "faith" (πίστεως) for a salvation ready to be revealed in the last time (1:5). Indeed, the refinement of their "faith" (πίστεως) through the fire of the trials they may suffer is so that it may be found for the worship of praise, glory, and honor at the revelation of Jesus Christ (1:7).

5:9b-14 (A'): Sufferings, Encouraging, and Bearing Witness

The audience hear the A' element (5:9b-14) of this chiastic unit as a chiastic pattern in itself:

a) knowing that the same kinds of sufferings are being undergone by your brotherhood throughout the world. The God of *all* grace, who called you for his eternal glory *in Christ* Jesus, after you have suffered briefly, will himself restore, confirm, strengthen, establish. To him be the might for the ages, amen! Through Silvanus, *to you* the faithful brother, as I reckon, through a few things I have written, encouraging and bearing witness that this is the true grace of God for which you are to remain firm (5:9b-12).
b) The chosen together in Babylon *greet* you (5:13a)
c) and Mark my son (5:13b).[9]

Christian lives" (Donelson, *I & II Peter*, 150). "The roar of a lion would scatter a flock of sheep in panic, so this threatening image coheres well with the shepherd-flock motif in 5:1-5. When a lion is on the prowl, neither the shepherd nor the sheep sleep, but both are alert and watchful" (Jobes, *1 Peter*, 314). "While this is the only place in the Bible that the devil is so identified, the figure of a lion does appear in the OT to describe the opponents of Israel" (Achtemeier, *1 Peter*, 341).

8. That these are the only occurrences of the verb "seek" (ζητέω) in 1 Peter enhances this connection.

9. "Although the name 'Mark' is common in the Greco-Roman world, the reference to 'Mark my son' has traditionally been understood as referring to the John Mark of Acts. This Mark was part of the early Jerusalem community (Acts 12:12) and accompanied Paul and Barnabas on early missionary journeys (12:25; 15:37, 39). He is also mentioned several times (Col 4:10; 2 Tim 4:11; Phlm 24) as part of the Pauline entourage. In later tradition Papias names him as the interpreter of Peter and, in that role, the immediate author of the Gospel of Mark. The Mark named in 1 Peter as 'my son' fits nicely in that tradition" (Donelson, *I & II Peter*, 156).

1 Peter, 2 Peter, and Jude

b') *Greet* one another with a kiss of love (5:14a).
a') Peace *to you all* who are *in Christ* (5:14b).

After the central and unparalleled c) sub-element, "and Mark my son" (5:13b), the audience experience a pivot of parallels from the b) to the b') sub-element involving the only occurrences in 1 Peter of the verb "greet." "The chosen together in Babylon greet [ἀσπάζεται] you" (5:13a) progresses to "greet [ἀσπάσασθε] one another" (5:14a). They then hear a progression of parallels from the a) to the a') sub-element involving the only occurrences in this sub-unit of the expressions "all," "in Christ," and "to you." "The God of all [πάσης] grace" (5:10), "eternal glory in Christ [ἐν Χριστῷ] Jesus" (5:10), and "to you [ὑμῖν] the faithful brother" (5:12) progress to "peace to you [ὑμῖν] all [πᾶσιν] who are in Christ [ἐν Χριστῷ]" (5:14b).

At this point the audience hear progressions, via the chiastic parallels, from the A (5:1-5a) to the A' (5:9b-14) element of this chiastic unit. "Among you [ὑμῖν]" (5:1, 2), "I encourage [παρακαλῶ]" (5:1), "witness [μάρτυς] of the suffering of Christ [Χριστοῦ]" (5:1), "in the glory [δόξης]" (5:1), and "crown of the glory [δόξης]" (5:4) occur in the A element. These occurrences progress to "sufferings [παθημάτων]" (5:9b), "eternal glory [δόξαν] in Christ [Χριστῷ]" (5:10), "to you [ὑμῖν]" (5:12, 14), "encouraging [παρακαλῶν] and bearing witness [ἐπιμαρτυρῶν]" (5:12), and "in Christ [Χριστῷ]" (5:14).

In addition, the audience experience the a) sub-element (5:9b-12) of this chiastic sub-unit (5:9b-14) as yet another chiastic pattern in itself:

(a) knowing that the same kinds of sufferings are being undergone by your *brotherhood* throughout the world. The *God* of all *grace* (5:9b-10a),
 (b) who called you for *his eternal* glory in Christ Jesus, after you have suffered briefly, will *himself* restore, confirm, strengthen, establish (5:10b).
 (b') To *him* be the might for the *ages*, amen (5:11)!
(a') Through Silvanus, to you the faithful *brother*, as I reckon, through a few things I have written, encouraging and bearing witness that this is the true *grace* of God for which you are to remain firm (5:12).

At the center of this chiastic sub-unit the audience experience a pivot of parallels from the (b) to the (b') sub-element involving the only occurrences in this sub-unit of the third person singular masculine pronoun and expressions for "eternal/ages." "His [αὐτοῦ] eternal [αἰώνιον] glory" (5:10b) and "himself [αὐτός]" (5:10b) progress to "to him [αὐτῷ] be the might of the ages [αἰῶνας]" (5:11). They then hear a progression of parallels from the (a) to the (a') sub-element involving the only occurrences in this subunit of expressions regarding "brother" and of the terms "God" and "grace." "Your brotherhood [ἀδελφότητι]" (5:9b) and "the God [θεός] of all grace

1 Peter 5:1-14

[χάριτος]" (5:10a) progress to "faithful brother [ἀδελφοῦ]" (5:12) and "the true grace [χάριν] of God [θεοῦ]" (5:12).

The audience are "knowing" (εἰδότες) that not with perishable things, silver or gold, have they been ransomed from their futile conduct inherited from ancestral fathers (1:18), but with the precious blood of Christ (1:19). Similarly, they are "knowing" (εἰδότες) that the same kinds of sufferings they are experiencing are being undergone by their brotherhood of believers throughout the world (5:9b). They are thus to appreciate that whereas their knowledge regarding the precious blood of Christ's sacrificial worship ransomed them from the idolatrous worship of their nonbelieving ancestors, their knowledge regarding their sufferings caused by nonbelievers unites them more closely with their fellow believers throughout the world.[10]

The "sufferings" (παθημάτων) which the audience and their fellow believers are undergoing (5:9b) are the "sufferings" (παθημάτων) of Christ of which Peter is a witness (5:1), the "sufferings" (παθήμασιν) of Christ in which they are sharing, but in which they may engage in the worship of rejoicing and exulting (4:13). They are to appreciate that the brotherhood of believers are undergoing these sufferings throughout the "world [κόσμῳ]" (5:9b), the "world" (κόσμου) before whose foundation Christ was foreknown by God but now manifested at the last of these times for the sake of the audience (1:20). In contrast to this external world as the place of sufferings, the "adornment" or "world" (κόσμος) of the wives, who are to be models for the audience, is not to be an external one (3:3), but rather the inner human being of the heart in the imperishableness of the gentle and quiet spirit, which is before God of great value as ethical worship (3:4).

To the audience who are to be humbled under the mighty hand of the God (5:6) who gives "grace" (χάριν) to the humble (5:5b), Peter promises that the God of all "grace" (χάριτος), who called them for his eternal glory in Christ Jesus, will give them the grace of restoring, confirming, strengthening, and establishing them, after they have suffered briefly (5:10).[11] That God "called" (καλέσας) the audience "for" (εἰς) his eternal glory in Christ Jesus reminds them that "you were called" (ἐκλήθητε) by God "to" (εἰς) this—to the ethical worship of returning blessing for insult, so that they might inherit a blessing from God (3:9). And it reminds them that "you were called" (ἐκλήθητε) by

---

10. That these are the only occurrences of the verb "know" (οἶδα) in 1 Peter enhances this connection.

11. "This grace is varied in its manifestations (4:10) so that 'all' covers every aspect of grace experienced by the believers from the time of their baptism onward" (Elliott, *1 Peter*, 864). "This, he concludes, is how God 'gives grace to the humble.' The benediction turns out to be a promise of victory or vindication" (Michaels, *1 Peter*, 302).

God "to" (εἰς) this (2:21a)—to endure in suffering for doing good, which is the grace of an ethical worship pleasing in the sight of God (2:20).

In addition, it reinforces the exhortation for the audience to proclaim, in and through both their liturgical and ethical worship, the virtues of the God who "called" (καλέσαντος) them out of darkness "for" (εἰς) his marvelous light (2:9). And it bolsters the exhortation for them, according to the Holy One who "called" (καλέσαντα) them, to become holy as he is holy (1:15). Becoming holy includes their liturgical worship in which "you call upon" (ἐπικαλεῖσθε) God as the Father who called them to be holy, as well as their ethical worship of conducting the time of their sojourning in reverent fear of God (1:17).

The audience are to appreciate that the eternal "glory" (δόξαν) in Christ Jesus for which the God of all grace called them (5:10) is the unfading crown of the "glory" (δόξης) their exemplary elders will attain (5:4) and the "glory" (δόξης) that is going to be revealed of which Peter is a sharer (5:1). It is the same "glory" (δόξαν) of eternal life that God gave Christ when he raised him from the dead (1:21). And it reminds the audience that once their faith has been refined through the fire of suffering trials, it may be found for the "glory" (δόξαν) of eternal life at the revelation of Jesus Christ (1:7). In response to this eternal glory Peter has already led the audience in doxological worship of the God who in all things may be "glorified" (δοξάζηται) through Jesus Christ, to whom is the "glory" (δόξα) for ages of the ages, amen! (4:11).

That God will restore, confirm, strengthen, and establish the audience after they have suffered "briefly [ὀλίγον]" (5:10) recalls that though they may "briefly" (ὀλίγον) now be saddened in various trials, they are nevertheless engaged in the worship of exulting in God (1:6) and for Jesus Christ (1:8).[12] The notice of the audience having "suffered" (παθόντας) briefly reinforces the exhortation for them to entrust to the faithful Creator their souls in good-doing as those who are "suffering" (πάσχοντες) according to the will of God (4:19). They are not to let anyone of them "suffer" (πασχέτω) for evildoing (4:15). Rather, they are to arm themselves with the same attitude as Christ who "suffered" (παθόντος) in the flesh, for the one "suffering" (παθών) in the flesh is separated from the sin that prevents proper worship of God (4:1). Indeed, Christ once concerning sins "suffered" (ἔπαθεν), so that he might lead the audience to the worship of God (3:18).

---

12. "Saying that the suffering will last a short time does not mean that it will only last for a brief interval during the earthly sojourn of believers. The short time period refers to the entire interval before eternal glory commences. The sufferings of this life will seem as if they lasted a little while when compared to the eternal glory that endures forever" (Schreiner, *1, 2 Peter*, 245). "Peter probably uses these four [restore, confirm, strengthen, establish] as a rhetorical crescendo to refer to the complete act of God at the consummation of all things" (Jobes, *1 Peter*, 316).

1 Peter 5:1-14

Furthermore, even if the audience should "suffer" (πάσχοιτε) on account of the righteousness of doing God's will, as part of their ethical worship, they are blessed by God (3:14). Christ "suffered" (ἔπαθεν) on behalf of the audience, leaving them a model of ethical worship to follow (2:21), as one who, though "suffering" (πάσχων), handed himself over to the God who judges righteously (2:23). That Christ offered up our sins in a sacrificial worship of atonement enables us believers, to sins having died, to the righteousness that serves as ethical worship of God to live both now and eternally (2:24). Indeed, if anyone in the audience "suffers" (πάσχων) sorrows unjustly (2:19), and if, doing good and "suffering" (πάσχοντες), the audience endure, then this is the grace of an ethical worship pleasing in the sight of God (2:20).

In response to the promise of the grace of restoring, confirming, strengthening, and establishing the audience from the God of all grace, who called them for his "eternal" (αἰώνιον) glory in Christ Jesus (5:10), Peter invites them to join him in an exuberant act of doxological worship: "To him be the might [κράτος] for the ages [αἰῶνας], amen!" (5:11). This echoes and reverberates with the previous exuberant act of doxological worship that in all things that the audience do in and through both their liturgical and ethical worship God may be glorified through Jesus Christ, to whom is the glory and the "might" (κράτος) for the "ages" (αἰῶνας) of the "ages" (αἰώνων), amen! (4:11). The audience are thus to appreciate that such doxological worship serves as a fitting response to their having been given new birth by God for the glory of eternal life through a living word of God that is abiding (1:23), indeed, abiding for "eternity [αἰῶνα]" (1:25).[13]

Peter has written this letter through Silvanus, whom he reckons as a faithful brother to the audience (5:12a).[14] That he is a "faithful" (πιστοῦ) brother closely associates him with the audience as those who through Christ are "faithful" (πιστούς) for God (1:21), those who are to entrust to the "faithful" (πιστῷ) Creator their souls in good-doing (4:19). And that Silvanus is a faithful "brother" (ἀδελφῷ) means that he is part of the "brotherhood" (ἀδελφότητι) of believers throughout the world who are undergoing the same kinds of sufferings as the audience (5:9b). The audience are thus to appreciate Silvanus's significant qualifications for his authoritative role in the communication of the letter to them.[15]

---

13. "The letter body is closed by a doxology. As the letter body began with a eulogy, a thankful praise of God, so it also closes with worshipful praise; everything that was said in the work comes from the praise of God and leads to it" (Feldmeier, *First Letter*, 252).

14. "Silas is mentioned often in Acts as Paul's partner in ministry. He most likely was the same person as the Silvanus mentioned in 2 Cor 1:19; 1 Thess 1:1; 2 Thess 1:1 and here" (Schreiner, *1, 2 Peter*, 247).

15. "The preposition διά (through) in epistolary closings often designates the

In continuity with the scriptural will of God, according to which it is "written" (γέγραπται), "You shall be holy, for I am holy (Lev 19:2)" (1:16), Peter declares that "I have written" (ἔγραψα) this letter to the audience (5:12a).[16] Through it he is "encouraging" (παρακαλῶν) the whole audience, as "I encourage" (παρακαλῶ) the elders among them (5:1). This recalls his exhortation that "I encourage" (παρακαλῶ) you as aliens and sojourners to keep away from the fleshly desires that are waging war against the soul (2:11), and they are to keep their conduct among the Gentiles praiseworthy, so that it might inspire these nonbelievers to the worship of glorifying God on the day of visitation (2:12).

The Peter who is a "witness" (μάρτυς) of the sufferings of Christ (5:1) wrote the letter as one "bearing witness" (ἐπιμαρτυρῶν) that this is the true "grace" (χάριν) of God, the God of all "grace [χάριτος]" (5:10) who gives "grace" (χάριν) to the humble (5:5), for which "you are to remain or stand firm [στῆτε]" (5:12). This includes that you oppose or "stand against" (ἀντίστητε) the devil (5:9). It reinforces the exhortation for the audience to be praiseworthy stewards of the varied "grace" (χάριτος) of God (4:10), the "grace" (χάριτος) of eternal life (3:7), so that in all the things that they do in and through both their liturgical and ethical worship God may be glorified through Jesus Christ (4:11). It resonates with the exhortation that they are to completely hope upon the "grace" (χάριν) to be borne by God to them, the "grace" (χάριτος) that the prophets indicated as for them (1:10), at the revelation of Jesus Christ (1:13). It is the "grace" (χάρις) that Peter prayed may be multiplied for the audience (1:2).

That the audience are to remain firm for this "true" (ἀληθῆ) "grace" (χάριν) of God (5:12) refers not only to the grace that comes from God but to the grace that is given to God in and through their worship. Having purified their souls in the obedience to the "truth [ἀληθείας]" (1:22) of having been given the divine grace of a new birth to eternal life (1:23) for sincere brotherly affection, they are from a clean heart to love one another constantly (1:22) as part of their ethical worship of God.[17] It is the "grace" (χάρις) of ethical worship of God, if on account of a conscience toward God

---

carrier of the letter" (Donelson, *I & II Peter*, 154). "Silvanus would have been intimate enough with the author and production of this letter that, carrying it from one place to the next, he could properly serve as a personal link between Peter and his audience and appropriately 'perform' the letter—reading it aloud, modulating his voice and gesticulating for emphasis" (Green, *1 Peter*, 182).

16. That these are the only occurrences of the verb "write" (γράφω) in 1 Peter enhances this connection.

17. That these are the only occurrences of expressions regarding "truth" in 1 Peter enhances this connection.

1 Peter 5:1-14

anyone of them bears up, suffering sorrows unjustly (2:19). Indeed, if doing good and suffering they endure, this is the "grace" (χάρις) of ethical worship pleasing in the sight of God (2:20).

Recalling that in the days of Noah an ark was furnished as grace from God "for the purpose of which" (εἰς ἥν) a few souls were saved (3:20), this is the true grace "for which" (εἰς ἥν) the audience are to remain firm (5:12) for the salvation of their souls (1:9) from the sufferings they share with Christ (4:1).[18] It is the true grace that comes from God to save their souls from unjust suffering as the true grace of a new birth given to them by God for eternal life (1:3, 23). But it is also the true grace they are to give to God in and through both their liturgical and ethical worship (2:19-20; 4:10-11). "True grace" thus characterizes the entire letter.[19]

The "chosen together" (συνεκλεκτή), the believers with Peter in "Babylon," a derogatory reference to Rome which characterizes this city as the cause of the audience being oppressed in exile like Israel of old (1:1; 2:11), greet the audience, as does Mark who relates to Peter, one of the elders (5:1), as a younger "son" (5:13).[20] This closely relates these fellow believers with

---

18. That these are the only occurrences of the prepositional phrase "for which" (εἰς ἥν) in 1 Peter, as part of the many occurrences of this preposition with a telic meaning throughout the letter, enhances this connection.

19. "In this verse the author succinctly condenses the heart of his message: those who have been reborn to new life through the resurrection of Jesus Christ and incorporated into the family of faith are what they are by the grace of God. Until their final salvation, they must now live in and through this grace as the graced people of God. Their challenge is to stand fast in the divine grace that shapes their past, present, and their future" (Elliott, *1 Peter*, 880).

20. For the unconvincing view that "the chosen together" refers to a single person, see Applegate, "Co-Elect," 587–604. "Jewish tradition had developed the pattern of calling Rome by the name Babylon. This tradition is probably reflected here, as it is in the book of Revelation. The use of the name 'Babylon' for Rome is an insult and a threat since it equates the historical fall of Babylon with a still-future fall of Rome" (Donelson, *I & II Peter*, 156). "'Babylon' has become a cipher for a world-power hostile to God—in this case, 'Rome,' though 'Babylon' is not so much identified with Rome as used as a brand to characterize what Rome has become. This recapitulates for us the perspective on suffering we find elsewhere in the letter, for it draws attention to the systemic character of harassment and the institutionalization of evil in patterns of sanctioned behavior. The association of the name 'Babylon' with the historical exile of Israel in the sixth century BC, a dispersion from which Israel never fully recovered, also reminds us that 1 Peter is a circular letter written to exiles of the dispersion, bringing us back full-circle to the beginning of the letter (1:1-2)" (Green, *1 Peter*, 183–84). "Rome equals Babylon becomes a beautiful symbol for the capital of the place of exile away from the true inheritance in heaven" (Davids, *First Epistle*, 203). "Just as God's people had been driven out of Jerusalem and sent into exile in Babylon, the capital city of their oppressors centuries before, Peter himself has been driven from Jerusalem by the Roman powers and is sojourning in exile in the capital city of his oppressors" (Jobes, *1 Peter*, 323).

the audience as "chosen" (ἐκλεκτοῖς) sojourners of the diaspora (1:1) and as part of a race "chosen" (ἐκλεκτόν) by God (2:9). Christ was similarly "chosen" (ἐκλεκτόν) and esteemed by God (2:4, 6) as the foundation upon which the audience, and those chosen together with them, are built as a spiritual house for a holy priesthood to offer up the worship of spiritual sacrifices acceptable to God through Jesus Christ (2:5).

Just as the chosen together with Peter, as well as Mark, "greet" (ἀσπάζεται) them (5:13), so the audience, gathered together as a liturgical assembly to listen to the letter, are to "greet" (ἀσπάσασθε) one another with a ritualistic kiss of love (5:14a). They are to greet "one another" (ἀλλήλους) with a kiss of "love" (ἀγάπης) as those who are to clothe themselves with humility toward "one another [ἀλλήλοις]" (5:5), who are to be hospitable to "one another" (ἀλλήλους) without complaining (4:9), and who from a clean heart are to "love" (ἀγαπήσατε) "one another" (ἀλλήλους) constantly (1:22). They are to greet one another with a kiss of love as those who are to keep "love" (ἀγάπην) for each other constant, because "love" (ἀγάπη) covers a multitude of sins (4:8), who are to "love" (ἀγαπᾶτε) the brotherhood of fellow believers (2:17), who are to "love" (ἀγαπᾶν) eternal life (3:10), and who "love" (ἀγαπᾶτε) the Christ they do not see (1:8). Their kiss of love, as part of their liturgical worship, thus coincides with their love for one another and for the Christ through whom they have eternal life, as part of their ethical worship.[21]

The final prayer greeting of the letter that "peace" (εἰρήνη) be to you all in Christ (5:14b) bolsters the exhortation for each of them to seek "peace" (εἰρήνην) and pursue it as part of their ethical worship (3:11), for the ears of the Lord are attentive to the supplication that is part of their liturgical worship (3:12). It forms a literary inclusion with the letter's initial prayer greeting that "peace" (εἰρήνη) be to you multiplied (1:2). The prayer that peace be to you "all" (πᾶσιν) reminds the audience that in "all" (πᾶσιν) the things they do in and through both their liturgical and ethical worship God may be glorified through Jesus Christ, to whom is the glory and might for the ages of the ages,

---

21. "In the Greco-Roman world a 'kiss' could be on the lips or on the cheek. In fact, the word φίλημα could even refer to a hug ... While the imperative to 'greet one another with a kiss of love' may refer to greetings in all moments and places, it is more likely that this is a liturgical moment. The letter is being read during the gathering of the community, perhaps in worship itself. The call for the kiss of love is a call to end the reading and to greet one another" (Donelson, *I & II Peter*, 156). "The 'kiss of love' is embodied theology" (Green, *1 Peter*, 186). "The epistle, itself, in fact, is a kind of 'kiss of love' from Peter and from Rome, as well as 'true grace from God.' The fact that it is accompanied by a formal expression of greeting as it circulates from place to place adds nothing to it, but merely dramatizes its intention. All that remains is for Peter to add his own explicit greeting" (Michaels, *1 Peter* 313).

1 Peter 5:1-14

amen! (4:11).²² And finally, the concluding, climactic prayer that peace be to you all "in Christ" (ἐν Χριστῷ), recalling the "in Christ" (ἐν Χριστῷ) conduct of their ethical worship (3:16), complements the prayer that the God of all grace, who called you for his eternal glory "in Christ" (ἐν Χριστῷ) Jesus, after you have suffered briefly, will himself restore, confirm, strengthen, establish (5:10). "To him be the might for the ages, amen!" (5:11).²³

Summary on 5:1-14

Peter encourages the elders (5:1) to "shepherd" the "flock" of God, "overseeing" not as under compulsion but willingly according to God, not for shameful profit but eagerly (5:2), not as lording it over the ones allotted, but becoming examples to the "flock" (5:3). This implies that the elders are to imitate and extend the shepherding role of Christ, as it recalls the affirmation that the audience like sheep were being led astray, but have turned now to Christ as the "shepherd" and "overseer" of their souls (2:25). As the suffering Christ left the audience a model to closely follow in his footsteps (2:21), so the elders are to become examples for the flock.

That all in the audience are to clothe themselves with humility toward "one another" (5:5) resonates with the exhortations for the audience to be hospitable for "one another" without complaining (4:9), and to love "one another" constantly (1:22) as part of their ethical worship. That to the humble God "gives grace" was confirmed when God raised Christ from the dead and "gave" him the glory of eternal life (1:21). It reinforces the exhortation for husbands to show honor to their wives as fellow heirs of the "grace" of eternal life that is given by God, so that the prayers that are part of the audience's liturgical worship may not be hindered (3:7).

In contrast to the idolatrous conduct of the Gentiles, which includes drunkenness and drinking bouts (4:3), the audience are to "be sober" and watchful (5:8). This reinforces the exhortation for them to "be sober" for the prayers that are part of their liturgical worship (4:7). It coincides with the exhortation for them, "being sober," to completely hope upon the grace

---

22. That these are the only occurrences of the dative masculine plural adjective "all" (πᾶσιν) in 1 Peter enhances this connection.

23. "In his conclusion he has echoed the 'grace and peace' greeting of 1:2b, first with his characterization of the whole epistle as 'true grace' in v 12 and now with a final wish of 'peace.' The idea of peace, although not the actual word, has played a major role in his argument. If 'love' is what believers should show toward each other, 'peace' is their goal in relation to their fellow citizens, even their enemies. Peace, like love and grace and all else to which the epistle aspires, both begins with God and comes from God" (Michaels, *1 Peter*, 313).

to be borne to them by God at the revelation of Jesus Christ (1:13). The audience's opponent the devil, roaring like a lion, is going around "seeking" someone to devour (5:8). In contrast, each member of the audience is to "seek" peace and pursue it (3:11), for the eyes of the Lord are upon the righteous and his ears attuned and attentive for the prayerful supplication that is part of the audience's liturgical worship (3:12).

The "sufferings" which the audience and their fellow believers are undergoing (5:9) are the "sufferings" of Christ of which Peter is a witness (5:1), the "sufferings" of Christ in which they are sharing, but in which they may engage in the worship of rejoicing and exulting (4:13). They are to appreciate that the brotherhood of believers are undergoing these sufferings throughout the "world" (5:9), the "world" before whose foundation Christ was foreknown by God but now manifested at the last of these times for the sake of the audience (1:20). In contrast to this external world as the place of sufferings, the "adornment" or "world" of the wives, who are to be models for the audience, is not to be an external one (3:3), but rather the inner human being of the heart in the imperishableness of the gentle and quiet spirit, which is before God of great value as ethical worship (3:4).

That God "called" the audience "for" his eternal glory in Christ Jesus (5:10) reminds them that "you were called" by God "to" this—to the ethical worship of returning blessing for insult, so that they might inherit a blessing from God (3:9). It reminds them that "you were called" by God "to" this (2:21a)—to endure in suffering for doing good, which is the grace of an ethical worship pleasing in the sight of God (2:20). It also reinforces the exhortation for the audience to proclaim, in and through both their liturgical and ethical worship, the virtues of the God who "called" them out of darkness "for" his marvelous light (2:9). And it bolsters the exhortation for them, according to the Holy One who "called" them, to become holy as he is holy (1:15). Becoming holy includes their liturgical worship in which "you call upon" God as the Father who called them to be holy, as well as their ethical worship of conducting the time of their sojourning in reverent fear of God (1:17).

The audience are to appreciate that the eternal "glory" in Christ Jesus for which the God of all grace called them (5:10) is the unfading crown of the "glory" their exemplary elders will attain (5:4) and the "glory" that is going to be revealed of which Peter is a sharer (5:1). It is the same "glory" of eternal life that God gave Christ when he raised him from the dead (1:21). And it reminds the audience that once their faith has been refined through the fire of suffering trials, it may be found for the "glory" of eternal life at the revelation of Jesus Christ (1:7). In response to this eternal glory Peter has already led the audience in doxological worship of the God who in all things

1 Peter 5:1-14

may be "glorified" through Jesus Christ, to whom is the "glory" for ages of the ages, amen! (4:11).

That God will restore, confirm, strengthen, and establish the audience after they have suffered "briefly" (5:10) recalls that though they may "briefly" now be saddened in various trials, they are nevertheless engaged in the worship of exulting in God (1:6) and for Jesus Christ (1:8). The notice of the audience having "suffered" briefly reinforces the exhortation for them to entrust to the faithful Creator their souls in good-doing as those who are "suffering" according to the will of God (4:19). They are not to let anyone of them "suffer" for evildoing (4:15). Rather, they are to arm themselves with the same attitude as Christ who "suffered" in the flesh, for the one "suffering" in the flesh is separated from the sin that prevents proper worship of God (4:1). Indeed, Christ once concerning sins "suffered," so that he might lead the audience to the worship of God (3:18).

Furthermore, even if the audience should "suffer" on account of the righteousness of doing God's will, as part of their ethical worship, they are blessed by God (3:14). Christ "suffered" on behalf of the audience, leaving them a model of ethical worship to follow (2:21), as one who, though "suffering," handed himself over to the God who judges righteously (2:23). That Christ offered up our sins in a sacrificial worship of atonement enables us believers, to sins having died, to the righteousness that serves as ethical worship of God to live both now and eternally (2:24). Indeed, if anyone in the audience "suffers" sorrows unjustly (2:19), and if, doing good and "suffering," the audience endure, then this is the grace of an ethical worship pleasing in the sight of God (2:20).

In response to the promise of the grace of restoring, confirming, strengthening, and establishing the audience from the God of all grace, who called them for his "eternal" glory in Christ Jesus (5:10), Peter invites them to join him in an exuberant act of doxological worship: "To him be the might for the ages, amen!" (5:11). This echoes and reverberates with the previous exuberant act of doxological worship that in all things that the audience do in and through both their liturgical and ethical worship God may be glorified through Jesus Christ, to whom is the glory and the "might" for the "ages" of the "ages," amen! (4:11). The audience are thus to appreciate that such doxological worship serves as a fitting response to their having been given new birth by God for the glory of eternal life through a living word of God that is abiding (1:23), indeed, abiding for "eternity" (1:25).

The Peter who is a "witness" of the sufferings of Christ (5:1) wrote the letter as one "bearing witness" that this is the true "grace" of God, the God of all "grace" (5:10) who gives "grace" to the humble (5:5), for which "you are to remain or stand firm" (5:12). This includes that you oppose or "stand against" the devil (5:9). It reinforces the exhortation for the audience to be praiseworthy stewards of the varied "grace" of God (4:10), the "grace" of eternal life (3:7), so that in all the things that they do in and through both their liturgical and ethical worship God may be glorified through Jesus Christ (4:11). It resonates with the exhortation that they are to completely hope upon the "grace" to be borne by God to them, the "grace" that the prophets indicated as for them (1:10), at the revelation of Jesus Christ (1:13). It is the "grace" that Peter prayed may be multiplied for the audience (1:2).

That the audience are to remain firm for this "true grace" of God (5:12), which characterizes the entire letter, refers not only to the grace that comes from God but to the grace that is given to God in and through their worship. Having purified their souls in the obedience to the "truth" (1:22) of having been given the divine grace of a new birth to eternal life (1:23) for sincere brotherly love, they are from a clean heart to love one another constantly (1:22) as part of their ethical worship of God. It is the "grace" of ethical worship of God, if on account of a conscience toward God anyone of them bears up, suffering sorrows unjustly (2:19). Indeed, if doing good and suffering they endure, this is the "grace" of ethical worship pleasing in the sight of God (2:20).

Just as the chosen together with Peter, as well as Mark, "greet" them (5:13), so the audience, gathered together as a liturgical assembly to listen to the letter, are to "greet" one another with a ritualistic kiss of love (5:14). They are to greet "one another" with a kiss of "love" as those who from a clean heart are to "love one another" constantly (1:22), who are to keep "love" for each other constant, because "love" covers a multitude of sins (4:8), who are to "love" the brotherhood of fellow believers (2:17), who are to "love" eternal life (3:10), and who "love" the Christ they do not see (1:8). Their kiss of love, as part of their liturgical worship, thus coincides with their love for one another and for the Christ through whom they have eternal life, as part of their ethical worship.

The final prayer greeting of the letter that "peace" be to you all in Christ (5:14) bolsters the exhortation for each of them to seek "peace" and pursue it as part of their ethical worship (3:11), for the ears of the Lord are attentive to the supplication that is part of their liturgical worship (3:12). It forms a literary inclusion with the letter's initial prayer greeting that "peace" be to you multiplied (1:2). And finally, the concluding, climactic prayer that peace be to you all "in Christ," recalling the "in Christ" conduct of their ethical worship (3:16), complements the prayer that the God of all grace, who called you for his eternal glory "in Christ" Jesus, after you have suffered briefly, will himself restore, confirm, strengthen, establish (5:10). "To him be the might for the ages, amen!" (5:11).

13

Summary and Conclusion on 1 Peter

*Worship for Life through
the Sufferings of Jesus Christ*

THE PRECEDING CHAPTERS HAVE provided detailed summary conclusions for each of the eleven chiastic units comprising 1 Peter. This final chapter presents a comprehensive overview of how this letter as a liturgical homily or sermon, through the rhetorical dynamics of its various chiastic structures, exhorts its audience to worship for life through the sufferings of Jesus Christ. The term "worship" is to be understood comprehensively as including not only liturgical or cultic worship but also the ethical or moral behavior that complements it, so that the result is a holistic way of worshiping God. The phrase "for life" indicates the goal of this worship as a participation in the risen life of Jesus Christ, for which believers have been given a new birth by God (1:3, 23). They have thus already begun to live this eternal life as they look forward to its full and final manifestation at the revelation of Jesus Christ at the end of time (1:5, 7, 13). And the phrase "through the sufferings of Jesus Christ" indicates that the suffering and death of Jesus Christ is both the model and means by which this worship for eternal life takes place.

The opening chiastic A unit (1:1–13) introduces the sender of the letter as Peter, characterized as an "apostle of Jesus Christ" (1:1a). The audience to whom the letter is sent are characterized as "the chosen sojourners of the diaspora," thus placing them in a situation of hope for God's final restoration (1:1b). After Peter's prayer greeting that *grace* be multiplied to them (1:2), he leads the audience in an act of worship in which they are invited to bless the God who gave believers a new birth for a living *hope* through the resurrection of Jesus Christ from the dead (1:3). At the center of this unit the audience, who are now engaged in the worship of *exulting* in God (1:6), are assured that the *refinement* of their faith, which through the fire of various trials is *refined*, is so that it may be found for the worship of praise, glory, and honor at the revelation of Jesus Christ (1:7), for whom they are also now *exulting* (1:8). In the climactic final element of this unit the audience are exhorted to completely *hope* upon the *grace* that is to be borne to them by God at the revelation of Jesus Christ (1:13) (ch. 2).

At the center of the chiastic B unit (1:14–25) the audience are affirmed as those who through Christ are *faithful for God*, who raised him from the dead and gave him glory, so that their *faith* and hope are *for God* (1:21). They then experience a progression of chiastic parallels involving their worship. As children of *obedience* (1:14), they are exhorted to become holy as God is holy (1:15–16), not only by calling upon God in their liturgical worship, but to conduct the time of their sojourning in the reverent fear of their ethical worship (1:17), as those ransomed from past idolatrous worship not with *perishable* things but with the precious sacrificial blood of Christ (1:18–20). Having purified their souls in the *obedience* to the truth for sincere brotherly affection, from a clean heart they are to perform the ethical worship of loving one another constantly (1:22). Such worship is motivated by their having been given new birth not from a *perishable* but *imperishable* seed, through a living word of God that is abiding for eternal life (1:23–25) (ch. 3).

At the center of the chiastic C unit (2:1–17), through a pivot of parallels, the audience are affirmed as a *people* called to possess a divine inheritance, so that they may perform the worship of proclaiming the virtues of the God who called them out of darkness for the marvelous light of eternal life, as those who were once not a *people* but now are God's *people* (2:9–10). They then experience a progression of chiastic parallels involving worship. As those having removed all *evil* and all *slanders* (2:1), they are being built up as a spiritual house for a holy priesthood to offer up the worship of spiritual sacrifices acceptable to God through Jesus Christ (2:5). They are thus to keep their conduct among the nonbelieving Gentiles praiseworthy, so that in what they *slander* the audience as *evildoers*, observing the praiseworthy works of their ethical worship, they may in turn offer the worship of glorifying God on the day of visitation (2:12). The audience are to be subject to every human institution on account of the Lord, honoring all, loving the brotherhood of believers, fearing God, honoring the king (2:13–17) (ch. 4).

At the center of the chiastic D unit (2:18–21a) the audience experience a pivot of parallels from the question of their *enduring* being mistreated while sinning, rather than *suffering* sorrows unjustly, to the affirmation of their *enduring* for doing good and *suffering* (2:19–20). They then experience a progression of chiastic parallels involving their ethical worship. The house

Summary and Conclusion on 1 Peter

servants, as models for the whole audience as a spiritual household of worship (2:5), are to be subject to their masters in all reverent fear with a conscience oriented to *God*, for this is the *grace* of ethical worship (2:18–19). Indeed, this is the *grace* of an ethical worship pleasing in the sight of *God*, for it is to this kind of worship that the audience were called (2:20c–21a) (ch. 5).

At the center of the chiastic E unit (2:21b–25) the audience hear that Christ, being insulted did not return insult, suffering, he did not threaten, but handed himself over as ethical worship to the God who judges righteously (2:23). They then experience a pivot of parallels from the Christ who did not do *sin* nor was deceit found *in his mouth* (2:22) to the Christ who the *sins* of us offered up as sacrificial worship *in his body* upon the tree, so that to *sins* having died, to the righteousness that serves as ethical worship we might live now and eternally (2:24). Finally, they experience a progression of parallels from the Christ who suffered on behalf of *you*, to you leaving a model to follow closely in his footsteps (2:21b), to the affirmation that like sheep you were being led astray, but you have turned now to the shepherd and overseer of *your* souls (2:25) (ch. 6).

At the center of the chiastic F unit (3:1–7) the audience hear a pivot of parallels in the exhortation that the adornment of wives is not to *be* an external one (3:3), but rather the inner human being of the heart in the imperishableness of the gentle and quiet spirit, which *is* before God of great value as ethical worship (3:4). They then experience a progression of parallels from *wives* being subject *to their own husbands* with conduct that is pure in reverent *fear* of God (3:1–2) to holy *wives* being subject *to their own husbands* (3:5). The audience may become children of the holy wife Sarah by doing good and not *fearing* any intimidation (3:6). Finally, husbands are to show honor to their wives as fellow heirs of the grace of eternal life so that the prayers which are part of the liturgical worship of the audience may not be hindered (3:7) (ch. 7).

After the central and pivotal F unit (3:1–7), unparalleled within the macrochiastic structure organizing the entire letter, the audience hear resonances, via the macrochiastic parallels, between the E (2:21b–25) and the E' (3:8–17) unit. In the E unit the audience hear that Christ did not *do* sin nor was *deceit* found in his mouth (2:22), *being insulted he did not return insult* (2:23), so that to sins having died, to *righteousness* we might live (2:24). Then, in the E' unit, they are exhorted not to return *insult for insult* (3:9) and to separate their lips from speaking *deceit* (3:10). They learn that the face of the Lord is upon those *doing* evil things (3:12), but even if they should suffer on account of *righteousness*, they are blessed by God (3:14).

At the center of the chiastic E' unit (3:8–17) the audience experience a pivot of parallels from the reference to the *fear* of those doing evil to the exhortation not to *fear* or be terrified (3:14). They then hear a progression of chiastic parallels regarding their worship. First, they are informed that the eyes of the *Lord* are upon the righteous and his ears attuned for the prayerful supplication that is part of their liturgical worship (3:12). Then they are exhorted to hold holy the Christ as *Lord* in their hearts (3:15) as part of the in Christ conduct which serves as ethical worship (3:16). For it is better for them to suffer for doing good as part of their ethical worship, if the will of God wants it, than for doing evil (3:17) (ch. 8).

With 1 Pet 3:18-22, the D′ unit within the macrochiastic structure embracing the entire letter, the audience hear resonances of the corresponding D unit (2:18-21a). In the D unit the audience are alerted that if on account of a *conscience* toward *God* anyone bears up, suffering sorrows unjustly (2:19), then this is the grace of an ethical worship pleasing in the sight of God (2:20). Then, in the D′ unit, they are informed that their baptism, a ritualistic part of their liturgical worship, is a pledge of a good *conscience* for *God*, through the resurrection of Jesus Christ (3:21).

At the center of the chiastic D′ unit (3:18-22) the audience experience a pivot of parallels in the reminder that at the time of Noah eight souls were *saved* through water (3:20b), which also as an antitype of baptism now *saves* them (3:21a). They then hear a progression of chiastic parallels involving their worship. First, they are informed that *Christ* once concerning sins suffered, so that he might lead them to the worship of *God* (3:18). Then, they are reminded that their baptism, as a ritualistic act of worship, involved a pledge of a good conscience for *God*, as those saved through the resurrection of Jesus *Christ* (3:21b), who is at the right of *God* in a divinely authoritative position to mediate their worship of God (3:22) (ch. 9).

With 1 Pet 4:1-11, the C′ unit within the macrochiastic structure embracing the entire letter, the audience hear resonances with the corresponding C unit (2:1-17). In the C unit the audience hear that Christ was a living stone rejected by *human beings* (2:4) and that as living stones they are being built up as a spiritual house for a holy priesthood, as also a holy *nation* (2:9), to offer up spiritual sacrifices acceptable to God *through Jesus Christ* (2:5). They are to keep away from fleshly *desires* (2:11), keeping their conduct among *Gentiles* praiseworthy (2:12), for those doing good are to silence the ignorance of foolish *human beings* (2:15). Then, in the C′ unit, the audience are not in the *desires* of *human beings* but in the will of God to spend their time (4:2), for sufficient time has passed for them to accomplish the purpose of the *Gentiles*, which includes their idolatrous *desires* (4:3). Though those who have died were once judged according to *human beings* (4:6), in all things that the audience do in both their liturgical and ethical worship God may be glorified *through Jesus Christ* (4:11).

Summary and Conclusion on 1 Peter

At the center of the chiastic C' unit (4:1-11) the audience experience a pivot of parallels in the exhortation for them to keep *love* for each other constant, because *love* covers a multitude of the sins which prevent true worship (4:8). They then hear a progression of chiastic parallels involving their worship. First, they are to arm themselves with the same attitude as the suffering *Christ*, for the one suffering is separated from the idolatrous sinfulness (4:1) that prevents proper worship in accord with the will of *God* (4:2). Then, as praiseworthy stewards of the varied grace of *God* (4:10), they are drawn into an epistolary act of doxological worship as those who, in and through all the things they do, glorify *God* through Jesus *Christ*, to whom is the glory and might for the ages of the ages, amen! (4:11) (ch. 10).

With 1 Pet 4:12-19, the B' unit within the macrochiastic structure embracing the entire letter, the audience hear resonances with the corresponding B unit (1:14-25). In the B unit the audience are affirmed as those who through Christ are *faithful* for God (1:21). Having purified their *souls* in the obedience to the truth for sincere brotherly love, they are exhorted from a clean heart to love one another constantly as part of their ethical worship (1:22). Then, in the B' unit, they are exhorted, as those who are suffering according to the will of God, to entrust to the *faithful* Creator their *souls* in the good-doing that serves as ethical worship (4:19).

At the center of the chiastic B' unit (4:12-19) the audience experience a pivot of parallels in the exhortation for them *not* to let anyone of them suffer *as* a murderer or thief or evildoer or *as* a troublemaker (4:15). But if *as* a Christian they suffer, they are *not* to be ashamed (4:16). They then hear a progression of chiastic parallels involving their worship. First, to the degree that they are sharing in the sufferings of the Christ they are to rejoice, so that at the revelation of his *glory* they may engage in the worship of rejoicing and exulting (4:13). If they are reproached in the *name* of Christ, they are blessed, because the Spirit of *glory* and of *God* rests upon them (4:14). Then, they are assured that anyone of them who suffers as a Christian is performing the ethical worship of *glorifying God* in this *name* (4:16). Consequently, those who are suffering according to the will of *God* are to entrust to the faithful Creator their souls in the good-doing that is part of their ethical worship (4:19) (ch. 11).

With 1 Pet 5:1-14, the A' unit within the macrochiastic structure embracing the entire letter, the audience hear resonances with the corresponding A unit (1:1-13). In the A unit the audience, as *chosen* sojourners (1:1), are greeted with a prayer that *peace* be multiplied to them (1:2). They are assured that they are being guarded through faith for a salvation ready to be *revealed* in the last time (1:5). Though *briefly* they may be saddened in various trials (1:6), they are *attaining* the end of their faith, salvation of souls (1:9). And it was *revealed* to the prophets that they were serving the audience (1:12). Then, in the A' unit, they are informed that Peter is a sharer in the glory that is going to be *revealed* (5:1), the unfading crown of which they will *attain* (5:4). After they have suffered *briefly*, the God of all grace will restore, confirm, strengthen, and establish them (5:10). Those *chosen together* as fellow believers, who are now with Peter, greet the audience (5:13), who receive from Peter a final prayer greeting of *peace* to all of them who are in Christ (5:14).

At the center of the chiastic A' unit (5:1-14) the audience experience a pivot of parallels in the exhortation for them to clothe themselves with *humility* toward one another, for God *opposes* the proud but to the *humble* gives grace (5:5). They are to be *humbled* then under the mighty hand of God (5:6) and *oppose* their *opponent*, the devil (5:8-9). They then hear a progression of chiastic parallels involving their worship. First, as a *witness* of the *sufferings* of *Christ* and sharer of the *glory* to be revealed (5:1), Peter *encourages* the elders to shepherd the flock according to God, so that it serves as ethical worship (5:2). Then, Peter leads the audience in an act of epistolary worship as he prays that the God of all grace, who called them for his eternal *glory* in *Christ* Jesus, after they have suffered briefly, as part of the *sufferings* undergone by all believers (5:9), will restore, confirm, strengthen, establish. To him be the might of the ages, amen! (5:10-11). Finally, Peter wrote the letter to *encourage* and bear *witness* that this is the grace of God for which they are to remain firm in and through their worship (5:12) (ch. 12).

In conclusion, listening to and experiencing the rhetorical dynamics of the various chiastic patterns throughout the letter of 1 Peter encourages its audience, and all of us as we identify with them, to practice a holistic way of worship. They are to complement their liturgical worship of presently exulting in God and for Christ with their ethical worship of doing good even when they suffer as Christians. They are being built up as a spiritual house for a holy priesthood to offer up the worship of spiritual sacrifices through Jesus Christ, as both the means and model for their worship. His sacrificial worship of offering up our sins for atonement in his body upon the tree is the means making it possible for us to follow his model of ethical worship through suffering, so that to righteousness we believers might live both now and eternally in and through our worship. In short, the letter of 1 Peter functions as a concerted encouragement for its audience to practice, both within and outside of the worshiping assembly, the worship for the eternal life for which we have been given new birth through the sufferings of Jesus Christ.

14

Introduction to 2 Peter

2 Peter: Worship in the Knowledge of Our Lord and Savior Jesus Christ

SIMILARLY AS FOR 1 Peter (see ch. 1), I aim to contribute to a better understanding of 2 Peter in a twofold way. First, I will demonstrate a completely new and comprehensive text-centered structure for 2 Peter, based on its nature as an epistolary homily or sermon composed of rhetorical strategies meant for an oral performance to be heard by its audience gathered together as a worshiping assembly. This structure consists of a series of five microchiastic units arranged in a cohesive and coherent macrochiastic framework embracing the entire letter. Rather than imposing thematic or conceptually based labels upon sections of the text of the letter, as is often done by scholars, my proposal seeks to be as rigorously text-centered as possible. It begins with and is governed by a close reading of or listening to the text, and thus is strictly based upon linguistic criteria within the text itself.

Second, I will present a new proposal for the unifying or organizing theme of 2 Peter in accord with its comprehensive chiastic structure as a key to its interpretation. The subtitle I have chosen for 2 Peter, "worship in the knowledge of our Lord and Savior Jesus Christ," articulates what the whole of 2 Peter, as an epistolary homily or sermon which presupposes that in all probability its audience have heard 1 Peter (see 2 Pet 3:1), is encouraging its audience to maintain. Just as for 1 Peter, the term "worship" is to be understood comprehensively as including not only liturgical but ethical worship.[1] One of the main ways 2 Peter expresses this holistic worship is the "godliness" (εὐσέβεια) based on faith, which is mentioned strategically near

---

1. On the common emphases shared by 1 and 2 Peter, see Green, "Narrating the Gospel," 262–77.

the beginning (2 Pet 1:3, 6, 7) and near the conclusion (3:11) of the letter as an exhortation to maintain proper worship.[2]

The phrase "in the knowledge of our Lord and savior Jesus Christ" refers first of all to the knowledge of Jesus Christ as the Lord and savior who through his divine power has given believers all things necessary for eternal life and the godliness that embraces holistic worship (1:3). But it also refers to the knowledge, provided specifically by 2 Peter itself, of Jesus Christ as the Lord and savior who has granted believers the grace of delaying his final coming as the patience allowing for all to repent (3:9), the patience that the audience are to consider as salvation (3:15). The letter thus climactically concludes first with the exhortation for the audience to "grow in the grace and knowledge of our Lord and savior Jesus Christ" (3:18a). And then, finally, in accord with 2 Peter's overall theme of maintaining proper worship, the audience are led to perform a noteworthy act of doxological worship of Jesus Christ as our Lord and savior—"To him the glory both now and for the day of eternity. Amen!" (3:18b).[3]

In the rest of this chapter I will introduce and explain the text-centered, linguistically based chiastic structures of 2 Peter, and then I will provide preliminary indications of its unifying main theme regarding worship. In subsequent chapters I will present a comprehensive interpretation in accord with the chiastic structures, which illustrate and confirm that 2 Peter is encouraging its implied audience to maintain their worship in the knowledge of our Lord and savior Jesus Christ.

The Five Microchiastic Units of 2 Peter

In what follows I will first demonstrate how the text of 2 Peter naturally divides itself into five distinct literary units based upon their microchiastic structures as determined by very precise linguistic parallels found objectively in the text. Second, I will demonstrate how these five units form a macrochiastic pattern based upon very precise linguistic parallels found objectively in the text of the chiastically paired units. Third, I will point out the

---

2. The term εὐσέβεια is very closely related to the term θεοσέβεια, which Spicq ("θεοσέβεια," 2:196) describes as used "with men and women who worship the true God and conform to his will. The meaning is as much moral as religious, connected with notions of purity, holiness, perfection, wisdom."

3. This focus on worship represents a new proposal for the main purpose and theme of 2 Peter. For past discussions of its main purpose or theme, see Bauckham, *Jude, 2 Peter*, 151–57; Kraftchick, *Jude, 2 Peter*, 81–83; Davids, *2 Peter and Jude*, 132–36; Green, *Jude and 2 Peter*, 150–59; Harvey and Towner, *2 Peter and Jude*, 16–19; Donelson, *I & II Peter*, 209–10.

Introduction to 2 Peter

various transitional words that connect a unit to the unit that immediately precedes it. These various transitional words, which occur at the conclusion of one unit and at the beginning of the following unit, indicate that the chiastic units are heard as a cohesive sequence. These various transitional words are italicized in the translations of the units below.

1. To Stir You Up by Reminder
To Make Every Effort for Godliness (1:1–15)

Granted godliness to become sharers of the divine nature[4]

A 1:1 Symeon Peter, slave and apostle of Jesus Christ [Ἰησοῦ Χριστοῦ], to those who have obtained a faith [πίστιν] just as precious to us in the righteousness [δικαιοσύνῃ] of our [ἡμῶν] God and savior [σωτῆρος] Jesus Christ [Ἰησοῦ Χριστοῦ]. ² May grace to you [ὑμῖν] and peace be multiplied in the acknowledgment of God and of Jesus [Ἰησοῦ] our [ἡμῶν] Lord [κυρίου].

B ³ᵃ As all things to us, the things toward life and godliness, his divine [θείας] power having granted [δεδωρημένης],

C ³ᵇ through the acknowledgment of the one calling us by his own glory and virtue,

B′ ⁴ through which things the precious and great things promised to us have been granted [δεδώρηται], so that through these things you may become sharers of the divine [θείας] nature, escaping the destruction from desire in the world.

A′ ⁵ For this very reason, applying every effort, supply to your faith [πίστει] virtue, to virtue knowledge, ⁶ to knowledge self-control, to self-control endurance, to endurance godliness, ⁷ to godliness brotherly affection, to brotherly affection love. ⁸ For these things, existing and increasing to you [ὑμῖν], make you neither useless nor fruitless for the acknowledgment of our [ἡμῶν] Lord [κυρίου] Jesus Christ [Ἰησοῦ Χριστοῦ], ⁹ for to whomever these things are not present, he is blind, being shortsighted, receiving forgetfulness of the cleansing of his sins of the past. ¹⁰ Therefore rather, brothers, make every effort your call and chosenness as firm to uphold, for, upholding these things, you will never stumble, ¹¹ for thus will be richly supplied to you [ὑμῖν] the entrance for the eternal kingdom

---

4. The main heading of each unit is intended to summarize the unit as it relates to its parallel unit within the overall macrochiastic structure of the letter, while the subheading of each unit is intended to summarize or characterize the microchiastic dimension of each unit. The translations of each unit are my own.

1 Peter, 2 Peter, and Jude

of our [ἡμῶν] Lord [κυρίου] and savior [σωτῆρος] Jesus Christ [Ἰησοῦ Χριστοῦ]. [12] Therefore I intend always to remind you about these things, even though you know and are confirmed in the present truth. [13] I consider it righteous [δίκαιον], as long as I am in this tent, to stir you up by a reminder, [14] knowing that imminent is the removal of my tent, just as also our [ἡμῶν] Lord [κύριος] Jesus Christ [Ἰησοῦς Χριστός] indicated to me. [15] I will also make every effort at all times to have *you*, after my departure, the memory of these things to uphold.

An A-B-C-B'-A' chiastic pattern secures the integrity and distinctness of this first unit (1:1-15). Several linguistic occurrences constitute the parallelism between the A (1:1-2) and A' (1:5-15) elements of this chiasm. First of all, these elements contain the only occurrences in 2 Peter of the term "faith"—"to those who have obtained a faith [πίστιν]" in 1:1 and "supply to your faith [πίστει]" in 1:5. And these elements contain the only occurrences in this unit of "Jesus/Jesus Christ" in 1:1 (2x), 2, 8, 11, 14; of the terms "righteousness/righteous"—δικαιοσύνη in 1:1 and δίκαιον in 1:13; of the pronoun "our"—ἡμῶν in 1:1, 2, 8, 11, 14; of the term "savior"—σωτῆρος in 1:1, 11; and of the dative plural pronoun "you"—ὑμῖν in 1:2, 8, 11.

The only occurrences in 2 Peter of the adjective "divine"—"his divine [θείας] power" in 1:3a and "the divine [θείας] nature" in 1:4, and of the verb "grant"—"having granted [δεδωρημένης]" in 1:3a and "to us have been granted [δεδώρηται]" in 1:4 determine the parallelism between the B (1:3a) and the B' (1:4) elements. And finally, the unparalleled central and pivotal C (1:3b) element contains the only occurrence in 2 Peter of the verb "call"— "the one calling [καλέσαντος] us."

2. By the Holy Spirit Human Beings Spoke Prophecy from God (1:16-21)

Knowing every prophecy of scripture
does not come about by one's own interpretation

A   [16] For not by following craftily devised myths, did we make known [ἐγνωρίσαμεν] to *you* the power and coming of our Lord Jesus Christ, but by having become [γενηθέντες] eyewitnesses of the majesty of that one.

    B   [17a] For he received from God the Father honor and glory, when a voice [φωνῆς] was conveyed [ἐνεχθείσης] to him such as this by the majestic glory,

C ¹⁷ᵇ "My Son, my beloved, is this one for whom I am well pleased."
B' ¹⁸ᵃ And this voice [φωνήν] we ourselves heard conveyed [ἐνεχθεῖσαν] from heaven,
A' ¹⁸ᵇ being with him on the holy mountain. ¹⁹ And we have as very firm the prophetic word, to which you are upholding well, if attending to it as a light appearing in a dreary place, until the day dawns and the morning star arises in your hearts, ²⁰ this first knowing [γινώσκοντες], that every prophecy of scripture does not come about [γίνεται] by one's own interpretation, ²¹ for not by the will of a human being has *prophecy* ever been conveyed, rather, brought along by the Holy Spirit, human beings spoke from God.

The expression "did we make known to you [ὑμῖν]" at the beginning of this unit in 1:16 recalls the expression that "I will also be eager at any time to have you [ὑμᾶς], after my departure, the memory of these things to uphold" at the conclusion of the preceding unit in 1:15. These occurrences of the second person plural pronoun "you" in reference to the audience serve as the transitional terms linking the first unit (1:1-15) to the second unit (1:16-21).

An A-B-C-B'-A' chiastic pattern secures the integrity and distinctness of this second unit (1:16-21). The only occurrences in this unit of expressions regarding "knowing" and "becoming" constitute the parallelism between the A (1:16) and the A' (1:18b-21) elements of this chiasm. "Did we make known [ἐγνωρίσαμεν] to you" and "having become [γενηθέντες] eyewitnesses" occur in 1:16, whereas "this first knowing [γινώσκοντες], that every prophecy of scripture does not come about [γίνεται] by one's own interpretation" occurs in 1:20. The only occurrences in this unit of the term "voice"—"when a voice [φωνῆς] was conveyed" in 1:17a and "this voice [φωνήν] we ourselves heard" in 1:18a—determine the parallelism between the B (1:17a) and the B' (1:18a) elements. Finally, the unparalleled central and pivotal C (1:17b) element contains the only occurrences in 2 Peter of the terms "son" (υἱός), "I" (ἐγώ), and "well pleased" (εὐδόκησα).

3. The Lord Knows How To Rescue the Godly from Trial (2:1-16)

False prophets blaspheming the way of truth will be destroyed

A 2:1 There came about indeed *false prophets* [ψευδοπροφῆται] among the people, as also among you there will be [ἔσονται] false teachers, who will introduce opinions of annihilation, even denying the Master who purchased them, bringing upon themselves imminent annihilation, ² and many will follow [ἐξακολουθήσουσιν] their debaucheries, because of whom the way [ὁδός] of truth will be blasphemed [βλασφημηθήσεται], ³ and in greed [πλεονεξίᾳ] they will exploit you with deceptive words, for whom the judgment [κρίμα] of long ago is not becoming idle and their annihilation is not becoming drowsy. ⁴ For if God did not spare sinning angels [ἀγγέλων] but, in chains of gloom casting them into Tartarus, handed them over to be kept [τηρουμένους] for judgment [κρίσιν], ⁵ and if he did not spare the ancient world, but as the eighth, Noah, a herald of righteousness, he guarded, having brought a deluge upon the world of the ungodly, ⁶ and if, having reduced the cities of Sodom and Gomorrah to ashes, he condemned them to ruin, having placed them as an example of the things intended for the ungodly,

B ⁷ and if the righteous [δίκαιον] Lot, oppressed by the conduct of the disgraceful in debauchery, he rescued [ἐρρύσατο],

B' ⁸ for in what was seen and heard the righteous [δίκαιος] one, residing among them day after day, tormented his righteous [δικαίαν] soul by the lawless works, 9a then the Lord knows how to rescue [ῥύεσθαι] the godly from trial,

A' ⁹ᵇ and to keep [τηρεῖν] the unrighteous to be punished at the day of judgment [κρίσεως], ¹⁰ especially those going after the flesh in desire of defilement and despising lordship, arrogant bold ones, they do not tremble, blaspheming [βλασφημοῦντες] glorious beings, ¹¹ whereas angels [ἄγγελοι], being [ὄντες] greater in strength and power, do not convey a blasphemous [βλάσφημον] judgment [κρίσιν] against them before the Lord. ¹² But these, like irrational animals born by nature for capture and destruction, among things they do not know, blaspheming [βλασφημοῦντες], in their destruction they will also be destroyed, ¹³ suffering harm as recompense for unrighteousness, considering revelry at day a delight, stains and blemishes, delighting in their deceits as they feast together with you, ¹⁴ having eyes full of adultery and unceasing from sin, seducing unstable souls, having a heart trained for greed [πλεονεξίας], accursed children, ¹⁵ abandoning the proper way [ὁδόν], they have been led astray, following [ἐξακολουθήσαντες] the way [ὁδῷ] of Balaam son of Bosor, who loved recompense for unrighteousness, ¹⁶ but he had a rebuke for his own transgression—a mute donkey *talking* with a voice of a human being restrained the madness of the prophet [προφήτου].

The term "false prophets" (ψευδοπροφῆται) at the beginning of this unit in 2:1 recalls the term "prophecy" (προφητεία) near the conclusion of the preceding unit in 1:21. These successive terms regarding true and

Introduction to 2 Peter

false prophecy thus serve as the transitional terms linking the second unit (1:16-21) to the third unit (2:1-16).

An A-B-B'-A' chiastic pattern secures the integrity and distinctness of this third unit (2:1-16). The following linguistic occurrences constitute the parallelism between the A (2:1-6) and A' (2:9b-16) elements of this chiasm: the only occurrences in 2 Peter of the noun "way"—"the way [ὁδός] of truth" in 2:2, "the proper way [ὁδόν]" in 2:15, and "the way [ὁδῷ)]" of Balaam" in 2:15; of expressions regarding blasphemy—"will be blasphemed" (βλασφημηθήσεται) in 2:2, "blaspheming [βλασφημοῦντες] glorious beings" in 2:10, "a blasphemous [βλάσφημον] judgment" in 2:11, and "blaspheming" (βλασφημοῦντες) in 2:12; of the term "greed"—"in their greed [πλεονεξίᾳ]" in 2:3 and "trained for greed [πλεονεξίας]" in 2:14; and of the term "angels"— "sinning angels [ἀγγέλων]" in 2:4 and "angels" (ἄγγελοι) in 2:11.

In addition, the A and A' elements contain the only occurrences in this unit of references to prophets—"false prophets" (ψευδοπροφῆται) in 2:1 and "madness of the prophet [προφήτου]" in 2:16; of the verb "to be"— "there will be [ἔσονται] false teachers" in 2:1 and "being [ὄντες] greater" in 2:11; of "follow"—"many will follow [ἐξακολουθήσουσιν]" in 2:2 and "following [ἐξακολουθήσαντες] the way of Balaam" in 2:15; of the verb "keep"—"to be kept [τηρουμένους]" in 2:4 and "to keep" (τηρεῖν) in 2:9b; and of "judgment"—"the judgment [κρίμα] of long ago" in 2:3, "for judgment [κρίσιν]" in 2:4, "day of judgment [κρίσεως]" in 2:9b, and "a blasphemous judgment [κρίσιν]" in 2:11.

The following linguistic occurrences determine the parallelism between the B (2:7) and B' (2:8-9a) elements: the only occurrences in 2 Peter of the verb "rescue"—"he rescued" (ἐρρύσατο) in 2:7 and "the Lord knows how to rescue [ῥύεσθαι] the godly from trial" in 2:9a; the only occurrences in this unit of the adjective "righteous"—"the righteous [δίκαιον] Lot" in 2:7, "the righteous [δίκαιον] one" in 2:8, and "his righteous [δικαίαν] soul" in 2:8.

4. Do Not Turn Back from the Holy Commandment (2:17-22)

Those promising freedom are themselves slaves of destruction

A   ¹⁷ These [οὗτοί] are waterless springs and mists driven by a storm, for whom [οἷς] the gloom of darkness has been kept.

B   ^{18a} For, *talking* bombastic things of futility, they are seducing with desires of the flesh, debaucheries, those [τούς] barely escaping,

B'   ^{18b} those [τούς] in error residing,

197

1 Peter, 2 Peter, and Jude

A' ¹⁹ promising freedom to them [αὐτοῖς], they themselves are existing as slaves of destruction, for by what someone has been overcome, to this he has been enslaved. ²⁰ For if, escaping the defilements of the world in the acknowledgment of our Lord and savior Jesus Christ, and again becoming entangled in these things, they are overcome, for them [αὐτοῖς] the last things have become worse than the first. ²¹ For it was better for them [αὐτοῖς] not to have acknowledged the way of righteousness than, acknowledging it, to turn back from the holy *commandment* handed over to them [αὐτοῖς]. ²² The saying of the true proverb has happened to them [αὐτοῖς]—"a dog returns to its own vomit," and "a bathed sow to wallowing in the mire."

The expression "talking [φθεγγόμενοι] bombastic things of emptiness" near the beginning of this unit in 2:18a echoes the expression of "a mute donkey talking [φθεγξάμενον] with a human voice" at the conclusion of the preceding unit in 2:16. These are the only occurrences of this verb in 2 Peter, which thus serve as the transitional terms linking the third unit (2:1–16) to the fourth unit (2:17–22).

An A-B-B'-A' chiastic pattern secures the integrity and distinctness of this fourth unit (2:17–22). The following linguistic occurrences constitute the parallelism between the A (2:17) and A' (2:19–22) elements of this chiasm: the only occurrences in this unit of demonstrative pronouns—"these [οὗτοί] are waterless springs" in 2:17, "to this [τούτῳ] he has been enslaved" in 2:19, and "becoming entangled in these things [τούτοις]" in 2:20; and of relative or personal pronouns in the dative plural—"for whom [οἷς] the gloom of darkness has been kept" in 2:17, "promising freedom to them [αὐτοῖς]" in 2:19, "for them [αὐτοῖς] the last things have become worse than the first" in 2:20, "for it was better for them [αὐτοῖς]" in 2:21, "the holy commandment handed over to them [αὐτοῖς]" in 2:21, and "the true proverb has happened to them [αὐτοῖς]" in 2:22. The only occurrences in this unit of the accusative masculine plural definite article determine the parallelism of the B (2:18a) and B' (2:18b) elements—"those [τούς] barely escaping" in 2:18a and "those [τούς] in error residing" in 2:18b.

Introduction to 2 Peter

5. By a Reminder I Am Stirring You Up
To Make Every Effort for Godliness (3:1–18)

Make every effort to be found faultless and flawless in peace

A   3:1 This is now, beloved, the second letter [ἐπιστολήν] I am writing [γράφω] to you [ὑμῖν], in which by a reminder I am stirring up your sincere mind, ² to remember the pronouncements foretold by the holy prophets and the *commandment* of the Lord [κυρίου] and savior through your apostles, ³ this first knowing, that they will come in the last days with mocking, mockers according to their own [ἰδίας] desires going ⁴ and saying, "Where is [ἐστιν] the promise of his coming? For from the time the fathers fell asleep, all things in the same manner are continuing from the beginning of creation." ⁵ For it escapes the notice of these maintaining this that heavens were from long ago and earth from water and through water has consisted by the word of God, ⁶ through which things the world at that time by water, being deluged, was annihilated. ⁷ But the heavens now [νῦν] and the earth by that same word have been stored up for fire, being kept for the day of judgment and annihilation [ἀπωλείας] of the ungodly human beings. ⁸ But let not this one thing escape the notice of you [ὑμᾶς], beloved, that one day before the Lord [κυρίῳ] is like a thousand years and a thousand years like one day. ⁹ The Lord [κύριος] does not delay the promise, as some consider [ἡγοῦνται] a delay, but is being patient [μακροθυμεῖ] for you, not wishing for any to be annihilated, but for all to make room for repentance. ¹⁰ᵃ But the day of the Lord [κυρίου] will come like a thief,

B   ¹⁰ᵇ on which the heavens with a rushing sound will pass away, the elements [στοιχεῖα], being burned [καυσούμενα], will be dissolved [λυθήσεται] and the earth and works on it will be found [εὑρεθήσεται] out. ¹¹ᵃ All these things thus being dissolved [λυομένων],

C   ¹¹ᴮ what sort of persons is it necessary to be existing in holy conduct and godliness,[5]

B'   ¹² awaiting and hastening the coming of the day of God, because of which the heavens, being set on fire, will dissolve [λυθήσονται], and the elements [στοιχεῖα], being burned [καυσούμενα], melt away. ¹³ But new heavens and a new earth according to what was promised by him, we are awaiting, in which righteousness dwells.

---

5. According to Davids, *2 Peter and Jude*, 105, the variant reading that omits "you" (ὑμᾶς) "makes good sense and is found in very ancient manuscripts." See also Metzger, *Textual Commentary*, 637; Green, *Jude and 2 Peter*, 335.

1 Peter, 2 Peter, and Jude

¹⁴ Therefore, beloved, awaiting these things, make every effort to be found [εὑρεθῆναι] faultless and flawless before him in peace

A' ¹⁵ and the patience [μακροθυμίαν] of our Lord [κυρίου] consider [ἡγεῖσθε] as salvation, just as also our beloved brother Paul, according to the wisdom given to him wrote [ἔγραψεν] to you, ¹⁶ as also in all letters [ἐπιστολαῖς], speaking in them about these things, in which are some things hard to understand, which the ignorant and unstable distort, as also the rest of the writings [γραφάς], toward their own [ἰδίαν] annihilation [ἀπώλειαν]. ¹⁷ You [ὑμεῖς] then, beloved, knowing beforehand, be on guard, so that, not being led astray by the error of the disgraceful, you may not fall from your own [ἰδίου] stability, ¹⁸ but grow in grace and knowledge of our Lord [κυρίου] and savior Jesus Christ. To him the glory both now [νῦν] and for the day of eternity. Amen!

The reference to the "commandment [ἐντολῆς] of the Lord" near the beginning of this unit in 3:2 recalls the "holy commandment [ἐντολῆς]" near the conclusion of the preceding unit in 2:21. These are the only occurrences of the noun "commandment" in 2 Peter, which thus serve as the transitional terms linking the fourth unit (2:17–22) to the fifth and final unit (3:1–18).

An A-B-C-B'-A' chiastic pattern secures the integrity and distinctness of this fifth unit (3:1–18). The following linguistic occurrences constitute the parallelism between the A (3:1–10a) and A' (3:15–18) elements of this chiasm: the only occurrences in 2 Peter of the noun "letter"—"the second letter [ἐπιστολήν]" in 3:1 and "in all letters [ἐπιστολαῖς]" in 3:16; of the verb "write"—"I am writing [γράφω]" in 3:1 and "wrote [ἔγραψεν] to you" in 3:15; of the adverb "now"—"the heavens now [νῦν]" in 3:7 and "to him the glory both now [νῦν] and for the day of eternity" in 3:18; and of expressions regarding "patience"—"being patient" (μακροθυμεῖ) in 3:9 and "the patience [μακροθυμίαν] of our Lord" in 3:15.

In addition, the A and A' elements contain the only occurrences in this unit of the second person plural pronoun—"to you [ὑμῖν]" in 3:1, "your [ὑμῶν] apostles" in 3:2, "of you [ὑμᾶς]" in 3:8, "toward you [ὑμᾶς]" in 3:9, "to you [ὑμῖν]" in 3:15, and "you [ὑμεῖς] then" in 3:17; of the term "Lord"—"the Lord [κυρίου] and savior" in 3:2, "before the Lord [κυρίῳ]" in 3:8, "the Lord [κύριος] does not delay" in 3:9, "the day of the Lord [κυρίου]" in 3:10, "our Lord [κυρίου]" in 3:15, 18; of the adjective "one's own"—"their own [ἰδίας] desires" in 3:3, "their own [ἰδίαν] annihilation" in 3:16, and "their own [ἰδίου] stability" in 3:17; of the third person singular indicative active of the verb "to be"—"where is [ἐστιν] the promise" in 3:4 and "in which are [ἐστιν] some things hard to understand" in 3:16; of the term "annihilation"—"annihilation

Introduction to 2 Peter

[ἀπωλείας] of the ungodly human beings" in 3:7 and "their own annihilation [ἀπώλειαν]" in 3:16; and of the verb "consider"—"as some consider [ἡγοῦνται] a delay" in 3:9 and "consider [ἡγεῖσθε] as salvation" in 3:16.

The following linguistic occurrences determine the parallelism between the B (3:10b-11a) and the B' (3:12-14) elements: the only occurrences in 2 Peter of the term "elements" (στοιχεῖα) in 3:10b, 12; of the verb "being burned" (καυσούμενα) in 3:10b, 12; of the verb "dissolve"—"will be dissolved" (λυθήσεται) in 3:10b, "being dissolved" (λυομένων) in 3:11a, and "will dissolve" (λυθήσονται) in 3:12; and of the verb "find"—"will be found [εὑρεθήσεται] out" in 3:10b and "be eager to be found [εὑρεθῆναι] faultless and flawless" in 3:14. Finally, the unparalleled central and pivotal C (3:11b) element contains the only occurrence in 2 Peter of the terms in the expression "what sort of persons is it necessary" (ποταποὺς δεῖ).

The Macrochiastic Structure of 2 Peter

Having illustrated the sequence of the various microchiastic structures operative in the five distinct units of 2 Peter, I will now demonstrate how these five main units form an A-B-C-B'-A' macrochiastic structure unifying and organizing the entire letter.

A: *To Stir You Up by Reminder To Make Every Effort* for *Godliness* (1:1-15)
A': *By a Reminder I Am Stirring You Up To Make Every Effort* for *Godliness* (3:1-18)

The parallelism between the A unit (1:1-15) and the A' unit (3:1-18) within the macrochiastic structure is indicated by the only occurrences in 2 Peter of "apostle" (ἀπόστολος) in 1:1 and "apostles" (ἀποστόλων) in 3:2; "grace" (χάρις) in 1:2 and "in the grace [χάριτι]" in 3:18; "peace" (εἰρήνη) in 1:2 and "in peace [εἰρήνῃ]" in 3:14; "for godliness [εὐσέβειαν]" in 1:3, "godliness [εὐσέβειαν], to godliness [εὐσεβείᾳ]" in 1:6-7, and "in holy conduct and godliness [εὐσεβείαις]" in 3:11; "great things promised [ἐπαγγέλματα]" in 1:4 and "what was promised [ἐπάγγελμα]" in 3:13; "so that [ἵνα]" in 1:4; 3:17; "knowledge [γνῶσιν], to knowledge [γνώσει]" in 1:5-6 and "in knowledge [γνώσει] of our Lord" in 3:18; "therefore" (διό) in 1:10, 12; 3:14; "brothers" (ἀδελφοί) in 1:10 and "our beloved brother [ἀδελφός] Paul" in 3:15; "make every effort" (σπουδάσατε) in 1:10; 3:14 and "I will make every effort" (σπουδάσω) in 1:15; "eternal [αἰώνιον] kingdom" in 1:11 and "eternity" (αἰῶνος) in 3:18; "about these things" (περὶ τούτων) in 1:12; 3:16; "to stir you up by a reminder" (διεγείρειν ὑμᾶς ἐν ὑπομνήσει) in 1:13 and "by a reminder I am stirring up your [διεγείρω ὑμῶν ἐν ὑπομνήσει] sincere disposition" in 3:1; and "just as also" (καθὼς καί) in 1:14; 3:15.

B: By the *Holy* Spirit Human Beings Spoke Prophecy from God (1:16–21)
B': Do Not Turn Back from the *Holy* Commandment (2:17–22)

The only occurrences in 2 Peter of the adjective "holy" in the singular provide the chiastic parallels between the B (1:16–21) and the B' (2:17–22) units. In the B unit "on the holy [ἁγίῳ] mountain" occurs in 1:18 and "by the holy [ἁγίου] Spirit" in 1:21. In the B' unit "the holy [ἁγίας] commandment" occurs in 2:21.[6]

C: The Lord Knows How To Rescue the Godly from Trial (2:1–16)

The C unit (2:1–16) functions as the unparalleled central and pivotal unit within the macrochiastic structure of 2 Peter. It assures the audience that the Lord knows how to rescue the godly from the trial (2:9) caused by the false prophets and teachers among them. Framed by references to prophets in 2:1 and 2:16, this unit provides the pivot from the theme of true prophecy in the B unit (1:16–21) to a further focus on the false prophets and teachers in the B' unit (2:17–22).

Outline of the Macrochiastic Structure of 2 Peter

A: 1:1–15: *To Stir You Up by Reminder* To *Make Every Effort* for *Godliness*
B: 1:16–21: By the *Holy* Spirit Human Beings Spoke Prophecy from God
C: 2:1–16: The Lord Knows How To Rescue the Godly from Trial
B': 2:17–22: Do Not Turn Back from the *Holy* Commandment
A': 3:1–18: *By a Reminder I Am Stirring You Up* To *Make Every Effort* for *Godliness*

Preliminary Indications of Worship as the Main Theme of 2 Peter

As previously mentioned, the subtitle chosen for 2 Peter, "worship in the knowledge of our Lord and savior Jesus Christ," articulates what I am proposing as the main theme of 2 Peter. In this section I will present an introductory overview of the indications that worship, understood in its most comprehensive and dynamic sense as including not only liturgical but ethical worship, serves as the main theme that organizes and unifies the whole of 2 Peter.[7]

---

6. The adjective "holy" occurs in the plural in 3:2, 11 of the letter's final unit.

7. For a somewhat superficial consideration of worship in 2 Peter, see Borchert, *Worship*, 199–202.

Introduction to 2 Peter

First of all, as a letter, 2 Peter is very closely linked to 1 Peter. In all probability 1 Peter is the first letter implied by the statement in 2 Peter that "this is now, beloved, the second letter I am writing to you in which by a reminder I am stirring up your sincere disposition" (3:1). The relative pronoun "which" in the phrase "in which" (ἐν αἷς) is plural, thus referring to both letters, underlining the close connection between them. Just as the letter of 1 Peter, so also the closely related letter of 2 Peter was intended to be publicly read to communities gathered together as worshiping assemblies.

Secondly, just as for 1 Peter, the author of 2 Peter performs acts of worship within the letter itself. Indeed, both letters begin with identical introductory prayer greetings: "May grace to you and peace be multiplied [χάρις ὑμῖν καὶ εἰρήνη πληθυνθείη]" (1 Pet 1:2; 2 Pet 1:2). Just as for 1 Peter (5:14), 2 Peter concludes with an act of worship. Following upon the final exhortation for the audience to grow in the grace and knowledge of our Lord and savior Jesus Christ (3:18a), the author closes the letter by leading the audience in a climactic communal doxology: "To him the glory both now and for the day of eternity. Amen!" (3:18b). These acts of epistolary worship at the beginning and conclusion of the letter thus place 2 Peter within a context of communal worship.

And thirdly, a consideration of the language regarding "acknowledgment" and "knowledge," a key concept in the subtitle chosen for 2 Peter—worship in the knowledge of our Lord and savior Jesus Christ—provides additional preliminary indications of this letter's prevalent concern for the dynamics of worship. The initial prayer greeting is pronounced within a context of the "acknowledgment" that alludes to public and communal worship—"May grace to you and peace be multiplied in the acknowledgment [ἐπιγνώσει] of God and of Jesus our Lord" (1:2). "Acknowledgment" here refers to the public act of worship in which believers acknowledge God's initial acknowledgment of them by choosing and calling them to faith. "In the acknowledgment of God and of Jesus our Lord" thus refers both to the prior divine acknowledgment of believers and to the subsequent human acknowledgment of their divine election in and through their worship.[8]

Through the "acknowledgment" (ἐπιγνώσεως) of the one calling believers by his own glory and virtue, believers have been divinely granted all things

---

8. "As in Heb 10:26, so in 2 Pet 1:2f., ἐπίγνωσις is used in an almost technical sense for the call to the Christian faith. Yet this knowledge must also be demonstrated in righteous conduct (2 Pet 1:8; 2:20f.; cf. Rom 1:28)" (Hackenberg, "ἐπίγνωσις," 2.25). "In contrast to γνῶσις, which is used in 2 Peter for knowledge which can be acquired and developed in the course of Christian life (1:5, 6; 3:18), ἐπίγνωσις always refers to that fundamental saving knowledge on which the whole of Christian life is based" (Bauckham, *Jude, 2 Peter*, 170). See also Picirelli, "Epignosis," 85–93.

1 Peter, 2 Peter, and Jude

necessary for eternal life and the "godliness" (εὐσέβειαν) that embraces both liturgical and ethical worship (1:3).[9] The audience are to supply to their faith "knowledge [γνῶσιν]" (1:5), a knowledge provided them by the letter itself. In the letter the author tells them to be first "knowing" (γινώσκοντες) that every prophecy of scripture does not come about by one's own interpretation (1:20), but by the holy Spirit (1:21). This is in contrast to the false prophets and teachers among them (2:1–16). These false teachers had previously escaped the defilements of the world in the "acknowledgment" (ἐπιγνώσει) of our Lord and savior Jesus Christ (2:20) in their communal worship as believing members of the community. But it was better for them not to have thus "acknowledged" (ἐπεγνωκέναι) the way of righteousness in their worship as Christians than, "acknowledging" (ἐπιγνοῦσιν) it, to turn back from the holy commandment handed over to them (2:21).

In addition, the letter itself tells the audience that they are to be first "knowing" (γινώσκοντες) that mockers will come (3:3) with the mockery of denying the final coming of our Lord and savior Jesus Christ (3:4). "Knowing beforehand" (προγινώσκοντες) through the letter that this will happen (3:17), the audience are to grow in the grace and "knowledge" (γνώσει) of our Lord and savior Jesus Christ (3:18). That is, they are to grow in the knowledge that the delay of his final coming amounts to the divine grace of the patience for repentance which they are to consider as salvation (3:15).

Provided with such knowledge of our Lord and savior Jesus Christ (3:18) through the letter, the audience are thus enabled to supply to their faith the "godliness" (εὐσέβειαν) that connotes proper worship (1:6), so that they will be prepared for the eschatological "acknowledgment" (ἐπίγνωσιν) of our Lord Jesus Christ (1:8) at his final coming. This acknowledgment is synonymous with their entrance into the eternal kingdom of our Lord and savior Jesus Christ (1:11). The letter also assures the audience that the Lord knows how to rescue them, as those who are "godly" (εὐσεβεῖς)—those who worship God properly both liturgically and ethically—from the trial presented to them by the improper worship of the false teachers (2:9). The letter thus provides the audience the knowledge they need for each of them to be persons existing in holy conduct and the "godliness" (εὐσεβείαις) that

---

9. As Witherington (*Letters*, 311) notes, εὐσέβεια "literally means 'good worship,' but it normally has the broader sense of 'piety' or 'godliness,' and in a pagan context it means giving the gods their due in respect and in sacrifice and perhaps also to some extent in living a life of virtue. In a Christian context it refers to the godliness that necessarily entails both honoring God in worship, and also in one's behavior." "But in general usage εὐσέβεια came to mean the actual worship paid to the gods in cultic activities rather than a reverent attitude, although outward actions were seen as the expression of inner attitudes" (Trebilco, *Ephesus*, 361).

Introduction to 2 Peter

refers to the authentic and proper way they are to worship (3:11) our Lord and savior Jesus Christ (3:18).

These preliminary indications that "worship in the knowledge of our Lord and savior Jesus Christ" expresses the main theme and concern embracing the whole of 2 Peter will be confirmed by the remainder of my exegetical investigation into its chiastic structures in the chapters to follow.

Summary

1. There are five distinct units in 2 Peter with each exhibiting its own microchiastic structure.

2. The five units comprising 2 Peter operate as a macrochiastic structure with two pairs of parallel units and with the pivot of the entire macrochiastic structure occurring as the unparalleled central C unit in 2:1–16.

3. The letter of 2 Peter is very closely related to the letter of 1 Peter, continuing but modifying and further developing 1 Peter's main theme concerning worship. That 2 Peter was heard by its audiences in a setting of worship, is framed by epistolary acts of worship (1:2; 3:18), and is concerned with language and concepts involving the dynamics of both liturgical and ethical worship provide preliminary indications that proper worship is its main organizing and unifying theme. More specifically, the subtitle, "worship in the knowledge of our Lord and savior Jesus Christ," expresses the central focus and main concern of 2 Peter.

15

2 Peter 1:1-15
To Stir You Up by Reminder To Make Every Effort for Godliness (A)

*Granted godliness to become
sharers of the divine nature*

A   1:1 Symeon Peter, slave and apostle of *Jesus Christ*, to those who have obtained a *faith* just as precious to us in the *righteousness* of *our* God and *savior Jesus Christ*. ² May grace to *you* and peace be multiplied in the acknowledgment of God and of *Jesus our Lord*.

    B   ³ᵃ As all things to us, the things toward life and Godliness, his *divine* power having *granted*,

        C   ³ᵇ through the acknowledgment of the one calling us by his own glory and virtue,

    B′   ⁴ through which things the precious and great things promised to us have been *granted*, so that through these things you may become sharers of the *divine* nature, escaping the destruction from desire in the world.

   A′   ⁵ For this very reason, applying every effort, supply to your *faith* virtue, to virtue knowledge, ⁶ to knowledge self-control, to self-control endurance, to endurance godliness, ⁷ to godliness brotherly affection, to brotherly affection love. ⁸ For these things, existing and increasing to *you*, make you neither useless nor fruitless for the acknowledgment of *our Lord Jesus Christ*, ⁹ for to whomever these things are not present, he is blind, being shortsighted, receiving forgetfulness of the cleansing of his sins of the past. ¹⁰ Therefore rather, brothers, make every effort your call and

2 Peter 1:1–15

chosenness as firm to uphold, for, upholding these things, you will never stumble, ¹¹ for thus will be richly supplied to *you* the entrance for the eternal kingdom of *our Lord* and *savior Jesus Christ*. ¹² Therefore I intend always to remind you about these things, even though you know and are confirmed in the present truth. ¹³ I consider it *righteous*, as long as I am in this tent, to stir you up by a reminder, ¹⁴ knowing that imminent is the removal of my tent, just as also *our Lord Jesus Christ* indicated to me. ¹⁵ I will also make every effort at all times to have *you*, after my departure, the memory of these things to uphold.¹

Audience Response to 1:1–15

1:1–2 (A): In the Righteousness of Our God and Savior Jesus Christ

The audience hear the A element (1:1–2) of this chiastic unit as a chiastic pattern in itself:

a) Symeon Peter, slave and apostle of *Jesus* Christ, to those who have obtained a faith just as precious to us *in* the righteousness of *our God* and savior *Jesus* Christ (1:1).
b) May grace to you and peace be multiplied (1:2a)
a') *in* the acknowledgment of *God* and of *Jesus our* Lord (1:2b).

After the audience hear the central and unparalleled b) sub-element, "may grace to you and peace be multiplied" (1:2a), they experience a pivot of chiastic parallels from the a) to the a') sub-element involving the only occurrences in this sub-unit of the terms "Jesus," "in," "our," and "God." "The apostle of Jesus [Ἰησοῦ] Christ" and "in [ἐν] the righteousness of our [ἡμῶν] God [θεοῦ] and savior Jesus [Ἰησοῦ] Christ" (1:1) progress to "in [ἐν] the acknowledgment of God [θεοῦ] and of Jesus [Ἰησοῦ] our [ἡμῶν] Lord" (1:2b).

The letter of 1 Peter presents itself as sent by "Peter, apostle of Jesus Christ" (1 Pet 1:1a). In continuity but development, 2 Peter presents itself as sent by "Symeon Peter, slave and apostle of Jesus Christ" (2 Pet 1:1a). The double name "Symeon Peter," which adds the Hebrew "Symeon," instead of the Greek "Simon," to the Greek nickname "Peter" (rock), emphasizes that 2 Peter is sent by the same "Peter" as 1 Peter—the Simon Peter who became the leader of the twelve apostles chosen by Jesus (Matt 10:2; Mark 3:16; Luke 6:14; John 6:68–70). The addition of "slave" (δοῦλος) to "apostle" (ἀπόστολος)—one sent by and with the authority of Jesus Christ, underlines not only Peter's humble submission to the lordship of Jesus Christ but also

1. For the establishment of 2 Pet 1:1–15 as a chiasm, see ch. 14.

his honor as a slave who speaks authoritatively on behalf of Jesus Christ. The apostle Peter who exhorted the audience of 1 Peter to be "slaves" (δοῦλοι) of God (1 Pet 2:16) presents himself to the audience of 2 Peter as a model slave of Jesus Christ, worthy of their attention as well as of their imitation.[2]

"Symeon Peter" is thus presented as the implied author of the letter of 2 Peter. Whether or not the historical author of 2 Peter is the same as the historical author of 1 Peter, and/or the same as the historical Simon Peter, the apostolic authority and status of the historical Simon Peter stand behind the letter. Although there is no consensus among scholars on the identity of the historical author of either 1 or 2 Peter, it is not out of the question that the historical Simon Peter functioned in some sense as the actual author, or at least as the direct authority for the composition of both of these letters.[3]

Having already referred to the geographical situation of the audience in 1 Peter, addressed as "the chosen sojourners of the diaspora, of Pontus, Galatia, Cappadocia, Asia, and Bithynia" (1 Pet 1:1b), Peter addresses the audience in 2 Peter as "those who have obtained a faith just as precious to us in the righteousness of our God and savior Jesus Christ" (2 Pet 1:1b).[4] The

---

2. "This introductory prescript in 2 Peter 1:1 reflects continuity with 1 Peter and tries to stress the continuity with the original apostle to the Jews" (Witherington, *Letters*, 293). "This double name is frequently used in the New Testament. But only here and in Acts 15:14 is the name 'Simon' spelled the way it is here (*Symeon* in place of the usual *Simon*). This form of the name is a fairly exact transliteration of the Hebrew, and since it is so rare, we would not expect someone writing in Peter's name to use it. But it makes perfectly good sense for Peter himself to spell it this way, since it would have been the form natural to him from birth" (Moo, *2 Peter and Jude*, 33). "We can hardly argue either for or against the authenticity of the letter on the basis of the reading Συμεών since the use of this less-common transliteration for the apostle's name could be viewed as either a mark of authenticity or as part of the pseudepigrapher's art. If this is an authentic epistle of Peter, the use of the name Simeon would be a trace of his bilingualism... The combined name 'Simeon Peter' recalls the earliest memory of the fisherman who became foundational for the life of the church (Matt. 16:16-18). Both antiquity and authority adhere to the name and by extension to this writing composed under that name" (Green, *Jude and 2 Peter*, 172).

3. See the commentaries for discussions of the authorship of 2 Peter. "The contemporary objections to Petrine authorship are not without their weaknesses, and we must not allow the volume of opinion to decide the case. The verdict of the early church was ambiguous at first, but the problem of literary style in comparison to 1 Peter accounts for the early doubts. The book was used early and, according to early witnesses, used widely. The book is decidedly dissimilar to later literature that went under the name of Peter... The concerns raised within the letter fit well within the struggles of the church of the first century, and we may reasonably affirm that Simeon Peter, the apostle, authored the book. The letter stands within the circle of early Christian theology and serves as a witness to the struggles and dangers that the faith faced during its youngest years" (Green, *Jude and 2 Peter*, 150).

4. "Although a specific church is not named as the recipient of the letter in the

2 Peter 1:1-15

audience of 2 Peter have "obtained" (λαχοῦσιν), that is, have been allotted by God,[5] a faith as precious to them as it is to "us," that is, to Peter and his associates, such as his fellow apostles as well as Silvanus, Mark, and the others who, as those believers "chosen together," have been with Peter in Rome (1 Pet 5:12-13). The audience are thus addressed as part of the brotherhood of believers throughout the world (5:9; 2:17) who share the same precious faith.

That their "faith" (πίστιν) is "just as precious [ἰσότιμον]" (2 Pet 1:1) to them as it is to the brotherhood of their fellow believers who are undergoing the same kinds of sufferings throughout the world reminds the audience that in their "faith" (πίστει) they are strong enough to oppose the devil (1 Pet 5:9). They recall that their "faith" (πίστιν) for God (1:21) is precious because it is based on the "precious" (τιμίῳ) sacrificial blood of Christ (1:19) with which they have been ransomed from their futile, idolatrous conduct inherited from their ancestors (1:18). And they remember that the refinement of their "faith" (πίστεως) in their various trials is "more precious" (πολυτιμότερον) than gold (1:7).

The audience of 2 Peter have graciously been allotted a faith just as precious to Peter and associated believers within a realm or sphere established by the "righteousness" (δικαιοσύνῃ) of our God and savior Jesus Christ (2 Pet 1:1). As the audience recall, Christ established this righteousness when he handed himself over to the God who judges "righteously [δικαίως]" (1 Pet 2:23), and offered up our sins in his body upon the tree, so that to sins having died, to "righteousness" (δικαιοσύνῃ) we might live (2:24). To the righteousness that connotes the accomplishment of God's will we believers might "live" (ζήσωμεν) not only now but for eternity, since we have been given new birth through a "living" (ζῶντος) word of God (1:23) that abides for eternity (1:25). Indeed, God has given believers new birth for a "living" (ζῶσαν) hope, a hope for eternal life, through the resurrection of Jesus Christ from the dead (1:3).[6]

Addressed as those who have been allotted by God with a "faith" (πίστιν) that is as precious to them as it is to all believers (2 Pet 1:1), the audience of 2 Peter recall that in the power of God they are among those being

---

introductory remarks, in 3:1 the author says, 'I write this second letter to you.' 1 Peter is the first letter that Peter wrote, and this seems to be a reference to that letter ... If the second letter is addressed to the same group, this gives us some suggestion about the general region that the letter was sent to" (Reese, *2 Peter and Jude*, 122).

5. BDAG, 581; Harrington, *2 Peter*, 240.

6. "It is Christ and his work that is the cause of their faith and their relationship with God. 'Righteousness' here refers generally to what Christ has done for us by dying and rising again; it is 'righteousness' because it is an expression of God's faithfulness to his promises" (Keating, *First and Second Peter*, 137).

guarded through this precious "faith" (πίστεως) for a "salvation" (σωτηρίαν) ready to be revealed in the last time (1 Pet 1:5). They are among those in the process of attaining the end of their "faith" (πίστεως), "salvation" (σωτηρίαν) of souls (1:9), and of growing up for "salvation" (σωτηρίαν) to the eternal life for which they have become "newborn infants" (2:2). This salvation from eternal death and for eternal life is part of the righteousness in which the audience have been allotted by God with a very precious faith. This is the righteousness to which they are to live now as believers enabled to do God's will and thus worship God properly, the righteousness established by the death and resurrection of the Jesus Christ of whom Symeon Peter is a slave and apostle, the Jesus Christ who is not only our "savior" (σωτῆρος) but our God (2 Pet 1:1).[7]

The introductory prayer greeting, "May grace to you and peace be multiplied" (1:2a), echoes the identical introductory prayer greeting in 1 Peter (1:2). But for the audience of 2 Peter the "grace" (χάρις) prayed for them has a more specific reference. First Peter presented them with the "true grace [χάριν] of God" in which they are to remain firm (5:12), epitomized as the "grace [χάριτος] of life" (3:7), the eternal life for which God, the "God of all grace [χάριτος]" (5:10; cf. 1:10, 13; 4:10; 5:5), gave believers new birth (1:3, 23). But this grace of divine initiative implies a corresponding grace of human response to it that takes place in and through the worship that includes good ethical conduct. This is the "grace" (χάρις) pleasing in the sight of God (2:19, 20). And the "peace [εἰρήνη]" (1 Pet 1:2; 2 Pet 1:2a) which the prayer couples with grace is not only God's gift of a profound and overall well-being with God and one another in Christ (1 Pet 5:14), but also the "peace" (εἰρήνην) they are to seek and pursue by their good conduct (3:11).

Peter prays that this grace and peace may be multiplied for the audience by God (2 Pet 1:2a) within a realm or sphere characterized as "the acknowledgment of God and of Jesus our Lord" (1:2b). At this point the audience experience a progression from their reception of a precious faith "in" (ἐν) the righteousness of "our" (ἡμῶν) God and savior Jesus Christ (1:1) to the prayer that grace and peace be multiplied to them "in" (ἐν) the acknowledgment of God and of Jesus "our" (ἡμῶν) Lord. "In the acknowledgment [ἐπιγνώσει] of God" refers, on the one hand, to God's acknowledgment of the audience by divinely allotting them a precious faith in and through the righteousness accomplished by Jesus Christ.[8] This is also Jesus' acknowledg-

---

7. "This does not, of course, mean that for Peter Jesus Christ has taken the place of the Old Testament God he has worshiped since childhood. It means, rather, that he has now come to understand that Jesus, along with the Father, is God" (Moo, *2 Peter, Jude*, 35). Callan, "Christology," 253–63; idem, "Soteriology," 549–59.

8. For "acknowledgment" as the meaning of ἐπίγνωσις here, see ch. 14.

2 Peter 1:1-15

ment of the audience as believers, since he has already been identified as "our God" (1:1). On the other hand, it also refers to the audience's acknowledgment, in and through their worship, of God and of Jesus Christ as not only "our God and savior" (1:1) but also "our" divine "Lord" (1:2).

1:3a (B): His Divine Power Granted All Things toward Life and Godliness

Symeon Peter continues to address his audience: "As all things to us, the things toward life and godliness, his divine power having granted" (1:3a). Whereas "to us" (ἡμῖν) previously referred to Peter and his associates in distinction to the audience whose faith is just as precious (1:1), now, with an emphatic "to us" (ἡμῖν), the audience are included among all of "us" believers, as they were included in the reference to Jesus Christ as "our" (ἡμῶν) God and savior (1:1) and as "our" (ἡμῶν) Lord (1:2b). That all things toward life and godliness have been divinely granted "to us" believers explains why the faith the audience share with their fellow believers is so precious. The reference to "his divine power [θείας δυνάμεως]," that is, the divine power of Jesus Christ as our "God" (θεοῦ) and "savior [σωτῆρος]" (1:1), reminds the audience that in the "power of God" (δυνάμει θεοῦ) they are being guarded through faith for a "salvation" (σωτηρίαν) ready to be revealed in the last time (1 Pet 1:5).[9]

That the divine power of Jesus Christ has granted to us believers all the things necessary toward attaining "life [ζωήν]" (2 Pet 1:3a) reminds the audience that as believers they are fellow heirs of the grace of "life [ζωῆς]" (1 Pet 3:7), the eternal "life" (ζωήν) they are to inherit by turning away from evil and doing good (3:9-11).[10] The divine power of Jesus Christ has granted all things necessary not only toward eternal life but toward the "godliness," literally, the "good worship" (εὐσέβειαν) that includes both the liturgical and ethical worship that accords with this eternal life for which believers have been given new birth (1:3, 23).[11] That the divine power of Jesus Christ has "granted" (δεδωρημένης) all these things exemplifies the grace that Peter prayed may be multiplied for the audience (2 Pet 1:2a).

---

9. "θεῖος ('divine') was a very flexible word, but here it must indicate, not that Christ possesses a divine or godlike power of his own, as though he were a second god, but that he shares in God's own power" (Bauckham, *Jude, 2 Peter*, 177).

10. "When Peter referred to 'life' (ζωήν), eternal life is intended" (Schreiner, *1, 2 Peter*, 291-92).

11. For more on this meaning of εὐσέβεια, see ch. 14.

1 Peter, 2 Peter, and Jude

1:3b (C): Through the Acknowledgment of the One Calling Us

All the things necessary toward attaining eternal life and godliness the divine power of Jesus Christ has granted to us believers (1:3a) "through the acknowledgment of the one calling us by his own glory and virtue" (1:3b). Peter prayed that grace and peace may be multiplied to the audience "in the acknowledgment" (ἐν ἐπιγνώσει) of God and of Jesus our Lord (1:2). But now the audience are to appreciate that it is "through the acknowledgment" (διὰ τῆς ἐπιγνώσεως) of the one calling us by his own glory and virtue that the divine power of Jesus Christ has granted us believers all the things necessary toward attaining eternal life and godliness. Here again "acknowledgment" conveys a double meaning. It refers not only to the divine acknowledgment of us believers by calling and allotting us a precious faith (1:1), but also to the human acknowledgment of the divine call by becoming believers through a public profession of faith. Thus, the human response of acknowledgment to the divine initiative of acknowledgment finds its expression in the communal worship of us believers.

The one "calling" (καλέσαντος) us by his own "glory" (δόξῃ) and "virtue [ἀρετῇ]" (1:3b) resonates with what the audience heard at the conclusion of 1 Peter: "The God of all grace, who called [καλέσας] you for his eternal glory [δόξαν] in Christ Jesus" (1 Pet 5:10). It recalls the exhortations for them to proclaim the "virtues" (ἀρετάς) of the God who "called" (καλέσαντος) them out of darkness for his marvelous light (2:9), and to become holy in all conduct according to the Holy One who "called" (καλέσαντα) them to be holy (1:15). But since it is through Christ that the audience are faithful for God, who raised him from the dead and gave him "glory" (δόξαν), so that their faith and hope are for God (1:21), they realize that "the one calling us by his own glory and virtue" refers to Jesus Christ, as our God and savior (2 Pet 1:1). Whereas his own "glory" refers to his resurrection, his "virtue" was preeminently exemplified in his sacrificial death for our sins by which he established the righteousness (1 Pet 2:24) in and through which we believers have been divinely allotted a very precious faith (2 Pet 1:1).[12]

---

12. "The common Greek noun ἀρετή is difficult to translate into English. The usual translation of 'virtue' does not convey the sense of power, capacity, and ability that the Greek word contains. 'Virtue' also does not convey the overall sense of moral excellence that the Greek word also contains. However, the various alternative translations of 'might,' 'excellence,' or 'goodness' all have their own problems" (Donelson, *I & II Peter*, 218).

2 Peter 1:1-15

1:4 (B'): These Things Granted To Become Sharers of Divine Nature

The audience then hear the purpose for the things they have been divinely granted: "through which things the precious and great things promised to us have been granted, so that through these things you may become sharers of the divine nature, escaping the destruction from desire in the world" (1:4). At this point, having heard the unparalleled central C element of this chiastic unit, "through the acknowledgment of the one calling us by his own glory and virtue" (1:3b), the audience experience a progression of parallels from the B to the B' element. "His divine [θείας] power having granted [δεδωρημένης]" (1:3a) progresses to "the precious and great things promised to us have been granted [δεδώρηται], so that through these things you may become sharers of the divine [θείας] nature" (1:4).

That "through which things," that is, all the things toward life and godliness (1:3a), the precious and great things "promised" (ἐπαγγέλματα) to us believers have been divinely granted (1:4a) reminds the audience that they have been privileged to receive the things prefigured or promised by the prophets of old. These prophets testified beforehand to the sufferings for Christ and the glories to follow (1 Pet 1:11). They were thus serving the things promised which now have been "announced" (ἀνηγγέλη) to the audience through those who "proclaimed good news" (εὐαγγελισαμένων) unto them (1:12). These "precious" (τίμια) and great things promised include especially the "precious" (τιμίῳ) sacrificial blood of Christ (1:19), which motivates the audience to undergo their own sufferings, resulting in the refinement of their faith as "more precious" (πολυτιμότερον) than gold (1:7). Indeed, they are privileged to have been divinely allotted the faith which is "equally precious" (ἰσότιμον) to all believers (2 Pet 1:1).

"Through these things [τούτων]," that is, not only the precious and great "things" (τά) promised and divinely granted to us (1:4a), but also the "things" (τά) toward life and godliness divinely granted to us (1:3a), the audience may become sharers of the divine nature (1:4b). That "you," the audience, "may become" (γένησθε) sharers of the divine nature resonates with the exhortations for "you" to "become" (γένησθε) zealots for the good (1 Pet 3:13), as "you become" (ἐγενήθητε) children of Sarah by doing good (3:6), and as "you become" (γενήθητε) holy as God is holy (1:15). The audience are exhorted to become "sharers" (κοινωνοί) of the divine nature by the Peter who is himself a "sharer" (κοινωνός) in the divine glory that is going to be revealed (5:1; cf. 4:13). They may thus become sharers of the "divine" (θείας) nature, because the "divine" (θείας) power of Jesus Christ, our "God" (θεοῦ) and savior (2 Pet 1:1), has granted them all the things

213

necessary toward attaining the eternal life (1:3a) that is part of the divine nature, the future eternal life they may already begin to live in and through their ethical worship.[13]

That the audience have everything they need to become sharers of the divine nature that includes eternal life allows them to escape the destruction of eternal death that results from desire "in the world [ἐν τῷ κόσμῳ]" (1:4). This reminds them that they have undergone the same kinds of sufferings due to evil desire as the brotherhood of their fellow believers "throughout the world [ἐν τῷ κόσμῳ]" (1 Pet 5:9). Their escape from the destruction of eternal death resulting from "desire" (ἐπιθυμίᾳ) in the world reminds them that they are now able to spend their time not in the evil "desires" (ἐπιθυμίαις) of human beings, but in the ethical worship that accords with the will of God (4:2-3). They have been enabled to keep away from the fleshly "desires" (ἐπιθυμιῶν) that are waging war against the soul (2:11), and not to be conformed to the "desires" (ἐπιθυμίαις) of their pre-Christian existence (1:14). In short, they are able to conduct their time in the world in the reverent fear that includes both the liturgical and ethical worship of the God who called them to be holy as he is holy (1:15-17).

That the audience may become sharers of the divine nature that includes eternal life and allows them to escape the "destruction" (φθορᾶς) of eternal death (2 Pet 1:4) resonates with the eternal quality of good ethical conduct described as the "imperishableness" (ἀφθάρτῳ) of the gentle and quiet spirit, which amounts to ethical worship since it is before God of great value (1 Pet 3:4). It reminds the audience that they have been given new birth not from a seed "perishable" (φθαρτῆς) but "imperishable" (ἀφθάρτου), through a living word of God (1:23) that abides for eternity (1:25). And it recalls that God has given believers new birth for a living hope through the resurrection of Jesus Christ from the dead (1:3), for an "imperishable" (ἄφθαρτον) inheritance of eternal life in heaven (1:4).[14]

13. "To share in divine nature is to become immortal and incorruptible" (Bauckham, *Jude, 2 Peter*, 181). With regard to the phrase "divine nature," Harrington (*2 Peter*, 244) notes, "Interpreters who are not persuaded by the alleged Hellenistic background of this phrase take it to refer to participation by humans in the heavenly court and its worship (as in Revelation 4-5)." See also Starr, *Sharers*; Hafemann, "Divine Nature," 80-99.

14. "φθορᾶς can hardly be anything else than the mortality which the Christian believer will escape when, at death or at the Parousia, he attains to an immortal form of life. It is in line with Pauline thought that this escape is an eschatological expectation, not a present experience, for in this life the Christian still participates in decay and mortality" (Bauckham, *Jude, 2 Peter*, 182). "Believers have already escaped the world's corruption in that they belong to God, but the full realization of such a liberation will be theirs on the day of resurrection" (Schreiner, *1, 2 Peter*, 295). "Since this escape from the corruption in the world that parallels participating in the divine nature is ethical, the character of the divine nature must also be ethical and not simply another way

1:5-15 (A'): For the Acknowledgment of Our Lord and Savior Jesus Christ

The audience hear the A' element (1:5-15) of this chiastic unit as a chiastic pattern in itself:
a) For this very reason, applying every *effort*, supply to your faith virtue, to virtue knowledge, to knowledge self-control, to self-control endurance, to endurance godliness, to godliness brotherly affection, to brotherly affection love. For these things, existing and increasing to you, make you neither useless nor fruitless for the acknowledgment of *our Lord Jesus Christ*, for to whomever these things are not present, he is blind, being shortsighted, receiving forgetfulness of the cleansing of his sins of the past. Therefore rather, brothers, *make every effort* your call and chosenness as firm to *uphold*, for, *upholding* these things, you will never stumble, for thus will be richly supplied to you the entrance for the eternal kingdom of *our Lord* and savior *Jesus Christ*. Therefore I intend always to *remind* you about *these things*, even though you know and are confirmed in the present truth (1:5-12).
b) I consider it righteous, as long as I am in this *tent* (1:13a),
c) to stir you up my reminder (1:13b),
b') knowing that imminent is the removal of my *tent* (1:14a),
a') just as also *our Lord Jesus Christ* indicated to me. I will also *make every effort* at all times to have you, after my departure, the *memory* of *these things* to *uphold* (1:14b-15).

After the central and unparalleled c) sub-element of this chiastic sub-unit, "to stir you up my reminder" (1:13b), the audience experience a pivot of parallels from the b) to the b') sub-element involving the only occurrences in 2 Peter of the term "tent." "As long as I am in this tent [σκηνώματι]" (1:13a) progresses to "the removal of my tent [σκηνώματός]" (1:14a). The audience then hear a progression of parallels from the a) to the a') sub-element involving several terms occurring only in this sub-unit. "Effort [σπουδήν]" (1:5), "our Lord Jesus Christ [κυρίου ἡμῶν Ἰησοῦ Χριστοῦ]" (1:8, 11), "make every effort [σπουδάσατε]" (1:10), "uphold" (ποιεῖσθαι) and "upholding [ποιοῦντες]" (1:10), "remind [ὑπομιμνῄσκειν]" (1:12), and "these things [τούτων]" (1:12) occur in the a) sub-element. These occurrences progress to "our Lord Jesus Christ [κύριος ἡμῶν Ἰησοῦς Χριστός]" (1:14b), "I will make every effort [σπουδάσω]" (1:15), "memory [μνήμην]" (1:15), "these things [τούτων]" (1:15), and "uphold [ποιεῖσθαι]" (1:15) in the a') sub-element.

---

of indicating immortality" (Davids, *2 Peter and Jude*, 176). See also Fornberg, *Early Church*, 88-89; Neyrey, *2 Peter, Jude*, 157.

1 Peter, 2 Peter, and Jude

At this point the audience hear progressions, via the chiastic parallels, from the A (1:1-2) to the A' (1:5-15) element of this chiastic unit. "Jesus Christ [Ἰησοῦ Χριστοῦ]" (1:1, twice), "faith [πίστιν]" (1:1), "righteousness [δικαιοσύνῃ]" (1:1), "our [ἡμῶν]" (1:1, 2), "savior [σωτῆρος]" (1:1), "to you [ὑμῖν]" (1:2), "Jesus [Ἰησοῦ]" (1:2) and "Lord [κυρίου]" (1:2) occur in the A element. These occurrences progress to "faith [πίστει]" (1:5), "to you [ὑμῖν]" (1:8, 11), "our Lord Jesus Christ [κυρίου ἡμῶν Ἰησοῦ Χριστοῦ]" (1:8, 11), "savior [σωτῆρος]" (1:11), "righteous [δίκαιον]" (1:13), and "our Lord Jesus Christ [κύριος ἡμῶν Ἰησοῦς Χριστός]" (1:14b) in the A' element.

In addition, the audience hear the a) sub-element (1:5-12) of this chiastic sub-unit (1:5-15) as yet another chiastic pattern in itself:

(a) For this very reason, applying every effort, *supply* to your faith virtue, to virtue knowledge, to knowledge self-control, to self-control endurance, to endurance godliness, to godliness brotherly affection, to brotherly affection love. For these things, existing and increasing to *you*, make you neither useless nor fruitless *for* the acknowledgment of *our Lord Jesus Christ*, for to whomever these things are not *present*, he is blind, being shortsighted, receiving forgetfulness of the cleansing of his sins of the past (1:5-9).

(b) Therefore rather, brothers, make every effort your call and chosenness as firm to *uphold* (1:10a),

(b') for, *upholding* these things, you will never stumble (1:10b),

(a') for thus will be richly *supplied* to *you* the entrance *for* the eternal kingdom of *our Lord* and savior *Jesus Christ*. Therefore I intend always to remind you about these things, even though you know and are confirmed in the *present* truth (1:11-12).

At the center of this chiastic sub-unit the audience experience a pivot of parallels from the (b) to the (b') sub-element involving the only occurrences in this sub-unit of the verb "uphold." "As firm to uphold [ποιεῖσθαι]" (1:10a) progresses to "upholding [ποιοῦντες] these things" (1:10b).[15] They then hear a progression of parallels from the (a) to the (a') sub-element involving the only occurrences in 2 Peter of the verbs "supply" and "be present," and in this sub-unit of the terms "to you," "for," and "our Lord Jesus Christ." "Supply [ἐπιχορηγήσατε] to your faith" (1:5), "increasing to you [ὑμῖν]" (1:8), "for [εἰς] the acknowledgment of our Lord Jesus Christ [κυρίου ἡμῶν Ἰησοῦ Χριστοῦ]" (1:8), and "these things are not present [πάρεστιν]" (1:9) progress to "will be richly supplied [ἐπιχορηγηθήσεται] to you [ὑμῖν] the entrance for [εἰς] the eternal kingdom" (1:11), "our Lord

---

15. In the context of 2 Peter (1:10, 15, 19), the basic Greek verb for "doing" or "making" (ποιέω) can justifiably be translated as "upholding."

2 Peter 1:1-15

[κυρίου ἡμῶν]" (1:11), "Jesus Christ [Ἰησοῦ Χριστοῦ]" (1:11), and "in the present [παρούσῃ] truth" (1:12).

"For this very reason," that is, so that the audience may become sharers of the divine nature (1:4), "applying every [πᾶσαν] effort," that is, accepting and using "all [πάντα] the things" the divine power has granted toward life and godliness (1:3), the audience are to supply to their faith virtue (1:5). Since God "supplies" (χορηγεῖ) the strength by which one may use divine gifts (1 Pet 4:11), with such divine assistance the audience are to "supply" (ἐπιχορηγήσατε) to their "faith" (πίστει), a "faith" (πίστιν) divinely allotted to them as equally precious to all believers (2 Pet 1:1), the virtue that will enhance its quality.[16] They are to supply to their faith the "virtue" (ἀρετήν) of Jesus Christ, the one calling them by his own glory and "virtue [ἀρετῇ]" (1:3). In other words, they are to add virtue to their faith by imitating the virtue of obedience to God's will that the suffering Christ demonstrated in his sacrificial death for us when he handed himself over to the God who judges righteously (1 Pet 2:23). With the same attitude as Christ the audience may behave not in the desires of human beings but in the will of God (4:1-2).

The audience are to supply to their faith not only the virtue demonstrated by Christ but the "knowledge" (γνῶσιν) concerning Christ (2 Pet 1:5). As the audience recall, believing husbands are to dwell together with their wives in accord with the "knowledge" (γνῶσιν) of the significance of Christ in God's plan for all believers (1 Pet 3:7). Christ was "foreknown" (προεγνωσμένου) by God before the foundation of the world but manifested at the last of these times for the sake of the believing audience (1:20), chosen sojourners according to the "foreknowledge" (πρόγνωσιν) of God for the obedience of Jesus Christ (1:2). That the audience are to supply knowledge concerning Christ to their faith reinforces the exhortation for them, as children of obedience, not to be conformed to evil desires, as they were in their former "ignorance" (ἀγνοίᾳ) of Christ (1:14). They are to add to their faith not only the knowledge they already have of Christ, but the knowledge they will gain in listening to the rest of the letter.

By humbling themselves under the "mighty" (κραταιάν) hand of God (5:6), and with the "might" (κράτος) whose source is God (4:11; 5:11), the audience are to supply to their knowledge as believers the power of "self-control [ἐγκράτειαν]" (2 Pet 1:6). This reinforces the exhortation for the audience to imitate the self-control of Christ (1 Pet 2:21), "who, being insulted did not return insult, suffering, he did not threaten, but handed himself over

---

16. "This call to build up virtues is explicitly dependent on the divine giving enumerated in the preceding verses" (Donelson, *1 & II Peter*, 220). "The indicative of God's gift precedes and undergirds the imperative that calls for human exertion" (Schreiner, *1, 2 Peter*, 296).

to the one who judges righteously" (2:23). They are to arm themselves with the same attitude as Christ (4:1), so as to spend their time not in the desires of human beings, the fleshly desires waging war against the soul (2:11), but in the self-control that accords with the will of God (4:2). Thus, rather than being conformed, as in their former ignorance of Christ, to evil desires (1:14), they are to add self-control to their knowledge of Christ (2 Pet 1:6).

In addition to self-control the audience are to supply to their faith "endurance [ὑπομονήν]" (1:6). This reminds the audience how it would not be to their credit if, sinning and being mistreated, "you endure" (ὑπομενεῖτε). But if, doing good and suffering, "you endure" (ὑπομενεῖτε), then this is the grace of ethical worship pleasing in the sight of God (1 Pet 2:20). As the audience recall, it is better to suffer for doing good, as a result of their good, in Christ, conduct (3:16) and in imitation of the endurance demonstrated by Christ (2:21–25), if the will of God wants it, than for doing evil (3:17). Indeed, those believers who are suffering according to the will of God are, like Christ, to entrust to the faithful Creator their souls in the endurance of good-doing (4:19).

Since the divine power of Christ has granted to believers all the things necessary toward eternal life and "godliness" (εὐσέβειαν), literally, "good worship," the holistic worship that includes both liturgical and ethical worship (2 Pet 1:3), the audience, in addition to endurance, are to supply to their faith "godliness [εὐσέβειαν]" (1:6). This is possible for them because Christ once concerning sins suffered, the righteous one on behalf of the unrighteous, so that he might lead the audience to God, thus enabling them to engage in the godliness of worshiping God both in their liturgical or cultic conduct as well as in their ethical or moral behavior (1 Pet 3:18).

Christ modeled the godliness the audience are to include as a quality of their faith when he performed the ethical worship of not returning insults when insulted or threats when suffering, but handing himself over to the God who judges righteously. This led to his cultic, sacrificial worship of offering up our sins in his body upon the tree. Consequently, to sins having died, we believers might live, both now and eternally, to the righteousness that serves as worship pleasing to God, or, in other words, "godliness" (2:23–24). Because Christ offered up our sins in his sacrificial death, the audience are able to perform the godliness of offering up spiritual sacrifices acceptable to God through Jesus Christ (2:5). They are able to be holy as God is holy through the godliness of calling upon God as Father in their liturgical worship and conducting the time of their sojourning in the reverential fear of their ethical worship (1:15–17).

Recalling that they have purified their souls in obedience to the truth of Christ for sincere "brotherly affection [φιλαδελφίαν]" (1:22), and that they are to be believers "having brotherly affection [φιλάδελφοι]" (3:8), the audience are to supply to their faith, in addition to godliness, "brotherly affection [φιλαδελφίαν]" (2 Pet 1:7). That this refers to affection for the brotherhood of believers is indicated by the reference to the Silvanus through whom Peter wrote his first letter as a "faithful brother" (πιστοῦ ἀδελφοῦ) to the audience (1 Pet 5:12). The audience already heard how closely related brotherly affection is to godliness when the exhortation for them to fear God was immediately preceded by the exhortation to love the "brotherhood [ἀδελφότητα]" (2:17). This includes the "brotherhood" (ἀδελφότητι) of believers throughout the world, who are undergoing the same kinds of sufferings as the audience (5:9).[17]

At the end of 1 Peter the audience heard that they are to greet one another within their worshiping assembly with a ritualistic kiss of "love [ἀγάπης]" (5:14). They were exhorted to keep "love" (ἀγάπην) for each other constant, because "love" (ἀγάπη) covers a multitude of the sins that vitiate the worship that is essential to godliness (4:8). And now they are exhorted to supply to their faith, in addition to brotherly affection, "love [ἀγάπην]" (2 Pet 1:7). The audience have been twice addressed as "beloved [ἀγαπητοί]" (1 Pet 2:11; 4:12), that is, as those who are loved by God as well as by fellow believers. They have been exhorted to "love" (ἀγαπᾶτε) the brotherhood of their fellow believers (2:17), indeed, to "love" (ἀγαπήσατε) one another constantly (1:22), as believers who "love" (ἀγαπᾶτε) the Jesus Christ they have not seen (1:8). As the climax to the qualities the audience are to supply to their faith, Christian love is thus the key to the godliness that combines the love of God/Christ in their liturgical worship with the love of fellow believers in their ethical worship.[18]

For "these things" (ταῦτα), that is, the qualities the audience are to supply to their faith (2 Pet 1:5-7), are part of all "these things" (τούτων) through which Christ's divine power has granted for us the attainment of eternal life and godliness (1:4). Existing and increasing to the audience, these things make them neither useless nor fruitless for the acknowledgment of our Lord Jesus Christ (1:8). That these things are to be existing and "increasing" (πλεονάζοντα) to "you" (ὑμῖν) articulates one of the preeminent ways the initial prayer greeting that grace to "you" (ὑμῖν) and peace be "multiplied"

---

17. According to Aasgaard, "Brotherly Advice," 253, the theme of Christian siblingship permeates 1 Peter.

18. Callan, "2 Peter 1:1-7," 632-40; Charles, "2 Peter 1:5-7," 55-72. "Peter used a literary form here that is called *sorites*, in which we have a step-by-step chain that culminates in a climax ... When we examine the chain of virtues in 2 Peter, it is doubtful that we should understand each virtue as actually building on the previous one" (Schreiner, *1, 2 Peter*, 297).

(πληθυνθείη) may be actualized (1:2a). That these things "make" (καθίστησιν) the audience neither useless nor fruitless for the acknowledgment of our Lord Jesus Christ will enable them to fulfill the climactic exhortation of 1 Peter—to "remain firm" (στῆτε) for the true "grace" (χάριν) of God (1 Pet 5:12). This includes the eschatological "grace" (χάριν) of eternal life to be borne to them by God at the revelation of Jesus Christ (1:13), and the "grace" (χάρις) they are to give in worship pleasing to God (2:19–20).

It is "in" (ἐν) the "acknowledgment" (ἐπιγνώσει) of God and of Jesus our Lord that grace and peace are to be multiplied to the audience (2 Pet 1:2). And it is "through" (διά) the "acknowledgment" (ἐπιγνώσεως) of the Christ calling us believers by his own glory and virtue that his divine power has granted us all the things necessary toward eternal life and godliness (1:3). Consequently, the qualities the audience are to supply to their faith (1:5–7) will make them neither useless nor fruitless "for" (εἰς) the eschatological "acknowledgment" (ἐπίγνωσιν) of our Lord Jesus Christ (1:8). This includes not only Christ's acknowledgment of believers by granting them a share in the divine nature of his eternal life (1:4), but also believers' acknowledgment of Christ by offering him the grace of a holistic worship, a godliness, pleasing to God. The eschatological result of the qualities the audience are to supply to their faith thus resonates with the refinement of their faith through suffering "for" (εἰς) eschatological acknowledgment—the praise, glory, and honor to be given by and to God at the revelation of Jesus Christ (1 Pet 1:7).

For to whomever "these things" (ταῦτα), that is, "these things" (ταῦτα) the audience are to supply to their faith (1:8), are not "present" (πάρεστιν) as an apparent part of his faith, he "is" (ἐστιν) blind, being shortsighted (1:9a). Without these things he is shortsighted with regard to the future goal of faith because they make the audience neither useless nor fruitless for the eschatological acknowledgment of our Lord Jesus Christ (1:8). In ironic contrast to the audience as believers who love the Christ they have not seen (1 Pet 1:8), any believer who lacks these qualities that are climaxed by love (2 Pet 1:5–7) will be blinded and shortsighted with regard to the prospect of seeing and being seen by the Christ they love that will take place at the eschatological acknowledgment of our Lord Jesus Christ.

As the audience recall, each believer has "received" (ἔλαβεν) a gift from the varied grace of God (1 Pet 4:10) for doxological worship, "so that in all things God may be glorified through Jesus Christ, to whom is glory and might for the ages of the ages, amen!" (4:11). But, in ironic contrast, the believer who does not supply his faith with the various qualities provided by God (2 Pet 1:5–7) is not only blind and shortsighted, but is "receiving" (λαβών) forgetfulness of the cleansing of his sins of the past (1:9).[19] Such "cleansing" (καθαρισμοῦ) of sins enables the audience to perform the ethical worship of loving one another constantly from a "clean" (καθαρᾶς) heart (1 Pet 1:22). That a believer who does not supply his faith with love (2 Pet 1:7) receives forgetfulness of the cleansing of his "sins" (ἁμαρτιῶν) of the past recalls the exhortation for the audience to keep love for each other constant, because love covers a multitude of the "sins" (ἁμαρτιῶν) that prevent proper worship (1 Pet 4:8). Indeed, Christ suffered concerning "sins" (ἁμαρτιῶν), so that he might lead the audience to the worship of God (3:18).

"Therefore rather," that is, rather than being blind and shortsighted (2 Pet 1:9), the audience are to make every effort, by upholding these things as firm, never to stumble (1:10)—a danger for the blind and shortsighted—on their way to entering into the eternal kingdom (1:11).[20] "These things" (ταῦτα) they are to uphold refers to "these things" (ταῦτα) that are to be present to every believer (1:9), "these things" (ταῦτα) that are to be existing and increasing to the audience as believers (1:8). That the audience are here addressed as "brothers [ἀδελφοί]" (1:10) highlights love and "brotherly affection" (φιλαδελφίαν) as the final qualities they are to supply to their faith (1:7). As those who are to supply these qualities to their faith by applying every "effort [σπουδήν]" (1:5), they are also to "make every effort" (σπουδάσατε) their call and chosenness as firm to uphold (1:10).

The "call" (κλῆσιν) the audience are to uphold as firm (1:10) refers to the divine call of Jesus our Lord "calling" (καλέσαντος) us believers by his own glory and "virtue [ἀρετῇ]" (1:3) to become sharers of the divine nature that includes eternal life (1:4). And the "chosenness" (ἐκλογήν) they are to uphold as firm (1:10) recalls that they are sojourners divinely "chosen [ἐκλεκτοῖς]" (1 Pet 1:1; cf. 5:13) for the worship made possible for them by the obedience and sprinkling of the blood of Jesus Christ (1:2). They are reminded that as a "chosen" (ἐκλεκτόν) race and royal priesthood they are to proclaim, through both their liturgical and ethical worship, the "virtues" (ἀρετάς) of the God who "called" (καλέσαντος) them out of darkness for his marvelous light (2:9). As living stones being built up as a spiritual house for a holy priesthood, they are to offer up the worship of spiritual

---

19. "As is usual in the Bible, the idea of 'forgetting' is not a mental process but a practical failure to take into account the true meaning and significance of something" (Moo, *2 Peter and Jude*, 48).

20. On the grammatical combination "therefore rather" (διὸ μᾶλλον), see Davids, *2 Peter and Jude*, 51; Green, *Jude and 2 Peter*, 200. "The 'stumbling' here is the opposite of 'receiving a rich welcome into the eternal kingdom of our Lord and Savior Jesus Christ' (v. 11)" (Moo, *2 Peter and Jude*, 49).

sacrifices acceptable to God through Jesus Christ (2:5), the cornerstone "chosen" (ἐκλεκτόν) and esteemed in the sight of God (2:4, 6).

"For thus," that is, by upholding the list of qualities the audience are to "supply" (ἐπιχορηγήσατε) to their faith (2 Pet 1:5), the entrance for the eternal kingdom will be richly "supplied" (ἐπιχορηγηθήσεται) by God (divine passive) to "you [ὑμῖν]" (1:11), recalling that these qualities are to be existing and increasing to "you [ὑμῖν]" (1:8). These qualities to be added to their faith make the audience neither useless nor fruitless not only "for" (εἰς) the eschatological acknowledgment of our Lord Jesus Christ (1:8) but "for" (εἰς) the eternal kingdom of our Lord and savior Jesus Christ (1:11). The reference to the entrance "for" the "eternal" (αἰώνιον) kingdom recalls the conclusion of 1 Peter, where the audience are designated as those whom God has called "for" (εἰς) his "eternal" (αἰώνιον) glory in Christ Jesus (1 Pet 5:10). Their entrance for the eternal "kingdom" (βασιλείαν) reminds the audience that they are a "royal" (βασίλειον) priesthood (2:9), a holy priesthood, who are to offer up the worship of spiritual sacrifices acceptable to God through Jesus Christ (2:5).

The audience have heard the opening prayer greeting that grace and peace be multiplied to them within the realm of their acknowledgment of and by Jesus as "our Lord [κυρίου ἡμῶν]" (2 Pet 1:2). They have been exhorted to supply to their faith the qualities that will make them neither useless nor fruitless for their eschatological acknowledgment of and by "our Lord" (κυρίου ἡμῶν) Jesus Christ (1:8), which will be consummated when they finally enter into the eternal kingdom of "our Lord" (κυρίου ἡμῶν) Jesus Christ (1:11). The promise that the entrance for the eternal kingdom of "our" (ἡμῶν) divine Lord and "savior" (σωτῆρος) Jesus Christ will be divinely supplied to them (1:11) thus deepens their appreciation for the precious faith divinely allotted to them within the righteousness of "our" (ἡμῶν) God and "savior" (σωτῆρος) Jesus Christ (1:1). In and through such precious faith they may become sharers of the divine nature (1:4) through all the things divinely granted them toward eternal life and the godliness that is good worship (1:3).

After "therefore rather" (διὸ μᾶλλον) introduced Peter's exhortation for his audience to uphold their call and chosenness as firm (1:10), a complementary "therefore I intend" (διὸ μελλήσω) introduces Peter's personal role in his audience's fulfillment of it, as he intends always to remind them about "these things [τούτων]" (1:12).[21] This recalls "these things" (ταῦτα)

---

21. "[T]he unusual and somewhat awkward use of the future of μέλλω creates a sense of ongoing reminder. Since Peter's death is assumed to be soon (1:14), this future reminder cannot be done in person. Hence the letter itself must function in this way" (Donelson, *I & II Peter*, 226).

2 Peter 1:1-15

the audience are to uphold so they will never stumble (1:10), "these things" (ταῦτα) as the qualities to be present to every believer (1:9), and "these things" (ταῦτα) as the qualities of faith to be existing and increasing to them (1:8). But it especially resonates with "these things" (τούτων) through which they may become sharers of the divine nature (1:4). These are all the things the divine power of Jesus Christ has granted to us believers toward eternal divine life and the godliness that is good worship (1:3).

Peter intends to remind the audience about these things even though they know and are "confirmed" (ἐστηριγμένους) in the present truth (1:12), as they look forward to the future fulfillment of the promise that the God who called them for his eternal glory in Christ Jesus will himself restore, "confirm" (στηρίξει), strengthen, establish (1 Pet 5:10). The audience are already confirmed in the "present" (παρούσῃ) truth, as believers to whom the qualities to be supplied to their faith (2 Pet 1:5-7) are "present [πάρεστιν]" (1:9). And that they are confirmed in the present "truth" (ἀληθείᾳ) recalls that they have purified their souls in obedience to the "truth" (ἀληθείας) for sincere brotherly affection, so that from a clean heart they may perform the ethical worship of loving one another constantly (1 Pet 1:22).[22]

In accord with the "righteousness" (δικαιοσύνῃ) established by our God and savior Jesus Christ (2 Pet 1:1), Peter considers it "righteous" (δίκαιον), as long as he is in this "tent," that is, his physical body, to stir his audience up by a reminder (1:13). Whereas baptism is not a "removal" (ἀπόθεσις) by God of the dirt of flesh (1 Pet 3:21), Peter knows that imminent is the "removal" (ἀπόθεσις) by God of his "tent," his physical flesh (2 Pet 1:14a).[23] In continuity with the Spirit of Christ that was in the prophets "indicating" (ἐδήλου) to them the Christ event (1 Pet 1:11), our Lord Jesus Christ "indicated" (ἐδήλωσέν) to Peter his imminent removal (2 Pet 1:14b).[24] That "our Lord" (κύριος ἡμῶν) Jesus Christ has already indicated this to Peter exemplifies the acknowledgment the audience can anticipate from "our Lord" (κυρίου ἡμῶν) Jesus Christ (1:8), when they finally enter into the eternal kingdom of "our Lord" (κυρίου ἡμῶν) and savior Jesus Christ (1:11).

22. "ἀλήθεια ('truth') was a widespread and frequent designation for the gospel from an early period" (Bauckham, *Jude, 2 Peter*, 198). "The truth that is present in the community probably includes the full content of the gospel and the full realities of the Christian life" (Donelson, *I & II Peter*, 226).

23. "The word σκήνωμα ('tent') functions as a metaphor for the body understood as a temporary dwelling as opposed to a permanent structure" (Harrington, *2 Peter*, 251). "While the language of 'tent' may suggest a dualism of real self and unreal body, it is actually used to evoke the temporary character of life" (Donelson, *I & II Peter*, 226).

24. "The general sense of the passage must be: 'I know that I am going to die soon—and this corresponds to Christ's prophecy'" (Bauckham, *Jude, 2 Peter*, 199).

Peter exhorted his audience to "make every effort" (σπουδάσατε) their call and chosenness as firm to "uphold" (ποιεῖσθαι), for "upholding" (ποιοῦντες) "these things" (ταῦτα), they will never stumble (1:10) on their way toward entrance into the eternal kingdom of our Lord and savior Jesus Christ (1:11). He now complements this by pledging his personal assurance that "I will also make every effort [σπουδάσω]" at all times to have you, after my departure, the memory of "these things" (τούτων) to "uphold [ποιεῖσθαι]" (1:15). That Peter will make every effort to have the audience at all times the "memory" (μνήμην) of "these things" (τούτων) to uphold thus emphatically reinforces his assertion that he intends always to "remind" (ὑπομιμνῄσκειν) them about "these things [τούτων]" (1:12).

This reference to the memory of "these things [τούτων]" (1:15) once again calls to the attention of the audience "these things" (τούτων) through which they may become sharers of the divine nature (1:4). These are all the things the divine power of Jesus Christ has granted us believers toward attaining eternal life and the godliness that combines ethical with liturgical worship (1:3). Peter has thus attuned his audience to hear in the letter itself, which appears to be his last (1:14), his determined effort to have them uphold the memory of these things, after his "departure" (ἔξοδον) from this life (1:15), for the sake of their ultimate "entrance" (εἴσοδος) into eternal life in the kingdom of our Lord and savior Jesus Christ (1:11).[25]

Summary on 1:1–15

Addressed as those who have been allotted by God with a "faith" that is as precious to them as it is to all believers (2 Pet 1:1), the audience of 2 Peter recall that in the power of God they are among those being guarded through this precious "faith" for a "salvation" ready to be revealed in the last time (1 Pet 1:5). They are among those in the process of attaining the end of their "faith," "salvation" of souls (1:9), and of growing up for "salvation" to the eternal life for which they have become "newborn infants" (2:2). This salvation from eternal death and for eternal life is part of the righteousness in which the audience have been allotted by God with a very precious faith. This is the righteousness to which they are to live now as believers enabled to do God's will and thus worship God properly, the righteousness established by the death

---

25. "The most obvious candidate for fulfilling the role of a perpetual reminder is the letter we know as 2 Peter" (Harrington, *2 Peter*, 252). "Most readers understand this verse as the articulation of the ultimate purpose of the letter. The letter is to serve as a permanent reminder" (Donelson, *I & II Peter*, 227). "At death one leaves (*exodus*) this world and, having remained true to the gospel, enters into (*eisodus*) the eternal kingdom of Jesus Christ" (Kraftchick, *Jude, 2 Peter*, 105–6).

and resurrection of the Jesus Christ of whom Symeon Peter is a slave and apostle, the Jesus Christ who is not only our "savior" but our God (2 Pet 1:1).

The introductory prayer greeting, "May grace to you and peace be multiplied" (1:2a), echoes the identical introductory prayer greeting in 1 Peter (1:2). But for the audience of 2 Peter the "grace" prayed for them has a more specific reference. First Peter presented them with the "true grace of God" in which they are to remain firm (5:12), epitomized as the "grace of life" (3:7), the eternal life for which God, the "God of all grace" (5:10; cf. 1:10, 13; 4:10; 5:5), gave believers new birth (1:3, 23). But this grace of divine initiative implies a corresponding grace of human response to it that takes place in and through the worship that includes good ethical conduct. This is the "grace" pleasing in the sight of God (2:19, 20).

Peter prays that this grace and peace may be multiplied for the audience by God (2 Pet 1:2a) within a realm or sphere characterized as "the acknowledgment of God and of Jesus our Lord" (1:2b). At this point the audience experience a progression from their reception of a precious faith "in" the righteousness of "our" God and savior Jesus Christ (1:1) to the prayer that grace and peace be multiplied to them "in" the acknowledgment of God and of Jesus "our" Lord. "In the acknowledgment of God" refers, on the one hand, to God's acknowledgment of the audience by divinely allotting them a precious faith in and through the righteousness accomplished by Jesus Christ. This is also Jesus' acknowledgment of the audience as believers, since he has already been identified as "our God" (1:1). On the other hand, it also refers to the audience's acknowledgment, in and through their worship, of God and of Jesus Christ as not only "our God and savior" (1:1) but also "our" divine "Lord" (1:2).

That the divine power of Jesus Christ has granted to us believers all the things necessary toward attaining "life" (1:3a) reminds the audience that as believers they are fellow heirs of the grace of "life" (1 Pet 3:7), the eternal "life" they are to inherit by turning away from evil and doing good (3:9–11). The divine power of Jesus Christ has granted all things necessary not only toward eternal life but toward the "godliness," literally, the "good worship" that includes both the liturgical and ethical worship that accords with this eternal life for which believers have been given new birth (1:3, 23). That the divine power of Jesus Christ has "granted" all these things exemplifies the grace that Peter prayed may be multiplied for the audience (2 Pet 1:2a).

Peter prayed that grace and peace may be multiplied to the audience "in the acknowledgment" of God and of Jesus our Lord (1:2). But the audience are to appreciate that it is "through the acknowledgment" of the one calling us by his own glory and virtue that the divine power of Jesus Christ has granted us believers all the things necessary toward attaining eternal life and godliness (1:3). Here again "acknowledgment" conveys a double meaning. It refers not only to the divine acknowledgment of us believers by calling and allotting us a precious faith (1:1), but also to the human acknowledgment of the divine call by becoming believers through a public profession of faith. Thus, the human response of acknowledgment to the divine initiative of acknowledgment finds its expression in the communal worship of us believers.

"Through these things," that is, not only the precious and great "things" promised and divinely granted to us (1:4a), but also the "things" toward life and godliness divinely granted to us (1:3a), the audience may become sharers of the divine nature (1:4b). That "you," the audience, "may become" sharers of the divine nature resonates with the exhortations for "you" to "become" zealots for the good (1 Pet 3:13), as "you become" children of Sarah by doing good (3:6), and as "you become" holy as God is holy (1:15). The audience are exhorted to become "sharers" of the divine nature by the Peter who is himself a "sharer" in the divine glory that is going to be revealed (5:1; cf. 4:13). They may thus become sharers of the "divine" nature, because the "divine" power of Jesus Christ, our "God" and savior (2 Pet 1:1), has granted them all the things necessary toward attaining the eternal life (1:3a) that is part of the divine nature, the future eternal life they may already begin to live in and through their ethical worship.

Since the divine power of Christ has granted to believers all the things necessary toward eternal life and "godliness," the holistic worship that includes both liturgical and ethical worship (1:3), the audience, in addition to virtue, knowledge (1:5), self-control, and endurance, are to supply to their faith "godliness" (1:6). This is possible for them because Christ once concerning sins suffered, the righteous one on behalf of the unrighteous, so that he might lead the audience to God, thus enabling them to engage in the godliness of worshiping God both in their liturgical or cultic conduct as well as in their ethical or moral behavior (1 Pet 3:18).

Christ modeled the godliness the audience are to include as a quality of their faith when he performed the ethical worship of not returning insults when insulted or threats when suffering, but handing himself over to the God who judges righteously. This led to his cultic, sacrificial worship of offering up our sins in his body upon the tree. Consequently, to sins having died, we believers might live, both now and eternally, to the righteousness that serves as worship pleasing to God, or, in other words, "godliness" (2:23-24). Because Christ offered up our sins in his sacrificial death, the audience are able to perform the godliness of offering up spiritual sacrifices acceptable to God through Jesus Christ (2:5). They are able to be holy as God is holy through the godliness of calling upon God as Father in

2 Peter 1:1–15

their liturgical worship and conducting the time of their sojourning in the reverential fear of their ethical worship (1:15–17).

At the end of 1 Peter the audience heard that they are to greet one another within their worshiping assembly with a ritualistic kiss of "love" (5:14). They were exhorted to keep "love" for each other constant, because "love" covers a multitude of the sins that vitiate the worship that is essential to godliness (4:8). And now they are exhorted to supply to their faith, in addition to brotherly affection, "love" (2 Pet 1:7). The audience have been twice addressed as "beloved" (1 Pet 2:11; 4:12), that is, as those who are loved by God as well as by fellow believers. They have been exhorted to "love" the brotherhood of their fellow believers (2:17), indeed, to "love" one another constantly (1:22), as believers who "love" the Jesus Christ they have not seen (1:8). As the climax to the qualities the audience are to supply to their faith, Christian love is thus the key to the godliness that combines the love of God/Christ in their liturgical worship with the love of fellow believers in their ethical worship.

It is "in" the "acknowledgment" of God and of Jesus our Lord that grace and peace are to be multiplied to the audience (2 Pet 1:2). And it is "through" the "acknowledgment" of the Christ calling us believers by his own glory and virtue that his divine power has granted us all the things necessary toward eternal life and godliness (1:3). Consequently, the qualities the audience are to supply to their faith (1:5–7) will make them neither useless nor fruitless "for" the eschatological "acknowledgment" of our Lord Jesus Christ (1:8). This includes not only Christ's acknowledgment of believers by granting them a share in the divine nature of his eternal life (1:4), but also believers' acknowledgment of Christ by offering him the grace of a holistic worship, a godliness, pleasing to God. The eschatological result of the qualities the audience are to supply to their faith thus resonates with the refinement of their faith through suffering "for" eschatological acknowledgment—the praise, glory, and honor to be given by and to God at the revelation of Jesus Christ (1 Pet 1:7).

As the audience recall, each believer has "received" a gift from the varied grace of God (4:10) for doxological worship, "so that in all things God may be glorified through Jesus Christ, to whom is glory and might for the ages of the ages, amen!" (4:11). But, in ironic contrast, the believer who does not supply his faith with the various qualities provided by God (2 Pet 1:5–7) is not only blind and shortsighted, but is "receiving" forgetfulness of the cleansing of his sins of the past (1:9). Such "cleansing" of sins enables the audience to perform the ethical worship of loving one another constantly from a "clean" heart (1 Pet 1:22). That a believer who does not supply his faith with love (2 Pet 1:7) receives forgetfulness of the cleansing of his "sins" of the past recalls the exhortation for the audience to keep love for each other constant, because love covers a multitude of the "sins" that prevent proper worship (1 Pet 4:8). Indeed, Christ suffered concerning "sins," so that he might lead the audience to the worship of God (3:18).

The "call" the audience are to uphold as firm (2 Pet 1:10) refers to the divine call of Jesus our Lord "calling" us believers by his own glory and "virtue" (1:3) to become sharers of the divine nature that includes eternal life (1:4). And the "chosenness" they are to uphold as firm (1:10) recalls that they are sojourners divinely "chosen" (1 Pet 1:1; cf. 5:13) for the worship made possible for them by the obedience and sprinkling of the blood of Jesus Christ (1:2). They are reminded that as a "chosen" race and royal priesthood they are to proclaim, through both their liturgical and ethical worship, the "virtues" of the God who "called" them out of darkness for his marvelous light (2:9). As living stones being built up as a spiritual house for a holy priesthood, they are to offer up the worship of spiritual sacrifices acceptable to God through Jesus Christ (2:5), the cornerstone "chosen" and esteemed in the sight of God (2:4, 6).

"For thus," that is, by upholding the list of qualities the audience are to "supply" to their faith (2 Pet 1:5), the entrance for the eternal kingdom will be richly "supplied" by God (divine passive) to "you" (1:11), recalling that these qualities are to be existing and increasing to "you" (1:8). These qualities to be added to their faith make the audience neither useless nor fruitless not only "for" the eschatological acknowledgment of our Lord Jesus Christ (1:8) but "for" the eternal kingdom of our Lord and savior Jesus Christ (1:11). The reference to the entrance "for" the "eternal" kingdom recalls the conclusion of 1 Peter, where the audience are designated as those whom God has called "for" his "eternal" glory in Christ Jesus (1 Pet 5:10). Their entrance for the eternal "kingdom" reminds the audience that they are a "royal" priesthood (2:9), a holy priesthood, who are to offer up the worship of spiritual sacrifices acceptable to God through Jesus Christ (2:5).

After "therefore rather" introduced Peter's exhortation for his audience to uphold their call and chosenness as firm (2 Pet 1:10), a complementary "therefore I intend" introduces Peter's personal role in his audience's fulfillment of it, as he intends always to remind them about "these things" (1:12). This recalls "these things" the audience are to uphold so they will never stumble (1:10), "these things" as the qualities to be present to every believer (1:9), and "these things" as the qualities of faith to be existing and increasing to them (1:8). But it especially resonates with "these things" through which they may become sharers of the divine nature (1:4). These are all the things the divine power of Jesus Christ has granted to us believers toward eternal divine life and the godliness that is good worship (1:3).

2 Peter 1:1-15

In accord with the "righteousness" established by our God and savior Jesus Christ (1:1), Peter considers it "righteous," as long as he is in this "tent," that is, his physical body, to stir his audience up by a reminder (1:13). Whereas baptism is not a "removal" by God of the dirt of flesh (1 Pet 3:21), Peter knows that imminent is the "removal" by God of his "tent," his physical flesh (2 Pet 1:14a). In continuity with the Spirit of Christ that was in the prophets "indicating" to them the Christ event (1 Pet 1:11), our Lord Jesus Christ "indicated" to Peter his imminent removal (2 Pet 1:14b). That "our Lord" Jesus Christ has already indicated this to Peter exemplifies the acknowledgment the audience can anticipate from "our Lord" Jesus Christ (1:8), when they finally enter into the eternal kingdom of "our Lord" and savior Jesus Christ (1:11).

The reference to the memory of "these things" (1:15) once again calls to the attention of the audience "these things" through which they may become sharers of the divine nature (1:4). These are all the things the divine power of Jesus Christ has granted us believers toward attaining eternal life and the godliness that combines ethical with liturgical worship (1:3). Peter has thus attuned his audience to hear in the letter itself, which appears to be his last (1:14), his determined effort to have them uphold the memory of these things, after his "departure" from this life (1:15), for the sake of their ultimate "entrance" into eternal life in the kingdom of our Lord and savior Jesus Christ (1:11).

16

2 Peter 1:16–21
By the Holy Spirit Human Beings Spoke Prophecy from God (B)

Knowing every prophecy of scripture does not come about by one's own interpretation

A   ¹⁶ For not by following craftily devised myths, did we *make known* to you the power and coming of our Lord Jesus Christ, but by having *become* eyewitnesses of the majesty of that one.
  B   ^{17a} For he received from God the Father honor and glory, when a *voice* was conveyed to him such as this by the majestic glory,
    C   ^{17b} "My Son, my beloved, is this one for whom I am well pleased."
  B' ^{18a} And this *voice* we ourselves heard conveyed from heaven,
A' ^{18b} being with him on the holy mountain. ¹⁹ And we have as very firm the prophetic word, to which you are upholding well, if attending to it as a light appearing in a dreary place, until the day dawns and the morning star arises in your hearts, ²⁰ this first *knowing*, that every prophecy of scripture does not *come about* by one's own interpretation, ²¹ for not by the will of a human being has prophecy ever been conveyed, rather, brought along by the Holy Spirit, human beings spoke from God.[1]

---

1. For the establishment of 2 Pet 1:16–21 as a chiasm, see ch. 14.

2 Peter 1:16-21

Audience Response to 1:16-21

1:16 (A): We Made Known to You by Having Become Eyewitnesses of Majesty

Not by following myths craftily devised by certain human beings, did "we," that is, Peter and his apostolic associates (cf. 1:1), make known to you the power and future coming of our Lord Jesus Christ (1:16a).[2] This was made known to "you" (ὑμῖν), the audience, the "you" (ὑμᾶς) who are to uphold the memory of the things Peter is reminding them in this letter (1:15). These successive occurrences of the second person plural pronoun "you" in reference to the audience thus serve as the transitional terms linking this chiastic unit (1:16-21) with the preceding one (1:1-15).

The power and future coming of our Lord Jesus Christ that "we made known" (ἐγνωρίσαμεν) to you (1:16a) is part of the "knowledge" (γνῶσιν) the audience are to supply to their faith (1:5) as a result of heeding what Peter is intent on reminding them about in the letter (1:12-15).[3] The divine "power" (δυνάμεως) of our Lord Jesus Christ granted us believers everything needed toward the attainment of eternal life and the godliness that is good worship (1:3). And now the audience are to know and remember that this "power" (δύναμιν) is also associated with the future coming of our Lord Jesus Christ. The audience are thus to realize that it is at this final coming of "our Lord Jesus Christ" that they will be part of the eschatological acknowledgment of and by "our Lord Jesus Christ" (1:8), and that the entrance for the eternal kingdom of "our Lord and savior Jesus Christ" will be richly supplied to them (1:11).

Peter and his associates made known to the audience the power and future coming of our Lord Jesus Christ, not by following myths craftily devised by human beings, but by having become, through divine grace, eyewitnesses of the majesty of that one (1:16). That they have "become" (γενηθέντες) eyewitnesses through divine grace reinforces the exhortation

---

2. "[T]he modifier 'cleverly devised' indicates that these myths did not come from divine revelation but from human creativity" (Donelson, *I & II Peter*, 231). On myths see also Neyrey, *2 Peter, Jude*, 175-76. "The Greek noun *mythos* has a variety of meanings: 'tale, story, legend, myth.' Here, as in the Pastorals (see 1 Tim 1:4; 4:7; 2 Tim 4:4; Titus 1:14), it carries a negative or pejorative sense" (Harrington, *2 Peter*, 255).

3. "The switch from the first-person singular in the previous section (1:12-15) to the first-person plural here is significant: Peter presents his case not simply as one who is at the end of life but also as a person who stands shoulder to shoulder with others ... The reference in 1:16 may therefore be to the *letter* that Peter penned with the cooperation of Silvanus, his amanuensis (1 Pet. 5:12), since indeed that correspondence introduced the topic of Christ's future 'revelation' (1 Pet. 1:5, 7, 13; 4:13; 5:1), albeit with different terminology [emphasis original]" (Green, *Jude and 2 Peter*, 218-19).

for the audience to "become" (γένησθε) sharers of the divine nature through all the things divinely granted to them (1:4). In ironic contrast to anyone in the audience who might be "blind, being shortsighted" (1:9), with regard to a future entrance into the eternal kingdom (1:11), Peter and his associates have become "eyewitnesses" of the divine majesty that prefigures the future and final coming of our Lord Jesus Christ.

1:17a (B): When a Voice Was Conveyed to Him by the Majestic Glory

The audience then begin to hear what Peter and his associates witnessed with regard to the majesty of our Lord Jesus Christ (1:16): "For he received from God the Father honor and glory, when a voice was conveyed to him such as this by the majestic glory" (1:17a). In ironic contrast to any "blind, shortsighted" member of the audience "receiving" (λαβών) forgetfulness of the cleansing by God of his sins of the past (1:9), our Lord Jesus Christ "received" (λαβών) from God the Father honor and glory. The "honor and glory" (τιμὴν καὶ δόξαν) Jesus Christ received from God the Father anticipates the "glory and honor" (δόξαν καὶ τιμήν) the refined faith of the audience will receive at the revelation, that is, the final coming, of Jesus Christ (1 Pet 1:7). He received this divine honor and glory when a unique voice was conveyed to him by the "majestic" (μεγαλοπρεποῦς) glory of God (2 Pet 1:17a), which revealed to the eyewitnesses the divine "majesty" (μεγαλειότητος) that indicates the divine power and future coming of our Lord Jesus Christ (1:16).

1:17b (C): My Son, My Beloved, Is This One for Whom I Am Well Pleased

The audience then hear the voice that God the Father conveyed regarding our Lord Jesus Christ (1:17a): "My Son, my beloved, is this one for whom I am well pleased" (1:17b). God the Father's declaration that Jesus is "my" (μου) Son is emphatically intensified with the additional designation of him as "my" (μου) "beloved" (ἀγαπητός), the one "for whom" (εἰς ὅν), that is, for whose present as well as future divine honor and glory at his final coming (1:16), God is well pleased. This reminds the audience that this is the divinely beloved Jesus whom, not having seen, "you love" (ἀγαπᾶτε) also, and "for whom" (εἰς ὅν), that is, for whose final coming, now not seeing, but believing, they are engaged in the worship of exulting with a joy indescribable and glorified (1 Pet 1:8).⁴ Indeed, they are to completely hope upon the grace to be divinely borne to them at the revelation, the final coming, of Jesus Christ (1:13).

The declaration that God the Father is well pleased with Jesus as his beloved Son is intensified by the emphatic use of the first person singular pronoun—"for whom I [ἐγώ] am well pleased" (2 Pet 1:17b).⁵ This reminds the audience of a similar emphatic use of the same pronoun in the scriptural declaration that "you shall be holy, for I [ἐγώ] am holy" (Lev 19:2 in 1 Pet 1:16).⁶ The audience are to be holy by calling upon God in their liturgical worship as the Father who impartially judges according to the work of each one, and by conducting the time of their sojourning in the reverent fear of God in their ethical worship (1:17). The Jesus for whom "I am well pleased" (εὐδόκησα) has provided the model and means for the audience to be holy through their worship. As an act of ethical worship, he handed himself over to the God who judges righteously, so that believers might live to the righteousness of ethical worship (2:23-24). And, as living stones built up as a spiritual house for a holy priesthood, the audience are enabled to offer up the worship of spiritual sacrifices "acceptable" (εὐπροσδέκτους) to God through Jesus Christ (2:5).

1:18a (B'): And This Voice We Ourselves Heard Conveyed from Heaven

The audience hear more about the unique voice conveyed to Jesus (2 Pet 1:17a): "And this voice we ourselves heard conveyed from heaven" (1:18a). At this point, after the central and unparalleled C element (1:17b), the audience experience a pivot of parallels from the B to the B' element of this chiastic unit. "When a voice [φωνῆς] was conveyed to him" (1:17a) progresses to "this voice [φωνήν] we ourselves heard conveyed" (1:18a).

The emphatic employment of the first person plural pronoun "we ourselves" in the assertion that "this voice we ourselves [ἡμεῖς] heard" further enhances the divine authority that Peter and his associates have for the benefit

---

4. That these are the only occurrences of the phrase "for whom" (εἰς ὅν) in 1 and 2 Peter enhances the significance of this connection.

5. "The author of 2 Peter may have added the emphatic ἐγώ ('I') to the form of the words which he knew in the tradition. It stresses that Jesus is the one whom *God* himself has selected to be his vicegerent. Thus the expectation of the Parousia is not a humanly contrived myth (v 16), but is firmly grounded in God's declared will as the apostles themselves heard it spoken [emphasis original]" (Bauckham, *Jude, 2 Peter*, 220).

6. That these are the only occurrences of the first personal singular pronoun "I" (ἐγώ) in 1 and 2 Peter facilitates this connection.

of the audience.⁷ As those who became eyewitnesses, they not only saw the divine majesty of Jesus (1:16), but also actually heard for themselves the divine voice regarding him conveyed from heaven (1:18a). That the voice heard was conveyed "from heaven" (ἐξ οὐρανοῦ) implies that it was conveyed by the Holy Spirit, as it recalls that the gospel was proclaimed to the audience by the Holy Spirit sent "from heaven [ἀπ' οὐρανοῦ]" (1 Pet 1:12). The audience are to appreciate the significance of the divine heavenly origin of the voice, since it is "in heaven" (ἐν οὐρανοῖς) that the imperishable inheritance to eternal life is being divinely kept for them (1:4). And it is "into heaven" (εἰς οὐρανόν) that the risen Christ went to sit at the right of God, with angels and authorities and powers having been subjected to him (3:22).

1:18b–21 (A'): Knowing That Every Prophecy Comes About by the Holy Spirit

The audience hear the A' element (1:18b–21) of this chiastic unit as a chiastic pattern in itself:
a) being with him on the *holy* mountain (1:18b),
  b) And we have as very firm the *prophetic* word (1:19a),
    c) to which you are upholding well, if attending to it as a light appearing *in* a dreary place (1:19b),
    c') until the day dawns and the morning star arises *in* your hearts (1:19c),
  b') this first knowing, that every *prophecy* of scripture does not come about by one's own interpretation, for not by the will of a human being has *prophecy* ever been conveyed (1:20–21a),
a') rather, brought along by the *Holy* Spirit, human beings spoke from God (1:21b).

At the center of this chiastic sub-unit the audience experience a pivot of parallels from the c) to the c') sub-element involving the only occurrences in 2 Peter of expressions regarding light followed by the preposition "in." "A light appearing in [ἐν] a dreary place" (1:19b) progresses to "the morning star arises in [ἐν] your hearts" (1:19c). The audience then hear a progression of parallels from the b) to the b') sub-element involving the only occurrences in 2 Peter of the terms "prophetic/prophecy." "The prophetic [προφητικόν] word" (1:19a) progresses to "every prophecy [προφητεία] of scripture" (1:20) and to "not by the will of a human being has prophecy [προφητεία] ever been conveyed" (1:21a). Finally, the audience hear a

---

7. "The unnecessary inclusion of the pronoun ἡμεῖς (we) makes the subject emphatic" (Donelson, *I & II Peter*, 230).

2 Peter 1:16-21

progression of parallels from the a) to the a') sub-element involving the only occurrences in this sub-unit of the adjective "holy." "On the holy [ἁγίῳ] mountain" (1:18b) progresses to "by the Holy [ἁγίου] Spirit" (1:21b).

And at this point the audience experience a progression, via the chiastic parallels, from the A (1:16) to the A' (1:18b-21) element of this chiastic unit. "Did we make known [ἐγνωρίσαμεν] to you" and "having become [γενηθέντες] eyewitnesses" (1:16) progress to "this first knowing [γινώσκοντες], that every prophecy of scripture does not come about [γίνεται] by one's own interpretation" (1:20).

That Peter and his associate apostles were with Jesus when the voice was conveyed to him "on the holy mountain" (1:18b) refers to the mountain where Jesus was temporarily transfigured into a glorious heavenly figure in an epiphany before the eyes of the apostles Peter, James, and John, as recorded in the gospel traditions (Matt 17:1-8; Mark 9:2-8; Luke 9:28-36). Each of these gospel accounts mentions the mountain and reports a heavenly voice very similar to the one in 2 Pet 1:17b.[8] The audience are presumed to have knowledge of this tradition. They are to appreciate that the temporary transfiguration of Jesus into a heavenly figure on the holy mountain foreshadowed not only his resurrection into the glory of the heavenly realm but also his future and final coming from the glory of heaven.[9]

In addition, "we," that is, all of us believers, have as very firm the prophetic word (1:19a), implying that the prophetic word contained in the OT scriptures is a more reliable basis than any craftily devised myths for knowing about the final coming of our Lord Jesus Christ (1:16). The audience are to appreciate that the very firm prophetic word adds to the authoritative reliability of what Peter and his apostolic associates saw and heard on the holy mountain as indicative of Christ's future and final coming (1:17-18). This "very firm" (βεβαιότερον) prophetic word thus provides the audience with a further basis to uphold their call and chosenness as "firm [βεβαίαν]" (1:10).[10]

---

8. "The announcement itself is a combination of Ps 2:7 and Isa 42:1 and comes closest to that in Matthew (17:5)" (Donelson, *I & II Peter*, 232-33). And note the reference to God's "holy mountain" in Ps 2:6. See also Bauckham, *Jude, 2 Peter*, 221.

9. Heil, *Transfiguration*; Neyrey, "Apologetic Use of the Transfiguration," 504-19. "Thus it appears that 2 Peter interprets the story of transfiguration not just as an epiphany, which it certainly is, but also as a promise of Jesus' return" (Donelson, *I & II Peter*, 232). "This understanding by Peter of the Transfiguration's meaning for the three eyewitnesses is supported by the record of the Synoptic Gospel writers (Mt 16:27—17:8; Mk 8:38—39:8; Lk 9:26-36). Each discourse follows Jesus' reference to his coming 'in the glory of his Father with his angels' with his prediction that 'some who are standing here will not taste death before they see the kingdom of God come with power' and then with the account of the Transfiguration" (Harvey and Towner, *2 Peter and Jude*, 62).

10. "Given that in Koine Greek the comparative was frequently used as if it were

The audience are upholding well with regard to the prophetic word, if they are attending to it as if it were a light appearing in a dreary place (1:19b). They have heard of the despair implicit in the rhetorical question of where will the ungodly and sinful one "appear" (φανεῖται), if the righteous one is only with difficulty saved in the final judgment (Prov 11:31 in 1 Pet 4:18). And now they hear of the hope implicit in the comparison of the prophetic word that indicates the future coming of Christ for final judgment with a light "appearing" (φαίνοντι) in a dreary place.

The audience are to attend to the prophetic word "until the day dawns and the morning star arises in your hearts" (1:19c). The "day" (ἡμέρα) that is to dawn refers to the day of Christ's future coming for final judgment. It resonates with the "day" (ἡμέρᾳ) of divine visitation for final judgment, when the praiseworthy works of the audience are to lead Gentiles to the worship of glorifying God (1 Pet 2:12). The morning star that is to "arise" (ἀνατείλῃ) in their hearts refers to the future coming of Christ, as it reminds the audience of the scriptural messianic prophecy that "a star will arise [ἀνατελεῖ] out of Jacob" (Num 24:17 LXX). That the morning star arises "in" (ἐν) your hearts internalizes the hope implicit in the comparison of the prophetic word with a light appearing "in" (ἐν) a dreary place (2 Pet 1:19b). And the morning star that will arise "in your hearts" (ἐν ταῖς καρδίαις ὑμῶν) at the final coming of Christ resonates with the exhortation for the audience to hold holy the Christ as Lord "in your hearts" (ἐν ταῖς καρδίαις ὑμῶν), always ready for an answer to all who ask you a word concerning the hope within you (1 Pet 3:15).[11]

Peter then adds to the knowledge "we made known" (ἐγνωρίσαμεν) to you (2 Pet 1:16)—"this first knowing [γινώσκοντες]," that every "prophecy" (προφητεία) of scripture, that is, the very firm "prophetic" (προφητικόν) word we believers have (1:19a), does not come about by one's own interpretation (1:20).[12] Just as Peter and his associates "became" (γενηθέντες) prophetic eyewitnesses not through their own effort but by the grace of God (1:16), so every scriptural prophecy, such as the one alluded to by the messi-

---

a superlative, the meaning could also be 'most certain/reliable' or 'completely certain'" (Davids, *2 Peter and Jude*, 207).

11. "When Jesus comes, we will not need the prophetic word to shine in a dark place—this sinful world. Then our hearts will be enlightened by the Morning Star himself, and that to which prophecy points will have arrived. It is not incompatible to speak of an eschatological event and its interior impact" (Schreiner, *1, 2 Peter*, 322).

12. Wolfe, "2 Peter 1:20 Reconsidered," 92–106; Callan, "Note on 2 Peter 1:19–20," 143–50; Porter and Pitts, "2 Peter 1:20," 165–71. "In the Mediterranean world, prophets were regularly understood as having to interpret the revelation that came to them. This verse denies that the prophecies contained in Scripture are the result of the interpretive process of the prophets" (Donelson, *I & II Peter*, 234).

anic morning star that is to arise (1:19c), does not "come about" (γίνεται) by one's own interpretation. The audience are thus to appreciate that creating a scriptural prophecy by one's "own" (ἰδίας) interpretation contradicts Christ calling us by the divine grace of his "own" (ἰδίᾳ) glory and virtue to eternal life and the godliness of good worship (1:3).

That every "prophecy" (προφητεία) of scripture does not come about by one's own interpretation (1:20) is further explained. For not by the will of a human being, and thus not by myths craftily devised by human beings (1:16), has "prophecy" (προφητεία) ever been "conveyed [ἠνέχθη]" (1:21a). This has already been confirmed for the audience, who have heard that the prophetic voice that was "conveyed" (ἐνεχθείσης) to Jesus (1:17) was "conveyed" (ἐνεχθεῖσαν) not from human beings but from heaven (1:18a).[13] That rather, brought along by the "Holy" (ἁγίου) Spirit, human beings spoke from God (1:21b) further authenticates Peter as an authoritative prophetic spokesman. Indeed, Peter was among those on the "holy" (ἁγίῳ) mountain (1:18b), who heard conveyed from heaven (1:18a), and thus by the Holy Spirit (cf. 1 Pet 1:12), the voice of God prophetically indicative of the final coming of Christ (2 Pet 1:17b).[14] The audience have thus been attuned to heed the prophetic authority of their author regarding the future and final coming of our Lord Jesus Christ (1:16).

Summary on 1:16-21

Peter and his associates made known to the audience the power and future coming of our Lord Jesus Christ, not by following myths craftily devised by human beings, but by having become, through divine grace, eyewitnesses of the majesty of that one (1:16). That they have "become" eyewitnesses through divine grace reinforces the exhortation for the audience to "become" sharers of the divine nature through all the things divinely granted to them (1:4). In ironic contrast to anyone in the audience who might be "blind, being shortsighted" (1:9), with regard to a future entrance into the eternal kingdom (1:11), Peter and his associates have become "eyewitnesses" of the divine majesty that prefigures the future and final coming of our Lord Jesus Christ.

The declaration that God the Father is well pleased with Jesus as his beloved Son is intensified by the emphatic use of the first person singular

---

13. "It should be noted that φέρειν (lit. 'to bear') was also used in vv 17-18 of the heavenly voice. The author's concern there to stress that the words at the Transfiguration came from God, is comparable with his concern here to stress that the words of OT prophecy also came from God" (Bauckham, *Jude, 2 Peter*, 233).

14. Bénétreau, "Évangile et prophétie," 174-91.

pronoun—"for whom *I* am well pleased" (1:17). This reminds the audience of a similar emphatic use of the same pronoun in the scriptural declaration that "you shall be holy, for *I* am holy" (Lev 19:2 in 1 Pet 1:16). The audience are to be holy by calling upon God in their liturgical worship as the Father who impartially judges according to the work of each one, and by conducting the time of their sojourning in the reverent fear of God in their ethical worship (1 Pet 1:17). The Jesus for whom "I am well pleased" has provided the model and means for the audience to be holy through their worship. As ethical worship, he handed himself over to the God who judges righteously, so that believers might live to the righteousness of ethical worship (2:23–24). And, as living stones built up as a spiritual house for a holy priesthood, the audience are enabled to offer up the worship of spiritual sacrifices "acceptable" to God through Jesus Christ (2:5).

The emphatic employment of the first person plural pronoun "we ourselves" in the assertion that "this voice *we ourselves* heard" (2 Pet 1:18) further enhances the divine authority that Peter and his associates have for the benefit of the audience. As those who became eyewitnesses, they not only saw the divine majesty of Jesus (1:16), but also actually heard for themselves the divine voice regarding him conveyed from heaven. That the voice heard was conveyed "from heaven" implies that it was conveyed by the Holy Spirit, as it recalls that the gospel was proclaimed to the audience by the Holy Spirit sent "from heaven" (1 Pet 1:12). The audience are to appreciate the significance of the divine heavenly origin of the voice, since it is "in heaven" that the imperishable inheritance to eternal life is being divinely kept for them (1:4). And it is "into heaven" that the risen Christ went to sit at the right of God, with angels and authorities and powers having been subjected to him (3:22).

"We," that is, all of us believers, have as very firm the prophetic word (2 Pet 1:19), implying that the prophetic word contained in the OT scriptures is a more reliable basis than any craftily devised myths for knowing about the final coming of our Lord Jesus Christ (1:16). The audience are to appreciate that the very firm prophetic word adds to the authoritative reliability of what Peter and his apostolic associates saw and heard on the holy mountain of Jesus' transfiguration into a heavenly figure, which foreshadowed not only his resurrection into the glory of the heavenly realm but also his future and final coming from the glory of heaven (1:17–18). This "very firm" prophetic word thus provides the audience with a further basis to uphold their call and chosenness as "firm" (1:10).

The audience are to attend to the prophetic word "until the day dawns and the morning star arises in your hearts" (1:19). The "day" that is to dawn refers to the day of Christ's future coming for final judgment. It resonates

2 Peter 1:16-21

with the "day" of divine visitation for final judgment, when the praiseworthy works of the audience are to lead Gentiles to the worship of glorifying God (1 Pet 2:12). The morning star that is to "arise" in their hearts refers to the future coming of Christ, as it reminds the audience of the scriptural messianic prophecy that "a star will arise out of Jacob" (Num 24:17 LXX). That the morning star arises "in" your hearts internalizes the hope implicit in the comparison of the prophetic word with a light appearing "in" a dreary place (2 Pet 1:19). And the morning star that will arise "in your hearts" at the final coming of Christ resonates with the exhortation for the audience to hold holy the Christ as Lord "in your hearts," always ready for an answer to all who ask you a word concerning the hope within you (1 Pet 3:15).

Peter then adds to the knowledge "we made known" to you (2 Pet 1:16)—"this first knowing," that every "prophecy" of scripture, that is, the very firm "prophetic" word we believers have (1:19), does not come about by one's own interpretation (1:20). Just as Peter and his associates "became" prophetic eyewitnesses not through their own effort but by the grace of God (1:16), so every scriptural prophecy, such as the one alluded to by the messianic morning star that is to arise (1:19), does not "come about" by one's own interpretation. The audience are thus to appreciate that creating a scriptural prophecy by one's "own" interpretation contradicts Christ calling us by the divine grace of his "own" glory and virtue to eternal life and the godliness of good worship (1:3).

Not by the will of a human being, and thus not by myths craftily devised by human beings (1:16), has "prophecy" ever been "conveyed" (1:21a). This has already been confirmed for the audience, who have heard that the prophetic voice that was "conveyed" to Jesus (1:17) was "conveyed" not from human beings but from heaven (1:18a). That rather, brought along by the "Holy" Spirit, human beings spoke from God (1:21b) further authenticates Peter as an authoritative prophetic spokesman. Indeed, Peter was among those on the "holy" mountain (1:18b), who heard conveyed from heaven (1:18a), and thus by the Holy Spirit (cf. 1 Pet 1:12), the voice of God prophetically indicative of the final coming of Christ (2 Pet 1:17b). The audience have thus been attuned to heed the prophetic authority of Peter regarding the future and final coming of our Lord Jesus Christ (1:16).

17

2 Peter 2:1–16
The Lord Knows How To Rescue the Godly from Trial (C)

*False prophets blaspheming
the way of truth will be destroyed*

A   2:1 There came about indeed false *prophets* among the people, as also among you there *will be* false teachers, who will introduce opinions of annihilation, even denying the Master who purchased them, bringing upon themselves imminent annihilation, ² and many will *follow* their debaucheries, because of whom the *way* of truth will be *blasphemed*, ³ and in *greed* they will exploit you with deceptive words, for whom the *judgment* of long ago is not becoming idle and their annihilation is not becoming drowsy. ⁴ For if God did not spare sinning *angels* but, in chains of gloom casting them into Tartarus, handed them over to be *kept* for *judgment*, ⁵ and if he did not spare the ancient world, but as the eighth, Noah, a herald of righteousness, he guarded, having brought a deluge upon the world of the ungodly, ⁶ and if, having reduced the cities of Sodom and Gomorrah to ashes, he condemned them to ruin, having placed them as an example of the things intended for the ungodly,

B   ⁷ and if the *righteous* Lot, oppressed by the conduct of the disgraceful in debauchery, he *rescued*,

B′   ⁸ for in what was seen and heard the *righteous* one, residing among them day after day, tormented his *righteous* soul by the lawless works, ⁹ᵃ then the Lord knows how to *rescue* the godly from trial,

2 Peter 2:1-16

A′ ⁹ᵇ and to *keep* the unrighteous to be punished at the day of *judgment*, ¹⁰ especially those going after the flesh in desire of defilement and despising lordship, arrogant bold ones, they do not tremble, *blaspheming* glorious beings, ¹¹ whereas *angels, being* greater in strength and power, do not convey a *blasphemous judgment* against them before the Lord. ¹² But these, like irrational animals born by nature for capture and destruction, among things they do not know, *blaspheming*, in their destruction they will also be destroyed, ¹³ suffering harm as recompense for unrighteousness, considering revelry at day a delight, stains and blemishes, delighting in their deceits as they feast together with you, ¹⁴ having eyes full of adultery and unceasing from sin, seducing unstable souls, having a heart trained for *greed*, accursed children, ¹⁵ abandoning the proper *way*, they have been led astray, *following* the *way* of Balaam son of Bosor, who loved recompense for unrighteousness, ¹⁶ but he had a rebuke for his own transgression—a mute donkey talking with a voice of a human being restrained the madness of the *prophet*.[1]

Audience Response to 2:1-16

2:1-6 (A): False Prophets Many Will Follow and the Way of Truth Will Be Blasphemed

The audience hear the A element (2:1-6) of this chiastic unit as a chiastic pattern in itself:

a) There came about indeed false prophets among the people, as also among you there will be false teachers, who will introduce opinions of *annihilation*, even denying the Master who purchased them, *bringing upon* themselves imminent *annihilation* (2:1),

b) and many will follow their debaucheries, because of *whom* the way of truth will be blasphemed (2:2),

c) and in greed they will exploit you with deceptive words (2:3a),

b′) for *whom* the judgment of long ago is not becoming idle (2:3b)

a′) and their *annihilation* is not becoming drowsy. For if God did not spare sinning angels but, in chains of gloom casting them into Tartarus, handed them over to be kept for judgment, and if he did not spare the ancient world, but as the eighth, Noah, a herald of righteousness, he guarded, *having brought* a deluge *upon* the world of the ungodly, and if, having reduced the cities of Sodom and Gomorrah to ashes, he

---

1. For the establishment of 2 Pet 2:1-16 as a chiasm, see ch. 14.

condemned them to ruin, having placed them as an example of the things intended for the ungodly (2:3c-6).

After the central and unparalleled c) sub-element, "and in greed they will exploit you with deceptive words" (2:3a), the audience experience a pivot of chiastic parallels from the b) to the b') sub-element involving the only occurrences in this sub-unit of the relative pronoun. "Because of whom [οὕς]" (2:2) progresses to "for whom [οἷς]" (2:3b). The audience then hear a progression of parallels from the a) to the a') sub-element involving the only occurrences in 2 Peter of the verb "bring upon" and in this sub-unit of the noun "annihilation." "Opinions of annihilation [ἀπωλείας]" (2:1) and "bringing upon [ἐπάγοντες] themselves imminent annihilation [ἀπώλειαν]" (2:1) progress to "their annihilation [ἀπώλεια] is not becoming drowsy" (2:3c) and "having brought a flood upon [ἐπάξας] the world of the ungodly" (2:5). Furthermore, the term "false prophets" (ψευδοπροφῆται) at the beginning of this sub-unit in 2:1 and the term "prophecy" (προφητεία) in 1:21 function as the transitional terms linking this C unit (2:1–16) to the preceding B unit (1:16–21).

And the audience hear the a') sub-element (2:3c–6) as yet another chiastic pattern in itself:
(a) and their annihilation is not becoming drowsy. For if God did not spare sinning angels but, in chains of gloom casting them into Tartarus, handed them over to be kept for *judgment* (2:3c–4),
　(b) and if he did not spare the ancient *world* (2:5a),
　　(c) but as the eighth, Noah, a herald of righteousness (2:5b),
　(b') he guarded, having brought a deluge upon the *world* of the ungodly (2:5c),
(a') and if, having reduced the cities of Sodom and Gomorrah to ashes, he *condemned* them to ruin, having placed them as an example of the things intended for the ungodly (2:6).

After the central and unparalleled (c) sub-element, "but as the eighth, Noah, a herald of righteousness" (2:5b), the audience experience a pivot of parallels from the (b) to the (b') sub-element involving the only occurrences in this sub-unit of the term "world." "Ancient world [κόσμου]" (2:5b) progresses to "the world [κόσμῳ] of the ungodly" (2:5c). They then hear a progression of parallels from the (a) to the (a') sub-element involving the only occurrences in this sub-unit of expressions for "judgment/condemnation." "To be kept for judgment [κρίσιν]" (2:4) progresses to "he condemned [κατέκρινεν] them to ruin" (2:6).

As part of the knowledge they are to add to their faith (1:5–6), the audience are to know that every "prophecy" (προφητεία) of scripture does not "come about" (γίνεται) by one's own interpretation (1:20), for not by the

2 Peter 2:1-16

will of a human being has true "prophecy" (προφητεία) ever been conveyed (1:21). And they are also to remember that there "came about" (ἐγένοντο) indeed "false prophets" (ψευδοπροφῆται) among the "people" (λαῷ), that is, their ancestors as the people of God (2:1). So also among "you," that is, among the audience as those who were once not a "people" (λαός) but now are God's "people [λαός]" (1 Pet 2:10), there will be "false teachers [ψευδοδιδάσκαλοι]" (2 Pet 2:1).[2]

These false teachers will introduce opinions that lead to eternal annihilation, even denying the Lord Jesus himself as the Master who purchased them as an act of redemption to save them from such annihilation (2:1). Just as house servants are to be subject in all reverent fear to their "masters [δεσπόταις]" (1 Pet 2:18), these false teachers, as also the audience, are not to deny but to be subject in all the reverent fear that connotes their holistic worship of this "Master" (δεσπότην), our Lord Jesus Christ.[3] These false teachers will thus contradict all the things toward eternal life and the godliness of good worship that the divine power of our Lord Jesus Christ granted us believers (2 Pet 1:2-3). Just as Peter's removal by God is "imminent [ταχινή]" (1:14), so these false teachers are bringing upon themselves "imminent" (ταχινήν) annihilation from God (2:1).

Whereas it was not by "following" (ἐξακολουθήσαντες) craftily devised myths that Peter and his associates made known to the audience the power and coming of our Lord Jesus Christ (1:16), many will "follow" (ἐξακολουθήσουσιν) the debaucheries of these false teachers (2:2). The reference to their "debaucheries" (ἀσελγείαις) links them to the "debaucheries" (ἀσελγείαις) of the ungodly Gentiles associated with the false worship of their "wanton idolatries" (1 Pet 4:3). Because of these false teachers the way of "truth" (ἀληθείας), that is, the way of living that includes both their liturgical and ethical worship in accord with the divine "truth" (ἀληθείᾳ) in which they are confirmed (2 Pet 1:12), will be blasphemed (2:2). And that the way of truth will be "blasphemed" (βλασφημηθήσεται) by these false teachers further associates them with the Gentiles who are surprised that the audience do not join their idolatrous behavior, as they

---

2. "The author predicts the coming of these false teachers, yet later in the chapter they appear to have already arrived (2:10b-22) . . . The oscillation between the present and the future in the letter in reference to the heretics appears to be rooted in the author's eschatology. The heretics will come in the last days (3:3-4), and their presence in the church is evidence that the last times have come (3:5-7)" (Green, *Jude and 2 Peter*, 238-39). "At this point in the argument 2 Peter has labeled his opponents 'false teachers,' but he has not forgotten the comparison with false prophets" (Davids, *2 Peter and Jude*, 218).

3. "'To deny' Christ is the opposite of 'to confess' him and thus is saying 'no' instead of 'amen'" (Green, *Jude and 2 Peter*, 240).

go on "blaspheming [βλασφημοῦντες]" (1 Pet 4:4), with its connotation of reviling or ridiculing, rather than properly worshiping, the God responsible for this way of truth.[4]

In the "greed" (πλεονεξίᾳ) that in the biblical tradition is often closely associated if not synonymous with idolatry, these false teachers will exploit the audience with deceptive words (2 Pet 2:3a).[5] With such deceptive "words" (λόγοις) these false teachers would mislead the audience into the false worship that contradicts their true worship based on the prophetic "word" (λόγον), to which the audience are upholding well (1:19). For "whom" (οἷς), that is, those false teachers because of "whom" (οὕς) the way of truth will be blasphemed (2:2), the divine judgment that was decided long ago is not becoming idle (2:3b). And their "annihilation" (ἀπώλεια), the imminent "annihilation" (ἀπώλειαν) they are bringing upon themselves with their opinions that will lead to their eternal "annihilation [ἀπωλείας]" (2:1), is not becoming drowsy, so that they will not escape it (2:3c).[6]

The audience were made aware that there is no credit or grace before God if they endure while "sinning" (ἁμαρτάνοντες) and being mistreated (1 Pet 2:20). Now they are reminded that God did not spare "sinning" (ἁμαρτησάντων) angels but, in chains of gloom casting them into Tartarus, handed them over to be kept for judgment (2 Pet 2:4).[7] In ironic contrast to Christ, who "handed himself over" (παρεδίδου) to the God who "judges" (κρίνοντι) righteously (1 Pet 2:23), God "handed over" (παρέδωκεν) the sinning angels to be kept for "judgment" (κρίσιν). And in ironic contrast

---

4. Hofius, "βλασφημία," 220. "The verb translated 'to blaspheme' could refer to slanderous and defaming speech against a person or against supernatural beings, but was also used widely in Greco-Roman, Jewish, and Christian literature to speak of reviling or defaming the Deity" (Green, *Jude and 2 Peter*, 243).

5. "Idolatry is a typical sin of the gentiles, a vain folly and an evil desire that leads to other sins and ought to be treated with the greatest vigilance since it evokes stern divine judgment. According to a range of texts in the Bible, so is greed. Idolatry involves trusting, loving, and serving gold and silver objects rather than the true and living God. So does greed" (Rosner, *Greed as Idolatry*, 174). "A life controlled by greed becomes a life that is no longer oriented towards God and his priorities" (Reese, *2 Peter and Jude*, 147).

6. "In the syntax of 2 Peter 'judgment' and 'destruction' become eerily personified. The present tense of the verbs also adds to threat. Judgment and destruction are actively waiting for their moment" (Donelson, *I & II Peter*, 240).

7. Billings, "Angels Who Sinned," 532-37. "In Greek myths Tartarus was the deepest part of Hades, where the Titans were imprisoned. Its role as a special place for the imprisonment of divine beings may explain its usage here for the destiny of angels" (Donelson, *I & II Peter*, 242). "The traditions about an angelic fall grew out of Gen. 6:1-4. The first readers of this letter have to be acquainted with these to interpret the author's reference" (Green, *Jude and 2 Peter*, 249).

to the eternal inheritance being divinely "kept" (τετηρημένην) in heaven "for" (εἰς) the audience (1 Pet 1:4), God handed over the sinning angels to be "kept" (τηρουμένους) "for" (εἰς) judgment. The audience are thus invited to liken the false teachers for whom the divine "judgment" (κρίμα) of long ago is not becoming idle (2 Pet 2:3) to the sinning angels whom God handed over to be kept for judgment (2:4).

The audience have obtained a precious faith in the "righteousness" (δικαιοσύνῃ) of our God and savior Jesus Christ (1:1). They are blessed by God if they should suffer on account of this "righteousness [δικαιοσύνην]" (1 Pet 3:14), the "righteousness" (δικαιοσύνῃ) to which they may now live because of Christ's sacrificial offering of himself for our sins (2:24). Since God guarded Noah, a herald of "righteousness" (δικαιοσύνης), as the eighth along with seven others (2 Pet 2:5), the audience are to be encouraged that God will likewise guard them from the destructive threat of the false teachers who are "bringing upon" (ἐπάγοντες) themselves imminent annihilation (2:1).[8] They are like the ancient world that God did not spare, "having brought" (ἐπάξας) a deluge upon the world of the ungodly (2:5). And, having reduced the cities of Sodom and Gomorrah to ashes, God "condemned" (κατέκρινεν) them to ruin, having placed them as an example of the things intended for the ungodly (2:6), among whom are the false teachers, who have been likened to the sinning angels God kept for "judgment [κρίσιν]" (2:4).

2:7 (B): If the Righteous Lot God Rescued

The series of past examples of how God has protected the godly from the ungodly continues: "and if the righteous Lot, oppressed by the conduct of the disgraceful in debauchery, he rescued" (2:7). The audience are to appreciate that just as God guarded Noah, a herald of "righteousness [δικαιοσύνης]" (2:5), so God rescued the "righteous" (δίκαιον) Lot, recalling that Peter considers it "righteous" (δίκαιον) to stir up the audience by a reminder (1:13). That Lot was oppressed by the "conduct" (ἀναστροφῆς) of the disgraceful in debauchery makes him relevant for the audience, whom God ransomed from the futile idolatrous "conduct" (ἀναστροφῆς) they inherited from their ancestors (1 Pet 1:18). And just as the righteous Lot was oppressed by the conduct of the disgraceful in "debauchery" (ἀσελγείᾳ), so the audience are in danger of following the "debaucheries" (ἀσελγείαις) of the false teachers (2 Pet 2:2).

---

8. "Noah is called the eighth presumably because, according to tradition (see 1 Pet 3:20), eight people—Noah and his wife, along with their three sons and their wives—were saved in the ark" (Donelson, *I & II Peter*, 244).

2:8-9a (B'): Then the Lord Knows How to Rescue the Righteous Godly from Trial

The audience continue to hear how the example of Lot is relevant for them: "for in what was seen and heard the righteous one, residing among them day after day, tormented his righteous soul by the lawless works, then the Lord knows how to rescue the godly from trial" (2:8-9a). At this point the audience experience a pivot of parallels from the B (2:7) to the B' (2:8-9a) element of this chiastic unit. "The righteous [δίκαιον] Lot" and "he rescued [ἐρρύσατο]" (2:7) progress to "the righteous [δίκαιος] one" (2:8), "his righteous [δικαίαν] soul" (2:8), and "the Lord knows how to rescue [ῥύεσθαι]" (2:9a).

For in what was seen and heard the "righteous" one, that is, the "righteous" Lot (2:7), residing among them, that is, those disgraceful in debauchery (2:7), day after day, tormented his "righteous" soul by their lawless works (2:8).[9] That Lot tormented his righteous "soul" (ψυχήν) by the lawless works likens him to the audience, who were encouraged to keep away from fleshly desires that are waging war against the "soul [ψυχῆς]" (1 Pet 2:11).[10] And that Lot tormented his righteous soul by the "lawless works" (ἀνόμοις ἔργοις) reminds the audience that they are to keep their conduct among the ungodly and lawless Gentiles praiseworthy, so that in what they slander the audience as evildoers, observing their "praiseworthy works" (καλῶν ἔργων), they may offer the worship of glorifying God on the day of visitation (2:12).

If God "rescued" (ἐρρύσατο) the righteous Lot (2 Pet 2:7), then the "Lord," that is, the divine "Lord" Jesus Christ who is coming with power (1:16), knows how to "rescue" (ῥύεσθαι) the godly from trial (2:9a). The "godly" (εὐσεβεῖς) include the audience, who are to add to their faith "godliness [εὐσέβειαν]" (1:6), the "godliness" (εὐσέβειαν) of good worship toward which the divine power of Jesus Christ our Lord has granted all things we believers need (1:3). The audience are thus to appreciate that the divine Lord knows how to rescue them from "trial" (πειρασμοῦ), as those who are not to be surprised at the burning among them, occurring to them for a "trial [πειρασμόν]" (1 Pet 4:12), and as those who may be briefly saddened in various "trials [πειρασμοῖς]" (1:6).[11]

---

9. Makujina, "The 'Trouble' with Lot in 2 Peter," 255-69. "The idea is that Lot's moral sensitivity made his life among the Sodomites unbearable, just as the life of faithful Christians among the false teachers and those influenced by them will become unbearable" (Harrington, 2 *Peter*, 267-68).

10. "The 'soul' could signify not merely the inner life of a human but the whole person" (Green, *Jude and 2 Peter*, 261).

11. "This portrait of Lot is sketched in order to draw a parallel with the experience

2 Peter 2:1-16

2:9b-16 (A'): Blaspheming and Following the Way of Balaam the Prophet

The audience hear the A' element (2:9b-16) of this chiastic unit as a chiastic pattern in itself:

a) and to keep the *unrighteous* to be punished at the *day* of judgment, especially those going after the flesh in desire of defilement and despising lordship, arrogant bold ones, they do not tremble, blaspheming glorious beings, whereas angels, being greater in strength and power, do not convey a blasphemous judgment against them before the Lord (2:9b-11).

b) But these, like irrational animals born by nature for capture and *destruction* (2:12a),

c) among things they do not know, blaspheming (2:12b),

b') in their *destruction* they will also be *destroyed* (2:12c),

a') suffering harm as recompense for *unrighteousness*, considering revelry at *day* a delight, stains and blemishes, delighting in their deceits as they feast together with you, having eyes full of adultery and unceasing from sin, seducing unstable souls, having a heart trained for greed, accursed children, abandoning the proper way, they have been led astray, following the way of Balaam son of Bosor who loved recompense for *unrighteousness*, but he had a rebuke for his own transgression—a mute donkey talking with a voice of a human being restrained the madness of the prophet (2:13-16).

After the central and unparalleled c) sub-element, "among things they do not know, blaspheming" (2:12b), the audience experience a pivot of chiastic parallels from the b) to the b') sub-element involving the only occurrences in this sub-unit of expressions regarding "destruction." "For capture and destruction [φθοράν]" (2:12a) progresses to "in their destruction [φθορᾷ] they will also be destroyed [φθαρήσονται]" (2:12c). They then hear a progression of chiastic parallels from the a) to the a') sub-element involving the only occurrences in 2 Peter of the terms "unrighteous/unrighteousness" and in this sub-unit of the term "day." "To keep the unrighteous [ἀδίκους] to be punished at the day [ἡμέραν] of judgment" (2:9b) progresses

---

of the readers of the letter. They too live among impious people. Their lives are also tortured by the lawlessness and immorality around them. Lot remained righteous. The obvious challenge to the readers is to do the same. This challenge comes with a promise that is implied in the story and made explicit in the assertion that follows. God saves righteous people who remain righteous in the midst of immorality" (Donelson, *I & II Peter*, 245). "Since the Flood and the judgment of Sodom and Gomorrah are prototypes of eschatological judgment, the situations of Noah and Lot are typical of the situation of Christians in the final evil days before the Parousia" (Bauckham, *Jude, 2 Peter*, 253).

to "suffering harm as recompense for unrighteousness [ἀδικίας], considering revelry at day [ἡμέρᾳ] a delight" (2:13) and "who loved recompense for unrighteousness [ἀδικίας]" (2:15).

At this point the audience also hear a progression of parallels from the A (2:1-6) to the A' (2:9b-16) element of this chiastic unit. The expressions "false prophets [ψευδοπροφῆται]" (2:1), "will be [ἔσονται]" (2:1), "will follow [ἐξακολουθήσουσιν]" (2:2), "way [ὁδός] of truth" (2:2), "will be blasphemed [βλασφημηθήσεται]" (2:2), "greed [πλεονεξίᾳ]" (2:3), "judgment [κρίμα]" (2:3), "angels [ἀγγέλων]" (2:4), and "to be kept [τηρουμένους] for judgment [κρίσιν]" (2:4) occur in the A element. These occurrences progress to "to keep [τηρεῖν]" (2:9b), "judgment [κρίσεως]" (2:9b), "blaspheming [βλασφημοῦντες]" (2:10, 12), "angels [ἄγγελοι]" (2:11), "being [ὄντες]" (2:11), "blasphemous judgment [βλάσφημον κρίσιν]" (2:11), "greed [πλεονεξίας]" (2:14), "proper way [ὁδόν]" (2:15), "following [ἐξακολουθήσαντες] the way [ὁδῷ] of Balaam" (2:15), and "madness of the prophet [προφήτου]" (2:16).

In addition, the audience hear the a) sub-element (2:9b-11) of the chiastic sub-unit (2:9b-16) as yet another chiastic pattern in itself:

(a) and to keep the unrighteous to be punished at the day of *judgment*, especially those going after the flesh in desire of defilement and despising *lordship*, arrogant bold ones, they do not tremble (2:9b-10a),

(b) *blaspheming* glorious beings (2:10b),

(c) whereas angels, being greater in strength and power (2:11a),

(b') do not convey a *blasphemous* (2:11b)

(a') *judgment* against them before the *Lord* (2:11c).

After the central and unparalleled (c) sub-element, "whereas angels, being greater in strength and power" (2:11a), the audience experience a pivot of chiastic parallels from the (b) to the (b') sub-element involving the only occurrences in the a) sub-element (2:9b-11) of expressions regarding "blasphemy." "Blaspheming [βλασφημοῦντες] glorious beings" (2:10b) progresses to "blasphemous [βλάσφημον]" (2:11b). They then hear a progression of chiastic parallels from the (a) to the (a') sub-element involving the only occurrences in the a) sub-element (2:9b-11) of the terms "lordship/ Lord" and "judgment." "The day of judgment [κρίσεως]" (2:9b) and "despising the lordship [κυριότητος]" (2:10a) progress to "judgment [κρίσιν] against them before the Lord [κυρίῳ]" (2:11c).[12]

The divine Lord knows how not only to rescue the godly audience from trial (2:9a), but also to "keep" (τηρεῖν) the unrighteous false teachers

---

12. For the preference of the variant "before the Lord" (παρὰ κυρίῳ), see Kraus, "Παρὰ κυρίου," 265-73; Green, *Jude and 2 Peter*, 289; Donelson, *I & II Peter*, 249.

among them to be punished at the day of "judgment [κρίσεως]" (2:9b), just as God handed sinning angels over to be "kept" (τηρουμένους) for "judgment [κρίσιν]" (2:4). The Lord knows how to punish especially those unrighteous false teachers who are "going" (πορευομένους) after the "flesh" (σαρκός) in "desire" (ἐπιθυμίᾳ) of defilement (2:10), in contrast to the audience, who are escaping the destruction from "desire" (ἐπιθυμίᾳ) in the world (1:4). Indeed, the audience have already been encouraged to keep away from "fleshly desires [σαρκικῶν ἐπιθυμιῶν]" (1 Pet 2:11), for sufficient time has passed for them to accomplish the purpose of the Gentiles, having "gone" (πεπορευμένους) in debaucheries, "desires" (ἐπιθυμίαις), drunkenness, carousing, drinking bouts, and the false worship of wanton idolatries (4:3). Now the audience are following the way of truth (2 Pet 2:2), which includes true liturgical and ethical worship.[13]

The false teachers are not only denying the divine Master (2:1), but despising the "lordship [κυριότητος]" (2:10) of the divine "Lord" (κύριος) who knows how to rescue the godly, who include the audience, from trial (2:9a). They are arrogant bold ones who do not tremble at blaspheming "glorious beings [δόξας]" (2:10), which include our Lord Jesus Christ and God the Father from whom he received honor and "glory" (δόξαν), so that he is now endowed with his own divine "glory [δόξῃ]" (1:3). This happened when God's heavenly voice was conveyed to him by the majestic "glory" (δόξης) at his transfiguration into a glorious heavenly being (1:17) on the holy mountain (1:18), which indicates his future coming in glory (1:16). That the false teachers do not tremble at "blaspheming" (βλασφημοῦντες), rather than reverently worshiping, glorious beings reinforces the warning that because of them the way of truth by which the audience worship these glorious heavenly beings will be "blasphemed [βλασφημηθήσεται]" (2:2).

In ironic contrast to the sinning "angels" (ἀγγέλων) whom God did not spare but handed over to be kept for "judgment [κρίσιν]" (2:4), those "angels" (ἄγγελοι) "being" (ὄντες) greater than the false teachers who "will be" (ἔσονται) among the audience (2:1) do not convey a blasphemous "judgment" (κρίσιν) against these false teachers before the Lord (2:11). That they are greater in the "strength" (ἰσχύϊ) that comes from God (cf. 1 Pet 4:11) and in divine "power" (δυνάμει) recalls the making known of the

13. "The expression πορεύομαι ὀπίσω (go after) commonly refers to following other gods in the LXX as opposed to following God or the Lord" (Green, *Jude and 2 Peter*, 266). "2 Peter has conformed the term for 'going after' to the language of the Greek OT, language that is used for going after other deities. This implies that, like Mammon, desire in the NT can function as a pagan deity did in the OT. The first charge against the teachers he opposes, then, is that they, like the fallen angels and like Sodom, have defiled themselves due to following, perhaps deifying, their desire, specifically their sexual desire" (Davids, *2 Peter and Jude*, 233).

divine "power" (δύναμιν) and coming of our Lord Jesus Christ (2 Pet 1:16). His divine "power" (δυνάμεως) granted us believers all the things necessary toward eternal life and the godliness of good worship (1:3).

In striking contrast to the false teachers who do not tremble at "blaspheming" (βλασφημοῦντες), rather than reverently worshiping, glorious beings (2:10), these angels do not convey a "blasphemous" (βλάσφημον) "judgment" (κρίσιν) against them before the "Lord [κυρίῳ]" (2:11). They thus provide the audience with an angelic model for likewise not conveying a blasphemous judgment against those who blaspheme glorious beings. The audience are to leave judgment of the blasphemous to their Lord. They are to be among the godly who engage in the godliness of good worship and whom the "Lord" (κύριος) knows how to rescue from trial, as well as to keep the unrighteous, such as the false teachers, to be punished at the day of "judgment [κρίσεως]" (2:9). Rather than following the way of the false teachers, the audience are to continue their true worship of glorious beings.

In contrast to the audience, who are escaping "destruction" (φθορᾶς) from desire in the world (1:4), these false teachers are like irrational animals born for capture and "destruction [φθοράν]" (2:12a).[14] Whereas they are among things "they do not know" (ἀγνοοῦσιν), "blaspheming [βλασφημοῦντες]" (2:12b), that is, "blaspheming" (βλασφημοῦντες) glorious beings (2:10), among whom are the Lord Jesus Christ, the audience are "knowing [γινώσκοντες]" (1:20) that the prophecy about the future and final coming of our Lord Jesus Christ (1:16) has a divine origin (1:21). That in the "destruction" (φθορᾷ) of the irrational animals to which they have been likened they will also be ultimately "destroyed [φθαρήσονται]" (2:12c) further warns the audience not to allow the false teachers to prevent them from the proper worship of glorious beings.[15]

The audience hear the a') sub-element (2:13-16) as yet another chiastic pattern in itself:

(a) suffering harm as *recompense for unrighteousness*, considering revelry at day a delight, stains and blemishes, delighting in their deceits as they feast together with you, *having* eyes full of adultery and unceasing from sin, seducing unstable souls, having a heart trained for greed, accursed children (2:13-14),

(b) abandoning the proper *way* (2:15a),

(c) they have been led astray (2:15b),

(b') following the *way* of Balaam son of Bosor (2:15c),

---

14. Callan, "Comparison of Humans to Animals," 101-13.

15. "These people are like animals. Thus they will share the fate of animals, although they will do so eschatologically" (Donelson, *I & II Peter*, 252).

(a') who loved *recompense for unrighteousness*, but he *had* a rebuke for his own transgression--a mute donkey talking with a voice of a human being restrained the madness of the prophet (2:15d-16).

After the central and unparalleled (c) sub-element, "they have been led astray" (2:15b), the audience experience a pivot of parallels from the (b) to the (b') sub-element involving the only occurrences in this sub-unit of the term "way." "Abandoning the proper way [ὁδόν]" (2:15a) progresses to "following the way [ὁδῷ] of Balaam" (2:15c). They then hear a progression of chiastic parallels from the (a) to the (a') sub-element involving the only occurrences in 2 Peter of the phrase "recompense for unrighteousness" and in this sub-unit of the verb "to have." "Suffering harm as recompense for unrighteousness [μισθὸν ἀδικίας]" (2:13) progresses to "loved recompense for unrighteousness [μισθὸν ἀδικίας]" (2:15d). And "having [ἔχοντες] eyes full of adultery" (2:14) progresses to "he had [ἔσχεν] a rebuke" (2:16).

That the false teachers are suffering harm as recompense for "unrighteousness [ἀδικίας]" (2:13a) recalls that the Lord knows how to keep the "unrighteous" (ἀδίκους) to be punished at the day of judgment (2:9).[16] In contrast to Peter, who "considers" (ἡγοῦμαι) it righteous to stir up the audience by reminder (1:13), the unrighteous false teachers, who are "considering" (ἡγούμενοι) revelry at "day" (ἡμέρᾳ) a delight (2:13b), are ironically to be punished at the "day" (ἡμέραν) of judgment. Metaphorically, they are the equivalent of the "stains and blemishes," the cultic as well as moral impurities, which disqualify them for proper worship, as those delighting in their deceits as they feast together, that is, join in the communal worship that includes the Lord's Supper, with the audience (2:13c).[17] That they are delighting in "their deceits" (ταῖς ἀπάταις αὐτῶν) resonates with the warning that many will follow "their debaucheries" (αὐτῶν ταῖς ἀσελγείαις), and that because of them the way of truth, which includes the godliness of good worship, will be blasphemed (2:2).

16. "The somewhat unusual meaning of ἀδικούμενοι as 'suffering harm' results from the wordplay with ἀδικία. The wordplay itself stresses the equity that is at the heart of divine justice ... As these people engage in the harm of ἀδικία now, so will this same harm be returned to them by God on the day of judgment" (Donelson, *I & II Peter*, 252).

17. "The rite we refer to as the Lord's Supper took place within the context of a feast (feasting and religion were closely intertwined; see 1 Cor. 11:17-34). The heretics Peter combats have transformed the Christian celebration into an event marked by cultural practices that are antithetical to authentic Christian feasting" (Green, *Jude and 2 Peter*, 280). "Just as spots and blemishes make a temple sacrifice unacceptable, these false teachers compromise the holiness of the community" (Donelson, *I & II Peter*, 253). "Indeed, since they were feasting with believers, they were turning the Lord's Supper into something deceitful. They were not there celebrating in the presence of their living Lord, but rather they were there indulging their own selves, having their own agendas, for Jesus was not their Lord" (Davids, *2 Peter and Jude*, 240).

Whereas the "eyes" (ὀφθαλμοί) of the Lord are upon the righteous (1 Pet 3:12) who worship him properly, the unrighteous false teachers have "eyes" (ὀφθαλμούς) full of adultery (2 Pet 2:14a). In contrast to believers, we who "have" (ἔχομεν) as very firm the prophetic word (1:19) which points to the final coming of our Lord Jesus Christ (1:16), the false teachers "have" (ἔχοντες) eyes full of the "adultery" which in the biblical tradition connotes idolatrous worship. They are unceasing from "sin [ἁμαρτίας]" (2:14b), forgetful of the divine cleansing of their "sins" (ἁμαρτιῶν) of the past (1:9), which qualified them for proper worship. That they are seducing unstable "souls [ψυχάς]" (2:14c) reinforces the exhortation for those who are suffering according to the will of God to entrust to the faithful Creator their "souls" (ψυχάς) in good-doing (1 Pet 4:19), as those who have purified their "souls" (ψυχάς) in obedience to the truth for the ethical worship of sincere brotherly affection and love (1:22).

In contrast to the audience who are to be attending to the prophetic word that points to the final coming of our Lord Jesus Christ (2 Pet 1:16) as a light appearing in a dreary place, until the day dawns and the morning star arises in your "hearts [καρδίαις]" (1:19), the false teachers are those having a "heart" (καρδίαν) trained for greed (2:14d). Not only are they "having" (ἔχοντες) eyes full of the adultery of idolatry (2:14a), but they are "having" (ἔχοντες) a heart trained for the greed associated with idolatry. That they have a heart trained for "greed" (πλεονεξίας) reinforces the warning that in idolatrous "greed" (πλεονεξίᾳ) they will exploit the audience with deceptive words (2:3) that would deter them from the godliness of good worship. And that the false teachers are accursed "children [τέκνα]" (2:14e) reinforces the exhortation for the audience, as "children" (τέκνα) of obedience (1 Pet 1:14), to become "children" (τέκνα) of Sarah, who obeyed Abraham as her lord, by doing good as part of their ethical worship.

In abandoning the proper "way" (ὁδόν), the false teachers have been led astray, "following" (ἐξακολουθήσαντες) the "way" (ὁδῷ) of Balaam son of Bosor (Num 22:5), who loved recompense for unrighteousness (2 Pet 2:15).[18]

---

18. For a discussion of the textual criticism involving the reading of Βοσόρ here, see Hays, "Textual Criticism in 2 Peter 2:15," 105–9. "Peter may be referring not to Balaam's father but the place from which he came. A city called Bosor was located in Syria, and according to Num. 23:7, Balaam came from Aram, the state around Damascus" (Green, *Jude and 2 Peter*, 289). "The word 'Bosor' likely derives from a pun on the word 'flesh' (*basar*) in Hebrew. Balaam was not a man of the Spirit but of the flesh. The false teachers, like Balaam, were not leading God's people in the righteous way but in the way of the flesh" (Schreiner, *1, 2 Peter*, 354). "In Num 22–24 Balaam is more positive than negative. He resists the request of King Balak to curse Israel. Later canonical accounts depict Balaam in a more negative light and suggest greed as motive (e.g., Deut 23:4–5; Neh 13:2; Philo, *Mos.* 1.264–300). Whatever part of the Balaam tradition is in play, the point in 2 Peter is clear.

This reinforces the warning that many will "follow" (ἐξακολουθήσουσιν) their debaucheries, because of whom the "way" (ὁδός) of truth will be blasphemed (2:2). In contrast to the audience, who like sheep were being "led astray" (πλανώμενοι), but have turned now to the Lord Jesus Christ as the shepherd and overseer of their souls (1 Pet 2:25), the false teachers have been "led astray [ἐπλανήθησαν]" (2 Pet 2:15) by despising the lordship of Jesus Christ (2:10), thus denying the Master who purchased them (2:1).

As those having a heart trained for idolatrous greed (2:14) and thus following the idolatrous way of Balaam, who in his greed loved "recompense for unrighteousness [μισθὸν ἀδικίας]" (2:15), the false teachers are ironically suffering harm as "recompense for unrighteousness [μισθὸν ἀδικίας]" (2:13). In following the way of Balaam, who "loved" (ἠγάπησεν) recompense for unrighteousness, the false teachers in their greed are following the idolatrous way of loving money more than God and the ways of God. In contrast, the audience, as those who are "loving" (ἀγαπᾶτε) Jesus Christ (1 Pet 1:8), are to "love" (ἀγαπήσατε) one another (1:22), "love" (ἀγαπᾶτε) the brotherhood (2:17), and "love" (ἀγαπᾶν) eternal life (3:10) as part of the godliness of good worship.

In ominous contrast to the false teachers "having" (ἔχοντες) eyes full of idolatrous adultery and unceasing from sin (2 Pet 2:14), Balaam, whose idolatrous way the false teachers are following (2:15), "had" (ἔσχεν) a divine rebuke for his own transgression (2:16). As the audience recall, the divine "voice" (φωνῆς) of God the Father was conveyed to the Lord Jesus Christ by the majestic glory (1:17), a "voice" (φωνήν) heard conveyed from heaven (1:18). In appropriate accord with this, a "mute" (ἄφωνον) donkey talking with a "voice" (φωνῇ) of a human being restrained the "madness" (παραφρονίαν), alliteratively resonating with the "transgression" (παρανομίας), of Balaam the prophet (2:16).[19]

That the mute donkey was talking with a divinely inspired voice of a "human being [ἀνθρώπου]" (2:16) accords with the fact that not by the will of a "human being" (ἀνθρώπου) has prophecy ever been conveyed, but rather, "human beings" (ἄνθρωποι) spoke from God (1:21). This voice of a human being is thus a prophetic voice spoken from God to rebuke

---

Some people out of greed engage in false prophecy" (Donelson, *I & II Peter*, 254). See also Miller, "Dogs, Adulterers, and the Way of Balaam," 123–44, 182–91.

19. "The word παραφρονίαν ('madness') is not found elsewhere in extant Greek literature. The author has probably used this form for the sake of its assonance with παρανομία ('offense'). The two words are closely connected, representing two aspects of Balaam's behavior in Num 22. His transgression was his determination to curse Israel for the sake of financial profit. His madness lay in supposing that he would be able to do so. His greed swayed his judgment and made the crime seem feasible" (Bauckham, *Jude, 2 Peter*, 269).

the false prophet Balaam.[20] And that this divine voice restrained the madness of the false "prophet" (προφήτου) Balaam reinforces the warning for the audience not to follow the idolatrous way of the false teachers, who, like "false prophets [ψευδοπροφῆται]" (2:1), are trying to deter them from following the way of truth (2:2) that includes the godliness of properly worshiping glorious beings (2:10).[21]

Summary on 2:1-16

False teachers will introduce opinions that lead to eternal annihilation, even denying the Lord Jesus himself as the Master who purchased them as an act of redemption to save them from such annihilation (2:1). Just as house servants are to be subject in all reverent fear to their "masters" (1 Pet 2:18), these false teachers, as also the audience, are not to deny but to be subject in all the reverent fear that connotes their holistic worship of this "Master," our Lord Jesus Christ. These false teachers will thus contradict all the things toward eternal life and the godliness of good worship that the divine power of our Lord Jesus Christ granted us believers (2 Pet 1:2-3).

Whereas it was not by "following" craftily devised myths that Peter and his associates made known to the audience the power and coming of our Lord Jesus Christ (1:16), many will "follow" the debaucheries of these false teachers (2:2). The reference to their "debaucheries" links them to the "debaucheries" of the ungodly Gentiles associated with the false worship of their "wanton idolatries" (1 Pet 4:3). Because of these false teachers the way of "truth," that is, the way of living that includes both their liturgical and ethical worship in accord with the divine "truth" in which they are confirmed (2 Pet 1:12), will be blasphemed (2:2). And that the way of truth will be "blasphemed" by these false teachers further associates them with the Gentiles who are surprised that the audience do not join their idolatrous behavior, as they go on "blaspheming" (1 Pet 4:4), with its connotation of reviling or ridiculing, rather than properly worshiping, the God responsible for this way of truth.

In the "greed" that in the biblical tradition is often closely associated if not synonymous with idolatry, these false teachers will exploit the audience with deceptive words (2 Pet 2:3a). With such deceptive "words" these false

---

20. "The story of Balaam's donkey shows that animals, which by nature are without speech, can actually speak true prophecies" (Donelson, *I & II Peter*, 255).

21. "Balaam is here called a 'prophet,' which, again, is not the term used in Numbers to describe him . . . In Peter's telling, one who is a spokesman for God as a prophet is countered by the dumb ass, whose mouth God opens" (Green, *Jude and 2 Peter*, 288).

teachers would mislead the audience into the false worship that contradicts their true worship based on the prophetic "word," to which the audience are upholding well (1:19). For "whom," that is, those false teachers because of "whom" the way of truth will be blasphemed (2:2), the divine judgment that was decided long ago is not becoming idle (2:3b). And their "annihilation," the imminent "annihilation" they are bringing upon themselves with their opinions that will lead to their eternal "annihilation" (2:1), is not becoming drowsy, so that they will not escape it (2:3c).

The audience have obtained a precious faith in the "righteousness" of our God and savior Jesus Christ (1:1). They are blessed by God if they should suffer on account of this "righteousness" (1 Pet 3:14), the "righteousness" to which they may now live because of Christ's sacrificial offering of himself for our sins (2:24). Since God guarded Noah, a herald of "righteousness," as the eighth along with seven others (2 Pet 2:5), the audience are to be encouraged that God will likewise guard them from the destructive threat of the false teachers who are "bringing upon" themselves imminent annihilation (2:1). They are like the ancient world that God did not spare, "having brought" a deluge upon the world of the ungodly (2:5). And, having reduced the cities of Sodom and Gomorrah to ashes, God "condemned" them to ruin, having placed them as an example of the things intended for the ungodly (2:6), among whom are the false teachers, who have been likened to the sinning angels God kept for "judgment" (2:4).

If God "rescued" the righteous Lot (2 Pet 2:7), then the "Lord," that is, the divine "Lord" Jesus Christ who is coming with power (1:16), knows how to "rescue" the godly from trial (2:9a). The "godly" include the audience, who are to add to their faith "godliness" (1:6), the "godliness" of good worship toward which the divine power of Jesus Christ our Lord has granted all things we believers need (1:3). The audience are thus to appreciate that the divine Lord knows how to rescue them from "trial," as those who are not to be surprised at the burning among them, occurring to them for a "trial" (1 Pet 4:12), and as those who may be briefly saddened in various "trials" (1:6).

The divine Lord also knows how to "keep" the unrighteous false teachers among them to be punished at the day of "judgment" (2 Pet 2:9b), just as God handed sinning angels over to be "kept" for "judgment" (2:4). The Lord knows how to punish especially those unrighteous false teachers who are "going" after the "flesh" in "desire" of defilement (2:10), in contrast to the audience, who are escaping the destruction from "desire" in the world (1:4). Indeed, the audience have already been encouraged to keep away from "fleshly desires" (1 Pet 2:11), for sufficient time has passed for them to accomplish the purpose of the Gentiles, having "gone" in debaucheries, "desires," drunkenness, carousing, drinking bouts, and the false worship of wanton idolatries (4:3). Now the audience are following the way of truth (2 Pet 2:2), which includes true liturgical and ethical worship.

The false teachers are not only denying the divine Master (2:1), but despising the "lordship" (2:10) of the divine "Lord" who knows how to rescue the godly, who include the audience, from trial (2:9a). They are arrogant bold ones who do not tremble at blaspheming "glorious beings" (2:10), which include our Lord Jesus Christ and God the Father from whom he received honor and "glory," so that he is now endowed with his own divine "glory" (1:3). This happened when God's heavenly voice was conveyed to him by the majestic "glory" at his transfiguration into a glorious heavenly being (1:17) on the holy mountain (1:18), which indicates his future coming in glory (1:16). That the false teachers do not tremble at "blaspheming," rather than reverently worshiping, glorious beings reinforces the warning that because of them the way of truth by which the audience worship these glorious heavenly beings will be "blasphemed" (2:2).

In ironic contrast to the sinning "angels" whom God did not spare but handed over to be kept for "judgment" (2:4), those "angels" "being" greater than the false teachers who "will be" among the audience (2:1) do not convey a blasphemous "judgment" against these false teachers before the Lord (2:11). That they are greater in the "strength" that comes from God (cf. 1 Pet 4:11) and in divine "power" recalls the making known of the divine "power" and coming of our Lord Jesus Christ (2 Pet 1:16). His divine "power" granted us believers all the things necessary toward eternal life and the godliness of good worship (1:3).

In contrast to the audience, who are escaping "destruction" from desire in the world (1:4), these false teachers are like irrational animals born for capture and "destruction" (2:12a). Whereas they are among things "they do not know," "blaspheming" (2:12b), that is, "blaspheming" glorious beings (2:10), among whom are the Lord Jesus Christ, the audience are "knowing" (1:20) that the prophecy about the future and final coming of our Lord Jesus Christ (1:16) has a divine origin (1:21). That in the "destruction" of the irrational animals to which they have been likened they will also be ultimately "destroyed" (2:12c) further warns the audience not to allow the false teachers to prevent them from the proper worship of glorious beings.

That the false teachers are suffering harm as recompense for "unrighteousness" (2:13a) recalls that the Lord knows how to keep the "unrighteous" to be punished at the day of judgment (2:9). In contrast to Peter, who "considers" it righteous to stir up the audience by reminder (1:13), the unrighteous false teachers, who are "considering" revelry at "day" a delight (2:13b), are ironically to be punished at the "day" of judgment. Metaphorically, they are the equivalent of the "stains and blemishes," the cultic as well

2 Peter 2:1-16

as moral impurities, which disqualify them for proper worship, as those delighting in their deceits as they feast together, that is, join in the communal worship that includes the Lord's Supper, with the audience (2:13c). That they are delighting in "their deceits" resonates with the warning that many will follow "their debaucheries," and that because of them the way of truth, which includes the godliness of good worship, will be blasphemed (2:2).

In ominous contrast to the false teachers "having" eyes full of idolatrous adultery and unceasing from sin (2:14), Balaam, whose idolatrous way the false teachers are following (2:15), "had" a divine rebuke for his own transgression (2:16). As the audience recall, the divine "voice" of God the Father was conveyed to the Lord Jesus Christ by the majestic glory (1:17), a "voice" heard conveyed from heaven (1:18). In appropriate accord with this, a "mute" donkey talking with a "voice" of a human being restrained the madness of Balaam the prophet (2:16).

That the mute donkey was talking with a divinely inspired voice of a "human being" (2:16) accords with the fact that not by the will of a "human being" has prophecy ever been conveyed, but rather, "human beings" spoke from God (1:21). This voice of a human being is thus a prophetic voice spoken from God to rebuke the false prophet Balaam. And that this divine voice restrained the madness of the false "prophet" Balaam reinforces the warning for the audience not to follow the idolatrous way of the false teachers, who, like "false prophets" (2:1), are trying to deter them from following the way of truth (2:2) that includes the godliness of properly worshiping glorious beings (2:10).

18

2 Peter 2:17–22
Do Not Turn Back from the Holy Commandment (B′)

*Those promising freedom
are themselves slaves of destruction*

A   ¹⁷ *These* are waterless springs and mists driven by a storm, for *whom* the gloom of darkness has been kept.
  B   ^{18a} For, talking bombastic things of futility, they are seducing with desires of the flesh, debaucheries, *those* barely escaping,
  B′   ^{18b} *those* in error residing,
A′   ¹⁹ promising freedom to *them*, they themselves are existing as slaves of destruction, for by what someone has been overcome, to *this* he has been enslaved. ²⁰ For if, escaping the defilements of the world in the acknowledgment of our Lord and savior Jesus Christ, and again becoming entangled in *these things*, they are overcome, for *them* the last things have become worse than the first. ²¹ For it was better for *them* not to have acknowledged the way of righteousness than, acknowledging it, to turn back from the holy commandment handed over to *them*. ²² The saying of the true proverb has happened to *them*—"a dog returns to its own vomit," and "a bathed sow to wallowing in the mire."[1]

---

1. For the establishment of 2 Pet 2:17–22 as a chiasm, see ch. 14.

2 Peter 2:17-22

Audience Response to 2:17-22

At this point, after the central and unparalleled C unit (2:1-16), the audience experience a pivotal progression of macrochiastic parallels from the B (1:16-21) to this B' (2:17-22) chiastic unit. In the B unit the audience were told about those who were with him (the Lord Jesus Christ) on the "holy" (ἁγίῳ) mountain (1:18), and that, brought along by the "Holy" (ἁγίου) Spirit, human beings spoke from God (1:21). This progresses to a warning in the B' unit about turning back from the "holy" (ἁγίας) commandment (2:21).

2:17 (A): These Waterless Springs for Whom the Gloom of Darkness Has Been Kept

Having heard "these" (οὗτοί) false teachers compared to irrational animals born by nature for capture and destruction (2:12), the audience now hear that "these" (οὗτοί) false teachers metaphorically are "waterless springs," which points to their uselessness, and "mists driven by a storm," which indicates their instability (2:17).[2] As the audience recall, the Lord knows how to "keep" (τηρεῖν) the unrighteous to be punished at the day of judgment (2:9), and God did not spare sinning angels but, in chains of "gloom" (ζόφου) casting them into Tartarus, handed them over to be "kept" (τηρουμένους) for judgment (2:4). Similarly, for these false teachers the "gloom" (ζόφος) of darkness has been "kept" (τετήρηται) by God (2:17).

2:18a (B): They Are Seducing Those Barely Escaping

Why the gloom of darkness has been kept for these false teachers (2:17) begins to be explained: "For, talking bombastic things of futility, they are seducing with desires of the flesh, debaucheries, those barely escaping" (2:18a). With the word "talking" (φθεγγόμενοι), the audience hear the transitional term that links this chiastic unit (2:17-22) with the previous unit (2:1-16), which concludes with a reference to a mute donkey "talking [φθεγξάμενον]" (2:16), the only other occurrence of this verb in 2 Peter. In ironic contrast to Balaam's mute donkey "talking" divine prophecy with a voice of a human being, these false teachers are "talking" bombastic things

---

2. "Whatever the cause, the point is clear: springs promise water. Waterless springs do not deliver on that promise. Mists promise a change in weather. Mists driven away by a storm do not produce that change. Thus these images specifically anticipate the broken promise of freedom in 2:19 and evoke in general the danger and seductions of false teachers" (Donelson, *I & II Peter*, 257-58).

of the "futility" (ματαιότητος) that connotes false worship, reminding the audience that they, on the other hand, have been ransomed by God from their past "futile" (ματαίας) idolatrous conduct (1 Pet 1:18).[3]

Having heard that the false teachers are "seducing" (δελεάζοντες) unstable souls (2 Pet 2:14), the audience now hear that they are "seducing" (δελεάζουσιν) with desires of the flesh, debaucheries, those barely escaping (2:18a). That they are seducing with "desires" (ἐπιθυμίαις) of the "flesh" (σαρκός) reminds the audience that, as those going after the "flesh" (σαρκός) in "desire" (ἐπιθυμίᾳ) of the defilement that renders them unworthy for proper worship and despising rather than worshiping divine lordship, they are being kept for punishment at the day of judgment (2:10). That they are seducing with "debaucheries" (ἀσελγείαις) reinforces the warning that many will follow their "debaucheries" (ἀσελγείαις; cf. 2:7), because of whom the way of truth that includes the godliness of good worship will be blasphemed (2:2). Whereas the false teachers are seducing with desires of the flesh those barely "escaping" (ἀποφεύγοντας), the audience may become sharers of the divine nature, "escaping" (ἀποφυγόντες) the destruction from "desire" (ἐπιθυμίᾳ) in the world (1:4).

2:18b (B'): Those in Error Residing

At this point the audience experience a pivot of parallels from the B to the B' element of this chiastic unit. "Those" (τούς) barely escaping" the seduction of the false teachers (2:18a) progresses to the further description of them as "those (τούς) in error residing" (2:18b). That those in "error" (πλάνῃ) residing are being seduced with desires of the flesh reminds the audience that they like sheep were once "being led astray" (πλανώμενοι) in error, but have now turned to the Lord Jesus Christ as the shepherd and overseer of their souls (1 Pet 2:25). And that those in error "residing" or "conducting" (ἀναστρεφομένους) themselves are being seduced toward idolatrous worship by the false teachers reinforces the exhortation for the audience in reverential fear of the God they call upon as Father in their liturgical worship to "conduct" (ἀναστράφητε) in proper ethical worship the time of their earthly sojourning (1:17).

---

3. "In the LXX the lying words of the prophets not authorized by God (Zech 10:2; Ezek 13:6ff.) and everything else connected with the pagan gods and their images was considered μάταιος ... In the NT the μάταια include every false worship directed toward the veneration of humankind rather than the true, living God" (Balz, "μάταιος," 2.396).

2:19-22 (A'): For Them the Last Things Have Become Worse Than the First

The audience hear the A' element (2:19-22) of this chiastic unit as a chiastic pattern in itself:
a) promising freedom to *them*, they themselves are existing as slaves of destruction (2:19a),
  b) for by what someone has been *overcome* (2:19b),
    c) to *this* he has been enslaved (2:19c).
      d) For if, escaping the defilements of the world in the acknowledgment of our Lord and savior Jesus Christ (2:20a),
    c') and again becoming entangled in *these things* (2:20b),
  b') they are *overcome* (2:20c),
a') for *them* the last things have become worse than the first. For it was better for *them* not to have acknowledged the way of righteousness than, acknowledging it, to turn back from the holy commandment handed over to *them*. The saying of the true proverb has happened to *them*—"a dog returns to its own vomit," and "a bathed sow to wallowing in the mire" (2:20d-22).

After the central and unparalleled d) sub-element, "For if, escaping the defilements of the world in the acknowledgment of our Lord and savior Jesus Christ" (2:20a), the audience experience a pivot of chiastic parallels from the c) to the c') sub-element involving the only occurrences in this sub-unit of the demonstrative pronoun. "To this [τούτῳ] he has been enslaved" (2:19c) progresses to "again becoming entangled in these things [τούτοις]" (2:20b). They then hear a progression of parallels from the b) to the b') sub-element involving the only occurrences in 2 Peter of the verb "overcome." "By what someone has been overcome [ἥττηται]" (2:19b) progresses to "they are overcome [ἡττῶνται]" (2:20c). Finally, the audience hear a progression of parallels from the a) to the a') sub-element involving the only occurrences in this sub-unit of the dative masculine plural personal pronoun. "Promising freedom to them [αὐτοῖς]" (2:19a) progresses to "from them [αὐτοῖς]" (2:20d, 21a) and "to them [αὐτοῖς]" (2:21d, 22).

At this point the audience experience a progression, via the chiastic parallels, from the A (2:17) to the A' (2:19-22) sub-element of this chiastic unit. "These [οὗτοί] are waterless springs" (2:17) progresses to "to this [τούτῳ] he has been enslaved" (2:19c) and "again becoming entangled in these things [τούτοις]" (2:20b). And "for whom [οἷς] the gloom of darkness has been kept" (2:17) progresses to "to them [αὐτοῖς]" (2:19a, 21d, 22) and "for them [αὐτοῖς]" (2:20d, 21a).

Although the false teachers are promising "freedom" (ἐλευθερίαν) to those they are seducing to idolatrous worship, they are "slaves" (δοῦλοι) of destruction (2:19a).[4] In contrast, the audience have been exhorted that they are to be "free" (ἐλεύθεροι) but not keep "freedom" (ἐλευθερίαν) as a cover for evil, but rather to be "slaves" (δοῦλοι) of God (1 Pet 2:16). Whereas the false teachers are "existing" (ὑπάρχοντες) as slaves of destruction, the things "existing" (ὑπάρχοντα) and increasing to the audience make them neither useless nor fruitless for the acknowledgment of our Lord Jesus Christ (2 Pet 1:8). And that the false teachers are existing as slaves of "destruction" (φθορᾶς) reinforces the assertion that in their "destruction" (φθορᾷ), the "destruction" (φθοράν) of irrational animals, they will be "destroyed" (φθαρήσονται) eternally (2:12), whereas the audience are escaping eternal "destruction" (φθορᾶς) from desire in the world (1:4). That by what someone is overcome, to this he has been "enslaved" (δεδούλωται), emphatically reinforces that the false teachers are "slaves" (δοῦλοι) of eternal destruction (2:19).

Through the "acknowledgment" (ἐπιγνώσεως) of the one calling us believers by his own glory and virtue (1:3), that is, in the "acknowledgment" (ἐπιγνώσει) of God and of Jesus our Lord (1:2), and for the final "acknowledgment" (ἐπίγνωσιν) of our Lord Jesus Christ (1:8), the audience are "escaping" (ἀποφυγόντες) the destruction from desire in the "world [κόσμῳ]" (1:4). As part of the audience, the false teachers, similarly, were "escaping" (ἀποφυγόντες) the "defilements" (μιάσματα) of the "world" (κόσμου) in the "acknowledgment" (ἐπιγνώσει) of our Lord and savior Jesus Christ (2:20a). But now these false teachers are those going after the flesh in desire of "defilement" (μιασμοῦ) and despising the lordship of Jesus Christ (2:10).[5]

That the false teachers, as part of the audience, once were escaping the defilements of the world in the acknowledgment of "our Lord and savior Jesus Christ [τοῦ κυρίου ἡμῶν καὶ σωτῆρος Ἰησοῦ Χριστοῦ]" (2:20a) reminds the audience that they have been promised the entrance for the eternal kingdom of "our Lord and savior Jesus Christ [τοῦ κυρίου ἡμῶν καὶ σωτῆρος Ἰησοῦ Χριστοῦ]" (1:11). This "acknowledgment" includes not only being "acknowledged" in and through receiving the grace of faith from the divine Lord, but also "acknowledging," in and through the godliness of good

---

4. Caulley, "They Promise Them Freedom," 129–38. "If 'freedom' was one of their catchwords, they could have given it a broad spectrum of significance: freedom from judgment, freedom from moral constraint, perhaps also freedom from fear of the powers of evil. But so far as we can tell, freedom from fear of eschatological judgment will have been the fundamental freedom" (Bauckham, *Jude, 2 Peter*, 275).

5. "The 'defilements' in the present verse, as the use of the cognate in 2:10 suggests, are acts that cross the moral boundary. These are deeds that can even be classified as vice or criminal offenses and not simply cultic defilement" (Green, *Jude and 2 Peter*, 301).

2 Peter 2:17-22

liturgical and ethical worship rather than the ungodly behavior of the false teachers, the divine Lord for the reception of his grace.

The audience hear the a') sub-element (2:20d-22) of this chiastic sub-unit (2:19-22) as a chiastic pattern in itself:
(a) for *them* the last things have become worse than the first. For it was better for *them* (2:20d-21a)
  (b) not to have *acknowledged* the way of righteousness (2:21b)
  (b') than, *acknowledging* it (2:21c),
(a') to turn back from the holy commandment handed over to *them*. The saying of the true proverb has happened to *them*—"a dog returns to its own vomit," and "a bathed sow to wallowing in the mire" (2:21d-22).

At the center of this chiastic sub-unit the audience experience a pivot of chiastic parallels from the (b) to the (b') sub-element involving the only occurrences in 2 Peter of the verb "acknowledge." "Not to have acknowledged [ἐπεγνωκέναι] the way of righteousness" (2:21b) progresses to "acknowledging [ἐπιγνοῦσιν] it" (2:21c). They then hear a progression of parallels from the (a) to the (a') sub-element involving the only occurrences in this sub-unit of the dative masculine plural personal pronoun. "For them [αὐτοῖς]" (2:20d, 21a) progresses to "to them [αὐτοῖς]" (2:21d, 22).

If the false teachers, again becoming entangled in "these things" (τούτοις), that is, in the defilements of the world, are "overcome" (ἡττῶνται), recalling that by what someone has been "overcome" (ἥττηται), to "this" (τούτῳ) he has been enslaved (2:19), then for them the last things have become worse than the first (2:20). For "them" (αὐτοῖς) the last things have become worse than the first, since as those for "whom" (οἷς) the gloom of darkness has been kept (2:17), they are existing as slaves of eternal destruction (2:19).

As part of the audience, the false teachers had acknowledged, in and through the godliness of good worship, the "way" (ὁδόν) of "righteousness [δικαιοσύνης]" (2:21). But now they are abandoning the proper "way" (ὁδόν) and following the erroneous "way" (ὁδῷ) of Balaam, who loved recompense for "unrighteousness [ἀδικίας]" (2:15). They thus cannot expect to be divinely guarded like Noah as a herald of "righteousness [δικαιοσύνης]" (2:5), since they have abandoned the precious faith obtained in the "righteousness" (δικαιοσύνῃ) of our God and savior Jesus Christ (1:1). Because of them the "way" (ὁδός) of truth that includes the godliness of good worship will be blasphemed (2:2).

The audience are to appreciate that it was better for the false teachers among them not to have acknowledged the way of righteousness than, acknowledging it, to turn back from the holy commandment handed over to them by God (2:21). Their turning back from the holy commandment "handed over" (παραδοθείσης) to them ironically likens them to the

263

sinning angels whom God "handed over" (παρέδωκεν) to be kept for judgment (2:4). And their turning back from the "holy" (ἁγίας) commandment of God underscores that they are not among those brought along by the "Holy" (ἁγίου) Spirit to speak true prophecy from God (1:21). The audience are rather to heed the divine voice Peter and his associates heard conveyed from heaven while being with the Jesus transfigured into a glorious heavenly figure on the "holy" (ἁγίῳ) mountain (1:18), the voice which prophetically indicates the power and final coming of our Lord Jesus Christ (1:16).[6]

The audience are not to be surprised at the sufferings that come their way as Christians, as if something strange were "happening" (συμβαίνοντος) to them (1 Pet 4:12). In contrast, to the surprise of the false teachers the saying of the "true" (ἀληθοῦς) proverb, associated with the way of "truth" (ἀληθείας) that will be blasphemed because of the false teachers (2 Pet 2:2), has "happened" (συμβέβηκεν) to them (2:22). That the saying of the true "proverb" (παροιμίας) has happened to them reminds the audience, through the noteworthy alliteration in the Greek terms, of the similarity between the false teachers and Balaam, who had a rebuke for his own "transgression [παρανομίας]" (2:16).[7]

In contrast to the audience, who like sheep were being led astray, but have "turned" (ἐπεστράφητε) now to Christ as the shepherd and overseer of their souls (1 Pet 2:25), the false teachers, in accord with the true proverb, are like a dog who "returns" (ἐπιστρέψας) to its own vomit (2 Pet 2:22). That they are like a dog who returns to its "own" (ἴδιον) vomit continues the resonance between the false teachers and Balaam, who had a rebuke for his "own" (ἰδίας) transgression (2:16). It reminds the audience that the false teachers are engaged in false prophecy based on one's "own" (ἰδίας) interpretation (1:20). In contrast, believers have been granted all things needed for eternal life and the godliness of good worship through the acknowledgment of the one, the Lord Jesus Christ, calling us by his "own" (ἰδίᾳ) glory and virtue (1:3). And that the false teachers are like a bathed sow who returns to wallowing in the "mire [βορβόρου]" (2:22) alliteratively resonates with

---

6. "Thus the 'holy commandment' would demand and produce 'the way of righteousness.' The details of how the holy commandment was handed over are not given because they do not need to be. This imagery of handing over the commandment fits with the role of eyewitnesses in 1:16–18 and the Petrine authorship of the letter itself. Second Peter assumes the coherence of its theology with apostolic tradition" (Donelson, *I & II Peter*, 262). "Receiving this 'commandment' was how one was initiated into the way of Jesus or the way of righteousness: one committed oneself to Jesus as Lord, and one learned what their new Lord called them to" (Davids, *2 Peter and Jude*, 251).

7. "The Greek term παροιμίας appears in the LXX to describe the proverbs of the book by the name (Prov. 1:1), but it was also used more widely of maxims in general" (Green, *Jude and 2 Peter*, 306).

2 Peter 2:17-22

and reinforces how they are following the improper way of "Balaam son of Bosor [Βαλαὰμ τοῦ Βοσόρ]" (2:15).[8]

Summary on 2:17-22

In ironic contrast to Balaam's mute donkey "talking" divine prophecy with a voice of a human being (2:16), these false teachers are "talking" bombastic things of the "futility" (2:17-18) that connotes false worship, reminding the audience that they, on the other hand, have been ransomed by God from their past "futile" idolatrous conduct (1 Pet 1:18). Having heard that the false teachers are "seducing" unstable souls (2 Pet 2:14), the audience now hear that they are "seducing" with desires of the flesh, debaucheries, those barely escaping (2:18). That they are seducing with "desires" of the "flesh" reminds the audience that, as those going after the "flesh" in "desire" of the defilement that renders them unworthy for proper worship and despising rather than worshiping divine lordship, they are being kept for punishment at the day of final judgment (2:10).

That the false teachers are seducing with "debaucheries" (2:18) reinforces the warning that many will follow their "debaucheries" (cf. 2:7), because of whom the way of truth that includes the godliness of good worship will be blasphemed (2:2). Whereas the false teachers are seducing with desires of the flesh those barely "escaping" (2:18), the audience may become sharers of the divine nature, "escaping" the destruction from "desire" in the world (1:4). That those in "error" residing are being seduced with desires

---

8. "The first image is probably derived directly from Prov 26:11: 'Like a dog that returns to its vomit is a fool who reverts to his folly.' For the most part, ancient Mediterranean people saw the dog as a disgusting animal. Few behaviors were more repulsive than a dog's tendency to eat its own vomit. The repulsiveness of the image is key to its force in 2 Peter. Apostasy is not only the profaning of the holy; it is also disgusting. There is no obvious source for the pig imagery ... Both images make the same point. The animal is cleansed, either by vomiting or washing. Once cleansed, it returns to the very thing that made it filthy" (Donelson, *I & II Peter*, 262-63). "As with the dog, the sow is unclean (Lev. 11:7; Deut. 14:8), and indeed, the two animals are sometimes classified together. These unclean beasts go right back to uncleanness. Peter emphasizes their return as an illustration of the heretics' conduct. They, once having known the Lord and his holy commandment, have denied the Lord (2:1), have been entangled in the defilements of the world again (2:20), and have turned away after having known the way of righteousness (2:21), forgetting that they have been purified from past sins (1:9)" (Green, *Jude and 2 Peter*, 307). "We probably should not overread the proverb and see an allusion to baptism in the original washing, since it refers to the washing of a pig" (Schreiner, *1, 2 Peter*, 363). "Many commentators see an allusion to baptism in the sow's 'washing,' but this theme is so integral to the pre-Christian proverb that its suggestion of baptism can be no more than a happy coincidence" (Bauckham, *Jude, 2 Peter*, 280).

of the flesh reminds the audience that they like sheep were once "being led astray" in error, but have now turned to the Lord Jesus Christ as the shepherd and overseer of their souls (1 Pet 2:25). And that those in error "residing" or "conducting" themselves are being seduced toward idolatrous worship by the false teachers reinforces the exhortation for the audience in reverential fear of the God they call upon as Father in their liturgical worship to "conduct" in proper ethical worship the time of their earthly sojourning (1:17).

Although the false teachers are promising "freedom" to those they are seducing to idolatrous worship, they are "slaves" of destruction (2 Pet 2:19a). In contrast, the audience have been exhorted that they are to be "free" but not keep "freedom" as a cover for evil, but rather to be "slaves" of God (1 Pet 2:16). Whereas the false teachers are "existing" as slaves of destruction, the things "existing" and increasing to the audience make them neither useless nor fruitless for the acknowledgment of our Lord Jesus Christ (2 Pet 1:8). And that the false teachers are existing as slaves of "destruction" reinforces the assertion that in their "destruction," the "destruction" of irrational animals, they will be "destroyed" eternally (2:12), whereas the audience are escaping eternal "destruction" from desire in the world (1:4). That by what someone is overcome, to this he has been "enslaved," emphatically reinforces that the false teachers are "slaves" of eternal destruction (2:19).

Through the "acknowledgment" of the one calling us believers by his own glory and virtue (1:3), that is, in the "acknowledgment" of God and of Jesus our Lord (1:2), and for the final "acknowledgment" of our Lord Jesus Christ (1:8), the audience are "escaping" the destruction from desire in the "world" (1:4). As part of the audience, the false teachers, similarly, were "escaping" the "defilements" of the "world" in the "acknowledgment" of our Lord and savior Jesus Christ (2:20a). But now these false teachers are those going after the flesh in desire of "defilement" and despising the lordship of Jesus Christ (2:10).

That the false teachers, as part of the audience, once were escaping the defilements of the world in the acknowledgment of "our Lord and savior Jesus Christ" (2:20) reminds the audience that they have been promised the entrance for the eternal kingdom of "our Lord and savior Jesus Christ" (1:11). This "acknowledgment" includes not only being "acknowledged" in and through receiving the grace of faith from the divine Lord, but also "acknowledging," in and through the godliness of good liturgical and ethical worship rather than the ungodly behavior of the false teachers, the divine Lord for the reception of his grace.

The audience are to appreciate that it was better for the false teachers among them not to have acknowledged the way of righteousness than, acknowledging it, to turn back from the holy commandment handed over to them by God (2:21). Their turning back from the holy commandment "handed over" to them ironically likens them to the sinning angels whom God "handed over" to be kept for judgment (2:4). And their turning back from the "holy" commandment of God underscores that they are not among those brought along by the "Holy" Spirit to speak true prophecy from God (1:21). The audience are rather to heed the divine voice Peter and his associates heard conveyed from heaven while being with the Jesus transfigured into a glorious heavenly figure on the "holy" mountain (1:18), the voice which prophetically indicates the power and final coming of our Lord Jesus Christ (1:16).

In contrast to the audience, who like sheep were being led astray, but have "turned" now to Christ as the shepherd and overseer of their souls (1 Pet 2:25), the false teachers, in accord with the true proverb, are like a dog who "returns" to its own vomit (2 Pet 2:22). That they are like a dog who returns to its "own" vomit continues the resonance between the false teachers and Balaam, who had a rebuke for his "own" transgression (2:16). It reminds the audience that the false teachers are engaged in false prophecy based on one's "own" interpretation (1:20). In contrast, believers have been granted all things needed for eternal life and the godliness of good worship through the acknowledgment of the one, the Lord Jesus Christ, calling us by his "own" glory and virtue (1:3).

19

2 Peter 3:1–18
By a Reminder I Am Stirring You Up to Make Every Effort for Godliness (A′)

*Make every effort to be found faultless
and flawless in peace*

A   3:1 This is now, beloved, the second *letter* I am *writing* to *you*, in which by a reminder I am stirring up your sincere mind, ² to remember the pronouncements foretold by the holy prophets and the commandment of the *Lord* and savior through *your* apostles, ³ this first knowing, that they will come in the last days with mocking, mockers according to their *own* desires going ⁴ and saying, "Where *is* the promise of his coming? For from the time the fathers fell asleep, all things in the same manner are continuing from the beginning of creation." ⁵ For it escapes the notice of these maintaining this that heavens were from long ago and earth from water and through water has consisted by the word of God, ⁶ through which things the world at that time by water, being deluged, was annihilated. ⁷ But the heavens *now* and the earth by that same word have been stored up for fire, being kept for the day of judgment and *annihilation* of the ungodly human beings. ⁸ But let not this one thing escape the notice of *you*, beloved, that one day before the *Lord* is like a thousand years and a thousand years like one day. ⁹ The *Lord* does not delay the promise, as some *consider* a delay, but is being *patient* for *you*, not wishing for any to be annihilated, but for all to make room for repentance. ¹⁰ᵃ But the day of the *Lord* will come like a thief,

B ¹⁰ᵇ on which the heavens with a rushing sound will pass away, the *elements*, being *burned*, will be *dissolved* and the earth and works on it will be *found* out. ¹¹ᵃ All these things thus being *dissolved*,
C ¹¹ᵇ what sort of persons is it necessary to be existing in holy conduct and godliness,
B′ ¹² awaiting and hastening the coming of the day of God, because of which the heavens, being set on fire, will *dissolve*, and the *elements*, being *burned*, melt away. ¹³ But new heavens and a new earth according to what was promised by him, we are awaiting, in which righteousness dwells. ¹⁴ Therefore, beloved, awaiting these things, make every effort to be *found* faultless and flawless before him in peace
A′ ¹⁵ and the *patience* of our *Lord consider* as salvation, just as also our beloved brother Paul, according to the wisdom given to him *wrote* to *you*, ¹⁶ as also in all *letters*, speaking in them about these things, in which *are* some things hard to understand, which the ignorant and unstable distort, as also the rest of the *writings*, toward their *own annihilation*. ¹⁷ *You* then, beloved, knowing beforehand, be on guard, so that, not being led astray by the error of the disgraceful, you may not fall from your *own* stability, ¹⁸ but grow in grace and knowledge of our *Lord* and savior Jesus Christ. To him the glory both *now* and for the day of eternity. Amen!¹

Audience Response to 3:1-18

At this point the audience hear a progression of macrochiastic parallels from the A (1:1-15) to this A′ (3:1-18) chiastic unit. "Apostle [ἀπόστολος] of Jesus Christ" (1:1), "grace [χάρις] to you and peace [εἰρήνη]" (1:2), "godliness [εὐσέβειαν]" and "to godliness [εὐσεβείᾳ]" (1:3, 6-7), "promised [ἐπαγγέλματα]" (1:4), "so that [ἵνα]" (1:4), "knowledge [γνῶσιν] to knowledge [γνώσει]" (1:5-6), "therefore [διό]" (1:10, 12), "brothers [ἀδελφοί]" (1:10), "make every effort [σπουδάσατε; σπουδάσω]" (1:10, 15), "about these things" [περὶ τούτων]" (1:12), "eternal [αἰώνιον] kingdom" (1:11), "to stir you up by a reminder [διεγείρειν ὑμᾶς ἐν ὑπομνήσει]" (1:13), and "just as also [καθὼς καί]" (1:14) occur in the A unit.

While "by a reminder I am stirring up your [διεγείρω ὑμῶν ἐν ὑπομνήσει] sincere disposition" (3:1), "your apostles [ἀποστόλων]" (3:2), "godliness [εὐσεβείαις]" (3:11), "promised [ἐπάγγελμα]" (3:13), "therefore [διό]" (3:14), "make every effort [σπουδάσατε]" (3:14), "in peace [εἰρήνη]"

---

1. For the establishment of 2 Pet 3:1-18 as a chiasm, see ch. 14.

(3:14), "brother [ἀδελφός] Paul" (3:15), "just as also [καθὼς καί]" (3:15), "about these things [περὶ τούτων]" (3:16), "so that [ἵνα]" (3:17), "in the grace [χάριτι] and knowledge [γνώσει]" (3:18), and "eternity [αἰῶνος]" (3:18) occur in the A' unit.

3:1–10a (A): The Lord Is Being Patient for You

The audience hear the A element (3:1–10a) of this chiastic unit as a chiastic pattern in itself:

a) This is now, *beloved*, the second letter I am writing to *you*, in which by a reminder I am stirring up your sincere mind, to remember the pronouncements foretold by the holy prophets and the commandment of the *Lord* and savior through *your* apostles, this first knowing, that they will come in the last days with mocking, mockers according to their own desires going and saying, "Where is the *promise* of his coming? For from the time the fathers fell asleep, all things in the same manner are continuing from the beginning of creation" (3:1–4).

b) For it *escapes the notice* of these maintaining this that *heavens* were from long ago and *earth* from water and through water has consisted by the *word* of God, through which things the world at that time by water, being deluged, was annihilated (3:5–6).

b') But the *heavens* now and the *earth* by that same *word* have been stored up for fire, being kept for the day of judgment and annihilation of the ungodly human beings. But let not this one thing *escape the notice* (3:7–8a)

a') of *you, beloved*, that one day before the *Lord* is like a thousand years and a thousand years like one day. The *Lord* does not delay the *promise*, as some consider a delay, but is being patient for *you*, not wishing for any to be annihilated, but for all to make room for repentance. But the day of the *Lord* will come like a thief (3:8b–10a).

At the center of this chiastic sub-unit the audience experience a pivot of parallels from the b) to the b') sub-element involving the only occurrences in 2 Peter of the verb "escape the notice" and in this sub-unit of the terms "heavens," "earth," and "word." "For it escapes the notice [λανθάνει] of these maintaining this" (3:5) progresses to "but let not this one thing escape the notice [λανθανέτω]" (3:8a). And "that heavens [οὐρανοί] were from long ago and earth [γῆ] from water and through water has consisted by the word [λόγῳ] of God" (3:5) progresses to "but the heavens [οὐρανοί] now and the earth [γῆ] by that same word [λόγῳ] have been stored up for fire" (3:7).

2 Peter 3:1-18

The audience then hear a progression of chiastic parallels from the a) to the a') sub-element involving the only occurrences in 2 Peter of the term "promise" and in this sub-unit of the terms, "beloved," "Lord," and the second person plural pronoun. "Beloved [ἀγαπητοί]" (3:1), "to you [ὑμῖν]" (3:1)," "your [ὑμῶν] sincere disposition" (3:1), "Lord [κυρίου]" (3:2), "your [ὑμῶν] apostles" (3:2), and "promise [ἐπαγγελία]" (3:4) occur in the a) sub-element. And "of you [ὑμᾶς]" (3:8b), "beloved [ἀγαπητοί]" (3:8b), "before the Lord [κυρίῳ]" (3:8b), "Lord [κύριος]" (3:9), "promise [ἐπαγγελίας]" (3:9), "for you [ὑμᾶς]" (3:9), and "of the Lord [κυρίου]" (3:10a) occur in the a') sub-element.

And the audience hear the a) sub-element (3:1-4) of this chiastic sub-unit (3:1-10a) as yet another chiastic pattern in itself:
(a) This is now, beloved, the second letter I am writing to you, *in which* by a reminder I am stirring up your sincere mind, to remember the pronouncements foretold by the holy prophets and the commandment of the Lord and savior through your apostles, this first knowing (3:1-3a),
  (b) that they will come in the last days with *mocking* (3:3b),
  (b') *mockers* according to their own desires going (3:3c)
(a') and saying, "Where is the promise of his coming? For *from the time* the fathers fell asleep, all things in the same manner are continuing from the beginning of creation" (3:4).

At the center of this chiastic sub-unit the audience experience a pivot of parallels from the (b) to the (b') sub-element involving the only occurrences in 2 Peter of expressions for "mocking/mockers." "That they will come in the last days with mocking [ἐμπαιγμονῇ]" (3:3b) progresses to "mockers [ἐμπαῖκται] according to their own desires going" (3:3c). They then hear a progression of chiastic parallels from the (a) to the (a') sub-element involving the only occurrences in this sub-unit of the feminine relative pronoun as the object of a preposition. "In which [ἐν αἷς]" (3:1) progresses to "from the time [ἀφ' ἧς]" (3:4).

That this is now the second letter Peter is writing to his audience, addressed as "beloved [ἀγαπητοί]" (3:1), reminds them of the way he addressed them in the first letter, 1 Peter.[2] In the first letter Peter exhorted the audience, "Beloved [ἀγαπητοί], I encourage you as aliens and sojourners to keep away from fleshly desires [σαρκικῶν ἐπιθυμιῶν] that are waging

---

2. "Since one of the principal contexts of moral exhortation was the family, we are not surprised to find that our author repeatedly appeals to the recipients of the letter as 'beloved' (cf. 1 Cor. 4:14; 10:14; 1 Pet. 2:11; 4:12). The address lends force to Peter's appeal and at the same time marks the solidarity of the readers with the author. They are those who are inside, within the circle of the family, and not those separated off, as were the heretics" (Green, *Jude and 2 Peter*, 309).

war against the soul" (1 Pet 2:11). Then in this second letter he warned the audience about the false teachers who are going after the "flesh" (σαρκός) in "desire" (ἐπιθυμίᾳ) of defilement and despising the lordship of Jesus Christ (2 Pet 2:10), and who are seducing with "desires" (ἐπιθυμίαις) of the "flesh" (σαρκός) those barely escaping (2:18). And in the first letter Peter advised the audience, "Beloved [ἀγαπητοί], do not be surprised at the burning among you, occurring to you for a trial [πειρασμόν]" (1 Pet 4:12). But in this second letter Peter assured his audience that the Lord knows how to rescue the godly from "trial [πειρασμοῦ]" (2 Pet 2:9).

The prepositional phrase "in which" (ἐν αἷς) with the relative pronoun in the plural refers to both the first and second letter. In both of which, as Peter says, "by a reminder I am stirring up your [διεγείρω ὑμῶν ἐν ὑπομνήσει] sincere mind" (3:1). This reinforces Peter's previous assertion that he considers it righteous as long as he is alive "to stir you up by a reminder" (διεγείρειν ὑμᾶς ἐν ὑπομνήσει), knowing that imminent is the removal of his "tent," his earthly life (1:13).[3] That he is stirring up the audience's sincere "mind" (διάνοιαν) reminds them of his exhortation in the first letter that "having girded up the loins of your mind [διανοίας], being sober, completely hope upon the grace that is to be borne to you at the revelation of Jesus Christ" (1 Pet 1:13), that is, at the final "coming of our Lord Jesus Christ" (2 Pet 1:16).

By a reminder Peter is stirring up the sincere mind of his audience (3:1) to remember the pronouncements foretold by the holy "prophets [προφητῶν]" (3:2). This refers especially to the prophetic pronouncements that point to the future coming of our Lord Jesus Christ for final judgment (1:16). It reminds the audience that we have as very firm the "prophetic" (προφητικόν) word, to which they are to attend until the "day" dawns, that is, the day of final judgment, and the "morning star arises," that is, the Lord Jesus Christ comes again (1:19). As the audience are to know, every "prophecy" (προφητεία) of scripture does not come about by one's own interpretation (1:20), for not by the will of a human being has "prophecy" (προφητεία) ever been conveyed, rather, brought along by the "Holy" (ἁγίου) Spirit, human beings, the "holy" (ἁγίων) prophets (3:2), spoke from God (1:21). The pronouncements foretold by the "holy" prophets thus reinforce the assertion that Peter and his associates witnessed on the "holy" (ἁγίῳ) mountain the majesty of the transfigured Jesus, which prefigured his final coming in glory (1:18).

---

3. According to Davids, *2 Peter and Jude*, 259, "reminding is an important function of oral mnemonic culture in that without having books available that one could read oneself it was important that critical stories and ideas be repeated, whether through having a letter such as this one read aloud in church or through having a teacher frequently repeat a teaching."

When the audience hear that they are to remember not only the pronouncements foretold by the "holy" prophets but also the "commandment" (ἐντολῆς) of the Lord and savior through your apostles (3:2), they hear the transitional word that links this chiastic unit (3:1-18) with the previous one (2:17-22). That unit concluded with the notice that it was better for the false teachers not to have acknowledged the way of righteousness than, acknowledging it, to turn back from the "holy" (ἁγίας) "commandment" (ἐντολῆς) handed over to them (2:21).[4]

Remembering the commandment of the "Lord and savior [κυρίου καὶ σωτῆρος]" (3:2) implies following the way of righteousness included in the acknowledgment, through liturgical and ethical worship, of "our Lord and savior" (κυρίου ἡμῶν καὶ σωτῆρος) Jesus Christ, in which we believers are escaping the defilements of the world that hinder our worship (2:20). It reinforces the exhortation for the audience to uphold their call and chosenness, for thus will be richly supplied to them the entrance for the eternal kingdom of "our Lord and savior" (κυρίου ἡμῶν καὶ σωτῆρος) Jesus Christ (1:11). It also reminds them that they have obtained a precious faith in the righteousness that implies following the way of righteousness of "our God and savior" (θεοῦ ἡμῶν καὶ σωτῆρος) Jesus Christ (1:1). And that they are to remember this commandment through your "apostles [ἀποστόλων]" (3:2) further reinforces the eyewitness testimony of Peter, an "apostle [ἀπόστολος]" (1:1), and his apostolic associates regarding the transfiguration of Jesus, which indicates his future coming for final judgment (1:16-18).

The audience have already heard how the participial clause, "this first knowing" (τοῦτο πρῶτον γινώσκοντες), introduced the notice that every prophecy of scripture does not come about by one's "own" (ἰδίας) interpretation (1:20). And now they hear the same clause, "this first knowing" (τοῦτο πρῶτον γινώσκοντες), introduce the notice that they will come in the last days with mocking, mockers according to their "own" (ἰδίας) desires going (3:3). What the audience are first of all to know about the mockery of false prophecy is part of the "knowledge" (γνῶσιν) they are to supply to their faith (1:5), the "knowledge" (γνώσει) to which they are to add self-control (1:6). And such knowledge is part of the things that equip the audience for the acknowledgment of our Lord Jesus Christ (1:8), the acknowledgment that takes place in and through the "godliness" of good worship (1:3, 6-7).

The audience's "first" (πρῶτον) knowing that mockers will come in the "last" (ἐσχάτων) days with mocking (3:3) associates such mockers with the

---

4. "As in 2:21, 'commandment' probably does not refer to a particular commandment or even to the general proclamation of the lordship of Jesus but to the call for obedience to the ethical demands of the Christian life. Thus the 'commandment' produces the life of righteousness (2:21; 3:13)" (Donelson, *I & II Peter*, 266).

false teachers for whom the "last" (ἔσχατα) things have become worse than the "first [πρώτων]" (2:20). That these mockers are "going" (πορευόμενοι) according to their own "desires [ἐπιθυμίας]" (3:3) numbers them among the unrighteous to be punished at the day of judgment (2:9), especially those "going" (πορευομένους) after the flesh in "desire" (ἐπιθυμίᾳ) of the defilement that prevents proper worship and despising rather than worshiping the lordship of Jesus Christ (2:10). The audience are thus to beware that following the false teaching of these mockers would return them to the time when they were accomplishing the purpose of the Gentiles, having "gone" (πεπορευμένους) in debaucheries, "desires" (ἐπιθυμίαις), drunkenness, carousing, drinking bouts, and the false worship of wanton idolatries (1 Pet 4:3).

The mocking of the false teachers is expressed in their saying, "Where is the promise of his coming [παρουσίας]?" (2 Pet 3:4).[5] But Peter has already provided that promise in making known to the audience the power and "coming" (παρουσίαν) of our Lord Jesus Christ, by having become an eyewitness of the majesty of Jesus during his transfiguration into a heavenly figure (1:16). In a further explanation of their questioning the promise of his coming the mocking false teachers also object that from the time the ancestral "fathers" (πατέρες) fell asleep in death, all things in the same manner are continuing from the beginning of creation (3:4). They have thus failed to realize the significance of the heavenly honor and glory the transfigured Jesus received from God the "Father" (πατρός), when a voice was conveyed to him such as this by the majestic glory, "My Son, my beloved, is this one for whom I am well pleased" (1:17). As the audience are to appreciate, the heavenly glory the transfigured Jesus received from God his Father is what promises his future and final coming in heavenly glory for the last judgment.

The audience have been warned that the false teachers will exploit them with deceptive "words" (λόγοις), but for these false teachers the judgment of "long ago" (ἔκπαλαι) is not becoming idle (2:3). Now the audience are to know that it escapes the notice of these false teachers maintaining that everything has continued in the same manner from the beginning of creation that the heavens were from "long ago" (ἔκπαλαι) and earth from water and through water has consisted by the "word" (λόγῳ) of "God [θεοῦ]" (3:5).[6] This recalls that we have as very firm the prophetic "word [λόγον]" (1:19a) through which human beings spoke from "God [θεοῦ]" (1:21), and

---

5. Adams, "Promise," 106–22. "Ironically, the mockers who are predicted to come in 'the last days' deny the very idea of last days" (Donelson, *I & II Peter*, 267).

6. "The imagery of the earth being created 'out of water and through water' probably refers, first of all, to the waters of chaos that are separated in Gen 1:6–7 and now reside above the firmament. However, the dual phrases may also include a reference to water as the, or one of the, constituent elements of creation" (Donelson, *I & II Peter*, 268).

to which the audience are to attend (1:19b). This is the prophetic word of God that points to the final judgment as the "day" that will dawn and to the final coming of the Lord Jesus as the "morning star" (1:19c).

Through "which things," that is, through water as the means and the word of God as the cause, the "world" (κόσμος) at one time by water, being "deluged" (κατακλυσθείς), was "annihilated [ἀπώλετο]" (3:6).[7] This recalls that God did not spare the ancient "world" (κόσμου), but "brought" (ἐπάξας) a "deluge" (κατακλυσμόν) upon the "world" (κόσμῳ) of the ungodly (2:5). The audience, who are escaping destruction from desire in the "world [κόσμῳ]" (1:4), are thus not to follow the ungodly false teachers who, although they were at one time escaping the defilements of the "world" (κόσμου) in the acknowledgment of our Lord and savior Jesus Christ (2:20), are now "bringing" (ἐπάγοντες) upon themselves imminent "annihilation [ἀπώλειαν]" (2:1).

But the "heavens" (οὐρανοί) now and the "earth" (γῆ) by that same "word" (λόγῳ), that is, by the "word" (λόγῳ) of God by which the "heavens" (οὐρανοί) were from long ago and the "earth" (γῆ) from water and through water has consisted (3:5), have been stored up for fire (3:7a).[8] They are being "kept" (τηρούμενοι) by God (divine passive) for the "day" (ἡμέραν) of "judgment" (κρίσεως) and "annihilation" (ἀπωλείας) of the ungodly human beings (3:7b). This reinforces the warning for the audience that for the false teachers the gloom of darkness has been "kept [τετήρηται]" (2:17), that the Lord knows how to "keep" (τηρεῖν) the unrighteous false teachers to be punished at the "day" (ἡμέραν) of "judgment [κρίσεως]" (2:9), and that like the sinning angels they are to be "kept" (τηρουμένους) for "judgment [κρίσιν]" (2:4). It thus bolsters the exhortation for the audience to continue to attend to the prophetic word of God until the "day" (ἡμέρα) of judgment dawns (1:19).

It also reinforces that for the false teachers the "judgment" (κρίμα) of long ago is not becoming idle and their "annihilation" (ἀπώλεια) is not

---

7. "The earth came out of water, but the water turned and destroyed the earth (3:6). God, the sustainer of the earth, is also the judge of the earth" (Green, *Jude and 2 Peter*, 320). "If δι' ὧν refers to both water and the word of God, there is a neat parallelism in all three vv in this section: by his word and by means of water God created the world (v 5); by his word and by means of water he destroyed it (v 6); by his word and by means of fire he will destroy it in the future (v 7)" (Bauckham, *Jude, 2 Peter*, 298).

8. "Although Iranian ideas may have had some influence on Jewish imagery, it probably is the story of Sodom and Gomorrah that inspires Jewish thinking on fire and judgment. Jewish imagery on final judgment is diverse and fluid; it never settles on one scenario. However, fire is one of the most common forces of destruction in these accounts (e.g., Deut 32:22; Isa 30:30; 66:15–16; Mal 4:1). The NT does not have many narratives of final judgment. However, fire is by far the most common tool of destruction and judgment in the NT" (Donelson, *I & II Peter*, 269–70). "The roots of the idea of a coming world destruction by fire are to be found in late OT and Jewish apocalyptic texts" (Harrington, *2 Peter*, 287).

becoming drowsy (2:3), as those bringing upon themselves imminent "annihilation" (ἀπώλειαν) through their opinions of "annihilation [ἀπωλείας]" (2:1). The audience are thus to beware that the false teachers, numbered among the "ungodly" (ἀσεβῶν) human beings to be annihilated by fire (3:7), stand in continuity with the "ungodly" (ἀσεβῶν) upon whom God brought the deluge (2:5), as well as the "ungodly" (ἀσεβέσιν) for whom the ruin of Sodom and Gomorrah, reduced to ashes by fire, was intended (2:6). The audience hear the a') sub-element (3:8b-10a) in the A element (3:1-10a) of this chiastic unit as yet another chiastic pattern in itself:

(a) of *you*, beloved, that one *day* before the Lord is like a thousand years and a thousand years like one *day* (3:8b).

  (b) The Lord does not *delay* the promise (3:9a),

  (b') as some consider a *delay* (3:9b),

(a') but is being patient for *you*, not wishing for any to be annihilated, but for all to make room for repentance. But the *day* of the Lord will come like a thief (3:9c-10a).

At the center of this chiastic sub-unit the audience experience a pivot of parallels from the (b) to the (b') sub-element involving the only occurrences in 2 Peter of expressions for "delay." "Does not delay [βραδύνει] the promise" (3:9a) progresses to "as some consider a delay [βραδύτητα]" (3:9b). They then hear a progression of chiastic parallels from the (a) to the (a') sub-element involving the only occurrences in this sub-unit of the second person plural pronoun and the term "day." "Of you [ὑμᾶς]" (3:8b), "one day [ἡμέρα]" (3:8b), and "like one day [ἡμέρα]" (3:8b) progress to "for you [ὑμᾶς]" (3:9c) and "the day [ἡμέρα] of the Lord" (3:10a).

In contrast to the false teachers of whom it "escapes the notice [λανθάνει]" (3:5), the audience are not to let this one thing "escape the notice" (λανθανέτω) of them, addressed as "beloved [ἀγαπητοί]" (3:8), the "beloved" (ἀγαπητοί) to whom Peter is writing this second letter (3:1). They are to take note that one day "before the Lord" (παρὰ κυρίῳ) is like a thousand years and a thousand years like one day (3:8).[9] They are thus to realize that the angels do not convey a blasphemous judgment against the false teachers "before the Lord" (παρὰ κυρίῳ) in order to allow them time for repentance (2:11).

The audience are to appreciate that the Lord does not delay the "promise" (ἐπαγγελίας), the "promise" (ἐπαγγελία) of the coming of the Lord Jesus Christ (3:4), as some consider a delay (3:9).[10] Rather, he is being patient

---

9. "The heart of this verse is a quote from Ps 90:4 (89:4 LXX)... Psalm 90:4 was also used in Jewish literature simply to note the gap between human time and divine time as a way of reminding people that they cannot calculate the ultimate mysteries of God's time. This seems to be the point in 2 Peter" (Donelson, *I & II Peter*, 273-74).

10. "The question about delay voiced by the heretics is part of the general fabric of

2 Peter 3:1-18

for "you [ὑμᾶς]" (3:9), the audience, those of "you" (ὑμᾶς) who are not to let this one thing escape the notice (3:8). That some, especially the false teachers, "consider" (ἡγοῦνται) a delay in the coming day of judgment resonates with their "considering" (ἡγούμενοι) revelry at day a delight (2:13). In contrast, Peter "considers" (ἡγοῦμαι) it righteous to stir up the audience by a reminder (1:13). The Lord is not wishing for "any" (τινες), including "some" (τινας) who consider a delay, to be "annihilated [ἀπολέσθαι]" (3:9) in such an "annihilation [ἀπωλείας]" (3:7) as the world was once "annihilated [ἀπώλετο]" (3:6).[11] This reinforces the warning not to follow the false teachers for whom their "annihilation" (ἀπώλεια) is not becoming drowsy (2:3), as those bringing upon themselves imminent "annihilation" (ἀπώλειαν) through their opinions which lead to "annihilation [ἀπωλείας]" (2:1).

But the "day" (ἡμέρα) of the "Lord" (κυρίου), the "Lord" (κυρίῳ) before whom one "day" (ἡμέρα) is like a thousand years and a thousand years like one "day [ἡμέρα]" (3:8), will come like a thief (3:10a).[12] This day of the Lord will be the "day" (ἡμέραν) of judgment and annihilation of the ungodly human beings (3:7), the "day" (ἡμέραν) of judgment at which the unrighteous are to be punished (2:9). This reinforces the exhortation for the audience not to let it escape their notice (3:8) that the "Lord" (κύριος) does not delay the promise of the coming of this day, as some consider a delay, but is being patient, not wishing for any to be annihilated, but for all to make room for repentance (3:9).[13]

3:10b-11a (B): The Earth and Works on It Will Be Found Out

What will take place on the day of the Lord that will come like a thief (3:10a) is further described: "on which the heavens with a rushing sound will pass away, the elements, being burned, will be dissolved and the earth and works on it will be found out. All these things thus being dissolved" (3:10b-11). On the day of the Lord's judgment the "heavens" (οὐρανοί), the "heavens" (οὐρανοί) that now have been stored up for fire (3:7), with a rushing sound will pass away (3:10b). The elements that constitute the universe, being burned by the fire, will be dissolved and the "earth" (γῆ), the "earth" (γῆ)'

reflection on divine judgment current during the era" (Green, *Jude and 2 Peter*, 328).

11. "It looks as if 2 Peter is saying that God does not wish even the 'scoffers' to perish (although our author does not have any expectation that they will repent) but rather wants even them to repent" (Davids, *2 Peter and Jude*, 281).

12. "The verb 'will come' (ἥξει) is first in the Greek text, emphasizing that the day will certainly come" (Schreiner, *1, 2 Peter*, 383).

13. "The verse may be highly ironic. The false teachers use God's patience as an argument against God, when it should lead them to repentance" (Schreiner, *1, 2 Peter*, 381).

that now by the word of God has been stored up for fire, being kept for the day of judgment and annihilation of the ungodly human beings (3:7), and the works on the earth will be found out (3:10b).[14]

The "works" (ἔργα) on the earth that will be found out on the day of the Lord's judgment (3:10b) include the lawless "works" (ἔργοις) such as those that tormented the righteous soul of Lot (2:8). This reinforces the exhortation for the audience to keep their conduct among the Gentiles praiseworthy, so that in what the Gentiles slander them as evildoers, observing the praiseworthy "works" (ἔργων) of the audience, the Gentiles may offer the worship of glorying God on the day of visitation (1 Pet 2:12), the day of the Lord's judgment. It reminds the audience that the God they call upon as Father in their liturgical worship is the one who impartially judges according to the "work" (ἔργον) of each one, so that in the reverential fear of their ethical worship they are to conduct the time of their sojourning on earth (1:17).

That the works on earth will be "found" (εὑρεθήσεται) out on the day of the Lord's judgment (2 Pet 3:10b) reinforces the exhortation for the audience to follow the model of Christ, who did not do sin nor was deceit "found" (εὑρέθη) in his mouth (1 Pet 2:22).[15] It reassures the audience that the refinement of their faith in various trials may be "found" (εὑρεθῇ) for praise and glory and honor at the revelation of Jesus Christ (1:7) on the day of the Lord's judgment. And that all these things are thus being "dissolved [λυομένων]" (2 Pet 3:11a) underlines for the audience that the elements presently comprising the universe will indeed be "dissolved" (λυθήσεται) on the day of the Lord's final judgment.

3:11b (C): It Is Necessary To Be Existing in Holy Conduct and Godliness

Since all these things, the elements comprising the universe (3:10), are being dissolved (3:11a), the audience are exhorted: "what sort of persons is it necessary to be existing in holy conduct and godliness" (3:11b). What sort of persons it is "necessary" (δεῖ), that is, in accord with God's will, for the audience to be recalls that they may briefly now, if "necessary" (δέον), be saddened in various trials (1 Pet 1:6). In contrast to the false teachers, who are "existing" (ὑπάρχοντες) as slaves of destruction (2 Pet 2:19), the audience are to be "existing" (ὑπάρχειν) in holy conduct and godliness. This recalls

---

14. Tresham, "2 Peter 3:10d," 55–79.

15. "The verb εὑρεθήσεται in this context, as in verse 14, suggests a judicial inquiry through which God will discover the deeds of humanity and will execute his judgment on the basis of what he finds" (Green, *Jude and 2 Peter*, 330).

that the things they are to supply to their faith, "existing" (ὑπάρχοντα) and increasing to them, make them neither useless not fruitless for the acknowledgment of our Lord Jesus Christ (1:8), which is to take place on the day of the Lord's final judgment.

In contrast to the "conduct" (ἀναστροφῆς) of the disgraceful in debauchery by which the righteous Lot was oppressed (2:7), the audience are to be persons existing in holy "conduct" (ἀναστροφαῖς) and godliness (3:11b). This "holy" (ἁγίαις) conduct accords with the pronouncements foretold by the "holy" (ἁγίων) prophets (3:2), the "holy" (ἁγίας) commandment of the Lord (2:21), and the true prophecy that human beings, brought along by the "Holy" (ἁγίου) Spirit, spoke from God (1:21). This is the God who, on the "holy" (ἁγίῳ) mountain (1:18), gave the Lord Jesus Christ the honor and glory that point to his future and final coming with honor and glory on the day of the Lord's last judgment (1:17). And that the audience are to be persons existing in "godliness" (εὐσεβείαις) reinforces the exhortation for them to supply to their faith "godliness [εὐσέβειαν]" (1:6), as the divine power of Jesus our Lord has granted us believers all the things necessary toward eternal life and the "godliness" (εὐσέβειαν) of good worship, both liturgical and ethical (1:3).[16]

3:12–14 (B′): Make Every Effort To Be Found Spotless and Blameless before Him

The audience hear the B′ element (3:12–14) of this chiastic unit as a chiastic pattern in itself:

a) *awaiting* and hastening the coming of the day of God (3:12a),

   b) because of which the *heavens*, being set on fire, will dissolve, and the elements, being burned, melt away (3:12b).

   b′) But new *heavens* and a new earth according to what was promised by him (3:13a),

a′) we are *awaiting*, in which righteousness dwells. Therefore, beloved, *awaiting* these things, make every effort to be found faultless and flawless before him in peace (3:13b–14).

At the center of this chiastic sub-unit the audience experience a pivot of chiastic parallels from the b) to the b′) sub-element involving the only occurrences in this sub-unit of the term "heavens." "Because of which

---

16. "The plural of ἀναστροφή indicates a variety of holy lifestyles, while the plural of εὐσέβεια indicates pious acts or 'godly acts.' The reference to εὐσέβεια, which is one of the virtues of 1:6, creates a terminological *inclusion* as the work moves toward its conclusion [emphasis original]" (Davids, *2 Peter and Jude: A Handbook*, 105).

1 Peter, 2 Peter, and Jude

the heavens [οὐρανοί]" (3:12b) progresses to "new heavens [οὐρανούς]" (3:13a). They then hear a progression of chiastic parallels from the a) to the a') sub-element involving the only occurrences in 2 Peter of the verb "await." "Awaiting [προσδοκῶντας] and hastening" (3:12a) progresses to "we are awaiting [προσδοκῶμεν]" (3:13b) and "awaiting [προσδοκῶντες] these things" (3:14).

At this point the audience also experience a progression of parallels from the B (3:10b-11a) to the B' (3:12-14) element of this chiastic unit. "The elements [στοιχεῖα], being burned [καυσούμενα], will be dissolved [λυθήσεται]" (3:10b), "will be found out [εὑρεθήσεται]" (3:10b), and "being dissolved [λυομένων]" (3:11a) in the B element progress to "will dissolve [λυθήσονται], and the elements [στοιχεῖα], being burned [καυσούμενα]" (3:12) and "to be found [εὑρεθῆναι] faultless and flawless" (3:14) in the B' element.

As those existing in holy conduct and godliness (3:11b), the audience are awaiting and hastening the "coming" (παρουσίαν) of the day of God (3:12a), in answer to the mockery of the false teachers who question the promise of his "coming [παρουσίας]" (3:4), the "coming" (παρουσίαν) of our Lord Jesus Christ (1:16). This "day" (ἡμέρας) of God is the "day" (ἡμέρα) of the Lord that will come like a thief (3:10), the "day" (ἡμέραν) of the judgment and annihilation of the ungodly human beings (3:7), and the "day" (ἡμέραν) of judgment at which the unrighteous are to be punished (2:9). That the audience are to await and hasten it reinforces the exhortation for them to attend to the prophetic word they hear in their liturgical worship until the "day" (ἡμέρα) dawns (1:19). It is the day of "the God" (τοῦ θεοῦ), "the God" (τοῦ θεοῦ) by whose word the heavens and earth has consisted (3:5), "the God" (τοῦ θεοῦ) in whose acknowledgment grace and peace may be multiplied (1:2), but also the day of our "God" (τοῦ θεοῦ) and savior Jesus Christ (1:1).[17]

Because of the day of God's judgment the "heavens" (οὐρανοί), being "set on fire [πυρούμενοι]" (3:12b), the "heavens" (οὐρανοί) now having been stored up for "fire [πυρί]" (3:7), will "dissolve" (λυθήσονται), and the "elements" (στοιχεῖα), being "burned" (καυσούμενα), will melt away (3:12b). This emphatically reinforces that on the day of the Lord the "heavens" (οὐρανοί) with a rushing sound will pass away. And the "elements" (στοιχεῖα), being "burned" (καυσούμενα), "will be dissolved [λυθήσεται]" (3:10), as indeed all things will be "dissolved [λυομένων]" (3:11a).

---

17. "Because God retards his judgment due to his desire that sinners should repent (3:9), this repentance will accelerate 'the coming of the day of God'... Although God is the one who effects the acceleration, he brings it to pass with reference to human repentance" (Green, *Jude and 2 Peter*, 334).

2 Peter 3:1–18

But new "heavens" (οὐρανούς), to replace the "heavens" (οὐρανοί) that will dissolve (3:12), and a new "earth" (γῆν), to replace the "earth" (γῆ) that has been stored up for fire (3:7), according to what was promised by God, we believers are awaiting, in which righteousness dwells (3:13).[18] In contrast to the false teachers, mockers "according" (κατά) to their own desires (3:3), we are awaiting new heavens and a new earth "according" (κατά) to what was promised by God. What was "promised" (ἐπάγγελμα) by God recalls the precious and great things "promised" (ἐπαγγέλματα) to us through which the audience may become sharers of the divine nature, escaping destruction from desire in the world (1:4).

"Awaiting" (προσδοκῶντας) and hastening the coming of the day of God (3:12), we believers are "awaiting" (προσδοκῶμεν) new heavens and a new earth in which God's "righteousness" (δικαιοσύνη) dwells (3:13). This recalls the way of "righteousness" (δικαιοσύνης) acknowledged—in and through the godliness of their good worship—by those who believe (2:21). It is the "righteousness" (δικαιοσύνης) of which Noah was a herald (2:5), and the "righteousness" (δικαιοσύνῃ) of our God and savior Jesus Christ in which the audience have obtained their precious faith (1:1).[19]

The audience are exhorted therefore as "beloved" (ἀγαπητοί), "awaiting" (προσδοκῶντες) these things, that is, the new heavens and new earth we are "awaiting [προσδοκῶμεν]" (3:13), while "awaiting" (προσδοκῶντας) and hastening the coming of the day of God (3:12), that they are to make every effort to be found faultless and flawless before God in peace (3:14). This follows upon their address as the "beloved" (ἀγαπητοί) who are to take note (3:8) that the Lord is being patient for all to make room for repentance (3:9), and the "beloved" (ἀγαπητοί) to whom Peter is writing this second letter as a reminder (3:1). That "therefore" (διό) they are to "make every effort" (σπουδάσατε) resonates with "therefore [διό]" (1:12) "I," Peter, will also "make every effort" (σπουδάσω) to have the audience through this second letter the memory of these things to uphold (1:15), and with "therefore" (διό) "you," the audience, are to "make every effort" (σπουδάσατε) their call and chosenness as firm to uphold (1:10).

When the heavens pass away, the earth and works on it will be "found" (εὑρεθήσεται) out (3:10); therefore, the audience are to make every effort to be "found" (εὑρεθῆναι) faultless and flawless before God in peace (3:14).

---

18. Adams, "Awaiting," 168–75. "The announcement of new heavens and a new earth recalls Isa 65:17 and 66:22 ... Everything is going to be destroyed, and there will be an entirely new heaven(s) and earth" (Donelson, *I & II Peter*, 278).

19. "At the heart of the difference between present and future worlds will be a moral discontinuity; the present world of corruption will be superseded by a future world of righteousness" (Stephens, *Annihilation*, 137).

To be found "faultless and flawless" (ἄσπιλοι καὶ ἀμώμητοι), in contrast to the false teachers, who are "stains and blemishes [σπίλοι καὶ μῶμοι]" (2:13), recalls the similar alliterative description of the precious blood of Christ, as of a lamb "flawless and faultless [ἀμώμου καὶ ἀσπίλου]" (1 Pet 1:19), cultic terminology for worthy sacrificial as well as ethical worship. As the audience are to appreciate, the worship offered by Christ is the model and means for them to be found faultless and flawless before God in and through the godliness of their good worship, both liturgical and ethical.[20] And the audience may be found faultless and flawless before God in "peace" (εἰρήνῃ), because Peter has offered the prayer greeting that grace and "peace" (εἰρήνη) may be multiplied to them in the acknowledgment that takes place in and through their worship of God and of Jesus our divine Lord (2 Pet 1:2).

3:15-18 (A'): The Patience of Our Lord Consider as Salvation

The audience hear the A' element (3:15-18) of this chiastic unit as a chiastic pattern in itself:

a) and the patience of *our Lord* consider as *salvation*, just as also our *beloved* brother Paul (3:15a),

  b) according to the wisdom given to him *wrote* to you, *as also in* all letters, speaking *in* them about these things (3:15b-16a),

  b') *in* which are some things hard to understand, which the ignorant and unstable distort, *as also* the rest of the *writings*, toward their own annihilation (3:16b).

a') You then, *beloved*, knowing beforehand, be on guard, so that, not being led astray by the error of the disgraceful, you may not fall from your own stability, but grow in grace and knowledge of *our Lord* and *savior* Jesus Christ. To him the glory both now and for the day of eternity. Amen! (3:17-18).

At the center of this chiastic sub-unit the audience experience a pivot of chiastic parallels from the b) to the b') sub-element involving the only occurrences in this sub-unit of terms for "writing," the expression "as also,"

---

20. "The believers' deportment should be such that they will not be found guilty before the Judge, thus imitating the example of the Lord, who was 'a lamb without defect or blemish' (1 Pet. 1:19)" (Green, *Jude and 2 Peter*, 337). "Although Christianity will develop a peculiar context for sacrificial imagery due to the centrality of the crucifixion and the notion that Jesus was a sacrifice (e.g., Heb 9:14; 1 Pet 1:19), the imagery itself and the use of such sacrificial language to refer to morality and ethics would not be strange to anyone in antiquity. The border between cult and personal ethics was porous" (Donelson, *I & II Peter*, 282). "The two words describe Christians as morally pure, metaphorically an unblemished sacrifice to God" (Bauckham, *Jude, 2 Peter*, 327).

and the preposition "in." "Wrote [ἔγραψεν] to you, as also in [ὡς καὶ ἐν] all letters, speaking in [ἐν] them" (3:15b-16a) progresses to "in [ἐν] which" and "as also [ὡς καί] the rest of the writings [γραφάς]" (3:16b). They then hear a progression of chiastic parallels from the a) to the a') sub-element involving the only occurrences in this sub-unit of "our Lord," "salvation/savior," and "beloved." "The patience of our Lord [κυρίου ἡμῶν] consider as salvation [σωτηρίαν], just as also our beloved [ἀγαπητός] brother Paul" (3:15a) progresses to "beloved [ἀγαπητοί]" (3:17) and "in grace and knowledge of our Lord [κυρίου ἡμῶν] and savior [σωτῆρος] Jesus Christ" (3:18).

And at this point the audience experience a progression of parallels from the A (3:1-10a) to the A' (3:15-18) element of this chiastic unit. "Letter [ἐπιστολήν]" (3:1), "I am writing [γράφω]" (3:1), "you [ὑμῖν]" (3:1), "Lord [κυρίου]" (3:2, 10a), "your [ὑμῶν]" (3:2), "their own [ἰδίας]" (3:3), "is [ἐστιν]" (3:4), "now [νῦν]" (3:7), "annihilation [ἀπωλείας]" (3:7), "you [ὑμᾶς]" (3:8, 9), "Lord [κυρίῳ]" (3:8), "Lord [κύριος]" (3:9), "consider [ἡγοῦνται]" (3:9), and "being patient [μακροθυμεῖ]" (3:9) occur in the A element. These occurrences progress to "patience [μακροθυμίαν]" (3:15), "Lord [κυρίου]" (3:15, 18), "consider [ἡγεῖσθε]" (3:15), "wrote [ἔγραψεν]" (3:15), "you [ὑμῖν]" (3:15), "letters [ἐπιστολαῖς]" (3:16), "are [ἐστιν]" (3:16), "writings [γραφάς]" (3:16), "their own [ἰδίαν] annihilation [ἀπώλειαν]" (3:16), "you [ὑμεῖς]" (3:17), "your own [ἰδίου]" (3:17), and "now [νῦν]" (3:18) in the A' element.

Since the "Lord" (κύριος) does not delay the promise, as some "consider" (ἡγοῦνται) a delay, but is being "patient" (μακροθυμεῖ) for the audience, not wishing for any to be annihilated, but for all to make room for repentance (3:9), the audience are to "consider" (ἡγεῖσθε) the "patience" (μακροθυμίαν) of our "Lord" (κυρίου) as salvation (3:15a). That they are to consider the Lord's patience for their repentance as "salvation" (σωτηρίαν) reminds the audience that, as infants who have been given new birth for eternal life (1 Pet 1:3, 23), they are to use this time for repentance to grow up for "salvation [σωτηρίαν]" (2:2). It reminds them that they are to be engaged in the worship of exulting (1:6-8) for the coming of our Lord Jesus Christ, as those attaining the end of their faith, "salvation" (σωτηρίαν) of souls (1:9), concerning which "salvation" (σωτηρίας) prophets sought and searched (1:10). And it reminds them that they are those who in the power of God are being guarded through faith for a "salvation" (σωτηρίαν) ready to be revealed in the last time (1:5), the day of the Lord God (2 Pet 3:10, 12).

The expression, "just as also [καθὼς καί] our beloved [ἀγαπητός] brother [ἀδελφός] Paul" (3:15a)," closely associates Paul with Peter, Christ, and the audience. It recalls the only previous occurrence in the letter of "just as also" in the expression that "just as also" (καθὼς καί) our Lord Jesus

Christ indicated to Peter the imminent removal of his earthly existence (1:14). It also recalls that God the Father declared Christ as his "beloved [ἀγαπητός]" (1:17), so that both Christ and Paul are considered "beloved." And it closely links the audience, addressed as "brothers [ἀδελφοί]" (1:10) and as "beloved [ἀγαπητοί]" (3:1, 8, 14), to both Peter and Paul as "our beloved brother."

In contrast to the false teachers, who are mockers "according" (κατά) to their own desires (3:3), but in continuity with "according" (κατά) to what was promised by God (3:13), Paul, "according" (κατά) to the wisdom given to him by God wrote to the audience (3:15b). That Paul "wrote" (ἔγραψεν) to "you" (ὑμῖν), as also in all his "letters" (ἐπιστολαῖς), speaking in them "about these things [περὶ τούτων]" (3:16a) adds his authority to that of Peter—"I" who am "writing" (γράφω) to "you" (ὑμῖν) this second "letter [ἐπιστολήν]" (3:1), as part of his intention to remind you "about these things [περὶ τούτων]" (1:12). And that Paul was "speaking" (λαλῶν) in his letters about these things, especially the things concerning the future coming of the Lord Jesus Christ for final judgment, lends to his letters the authority of true prophecy that human beings "spoke" (ἐλάλησαν) from God (1:21).

That in Paul's letters "are" (ἐστιν) some things hard to understand (3:16b) resonates with the misunderstanding of the false teachers, who in their mockery ask, "Where is [ἐστιν] the promise of his coming?" (3:4).[21] Although Paul wrote to the audience, "as also" (ὡς καί) in all his letters (3:16a), the ignorant and unstable, such as the false teachers, distort Paul's letters, "as also" (ὡς καί) the rest of the "writings [γραφάς]" (3:16b) of the "scripture" (γραφῆς) that contains divine prophecy (1:20). That they do this toward their "own" (ἰδίαν) "annihilation [ἀπώλειαν]" (3:16b) reinforces for the audience the warning that the mocking false teachers, who are going according to their "own" (ἰδίας) desires (3:3), are being kept for the day of judgment and "annihilation" (ἀπωλείας) of the ungodly human beings (3:7).

The audience are again addressed as "beloved [ἀγαπητοί]" (3:17), the "beloved" (ἀγαπητοί) awaiting new heavens and a new earth (3:14), the "beloved" (ἀγαπητοί) who are to take note (3:8) that the delay of the coming of the Lord is for their repentance (3:9), and the "beloved" (ἀγαπητοί) to whom Peter is writing this second letter as a reminder (3:1). They are those "knowing beforehand [προγινώσκοντες]" (3:17), as those "this first knowing [πρῶτον γινώσκοντες]" that mocking false teachers will come in the last days (3:3). Therefore, they are to "be on guard" (φυλάσσεσθε), with the

---

21. "The reference is probably therefore to passages which are liable to be misunderstood unless they are interpreted in the light of the rest of Paul's teaching and of the apostolic teaching generally, rather than to passages which are simply obscure" (Bauckham, *Jude, 2 Peter*, 331).

divine help of the God who "guarded" (ἐφύλαξεν) Noah (2:5), so that, not being led astray by the error of the disgraceful, they may not fall from their own stability (3:17).

The letter's final exhortation, that the audience may not fall from their own stability, is introduced by the conjunction "so that [ἵνα]" (3:17). This reinforces the letter's initial exhortation, introduced by the only other occurrence in the letter of this conjunction, "so that" (ἵνα), through the things granted to the audience toward eternal life and the godliness of good worship (1:3), they may become sharers of divine nature (1:4).

Like the righteous Lot, oppressed by the conduct of the "disgraceful" (ἀθέσμων) in debauchery (2:7), the audience are not to be led astray by the "error" (πλάνῃ) of the "disgraceful" (ἀθέσμων) false teachers (3:17), like those in "error" (πλάνῃ) residing, who are barely escaping (2:18) those seducing "unstable" (ἀστηρίκτους) souls (2:14). The ignorant and "unstable" (ἀστήρικτοι) false teachers distort the letters of Paul toward their "own" (ἰδίαν) annihilation (3:16), going according to their "own" (ἰδίας) desires (3:3). In contrast, the audience are not to fall from their "own" (ἰδίου) "stability [στηριγμοῦ]" (3:17), based on the acknowledgment of the divine Lord calling us by his "own" (ἰδίᾳ) glory and virtue (1:3).

As those previously exhorted to "grow" (αὐξηθῆτε) up for salvation (1 Pet 2:2), the audience are to "grow" (αὐξάνετε) in "grace" (χάριτι) and knowledge of our Lord and savior Jesus Christ (2 Pet 3:18a), aided by Peter's initial prayer that "grace" (χάρις) be multiplied to them in the acknowledgment of God and of Jesus Christ our Lord (1:2). The knowledge of "our Lord" (κυρίου ἡμῶν) and "savior" (σωτῆρος) Jesus Christ in which they are to grow includes especially the knowledge that the delay of his future coming for final judgment is to be considered his patience for repentance (3:9). This is the patience of "our Lord" (κυρίου ἡμῶν), which they are to consider as "salvation [σωτηρίαν]" (3:15).

The audience may grow in the "knowledge of our Lord and savior Jesus Christ [γνώσει τοῦ κυρίου ἡμῶν καὶ σωτῆρος Ἰησοῦ Χριστοῦ]" (3:18a) in the "acknowledgment" (ἐπιγνώσει), in and through the godliness of their good worship as believers, "of our Lord and savior Jesus Christ [τοῦ κυρίου ἡμῶν καὶ σωτῆρος Ἰησοῦ Χριστοῦ]" (2:20). That the delay of his final coming is to be considered as his patience for repentance and salvation serves as the "knowledge" (γνῶσιν) they are to supply to their faith (1:5) for the eschatological "acknowledgment" (ἐπίγνωσιν) of our Lord Jesus Christ (1:8) at his final coming. And this is so that the eschatological entrance for the eternal kingdom "of our Lord and savior Jesus Christ" (τοῦ κυρίου ἡμῶν καὶ σωτῆρος Ἰησοῦ Χριστοῦ) will be richly supplied to them (1:11) at his final coming.

In the first letter the audience were twice invited to join Peter in doxological worship—"to him be the might for the ages [αἰῶνας], amen!" (1 Pet 5:11) and "to whom is the glory [δόξα] and the might for the ages of the ages [αἰῶνας τῶν αἰώνων], amen!" (4:11). And now they are again invited to join him in the exuberant doxology that climactically closes the second letter in resonance with the first letter—"to him the glory [δόξα] both now and for the day of eternity [αἰῶνος]. Amen!" (2 Pet 3:18b). This worshipful acknowledgment of "glory" to our Lord and savior Jesus Christ (3:18) stands in stark contrast to the false teachers, who despise his lordship, blaspheming rather than worshiping "glorious beings [δόξας]" (2:10). It serves as a worshipful acknowledgment of the majestic "glory" (δόξαν) of the divine voice that prophetically indicated the future coming in glory of our Lord Jesus Christ (1:17), as the one calling all of us believers by his own "glory [δόξῃ]" (1:3).

The worshipful acknowledgment of glory to our Lord and savior Jesus Christ is both "now" (νῦν), the time "now" (νῦν) when the heavens and the earth have been stored up for fire (3:7), as well as for the "day" (ἡμέραν) of eternity (3:18). This is the "day" (ἡμέρας) of God (3:12), the "day" (ἡμέρα) of the Lord (3:10), the "day" (ἡμέραν) of judgment (3:7; 2:9), the "day" (ἡμέρα) that dawns at the final coming of our Lord Jesus Christ (1:19). It is the day of "eternity" (αἰῶνος), as the day when the entrance for the "eternal" (αἰώνιον) kingdom of our Lord and savior Jesus Christ will be richly supplied to the audience (1:11). And so the audience, gathered together as a worshiping assembly to listen to the letter, are invited to complete Peter's climactic doxological act of worship by affirmatively adding their own resounding "Amen!" (3:18).[22]

Summary on 3:1-18

By a reminder Peter is stirring up the sincere mind of his audience (3:1) to remember the pronouncements foretold by the holy "prophets" (3:2). This refers especially to the prophetic pronouncements that point to the future coming of our Lord Jesus Christ for final judgment (1:16). It reminds the audience that we have as very firm the "prophetic" word, to which they are to attend until the "day" dawns, that is, the day of final judgment, and the "morning star arises," that is, the Lord Jesus Christ comes again (1:19). As

---

22. "This doxology is one of the very few dedicated specifically to Jesus Christ (see 2 Tim. 4:18; Rev. 1:5-6). Its presence at the end of this letter provides evidence of Peter's high Christology. His high Christology is suggested in the first part of this verse as well as at the beginning of this letter, where he ascribes to Christ the divine titles 'God,' 'Savior,' and 'Lord' (1:1-2)" (Green, *Jude and 2 Peter*, 344).

the audience are to know, every "prophecy" of scripture does not come about by one's own interpretation (1:20), for not by the will of a human being has "prophecy" ever been conveyed, rather, brought along by the "Holy" Spirit, human beings, the "holy" prophets (3:2), spoke from God (1:21). The pronouncements foretold by the "holy" prophets thus reinforce the assertion that Peter and his associates witnessed on the "holy" mountain the majesty of the transfigured Jesus, which prefigured his final coming in glory (1:18).

Remembering the commandment of the "Lord and savior" (3:2) implies following the way of righteousness included in the acknowledgment, through liturgical and ethical worship, of "our Lord and savior" Jesus Christ, in which we believers are escaping the defilements of the world that hinder our worship (2:20). It reinforces the exhortation for the audience to uphold their call and chosenness, for thus will be richly supplied to them the entrance for the eternal kingdom of "our Lord and savior" Jesus Christ (1:11). It also reminds them that they have obtained a precious faith in the righteousness that implies following the way of righteousness of "our God and savior" Jesus Christ (1:1). And that they are to remember this commandment through your "apostles" (3:2) further reinforces the eyewitness testimony of Peter, an "apostle" (1:1), and his apostolic associates regarding the transfiguration of Jesus, which indicates his future coming for final judgment (1:16–18).

The audience have already heard how the participial clause, "this first knowing," introduced the notice that every prophecy of scripture does not come about by one's "own" interpretation (1:20). And now they hear the same clause, "this first knowing," introduce the notice that they will come in the last days with mocking, mockers according to their "own" desires going (3:3). What the audience are first of all to know about the mockery of false prophecy is part of the "knowledge" they are to supply to their faith (1:5), the "knowledge" to which they are to add self-control (1:6). And such knowledge is part of the things that equip the audience for the acknowledgment of our Lord Jesus Christ (1:8), the acknowledgment that takes place in and through the "godliness" of good worship (1:3, 6–7).

The mocking of the false teachers is expressed in their saying, "Where is the promise of his coming?" (3:4). But Peter has already provided that promise in making known to the audience the power and "coming" of our Lord Jesus Christ, by having become an eyewitness of the majesty of Jesus during his transfiguration into a heavenly figure (1:16). In a further explanation of their questioning the promise of his coming the mocking false teachers also object that from the time the ancestral "fathers" fell asleep in death, all things in the same manner are continuing from the beginning of creation (3:4). They have thus failed to realize the significance of the heavenly honor and glory the transfigured Jesus received from God the "Father," when a voice was conveyed to him such as this by the majestic glory, "My Son, my beloved, is this one for whom I am well pleased" (1:17). As the audience are to appreciate, the heavenly glory the transfigured Jesus received from God his Father is what promises his future and final coming in heavenly glory for the last judgment.

But the "day" of the "Lord," the "Lord" before whom one "day" is like a thousand years and a thousand years like one "day" (3:8), will come like a thief (3:10a). This day of the Lord will be the "day" of judgment and annihilation of the ungodly human beings (3:7), the "day" of judgment at which the unrighteous are to be punished (2:9). This reinforces the exhortation for the audience not to let it escape their notice (3:8) that the "Lord" does not delay the promise of the coming of this day, as some consider a delay, but is being patient, not wishing for any to be annihilated, but for all to make room for repentance (3:9).

The "works" on the earth that will be found out on the day of the Lord's judgment (3:10b) include the lawless "works" such as those that tormented Lot (2:8). This reinforces the exhortation for the audience to keep their conduct among the Gentiles praiseworthy, so that in what the Gentiles slander them as evildoers, observing the praiseworthy "works," the Gentiles may offer the worship of glorying God on the day of visitation (1 Pet 2:12). It reminds them that the God they call upon as Father in their liturgical worship is the one who impartially judges according to the "work" of each one, so that in the reverential fear of their ethical worship they are to conduct the time of their sojourning on earth (1:17). That the works on earth will be "found" out on the day of the Lord's judgment reinforces the exhortation for the audience to follow the model of Christ, who did not do sin nor was deceit "found" in his mouth (2:22). It reassures them that the refinement of their faith in various trials may be "found" for praise and glory and honor at the revelation of Jesus Christ (1:7) on the day of the Lord's judgment.

In contrast to the "conduct" of the disgraceful in debauchery by which the righteous Lot was oppressed (2 Pet 2:7), the audience are to be persons existing in holy "conduct" and godliness (3:11b). This "holy" conduct accords with the pronouncements foretold by the "holy" prophets (3:2), the "holy" commandment of the Lord (2:21), and the true prophecy that human beings, brought along by the "Holy" Spirit, spoke from God (1:21). This is the God who, on the "holy" mountain (1:18), gave the Lord Jesus Christ the honor and glory that point to his future and final coming with honor and glory on the day of the Lord's last judgment (1:17). And that the audience are to be persons existing in "godliness" reinforces the exhortation for them to supply to their faith "godliness" (1:6), as the divine power of Jesus our

2 Peter 3:1-18

Lord has granted us believers all the things necessary toward eternal life and the "godliness" of good worship, both liturgical and ethical (1:3).

When the heavens pass away, the earth and works on it will be "found" out (3:10); therefore, the audience are to make every effort to be "found" faultless and flawless before God in peace (3:14). To be found "faultless and flawless," in contrast to the false teachers, who are "stains and blemishes" (2:13), recalls the similar alliterative description of the precious blood of Christ, as of a lamb "flawless and faultless" (1 Pet 1:19), cultic terminology for worthy sacrificial as well as ethical worship. As the audience are to appreciate, the worship offered by Christ is the model and means for them to be found faultless and flawless before God in and through the godliness of their good worship, both liturgical and ethical. And the audience may be found faultless and flawless before God in "peace," because Peter has offered the prayer greeting that grace and "peace" may be multiplied to them in the acknowledgment that takes place in and through their worship of God and of Jesus our divine Lord (2 Pet 1:2).

Since the "Lord" does not delay the promise, as some "consider" a delay, but is being "patient" for the audience, not wishing for any to be annihilated, but for all to make room for repentance (3:9), the audience are to "consider" the "patience" of our "Lord" as salvation (3:15a). That they are to consider the Lord's patience for their repentance as "salvation" reminds the audience that, as infants who have been given new birth for eternal life (1 Pet 1:3, 23), they are to use this time for repentance to grow up for "salvation" (2:2). It reminds them that they are to be engaged in the worship of exulting (1:6-8) for the coming of our Lord Jesus Christ, as those attaining the end of their faith, "salvation" of souls (1:9), concerning which "salvation" prophets sought and searched (1:10). And it reminds them that they are those who in the power of God are being guarded through faith for a "salvation" ready to be revealed in the last time (1:5), the day of the Lord God (2 Pet 3:10, 12).

That Paul "wrote" to "you," as also in all his "letters," speaking in them "about these things" (3:16a) adds his authority to that of Peter—"I" who am "writing" to "you" this second "letter" (3:1), as part of his intention to remind you "about these things" (1:12). And that Paul was "speaking" in his letters about these things, especially the things concerning the future coming of the Lord Jesus Christ for final judgment, lends to his letters the authority of true prophecy that human beings "spoke" from God (1:21). Although Paul wrote to the audience, "as also" in all his letters (3:16a), the ignorant and unstable, such as the false teachers, distort Paul's letters, "as also" the rest of the "writings" (3:16b) of the "scripture" that contains divine prophecy (1:20). That they do this toward their "own annihilation" (3:16b) reinforces for the audience the warning that the mocking false teachers, who are going according to their "own" desires (3:3), are being kept for the day of judgment and "annihilation" of the ungodly human beings (3:7).

The audience are to grow in the "knowledge of our Lord and savior Jesus Christ" (3:18a) in the "acknowledgment," in and through the godliness of their good worship as believers, "of our Lord and savior Jesus Christ" (2:20). That the delay of his final coming is to be considered as his patience for repentance and salvation serves as the "knowledge" they are to supply to their faith (1:5) for the eschatological "acknowledgment" of our Lord Jesus Christ (1:8) at his final coming. And this is so that the eschatological entrance for the eternal kingdom "of our Lord and savior Jesus Christ" will be richly supplied to them (1:11) at his final coming.

In the first letter the audience were twice invited to join Peter in doxological worship—"to him be the might for the ages, amen!" (1 Pet 5:11) and "to whom is the glory and the might for the ages of the ages, amen!" (4:11). And now they are again invited to join him in the exuberant doxology that climactically closes the second letter in resonance with the first letter—"to him the glory both now and for the day of eternity. Amen!" (2 Pet 3:18b). This worshipful acknowledgment of "glory" to our Lord and savior Jesus Christ (3:18) stands in stark contrast to the false teachers, who despise his lordship, blaspheming rather than worshiping "glorious beings" (2:10). It serves as a worshipful acknowledgment of the majestic "glory" of the divine voice that prophetically indicated the future coming in glory of our Lord Jesus Christ (1:17), as the one calling all of us believers by his own "glory" (1:3).

The worshipful acknowledgment of glory to our Lord and savior Jesus Christ is both "now," the time "now" when the heavens and the earth have been stored up for fire (3:7), as well as for the "day" of eternity (3:18). This is the "day" of God (3:12), the "day" of the Lord (3:10), the "day" of judgment (3:7; 2:9), the "day" that dawns at the final coming of our Lord Jesus Christ (1:19). It is the day of "eternity," as the day when the entrance for the "eternal" kingdom of our Lord and savior Jesus Christ will be richly supplied to the audience (1:11). And so the audience, gathered together as a worshiping assembly to listen to the letter, are invited to complete Peter's climactic doxological act of worship by affirmatively adding their own resounding "Amen!" (3:18).

20

Summary and Conclusion on 2 Peter

*Worship in the Knowledge
of Our Lord and Savior Jesus Christ*

THE PRECEDING CHAPTERS HAVE provided detailed summary conclusions for each of the five chiastic units comprising 2 Peter. This final chapter presents a comprehensive overview of how this letter as a liturgical homily or sermon, through the rhetorical dynamics of its various chiastic structures, exhorts its audience to worship in the knowledge of our Lord and savior Jesus Christ. As they await the final coming of our Lord Jesus Christ, the audience, who have been given everything necessary for "godliness" (1:3), are to practice the "godliness" (3:11), that is, the "good worship" (εὐσέβεια) that includes liturgical worship and the ethical or moral behavior that complements it. They are to practice this worship and thereby grow in the "knowledge" (3:18) that in delaying his final coming, our Lord Jesus Christ is being patient so that all have time for repentance (3:9). With this knowledge they are to consider such patience as the "salvation" (3:15) they celebrate in, through, and for the worshipful acknowledgment (1:2, 3, 8) of our Lord and "savior" Jesus Christ (1:11; 2:20; 3:18).

The opening chiastic A unit (1:1–15) introduces the sender of the letter as Symeon Peter, characterized as "slave and apostle of *Jesus Christ*" (1:1a). The audience to whom the letter is sent are characterized as "those who have obtained a *faith* just as precious to us in the *righteousness* of *our* God and *savior Jesus Christ*" (1:1b). At the pivotal center of the unit the audience are reminded that his *divine* nature has *granted* us all things necessary toward eternal life and godliness, through the acknowledgment in worship of the one calling us by his own glory and virtue, so that through the things *granted* to us the audience may become sharers of the *divine* nature (1:3–4).

291

In the climactic final element of this unit the audience are to supply to their *faith* the things that will prepare them for the acknowledgment of *our Lord Jesus Christ* (1:5-8), so that there will be supplied to them the entrance for the eternal kingdom of *our Lord and savior Jesus Christ* (1:11). Therefore, Peter considers it *righteous* to stir them up by a reminder in and through this letter (1:13) (ch. 15).

At the center of the chiastic B unit (1:16-21) the audience hear the *voice* that was conveyed to our Lord Jesus Christ by God the Father, "My Son, my beloved, is this one for whom I am well pleased" (1:17). This was the *voice* Peter and his associates themselves heard conveyed from heaven on the holy mountain where Jesus was transfigured into a heavenly figure as a prefigurement of his final coming in glory (1:18). They then experience a progression of chiastic parallels involving the testimony and prophecy that confirms this final coming. Peter and his associates *made known* to the audience the power and coming of our Lord Jesus Christ by having *become* eyewitnesses of his divine majesty (1:16). And the audience are to be first *knowing* that every prophecy of scripture, especially the prophetic word to which they are attending until the day of his final coming (1:19), does not *come about* by one's own interpretation, for not by the will of a human being has prophecy ever been conveyed, rather, brought along by the Holy Spirit, human beings spoke from God (1:20-21) (ch. 16).

At the center of the chiastic C unit (2:1-16) the audience are assured that if the *righteous* Lot, oppressed by the conduct of the disgraceful in debauchery, God *rescued* (2:7), for in what was seen and heard the *righteous* one tormented his *righteous* soul by the lawless works, then the Lord knows how to *rescue* the godly, including the audience, from the trial presented to them by the false teachers (2:8-9a). They then experience a progression of chiastic parallels involving the coming final judgment. The false teachers, like the *false prophets* that appeared among the people, deny the divine Master (2:1). Many will *follow* their debaucheries, because of whom the *way* of truth will be *blasphemed*, but for whom the same *judgment* as for sinning angels has been *kept* by God (2:1-6). Indeed, the Lord *keeps* the unrighteous for punishment at the day of *judgment*, especially those despising divine lordship and *blaspheming* the glorious beings that include God and our Lord Jesus Christ. Abandoning the proper *way*, they have been led astray, *following* the *way* of Balaam, the *prophet*, whom the voice of God rebuked (2:9b-16) (ch. 17).

After the central and pivotal C unit (2:1-16), unparalleled within the macrochiastic structure organizing the entire letter, the audience hear resonances, via the macrochiastic parallels, between the B (1:16-21) and the B' (2:17-22) unit. In the B unit the audience are assured that Peter and his

Summary and Conclusion on 2 Peter

associates witnessed the prefigurement of the final coming of our Lord Jesus Christ on the *holy* mountain (1:18), and that not by the will of a human being has prophecy ever been conveyed, rather, brought along by the *Holy* Spirit, human beings spoke from God (1:21). Then, in the B' unit, they are warned about the false teachers who turned back from the *holy* commandment handed over to them (2:21).

At the center of the chiastic B' unit (2:17-22) the audience are warned that the false teachers are seducing *those* barely escaping, *those* in error residing (2:18). They then experience a progression of chiastic parallels indicating how the false teachers have turned away from the godliness of good worship. First, they hear that *these* false teachers are waterless springs and mists driven by a storm, for *whom* the gloom of darkness has been kept by God (2:17). Then they hear that the false teachers, at one time escaping the defilements of the world in the acknowledgment, in and though their participation in communal worship, of our Lord Jesus Christ, have now once again become enslaved by their own destructive ways of the past. It was better for *them* not to have acknowledged the way of righteousness than, acknowledging it, to turn back from the holy commandment handed over to *them* (2:19-22) (ch. 18).

With 2 Pet 3:1-18, the A' unit within the macrochiastic structure embracing the entire letter, the audience hear resonances with the corresponding A unit (1:1-15). In the A unit Peter reminds the audience that they have been given all things needed for the *godliness* of good worship (1:3), the *godliness* they are to supply, along with *knowledge*, to their faith (1:5). For thus will be richly supplied to them the entrance for the *eternal* kingdom of our Lord and savior Jesus Christ (1:11). Therefore, Peter is *stirring them up by a reminder* in and through this letter (1:13). Then, in the A' unit, the audience hear that Peter *by a reminder is stirring up their* sincere mind in both letters (1 and 2 Peter) he has written to them (3:1). In view of the Lord's delay in coming as his patience for repentance (3:9), the audience are to be persons who practice the *godliness* of good worship, both liturgical and ethical (3:11). They are to grow in this *knowledge* of our divine Lord and savior Jesus Christ, whom they worship by acknowledging his glory both now and for the day of *eternity*, the day of his future coming for final judgment (3:18).

After hearing at the center of the chiastic A' unit (3:1-18) that they are to be persons who practice the godliness of good worship (3:11b), the audience experience a pivot of chiastic parallels. First, they hear that the heavens will pass away, the *elements* being *burned*, will be *dissolved* and the earth and works on it will be *found* out, as all these things will be *dissolved* (3:10b-11a). Then, because of the coming day of God on which the heavens will *dissolve* and the *elements*, being *burned*, melt away, they are to make every effort to be *found* faultless and flawless, in and through their liturgical and ethical worship, before God (3:12–14). They then experience a progression of parallels involving the godliness of their good worship in view of the delay in the final coming. First, they are to appreciate that the *Lord* does not delay the promise of his coming as some *consider* a delay, but is being *patient* to make room for repentance (3:1–10a). Then the *patience* of the *Lord* they are to *consider* as salvation, as they grow in grace and knowledge of our *Lord* and savior Jesus Christ, the focus of their worship (3:15–18) (ch. 19).

In conclusion, listening to and experiencing the rhetorical dynamics of the various chiastic patterns throughout the letter of 2 Peter encourages its audience, and all of us as we identify with them, to practice the godliness of good liturgical and ethical worship as those awaiting new heavens and a new earth (3:13). They are to practice this worship in the knowledge of our Lord and savior Jesus Christ. This knowledge preeminently includes knowing that the delay of the future coming of our divine Lord for final judgment is to provide patience for repentance, a patience they are to consider as salvation (3:9–15). The audience are among those who have obtained a precious faith in the righteousness of our God and savior Jesus Christ (1:1). Peter has stirred them up by a reminder, in and through the letter, to grow in grace and knowledge of our divine Lord and savior Jesus Christ, to whom they are invited to offer the worship of glorifying both now and for the day of eternity (3:18), the day of his future and final coming for their entrance into the eternal kingdom (1:11).

21

Introduction to Jude

Jude: Worship in the Mercy and Love of God through Our Lord Jesus Christ

JUST AS PREVIOUSLY FOR 1 and 2 Peter, I aim to contribute to a better understanding of Jude in a twofold way. First, I will demonstrate a completely new and comprehensive text-centered structure for Jude, based on its nature as an epistolary homily or hortatory sermon composed of rhetorical strategies meant for an oral performance to be heard by its audience gathered together as a worshiping assembly. This structure consists of a series of four microchiastic units arranged in a cohesive and coherent macrochiastic framework embracing the entire letter. My proposal seeks to be as rigorously text-centered as possible. It begins with and is governed by a close reading of or listening to the text, and thus is strictly based upon linguistic criteria within the text itself.[1]

Second, I will present a new proposal for the unifying or organizing theme of Jude in accord with its comprehensive chiastic structure as a key to its interpretation. The subtitle I have chosen for Jude, "worship in the mercy and love of God through our Lord Jesus Christ," articulates what the whole of Jude, as an epistolary homily or hortatory sermon, is encouraging its audience to maintain. Just as for 1 and 2 Peter, the term "worship" is to be understood comprehensively as including not only liturgical but ethical worship. Occurrences of the terms "mercy" and "love of God" form a

---

1. For some recent discussions of Jude, see Charles, "Angels," 39–48; idem, "Jude's Use," 130–45; idem, "Literary Artifice," 106–24; idem, *Literary Strategy*; idem, "Those," 109–24; Joubert, "Facing the Past," 56–70; idem, "Language," 335–49; idem, "Persuasion," 75–87; Reed and Reese, "Verbal Aspect," 181–200; Reese, "Holiness," 326–34; Thurén, "Hey Jude," 451–65; Webb, "Eschatology," 139–51. For a recent discussion of the relationship between 2 Peter and Jude, see Mathews, "Literary Relationship," 47–66.

literary inclusion embracing the entire letter. The letter begins with an act of worship which prays that "mercy" and "love" be multiplied by God for the audience (Jude 1:2). It closes with an exhortation for the audience to keep themselves in the "love of God," awaiting the "mercy" of "our Lord Jesus Christ" (1:21). After further exhortations regarding mercy (1:22–23), the letter ends with a climactic act of doxological worship to the only "God" our savior "through Jesus Christ our Lord" (1:25).

In the rest of this chapter I will introduce and explain the text-centered, linguistically based chiastic structures of Jude. In subsequent chapters I will present a comprehensive interpretation in accord with the chiastic structures, which illustrate and confirm that Jude is encouraging its implied audience to maintain their worship in the mercy and love of God through our Lord Jesus Christ.

The Four Microchiastic Units of Jude

In what follows I will first demonstrate how the text of Jude naturally divides itself into four distinct literary units based upon their microchiastic structures as determined by very precise linguistic parallels found objectively in the text. Second, I will demonstrate how these four units form a macrochiastic pattern based upon very precise linguistic parallels found objectively in the text of the chiastically paired units. Third, I will point out the various transitional words that connect a unit to the unit that immediately precedes it. These various transitional words, which occur at the conclusion of one unit and at the beginning of the following unit, indicate that the chiastic units are heard as a cohesive sequence. These various transitional words are italicized in the translations of the units below.

1. May the Mercy and Love of God Be Multiplied to You (1:1–4)

Necessity to write about those perverting
the grace of God and denying the Lord[2]

A   1:1 Jude, a slave of Jesus Christ [Ἰησοῦ Χριστοῦ] and brother of James, to those who are called, beloved in God [θεῷ] the Father and kept for Jesus Christ [Ἰησοῦ Χριστῷ].

---

2. The main heading of each unit is intended to summarize the unit as it relates to its parallel unit within the overall macrochiastic structure of the letter, while the subheading of each unit is intended to summarize or characterize the microchiastic dimension of each unit. The translations of each unit are my own.

Introduction to Jude

B   ² May mercy to you and peace and love be multiplied! ³ᵃ Beloved, exercising every eagerness to write to you [γράφειν ὑμῖν] about our common salvation,

C   ³ᵇ I had the necessity

B′   ³ᶜ to write to you [γράψαι ὑμῖν], exhorting to contend for the faith once for all handed down to the holy ones.

A′   ⁴ For certain persons have sneaked in, long ago written down for this condemnation, ungodly ones, perverting the grace of our God [θεοῦ] into debauchery and denying our only Master and *Lord*, Jesus Christ [Ἰησοῦν Χριστόν].

An A-B-C-B′-A′ chiastic pattern secures the integrity and distinctness of this first unit (1:1–4). The only occurrences in this unit of the titles "Jesus Christ" and "God"—"of Jesus Christ [Ἰησοῦ Χριστοῦ]" and "for Jesus Christ [Ἰησοῦ Χριστῷ]" in 1:1, "Jesus Christ [Ἰησοῦν Χριστόν]" in 1:4, "in God [θεῷ]" in 1:1, and "of our God [θεοῦ]" in 1:4—constitute the parallelism between the A (1:1) and A′ (1:4) elements of this chiasm. The only occurrences in Jude of the expression "to write to you"—"to write to you [γράφειν ὑμῖν]" in 1:3a and "to write to you [γράψαι ὑμῖν]" in 1:3c—determine the parallelism between the B (1:2–3a) and B′ (1:3c) elements. And finally, the unparalleled central and pivotal C (1:3b) element contains the only occurrence in Jude of the term "necessity"—"I had the necessity [ἀνάγκην]."

2. Some Are Kept under Gloom for Judgment (1:5–11)

Do not follow those undergoing divine punishment and do not judge

A   ⁵ I want to remind you, having known all these things once for all, that the *Lord*, having saved a people from the land of Egypt, later annihilated [ἀπώλευεν] those not believing,

B   ⁶ and that the angels [ἀγγέλους] not keeping to the domain of themselves but [ἀλλά] leaving behind their own dwelling he has kept in everlasting chains under gloom for the judgment [κρίσιν] of the great day,

C   ⁷ᵃ as also Sodom and Gomorrah and the cities round about them, in the same manner as these, indulging in sexual immorality and going after a different flesh [σαρκός],

D   ⁷ᵇ are displayed as an example, undergoing a punishment of eternal fire.

1 Peter, 2 Peter, and Jude

    C'   ^{8a} Likewise however, also these dreamers not only defile flesh [σάρκα]

    B'   ^{8b} but reject lordship and blaspheme glorious beings. ⁹ Yet even Michael the archangel [ἀρχάγγελος], when, disputing with the devil, argued about the body of Moses, did not dare to bring a judgment [κρίσιν] of blasphemy but [ἀλλά] said, "May the Lord rebuke you." ¹⁰ But *these* do not know whatever things they blaspheme, yet whatever things they naturally, like irrational animals, understand; in these things they are being destroyed.

    A'   ¹¹ Woe to them! For in the way of Cain they have gone and to the wandering of Balaam's recompense they abandoned themselves and in the rebellion of Korah they are annihilated [ἀπώλοντο].

The reference to "the Lord [κύριον]" at the beginning of this unit in 1:5 recalls and resonates with the expression, "denying our only Master and Lord [κύριος], Jesus Christ," at the conclusion of the preceding unit in 1:4. These occurrences of the term "Lord" in reference to Jesus Christ serve as the transitional terms linking the first unit (1:1–4) to the second unit (1:5–11).

An A-B-C-D-C'-B'-A' chiastic pattern secures the integrity and distinctness of this second unit (1:5–11). The only occurrences in Jude of the verb "annihilate"—"later annihilated [ἀπώλεσεν] those not believing" in 1:5 and "they are annihilated [ἀπώλοντο]" in 1:11—constitute the parallelism between the A (1:5) and the A' (1:11) elements of this chiasm. The only occurrences in Jude of references to "angels"—"angels [ἀγγέλους] not keeping to their own domain" in 1:6 and "Michael the archangel [ἀρχάγγελος]" in 1:9, of the conjunction "but"—"but [ἀλλά] leaving behind" in 1:6 and "but [ἀλλά] said" in 1:9, and in this unit of the term "judgment"—"for the judgment [κρίσιν]" in 1:6 and "judgment [κρίσιν] of blasphemy" in 1:9—determine the parallelism between the B (1:6) and the B' (1:8b–10) elements.

The only occurrences in this unit of the term "flesh"—"a different flesh [σαρκός]" in 1:7a and "defile flesh [σάρκα]" in 1:8a—establish the parallelism between the C (1:7a) and the C' (1:8a) elements. And finally, the unparalleled central and pivotal D (1:7b) element contains the only occurrence in Jude of the terms "displayed," "example," "undergoing," and "punishment" in the expression "are displayed [πρόκεινται] as an example [δεῖγμα], undergoing [ὑπέχουσαι] a punishment [δίκην] of eternal fire."

Introduction to Jude

3. Judgment of the Ungodly for Whom the Gloom Has Been Kept (1:12-20)

Build up yourselves in your most holy faith praying in the Holy Spirit

A   ¹² *These* are [Οὗτοί εἰσιν] dangerous reefs at your love feasts, feasting together without reverence, shepherding themselves [ἑαυτούς], clouds without water carried along by winds, autumn trees without fruit, twice having died, uprooted, ¹³ wild waves of the sea, foaming up things shameful of themselves [ἑαυτῶν], wandering stars for whom the gloom of the darkness for ages has been kept. ¹⁴ Enoch, the seventh from Adam, even prophesied to these, saying [λέγων], "Behold, the Lord [κύριος] has come with his holy [ἁγίαις] myriads,

B   ¹⁵ᵃ to exercise judgment against all [πάντων] and to convict every soul about [περί] all [πάντων] of their deeds of ungodliness in which [ὧν] they acted ungodly

B'   ¹⁵ᵇ and about [περί] all [πάντων] of the harsh things which [ὧν] ungodly sinners spoke against him" (*1 En.* 1:9).

A'   ¹⁶ These are [Οὗτοί εἰσιν] discontented grumblers according to the desires of themselves [ἑαυτῶν] going, and their mouth speaks bombastic things, enchanting people for the sake of gain. ¹⁷ But you, beloved, remember the pronouncements said beforehand by the apostles of our Lord [κυρίου] Jesus Christ, ¹⁸ for they said [ἔλεγον] to you, "In the end time there will be mockers according to the desires of themselves [ἑαυτῶν] going for ungodly things." ¹⁹ These are [Οὗτοί εἰσιν] the ones causing divisions, worldly-minded, not having the Spirit. ²⁰ But you, beloved, building up *yourselves* [ἑαυτούς] in your most holy [ἁγιωτάτῃ] faith, in the Holy [ἁγίῳ] Spirit praying.

The demonstrative pronoun "these" (οὗτοι) in reference to the ungodly intruders (see 1:4) at the beginning of this unit in 1:12 recalls "these" (οὗτοι) in reference to the same ungodly intruders near the conclusion of the preceding unit in 1:10. These successive occurrences of the same demonstrative pronoun thus serve at the transitional terms linking the second unit (1:5-11) to the third unit (1:12-20).

An A-B-B'-A' chiastic pattern secures the integrity and distinctness of this third unit (1:12-20). The following linguistic occurrences constitute the parallelism between the A (1:12-14) and A' (1:16-20) elements of this chiasm: the only occurrences in this unit of "these are"—"these are [οὗτοί εἰσιν] dangerous reefs" in 1:12, "these are [οὗτοί εἰσιν] discontented grumblers" in 1:16, and "these are [οὗτοί εἰσιν] the ones causing divisions" in 1:19; of

299

the plural reflexive pronoun—shepherding themselves [ἑαυτούς] in 1:12, "things shameful of themselves [ἑαυτῶν]" in 1:13, "the desires of themselves [ἑαυτῶν]" in 1:16 and 1:18, and "building yourselves [ἑαυτούς] up" in 1:20; of the verb "say"—"saying [λέγων]" in 1:14 and "they said [ἔλεγον]" in 1:18; of "Lord"—"the Lord [κύριος] has come" in 1:14 and "of our Lord [κυρίου] Jesus Christ" in 1:17; and of "holy"—"his holy [ἁγίαις] myriads" in 1:14 and "your most holy [ἁγιωτάτῃ] faith, in the holy [ἁγίῳ] Spirit" in 1:20.

The following linguistic occurrences determine the parallelism between the B (1:15a) and B' (1:15b) elements: the only occurrences in this unit of "all" and "about all"—"against all [πάντων]" in 1:15a and "about all [περὶ πάντων]" in 1:15a and in 1:15b; and of the relative pronoun "which"—"in which [ὧν] they acted" in 1:15a and "which [ὧν] ungodly sinners spoke" in 1:15b.

4. Keep Yourselves in the Love of God Awaiting the Mercy of Our Lord (1:21–25)

Have mercy on others for the glory of God through our Lord Jesus Christ

A   ²¹ keep *yourselves* in the love of God [θεοῦ], awaiting the mercy of our [ἡμῶν] Lord [κυρίου] Jesus Christ [Ἰησοῦ Χριστοῦ] for eternal life.

B   ²² And on those disputing have mercy [ἐλεᾶτε],

C   ²³ᵃ some save, snatching them out of fire,

B' ²³ᵇ on others have mercy [ἐλεᾶτε] in reverence, hating even the tunic stained from the flesh.³

A' ²⁴ To the one who is able to guard you from stumbling and cause you to stand before his glory without blemish in exultation, ²⁵ to the only God [θεῷ] our [ἡμῶν] savior through Jesus Christ [Ἰησοῦ Χριστοῦ] our [ἡμῶν] Lord [κυρίου], glory, majesty, might, and authority before every age and now and for all ages. Amen!

The exhortation to "keep yourselves [ἑαυτούς] in the love of God" at the beginning of this unit in 1:21 recalls "building up yourselves [ἑαυτούς]" in 1:20 at the conclusion of the preceding unit. These successive occurrences of the same reflexive pronoun thus serve as the transitional terms linking the third unit (1:12–20) to the fourth unit (1:21–25).

An A-B-C-B'-A' chiastic pattern secures the integrity and distinctness of this fourth unit (1:21–25). The following linguistic occurrences constitute the parallelism between the A (1:21) and A' (1:24–25) elements of this

---

3. This choice from the several textual variants for Jude 1:22–23 is based on Metzger, *Textual Commentary*, 658–61.

Introduction to Jude

chiasm: the only occurrences in this unit of "God"—"the love of God [θεοῦ]" in 1:21 and "to the only God [θεῷ]" in 1:25; of "our" and of "our Lord Jesus Christ"—"our Lord Jesus Christ [τοῦ κυρίου ἡμῶν Ἰησοῦ Χριστοῦ]" in 1:21, "our [ἡμῶν] savior" in 1:25, and "Jesus Christ our Lord [Ἰησοῦ Χριστοῦ τοῦ κυρίου ἡμῶν]" in 1:25. The only occurrences in Jude of the verb "have mercy" determine the parallelism between the B (1:22) and the B' (1:23b) elements—"on those disputing have mercy [ἐλεᾶτε]" in 1:22 and "on others have mercy [ἐλεᾶτε] in reverence" in 1:23b. Finally, the central and unparalleled C (1:23a) element contains the only occurrence in Jude of the verb "snatch"—"some save, snatching [ἁρπάζοντες] them out of fire."

The Macrochiastic Structure of Jude

Having illustrated the sequence of the various microchiastic structures operative in the four distinct units of Jude, I will now demonstrate how these four main units form an A-B-B'-A' macrochiastic structure unifying and organizing the entire letter.

A: May the *Mercy* and *Love* of *God* Be Multiplied to You (1:1-4)
A': Keep Yourselves in the *Love* of *God* Awaiting the *Mercy* of our Lord (1:21-25)

The parallelism between the A unit (1:1-4) and the A' unit (1:21-25) within the macrochiastic structure is indicated by the only occurrences in Jude of "God"—"in God [θεῷ]" in 1:1, "of God [θεοῦ]" in 1:4 and 1:21, and "to God [θεῷ]" in 1:25; of the noun "mercy"—"mercy [ἔλεος] to you" in 1:2 and "the mercy [ἔλεος] of our Lord" in 1:21; of the noun "love"—"love" (ἀγάπη) in 1:2 and "love [ἀγάπη] of God" in 1:21; and of "only"—"only [μόνον] Master" in 1:4 and "only [μόνῳ] God" in 1:25.

B: Some Are Kept under *Gloom* for *Judgment* (1:5-11)
B': *Judgment* of the Ungodly for Whom the *Gloom* Has Been Kept (1:12-20)

The only occurrences in Jude of the terms "gloom" and "judgment" provide the chiastic parallels between the B (1:5-11) and the B' (1:12-20) units. In the B unit "gloom [ζόφον] for the judgment [κρίσιν]" occurs in 1:6 and "judgment [κρίσιν] of blasphemy" in 1:9. In the B' unit "the gloom [ζόφος] of the darkness" occurs in 1:13 and "to exercise judgment [κρίσιν]" in 1:15.

Outline of the Macrochiastic Structure of Jude

A: 1:1-4: May the *Mercy* and *Love* of *God* Be Multiplied to You
B: 1:5-11: Some Are Kept under *Gloom* for *Judgment*

B': 1:12–20: *Judgment* of the Ungodly for Whom the *Gloom* Has Been Kept

A': 1:21–25: Keep Yourselves in the *Love* of *God* Awaiting the *Mercy* of our Lord

Summary

1. There are four distinct units in Jude with each exhibiting its own microchiastic structure.

2. The four units comprising Jude operate as a macrochiastic structure with two pairs of parallel units.

3. The letter of Jude encourages its audience to maintain a liturgical and ethical worship in the mercy and love of God through our Lord Jesus Christ.

22

Jude 1:1-4
May the Mercy and Love of God Be Multiplied to You (A)

Necessity to write about those perverting the grace of God and denying the Lord

A   1:1 JUDE, A slave of *Jesus Christ* and brother of James, to those who are called, beloved in God the Father and kept for *Jesus Christ*.
B   ² May mercy to you and peace and love be multiplied! 3a Beloved, exercising every eagerness to *write to you* about our common salvation,
C   ³ᵇ I had the necessity
B'   ³ᶜ to *write to you*, exhorting to contend for the faith once for all handed down to the holy ones.
A'   ⁴ For certain persons have sneaked in, long ago written down for this condemnation, ungodly ones, perverting the grace of our *God* into debauchery and denying our only Master and Lord, *Jesus Christ*.[1]

Audience Response to 1:1-4

1:1 (A): Slave of Jesus Christ to Those Beloved in God and Kept for Jesus Christ

The letter presents itself as sent by "Jude, a slave of Jesus Christ and brother of James" (1:1a). That Jude is a "slave" (δοῦλος) of Jesus Christ indicates not only his humble submission to the lordship of Jesus Christ but also his

1. For the establishment of Jude 1:1-4 as a chiasm, see ch. 21.

honor as a slave who speaks authoritatively on behalf of Jesus Christ.[2] It is part of his service as a slave of Jesus Christ to address his audience gathered together as a worshiping assembly to hear his epistolary homily. And that he identifies himself as "brother of James," who along with Jude was also a brother of Jesus, adds to his authority, as it associates him with the James who was leader of the Jerusalem church.[3]

The recipients of the letter are characterized as those who have been "called" (κλητοῖς), further specified as those who have been and still are "beloved" (ἠγαπημένοις) within a realm established by God the Father, and as those who have been and still are being "kept" (τετηρημένοις) for Jesus Christ (1:1b).[4] Identified as those being kept safe for the future and final coming of Jesus Christ, the audience have been attuned to heed what Jude, authorized as a slave of Jesus Christ, has to communicate to them.

1:2-3a (B): All Eagerness to Write to You about Our Common Salvation

The audience then receive an introductory prayer greeting followed by a further address from Jude: "May mercy to you and peace and love be multiplied! Beloved, exercising all eagerness to write to you about our common salvation" (1:2-3a). As those who are called, "beloved" (ἠγαπημένοις) in

---

2. "Since Jude is the slave-agent of Jesus Christ, the one who holds the highest status according to Christian thought, we should understand his self-designation as a claim to authority, divine commission, and perhaps even inspiration. Standing behind him is Christ himself . . . His weighty words are not those of low honor. They could not be easily dismissed by members of the church who had come under the influence of the heretics" (Green, *Jude and 2 Peter*, 45-46).

3. "There is little debate about which James is intended here. It is probably true that only James the brother of Jesus would be so named without further explanation. . . . The author does not name his father or even his brother Jesus but James. Thus it must be James's position as leader of the church in Jerusalem that is being evoked here. The author wants to speak from within that special authority" (Donelson, *Jude*, 170).

4. "[I]n the NT καλεῖν ('to call') becomes a technical term for the process of Christian salvation" (Bauckham, *Jude, 2 Peter*, 26). "The phrase in Jude is couched as being 'loved in God the Father,' not 'by God.' However, with this locative syntax the author is probably not denying that these called ones are loved by God; rather, the author is placing them in God's presence, in the location wherein God's blessings, promises, and warnings are and will take effect . . . Thus, as the letter of Jude opens upon the dangers of the Christian life in the arguments that follow, it does so with an evocation of God's love and keeping. Those same persons who are threatened by impiety are being kept safe by God for Jesus Christ. The syntax of keeping 'for' Jesus Christ rather than 'by' means that it is God who is the keeper. And God is keeping for Jesus because it is in Jesus where mercy lies (v. 21)" (Donelson, *Jude*, 171).

Jude 1:1-4

God the Father and kept safe and secure for the final coming of Jesus Christ (1:1), the audience have already experienced not only the mercy and peace but especially the "love" (ἀγάπη) that comes from God. In an epistolary act of worship, Jude prays that God may grant his audience an increased experience of this divine mercy, peace, and love with the implication that this is what is to happen in and through their listening to the letter (1:2).[5]

Jude reinforces the implication that the prayer for a divine increase of the mercy "to you" (ὑμῖν) and peace and love (1:2) may begin to be fulfilled through the letter itself. He further addresses his audience as "beloved" (ἀγαπητοί), not only "beloved" (ἠγαπημένοις) in God (1:1) but also by Jude, who is exercising all eagerness to write this letter "to you" (ὑμῖν) about our common salvation (1:3a). The audience are to appreciate that they share a common salvation with Jude, a slave of Jesus Christ (1:1a), and with all other believers, as those who have been called and are being kept safe for the final coming of Jesus Christ (1:1b).

1:3b (C): I Had the Necessity

Jude offers the motivation for his letter: "I had the necessity" (1:3b). As a divinely authorized slave in humble submission to Jesus Christ (1:1), Jude has been led by the "necessity" (ἀνάγκην) that is dictated by God's plan for the salvation Jude shares in common with his audience and all other believers (1:3a).[6]

1:3c (B'): To Write to You to Contend for the Faith

Jude was driven by a divinely dictated necessity "to write to you, exhorting to contend for the faith once for all handed down to the holy ones" (1:3c). After the central and unparalleled C element, "I had the necessity" (1:3b), the audience experience a pivot of chiastic parallels from the B (1:2–3a) to the B'

---

5. "The blessings that Jude emphasizes are woven into the fabric of his epistle and, therefore, this wish-prayer serves as an introduction to the fundamental themes he will take up" (Green, *Jude and 2 Peter*, 50). "In this salutation Jude has set a tone. His readers are in a secure position. They are not only receiving God's love and protection, but Jude is praying that this mercy, peace, and love that they have received will be multiplied ... Thus, its rhetorical function includes both joining with the church and setting the stage for contrasting them with the interlopers" (Davids, *2 Peter and Jude*, 40–41).

6. According to Strobel, "ἀνάγκη," 78, "necessity" (ἀνάγκη) "in the Greek-speaking world had the special sense of fateful, divinely ordered *necessity*, but which was in the NT combined with a conviction of the providence and purposeful action of God for salvation" (emphasis original).

element of this chiastic unit. "Mercy to you [ὑμῖν]" (1:2) and "to write to you [γράφειν ὑμῖν]" (1:3a) progress to "to write to you [γράψαι ὑμῖν]" (1:3c).[7]

Jude's "exercising" (ποιούμενος) of all eagerness to write to his audience about their common salvation (1:3a) is further specified by the divine necessity (1:3b) he had to write to them, "exhorting" (παρακαλῶν) them to contend for the faith in this salvation, the faith once for all handed down to the holy ones (1:3c).[8] The audience are thus alerted to the need for them to fight for the faith they have been privileged to receive. As those who are called, beloved in God the Father and kept safe for the final coming of Jesus Christ (1:1b), the audience are to appreciate that they are numbered among the "holy ones" (ἁγίοις), those who are to keep themselves separate from what is profane in their environment, so that they may devote themselves to the proper worship of God.

1:4 (A'): Perverting the Grace of Our God and Denying Jesus Christ

The audience hear the reason they are being encouraged to contend for the faith (1:3): "For certain persons have sneaked in, long ago designated for this condemnation, ungodly ones, perverting the grace of our God into debauchery and denying our only Master and Lord, Jesus Christ" (1:4). At this point the audience experience a progression, via the chiastic parallels, from the A to the A' element of this chiastic unit. "Beloved in God [θεῷ] the Father and kept for Jesus Christ [Ἰησοῦ Χριστῷ]" (1:1) progresses to "perverting the grace of our God [θεοῦ]" and "denying our only Master and Lord, Jesus Christ [Ἰησοῦν Χριστόν]" (1:4).

The audience are alerted that certain persons, in alliterative contrast and as a threat to the faith once for all "handed down" (παραδοθείσῃ) to the holy ones (1:3c), have "sneaked in" (παρεισέδυσαν) to their community (1:4a).[9] But the audience are assured that these intruders were long ago "writ-

---

7. On the use of the present infinitive for "to write" in 1:3a but the aorist in 1:3c, Bauckham (*Jude, 2 Peter*, 30) notes that "the distinction will be between the general intention of writing and the concrete action actually carried out."

8. "The present participle παρακαλῶν, translated here as 'exhort,' is an important indication of the genre of the body of the letter: It is an exhortation" (Harrington, *Jude*, 189). "The description of the faith as that which is handed down suggests its divine origin, and the finality of that revelation is underscored by Jude's description of the faith as that which was 'once and for all' (ἅπαξ) delivered to the saints" (Green, *Jude and 2 Peter*, 57).

9. "While they are 'outsiders' to the community that is addressed by Jude, they seem to have been Christians who intruded themselves into the community. On the

Jude 1:1-4

ten down" (προγεγραμμένοι) in accord with God's scriptural plan for this condemnation (1:4b), whereas the audience are "beloved" (ἠγαπημένοις) in God and "kept" (τετηρημένοις) for Jesus Christ (1:1). That the intruders were long ago divinely "written down" for this condemnation reinforces the divine necessity for Jude to "write" (γράψαι) to the audience (1:3c). Jude thus adds his timely and contemporary writing, which was to be heard by his audience gathered for communal worship, to the scriptural writings in which they, as a worshiping assembly, have often heard what was long ago written down.[10]

As "ungodly ones [ἀσεβεῖς]" (1:4c), these intruders do not properly worship God, whereas the audience, as among the "holy ones" (ἁγίοις), are set apart for the proper holistic worship of God (1:3c).[11] The ungodly intruders are perverting the grace of our God and denying our only Master and Lord, Jesus Christ (1:4d).[12] But, as a slave submitted to the lordship of Jesus Christ (1:1a), Jude is exhorting the audience to counter this perversion and denial by responding appropriately as holy ones to the grace of being beloved in God and kept safe for Jesus Christ (1:1b) with communal worship that liturgically confesses and is ethically lived out in humble submission to the lordship of Jesus Christ.[13]

---

basis of this phrase it has become customary among commentators to refer to Jude's opponents as the 'intruders'" (Harrington, *Jude*, 190).

10. "Although the language of judgment in Jude suggests the heavenly books where judgment is written down, the far simpler reading is that it is the prophetic books of the Old Testament and other Jewish texts, especially *1 Enoch*, that are being called upon here" (Donelson, *Jude* 175).

11. "To be 'godless' is to commit the fundamental sin because of living without reckoning with God. The godless live as if God does not exist, so they do not honor him as their Lord and Master" (Schreiner, *Jude*, 439).

12. "For Jude, κύριος is the title of Jesus' divine authority as the one who exercises the divine function of judgment; in v 4 he adds δεσπότης to convey the thought that, as Christians, the false teachers belong to Jesus as his slaves whom he has bought. They are both disowning him as Master and flouting his authority as universal Judge" (Bauckham, *Jude, 2 Peter*, 39).

13. "Within Christian vocabulary, 'grace' points to God's saving work through Christ Jesus and also includes his continuous activity that enables his people to do his will ... Jude spotlights the heretics' denial of Christ by employing a verb (ἀρνούμενοι) that, in the papyri, commonly refers to a verbal denial or repudiation. As such, it is the opposite of 'confess'" (Green, *Jude and 2 Peter*, 59-60). With regard to "our only Master and Lord" as a divine title, Bauckham (*Jude, 2 Peter*, 39) states, "Early Christianity took over this usage, especially in prayer and liturgical formulae."

Summary on 1:1-4

In an epistolary act of worship, Jude prays that God may grant his audience an increased experience of his divine mercy, peace, and love with the implication that this is what is to happen in and through their listening to the letter (1:2). Jude reinforces the implication that the prayer for a divine increase of the mercy "to you" and peace and love (1:2) may begin to be fulfilled through the letter itself. He further addresses his audience as "beloved," not only "beloved" in God (1:1) but also by Jude, who is exercising all eagerness to write this letter "to you" about our common salvation (1:3a). The audience are to appreciate that they share a common salvation with Jude, a slave of Jesus Christ (1:1a), and with all other believers, as those who have been called and are being kept safe for the final coming of Jesus Christ (1:1b).

Jude's "exercising" of all eagerness to write to his audience about their common salvation (1:3a) is further specified by the divine necessity (1:3b) he had to write to them, "exhorting" them to contend for the faith in this salvation, the faith once handed down to the holy ones (1:3c). The audience are thus alerted to the need for them to fight for the faith they have been privileged to receive. As those who are called, beloved in God the Father and kept safe for the final coming of Jesus Christ (1:1b), the audience are to appreciate that they are numbered among the "holy ones," those who are to keep themselves separate from what is profane in their environment, so that they may devote themselves to the proper holistic worship of God.

The ungodly intruders who have sneaked in are perverting the grace of our God and denying our only Master and Lord, Jesus Christ (1:4). But, as a slave submitted to the lordship of Jesus Christ (1:1a), Jude is exhorting the audience to counter this perversion and denial by responding appropriately as holy ones to the grace of being beloved in God and kept safe for Jesus Christ (1:1b) with communal worship that liturgically confesses and is ethically lived out in humble submission to the lordship of Jesus Christ.

23

Jude 1:5-11
Some Are Kept under Gloom for Judgment (B)

Do not follow those undergoing divine punishment and do not judge

A   ⁵ I want to remind you, having known all these things once for all, that the Lord, having saved a people from the land of Egypt, later *annihilated* those not believing,
  B   ⁶ and that the *angels* not keeping to the domain of themselves *but* leaving behind their own dwelling he has kept in everlasting chains under gloom for the *judgment* of the great day,
    C   ⁷ᵃ as also Sodom and Gomorrah and the cities round about them, in the same manner as these, indulging in sexual immorality and going after a different *flesh*,
      D   ⁷ᵇ are displayed as an example, undergoing a punishment of eternal fire.
    C′   ⁸ᵃ Likewise however, also these dreamers not only defile *flesh*
  B′   ⁸ᵇ but reject lordship and blaspheme glorious beings. ⁹ Yet even Michael the *archangel*, when, disputing with the devil, argued about the body of Moses, did not dare to bring a *judgment* of blasphemy *but* said, "May the Lord rebuke you." ¹⁰ But these do not know whatever things they blaspheme, yet whatever things they naturally, like irrational animals, understand; in these things they are being destroyed.

1 Peter, 2 Peter, and Jude

A′ ¹¹ Woe to them! For in the way of Cain they have gone and to the wandering of Balaam's recompense they abandoned themselves and in the rebellion of Korah they are *annihilated*.¹

Audience Response to 1:5-11

1:5 (A): The Lord Annihilated Those Not Believing

The audience receive further elaboration regarding the purpose of the letter: "I want to remind you, having known all these things once for all, that the Lord, having saved a people from the land of Egypt, later annihilated those not believing" (1:5).² That Jude wants to remind "you" (ὑμᾶς) further explains the necessity he had to write this letter to "you [ὑμῖν]" (1:3), the audience. That the audience have known all these things "once for all" (ἅπαξ) resonates with the faith "once for all" (ἅπαξ) handed down to them as holy ones (1:3), the faith now threatened by certain persons who have sneaked in (1:4). With the word "Lord" (κύριος) at the beginning of this unit the audience hear the transitional term that links this unit (1:5-11) to the preceding unit (1:1-4), which concludes with a reference to our only Master and "Lord" (κύριον), Jesus Christ (1:4). The implication for the audience is that Jesus Christ was the divine Lord who saved the people of Israel from the land of Egypt.³

---

1. For the establishment of Jude 1:5-11 as a chiasm, see ch. 21.

2. For the choice of the variant reading in which "once for all" (ἅπαξ) modifies "having known" rather than "saved," see Bauckham, *Jude, 2 Peter*, 43; Schreiner, *Jude*, 443; Metzger, *Textual Commentary*, 657-58; Flink, "Reconsidering," 99-106. For the choice of the reading "Lord" (κύριος) rather than "Jesus" (Ἰησοῦς), Bauckham (*Jude, 2 Peter*, 43) notes that "κύριος should be preferred since it could have given rise to the other readings as attempts to resolve the ambiguity in κύριος." See also Davids, *2 Peter and Jude*, 48.

3. "Jude's Jewish source material clearly contained the word 'Lord' (κύριος) as a title for God. But three factors suggest that Jude intended his readers to understand it as a reference to Christ. First, Jude makes the same substitution in verse 14. Second, he has just referred to the 'Lord Jesus Christ' in verse 4, and three other times he explicitly connects Jesus Christ with the title 'Lord' (vv. 17, 21, 25). Third, the New Testament includes other references to the activity of the pre-existent Christ (e.g., 1 Cor 10:4, 9; Phil 2:6)" (Kraftchick, *Jude*, 37). "Most scholars doubt that the reference could be to Jesus on internal grounds, arguing that God led Israel out of Egypt and destroyed the wicked angels. A reference to Jesus Christ, however, is not as strange as some suggest. Paul saw Christ as present with Israel in the wilderness (1 Cor 10:4, 9), and so it is possible to think Jude believed that Jesus Christ delivered Israel out of Egypt" (Schreiner, *Jude*, 444). See also Bartholomä, "Did Jesus Save the People?" 143-58.

Jude 1:5-11

The audience are reminded that our common "salvation" (σωτηρίας) as believers who are holy ones (1:3) stands in continuity with that of the chosen people of Israel, whom the divine Lord Jesus Christ "saved" (σώσας) from the land of Egypt (1:5). That the divine Lord later annihilated those not "believing [πιστεύσαντας]" (1:5) reinforces the exhortation for the audience to contend for the "faith" (πίστει) once for all handed down to them as holy ones (1:3). It further warns the audience to beware of these intruders, who are perverting the grace of our God into debauchery and denying our only Master and Lord, Jesus Christ (1:4). The implication is that these ungodly ones, long ago written down for this condemnation (1:4), are destined for a similar annihilation as those not believing. The audience are thus to realize that our common salvation does not preclude a later annihilation for those not believing.

1:6 (B): Angels under Gloom for the Judgment of the Great Day

The audience are reminded of further activity on the part of the divine Lord: "and that the angels not keeping to the domain of themselves but leaving behind their own dwelling he has kept in everlasting chains under gloom for the judgment of the great day" (1:6). In contrast to the audience, who have been "kept" (τετηρημένοις) safe for Jesus Christ (1:1), the angels not "keeping" (τηρήσαντας) to the domain of themselves but leaving behind their own dwelling the divine Lord Jesus Christ has "kept" (τετήρηκεν) in everlasting chains. The audience are to draw a comparison between these angels whom the divine Lord has kept under gloom for the "judgment" (κρίσιν) of the great day of his final coming and the intruders who have sneaked in, long ago written down for this "judgment" or "condemnation [κρίμα]" (1:4). They are like the angels who have not kept to their own domain but left behind their own dwelling.[4]

1:7a (C): Going after a Different Flesh

The audience are then reminded to whom these angels can further be compared: "as also Sodom and Gomorrah and the cities round about them, in

---

4. "We can be almost certain that Jude referred here to the sin of the angels in Gen 6:1-4. The sin the angels committed, according to Jewish tradition, was sexual intercourse with the daughters of men" (Schreiner, *Jude*, 447-48). "To keep one's proper station in society was a high value during the era when Jude wrote. In a stratified society where status and position were marked by both clothing and positions in banquets and the theater, the accusation that these beings had moved outside their proper sphere or realm would have been understood as a transgression without any further mention of their sin" (Green, *Jude and 2 Peter*, 69).

the same manner as these, indulging in sexual immorality and going after a different flesh" (1:7a). In the same manner as these, that is, as the angels not keeping to their own domain but "leaving behind" (ἀπολιπόντας) their own dwelling (1:6), Sodom and Gomorrah and the cities round about them were indulging in sexual immorality and "going after" (ἀπελθοῦσαι ὀπίσω) a different flesh.[5] The implication for the audience is that in perverting the grace of our God into debauchery and denying our only Master and Lord, Jesus Christ, the ungodly intruders who have sneaked in (1:4) can be compared not only to these angels but also to Sodom and Gomorrah and the cities round about them.[6]

1:7b (D): An Example of the Punishment of Eternal Fire

Sodom and Gomorrah and the cities round about them "are displayed as an example, undergoing a punishment of eternal fire" (1:7b). Like the angels kept in "everlasting" (ἀϊδίοις) chains under gloom for the judgment of the great day (1:6), Sodom and Gomorrah and the cities round about them are undergoing a punishment of "eternal" (αἰωνίου) fire. This punishment serves as an "example" (δεῖγμα), through an alliterative wordplay, of the "condemnation" (κρίμα) for which the ungodly intruders have long ago been written down (1:4). It thus reinforces the exhortation for the audience to contend for the faith (1:3) threatened by the ungodly intruders who have sneaked in.

1:8a (C'): Also These Dreamers Defile Flesh

The implicit comparisons involving the ungodly intruders begin to be made explicit for the audience: "Likewise however, also these dreamers not only defile flesh" (1:8a). At this point, after the central and unparalleled D element of this chiastic unit, "are displayed as an example, undergoing a punishment of eternal fire" (1:7b), the audience experience a pivot of chiastic parallels from the C to the C' element of this chiastic unit. "Going after a different flesh [σαρκός]" (1:7a) progresses to "defile flesh [σάρκα]" (1:8a).

---

5. For an unconvincing argument that "these" in 1:7 refers to "certain persons" in 1:4 rather than to "angels" in the preceding verse in 1:6, see Kruger, "τούτοις in Jude 7," 119-32. As Donelson (*Jude*, 178) notes, "a more natural reading understands the angels as the antecedent."

6. "Whereas in Jude 6 the rebellious angels of Gen 6:1-4/*1 Enoch* 6-11 wanted to have sexual relations with human women, in Jude 7 the human men of Genesis 19 wanted (knowingly or not) to have sexual relations with angels" (Harrington, *Jude*, 197).

Jude 1:5-11

The ungodly intruders (1:4), derogatorily referred to as simply "these dreamers [ἐνυπνιαζόμενοι]," suggesting that they lack a true authoritative basis, thus being equivalent to false prophets (1:8a), are alliteratively linked to the cities "indulging in sexual immorality [ἐκπορνεύσασαι]" (1:7a).[7] Similar to these wicked cities which violated both hospitality and morality in abusing the divine messengers who visited them (Gen 19:4-11), thus going after a "different flesh" (Jude 1:7a), these intruding dreamers who pervert the grace of God into debauchery (1:4) also "defile flesh" (1:8a). That they "defile" (μιαίνουσιν) flesh connotes cultic contamination which prevents proper worship. The audience are thus to beware of the danger these intruding dreamers present to both their liturgical and ethical worship.[8]

1:8b-10 (B'): Michael the Archangel Did Not Bring a Judgment of Blasphemy

The audience hear the B' element (1:8b-10) of this chiastic unit as a chiastic pattern in itself:
a) but reject lordship and *blaspheme* glorious beings. Yet even Michael the archangel, when, disputing with the devil, argued about the body of Moses, did not dare to bring a judgment of *blasphemy* but said (1:8b-9a),
b) "May the Lord rebuke you" (1:9b).
a') But these do not know whatever things they *blaspheme*, yet whatever things they naturally, like irrational animals, understand; in these things they are being destroyed (1:10).

After the central and unparalleled b) sub-element, "May the Lord rebuke you" (1:9b), the audience experience a pivot of chiastic parallels from the a) to the a') sub-element involving the only occurrences in Jude of expressions for "blasphemy." "They blaspheme [βλασφημοῦσιν] glorious

---

7. "Jude's identification of the heretics as 'dreamers' opens the window on his rhetorical strategy. Since the errorists claimed divine inspiration, Jude made his appeal to established revelation (vv. 3-4) in his attempt to dissuade his readers from their perspectives" (Green, *Jude and 2 Peter*, 74-75). "In antiquity dreams are a well-known source of visions and revelations. However, revelations based solely on dreams were often suspect. This is apparently the sense here" (Donelson, *Jude*, 183). "The reference, as most modern commentators agree, is to dreams as the medium of prophetic revelation . . . often in the OT of the dreams of false prophets" (Bauckham, *Jude, 2 Peter*, 55).

8. "This verb, meaning 'defile' or 'stain,' is always used in a literal or metaphorical cultic sense in the NT, e.g., John 18:28; Titus 1:15; Heb 12:15 . . . Not only (μὲν) do they stain or defile the flesh (which could refer to their own human flesh or also include the flesh of other beings that are involved)—this is on a physical plane—but they also (δὲ), like the corrupted angels and others who were mentioned previously, do things on what we might term a spiritual plane" (Davids, *2 Peter and Jude: A Handbook*, 13).

beings" (1:8b) and "a judgment of blasphemy [βλασφημίας]" (1:9a) progress to "whatever things they blaspheme [βλασφημοῦσιν]" (1:10). In addition, at this point, the audience hear a progression, via the chiastic parallels, from the B to the B' element of this chiastic unit. "The angels [ἀγγέλους]," "but [ἀλλά] leaving behind," and "judgment [κρίσιν] of the great day" (1:6) progress to "the archangel [ἀρχάγγελος]," "a judgment [κρίσιν] of blasphemy," and "but [ἀλλά] said" (1:9).

These intruding dreamers not only defile flesh (1:8a) but reject "lordship [κυριότητα]" (1:8b), resonating with their denying our only Master and "Lord" (κύριον), Jesus Christ (1:4), the divine "Lord" (κύριος) who saved the people of Israel from the land of Egypt (1:5). They blaspheme the glorious heavenly beings involved in proper worship (1:8b)—angels, God the Father, and the divine Lord Jesus Christ (1:1, 4). Yet, in contrast to the "angels" (ἀγγέλους) not keeping to their own domain (1:6), Michael the "archangel" (ἀρχάγγελος), when, disputing with the devil, argued about the body of Moses, did not bring a "judgment" (κρίσιν) of blasphemy against him (1:9a). The archangel thus kept to his own domain by leaving "judgment" (κρίσιν) to the divine Lord on the great day (1:6). He merely said to the devil, "May the Lord rebuke you" (1:9b; cf. Zech 3:2 LXX), which amounts to a prayer that accords with proper worship. The audience likewise are not to bring a judgment of blasphemy against the ungodly dreamers, but leave such judgment to the divine Lord in accord with their proper worship.[9]

In contrast to these dreamers who do not "know" (οἴδασιν) whatever things they blaspheme (1:10a), the audience have "known" (εἰδότας) all these things once for all (1:5), the things regarding the faith once for all handed down to them, the faith for which they are to contend (1:3).[10] Ironically, whatever things these dreamers naturally, like irrational animals, understand; in these very things they are being destroyed (1:10b).[11] Consequently, the audience are, in accord with their proper worship, neither to judge nor to follow them on their path to destruction.

---

9. According to Donelson, *Jude*, 184, "the story of the conflict between Michael and the devil over the body of Moses circulates in several versions. The version most likely suggested in Jude is the devil's dispute of Moses' right to a proper burial because Moses killed the Egyptian. Michael argues with the devil, eventually calling upon the Lord to rebuke the devil. The initial force of the citation is to affirm Michael as exemplary in his refusal to presume the right to judge the devil for slandering Moses."

10. "What they do not know is the world of the angels" (Harrington, *Jude*, 198). "The opponents show no honor towards those who serve in the presence of God's glory" (Reese, *2 Peter and Jude*, 48).

11. "The verb φθείρονται may mean 'are destroyed' in the sense of suffering eternal punishment" (Green, *Jude and 2 Peter*, 85).

1:11 (A′): They Are Annihilated

The audience are then advised about what is in store for these ungodly dreamers: "Woe to them! For in the way of Cain they have gone and to the wandering of Balaam's recompense they abandoned themselves and in the rebellion of Korah they are annihilated" (1:11). At this point, the audience hear a progression, via the chiastic parallels, from the A to the A′ element of this chiastic unit. "He later annihilated [ἀπώλεσεν] those not believing" (1:5) progresses to "they are annihilated [ἀπώλοντο]" (1:11).

These ungodly dreamers have subjected themselves to the sad situation of the "woe" of divine judgment prophetically pronounced by Jude (1:11a).[12] They stand in a climactic continuity with three negative OT examples of those whose conduct blasphemed rather than offered proper ethical worship to God. The three negative comparisons increase in intensity from "in the way [ὁδῷ] of Cain they have gone [ἐπορεύθησαν]" to "to the wandering [πλάνῃ] of Balaam's recompense they abandoned themselves [ἐξεχύθησαν]" to "in the rebellion [ἀντιλογίᾳ] of Korah they are annihilated [ἀπώλοντο]" (1:11b).[13] Just as the divine Lord "annihilated" (ἀπώλεσεν) those not believing (1:5), these ungodly dreamers are destined to be "annihilated [ἀπώλοντο]."[14] This reinforces the exhortation for the audience to contend for the faith (1:3), in accord with their proper worship, by neither judging nor following these unbelieving, ungodly dreamers who are currently on a

---

12. "The use of a woe implies prophetic consciousness on the part of the speaker or writer, as one authorized to announce divine judgment, and the prophetic character of v 11 is confirmed by the three aorist verbs, representing the Semitic use of a 'prophetic perfect'" (Bauckham, *Jude, 2 Peter*, 78).

13. "All have in common that in Second Temple Jewish tradition they taught evil to others and they were punished, Cain by banishment, Balaam by being killed by Israel (Num 31:8), and Korah by divine judgment (Num 16:31-35). They are joined in a paratactic construction by καὶ for rhetorical effect" (Davids, *2 Peter and Jude*, 17). "We have argued that in the cases of Cain and Balaam, Jude has referred primarily to their sins, though perhaps also hinted at their judgment. In the case of Korah, however, he refers explicitly to Korah's judgment. This is not likely to be because he sees Korah as the most heinous sinner of the three. It is more probably because the exceptional character of Korah's fate made it a much more striking example of divine judgment than those of Cain and Balaam. This will also explain why Jude has placed Korah last, out of chronological order. The sequence of three clauses reaches a climax in the final word ἀπώλοντο ('have perished'). Although Korah was sometimes thought to have been consumed by the fire, he was usually held to have shared the fate of Dathan and Abiram, when the earth swallowed them up and they went down alive to Sheol" (Bauckham, *Jude, 2 Peter*, 84).

14. "In describing their end, Jude uses the aorist tense in a perfective sense, indicating that their doom is already a certainty" (Green, *Jude and 2 Peter*, 93). See also Bauckham, *Jude, 2 Peter*, 84.

course that will certainly end in their eternal annihilation in the judgment of the great day (1:6).

Summary on 1:5–11

The audience are reminded that our common "salvation" as believers who are holy ones (1:3) stands in continuity with that of the chosen people of Israel, whom the divine Lord Jesus Christ "saved" from the land of Egypt (1:5). That the divine Lord later annihilated those not "believing" (1:5) reinforces the exhortation for the audience to contend for the "faith" once for all handed down to them as holy ones (1:3). It further warns the audience to beware of these intruders, who are perverting the grace of our God into debauchery and denying our only Master and Lord, Jesus Christ (1:4). The implication is that these ungodly ones, long ago written down for this condemnation (1:4), are destined for a similar annihilation as those not believing. The audience are thus to realize that our common salvation does not preclude a later annihilation for those not believing.

In the same manner as the angels not keeping to the domain of themselves but "leaving behind" their own dwelling (1:6), Sodom and Gomorrah and the cities round about them were indulging in sexual immorality and "going after" a different flesh (1:7a). The implication for the audience is that in perverting the grace of our God into debauchery and denying our only Master and Lord, Jesus Christ, the ungodly intruders who have sneaked in (1:4) can be compared not only to these angels but also to Sodom and Gomorrah and the cities round about them. Like the angels kept in "everlasting" chains under gloom for the judgment of the great day (1:6), Sodom and Gomorrah and the cities round about them are undergoing a punishment of "eternal" fire. This punishment serves as an example (1:7b) of the condemnation for which the ungodly intruders have long ago been written down (1:4). It thus reinforces the exhortation for the audience to contend for the faith (1:3) threatened by the ungodly intruders who have sneaked in.

Similar to the wicked cities which violated both hospitality and morality in abusing the divine messengers who visited them (Gen 19:4–11), thus going after a "different flesh" (Jude 1:7a), these intruding dreamers who pervert the grace of God into debauchery (1:4) also "defile flesh" (1:8a). That they "defile" flesh connotes cultic contamination which prevents proper worship. The audience are thus to beware of the danger these intruding dreamers present to both their liturgical and ethical worship.

These intruding dreamers not only defile flesh (1:8a) but reject "lordship" (1:8b), resonating with their denying our only Master and "Lord,"

Jesus Christ (1:4), the divine "Lord" who saved the people of Israel from the land of Egypt (1:5). They blaspheme the glorious heavenly beings involved in proper worship (1:8b)—angels, God the Father, and the divine Lord Jesus Christ (1:1, 4). Yet, in contrast to the "angels" not keeping to their own domain (1:6), Michael the "archangel," when, disputing with the devil, argued about the body of Moses, did not bring a "judgment" of blasphemy against him (1:9a). The archangel thus kept to his own domain by leaving "judgment" to the divine Lord on the great day (1:6). He merely said to the devil, "May the Lord rebuke you" (1:9b; cf. Zech 3:2 LXX), which amounts to a prayer that accords with proper worship. The audience likewise are not to bring a judgment of blasphemy against the ungodly dreamers, who are on their way to being destroyed (1:10), but leave such judgment to the divine Lord in accord with their proper worship.

These ungodly dreamers have subjected themselves to the sad situation of the "woe" of divine judgment prophetically pronounced by Jude (1:11a). They stand in a climactic continuity with three negative OT examples of those whose conduct blasphemed rather than offered proper ethical worship to God. The three negative comparisons increase in intensity from "in the way of Cain they have gone" to "to the wandering of Balaam's recompense they abandoned themselves" to "in the rebellion of Korah they are annihilated" (1:11b). Just as the divine Lord "annihilated" those not believing (1:5), these ungodly dreamers are destined to be "annihilated." This reinforces the exhortation for the audience to contend for the faith (1:3), in accord with their proper worship, by neither judging nor following these unbelieving, ungodly dreamers who are currently on a course that will certainly end in their eternal annihilation in the judgment of the great day (1:6).

24

Jude 1:12-20

Judgment of the Ungodly for Whom the Gloom Has Been Kept (B')

*Build up yourselves in your most
holy faith praying in the Holy Spirit*

A   ¹² *These are* dangerous reefs at your love feasts, feasting together without reverence, shepherding *themselves*, clouds without water carried along by winds, autumn trees without fruit, twice having died, uprooted, ¹³ wild waves of the sea, foaming up things shameful of *themselves*, wandering stars for whom the gloom of the darkness for ages has been kept. ¹⁴ Enoch, the seventh from Adam, even prophesied to these, saying, "Behold, the *Lord* has come with his *holy* myriads,

  B   ^{15a} to exercise judgment against *all* and to convict every soul *about all* of their deeds of ungodliness in *which* they acted ungodly

    B'   ^{15b} and *about all* of the harsh things *which* ungodly sinners spoke against him" (*1 En.* 1:9).

A'   ¹⁶ *These are* discontented grumblers according to the desires of *themselves* going, and their mouth speaks bombastic things, enchanting people for the sake of gain. ¹⁷ But you, beloved, remember the pronouncements said beforehand by the apostles of our *Lord* Jesus Christ, ¹⁸ for they *said* to you, "In the end time there will be mockers according to the desires of *themselves* going for ungodly things." ¹⁹ *These are* the ones causing divisions, worldly-minded, not having the Spirit. ²⁰ But

Jude 1:12–20

you, beloved, building up *yourselves* in your most *holy* faith, in the *Holy Spirit* praying.[1]

Audience Response to 1:12–20

At this point, the audience experience a pivotal progression of macrochiastic parallels from the B (1:5–11) to this B' (1:12–20) chiastic unit. In the B unit the audience heard about the angels the Lord "has kept in everlasting chains under gloom [ζόφον] for the judgment [κρίσιν] of the great day" (1:6), and that Michael the archangel "did not dare to bring a judgment [κρίσιν] of blasphemy" against the devil (1:9). This progresses to their hearing in the B' unit about these "wandering stars for whom the gloom [ζόφος] of the darkness for ages has been kept" (1:13), and that the Lord has come "to exercise judgment [κρίσιν] against all" (1:15).

1:12–14 (A): These Are the Ones for Whom the Lord Has Come with His Holy Myriads

The audience hear the A element (1:12–14) of this chiastic unit as a chiastic pattern in itself:

a) *These* are dangerous reefs at your love feasts, feasting together without reverence (1:12a),
  b) shepherding *themselves* (1:12b),
    c) clouds without water carried along by winds, autumn trees without fruit, twice having died, *uprooted* (1:12c),
      d) wild waves of the sea (1:13a),
    c') *foaming up* (1:13b)
  b') things shameful of *themselves*, wandering stars for whom the gloom of the darkness for ages has been kept (1:13c).
a') Enoch, the seventh from Adam, even prophesied to *these*, saying, "Behold, the Lord has come with his holy myriads [1 En. 1:9]" (1:14).

After the central the unparalleled d) sub-element, "wild waves of the sea" (1:13a), the audience experience a pivot of chiastic parallels from the c) to the c') sub-element involving the only occurrences in Jude of alliterative neuter plural participles. "Uprooted [ἐκριζωθέντα]" (1:12c) progresses to "foaming up [ἐπαφρίζοντα]" (1:13b). They then hear a progression of chiastic parallels from the b) to the b') sub-element involving the only occurrences in this sub-unit of the plural reflexive pronoun. "Shepherding themselves

---

1. For the establishment of Jude 1:12–20 as a chiasm, see ch. 21.

1 Peter, 2 Peter, and Jude

[ἑαυτούς]" (1:12b) progresses to "things shameful of themselves [ἑαυτῶν]" (1:13c). Finally, they hear a progression of chiastic parallels from the a) to the a′) sub-element involving the only occurrences in this sub-unit of the plural demonstrative pronoun. "These [οὗτοι] are dangerous reefs" (1:12a) progresses to "prophesied to these [τούτοις]" (1:14). In addition, when the audience hear the term "these" at the beginning of this unit (1:12), they hear the transitional term that links this unit (1:12-20) with the preceding unit (1:5-11), which contains the term "these" (οὗτοι) near its conclusion (1:10).

The audience have been warned that certain ungodly persons have sneaked in among them, who pervert rather than acknowledge the grace of our God through proper worship and deny rather than venerate our only Master and Lord, Jesus Christ (1:4). "These" (οὗτοι) dreamers not only defile flesh but reject lordship and blaspheme glorious beings (1:8), behavior not in accord with proper worship. Indeed, "these" (οὗτοι) do not even know whatever things they blaspheme (1:10), so that they are ignorant of the things involved in true and proper worship. And now the audience are further warned that "these" (οὗτοί) are dangerous reefs at their "love feasts [ἀγάπαις]" (1:12a), the communal meals connected to their worship, meant to promote the "love" (ἀγάπη) that Jude prayed may be multiplied among them (1:2).[2] The audience are to beware that these "dangerous reefs" represent a threat capable of seriously damaging their communal worship.[3]

---

2. According to BDAG, 7, the term "love feasts" here refers to "a common meal eaten by early Christians in connection with their worship, for the purpose of fostering and expressing mutual affection and concern . . . Paul implicitly refers to it 1 Cor 11:17ff." "Although we cannot reconstruct many details about early Christian communal meals, in Jude's time 'love feasts' probably included both a celebration of the Eucharist and a communal meal" (Donelson, *Jude*, 187). "Jude raises the alarm that the heretics participate in the 'love-feasts' of the church, the time when the church celebrates the Lord's Supper. The ethical characteristic that marked the early Christian feasts was 'love,' the principal virtue of the Christian community that reflected the very nature of God himself. The virtue of love was so dominant in both the consciousness and experience of the community that, by extension, the sacred meal came to be known as an ἀγάπη. Jude is the first witness that we have of this use of the term, which became very prevalent in the early church" (Green, *Jude and 2 Peter*, 94). See also Bauckham, *Jude, 2 Peter*, 85.

3. According to Davids, *2 Peter and Jude: a Handbook*, 19, the feminine noun "dangerous reefs" (σπιλάδες) is an example of a *constructio ad sensum* in which the masculine article (οἱ) is used "despite the fact that the noun is feminine because the subject is οὗτοί." "The image of 'dangerous reefs' is a natural one for the world gathered around the Mediterranean Sea, where there were many submerged rocks. The image also fits with the accusation that heretics are in the midst of the community. These impious people are hidden beneath the water or beneath the facade of being a good member of the community; thus they can inflict great damage" (Donelson, *Jude*, 187).

Jude 1:12-20

These "dangerous reefs" threaten the proper worship of the audience, since they are feasting together in the shared communal meals of the love feasts "without reverence," that is, without the reverence of God appropriate to proper worship (1:12a).[4] Although they are feasting together with the audience, they are "shepherding themselves" (1:12b) rather than others, thus contradicting the love for others connoted by and celebrated within the love feasts.[5] Not only are they feasting together "without reverence" (ἀφόβως), but they are metaphorical clouds "without water [ἄνυδροι]" (cf. Prov 25:14) and autumn trees "without fruit [ἄκαρπα]" (1:12c), and thus of no benefit for the communal worship of the audience. That they are "carried along by winds," "twice," that is, with an emphatic completeness, "having died," and are "uprooted" suggests an utter instability that underlines their worthlessness for the audience as a worshiping assembly.

Not only are these ungodly intruders dangerous reefs at the audience's love feasts, who are shepherding "themselves [ἑαυτούς]" (1:12b), but they are wild waves of the sea, foaming up things shameful of "themselves [ἑαυτῶν]" (1:13; cf. Isa 57:20), further indicating how they are contradicting the love for others connected with the love feasts.[6] That they produce shameful things which do not honor God underscores how they are feasting together without proper reverence for God (1:12a). Furthermore, these ungodly intruders are "wandering" (πλανῆται) stars, recalling that to the "wandering" (πλάνη) of Balaam's recompense they have abandoned themselves (1:11), for whom the "gloom" (ζόφος) of the darkness for "ages" (αἰῶνα) has been "kept [τετήρηται]" (1:13).[7] And so they are like the angels not "keeping" (τηρήσαντας) to the domain of "themselves" (ἑαυτῶν) but leaving behind their own dwelling, whom the divine Lord has "kept" (τετήρηκεν) in "everlasting" (ἀϊδίοις) chains under "gloom" (ζόφον) for the judgment of the great day (1:6).

---

4. "These hidden reefs feast with the community, but they do so without proper reverence. Though no details of either the feasts or the irreverent behavior of these people is given, this imagery assumes that these people are members of the community. They participate in the communal meals. What distinguishes them is that they do so improperly" (Donelson, *Jude*, 187).

5. "The reference to shepherds indicates that the opponents were leaders, claiming that they had the ability to guide and lead God's people. But they had no concern for anyone but themselves" (Schreiner, *Jude*, 466).

6. With regard to Jude 1:12, Davids (*2 Peter and Jude*, 19) notes, "This and the following verse need to be read aloud in Greek to appreciate the rhetorical effect of the repeated sounds that builds toward the end of verse 12 and continues into verse 13."

7. "They have rushed, not to obey God, but into Balaam's error; they are stars, but not shining where God has commanded them, but wandering or erring stars" (Davids, *2 Peter and Jude*, 74).

Enoch (cf. Gen 5:18-24), whose authoritative status is enhanced as being the seventh generation from Adam, even prophesied to these ungodly intruders, "saying" (λέγων), "Behold, the Lord [κύριος] has come with his holy myriads" (1:14; cf. *1 En.* 1:9).[8] This prophetic pronouncement of judgment thus accords with the archangel Michael's prayer for judgment, when to the devil he "said" (εἶπεν), "May the Lord [κύριος] rebuke you" (1:9). This refers to our "Lord" (κύριον) Jesus Christ (1:4), the "Lord" (κύριος) who annihilated those not believing (1:5).[9] And so Enoch's prophetic pronouncement of judgment from the Lord who will come with his "holy" (ἁγίαις) myriads against these ungodly intruders who threaten to harm proper communal worship further encourages the audience to contend for the faith once for all handed down to them as among the "holy ones [ἁγίοις]" (1:3).

1:15a (B): Judgment against All about All of Their Deeds of Ungodliness

Enoch prophesied that the Lord has come with his holy myriads (1:14) "to exercise judgment against all and to convict every soul about all of their deeds of ungodliness in which they acted ungodly" (1:15a). That the Lord will come to "exercise" (ποιῆσαι) judgment against the ungodly and to convict "every" (πᾶσαν) soul of ungodliness reinforces the exhortation for the audience to contend for the faith, the reason Jude is "exercising" (ποιούμενος) "every" (πᾶσαν) eagerness to write the letter (1:3). That the Lord will come to exercise "judgment" (κρίσιν) against all not only serves as the answer to the prayer for divine judgment by the archangel Michael, who did not dare to bring a "judgment" (κρίσιν) against the devil (1:9), but broadens the scope of the "judgment" (κρίσιν) for which the divine Lord has kept the sinning angels (1:6) to include all who act ungodly.

On the one hand, Enoch's prophetic pronouncement of judgment (1:14-15a) further assures the audience that these dangerous intruders to their proper worship (1:12), for whom the gloom of the darkness for ages has been divinely kept (1:13), are destined to be divinely judged and convicted for their ungodliness that contradicts authentic communal worship.

---

8. "While Enoch is seventh only if Adam is counted, this is the traditional counting (see *1 En.* 60.8; 93.3). The designation as the seventh obviously enhances Enoch's status as a prophet" (Donelson, *Jude*, 189).

9. "Jude refers to Jesus Christ as 'Lord' (vv. 4, 17, 21, 25), and it is his coming that is in view ... Jude alters the present 'comes' of the Greek of 1 En. 1.9 to the aorist ἦλθεν, which here has a future sense, perhaps representing the Semitic prophetic perfect" (Green, *Jude and 2 Peter*, 105). For an argument that Jude made use of an Aramaic version of *1 Enoch*, see Mazich, "The Lord Will Come," 276-81.

Jude 1:12-20

On the other hand, it warns the audience to beware of the influence of these dangerous intruders to their communal worship, lest the audience themselves be convicted of ungodliness by the Lord who will come to exercise judgment against all.

1:15b (B'): About All of the Harsh Things of Ungodly Sinners

According to the prophecy of Enoch, the divine Lord will come (1:14) to exercise judgment against all and to convict every soul about all of their deeds of ungodliness in which they acted ungodly (1:15a) "and about all of the harsh things which ungodly sinners spoke against him" (1:15b). At this point, the audience experience a pivot of parallels from the B to the B' element of this chiastic unit. "Against all [πάντων]," "about [περί] all [πάντων] of their deeds," and "in which [ὧν] they acted ungodly" (1:15a) progress to "about [περί] all [πάντων] of the harsh things which [ὧν] ungodly sinners spoke" (1:15b).

In reciprocal recompense for "all" (πάντων) of the harsh things which ungodly sinners spoke "against" (κατά) him (1:15b), the divine Lord will come to exercise judgment "against" (κατά) "all" (πάντων) of them (1:15a). He will convict every soul among the "ungodly" (ἀσεβεῖς) sinners with regard to their deeds of "ungodliness" (ἀσεβείας) in which they "acted ungodly [ἠσέβησαν]" (1:15a), thus contradicting the godliness that is to characterize proper worship.[10] The audience are thus further warned to beware of these "ungodly ones" (ἀσεβεῖς) who have sneaked in among them (1:4), and who are threatening to seriously harm their communal worship through their self-centered, death-bringing, and thus ungodly behavior (1:12–13), because they are included among the "ungodly" (ἀσεβεῖς) sinners destined for a divine judgment against them.

1:16–20 (A'): These Are the Ones Not Having the Holy Spirit

The audience hear the A' element (1:16–20) of this chiastic unit as a chiastic pattern in itself:
a) *These are* discontented grumblers according to the desires of *themselves* going, and their mouth speaks bombastic things, enchanting people for the sake of gain. *But you, beloved*, remember the pronouncements said

---

10. "The false teachers are best described as ungodly. They lived their lives in disregard of God, as if he were not the sovereign and mighty God who deserves praise and honor and thanksgiving" (Schreiner, *Jude*, 472). "These 'godless sinners' will be judged not only for their deeds but also for their words, both of which demonstrate that they did not revere God and had set themselves against him" (Green, *Jude and 2 Peter*, 107).

beforehand by the apostles of our Lord Jesus Christ, for they said to you, "In the end time there will be mockers according to the desire of *themselves* going (1:16–18b)

b) for ungodly things" (1:18c).

a') *These are* the ones causing divisions, worldly-minded, not having the Spirit. *But you, beloved*, building up *yourselves* in your most holy faith, in the Holy Spirit praying (1:19–20).

After the central and unparalleled b) sub-element, "for ungodly things" (1:18c), the audience experience a pivot of chiastic parallels from the a) to the a') sub-element involving the only occurrences in Jude of the address "but you, beloved [ὑμεῖς δέ, ἀγαπητοί]" (1:17, 20), and in this sub-unit of "these are" as well as of the plural reflexive pronoun. "These are [οὗτοι εἰσιν] discontented grumblers, going according to the desires of themselves [ἑαυτῶν]" (1:16, 18) progresses to "these are [οὗτοι εἰσιν] the ones causing divisions" (1:19) and "building up yourselves [ἑαυτούς]" (1:20).

At this point, the audience also experience a progression, via the chiastic parallels, from the A (1:12–14) to the A' (1:16–20) element of this chiastic unit. "These are [οὗτοι εἰσιν] dangerous reefs" (1:12) progresses to "these are [οὗτοι εἰσιν] discontented grumblers" (1:16) and "these are [οὗτοι εἰσιν] the ones causing divisions" (1:19). "Shepherding themselves [ἑαυτούς]" (1:12) and "foaming up things shameful of themselves [ἑαυτῶν]" (1:13) progress to "according to the desires of themselves [ἑαυτῶν]" (1:16, 18) and "building up yourselves [ἑαυτούς]" (1:20). Enoch "saying" (λέγων) that the "Lord" (κύριος) has come with his "holy" (ἁγίαις) myriads (1:14) progresses to the apostles of our "Lord" (κυρίου) Jesus Christ (1:17) "said" (ἔλεγον) to you (1:18) and to "in your most holy [ἁγιωτάτῃ] faith, in the holy [ἁγίῳ] Spirit praying" (1:20).

In addition, the audience experience the a) sub-element (1:16–18b) as yet another chiastic pattern in itself:

(a) These are discontented grumblers *according to the desires of themselves going*, and their mouth speaks bombastic things, enchanting people for the sake of gain (1:16).

  (b) But *you*, beloved, remember the pronouncements *said beforehand* (1:17a)

    (c) by the apostles of our Lord Jesus Christ (1:17b),

  (b') for they *said to you* (1:18a),

(a') "In the end time there will be mockers *according to the desires of themselves going*" (1:18b).

After the central and unparalleled (c) sub-element, "by the apostles of our Lord Jesus Christ" (1:17b), the audience experience a pivot of parallels from the (b) to the (b') sub-element involving the only occurrences in

Jude 1:12-20

this chiastic sub-unit of the second person plural pronoun and of verbs for "saying." "But you [ὑμεῖς]" and "said beforehand [προειρημένων]" (1:17a) progress to "they said [ἔλεγον] to you [ὑμῖν]" (1:18a). Finally, the audience hear a progression of parallels from the (a) to the (a') sub-element involving the only occurrences in Jude of the expression "according to the desires of themselves going." "Discontented grumblers according to the desires of themselves going [κατὰ τὰς ἐπιθυμίας ἑαυτῶν πορευόμενοι]" (1:16) progresses to "mockers according to the desires of themselves going [κατὰ τὰς ἑαυτῶν ἐπιθυμίας πορευόμενοι]" (1:18b).

That "these are" (οὗτοί εἰσιν) discontented grumblers (1:16) further develops the description of the ungodly intruders as "these are" (οὗτοί εἰσιν) dangerous reefs at the love feasts (1:12) of the audience's communal worship.[11] Not only are they selfishly shepherding "themselves [ἑαυτούς]" (1:12) and foaming up things shameful of "themselves [ἑαυτῶν]" (1:13), but they are going according to the desires of "themselves [ἑαυτῶν]" (1:16). These discontented grumblers who have "gone" (ἐπορεύθησαν) in the misguided way of the discontented grumbler, Cain (1:11), are "going" (πορευόμενοι) according to the desires of themselves. That their mouth "speaks" (λαλεῖ) bombastic things (1:16) underlines their being ungodly sinners who "spoke" (ἐλάλησαν) against the divine Lord (1:15). And that these discontented grumblers are enchanting people for the sake of "gain [ὠφελείας]" (1:16) resonates alliteratively with their deeds of "ungodliness [ἀσεβείας]" (1:15) that contradict the godliness of proper worship.[12]

Jude previously expressed his desire to "remind" (ὑπομνῆσαι) "you" (ὑμᾶς), his "beloved" (ἀγαπητοί) audience (1:3), that the divine "Lord" (κύριος), who saved a people from the land of Egypt, later annihilated those not believing (1:5). And now again addressing his audience, "but you [ὑμεῖς], beloved [ἀγαπητοί]," he exhorts them to "remember" (μνήσθητε) the pronouncements said beforehand by the apostles of our "Lord" (κυρίου) Jesus Christ (1:17). This is the same "Lord" (κύριον) Jesus Christ whom the ungodly intruders are denying (1:4) to the detriment of the audience's proper communal worship.

---

11. "Grumblers and their grumbling are an essential part of the wilderness narratives (e.g., Exod 15:24; 16:2-12; Num 14:27-29). The word 'grumbler' may even recall the grumbling that was part of Korah's rebellion mentioned in Jude 11 (Num 16:11) or the disbelief in the wilderness mentioned in Jude 5" (Donelson, *Jude*, 191).

12. "'Grumbling' was considered a vice in the wider Greco-Roman world as well and was understood as the opposite of thankfulness to the gods . . . The heretics were in the 'business' of religion, yet showed no true piety toward God" (Green, *Jude and 2 Peter*, 108, 111).

1 Peter, 2 Peter, and Jude

The apostles prophetically predicted to the audience that in the end time there will be mockers according to the desires of themselves going for ungodly things (1:18).[13] This not only confirms that these discontented grumblers are the prophesied end-time mockers, but underscores their ungodly self-centeredness. As discontented grumblers, these are going according to the "desires of themselves [ἐπιθυμίας ἑαυτῶν]" (1:16), but as the end-time mockers, these are going according to the, literally, "of themselves desires" (ἑαυτῶν ἐπιθυμίας), with an emphatic accent on their own selfish desires (1:18). That these are selfishly going for "ungodly things" (ἀσεβειῶν) reinforces the warning that these "ungodly ones [ἀσεβεῖς]" (1:4) are destined for a divine judgment in which they will be convicted with regard to all of their deeds of "ungodliness" (ἀσεβείας) in which they "acted ungodly" (ἠσέβησαν) as "ungodly" (ἀσεβεῖς) sinners who spoke against the divine Lord (1:15). Their selfish going for ungodly things thus further underlines how they are contradicting the godliness necessary for authentic worship.[14]

The audience have heard the ungodly intruders denigrated as "these are" (οὗτοί εἰσιν) dangerous reefs at your love feasts (1:12). And they have heard that "these are" (οὗτοί εἰσιν) the discontented grumblers (1:16). Now they hear that "these are" (οὗτοί εἰσιν) the ungodly ones causing divisions, who are worldly-minded (1:19), and thus damaging the audience's proper communal worship. In contrast to Jude, who "had" (ἔσχον) the necessity in accord with the divine will, to write to the audience (1:3), these ungodly ones are not "having" (ἔχοντες) the divine Spirit (1:19) essential for authentic worship.

The audience were exhorted, "but you, beloved" (ὑμεῖς δέ, ἀγαπητοί), to remember the prophetic pronouncements by the apostles of our Lord Jesus Christ (1:17). And now they are exhorted, "but you, beloved" (ὑμεῖς δέ, ἀγαπητοί), to build up themselves in their most holy faith by their worship of praying in the Holy Spirit (1:20). In contrast to the ungodly intruders, who are selfishly shepherding "themselves [ἑαυτούς]" (1:12), foaming up things shameful of "themselves [ἑαυτῶν]" (1:13), and who are according to the desires of "themselves" (ἑαυτῶν) "going [πορευόμενοι]" (1:16, 18), the audience are to build up "themselves" (ἑαυτούς) in the Holy Spirit "praying" (προσευχόμενοι).[15]

---

13. "The argument is not that these are the last times and thus the beloved should be alert for mockers but its reverse. These mockers are a sign of the end" (Donelson, *Jude*, 194).

14. "The evil desires (ἐπιθυμίας) were rooted in their lack of piety: true religion and right conduct are linked in Jude's mind. The fact that they lived according to no higher values than their own desires was clear evidence of their impiety" (Green, *Jude and 2 Peter*, 116).

15. "Jude does not mean that each of his readers should build himself up—which

Jude 1:12-20

That the audience are to build up themselves in their "most holy" (ἁγιωτάτῃ) "faith [πίστει]" (1:20) reinforces the exhortation for them to contend against these ungodly ones for the "faith" (πίστει) once for all handed down to them as "holy ones [ἁγίοις]" (1:3). These ungodly intruders, who do not have the "Spirit [πνεῦμα]" (1:19) essential for authentic worship, are destined for a divine judgment against them to be exercised by the Lord who will come with his "holy" (ἁγίαις) myriads (1:14). But the audience may avoid the fate of these ungodly sinners by being those engaged in authentic and proper communal worship, in other words, by being those in the "Holy" (ἁγίῳ) "Spirit" (πνεύματι) praying (1:20).[16]

Summary on 1:12-20

The audience have been warned that certain ungodly persons have sneaked in among them, who pervert rather than acknowledge the grace of our God through proper worship and deny rather than venerate our only Master and Lord, Jesus Christ (1:4). "These" dreamers not only defile flesh but reject lordship and blaspheme glorious beings (1:8), behavior not in accord with proper worship. Indeed, "these" do not even know whatever things they blaspheme (1:10), so that they are ignorant of the things involved in true and proper worship. And now the audience are further warned that "these" are dangerous reefs at their "love feasts" (1:12a), the communal meals connected to their worship, meant to promote the "love" that Jude prayed may be multiplied among them (1:2). The audience are to beware that these "dangerous reefs" represent a threat capable of seriously damaging their communal worship.

These "dangerous reefs" threaten the proper worship of the audience, since they are feasting together in the shared communal meals of the love feasts "without reverence," that is, without the reverence of God appropriate to proper worship (1:12a). Although they are feasting together with the audience, they are "shepherding themselves" (1:12b) rather than others, thus contradicting the love for others connoted by and celebrated within the love feasts. Not only are they feasting together "without reverence," but they are metaphorical clouds "without water" (cf. Prov 25:14) and autumn trees "without fruit" (1:12c), and thus of no benefit for the communal worship of

---

would be contrary to the ordinary Christian use of the metaphor—but that all should contribute to the spiritual growth of the whole community" (Bauckham, *Jude, 2 Peter*, 112–13).

16. "Jude seems to envision 'praying in the Spirit' as an act supportive of the tradition... Thus because of its context, 'praying in the Spirit' has to do with honoring God, not denying the Lord, and acclaiming authority, not flouting it" (Neyrey, *2 Peter, Jude*, 90).

the audience. That they are "carried along by winds," "twice," that is, with an emphatic completeness, "having died," and are "uprooted" suggests an utter instability that underlines their worthlessness for the audience as a worshiping assembly.

Not only are these ungodly intruders dangerous reefs at the audience's love feasts, who are shepherding "themselves" (1:12b), but they are wild waves of the sea, foaming up things shameful of "themselves" (1:13; cf. Isa 57:20), further indicating how they are contradicting the love for others connected with the love feasts. That they produce shameful things which do not honor God underscores how they are feasting together without proper reverence of God (1:12a). Furthermore, these ungodly intruders are "wandering" stars, recalling that to the "wandering" of Balaam's recompense they have abandoned themselves (1:11), for whom the "gloom" of the darkness for "ages" has been "kept" (1:13). And so they are like the angels not "keeping" to the domain of "themselves" but leaving behind their own dwelling, whom the divine Lord has "kept" in "everlasting" chains under "gloom" for the judgment of the great day (1:6).

In reciprocal recompense for "all" of the harsh things which ungodly sinners spoke "against" him (1:15b), the divine Lord will come to exercise judgment "against all" of them (1:15a). He will convict every soul among the "ungodly" sinners with regard to their deeds of "ungodliness" in which they "acted ungodly" (1:15a), thus contradicting the godliness that is to characterize proper worship. The audience are thus further warned to beware of these "ungodly ones" who have sneaked in among them (1:4), and who are threatening to seriously harm their communal worship through their self-centered, death-bringing, and thus ungodly behavior (1:12–13), because they are included among the "ungodly" sinners destined for a divine judgment against them.

That "these are" discontented grumblers (1:16) further develops the description of the ungodly intruders as "these are" dangerous reefs at the love feasts (1:12) of the audience's communal worship. Not only are they selfishly shepherding "themselves" (1:12) and foaming up things shameful of "themselves" (1:13), but they are going according to the desires of "themselves" (1:16). These discontented grumblers who have "gone" in the misguided way of the discontented grumbler, Cain (1:11), are "going" according to the desires of themselves. That their mouth "speaks" bombastic things (1:16) underlines their being ungodly sinners who "spoke" against the divine Lord (1:15). And that these discontented grumblers are enchanting people for the sake of "gain" (1:16) resonates with their deeds of "ungodliness" (1:15) that contradict the godliness of proper worship.

Jude 1:12-20

The audience were exhorted, "but you, beloved," to remember the prophetic pronouncements by the apostles of our Lord Jesus Christ (1:17). And they were again exhorted, "but you, beloved," to build up themselves in their most holy faith by their worship of praying in the Holy Spirit (1:20). In contrast to the ungodly intruders, who are selfishly shepherding "themselves" (1:12), foaming up things shameful of "themselves" (1:13), and who are according to the desires of "themselves going" (1:16, 18), the audience are to build up "themselves" in the Holy Spirit "praying."

That the audience are to build up themselves in their "most holy faith" (1:20) reinforces the exhortation for them to contend against these ungodly ones for the "faith" once for all handed down to them as "holy ones" (1:3). These ungodly intruders, who do not have the "Spirit" (1:19) essential for authentic worship, are destined for a divine judgment against them to be exercised by the Lord who will come with his "holy" myriads (1:14). But the audience may avoid the fate of these ungodly sinners by being those engaged in authentic and proper communal worship, in other words, by being those in the "Holy Spirit" praying (1:20).

25

Jude 1:21-25
Keep Yourselves in the Love of God Awaiting the Mercy of Our Lord (A')

Have mercy on others for the glory of God through our Lord Jesus Christ

A   ²¹ keep yourselves in the love of *God*, awaiting the mercy of *our Lord Jesus Christ* for eternal life.
  B   ²² And on those disputing *have mercy*,
    C   ²³ᵃ save some, snatching them out of fire,
  B'   ²³ᵇ on others *have mercy* in reverence, hating even the tunic stained from the flesh.
A'   ²⁴ To the one who is able to guard you from stumbling and cause you to stand before his glory without blemish in exultation, ²⁵ to the only *God our* savior through *Jesus Christ our Lord*, glory, majesty, might, and authority before every age and now and for all ages. Amen![1]

Audience Response to 1:21-25

At this point, the audience experience a progression of macrochiastic parallels from the A (1:1-4) to this A' (1:21-25) chiastic unit. In the A unit the audience were addressed as "beloved in God [θεῷ]" (1:1) for whom Jude prayed that "mercy" (ἔλεος) and "love" (ἀγάπη) may be multiplied (1:2), before warning them of the ungodly ones who are perverting the grace of our "God"

---

1. For the establishment of Jude 1:21-25 as a chiasm, see ch. 21.

(θεοῦ) and denying our "only" (μόνον) Master and Lord (1:4). This progresses in the A' unit to the exhortation for the audience to keep themselves in the "love" (ἀγάπῃ) of "God" (θεοῦ), awaiting the "mercy" (ἔλεος) of our Lord Jesus Christ (1:21), and to the worship of the "only God" (μόνῳ θεῷ) our savior (1:25). In addition, when the audience hear the first word of this A' unit, "yourselves [ἑαυτούς]" (1:21), they hear the transitional term that links this unit to the preceding unit (1:12-20), which concluded with a reference to the audience as building up "yourselves [ἑαυτούς]" (1:20).

1:21 (A): In the Love of God Awaiting the Mercy of Our Lord Jesus Christ

As those who are building up themselves in their most holy faith through their proper worship of praying in the Holy Spirit (1:20), the "beloved" (ἀγαπητοί) audience (1:17, 20), those called "beloved" (ἠγαπημένοις) in "God" (θεῷ) the Father (1:1), are to keep themselves in the "love" (ἀγάπῃ) of "God [θεοῦ]" (1:21a). This accords with the worship that takes place in their "love feasts [ἀγάπαις]" (1:12), whose very purpose is being threatened by the ungodly ones, who are perverting the grace of our "God [θεοῦ]" (1:4). The audience may thereby contribute to the fulfillment of Jude's initial prayer that "love" (ἀγάπη) be multiplied for them (1:2). In contrast to the ungodly ones, for whom the gloom of the darkness for ages has been "kept [τετήρηται]" (1:13), and to the angels not "keeping" (τηρήσαντας) to their own domain, whom the Lord has "kept" (τετήρηκεν) in everlasting chains under gloom for the judgment of the great day (1:6), the audience are to "keep" (τηρήσατε) themselves in the love of God. This accords with their being called beloved in God the Father and "kept" (τετηρημένοις) for Jesus Christ (1:1).[2]

The audience have been exhorted to remember the pronouncements by the apostles of "our Lord Jesus Christ [κυρίου ἡμῶν Ἰησοῦ Χριστοῦ]" (1:17) that in the end time there will be mockers going according to the desires of themselves for ungodly things (1:18). The audience are now exhorted to keep themselves in the love of God, as those awaiting the divine "mercy" (ἔλεος), the "mercy" (ἔλεος) Jude prayed may be multiplied for them (1:2), of "our Lord Jesus Christ" (κυρίου ἡμῶν Ἰησοῦ Χριστοῦ) for eternal life (1:21). This is in contrast to the ungodly ones, who are denying

---

2. "God keeps his own, and yet believers must keep themselves in God's love. Jude represented well the biblical tension between divine sovereignty and human responsibility. On the one hand, believers only avoid apostasy because of the grace of God. On the other hand, the grace of God does not cancel out the need for believers to exert all their energy to remain in God's love" (Schreiner, *Jude*, 484).

"our Lord Jesus Christ [κύριον ἡμῶν Ἰησοῦν Χριστόν]" (1:4). And in contrast to the punishment of "eternal" (αἰωνίου) fire awaiting not only Sodom and Gomorrah and the cities around them, but also the ungodly ones who are like them (1:7), the audience are awaiting the mercy of our Lord Jesus Christ for "eternal" (αἰώνιον) life.³

1:22 (B): On Those Disputing Have Mercy

As is most appropriate for those awaiting the divine "mercy" (ἔλεος) of our Lord Jesus Christ for eternal life (1:21), the audience are to "have mercy" (ἐλεᾶτε) on those disputing (1:22). "Those disputing" refers to the ungodly ones, who, as discontented grumblers (1:16) and mockers going after the ungodly things (1:18) that contradict proper worship, are causing divisions among the audience (1:19). As those not having the Spirit needed for proper worship, those disputing are distinguished from the audience engaged in the authentic worship of praying in the Holy Spirit (1:20). Much like the archangel Michael, who, when "disputing" (διακρινόμενος) with the devil, left judgment of him to the divine Lord (1:9), the audience, as recipients of divine mercy, are to have mercy on those "disputing" (διακρινομένους), rather than judging them.⁴

1:23a (C): Some Save Snatching Them out of Fire

By having mercy on those disputing (1:22), rather than judging them, the audience may "save" (σῴζετε) some of them, snatching them out of fire (1:23a). They may thereby extend to these ungodly disputers the salvific activity of the divine Lord who "saved" (σώσας) a people from the land of Egypt (1:5). By snatching them out of "fire" (πυρός), they will save them from the punishment of eternal "fire" (πυρός) that awaits Sodom and Gomorrah and

---

3. "Eternal life, i.e. the resurrection life of the age to come, is the gift which Christ in his mercy will bestow on the faithful Christians at the Parousia" (Bauckham, *Jude, 2 Peter*, 114). "To be sure, Jude's concern is not simply to inform them about a bright future. His call to await this event also implies that in the hope of eternal life, they should continue to avoid the way of the heretics" (Green, *Jude and 2 Peter*, 124).

4. "It is simplest to read the διακρινομένους as 'those who dispute' and to understand the verses as advising the loyal beloved to show mercy on these impious people" (Donelson, *Jude*, 199). "The meaning, 'those who dispute,' makes good sense in the context. Jude refers to those who will not accept the rebuke of their fellow-Christians, but argue against it, trying to justify their behavior by means of the antinomian doctrines which the false teachers were propagating. The people in question will be either the false teachers themselves or disciples of theirs" (Bauckham, *Jude, 2 Peter*, 115).

Jude 1:21-25

the immoral cities around them (1:7). Those disputers whom the audience save by having mercy on them may thus join the audience in the proper worship of praying in the Holy Spirit (1:20), as they await the mercy of our Lord Jesus Christ for eternal life (1:21).

1:23b (B'): On Others Have Mercy in Reverence

The audience are to have mercy on those disputing (1:22), since they may save some of them from the fire of eternal punishment (1:23a), but "on others have mercy in reverence, hating even the tunic stained from the flesh" (1:23b). At this point, after the central and unparalleled C element, "some save, snatching them out of fire" (1:23a), the audience experience a pivot of chiastic parallels from the B to the B' element of this chiastic unit. "On those disputing have mercy [ἐλεᾶτε]" (1:22) progresses to "on others have mercy [ἐλεᾶτε] in reverence" (1:23b).

By having mercy on those disputing (1:22), the audience may save some of them (1:23a). But on others, whom the audience may not be able to save, they are still to have mercy, albeit in "reverence" (φόβῳ) of God (1:23b), making sure to preserve their proper worship from the threat of these ungodly disputers, these "dangerous reefs" at their love feasts, who are feasting together in an improper worship "without reverence" (ἀφόβως) of God (1:12). The audience are to hate even the tunic, symbolic of the behavior of these ungodly disputers, which is "stained from the flesh [σαρκός]"— cultic terminology metaphorically indicating their unworthiness for proper worship (1:23b).[5] This recalls that, like those going after a different "flesh" (σαρκός) in immorality (1:7), these ungodly dreamers "defile flesh [σάρκα]," reinforcing how they have disqualified themselves for proper worship (1:8). That their tunic is "stained" (ἐσπιλωμένον) serves as an alliterative wordplay underlining that these ungodly ones are "dangerous reefs" (σπιλάδες) threatening to destroy the audience's proper communal worship (1:12).[6]

---

5. "Showing love for the sinner does not exclude an intense hatred for the corruption brought about by sin. Furthermore, believers need to beware of getting too entangled with some who sin, lest the sinner influence them rather than vice versa" (Schreiner, *Jude*, 489). "Nevertheless, there is no question of abandoning such people to their fate. That Jude continues to hope for their salvation is suggested not only by ἐλεᾶτε ('have mercy'), but also by the source of his picture of the soiled garments in Zech 3:3-4. Joshua's 'filthy garments' were removed and replaced by clean ones, as a symbol of God's forgiveness (3:4-5). Similarly, if Jude's opponents will abandon their sin and all that is associated with it, forgiveness is available for them" (Bauckham, *Jude, 2 Peter*, 117).

6. On the three commands in 1:22-23 Donelson (*Jude*, 199-200) explains, "The first command, to show mercy on those who are disputing, summarizes the intent of the verses. This is a basic norm that should drive all relationships with the impious

1:24–25 (A′): To the Only God Our Savior through Jesus Christ Our Lord

The audience hear the A′ element (1:24–25) of this chiastic unit as a chiastic pattern in itself:
a) To the one who is able to guard you from stumbling and cause you to stand before his *glory* without blemish in exultation (1:24),
 b) to the only God *our* savior (1:25a)
 b′) through Jesus Christ *our* Lord (1:25b),
a′) *glory*, majesty, might, and authority before every age and now and for all ages. Amen! (1:25c).

At the center of this chiastic sub-unit the audience experience a pivot of parallels from the b) to the b′) sub-element involving the only occurrences in this sub-unit of the plural personal pronoun "our." "The only God our [ἡμῶν] savior" (1:25a) progresses to "Jesus Christ our [ἡμῶν] Lord" (1:25b). They then hear a progression of chiastic parallels from the a) to the a′) sub-element involving the only occurrences in this sub-unit of the word "glory." "Before his glory [δόξης]" (1:24) progresses to "glory" (δόξα) to God for all ages (1:25c).

The audience have been warned that the ungodly disputers, the "dangerous reefs" at the worship of the audience's love feasts, are feasting together in a false worship without proper reverence for God (1:12). But as a stellar illustration of true worship with proper reverence for God, Jude leads his audience, gathered together as a worshiping assembly to listen to the letter, in a climactic act of doxological worship.[7] The doxology begins

---

and their followers. The beloved should be merciful toward them all. The second and third commands can be read as examples of two different ways this mercy might be displayed. The beloved will save some of these people . . . from eternal fire. The third command assumes that some of these people will be more resistant to this saving. Since the call to hate garments stained by the flesh is connected to Zech 3:3–5 and given the general use of clothing imagery and the staining power of the flesh, the imagery here must refer to people who have sins to which they are powerfully attached. These people are dangerous because their sins can stain others . . . They are dangerous to the beloved. Nevertheless, the beloved should show mercy to them." For different interpretations of these verses, see Winter, "Jude 22–23," 215–22; Allen, "New Possibility," 133–43.

7. "The formulaic and repetitive style of this doxology (and of all doxologies) raises the possibility that it originated from the dynamics of liturgy and not from the hand of the author of Jude. In particular, the expansiveness of this doxology seems to reflect the elaborating forces of worship. Thus some readers prefer to see this doxology more as a reflection of early Christian worship than as a final articulation of the theology of the author of the letter. However, even if this doxology was taken in its entirety from the worship tradition of the author or the readers, its themes and images cohere nicely with the rest of the letter" (Donelson, *Jude*, 201–2). "The peculiarity of Jude's letter-ending is the lack of any personal greetings or specifically epistolary conclusion.

Jude 1:21-25

with an address to God as the one who is able to "guard" (φυλάξαι) the audience, who have been "kept" (τετηρημένοις) by God for Jesus Christ (1:1), from stumbling (1:24a), especially by being influenced by the ungodly ones among them (1:4). The doxology continues by leading the audience to acknowledge that God is able also to cause them to stand before his heavenly "glory" (δόξης) without blemish in exultation (1:24b).[8] This is in contrast to the ungodly dreamers who contradict proper worship by blaspheming the "glorious beings" (δόξας) that are a central part of it (1:8).

The ungodly dreamers "defile" (μιαίνουσιν) flesh (1:8), a metaphor for their immorality, and wear a tunic that is "stained" (ἐσπιλωμένον) from the flesh (1:23), clothing representative of their immoral behavior. This renders them unworthy to offer true cultic worship. But in their act of doxological worship the audience acknowledge that God is able to cause them to stand before his heavenly glory "without blemish" (ἀμώμους), thus rendering them worthy to offer true cultic worship, the heavenly worship in joyful "exultation" (ἀγαλλιάσει) of God (1:24b).[9] They are able to stand before God's heavenly glory "without blemish" (ἀμώμους) in their moral behavior, because God is able to guard them so that they can stand "without stumbling" (ἀπταίστους) over the immoral behavior of the ungodly ones among them (1:24).

The doxology continues by leading the audience to acknowledge, through this act of true and proper worship, that the one who is able to guard them from stumbling and cause them to stand before his glory without blemish in exultation (1:24) is the "only [μόνῳ] God [θεῷ] our [ἡμῶν] savior" (1:25a).[10] This is in contrast to the ungodly ones, who contradict true and proper worship by perverting the grace of "our God" (θεοῦ ἡμῶν) into debauchery and denying "our" (ἡμῶν) "only" (μόνον) Master and Lord,

---

He ends as he might have ended a spoken homily, with a liturgical doxology" (Bauckham, *Jude, 2 Peter*, 121).

8. "Jude, however, looks beyond the present moment and praises God for his ability to make them stand morally pure before him in judgment" (Green, *Jude and 2 Peter*, 133). "The background of this imagery is the presentation of the sacrificial animal before the altar. Only an animal determined by the priests to be without blemish can be an offering. In early Christian literature this imagery is not used to discuss the cleanness of sacrificial animals but of humans about to be judged by God" (Donelson, *Jude*, 203).

9. "They will stand there unblemished because they have kept themselves and God has kept them. And they will stand there in public celebration. The picture is that of a festival in the presence of God, a sea of people singing, praising, and dancing in joyous celebration in the very presence of the God they had served on earth" (Davids, *2 Peter and Jude*, 111). "Here, in the context of the cultic picture, the eschatological joy is represented as a cultic festival" (Bauckham, *Jude, 2 Peter*, 122-23).

10. "Although the confession of the unity of God is often framed against the polytheism and idolatry of the ancient world, Jude's proclamation that he is one becomes the foundation for worship" (Green, *Jude and 2 Peter*, 134).

Jesus Christ (1:4). This worship of the only God "our savior" (σωτῆρι ἡμῶν) reminds the audience of "our" (ἡμῶν) common "salvation" (σωτηρίας), the purpose for writing the letter to them (1:3). The audience are to appreciate that the worship of God as "our savior," the divine savior who is the focus of the true and proper worship of all of us believers, takes place through our divine Lord Jesus Christ, who "saved" (σώσας) a people from Egypt (1:5).

The reverent acknowledgment of the only God our savior (1:25a) is addressed "through Jesus Christ our Lord [Ἰησοῦ Χριστοῦ τοῦ κυρίου ἡμῶν]" (1:25b), the mediator of this act of doxological worship, which the audience are appropriately offering as those awaiting the mercy of "our Lord Jesus Christ" (τοῦ κυρίου ἡμῶν Ἰησοῦ Χριστοῦ) for eternal life (1:21).[11] This stands in poignant contrast to the ungodly ones, who deny "our" (ἡμῶν) only Master and "Lord [κύριον], Jesus Christ [Ἰησοῦν Χριστόν]" (1:4). Ironically, they represent the end-time mockers who go for the ungodly things that contradict true and proper worship (1:18), as predicted by the apostles of "our Lord Jesus Christ [τοῦ κυρίου ἡμῶν Ἰησοῦ Χριστοῦ]" (1:17).

In appropriate reciprocation to the only God our savior (1:25a) who is able to cause the audience to stand before his "glory" (δόξης) without blemish in worshipful exultation (1:24), the audience are led to acknowledge, through their act of doxological worship, God's "glory" (δόξα), reinforced by the rhetorical triplet of his divine majesty, might, and authority (1:25c).[12] In contrast to the ungodly ones as wandering stars for whom the gloom of the darkness for "ages" (αἰῶνα) has been kept by God (1:13), the audience acknowledge the glory of God before every "age" (αἰῶνος) and now and for all "ages [αἰῶνας]" (1:25c). Finally, the audience are invited to join Jude in bringing this stirring act of doxological worship to its proper conclusion with their resounding and reverberating liturgical refrain of "Amen!" (1:25c).[13] And so with Jude they affirm that this exhilarating doxology is the

11. As Green (*Jude and 2 Peter*, 135) notes, "the NT envisions Christ's mediatorial role in worship (Heb. 13:15; 1 Pet. 2:5; and cf. Rom. 15:16). All praise and honor are acceptable to God only through Christ, a fact that underscores God's transcendence."

12. "Jude's doxology is not a random collection of stereotypical language but rather a carefully selected locus of divine attributes that highlights his grandeur and ruling power" (Green, *Jude and 2 Peter*, 135). "Drawing on traditional liturgical material, he pictures the last day as the eschatological festival of worship, in which the achievement of God's purposes for his people will take the form of his presentation of them as perfect sacrifices in his heavenly sanctuary, offered up to the glory of God amid the jubilation of the worshipers. All Jude's concerns in the letter, to combat the false teaching for the sake of the health of the church and the Christian obedience of its members, are finally aimed at this goal: that they should in the end be found fit to be a sacrificial offering to God" (Bauckham, *Jude, 2 Peter*, 124).

13. "The final 'amen' is both standard and effective. It is a nice liturgical way to assert that what was just said to be true is indeed true" (Donelson, *Jude*, 204). "As the letter is

kind of true worship in proper reverence for God that they are to uphold against the dangerous threat of the ungodly ones, who are feasting together with them in their communal worship but without a proper reverence for God (1:12).[14]

Summary on 1:21-25

As those who are building up themselves in their most holy faith through their proper worship of praying in the Holy Spirit (1:20), the "beloved" audience (1:17, 20), those called "beloved" in "God" the Father (1:1), are to keep themselves in the "love" of "God" (1:21a). This accords with the worship that takes place in their "love feasts" (1:12), whose very purpose is being threatened by the ungodly ones, who are perverting the grace of our "God" (1:4). The audience may thereby contribute to the fulfillment of Jude's initial prayer that "love" be multiplied for them (1:2). In contrast to the ungodly ones, for whom the gloom of the darkness for ages has been "kept" (1:13), and to the angels not "keeping" to their own domain, whom the Lord has "kept" in everlasting chains under gloom for the judgment of the great day (1:6), the audience are to "keep" themselves in the love of God. This accords with their being called beloved in God the Father and "kept" for Jesus Christ (1:1).

The audience have been exhorted to remember the pronouncements by the apostles of "our Lord Jesus Christ" (1:17) that in the end time there will be mockers going according to the desires of themselves for ungodly things (1:18). The audience are now exhorted to keep themselves in the love of God, as those awaiting the divine "mercy," the "mercy" Jude prayed may be multiplied for them (1:2), of "our Lord Jesus Christ" for eternal life (1:21). This is in contrast to the ungodly ones, who are denying "our Lord Jesus Christ" (1:4). And in contrast to the punishment of "eternal" fire awaiting not only Sodom and Gomorrah and the cities around them, but also the

---

read to the gathered believers, Jude's hope is for the congregation to join in and recite the 'Amen!,' thereby affirming again their faith in this God and commitment to his way alone" (Green, *Jude and 2 Peter*, 137). "'Amen' is not simply a rote liturgical response, nor the way a person indicated that a prayer or other liturgical piece was ending, but the response by which the congregation made a prayer or doxology their own . . . not as something read aloud by the messenger but as a response of the congregation, affirming the honor of the God whom they served in Jesus Christ" (Davids, *2 Peter and Jude*, 116).

14. "The shift from condemnation to mercy that began in verse 22 and the shift from attacking the impious to exhorting the beloved that began in verse 20 culminate in this rather eloquent doxology. For all the dangers of the impious and the temptations to sin that come with them, these verses affirm that God can protect the beloved from sin and present them blameless before God's glory" (Donelson, *Jude*, 204).

ungodly ones who are like them (1:7), the audience are awaiting the mercy of our Lord Jesus Christ for "eternal" life.

As is most appropriate for those awaiting the divine "mercy" of our Lord Jesus Christ for eternal life (1:21), the audience are to "have mercy" on those disputing (1:22). "Those disputing" refers to the ungodly ones, who, as discontented grumblers (1:16) and mockers going after the ungodly things (1:18) that contradict proper worship, are causing divisions among the audience (1:19). As those not having the Spirit needed for proper worship, those disputing are distinguished from the audience engaged in the authentic worship of praying in the Holy Spirit (1:20). Much like the archangel Michael, who, when "disputing" with the devil, left judgment of him to the divine Lord (1:9), the audience, as recipients of divine mercy, are to have mercy on those "disputing," rather than judging them.

By having mercy on those disputing (1:22), the audience may save some of them (1:23a). But on others, whom the audience may not be able to save, they are still to have mercy, albeit in "reverence" of God (1:23b), making sure to preserve their proper worship from the threat of these ungodly disputers, these "dangerous reefs" at their love feasts, who are feasting together in an improper worship "without reverence" of God (1:12). The audience are to hate even the tunic, symbolic of the behavior of these ungodly disputers, which is "stained from the flesh"—cultic terminology metaphorically indicating their unworthiness for proper worship (1:23b). This recalls that, like those going after a different "flesh" in immorality (1:7), these ungodly dreamers "defile flesh," reinforcing how they have disqualified themselves for proper worship (1:8).

As a stellar illustration of true worship with proper reverence for God, Jude leads his audience, gathered together as a worshiping assembly to listen to the letter, in a climactic act of doxological worship. The doxology begins with an address to God as the one who is able to "guard" the audience, who have been "kept" by God for Jesus Christ (1:1), from stumbling (1:24a), especially by being influenced by the ungodly ones among them (1:4). The doxology continues by leading the audience to acknowledge that God is able also to cause them to stand before his heavenly "glory" without blemish in exultation (1:24b). This is in contrast to the ungodly dreamers who contradict proper worship by blaspheming the "glorious beings" that are a central part of it (1:8).

The ungodly dreamers "defile" flesh (1:8), a metaphor for their immorality, and wear a tunic that is "stained" from the flesh (1:23), clothing representative of their immoral behavior. This renders them unworthy to offer true cultic worship. But in their act of doxological worship the audience acknowledge that God is able to cause them to stand before his heavenly glory "without blemish," thus rendering them worthy to offer true cultic worship, the heavenly worship in joyful "exultation" of God (1:24b). They are able to stand before God's heavenly glory "without blemish" in their moral behavior, because God is able to guard them so that they can stand "without stumbling" over the immoral behavior of the ungodly ones among them (1:24).

The doxology continues by leading the audience to acknowledge, through this act of true and proper worship, that the one who is able to guard them from stumbling and cause them to stand before his glory without blemish in exultation (1:24) is the "only God our savior" (1:25a). This is in contrast to the ungodly ones, who contradict true and proper worship by perverting the grace of "our God" into debauchery and denying "our only" Master and Lord, Jesus Christ (1:4). This worship of the only God "our savior" reminds the audience of "our" common "salvation," the purpose for writing the letter to them (1:3). The audience are to appreciate that the worship of God as "our savior," the divine savior who is the focus of the true and proper worship of all of us believers, takes place through our divine Lord Jesus Christ, who "saved" a people from Egypt (1:5).

The reverent acknowledgment of the only God our savior (1:25a) is addressed "through Jesus Christ our Lord" (1:25b), the mediator of this act of doxological worship, which the audience are appropriately offering as those awaiting the mercy of "our Lord Jesus Christ" for eternal life (1:21). This stands in poignant contrast to the ungodly ones, who deny "our" only Master and "Lord, Jesus Christ" (1:4). Ironically, they represent the end-time mockers who go for the ungodly things that contradict true and proper worship (1:18), as predicted by the apostles of "our Lord Jesus Christ" (1:17).

In appropriate reciprocation to the only God our savior (1:25a) who is able to cause the audience to stand before his "glory" without blemish in worshipful exultation (1:24), the audience are led to acknowledge, through their act of doxological worship, God's "glory," reinforced by the rhetorical triplet of his divine majesty, might, and authority (1:25c). In contrast to the ungodly ones as wandering stars for whom the gloom of the darkness for "ages" has been kept by God (1:13), the audience acknowledge the glory of God before every "age" and now and for all "ages" (1:25c). Finally, the audience are invited to join Jude in bringing this stirring act of doxological worship to its proper conclusion with their resounding and reverberating liturgical refrain of "Amen!" (1:25c). And so with Jude they affirm that this exhilarating doxology is the kind of true worship in proper reverence for God that they are to uphold against the dangerous threat of the ungodly ones, who are feasting together with them in their communal worship but without a proper reverence for God (1:12).

26

Summary and Conclusion on Jude

*Worship in the Mercy and Love of God
through Our Lord Jesus Christ*

THE PRECEDING CHAPTERS HAVE provided detailed summary conclusions for each of the four chiastic units comprising the letter of Jude. This final chapter presents a comprehensive overview of how this letter as a liturgical homily or sermon, through the rhetorical dynamics of its various chiastic structures, exhorts its audience to "worship in the mercy and love of God through our Lord Jesus Christ." The worship theme of the letter begins with an initial prayer for the audience beloved in God: "May mercy to you and peace and love be multiplied!" (1:2). After warning his audience about some ungodly ones among them, who are perverting the grace of our God into debauchery and denying our only Master and Lord, Jesus Christ (1:4), Jude exhorts them to keep themselves in the love of God (1:21a). As those awaiting the mercy of our Lord Jesus Christ for eternal life (1:21b), they are to have mercy on the ungodly disputers among them while maintaining their own proper reverence for God in their communal worship (1:22–23). In their properly reverent worship they are to glorify the only God our savior through Jesus Christ our Lord (1:25).

The opening chiastic A unit (1:1–4) introduces the sender of the letter as Jude, characterized as "a slave of *Jesus Christ* and brother of James" (1:1a). The audience to whom the letter is sent are characterized as "those who are called, beloved in *God* the Father and kept for *Jesus Christ*" (1:1b). At the pivotal center of the unit the audience are informed that in his eagerness to *write* to them about their common salvation (1:2), Jude had the necessity to *write* to them, exhorting them to contend for the faith once for all handed down to the holy ones (1:3). In the climactic final element of this

Summary and Conclusion on Jude

unit the audience are warned of certain ungodly persons who have sneaked in among them, perverting the grace of our *God* and denying our only Master and Lord, *Jesus Christ* (1:4) (ch. 22).

At the center of the chiastic B unit (1:5-11) the audience are warned that these ungodly dreamers who defile *flesh*, rendering them unworthy for proper worship (1:8a), are destined to undergo a punishment of eternal fire (1:7b), like Sodom and Gomorrah and the cities around them, who, in their immorality went after a different *flesh* (1:7a). They then experience a progression of chiastic parallels warning them that, like the fallen *angels* whom God has kept for the *judgment* of the great day (1:6), the ungodly ones are on their way to being destroyed in the *judgment* of God for which the *archangel* Michael prayed (1:8b-10). Finally, the audience, reminded that the divine Lord who saved a people from the land of Egypt later *annihilated* those not believing (1:5), are warned that the ungodly ones are likewise on their way to being *annihilated* by God like those in the rebellion of Korah (1:11) (ch. 23).

With the B' unit (1:12-20) the audience hear resonances, via the macrochiastic parallels, with the B unit (1:5-11). In the B unit the audience hear that God has kept the fallen angels in everlasting chains under *gloom* for the *judgment* of the great day (1:6), but that the archangel Michael did not dare to bring a *judgment* of blasphemy against the devil, thus leaving judgment to God (1:9). Then in the B' unit they hear the ungodly ones described as wandering stars for whom the *gloom* of the darkness for ages has been kept by God (1:13). And they are advised that Enoch prophesied that the divine Lord will come to exercise *judgment* against all (1:14-15).

At the center of the chiastic B' unit (1:12-20) the audience are warned that the divine Lord will come to exercise judgment against *all* and to convict every soul *about all* of their deeds of ungodliness in *which* they acted ungodly and *about all* of the harsh things *which* ungodly sinners spoke against him (1:15). They then experience a progression of chiastic parallels involving the false and improper worship of "these" self-centered ungodly ones among them. First, they hear that *these are* dangerous reefs at their love feasts, feasting together in the communal worship but without proper reverence for God, shepherding *themselves* (1:12) and foaming up things shameful of *themselves* (1:13). Then they hear that *these are* discontented grumblers according to the desires of *themselves* going (1:16), and that *these are* the ones causing divisions, not having the Spirit necessary for true and proper communal worship (1:19). But the beloved audience are to build up *themselves* in their most holy faith, in the true and proper communal worship of praying in the Holy Spirit (1:20) (ch. 24).

With Jude 1:21-25, the A' unit within the macrochiastic structure embracing the entire letter, the audience hear resonances with the corresponding A unit (1:1–4). In the A unit Jude addresses his audience as beloved in *God* (1:1) and, in an initial act of epistolary worship, prays that *mercy* and peace and *love* be multiplied for them (1:2). He warns that certain ungodly persons have sneaked in among them, perverting the grace of our *God* and denying our *only* Master and Lord, Jesus Christ (1:4), thus disqualifying themselves for true and proper worship. Then, in the A' unit, the audience are exhorted to keep themselves in the *love* of *God*, awaiting the *mercy* of our Lord Jesus Christ for eternal life (1:21). Finally, they are invited, in a climactic and concluding act of epistolary worship, to join Jude in a true and proper doxology to the *only God* our savior through Jesus Christ our Lord (1:25).

At the center of the chiastic A' unit (1:21–25) the audience are exhorted to *have mercy* on the ungodly disputers, some of whom they may save, snatching them out of the eternal fire, but on others they are to *have mercy* with due reverence for God, thus maintaining their true and proper communal worship (1:22–23). Finally, the audience, who are to keep themselves in the love of *God*, awaiting the mercy of *our Lord Jesus Christ* for eternal life (1:21) at his final coming, are to join Jude in a true and proper act of doxological worship to the one who is able to cause them to stand before his glory without any moral blemish, like a sacrificial offering, in worshipful exultation (1:24). They are to affirm with Jude that to the only *God our* savior through *Jesus Christ our Lord* is divine glory, majesty, might, and authority before every age and now and for all ages. Amen! (1:25) (ch. 25).

In conclusion, listening to and experiencing the rhetorical dynamics of the various chiastic patterns throughout the letter of Jude encourages its audience, and all of us as we identify with them, to practice a true and proper worship in the mercy and love of God through our Lord Jesus Christ. Such worship is characterized by a selfless ethical lifestyle that seeks to unite rather than divide fellow believers. It is expressed liturgically by believers who appreciate the love and mercy they have received as the grace of God through our Lord Jesus Christ. They build up themselves in their most holy faith by their communal worship of praying in the Holy Spirit, thereby keeping themselves in the love of God as they await the mercy of our Lord Jesus Christ for eternal life at his final coming. Such worship is epitomized by the letter's climactic act of a magnificent doxological worship in which all of us believers are invited to share: "To the one who is able to guard you from stumbling and cause you to stand before his glory without blemish in exultation, to the only God our savior through Jesus Christ our Lord, glory, majesty, might, and authority before every age and now and for all ages. Amen!" (1:24–25).

Bibliography

Aasgaard, Reidar. "'Brotherly Advice': Christian Siblingship and New Testament Paraenesis." In *Early Christian Paraenesis in Context*, edited by James Starr and Troels Engberg-Pedersen, 237–66. BZNW 125. Berlin: de Gruyter, 2004.
Abernathy, David. "Exegetical Considerations in 1 Peter 2:7–9." *Notes* 15 (2001) 24–39.
Achtemeier, Paul J. *1 Peter*. Hermeneia. Minneapolis: Fortress, 1996.
Adams, Edward. "Does Awaiting 'New Heavens and a New Earth' (2 Pet 3.13) Mean Abandoning the Environment?" *ExpTim* 121 (2010) 168–75.
———. "'Where is the Promise of His Coming?' The Complaint of the Scoffers in 2 Peter 3.4." *NTS* 51 (2005) 106–22.
Allen, Joel S. "A New Possibility for the Three-Clause Format of Jude 22–3." *NTS* 44 (1998) 133–43.
Applegate, J. K. "The Co-Elect Woman of 1 Peter." *NTS* 38 (1992) 587–604.
Balch, David L. *Let Wives Be Submissive: The Domestic Code in 1 Peter*. SBLMS 26. Chico, CA: Scholars, 1981.
Balz, Horst. "μάταιος." *EDNT* 2.396.
Bandstra, A. J. "'Making Proclamation to the Spirits in Prison': Another Look at 1 Peter 3:19." *CTJ* 38 (2003) 120–24.
Bartholomä, P. F. "Did Jesus Save the People out of Egypt? A Re-Examination of a Textual Problem in Jude 5." *NovT* 50 (2008) 143–58.
Batten, Alicia J. "Neither Gold Nor Braided Hair (1 Timothy 2.9; 1 Peter 3.3): Adornment, Gender and Honour in Antiquity." *NTS* 55 (2009) 484–501.
Bauckham, Richard J. *Jude, 2 Peter*. WBC 50. Nashville: Nelson, 1983.
Beckman, J. C. "Live a Fear-of-God Lifestyle, Ransomed Ones: 1 Peter 1:17–21." *Stulos Theological Journal* 10 (2002) 77–98.
Bénétreau, S. "Évangile et prophétie: Un texte original (1 P 1,10–12) peut-it éclairer un texte difficile (2 P 1,16–21)?" *Bib* 86 (2005) 174–91.
Billings, B. S. "'The Angels Who Sinned . . . He Cast into Tartarus' (1 Peter 2:4): Its Ancient Meaning and Present Relevance." *ExpTim* 119 (2008) 532–37.
Blomberg, Craig L. "The Structure of 2 Corinthians 1–7." *CTR* 4 (1989) 3–20.
Borchert, Gerald L. *Worship in the New Testament: Divine Mystery and Human Response*. St. Louis: Chalice, 2008.
Breck, John. "Biblical Chiasmus: Exploring Structure for Meaning." *BTB* 17 (1987) 70–74.
Brouwer, Wayne. *The Literary Development of John 13–17: A Chiastic Reading*. SBLDS 182. Atlanta: Society of Biblical Literature, 2000.

Bibliography

Brown, Jeannine K. "Just a Busybody? A Look at the Greco-Roman Topos of Meddling for Defining ἀλλοτριεπίσκοπος in 1 Peter 4:15." *JBL* 125 (2006) 549–68.

Callan, Terrance. "The Christology of the Second Letter of Peter." *Bib* 82 (2001) 253–63.

———. "Comparison of Humans to Animals in 2 Peter 2,10b–22." *Bib* 90 (2009) 101–13.

———. "A Note on 2 Peter 1:19–20." *JBL* 125 (2006) 143–50.

———. "The Soteriology of the Second Letter of Peter." *Bib* 82 (2001) 549–59.

———. "The Syntax of 2 Peter 1:1–7." *CBQ* 67 (2005) 632–40.

Campbell, D. N., and Fika J. Van Rensburg. "A History of the Interpretation of 1 Peter 3:18–22." *Acta Patristica et Byzantina* 19 (2008) 73–96.

Campbell, R. Alastair. *The Elders: Seniority in Early Christianity.* Edinburgh: T&T Clark, 1994.

Caulley, Thomas Scott. "The *Chrestos/Christos* Pun (1 Pet 2:3) in P^{72} and P^{125}." *NovT* 53 (2011) 376–87.

———. "'They Promise Them Freedom': Once Again, the ψευδοδιδάσκαλοι in 2 Peter." *ZNW* 99 (2008) 129–38.

Charles, J. Daryl. "The Angels Under Reserve in 2 Peter and Jude." *BBR* 15 (2005) 39–48.

———. "Jude's Use of Pseudepigraphical Source-Material as Part of a Literary Strategy." *NTS* 37 (1991) 130–45.

———. "The Language and Logic of Virtue in 2 Peter 1:5–7." *BBR* 8 (1998) 55–73.

———. "Literary Artifice in the Epistle of Jude." *ZNW* 82 (1991) 106–24.

———. *Literary Strategy in the Epistle of Jude.* Scranton, PA: University of Scranton Press, 1993.

———. "'Those' and 'These': The Use of the Old Testament in the Epistle of Jude." *JSNT* 38 (1990) 109–24.

Davids, Peter H. *The First Epistle of Peter.* NICNT. Grand Rapids: Eerdmans, 1990.

———. *The Letters of 2 Peter and Jude.* Pillar New Testament Commentary. Grand Rapids: Eerdmans, 2006.

———. *2 Peter and Jude: A Handbook on the Greek Text.* BHGNT. Waco, TX: Baylor University Press, 2011.

Deselaers, P. "'Der verborgene Mensch des Herzens' (1 Petr 3,4): Ein Leitbild biblischer Anthropologie." *BL* 81 (2008) 281–84.

DeSilva, David A. "X Marks the Spot? A Critique of the Use of Chiasmus in Macro-Structural Analyses of Revelation." *JSNT* 30 (2008) 343–71.

Dewey, Joanna. "Mark as Aural Narrative: Structures as Clues to Understanding." *Sewanee Theological Review* 36 (1992) 45–56.

Doering, Lutz. "First Peter as Early Christian Diaspora Letter." In *The Catholic Epistles and Apostolic Tradition,* edited by Karl-Wilhelm Niebuhr and Robert W. Wall, 215–36. Waco, TX: Baylor University Press, 2009.

Donelson, Lewis R. *I & II Peter and Jude: A Commentary.* NTL. Louisville: Westminster John Knox, 2010.

Dryden, J. de Waal. *Theology and Ethics in 1 Peter: Paranetic Strategies for Christian Character Formation.* WUNT 2/209. Tübingen: Mohr Siebeck, 2006.

Dubis, Mark. *1 Peter: A Handbook on the Greek Text.* BHGNT. Waco, TX: Baylor University Press, 2010.

———. *Messianic Woes in First Peter: Suffering and Eschatology in 1 Peter 4:12–19.* Studies in Biblical Literature 33. New York: Lang, 2002.

Dupont-Roc. R. "Le jeu de prepositions en 1 Pierre 1,1-12: De l'espérance finale à la joie dans les épreuves présentes." *EstBíb* 53 (1995) 201-12.
Elliott, John Hall. *1 Peter: A New Translation with Introduction and Commentary*. AB 37B. New York: Doubleday, 2000.
Engel, W. "Christus Victor: Eine Untersuchung zu Gattung und Struktur des vorliterarischen Christushymnus 1Petr 3, 18-22." *PzB* 7 (1998) 137-47.
Feldmeier, Reinhard. *The First Letter of Peter: A Commentary on the Greek Text*. Waco, TX: Baylor University Press, 2008.

———. "Salvation and Anthropology in First Peter." In *The Catholic Epistles and Apostolic Tradition*, edited by Karl-Wilhelm Niebuhr and Robert W. Wall, 203-13. Waco, TX: Baylor University Press, 2009.

Flink, Timo. "Reconsidering the Text of Jude 5, 13, 15, and 18." *Filología Neotestamentaria* 20 (2007) 95-125.
Forbes, Greg. "Children of Sarah: Interpreting 1 Peter 3:6b." *BBR* 15 (2005) 105-9.
Fornberg, Tord. *An Early Church in a Pluralistic Society: A Study of 2 Peter*. ConBNT 9. Lund, Swe.: Gleerup, 1987.
Giesen, Heinz. "Christi Leiden—Voraussetzung und Bedingung christlichen Lebens und Heils auch für Verstorbene (1 Petr 4, 1-6)." *SNTSU* 25 (2000) 176-218.
Gréaux, E. J. "The Lord Delivers Us: An Examination of the Function of Psalm 34 in 1 Peter." *RevExp* 106 (2009) 603-13.
Green, Gene L. *Jude and 2 Peter*. BECNT. Grand Rapids: Baker, 2008.
Green, Joel B. *1 Peter*. Two Horizons New Testament Commentary. Grand Rapids: Eerdmans, 2007.

———. "Narrating the Gospel in 1 and 2 Peter." *Int* 60 (2006) 262-77.

Hackenberg, Wolfgang. "ἐπίγνωσις." *EDNT* 2.25.
Hafemann, Scott. "'Divine Nature' in 2 Pet 1, within its Eschatological Context." *Bib* 94 (2013) 80-99.
Harvey, Robert, and Philip Towner. *2 Peter and Jude*. IVPNTC 18. Downers Grove, IL: InterVarsity, 2009.
Hays, C. M. "A Fresh Look at Βοσόρ: Textual Criticism in 2 Peter 2:15." *Filología Neotestamentaria* 17 (2004) 105-9.
Heil, John Paul. "The Chiastic Structure and Meaning of Paul's Letter to Philemon." *Bib* 82 (2001) 178-206.

———. *Colossians: Encouragement to Walk in All Wisdom as Holy Ones in Christ*. SBLECL 4. Atlanta: Society of Biblical Literature, 2010.

———. *Ephesians: Empowerment to Walk in Love for the Unity of All in Christ*. Studies in Biblical Literature 13. Atlanta: Society of Biblical Literature, 2007.

———. *Hebrews: Chiastic Structures and Audience Response*. CBQMS 46. Washington: Catholic Biblical Association, 2010.

———. *The Letter of James: Worship To Live By*. Eugene, OR: Cascade, 2012.

———. *Philippians: Let Us Rejoice in Being Conformed to Christ*. SBLECL 3. Atlanta: Society of Biblical Literature, 2010.

———. *The Transfiguration of Jesus: Narrative Meaning and Function of Mark 9:2-8, Matt 17:1-8 and Luke 9:28-36*. AnBib 144. Rome: Editrice Pontificio Istituto Biblico, 2000.

———. *Worship in the Letter to the Hebrews*. Eugene, OR: Cascade, 2011.

Bibliography

Herzer, J. "Alttestamentliche Prophetie und die Verkündigung des Evangeliums: Beobachtungen zur Stellung und zur hermeneutischen Funktion von 1Petr 1,10-12." *BTZ* 14 (1997) 14–22.

Hofius, Otfried. "βλασφημία." *EDNT* 1.219–21.

Holloway, Paul Andrew. "*Nihil Inopinati Accidisse*—'Nothing Unexpected Has Happened': A Cyrenaic Consolatory *Topos* in 1 Pet 4.12ff." *NTS* 48 (2002) 433–48.

Horrell, David G. *1 Peter*. New Testament Guides. London: T&T Clark, 2008.

———. "The Label Χριστιανός: 1 Peter 4:16 and the Formation of Christian Identity." *JBL* 126 (2007) 361–81.

———. "'Race,' 'Nation,' 'People': Ethnic Identity-Construction in 1 Peter 2:9." *NTS* 58 (2012) 123–43.

Howe, F. R. "Christ, the Building Stone, in Peter's Theology." *BSac* 157 (2000) 35–43.

Jobes, Karen H. *1 Peter*. BECNT. Grand Rapids: Baker, 2005.

———. "Got Milk? Septuagint Psalm 33 and the Interpretation of 1 Peter 2:1–3." *WTJ* 64 (2002) 1–14.

———. "The Septuagint Textual Tradition in 1 Peter." In *Septuagint Research: Issues and Challenges in the Study of the Greek Jewish Scriptures*, edited by Wolfgang Kraus and R. Glenn Wooden, 311–33. SBLSCS 53. Atlanta: Society of Biblical Literature, 2006.

Jodoin, D. "Au coeur de la dispersion, un appel personnel à la suite du Christ: lecture narratologique de 1 P 2,18–25." *LTP* 65 (2010) 515–30.

Joubert, Stephan J. "Facing the Past: Transtextual Relationships and Historical Understanding in the Letter of Jude." *BZ* 42 (1998) 56–70.

———. "Language, Ideology and the Social Context of the Letter of Jude." *Neot* 24 (1990) 335–49.

———. "Persuasion in the Letter of Jude." *JSNT* 58 (1995) 75–87.

Keating, Daniel. *First and Second Peter, Jude*. CCSS. Grand Rapids: Baker, 2011.

Kiley, Mark. "Like Sara: The Tale of Terror Behind 1 Peter 3:6." *JBL* 106 (1987) 689–92.

Klumbies, Paul-Gerhard. "Die Verkündigung unter Geistern und Toten nach 1Petr 3,19f. und 4,6." *ZNW* 92 (2001) 207–28.

Kraftchick, Steven J. *Jude, 2 Peter*. ANTC. Nashville: Abingdon, 2002.

Kratz, Reinhard. "φυλακή." *EDNT* 3.441.

Kraus, T. J. "Παρὰ κυρίου, παρὰ κυρίῳ oder *omit* in 2Petr 2,11: Textkritik und Interpretation vor dem Hintergrund juristischer Diktion und der Verwendung von παρά." *ZNW* 91 (2000) 265–73.

Kremer, Jacob. "ἀναφέρω." *EDNT* 1.94.

Kruger, M. A. "τούτοις in Jude 7." *Neot* 27 (1993) 119–32.

LaVerdiere, Eugene A. "A Grammatical Ambiguity in 1 Pet 1:23." *CBQ* 36 (1974) 89–94.

Makujina, J. "The 'Trouble' with Lot in 2 Peter: Locating Peter's Source for Lot's Torment." *WTJ* 60 (1998) 255–69.

Man, Ronald E. "The Value of Chiasm for New Testament Interpretation." *BSac* 141 (1984) 146–57.

Marshall, I. Howard. *1 Peter*. Downers Grove, IL: InterVarsity, 1991.

Mathews, M. D. "The Literary Relationship of 2 Peter and Jude: Does the Synoptic Tradition Resolve This Synoptic Problem?" *Neot* 44 (2010) 47–66.

Mazich, Edward. "'The Lord Will Come with His Holy Myriads': An Investigation of the Linguistic Source of the Citation of 1 Enoch 1,9 in Jude 14b-15." *ZNW* 94 (2003) 276–81.

Mbuvi, Andrew Mūtūa. *Temple, Exile and Identity in 1 Peter*. LNTS 345. London: T&T Clark, 2007.
McCartney, Dan. G. "λογικός in 1 Peter 2,2." *ZNW* 82 (1991) 128-32.
Metzger, Bruce Manning. *A Textual Commentary on the Greek New Testament: Second Edition*. Stuttgart: Deutsche Bibelgesellschaft, 1994.
Michaels, J. Ramsey. *1 Peter*. WBC 49. Nashville: Nelson, 1988.
Milinovich, Timothy. *Now Is the Day of Salvation: An Audience-Oriented Study of 2 Corinthians 5:16-6:2*. Eugene, OR: Wipf and Stock, 2011.
Miller, D. G. "The Resurrection as the Source of Living Hope: An Exposition of 1 Peter 1:3." *HBT* 17 (1995) 132-40.
Miller, T. A. "Dogs, Adulterers, and the Way of Balaam: The Forms and Socio-Rhetorical Function of the Polemical Rhetoric in 2 Peter." *IBS* 22 (2000) 123-44, 182-91.
Moo, Douglas, J. *2 Peter and Jude: The NIV Application Commentary*. Grand Rapids: Zondervan, 1996.
Neyrey, Jerome H. "The Apologetic Use of the Transfiguration in 2 Peter 1:16-21." *CBQ* 42 (1980) 504-19.
———. *2 Peter, Jude*. AB 37C. New York: Doubleday, 1993.
Page, Sydney H. T. "Obedience and Blood-Sprinkling in 1 Peter 1:2." *WTJ* 72 (2010) 291-98.
Palzkill, Elisabeth. "προσέρχομαι." *EDNT* 3.163-64.
Panning, A. J. "What Has Been Determined (ἐτέθησαν) in 1 Peter 2:8?" *Wisconsin Lutheran Quarterly* 98 (2001) 48-52.
Paschke, Boris A. "The Roman *Ad Bestias* Execution as a Possible Historical Background for 1 Peter 5.8." *JSNT* 28 (2006) 489-500.
Picirelli, Robert. "The Meaning of 'Epignosis.'" *EvQ* 47 (1975) 85-93.
Pierce, C. T. "Reexamining Christ's Proclamation to the Spirits in Prison: Punishment Traditions in the Book of Watchers and Their Influence on 1 Peter 3:18-22." *Hen* 28 (2006) 27-42.
Piper, J. "The Beautiful Faith of Fearless Submission (1 Pet 3:1-7)." *Journal for Biblical Manhood and Womanhood* 13 (2008) 48-52.
Porter, Stanley E., and A. W. Pitts. "τοῦτο πρῶτον γινώσκοντες ὅτι in 2 Peter 1:20 and Hellenistic Epistolary Covention." *JBL* 127 (2008) 165-71.
Punt, J. "Subverting Sarah in the New Testament: Galatians 4 and 1 Peter 3." *Scriptura* 95 (2007) 45-50.
Reed, Jeffrey T., and Ruth Anne Reese. "Verbal Aspect, Discourse Prominence, and the Letter of Jude." *Filología Neotestamentaria* 9 (1996) 181-200.
Reese, Ruth Anne. "Holiness and Ecclesiology in Jude and 2 Peter." In *Holiness and Ecclesiology in the New Testament*, edited by Kent E. Brower and Andy Johnson, 326-42. Grand Rapids: Eerdmans, 2007.
———. *2 Peter and Jude*. THNTC. Grand Rapids: Eerdmans, 2007.
Richards, E. Randolph. "Silvanus Was Not Peter's Secretary: Theological Bias in Interpreting διὰ Σιλουανοῦ . . . ἔγραψα in 1 Peter 5:12." *JETS* 43 (2000) 417-32.
Rosner, Brian S. *Greed as Idolatry: The Origin and Meaning of a Pauline Metaphor*. Grand Rapids: Eerdmans, 2007.
Sargent, Benjamin. "Chosen through Sanctification (1 Pet 1, 2 and 2 Thess 2, 13). The Theology or Diction of Silvanus?" *Bib* 94 (2013) 117-20.
Schelkle, K. H. *Die Petrusbriefe. Der Judasbrief*. Freiburg, Ger.: Herder, 1963.
Schreiner, Thomas R. *1, 2 Peter, Jude*. NAC 37. Nashville: B&H, 2003.

Bibliography

Seland, Torrey. "The 'Common Priesthood' of Philo and 1 Peter: A Philonic Reading of 1 Peter 2.5, 9." *JSNT* 57 (1995) 87–119.

Selwyn, Edward Gordon. *The First Epistle of St. Peter: The Greek Text with Introduction, Notes and Essays*. London: Macmillan, 1946.

Senior, Donald P., and Daniel J. Harrington. *1 Peter, Jude and 2 Peter*. SP 15. Collegeville, MN: Liturgical, 2003.

Siegert, Folker. "Christus, der 'Eckstein', und sein Unterbau: Eine Entdeckung an 1 Petr 2.6f." *NTS* 50 (2004) 139–46.

Slaughter, J. R. "Sarah as a Model for Christian Wives (1 Pet 3:5–6)." *BSac* 153 (1996) 357–65.

———. "Submission of Wives (1 Pet 3:1a) in the Context of 1 Peter." *BSac* 153 (1996) 63–74.

———. "Winning Unbelieving Husbands to Christ (1 Pet 3:1b-4)." *BSac* 153 (1996) 199–211.

Spencer, A. B. "Peter's Pedagogical Method in 1 Peter 3:6." *BBR* 10 (2000) 107–19.

Spicq, Ceslas. *Theological Lexicon of the New Testament*. Translated and edited by James D. Ernest. 3 vols. Peabody, MA: Hendrickson, 1994.

Starr, James M. *Sharers in the Divine Nature: 2 Peter 1:4 in Its Hellenistic Context*. ConBNT 33. Stockholm: Almquist & Wiksell, 2000.

Stenschke, Christoph. "'. . . das auserwählte Geschlecht, die königliche Priesterschaft, das heilige Volk' (1 Petr 2.9): Funktion und Bedeutung der Ehrenbezeichnungen Israels im 1.Petrusbrief." *Neot* 29 (2008) 119–46.

Stephens, Mark B. *Annihilation or Renewal? The Meaning and Function of New Creation in the Book of Revelation*. WUNT 2/307. Tübingen: Mohr Siebeck, 2011.

Strobel, August. "ἀνάγκη." *EDNT* 1.77–79.

Thomas, Kenneth J., and Margaret Orr Thomas. *Structure and Orality in 1 Peter: A Guide for Translators*. UBS Monograph 10. New York: United Bible Societies, 2006.

Thomson, Ian H. *Chiasmus in the Pauline Letters*. JSNTSup 111. Sheffield, UK: Sheffield Academic, 1995.

Thurén, Lauri. "Hey Jude! Asking for the Original Situation and Message of a Catholic Epistle." *NTS* 43 (1997) 451–65.

Tite, Philip L. "The Compositional Function of the Petrine Prescript: A Look at 1 Pet 1:1–3." *JETS* 39 (1996) 47–56.

———. "Nurslings, Milk and Moral Development in the Greco-Roman Context: A Reappraisal of the Paraenetic Utilization of Metaphor in 1 Peter 2.1–3." *JSNT* 31 (2009) 371–400.

Trebilco, Paul R. *The Early Christians in Ephesus from Paul to Ignatius*. Grand Rapids: Eerdmans, 2004.

———. *Self-Designations and Group Identity in the New Testament*. Cambridge: Cambridge University Press, 2012.

Tresham, A. K. "A Test Case for Conjectural Emendation: 2 Peter 3:10d." *Master's Seminary Journal* 21 (2010) 55–79.

Van Rensburg, Fika J. "The Referent of *Egeusasthe* (You Have Tasted) in 1 Peter 2:3." *AcT* 29 (2009) 103–19.

Van Rensburg, Fika J., and Steve Moyise. "Isaiah in 1 Peter 3:13–17: Applying Intertextuality to the Study of the Old Testament in the New." *Scriptura* 80 (2002) 275–86.

Watson, Duane F. "Spiritual Sobriety in 1 Peter." *ExpTim* 122 (2011) 539–42.

Bibliography

Webb, Robert L. "The Eschatology of the Epistle of Jude and Its Rhetorical and Social Functions." *BBR* 6 (1996) 139–51.

Welch, John W. "Chiasmus in the New Testament." In *Chiasmus in Antiquity: Structures, Analyses, Exegesis*, edited by John W. Welch, 211–49. Hildesheim, Ger.: Gerstenberg, 1981.

———. "Criteria for Identifying and Evaluating the Presence of Chiasmus." In *Chiasmus Bibliography*, edited by John W. Welch and Daniel B. McKinlay, 157–74. Provo, UT: Research, 1999.

Williams, Martin. *The Doctrine of Salvation in the First Letter of Peter*. SNTSMS 149. Cambridge: Cambridge University Press, 2011.

Wilson, Mark. *The Victor Sayings in the Book of Revelation*. Eugene, OR: Wipf and Stock, 2007.

Winter, Sarah C. "Jude 22–23: A Note on the Text and Translation." *HTR* 87 (1994) 215–22.

Witherington, Ben, III. *Letters and Homilies for Hellenized Christians Volume II: A Socio-Rhetorical Commentary on 1–2 Peter*. Downers Grove, IL: InterVarsity, 2007.

———. *New Testament Rhetoric: An Introductory Guide to the Art of Persuasion in and of the New Testament*. Eugene, OR: Wipf and Stock, 2009.

———. *What's in the Word: Rethinking the Socio-Rhetorical Character of the New Testament*. Waco, TX: Baylor University Press, 2009.

Wolfe, B. P. "The Prophets' Understanding or Understanding the Prophets? 2 Peter 1:20 Reconsidered." *Baptist Review of Theology* 8 (1998) 92–106.

Scripture Index

Old Testament

Genesis
5:18–24	322
19:4–11	313, 316
23:4 LXX	77

Exodus
19:6	72, 81
23:22	72, 81

Leviticus
19:2	8, 47, 48, 49, 59, 61, 69, 101, 104, 178, 233, 238

Numbers
22:5	252
24:17 LXX	236, 239

Deuteronomy
21:23	91

Psalms
8:7 LXX	134
33:9 LXX	9, 64, 65, 67
33:13–17 LXX	14, 110, 111, 116, 116n10
33:17 LXX	116
54:23 LXX	172
109:1 LXX	133
117:22 LXX	9, 64, 65, 70, 71

Proverbs
3:25	105
3:34 LXX	18, 167, 171
11:31 LXX	17, 154, 159, 161, 236
25:14	321, 327

Hosea
2:25	74

Haggai
2:9	73

Zechariah
3:2 LXX	314, 317

Malachi
3:17	73

Isaiah
8:12	118
8:13	118
8:14	9, 64, 65, 70
28:16	9, 64, 65, 70, 71, 159
40:6	8, 48, 57, 59, 63
40:8	8, 48, 57, 59, 63
43:20	72, 81
43:21	73
53:4	92n7

1 Peter, 2 Peter, and Jude

Isaiah (cont.)

53:5	93, 93n12	53:11	92n7
53:9	12, 90	53:12	91, 92n9
		57:20	321, 328

Old Testament Pseudepigrapha

1 Enoch

1:9   299, 318, 319, 322

New Testament

Matthew

4:18	29
10:2	29, 207
17:1–8	235

Mark

1:16	29
3:16	29, 207
9:2–8	235

Luke

6:14	29, 207
9:28–36	235

John

1:40	29
6:68–70	29, 207

Hebrews

9:28   92n9

1 Peter

1:1–13	6–8, 20, 23, 27–46, 49, 168, 185, 189
1:1–12	37n18, 43, 46
1:1–6	7, 28–34, 36
1:1–3	33n12
1:1–2	24, 25, 28, 29, 32
1:1	6, 7, 20, 23, 27, 28, 29, 30, 31, 32, 33, 34, 37, 39, 43, 45, 46, 49, 51, 52, 61, 67, 69, 72, 77, 81, 102, 129, 168, 179, 180, 185, 189, 207, 208, 221, 228
1:2	6, 7, 20, 24, 25, 27, 28, 29, 30, 31, 32, 33, 34, 37, 39, 41, 42, 44, 45, 46, 49, 52, 53, 54, 55, 58, 61, 62, 67, 69, 70, 84, 102, 106, 109, 115, 124, 129, 147, 148, 152, 168, 178, 180, 184, 185, 189, 203, 210, 217, 221, 228
1:3–6	28, 31
1:3–4	31, 32
1:3	5, 6, 7, 24, 25, 27, 28, 29, 32, 33, 34, 35, 37, 38, 39, 40, 44, 45, 46, 49, 50, 55, 56, 58, 59, 62, 66, 67, 68, 73, 92, 93, 96, 97, 102, 106, 109, 113, 114, 115, 120, 122, 123, 124, 129, 131, 133, 135, 136, 142, 144, 151, 169, 172, 179, 185, 209, 210, 211, 214, 225, 283, 289
1:4–6	32
1:4	6, 7, 27, 29, 31, 32, 33, 34, 35, 37, 39, 41, 42, 43, 44, 45, 46, 51, 54, 55, 58, 60, 61, 63, 73, 77, 102, 129, 134, 135, 141, 150, 214, 234, 238, 245
1:5	5, 6, 7, 20, 27, 29, 33, 34, 34n15, 35, 37, 38, 39, 40, 41, 42, 43, 44, 45, 53, 55, 62, 67, 73, 120, 131,

Scripture Index

160, 162, 165, 168, 169, 172, 173, 185, 189, 210, 211, 224, 283, 289
1:6–8   40, 283, 289
1:6–7   45
1:6   6, 7, 20, 26, 27, 34, 34n15, 35, 36, 37, 38, 39, 40, 42, 43, 44, 45, 46, 50, 53, 55, 56, 60, 61, 62, 85, 87, 90, 95, 101, 108, 147, 156, 163, 164, 166, 168, 169, 176, 183, 186, 189, 246, 255, 278
1:7–13   7, 36–44
1:7–9   36, 37, 43, 46
1:7   5, 6, 7, 8, 25, 27, 34, 35, 36, 37, 38, 39, 40, 42, 43, 44, 45, 46, 51, 53, 55, 59, 61, 63, 67, 69, 71, 73, 78, 79, 82, 84, 85, 87, 90, 95, 101, 106, 108, 112, 142, 149, 151, 153, 156, 164, 170, 173, 176, 182, 185, 186, 209, 213, 220, 227, 232, 278, 288
1:8–9   37, 38, 131
1:8   6, 7, 26, 27, 36, 37, 38, 39, 40, 42, 43, 44, 46, 50, 54, 55, 56, 58, 60, 61, 62, 68, 71, 77, 78, 79, 82, 95, 97, 114, 145, 149, 152, 156, 161, 163, 164, 166, 169, 176, 180, 183, 184, 186, 219, 220, 227, 233, 253
1:9   6, 7, 20, 21n16, 27, 34n15, 37, 40, 41, 43, 44, 46, 55, 57, 67, 77, 95, 97, 112, 130, 131, 135, 144, 161, 162, 163, 165, 166, 168, 170, 173, 179, 189, 210, 220, 224, 283, 289
1:10–12   43, 46
1:10–11   90
1:10   6, 7, 25, 27, 34n15, 36, 37, 41, 44, 46, 54, 60, 63, 67, 84, 131, 147, 160, 162, 165, 178, 184, 210, 225, 283, 289
1:11–13   36, 41
1:11–12   41
1:11   7, 25, 27, 36, 37, 42, 43, 55, 67, 70, 102, 156, 160, 164, 169, 213, 223, 229
1:12–13   41
1:12   7, 20, 28, 36, 37, 41, 41n26, 42, 43, 49, 54, 60, 67, 70, 75, 94, 97, 102, 129, 132, 134, 143, 147, 151, 161, 168, 190, 213, 234, 237, 238, 239

1:13   5, 7, 25, 28, 36, 37, 42, 43, 44, 46, 49, 50, 56, 61, 62, 67, 84, 104, 112, 144, 147, 148, 151, 152, 156, 164, 171, 172, 178, 182, 184, 185, 186, 210, 220, 225, 233, 272
1:14–25   8–9, 10, 20, 23, 47–63, 66, 155, 186, 189
1:14–20   8, 48–54, 57
1:14   8, 9, 21n17, 47, 48, 49, 50, 51, 52, 53, 57, 58, 59, 60, 61, 67, 74, 77, 78, 81, 105, 108, 161, 186, 214, 217, 218, 252
1:15–17   214, 218, 227
1:15–16   48, 186
1:15   8, 47, 49, 50, 51, 52, 54, 57, 59, 60, 61, 69, 74, 77, 81, 87, 88, 100, 104, 105, 107, 108, 112, 114, 117, 120, 122, 123, 124, 125, 170, 176, 182, 212, 213, 226
1:16   8, 9, 47, 49, 54, 57, 59, 61, 69, 71, 74, 81, 87, 88, 101, 104, 114, 120, 125, 178, 233, 238
1:17–19   48, 50
1:17   8, 47, 50, 51, 53, 54, 61, 62, 70, 72, 77, 80, 81, 82, 84, 91, 96, 100, 105, 107, 109, 118, 121, 122, 125, 140, 141, 143, 147, 150, 160, 170, 176, 182, 186, 233, 238, 260, 266, 278, 288
1:18–20   186
1:18–19   50
1:18   8, 47, 50, 51, 52, 53, 54, 57, 58, 61, 62, 66, 68, 69, 70, 74, 77, 80, 81, 94, 97, 100, 101, 107, 108, 122, 125, 175, 209, 245, 260, 265
1:19   8, 9, 47, 52, 53, 54, 57, 59, 61, 67, 69, 70, 80, 101, 103, 108, 120, 125, 148, 152, 175, 209, 213, 282, 289
1:20   8, 47, 48, 53, 54, 60, 62, 63, 101, 106, 108, 170, 175, 182, 217
1:21   8, 9, 21, 25, 47, 54, 55, 56, 60, 62, 63, 70, 80, 104, 120, 133, 134, 136, 144, 149, 151, 153, 155, 156, 163, 164, 169, 170, 171, 173, 176, 177, 181, 182, 186, 189, 209, 212
1:22–25   8, 56–60

353

1 Peter, 2 Peter, and Jude

1 Peter (cont.)

1:22–23	57
1:22	8, 9, 21, 47, 57, 58, 59, 60, 62, 63, 77, 79, 95, 97, 100, 101, 108, 112, 114, 120, 130, 135, 145, 147, 152, 155, 161, 163, 166, 171, 178, 180, 181, 184, 186, 189, 218, 219, 221, 223, 227, 252, 253
1:23–25	186
1:23	5, 8, 9, 47, 57, 58, 59, 60, 62, 63, 66, 68, 72, 81, 93, 96, 97, 102, 113, 120, 122, 124, 129, 131, 135, 142, 143, 144, 151, 177, 178, 179, 183, 184, 185, 209, 210, 211, 214, 225, 283, 289
1:24	8, 9, 10, 47, 57, 59, 63, 66, 71, 77, 129, 135, 149, 153
1:25	8, 47, 57, 59, 60, 63, 67, 68, 80, 102, 115, 120, 129, 135, 143, 149, 151, 153, 161, 177, 183, 209, 214
2:1–17	9–11, 21, 23, 64–82, 84, 138, 186, 188
2:1–9	10, 65–73, 76
2:1–3	65, 66
2:1	9, 10, 22n20, 64, 66, 68, 76, 77, 79, 80, 91, 95, 114, 121, 132, 135, 186
2:2	9, 10, 64, 66, 67, 69, 72, 73, 76, 80, 91, 95, 131, 162, 165, 210, 224, 283, 285, 289
2:3	9, 10, 64, 67, 68, 76, 78, 79, 80, 82, 115, 120
2:4–5	65, 66
2:4	9, 10, 20n13, 21, 64, 68, 69, 71, 72, 73, 76, 78, 79, 80, 81, 82, 86, 88, 93, 97, 101, 103, 108, 128, 129, 134, 135, 138, 140, 144, 150, 151, 180, 188, 222, 228
2:5–8	65, 66, 70
2:5	9, 10, 21, 25, 64, 69, 71, 72, 76, 80, 81, 84, 92, 93, 96, 105, 108, 113, 117, 120, 124, 125, 128, 129, 133, 135, 136, 138, 141, 144, 148, 151, 152, 160, 161, 165, 171, 180, 186, 187, 188, 218, 222, 226, 228, 233, 238
2:6–7	72, 73, 80, 81
2:6	9, 20n13, 64, 70, 71, 72, 79, 81, 121, 159, 172, 180, 222, 228
2:7–8	70, 71, 90, 95
2:7	9, 10, 64, 70, 71, 76, 79, 105, 106, 108, 117, 124
2:8–9	65, 66
2:8	9, 64, 66, 71, 72, 80, 99, 107, 130, 142, 161
2:9–10	77, 186
2:9	9, 10, 20n13, 21, 64, 72, 73, 74, 75, 76, 77, 81, 87, 88, 114, 120, 125, 138, 141, 151, 176, 180, 182, 188, 212, 221, 222, 228
2:10	9, 10, 64, 74–75, 78, 79, 81, 94, 97, 132, 155, 243
2:11–17	10, 75–80
2:11	10, 21, 21n16, 65, 75, 76, 77, 81, 94, 97, 114, 130, 133, 135, 136, 138, 140, 150, 155, 163, 166, 169, 178, 179, 188, 214, 218, 219, 227, 246, 249, 255, 272
2:12–13	75, 76
2:12	10, 21, 25, 65, 75, 76, 77, 78, 79, 80, 81, 82, 83, 86, 94, 97, 99, 100, 103, 105, 107, 108, 109, 114, 121, 122, 123, 125, 134, 136, 138, 140, 141, 142, 143, 145, 148, 149, 150, 151, 152, 155, 158, 160, 163, 165, 166, 178, 186, 188, 236, 239, 246, 278, 288
2:13–17	186
2:13	10, 65, 75, 76, 78, 79, 82, 83, 99, 105, 106, 108, 115, 120, 134, 136, 158, 171
2:14–15	76
2:14	10, 65, 76, 78, 82, 86, 123, 158
2:15	10, 21, 65, 76, 78, 79, 82, 86, 101, 103, 104, 105, 108, 109, 122, 138, 140, 150, 162, 163, 165, 166, 188
2:16	10, 65, 76, 79, 82, 84, 85, 87, 121, 125, 143, 145, 208, 262, 266
2:17	10, 11, 65, 76, 79, 80, 82, 84, 85, 87, 105, 109, 114, 118, 125, 145, 151, 180, 184, 209, 219, 227, 253
2:18–21	11, 12, 21–22, 23, 83–88, 90, 126, 186, 188
2:18–19	11, 83–85, 86, 187

2:18   11, 83, 84, 85, 87, 99, 100, 105, 107, 109, 113, 115, 118, 121, 134, 136, 171, 243, 254
2:19–20   11, 85, 86, 179, 186, 220
2:19   11, 22, 25, 83, 85, 87, 90, 91, 95, 96, 117, 121, 122, 125, 127, 133, 136, 143, 145, 148, 152, 157, 177, 179, 183, 184, 188, 210, 225
2:20–21   11, 86–87, 187
2:20   11, 12, 25, 83, 85, 86, 90, 91, 95, 96, 105, 109, 113, 117, 122, 128, 133, 135, 136, 148, 152, 157, 163, 165, 166, 176, 177, 179, 182, 183, 184, 188, 210, 218, 225, 244
2:21–25   12, 13, 22, 23, 89–97, 100, 111, 140, 150, 187, 218
2:21–24   31n7
2:21   11, 12, 25, 83, 87, 88, 89–90, 91, 94, 95, 97, 113, 117, 120, 122, 123, 124, 125, 127, 128, 135, 139, 146, 150, 152, 170, 176, 177, 181, 182, 183, 187, 217
2:22   12, 22, 89, 90–91, 92, 96, 111, 114, 115, 123, 128, 139, 146, 150, 152, 162, 165, 187, 278, 288
2:23–24   218, 226, 233, 238
2:23   12, 22, 25, 89, 91, 93, 95, 96, 111, 113, 115, 117, 123, 124, 125, 128, 140, 143, 146, 150, 152, 160, 163, 177, 183, 187, 209, 217, 218, 244
2:24–25   12, 93–95
2:24   12, 22, 25, 89, 91–93, 93n12, 96, 97, 111, 117, 124, 128, 129, 134, 135, 140, 144, 146, 150, 151, 152, 162, 165, 177, 183, 187, 209, 212, 245, 255
2:25   12, 13, 21n16, 89, 94, 95, 97, 100, 130, 131, 135, 163, 166, 170, 172, 181, 187, 253, 260, 264, 266, 267
3:1–7   13–14, 22, 23, 26, 98–109, 111, 187
3:1–2   13, 99–100, 104, 187
3:1   13, 98, 99, 103, 104, 105, 106, 107, 108, 122, 125, 130, 134, 136, 142, 147, 161, 171
3:2   13, 98, 100, 101, 102, 104, 106, 107, 109, 118, 121, 122, 125, 147
3:3   13, 14, 98, 100–101, 102, 104, 108, 175, 182, 187

3:4   13, 14, 21n18, 98, 101–3, 104, 108, 119, 121, 175, 182, 187, 214
3:5–7   13, 103–7
3:5   13, 98, 103, 104, 108, 119, 133, 134, 136, 171, 187
3:6   13, 98, 103, 105, 108, 109, 115, 117, 118, 119, 120, 122, 124, 133, 136, 163, 166, 170, 187, 213, 226
3:7   13, 14, 25, 98, 103, 104, 106, 107, 109, 114, 124, 129, 135, 145, 148, 151, 152, 171, 178, 181, 184, 187, 210, 211, 217, 225
3:8–17   13–14, 15, 22, 23, 110–25, 187
3:8–13   15, 111–17, 119
3:8–11   111, 112
3:8–9   112
3:8   13, 110, 112, 119, 123, 144, 161, 219
3:9–11   211, 225
3:9   13, 14, 15, 22, 110, 111, 112, 113, 114, 115, 116, 119, 123, 142, 175, 182, 187
3:10–12   116n10
3:10–11   112, 115
3:10   13, 15, 22, 110, 111, 112, 114, 115, 116, 119, 122, 129, 135, 140, 148, 150, 180, 184, 187, 253
3:11   13, 15, 20n13, 22, 110, 111, 112, 115, 116, 119, 122, 124, 173, 180, 182, 184, 210
3:12–13   111
3:12   13, 15, 22, 110, 111, 112, 115, 116, 119, 124, 128, 157, 161, 164, 170, 173, 180, 182, 184, 187, 188, 252
3:13   13, 15, 110, 112, 116, 117, 119, 122, 124, 170, 213, 226
3:14   13, 15, 22, 110, 111, 117–18, 121, 123, 124, 125, 156, 162, 177, 183, 187, 188, 245, 255
3:15–17   15, 118–23
3:15   13, 15, 110, 118, 119, 120, 121, 122, 125, 128, 142, 169, 172, 188, 236, 239
3:16–17   118, 119
3:16   13, 15, 22n19, 110, 118, 119, 121, 122, 123, 125, 133, 136, 143, 145, 159, 181, 184, 188, 218

355

1 Peter, 2 Peter, and Jude

1 Peter (cont.)

3:17   13, 15, 110, 119, 122, 123, 125, 127, 128, 135, 140, 150, 157, 162, 163, 165, 166, 188, 218
3:18–22   15–16, 17, 21–22, 23, 126–36, 138, 188
3:18–20   16, 127–30, 132
3:18   15, 16, 25, 126, 127, 128, 129, 130, 131, 132, 133, 134, 135, 139, 144, 146, 149, 151, 152, 157, 161, 162, 164, 165, 176, 183, 188, 218, 221, 226, 228
3:19   15, 16, 126, 127, 129, 132, 133, 135, 141, 150
3:20   15, 16, 21n16, 126, 127, 130–31, 132, 133, 135, 161, 163, 166, 179, 188
3:21–22   16, 132–34
3:21   15, 16, 17, 22, 126, 127, 131–32, 133, 135, 136, 138, 162, 165, 188, 223, 229
3:22   15, 16, 126, 133, 134, 136, 141, 150, 171, 188, 234, 238
4:1–11   16–17, 18, 21, 23, 137–53, 155, 188, 189
4:1–6   17, 138–44, 146
4:1–2   138, 139, 143, 151, 217
4:1   16, 17, 25, 137, 138, 139, 140, 146, 147, 149, 150, 152, 162, 165, 176, 179, 183, 189, 218
4:2–3   214
4:2   16, 17, 21, 137, 138, 139, 140, 141, 143, 147, 150, 151, 162, 165, 188, 189, 218
4:3–6   139, 142
4:3   16, 21, 137, 138, 139, 141, 150, 172, 181, 188, 243, 249, 254, 256, 274
4:4   16, 137, 141, 142, 151, 156, 244, 254
4:5–6   142
4:5   16, 137, 142, 143, 151, 160
4:6   16, 17, 21, 137, 138, 139, 142, 143, 144, 147, 151, 157, 161, 164, 170, 188
4:7–8   17, 144–45

4:7   16, 137, 144, 145, 148, 151, 161, 172, 181
4:8   16, 17, 137, 145–46, 147, 148, 151, 152, 155, 162, 165, 180, 184, 189, 219, 221, 227, 228
4:9–11   17, 146–49
4:9–10   146
4:9   16, 137, 146, 147, 171, 180, 181
4:10–11   179
4:10   16, 17, 25, 137, 146, 147, 148, 152, 178, 184, 189, 210, 220, 225, 227
4:11   16, 17, 18, 21, 24, 25, 137, 138, 146, 147, 148, 149, 152, 153, 155, 160, 161, 164, 165, 172, 176, 177, 178, 181, 183, 184, 188, 189, 217, 220, 227, 249, 256, 286, 290
4:12–19   17–18, 19, 20, 23, 154–66, 168, 189
4:12–14   155–57, 159
4:12   17, 154, 155, 156, 157, 169, 219, 227, 246, 255, 264, 272
4:13   17, 18, 25, 154, 155, 156, 157, 159, 160, 161, 164, 165, 169, 175, 182, 189, 213, 226
4:14   17, 18, 25, 154, 155, 156, 157, 158, 159, 160, 164, 165, 189
4:15   17, 18, 26, 154, 157–58, 159, 176, 183, 189
4:16–19   159–63
4:16–17   159
4:16   17, 18, 25, 26, 154, 158–59, 160, 161, 164, 165, 189
4:17   17, 18, 154, 159, 160, 161, 165
4:18   17, 154, 159, 161, 162, 163, 165, 236
4:19   17, 18, 19, 21, 154, 155, 159, 162, 163, 165, 166, 168, 176, 177, 183, 189, 218, 252
5:1–14   18–19, 20, 23, 167–84, 189, 190
5:1–5   168–71, 174
5:1   18, 19, 20, 25, 167, 168, 169, 170, 171, 174, 175, 176, 178, 179, 181, 182, 183, 190, 213, 226
5:2–3   168
5:2   18, 19, 167, 169, 170, 171, 174, 181, 190

Scripture Index

5:3-4	168
5:3	18, 167, 169, 170, 181
5:4-5	168
5:4	18, 20, 25, 167, 168, 169, 170, 174, 176, 182, 190
5:5	18, 19, 25, 167, 169, 171, 172, 173, 175, 178, 180, 181, 183, 190, 210, 225
5:6-9	19, 171-73
5:6	18, 19, 167, 172, 190, 217
5:7-9	19
5:7	18, 167, 172
5:8-9	190
5:8	18, 19, 167, 172, 173, 181, 182
5:9-14	173-81
5:9-12	173, 174
5:9-10	174
5:9	19, 25, 167, 172, 173, 174, 175, 177, 178, 182, 184, 190, 209, 214, 219
5:10-11	19, 190
5:10	19, 20, 25, 167, 168, 174, 175, 176, 177, 178, 181, 182, 183, 184, 190, 210, 212, 222, 223, 225, 228
5:11	19, 24, 167, 174, 177, 181, 183, 184, 217, 286, 290
5:12-13	209
5:12	19, 21n15, 24, 25, 168, 174, 175, 177, 178, 179, 183, 184, 190, 210, 219, 220, 225
5:13	19, 20, 168, 173, 174, 179, 180, 184, 190, 221, 228
5:14	19, 20, 24, 168, 174, 180, 184, 190, 203, 210, 219, 227

2 Peter

1:1-15	193-94, 195, 201, 202, 206-29, 231, 269, 291, 293
1:1-2	194, 207-11, 216
1:1	193, 194, 201, 206, 207, 208, 209, 210, 211, 212, 213, 216, 217, 222, 223, 224, 225, 226, 229, 231, 245, 255, 263, 269, 273, 280, 281, 287, 291, 294
1:2-3	243, 254
1:2	193, 194, 201, 203, 205, 206, 207, 210, 211, 212, 216, 220, 222, 225, 227, 262, 266, 269, 280, 282, 285, 289, 291
1:3-4	291
1:3	192, 193, 194, 201, 204, 206, 211-12, 213, 214, 217, 218, 220, 221, 222, 223, 224, 225, 226, 227, 228, 229, 231, 237, 239, 246, 249, 250, 255, 256, 262, 264, 266, 267, 269, 273, 279, 285, 286, 287, 289, 290, 291, 293
1:4	193, 194, 201, 206, 213-14, 217, 219, 220, 221, 222, 223, 224, 226, 227, 228, 229, 232, 237, 249, 250, 255, 256, 260, 262, 265, 266, 269, 275, 281, 285
1:5-15	194, 215-24
1:5-12	215, 216
1:5-9	216
1:5-8	292
1:5-7	219, 220, 223, 227
1:5-6	201, 242, 269
1:5	193, 194, 204, 206, 215, 216, 217, 221, 222, 226, 228, 231, 285, 287, 290, 293
1:6-7	201, 269, 273, 287
1:6	192, 193, 204, 206, 217, 218, 226, 246, 255, 273, 279, 287, 288
1:7	192, 193, 206, 219, 221, 227
1:8	193, 194, 204, 206, 215, 216, 219, 220, 221, 222, 223, 227, 228, 229, 231, 262, 266, 273, 279, 285, 287, 290, 291
1:9	193, 206, 216, 221, 223, 227, 228, 232, 237, 252
1:10	193, 201, 206-7, 215, 216, 216n15, 221, 222, 223, 224, 228, 235, 238, 269, 281, 284
1:11-12	216
1:11	193, 194, 201, 204, 207, 215, 216, 217, 221, 222, 223, 224, 228, 229, 231, 232, 237, 262, 266, 269, 273, 285, 286, 287, 290, 291, 292, 293, 294
1:12-15	231
1:12	194, 201, 207, 215, 217, 222, 223, 224, 228, 243, 254, 269, 281, 284, 289

1 Peter, 2 Peter, and Jude

2 Peter *(cont.)*

1:13   194, 201, 207, 215, 216, 223, 229, 245, 251, 256, 269, 272, 277, 292, 293
1:14–15   215
1:14   194, 201, 207, 215, 216, 223, 224, 229, 243, 269, 284
1:15   194, 195, 201, 207, 215, 216n15, 224, 229, 231, 269, 281
1:16–21   194–95, 197, 202, 230–39, 242, 259, 292
1:16–18   273, 287
1:16   194, 195, 230, 231–32, 234, 235, 236, 237, 238, 239, 243, 246, 249, 250, 252, 254, 255, 256, 264, 267, 272, 274, 280, 286, 287, 292
1:17–18   235, 238
1:17   194, 195, 230, 232–33, 235, 237, 238, 239, 249, 253, 256, 257, 274, 279, 284, 286, 288, 290, 292
1:18–21   195, 234–37
1:18   195, 202, 230, 233–34, 235, 237, 238, 239, 253, 256, 257, 259, 264, 267, 272, 279, 287, 288, 292, 293
1:19   195, 216n15, 230, 234, 235, 236, 237, 238, 239, 244, 252, 255, 272, 274, 275, 280, 286, 290, 292
1:20–21   234, 292
1:20   195, 204, 230, 234, 235, 236, 237, 239, 242, 250, 256, 264, 267, 272, 273, 284, 287, 289, 291
1:21   195, 196, 202, 204, 230, 234, 235, 237, 239, 242, 243, 250, 253, 256, 257, 259, 264, 267, 272, 274, 279, 284, 287, 288, 289, 293
2:1–16   195–97, 198, 202, 204, 205, 240–57, 259, 292
2:1–6   197, 241–45, 248, 292
2:1   195, 196, 197, 202, 240, 241, 242, 243, 244, 245, 248, 249, 253, 254, 255, 256, 257, 275, 276, 277, 292
2:2   195–96, 197, 240, 241, 242, 243, 244, 245, 248, 249, 251, 253, 254, 255, 256, 257, 260, 263, 264, 265
2:3–6   240–41
2:3–4   242
2:3   196, 197, 240, 241, 242, 244, 245, 248, 252, 254, 255, 274, 276, 277

2:4   196, 197, 240, 242, 244, 245, 248, 249, 255, 256, 259, 264, 267, 275
2:5   196, 240, 242, 245, 255, 263, 275, 276, 281, 285
2:6   196, 240, 242, 245, 255, 276
2:7   196, 197, 219, 240, 245, 246, 255, 260, 265, 279, 285, 288, 292
2:8–9   197, 246, 292
2:8   196, 197, 240, 246, 278, 288
2:9–16   197, 247–54, 292
2:9–11   247, 248
2:9–10   248
2:9   196, 197, 202, 204, 240–41, 246, 248, 249, 250, 251, 255, 256, 259, 272, 274, 275, 277, 280, 286, 288, 290
2:10   196, 241, 248, 249, 250, 253, 254, 255, 256, 257, 260, 262, 265, 266, 272, 274, 286, 290
2:11   196, 197, 241, 248, 249, 250, 256, 276
2:12   196, 197, 241, 247, 248, 250, 256, 259, 262, 266
2:13–16   247, 250–51
2:13–14   250
2:13   196, 241, 248, 251, 253, 256, 257, 277, 282, 289
2:14   196, 197, 241, 248, 251, 252, 253, 257, 260, 265, 285
2:15–16   251
2:15   196, 197, 241, 248, 250, 251, 252, 253, 257, 263, 265
2:16   196, 197, 198, 202, 241, 248, 251, 253, 257, 259, 264, 265, 267
2:17–22   197–98, 200, 202, 258–67, 273, 292, 293
2:17–18   265
2:17   197, 198, 258, 259, 261, 263, 275, 293
2:18   197, 198, 258, 259–60, 265, 272, 285, 293
2:19–22   198, 261–65, 293
2:19   198, 258, 261, 262, 263, 266, 278
2:20–22   261, 263
2:20–21   263
2:20   198, 204, 258, 261, 262, 263, 266, 273, 274, 275, 285, 287, 290
2:21–22   263

Scripture Index

2:21	198, 200, 202, 204, 258, 259, 261, 263, 267, 273, 279, 281, 288, 293
2:22	198, 258, 261, 263, 264, 267
3:1–18	199–201, 202, 268–90, 293
3:1–10	200, 270–77, 283, 294
3:1–4	270, 271
3:1–3	271
3:1	191, 199, 200, 201, 203, 268, 269, 271, 272, 276, 281, 283, 284, 286, 289, 293
3:2	199, 200, 201, 268, 269, 271, 272, 273, 279, 283, 286, 287, 288
3:3	199, 200, 204, 268, 271, 273, 274, 281, 283, 284, 285, 287, 290
3:4	199, 200, 204, 268, 271, 274, 276, 280, 283, 284, 287
3:5–6	270
3:5	199, 268, 270, 274, 275, 276, 280
3:6	199, 268, 275, 277
3:7–8	270
3:7	199, 200, 201, 268, 270, 275, 276, 277, 278, 280, 281, 283, 284, 286, 288, 290
3:8–10	270, 276
3:8	199, 200, 268, 270, 271, 276, 277, 281, 283, 284, 288
3:9–15	294
3:9–10	276
3:9	192, 199, 200, 201, 268, 271, 276, 277, 281, 283, 284, 285, 288, 289, 291, 293
3:10–11	201, 277–78, 280, 293
3:10	199, 200, 201, 268–69, 271, 276, 277, 278, 280, 281, 283, 286, 288, 289, 290
3:11	192, 199, 201, 205, 269, 278–79, 280, 288, 291, 293
3:12–14	201, 279–82, 294
3:12	199, 201, 269, 279, 280, 281, 283, 286, 289, 290
3:13–14	279
3:13	199, 201, 269, 279, 280, 281, 284, 294
3:14	200, 201, 269, 270, 280, 281, 283, 284, 289
3:15–18	200, 282–86, 294
3:15–16	282, 283
3:15	192, 200, 201, 204, 269, 270, 282, 283, 284, 285, 289, 291
3:16	200, 201, 269, 270, 282, 283, 284, 285, 289
3:17–18	282
3:17	200, 201, 204, 269, 270, 283, 284, 285
3:18	192, 200, 201, 203, 204, 205, 269, 270, 283, 285, 286, 290, 291, 293, 294

Jude

1:1–4	296–97, 298, 301, 303–8, 310, 330, 340, 342
1:1	296, 297, 303–4, 305, 306, 307, 308, 311, 314, 317, 330, 331, 335, 337, 338, 340, 342
1:2–3	297, 304–5
1:2	296, 297, 301, 303, 305, 306, 308, 320, 327, 330, 331, 337, 340, 342
1:3	297, 303, 305–6, 307, 308, 310, 311, 312, 314, 315, 316, 317, 322, 325, 326, 327, 329, 336, 339, 340
1:4	297, 298, 299, 301, 303, 306–7, 308, 310, 311, 312, 313, 314, 316, 317, 320, 322, 323, 325, 326, 327, 328, 331, 332, 335, 336, 337, 338, 339, 340, 341, 342
1:5–11	297–98, 299, 301, 309–17, 319, 320, 341
1:5	297, 298, 309, 310–11, 314, 315, 316, 317, 322, 325, 332, 336, 339, 341
1:6	297, 298, 301, 309, 311, 312, 314, 316, 317, 319, 322, 328, 331, 337, 341
1:7	297, 298, 309, 311–12, 313, 316, 332, 333, 338, 341
1:8–10	298, 313–14, 341
1:8–9	313
1:8	298, 309, 312–13, 314, 316, 317, 320, 327, 333, 335, 338, 341
1:9	298, 301, 309, 313, 314, 317, 319, 322, 332, 338, 341
1:10	298, 299, 309, 313, 314, 317, 320, 327
1:11	298, 310, 315–16, 317, 321, 325, 328, 341

Jude (cont.)

1:12–20	299–300, 301, 302, 318–29, 331, 341
1:12–14	299, 319–22, 324
1:12–13	323, 328
1:12	299, 300, 318, 319, 320, 321, 322, 324, 325, 326, 327, 328, 329, 331, 333, 334, 337, 338, 339, 341
1:13	299, 300, 301, 318, 319, 320, 321, 322, 324, 325, 326, 328, 329, 331, 336, 337, 339, 341
1:14–15	322, 341
1:14	299, 300, 318, 319, 320, 322, 323, 324, 327, 329
1:15	299, 300, 301, 318, 319, 322–23, 325, 326, 328, 341
1:16–20	299, 323–27
1:16–18	323–24
1:16	299, 300, 318, 324, 325, 326, 328, 329, 332, 338, 341
1:17	299, 300, 318, 324, 325, 326, 329, 331, 336, 337, 339
1:18	299, 300, 318, 324, 325, 326, 329, 331, 332, 336, 337, 338, 339
1:19–20	324
1:19	299, 318, 324, 326, 327, 329, 332, 338, 341
1:20	299, 300, 318–19, 324, 326, 327, 329, 331, 332, 333, 337, 338, 341
1:21–25	300–301, 302, 330–39, 341, 342
1:21	296, 300, 301, 330, 331–32, 333, 336, 337, 338, 339, 340, 342
1:22–23	296, 340, 342
1:22	300, 301, 330, 332, 333, 338
1:23	300, 301, 330, 332–33, 335, 338
1:24–25	300, 334–37, 342
1:24	300, 330, 334, 335, 336, 338, 339, 342
1:25	296, 300, 301, 330, 331, 334, 335, 336, 339, 340, 342

Author Index

Aasgaard, Reidar, 219n17
Abernathy, David, 73n20
Achtemeier, Paul J., 4n5, 5n8, 24n23,
    35n17, 40n24, 43n29, 52n10,
    56n19, 59n26, 60n29, 66n2,
    68n8, 69n11, 70n13, 72n18,
    72n19, 75n26, 78n30, 79n33,
    84n2, 85n6, 94n15, 99n3, 101n7,
    101n8, 102n9, 103n11, 106n14,
    106n16, 116n10, 116n11,
    119n14, 121n18, 130n8, 130n9,
    131n10, 133n12, 134n14, 140n5,
    141n6, 148n26, 149n29, 156n2,
    164n15, 173n7
Adams, Edward, 274n5, 281n18
Allen, Joel S., 334n6
Applegate, J. K., 179n20

Balch, David L., 75n26
Balz, Horst, 52n10, 260n3
Bandstra, A. J., 129n7
Bartholomä, P. F., 310n3
Batten, Alicia J., 101n8
Bauckham, Richard J., 192n3, 203n8,
    211n9, 214n13, 214n14, 223n22,
    223n24, 233n5, 235n8, 237n13,
    247n11, 253n19, 262n4, 265n8,
    275n7, 282n20, 284n21, 304n4,
    306n7, 307n12, 307n13, 310n2,
    313n7, 315n12, 315n13, 315n14,
    320n2, 327n15, 332n3, 332n4,
    333n5, 335n7, 335n9, 336n12
Beckman, J. C., 56n20
Bénétreau, S., 237n14
Billings, B. S., 244n7
Blomberg, Craig L., 2n1

Borchert, Gerald L., 23n21, 202n7
Breck, John, 5n9
Brouwer, Wayne, 2n1, 3n2
Brown, Jeannine K., 158n8

Callan, Terrance, 210n7, 219n18,
    236n12, 250n14
Campbell, D. N., 134n16
Campbell, R. Alastair, 169n2
Caulley, Thomas Scott, 67n6, 262n4
Charles, J. Daryl, 219n18, 295n1

Davids, Peter H., 44n30, 179n20,
    182n3, 199n5, 215n14, 221n20,
    236n10, 243n2, 249n13, 251n17,
    264n6, 272n3, 277n11, 279n16,
    305n5, 310n2, 313n8, 315n13,
    320n3, 321n6, 321n7, 335n9,
    337n13
Deselaers, P., 102n9
DeSilva, David A., 2n1
Dewey, Joanna, 3n3
Doering, Lutz, 30n4
Donelson, Lewis R., 4n5, 31n8, 40n23,
    43n30, 49n3, 51n7, 52n12,
    53n13, 54n16, 57n22, 59n27,
    66n3, 69n10, 70n12, 72n17,
    75n25, 79n32, 84n3, 94n15,
    99n3, 105n12, 106n14, 107n18,
    113n3, 113n5, 116n11, 117n12,
    119n14, 120n16, 129n6, 129n7,
    130n9, 133n13, 134n15, 141n6,
    144n13, 144n15, 148n24, 156n3,
    156n5, 158n8, 160n11, 160n12,
    172n6, 173n7, 173n9, 178n15,
    179n20, 180n21, 192n3, 212n12,

1 Peter, 2 Peter, and Jude

217n16, 222n21, 223n22,
223n23, 224n25, 231n2, 234n7,
235n8, 235n9, 236n12, 244n6,
244n7, 245n8, 247n11, 248n12,
250n 15, 251n16, 251n17,
253n18, 254n20, 259n2, 264n6,
265n8, 273n4, 274n5, 274n6,
275n8, 276n9, 281n18, 282n20,
304n3, 304n4, 307n10, 312n5,
313n7, 314n9, 320n2, 320n3,
321n4, 322n8, 325n11, 326n13,
332n4, 333n6, 334n7, 335n8,
336n13, 337n14
Dryden, J. de Waal, 32n9
Dubis, Mark, 32n10, 66n2, 91n5,
141n8, 163n15
Dupont-Roc. R., 37n18

Elliott, John Hall, 4n5, 5n8, 24n22,
24n23, 24n24, 31n8, 33n11,
33n13, 38n19, 40n22, 43n30,
49n2, 50n4, 50n5, 50n6, 51n9,
52n12, 55n18, 57n21, 59n26,
59n27, 66n2, 71n15, 74n23,
77n27, 77n28, 78n29, 78n31,
85n6, 93n11, 94n14, 100n6,
102n10, 105n13, 106n15,
106n16, 107n18, 112n2, 114n6,
116n9, 123n23, 132n11, 133n13,
134n15, 140n3, 141n6, 144n14,
146n18, 148n23, 148n25, 156n4,
157n6, 159n10, 160n11, 164n15,
169n3, 172n6, 175n11, 179n19
Engel, W., 134n16

Feldmeier, Reinhard, 33n13, 34n14,
51n8, 56n20, 74n24, 84n4, 90n3,
114n8, 120n16, 140n5, 177n13
Flink, Timo, 310n2
Forbes, Greg, 105n14
Fornberg, Tord, 215n14

Gréaux, E. J., 116n11
Giesen, Heinz, 144n14
Green, Gene L., 192n3, 199n5, 208n2,
208n3, 221n20, 231n3, 243n2,
243n3, 244n4, 244n7, 246n10,
248n12, 249n13, 251n17,
252n18, 254n21, 262n5, 264n7,
265n8, 271n2, 275n7, 277n10,
278n15, 280n17, 282n20,
286n22, 304n2, 305n5, 306n8,
307n13, 311n4, 313n7, 314n11,
315n14, 320n2, 322n9, 323n10,
325n12, 326n14, 332n3, 335n8,
335n10, 336n11, 336n12, 337n13
Green, Joel B., 32n10, 53n15, 84n3,
94n13, 149n28, 178n15, 179n20,
180n21

Hackenberg, Wolfgang, 203n8
Hafemann, Scott, 214n13
Harrington, Daniel J., 209n5, 214n13,
223n23, 224n25, 231n2, 246n9,
275n8, 306n8, 307n9, 312n6,
314n10
Harvey, Robert, 192n3, 235n9
Hays, C. M., 252n18
Heil, John Paul, 4n6, 92n9, 235n9
Herzer, J., 43n28
Hofius, Otfried, 244n4
Holloway, Paul Andrew, 156n2
Horrell, David G., 4n5, 73n22, 158n9
Howe, F. R., 72n17

Jobes, Karen H., 4n5, 5n8, 29n3, 30n4,
30n5, 34n15, 44n31, 53n14,
54n15, 67n6, 68n7, 70n13,
72n16, 92n9, 95n16, 99n4,
105n12, 113n5, 116n10, 116n11,
129n7, 131n10, 132n11, 133n12,
141n7, 142n9, 145n18, 147n19,
147n22, 149n28, 157n7, 162n13,
173n7, 176n12, 179n20
Jodoin, D., 95n16
Joubert, Stephan J., 295n1

Keating, Daniel, 209n6
Kiley, Mark, 105n14
Klumbies, Paul-Gerhard, 134n16
Kraftchick, Steven J., 192n3, 224n25,
310n3
Kratz, Reinhard, 130n7
Kraus, T. J., 248n12
Kremer, Jacob, 92n9
Kruger, M. A., 312n5

Author Index

LaVerdiere, Eugene A., 59n26

Makujina, J., 246n9
Man, Ronald E., 5n9
Marshall, I. Howard, 38n19, 92n9
Mathews, M. D., 295n1
Mazich, Edward, 322n9
Mbuvi, Andrew Mūtūa, 24n24, 31n7,
  52n11, 58n23, 58n25, 70n13,
  107n18
McCartney, Dan. G., 66n2
Metzger, Bruce Manning, 199n5,
  300n3, 310n2
Michaels, J. Ramsey, 32n9, 38n19,
  38n20, 39n21, 40n24, 44n31,
  44n32, 50n5, 52n12, 54n15,
  54n16, 54n17, 56n20, 58n24,
  60n28, 60n29, 67n4, 68n9,
  70n13, 71n14, 73n21, 73n22,
  74n24, 75n26, 79n33, 84n4,
  85n7, 87n8, 93n10, 100n6,
  103n11, 107n17, 113n4, 113n5,
  114n7, 116n10, 117n12, 121n19,
  121n20, 139n2, 143n11, 143n12,
  146n18, 148n24, 149n27, 158n9,
  160n11, 162n13, 164n15, 170n4,
  175n11, 180n21, 181n23
Milinovich, Timothy, 2n1
Miller, D. G., 32n10
Miller, T. A., 253n18
Moo, Douglas, J., 208n2, 210n7,
  221n19, 221n20
Moyise, Steve, 118n13

Neyrey, Jerome H., 215n14, 231n2,
  235n9, 327n16

Page, Sydney H. T., 30n6
Palzkill, Elisabeth, 68n8
Panning, A. J., 72n17
Paschke, Boris A., 172n7
Picirelli, Robert, 203n8
Pierce, C. T., 134n16
Piper, J., 107n18
Pitts, A. W., 236n12
Porter, Stanley E., 236n12
Punt, J., 105n14

Reed, Jeffrey T., 295n1
Reese, Ruth Anne, 209n4, 244n5,
  295n1, 314n10
Richards, E. Randolph, 29n3
Rosner, Brian S., 244n5

Sargent, Benjamin, 29n3
Schelkle, K. H., 92n9
Schreiner, Thomas R., 4n5, 33n11,
  34n16, 38n19, 51n9, 53n13,
  67n5, 69n10, 71n15, 72n19,
  91n5, 92n7, 94n13, 99n3,
  120n15, 122n21, 128n3, 129n7,
  132n11, 144n14, 145n18, 157n7,
  162n13, 163n14, 176n12,
  177n14, 211n10, 214n14,
  217n16, 219n18, 236n11,
  252n18, 265n8, 277n12, 277n13,
  307n11, 310n2, 310n3, 311n4,
  321n5, 323n10, 331n2, 333n5
Seland, Torrey, 73n20
Selwyn, Edward Gordon, 34n15
Senior, Donald P., 4n5, 41n25, 58n23,
  78n30, 90n2, 100n5, 106n15,
  121n20, 129n7, 140n3, 145n17,
  145n18, 148n24
Siegert, Folker, 71n16
Slaughter, J. R., 100n6, 103n11,
  105n14
Spencer, A. B., 105n14
Spicq, Ceslas, 192n2
Starr, James M., 214n13
Stenschke, Christoph, 73n20
Stephens, Mark B., 281n19
Strobel, August, 305n6

Thomas, Kenneth J., 4n4
Thomas, Margaret Orr, 4n4
Thomson, Ian H., 2n1
Thurén, Lauri, 295n1
Tite, Philip L., 33n12, 68n7
Towner, Philip, 192n3, 235n9
Trebilco, Paul R., 79n34, 158n9,
  204n9
Tresham, A. K., 278n14

Van Rensburg, Fika J., 67n6, 118n13, 134n16

Watson, Duane F., 44n30
Webb, Robert L., 295n1
Welch, John W., 2n1
Williams, Martin, 34n14

Wilson, Mark, 2n1
Winter, Sarah C., 334n6
Witherington, Ben, III, 4n4, 4n5, 23n21, 29n3, 42n27, 128n4, 149n29, 204n9, 208n2
Wolfe, B. P., 236n12

www.ingramcontent.com/pod-product-compliance
Lightning Source LLC
Chambersburg PA
CBHW021338300426
44114CB00012B/998